Economic Development

Economic

GERALD M. MEIER
Associate Professor of Economics
Wesleyan University

ROBERT E. BALDWIN
Assistant Professor of Economics
Harvard University

Development

THEORY,
HISTORY,
POLICY

ROBERT E. KRIEGER PUBLISHING COMPANY
HUNTINGTON, NEW YORK
1976

Original Edition 1957
Seventh Printing, June, 1966
Reprint 1976

Printed and Published by
ROBERT E. KRIEGER PUBLISHING CO., INC.
645 NEW YORK AVENUE
HUNTINGTON, NEW YORK 11743

Printed in the United States of America

Library of Congress Cataloging in Publication Data

Meier, Gerald M.
    Economic development.

    Reprint of the ed. published by Wiley, New York.
    1. Economic development.   I. Baldwin, Robert
E. joint author.   II. Title.
[HD82.M43 1975]   338.91   75-11875
ISBN 0-88275-299-5

Preface to 1976 Reprint

The original edition of this book may lay claim to having been the first "real" textbook in economic development. We deliberately adopted a panoramic approach—combining the themes of theory, history, and policy, and applying them to both the poor countries and the rich countries in a phase of mature capitalism.

The themes remain significant. Subsequent books in economic development have become narrower and more specialized. But we hope the broad approach in this book retains value. We believe that the history of thought and history of development sections in the present volume have become evermore significant for presenting the wider perspectives not available in later works.

We also emphasized the relation between international trade and development, and from the time of this book's first appearance until 1968 only five books were published on this topic. The issues raised have again come to the forefront of international policymaking.

The contrast between poor and rich countries has acquired even greater interest—as new theories of international polarization and stagflation in the world economy have been more recently propounded.

Above all, this book emphasizes fundamental principles that we believe should not be lost sight of in the intricacies of development programming and in the specialized plethora of more volumes and numerous country studies that now exist. We remain hopeful that the general synthesis offered in this volume will be useful for both students and practitioners of economic development.

G.M.M.
R.E.B.

July 1976

Preface

This book examines the problems of accelerating development in poor countries and maintaining development in rich countries. From the viewpoints of theory, history, and policy it attempts to explain the forces that give long-period growing power to an economy.

In response to the practical importance of development problems, many economists are now rethinking economic theory and economic history in terms of development. Since these reconsiderations, however, have proceeded in various directions and have yielded a wide range of contributions, one may not, on first glance, see any unity to the subject of economic development, but merely an assortment of fragmentary ideas and heterogeneous observations. We hope this book corrects such an impression. For our aim is to combine and expand the more important of these contributions into an orderly discussion that conveys some notion of the "logic" of the development process.

To accomplish this, we must first know what we are looking for: we must be able to ask intelligent questions. Accordingly, a considerable part of our discussion attempts to establish an analytical framework within which we may discover the interconnections among the strategic variables in the process of development.

Theories of development have long been of interest, and classical,

Marxian, neo-classical, and Keynesian economists have all contributed to the subject. Part 1 of this book reviews the most significant aspects of these analytical systems. We shall give particular attention to the writings of Adam Smith, David Ricardo, Karl Marx, Alfred Marshall, Joseph Schumpeter, and representatives of the present group of post-Keynesians who are concerned with the theory of economic growth. After having set forth the leading ideas of these writers, we shall then compare and synthesize them.

To allow perspective and furnish a proving ground for the preceding theoretical discussion, Part 2 examines the historical role of Britain as the "center" of the nineteenth century world economy and concentrates on some features of the extensive spread of development through the world economy during the past century. This discussion, which is intended to be a systematic survey rather than a detailed chronology, also serves to emphasize the quantitative aspects of development and to link together the domestic and international features of development.

The historical survey leads us to current problems. Differential rates of development in the past have resulted in the widely varying levels of development currently attained by various countries. At the extreme levels are the poor countries and the rich countries. For the poor countries, the predominant problem is to accelerate development—to increase the rate of growth in real national income. For the rich countries, the objective now is to maintain a suitable rate of development so that full employment may be achieved over the long run without chronic deflation or inflation. Parts 3 and 4 discuss these respective problems and their policy implications.

Thus, this study considers the following major questions:

(1) What are the principal determinants of economic development? (Part 1)

(2) What has been the influence of these determinants in the past? (Part 2)

(3) What problems are now associated with the objective of accelerating development in poor countries? (Part 3)

(4) What problems are now associated with the objective of maintaining a suitable rate of development in rich countries? (Part 4)

Although our emphasis is on a general framework of analysis in economic terms, we realize that other disciplines can contribute much to an understanding of the development process. We have therefore tried to give at least some attention to the contributions of other subjects—especially history to explain the "why" of the past, psychology and sociology to explain the value structures, motivations, and attitudes in different cultures, and political science to differentiate between the possible and the feasible, discover power relations, and indicate means of control. Furthermore, we have so arranged the contents that they may be readily supplemented by additional readings—listed in the Appendices—on sociocultural issues, actual development programs and plans of various countries, and case studies of development in individual countries.

In its entirety this book is designed for use in courses in economic development (or economic growth or economic change). It is addressed primarily to students majoring in economics and to beginning graduate students. Parts of the book should also be useful for courses in international economics, economic history, and comparative economic systems.

Although the authors have collaborated throughout, Professor Meier is responsible for "Studying Economic Development," Chapter 5, and Chapters 7 to 21; and Professor Baldwin is responsible for Chapters 1 to 4, 6, and 22 to 25.

We appreciate the suggestions offered by our students who were our first readers. For their helpful comments, we are also indebted to Professors Henry Broude, Evsey Domar, James Duesenberry, Gottfried Haberler, Burton Hallowell, David McClelland, William Parker, Arthur Smithies, and Kossuth Williamson. Professor A. H. Imlah kindly made available his revised estimates of Britain's terms of trade.

Professor Meier gratefully remembers his attendance at the 1955 conference of the Merrill Center for Economics where several conferees first suggested some of the thoughts of the book. The Wesleyan Research Committee provided for the helpful secretarial services of Mrs. Evelyn Place and Mrs. E. B. Carling.

Our gratitude is also expressed to the many publishers who have extended permission to quote from copyrighted materials; specific references are made in the footnotes. Thanks are due also for permission to republish some parts of articles already in print in *Economia Internazionale, Weltwirtschaftliches Archiv,* and *The Manchester School of Economic and Social Studies.*

Above all, we are indebted to our wives who were truly our other co-authors—and more.

G.M.M.
R.E.B.

Middletown, Conn.
Cambridge, Mass.
June, 1957

Contents

ix

PART 2
HISTORICAL OUTLINES OF ECONOMIC DEVELOPMENT

INTRODUCTORY

PART 3
ACCELERATING DEVELOPMENT IN POOR COUNTRIES

INTRODUCTORY

PART 4

MAINTAINING DEVELOPMENT IN RICH COUNTRIES

INTRODUCTORY

Charts

Tables

Studying
Economic Development

"Few problems are more fascinating, more important, or more neglected than the rates at which development proceeds in successive generations in different countries."[1] For two decades this observation by Wesley Clair Mitchell went unheeded as the Great Depression of the 1930's and the war economy of the 1940's diverted economists' attention to more immediate short-term economic problems. Now, however, the subject of development is at the very forefront of economic thought, and issues of development are of vital significance in poor and rich countries alike.

To the rich industrial countries, during the 1930's, the Keynesian analysis addressed a double-pronged message: a condemnation of the wastage of resources resulting from cyclical unemployment, and a warning against the deeper-rooted dangers of "secular stagnation." These two interrelated problems have been woven into the more general discussion of economic growth which is a major topic in post-Keynesian analysis. Now, considering countries in the more advanced phases of capitalistic development, economists are attempting to spell out the

[1] W. C. Mitchell, *Business Cycles,* National Bureau of Economic Research, New York, 1927, 416.

1

precise conditions necessary for the maintenance of steady growth and the avoidance of chronic problems of general overproduction or under-production.

Maintaining development is a problem for rich countries, but accelerating development is an even more pressing matter for poor countries. Most people consider the world's greatest economic problem to be the acute poverty of the majority of the world's population. Humanitarian, economic, and political interests combine to plead the claims of development in poor countries with increasing frequency and urgency.

1. What Is Economic Development?

No single definition of "economic development" is entirely satisfactory. There is a tendency to use the terms economic development, economic growth, and secular change interchangeably. Although it is possible to draw some fine distinctions among these terms, they are in essence synonymous. But just what, we may ask, is the content behind such a term as economic development?

A concise answer may be as follows: economic development is a process whereby an economy's real national income increases over a long period of time. And, if the rate of development is greater than the rate of population growth, then per capita real income will increase. "Process" implies the operation of certain forces; these forces operate over the long period and embody changes in certain variables. Details of the process vary under diverse conditions in space and time. But there are some basic common features. And the general result of the process is growth in an economy's national product—in itself a particular long-run change.

When we focus only on the growth in national product, we are taking a comprehensive view of the end result of the development process. If, however, we examine the process in more detail, we observe that many other changes, each of a particular character, accompany the rise in output. We can classify the most important of these as changes in fundamental factor supplies and changes in the structure of demand for products.[2]

Particular changes in factor supplies comprise: (1) the discovery of additional resources, (2) capital accumulation, (3) population growth, (4) introduction of new and better techniques of production, (5) improvement in skills, and (6) other institutional and organizational modifications.

Particular changes in the structure of demand for products are asso-

[2] T. W. Schultz, *Economic Organization of Agriculture,* McGraw-Hill Book Co., New York, 1953, 5.

ciated with developments in (1) size and age composition of population, (2) level and distribution of income, (3) tastes, and (4) other institutional and organizational arrangements.

It is possible, therefore, to interpret economic development in terms of specific developments in factor supplies and product demands. The subject matter of this book combines both the general and specific views of economic development. It considers not only the general end result of the developmental process—the increase in real national income—but also, what is more significant, the underlying detailed changes that determine this result.

In defining economic development as a process whereby an economy's real national income increases over a long period of time, we should underscore for special attention the words "process," "real national income," and "long period."

If we view economic development as a process, then it is not sufficient merely to cite and classify a list of separate developments, or even to examine each development individually. This is at best only a prelude to the much more important task of establishing causal relations among these developments. For only on the basis of such interconnections can we specify the consequences to be expected from certain changes. To achieve our major objective of explaining how a variety of particular changes determine the course of real national income we must get behind surface appearances and attempt to understand the process whereby real national income actually increases.

"Real national income" refers to the country's total output of final goods and services,[3] expressed not in money terms but in real terms: the money expression of national income must be corrected by an appropriate price index of both consumer and capital goods. "National income," however, might refer to gross national product or net national product. In measuring economic development, we want the most inclusive measure of the final goods and services produced, but we must also allow for the wastage of machinery and other capital goods during the process of production. Since gross national product makes no allowance for capital replacements, a better measure is net national product which includes final consumer goods and services plus only the net additions to capital goods. When, therefore, we say that a country experiences development if its real national income rises over the long period, we should remember that "real national income" is being used

---

[3] In a closed economy national income and total output are identical. In an economy open to foreign trade, however, national income will be greater than total output if the country is receiving income from foreign investments or is receiving gifts and grants from abroad.

as a short expression for "net national product corrected for price changes."[4]

From the standpoint of economic development, the increase in net national product must be a sustained increase. A short-period expansion, such as occurs within a business cycle, is of secondary consequence—a minor wave compared with the deep upsurge of a rising tide. Instead, what is significant is the underlying upward trend in net national product. Although the upward trend means that each successive cyclical peak and trough is generally at a higher level of real national output than the preceding peak and trough, respectively, it is the increase in real national income between cycles—rather than the increase within a cycle—that denotes development. Accordingly, the relevant time units are decades (in which secular trends are measured) rather than years (in which individual cycles are measured). Since the major business cycle is normally of 6 to 13 years' duration, we may consider a sustained movement as spanning a period of at least 25 years' duration.

Many people choose to interpret development as meaning something more than merely an increase in aggregate output; they believe that it should also denote a rising standard of living. Such a view requires economic development to be defined as a process whereby the real per capita income of a country increases over the long period. By relating development to the problem of removing poverty, many would use as the test of development an increase in real per capita income.[5] For, if the criterion is only an increase in real national income, then a situation is possible in which real national income rises, but the standard of living does not. This would happen whenever population growth surpasses the increase in national output, with the result that real per capita income falls; or, if the increase in national income is paralleled by an equal increase in population, real per capita income would remain constant.

[4] For a discussion of the problems connected with this measurement, see S. Kuznets, "Measurement of Economic Growth," in National Bureau of Economic Research, *Problems in the Study of Economic Growth,* National Bureau of Economic Research, New York, 1949, 137–172.

[5] Some, like Viner, would add the requirement that the absolute number of people below a minimum level of real income should also diminish at the same time that real per capita income increases. Otherwise it is conceivable that if there is a substantial increase in population "the numbers of those living at the margin of subsistence or below . . . may have grown steadily consistently with a rise in the average income of the population as a whole." J. Viner, *International Trade and Economic Development,* The Clarendon Press, Oxford, 1953, 100.

We should recognize, however, that this is a value judgment about the distribution of income. The normative elements of economic development are discussed later.

There is little point in debating whether the definition of development should focus on an increase in real national income or real per capita income, since the per capita index can always be found by dividing the national income by population. Nevertheless there are some reasons for emphasizing real national income. First, a larger real national income is normally a prerequisite for an increase in real per capita income.[6] Although the desire to reduce mass poverty by raising per capita real income may account for our concern with development in poor countries, we must recognize that population is growing rapidly in many of these countries, so that a considerable increase in national income is needed if per capita income is to rise. Moreover, as Part 4 shows, it is not per capita income, which is already high, that is most relevant for the problems confronting rich countries such as the United States and Britain. Instead, their problem is to maintain steady growth in national income so as to avoid chronic deflation or inflation. An increase in national income may therefore be suggested as the most relevant, as well as most convenient, single measure of development for both poor and rich countries.

Second, if an increase in per capita income were taken as the measure of development, we would be in the awkward position of having to say that a country had not developed if its real national income had risen, but population had also risen at the same rate. For instance, if over a given period, country A's national income quadrupled, and country B's national income only doubled, but population growth prevented per capita income from rising in either country, then by the per capita criterion we would have to say that neither country had developed. Yet it does some violence to our ordinary notions of development to deny that country A developed more than country B.

Third, and most importantly, if per capita income is the measurement, the population problem may be concealed, since population has already been divided out. The field of inquiry is then unduly narrowed. As Kuznets warns, "the choice of per-capita, per-unit, or any similar single measure to gauge the rate of economic growth . . . carries with it the danger of neglecting the denominator of the ratio. In a sense such neglect is an inevitable consequence of the operation: we divide national product by total population largely to eliminate changes in

[6] The only exceptions would be in instances where population steadily diminished in absolute numbers, and real national income remained constant (because the proportion of the population which is employed became larger, or hours of work increased, or productivity rose), or real national income fell by less than the decrease in population. But over a long time period an absolutely declining population is distinctly rare.

the former 'produced' by mere changes in the latter . . . . To put it bluntly, in insisting on gauging economic growth by such per-unit measures, economists are treating the population factor either as an extremely simple variable that can be handled by mere division . . . , or, what is worse, as an exogenous factor, beyond the ken of the economist as a student of economic growth . . . . In arguing for the total volume of national product rather than the per-capita, I am suggesting a change that should symbolize and give effect to the real widening of the field of required attention."[7] Thus, instead of jumping immediately to per capita income (the quotient), we may analyze problems of development more thoroughly if we give explicit attention to both national income (the numerator) and population (the denominator).

If we adopt an increase in real national income as the basic criterion of development, we can, of course, always go beyond this and consider whether real per capita income also rises by simply comparing the amount of development, that is, the increase in real national income, with the change in population. Once we give attention to real per capita income, however, it is easy to slide over to the view that economic development means "economic progress" or an increase in economic welfare. When the growth in real national income is compared with population growth, and an increase in real per capita income is found, it is tempting to say that this constitutes progress away from poverty towards a better standard of living. But at this point the term "economic development" no longer denotes only a quantitative concept but also a qualitative one. The expression is then no longer a descriptive term but rather a prescriptive term. When it includes the notion of economic progress or economic welfare, the definition of development becomes a "persuasive definition," implying that development is a desirable objective.

Now, almost everyone would agree that real national income and real per capita income are highly significant for economic welfare. On the basis of the rather obvious assumption that more goods and services are preferred to less, we may consider an increase in real national income as a necessary condition for an increase in economic welfare. But it is not by itself a sufficient condition. As real per capita income rises, it is possible that the rich are getting richer, or the poor are getting poorer—indeed, any distribution of income may accompany the increase in per capita income. But a judgment regarding economic welfare involves a judgment regarding the desirability of a particular distribution

[7] S. Kuznets, "Problems in Comparison of Economic Trends," in S. Kuznets, W. E. Moore, J. J. Spengler (eds.), *Economic Growth: Brazil, India, Japan,* Duke University Press, Durham, 1955, 12–13.

of income, and this is a value judgment dependent on the ethical predilections of the individual. It cannot, therefore, be definitely said that economic welfare has increased even if real national income and real per capita income have risen, unless the resultant distribution of income is also considered good.

Further, we should be cautious about identifying an expansion in total output or per capita output with enrichment because the composition of the total output is also important. An expansion of total output could be accompanied by a depletion of natural resources, or it could be composed only of a larger stockpile of military equipment, or it could consist merely in a greater output of capital goods while there is a possible reduction in output of consumer goods. Whether a larger total output contributes to the "sum of individual enjoyments and satisfactions" depends as much on what is produced and its quality as it does on the quantity produced. This problem is usually met by assuming that what is produced is valued in terms of its satisfaction of either consumers' desires or the wishes of the economy's planners, and that quality does not deteriorate. Moreover, for comparisons over a long time period, changes in consumers' tastes also have to be ignored or else treated in a complicated and indirect manner.[8]

From a welfare point of view, we must also consider not only what is produced but how it is produced. A recognition of changes in working conditions may make it impossible to link a rise in real per capita income with an increase in economic welfare. Even though real national output grows, the real costs—the "pain and sacrifice"—and the social costs involved in producing this larger output may also have risen. The expansion in output may have resulted, for example, from additional hours of work; if leisure is deemed desirable, then the increase in national output is not an unmixed blessing. Similarly, there may have been a deterioration in the conditions associated with the variety of work, personnel relationships, or provisions for health, safety, and comfort.

If considerations of the distribution of income, composition of total output, change in tastes, and character of working conditions make it difficult to equate development with economic welfare, how much more difficult is it to identify development with social welfare in general? It is quite possible that, even if development satisfied all the conditions necessary to promote economic welfare, this need not also promote social welfare. For economic welfare is but a part of social welfare, and, since the process of development has a profound impact on social institutions, habits, and beliefs, it is likely to introduce powerful causes of dis-

[8] Cf. P. A. Samuelson, "'Evaluation of Real National Income," *Oxford Economic Papers,* 2, No. 1, 1–29 (Jan. 1950); A. C. Pigou, "Real Income and Economic Welfare," *ibid.,* 3, No. 1, 16–20 (Feb. 1951).

content. Some aspects of human welfare might suffer if relations that were once personal become impersonal, the continuity in one's way of living is disrupted, and the support and assurance of a stable community disappear.[9]

Summarizing, we may say that the analysis of economic development centers on an increase in real national income and the particular changes that accompany such an over-all increase. Having measured the amount of development by the increase in real national income, we may then confront it with changes in population and consider real per capita income. Although an increase in output per head is in itself a significant achievement, nevertheless we cannot equate this with an increase in economic welfare, let alone social welfare, without additional considerations. To specify an optimum rate of development we must make value judgments regarding income distribution, composition of output, tastes, real costs, and other particular changes that are associated with the over-all increase in real income.[10]

For purposes of classifying countries as "poor" or "rich," we may compare the amount of development with population and use per capita real income. In a ranking of countries of the world by real per capita income, the poor countries would be at the bottom of the list. The extent of development has been limited in these countries relative to their populations, so that real per capita income has remained low. Rich countries, in contrast, are at the top of a ranking of countries of the world by real per capita income: development in these countries has been intensive relative to population growth, so that real per capita income is high.

The poor countries are commonly called "underdeveloped" countries. This term, however, is subject to various ambiguous interpretations.[11] The term also suggests that a country ought to be developed, or is capable of being developed. Yet there may be considerable disagreement about this. Because of the ambiguities involved in using the term "underdeveloped," and because we wish to focus on low per capita real in-

[9] For these and other causes of discontent which may accompany development, see E. H. Phelps Brown, *Economic Growth and Human Welfare,* Ranjit Printers and Publishers, Delhi, 1953, Chapter II; J. M. Clark, "Common and Disparate Elements in National Growth and Decline," in National Bureau of Economic Research, *op. cit.,* 24–28; S. H. Frankel, *Some Conceptual Aspects of International Economic Development of Underdeveloped Territories,* International Finance Section, Princeton University, Princeton, May 1952, 16–25.

[10] One may readily think of other value judgments that may have to be made, for instance, judgments regarding the degree of political freedom or the type and extent of government planning that should exist.

[11] Cf. S. Kuznets, "Toward a Theory of Economic Growth," in R. Lekachman (ed.), *National Policy for Economic Welfare at Home and Abroad,* Doubleday & Co., New York, 1955, 99.

come, we may better adopt the less confusing term "poor country." In doing this, however, we avoid calling a country poor merely because it is a young country (Canada, for example), or because it has a low ratio of industrial output to total output (New Zealand, for example). Nor are the terms "rich" and "poor" intended to describe anything but the performance of the country's economy; "poor" should have no invidious connotation regarding any other aspect of the country's culture.

The large absolute gap in per capita income between the rich and the poor countries can be observed in Table A which is based on national income estimates for 70 countries. Table B also shows the differences among various regions of the world according to population and income.

TABLE A. WORLD INCOME DISTRIBUTION IN 1949
(U. S. Dollars of 1949 Purchasing Power)

	Per Cent of World Income	Per Cent of World Population	Per Capita Income
High-income countries	67	18	$915
Middle-income countries	18	15	310
Low-income countries	15	67	54

Source: R. Nurkse, *Problems of Capital Formation in Underdeveloped Countries,* Basil Blackwell, Oxford, 1953, 63. Compiled from Statistical Office of the United Nations, "National and Per Capita Incomes of 70 Countries, 1949," *Statistical Papers,* Series E, No. 1, New York, Oct. 1950.

This coverage excludes about 400 million of world population for whom no national income estimates are available, but who are undoubtedly in poor countries.

The high-income countries are the United States, Canada, Western European countries, Australia, and New Zealand. The middle-income group includes Argentina, Uruguay, South Africa, Israel, and some Eastern European countries, especially Russia. The lowest-income group includes the poor countries that make up most of Asia, Africa, the Near and Middle East, Southeast Europe, the Caribbean, and much of Central and South America. It is a startling observation that, of the two billion people in the countries for which estimates of national income were available in 1949, over two-thirds had per capita income of less than $55.[12] The great majority of the world's people is in a constant struggle against poverty.

[12] These quantitative comparisons are subject to several conceptual and statistical criticisms. But, even if full allowance is made for downward biases, the range of differences is still very large.

For a full discussion of the uses of national income estimates in poor countries and the intercomparability of national income statistics, see the papers by S. H. Frankel, F. Benham, V. K. R. V. Rao, and D. Creamer in International Association for Research in Income and Wealth, *Income and Wealth,* Series III, Bowes and Bowes, London, 1953.

TABLE B. DISTRIBUTION OF WORLD POPULATION
AND INCOME, 1949

	Per Cent of World Population	Per Cent of World Income	Relative Income per Capita (World = 100)
United States	6.5	40.9	626
Western Europe*	10.0	21.5	214
U.S.S.R.	8.4	11.2	133
Other Europe	6.4	6.0	94
Latin America	6.6	4.4	66
Africa	8.6	2.0	24
Asia	52.4	10.5	20

* Includes Western, Central, and Northern Europe.

Source: S. Kuznets, "Quantitative Aspects of the Economic Growth of Nations," *Economic Development and Cultural Change, V,* No. 1, 17 (Oct. 1956).

Not only is there a wide disparity in the current income levels of poor and rich countries, but we may also infer that this disparity has increased during the past century. The secular rise in per capita income in many poor countries over the last century must have been at a much lower rate than in the rich countries, and the international differences in per capita income are now absolutely greater, and probably also relatively greater, than they were a century ago.[13]

Besides the contrasts in per capita income, Table C also shows international differences in various other measures related to a country's level of development. In all these measures the differences between rich and poor countries are striking.

Finally, we may broadly estimate that in the richest countries the rate of increase in national income is now about 25 per cent to 30 per cent every 10 years, whereas in poor countries it is generally less than 15 per cent every 10 years. And in many poor countries the rate of increase in national income is almost completely offset by a nearly equivalent increase in population, so that the rate of increase in per capita income is much less than in rich countries.

2. Why Study Economic Development?

Adam Smith truly set the stage for issues that were to dominate subsequent economic thought when he entitled his classic *An Inquiry into the Nature and Causes of the Wealth of Nations.* Ever since, economists have continued to inquire why countries develop at varying rates. The

[13] Kuznets, "Toward a Theory of Economic Growth," *op. cit.,* 27.

TABLE C. INTERNATIONAL DIFFERENCES IN PER CAPITA INCOME AND RELATED MEASURES, 53 COUNTRIES, 1939

	Groups of Countries by Per Capita Income		
	I	II	III
1. Per capita income (U. S. A. $)	461	154	41
2. Per cent of total population	20	16	64
3. Per cent of total income	64	18	18
4. Per capita income (index)	100	33	9
5. Average population type	1.1	1.5	2.9
6. Expectation of life at birth (index)	100	82	63
7. Physicians per 1000 population (index)	100	73	16
8. Per cent literate (index)	100	77	20
9. Per cent of total income from non-agricultural industries	84	71	59
10. Average income of population dependent on agriculture (index)	100	39	8
11. Investment in industry per worker (index)	100	39	11
12. Energy consumed per day (horsepower hours per capita, index)	100	24	5
13. Miles of railroads (per 1000 square miles of area, index)	100	72	32
14. Annual freight carried (ton miles per capita, index)	100	60	4
15. Daily per capita food supply (indexes)			
All foods (calories)	100	92	72
Animal proteins (ounces)	100	56	18
Fats (ounces)	100	57	32
16. Net annual consumption of textiles (pounds per capita, index)	100	40	26

Notes: All entries, except for line 9, from *Point Four* (U. S. Department of State, publication 3719, Jan. 1950, Appendix C, 103–124).

Groups of countries distinguished in the columns of the table are by size of per capita income. The following countries, arranged in declining order of per capita income, are included in each group:

I (per capita income over $200): U.S., Germany, United Kingdom, Switzerland, Sweden, Australia, New Zealand, Canada, Netherlands, Denmark, France, Norway, Belgium, Eire, Argentina.

II (per capita income from $101 through $200): Union of South Africa, Finland, Chile, Austria, U.S.S.R., Italy, Greece, Czechoslovakia, Hungary, Bulgaria.

III (per capita income from $22 through $50): Haiti, Nicaragua, Guatemala, Bolivia, Honduras, El Salvador, Brazil, Ecuador, Paraguay, India, Philippines, China, Indonesia. (per capita income from $51 through $100): Cuba, Yugoslavia, Poland, Japan, Venezuela, Egypt, Palestine, Costa Rica, Colombia, Peru, Panama, Ceylon, Mexico, Uruguay, Dominican Republic.

All averages used in the table are, unless otherwise indicated, weighted arithmetic means. For entries other than income and population type data may be for fewer countries, especially in group III, than listed above.

Population types are identified as follows:

Type 1. Low growth potential. Birth rates below 25 per thousand. Low death rates. Small natural increase with prospect of relatively stationary population in the future.

Type 2. Transitional growth. Birth rates 25–35 per thousand. Both birth and death rates generally falling. Rapid population growth.

Type 3. High growth potential. Birth rates over 35 per thousand. Death rates (but not birth rates) generally declining. Rapid growth in absence of civil disturbance, famine, and epidemic.

The entries in line 5 are unweighted arithmetic means of entries for each country, given separately in the source.

Source: S. Kuznets, "International Differences in Income Levels: Some Reflections on Their Causes," *Economic Development and Cultural Change, II,* No. 1, 5–6 (April 1953).

nineteenth-century development of Britain, Germany, and the United States posed many questions about the nature and causes of industrial capitalism. At the same time, there was the marked contrast with large areas of the world that remained in a condition of relative economic stagnation. The twentieth century, in turn, has raised the question why the rate of development in many countries has slowed down. It has also confronted liberal capitalist nations with the challenging problem of rapid development in Russia.

The study of economic development is now of immense practical importance. A study of the Poverty of Nations has even more urgency than a study of the Wealth of Nations. Not only because there are many countries with widespread poverty but also because these very countries are experiencing phenomenal growth in their populations, and are developing only enough to keep up with the population growth with little left over for a rise in per capita income. Recognizing that the disparities in levels of living between rich and poor countries are greater than ever before, and that two-thirds of the world's population receive less than one-sixth of world income, poor countries are now extremely self-conscious about their low income levels. There is a clamor for development, and the issue of development in poor countries has definitely become a major political problem. "What is novel today is that the underdeveloped areas of the world have made of economic development a high ideal. They have associated it . . . with political independence, a sense of sovereignty, thought of as a means to redress long-felt inferiority and chagrin. And, aside from pride and power, they are filled with a feeling that it is practical and possible to overcome the persistent hunger, the preventable disease, death and misery which, among them, is commonplace."[14]

Whether or not development can be identified with an increase in economic or human welfare, the simple fact is that many people in poor countries want real national income to grow. Few, if any, leaders in the poor countries have shied away from development in the belief that higher standards of living would be bad for their peoples. Directly and through the United Nations, the governments of these countries have challenged economists to show how higher levels of living can be attained. Many, who believe that development is desirable, are turning to the study of economic development to find the policy measures that development requires and the criteria by which to judge the merits and demerits of the various policies now being propounded.

The development ferment is also receiving serious attention outside

[14] Editorial in *Economic Development and Cultural Change, I,* No. 2, 83 (June 1952).

the poor countries. The fact that accelerated development in the poor countries is also in the interest of the more developed countries has become increasingly recognized in the foreign policy of the United States and Britain. Encouragement of development is a prominent feature of American and British foreign policy in order to confine the spread of communism, to expand trade between industrial nations of the free world and the poor countries, and to lead the new expressions of nationalism into democratic pro-Western forms.

Rich countries are also concerned with their own development even though the problem of alleviating poverty is relatively less pressing. Economists, businessmen, and government officials in rich countries increasingly recognize that their countries must maintain a sufficiently high rate of development if deep depressions are to be avoided and the possibility of secular stagnation averted. Unless the rate of development is sufficiently high, a rich country may suffer from general overproduction and face a long-run problem of unemployment.

Finally, another reason for studying economic development is that, by investigating long-period changes, we can offset our usual preoccupation with only short-term problems. Concentration on short-run issues narrows our vision of broader processes. Our disagreements on short-run issues also frequently stem from diverse and obscure views about development. We should realize that we cannot fully appreciate many short-period problems without giving some attention to the long-period setting in which they are embedded.

Consider, for instance, the efforts to relax the static assumptions and the short-run character of Keynesian analysis;[15] or the attempts to incorporate business cycle analysis into the setting of economic growth;[16] or those studies that judge the economic effects of monopoly in terms of the economy's growth instead of merely in terms of the possible deviations from a once-for-all optimum allocation of resources.[17] Indeed, the division of economic problems into one set labeled "short-run" and

[15] See, among others, Joan Robinson, "The Generalization of the General Theory," in *The Rate of Interest and Other Essays,* Macmillan and Co., Ltd., London, 1952, 67–142.

[16] J. R. Hicks, *A Contribution to the Theory of the Trade Cycle,* Oxford University Press, Oxford, 1950; R. F. Harrod, "Supplement on Dynamic Theory," in *Economic Essays,* Macmillan and Co., Ltd., London, 1952; W. Fellner, *Trends and Cycles in Economic Activity,* Henry Holt & Co., New York, 1956; D. Hamberg, *Economic Growth and Instability,* W. W. Norton & Co., New York, 1956.

[17] Cf. J. K. Galbraith, *American Capitalism,* Houghton Mifflin, Boston, 1952, Chapter VII; A. D. H. Kaplan, *Big Enterprise in a Competitive Society,* The Brookings Institution, Washington, D.C., 1954; E. S. Mason, "The New Competition," *Yale Review, XLIII,* 37–48 (Sept. 1953); P. Wiles, "Growth versus Choice," *Economic Journal, LXVI,* No. 262, 244–255 (June 1956).

another set labeled "long-run" is usually artificial. Time does not stop arbitrarily: the short period merges into the long period, and short-run problems have their long-term implications. Our study of development is thus significant in having general relevance to the larger area of economic phenomena.[18]

3. How Can Economic Development Be Understood?

We have already seen in broad outline that we want to analyze how and why there may be a sustained increase in a country's real national income. It is commonly stated that the level of national output at any given time is determined by the supply of resources, available techniques, the organization of markets, the institutional framework of economic life, and the psychological attributes of the population. But this is only a starting point. These "empty boxes" must be filled. Even then, they are only the immediate determinants of real national income; there are other factors underlying these proximate determinants. These too deserve attention. And there remains the much more important task of understanding the causal connections between these determinants and national income not only at a given moment but also over a period of time.

One basic issue is the extent to which we can explain development only in economic terms. It is clear that a full interpretation of development requires considerations of non-economic factors. An economy is not a mechanical system. And economic forces do not operate as "natural forces"; they must be considered within a sociocultural matrix. This is particularly true for problems of development in which political, sociological, and psychological factors are highly relevant. The type of government, the legal system, the standards of education and health, the role of family, the role of religion—all these influence a country's development. Even though there is much to be said in primarily economic terms, we should also become aware of the questions regarding development that we wish to ask of other disciplines and the aspects of development that might be explored further in non-economic terms.

But how can we best begin to understand the economic aspects of the nature, causes, and problems of development? If, as some maintain, economic development includes all economic history and economic theory, is not the scope too overpowering and the materials too varied to allow the discovery of any unity?

Fortunately, there is a source of consolation. If we interpret develop-

---

[18] Cf. Alfred Marshall, "Mechanical and Biological Analogies in Economics," in *Memorials of Alfred Marshall* (A. C. Pigou, ed.), Macmillan and Co., Ltd., London, 1925, 312–318.

ment as a process, then various materials begin to fall into place, and some common elements appear. For to view development as a process is to examine it as a form of progressive action, a working-out of certain principal forces that lead to certain results. There is much structure or "logic" in economic development. This may furnish a general framework of analysis within which to fit individual case studies of development, and thus assess the significance of particular events.

Our fundamental objective, therefore, is to get beneath the surface of particular events in order to make the process of development intelligible. We must try to understand the operation of the major forces determining development; we cannot merely describe the organization of an economy, or simply present a descriptive narrative of the movements in an economy's history. In other words, instead of being content with only the "story" of development, we must go beyond this and try to knit together the "plot" of development.

The distinction between a "story" and a "plot" has been aptly made by E. M. Forster in his discussion of the novel. Even though we are not students of the novel, nevertheless the relevance of the distinction is worth emphasizing for our study. A story, says Forster, is "a narrative of events arranged in their time-sequence. A plot is also a narrative of events, the emphasis falling on causality. 'The king died and then the queen died,' is a story. 'The king died, and then the queen died of grief' is a plot. The time-sequence is preserved, but the sense of causality overshadows it. Or again: 'The queen died, no one knew why, until it was discovered that it was through grief at the death of the king.' This is a plot with a mystery in it, a form capable of high development. It suspends the time-sequence, it moves as far away from the story as its limitations will allow. Consider the death of the queen. If it is in a story we say 'and then?' If it is in a plot we ask 'why?' That is the fundamental difference between these two aspects of the novel."[19]

It is also the fundamental difference between the two ways in which economic development can be examined. Just as a novel becomes more significant when it has a plot, so too does the study of economic development become more instructive when the emphasis falls on causality, rather than simple description. In examining the historical course of a country's development, we would not find it very rewarding merely to say "this happened" and then "that happened." We must try to understand why it happened. The course of development contains a plot, and we should try to discover the hidden interconnections.

We shall do well, therefore, to begin our study by attempting to estab-

[19] E. M. Forster, *Aspects of the Novel*, Edward Arnold and Co., London, 1949, 82–83.

lish some theoretical fundamentals. Without theory, no matter how voluminous are the facts we may have about a country's development, we shall be unable to make sense out of them. From a jumble of facts, we want to construct a sensible pattern. To do this we need a framework of analysis—a set of right questions to ask of the facts.

These questions have been considered by many famous economists— Adam Smith (1723–1790), David Ricardo (1772–1823), Karl Marx (1818–1883), Alfred Marshall (1842–1924), Joseph Schumpeter (1883–1950), and several contemporary economists. In Part 1, we shall become familiar with these theoretical contributions and incorporate their most significant elements into a broader discussion of the development process. We do not seek a single general theory of development; this is probably impossible. But we should like to focus on a number of theorems of general economic theory which are especially relevant to understanding economic development.

Having established a theoretical foundation, we may then acquire perspective by investigating in Part 2 some historical features of development. Here theory, by providing some dominant concepts and revealing some relationships, will help to orient us to the variety of data and will help to illuminate the historical facts. Past experience, in turn, will provide some test of the validity of the theory.

Against the theoretical and historical background, we may then examine systematically the problems of development that currently confront the poor countries (Part 3), and the rich countries (Part 4). And we may evaluate the various measures of public policy designed to meet these problems.

PART 1

Theories

of

Economic

Development

"*The store is rich and the steward is bounteous. So far from being an isolated study of abstract doctrines, political economy is treated from first to last as a branch of the study of mankind . . . . The laws of wealth unfold themselves like the incidents in a well-laid plot.*"

—FRANCIS W. HIRST

SINCE WE ARE ALL TOO MUCH AFFECTED by the times in which we live and are too prone to generalize from transitory circumstances, we are not likely to gain a clear understanding of economic development if we simply start with existing conditions and attempt to disentangle the major factors currently at work. A better approach might be to examine what the great thinkers of the past have contributed to the subject. Then we can attempt to determine in what respects they were right or wrong in the light of subsequent history.

In this manner, we can free ourselves, at least partially, from the confines of our own times. And, by sharpening our long-run perspective, we can better equip ourselves for an analysis of the diverse conditions of the present. From a careful survey of the major schools of thought on the causes, problems, and possibilities of development, we can better formulate our own views concerning development. By examining systems as a whole, we can study the various ideas about development within their historical milieu, and we can evaluate more easily the relevance of many traditional conclusions for present-day situations. Further, a more intelligent and more explicit basis for making policy judgments might also be gained. Ideas that have continued to live independently after the analysis upon which they were based has been destroyed can be exposed for what they are, and the solid reasons for differences in opinions about development possibilities can be brought into the open.

In this Part we shall examine and appraise the ideas on development of the five following major groups of theorists: (1) the classical economists, (2) the Marxists, (3) the neo-classical theorists, (4) Schumpeter, and (5) the post-Keynesians. Instead of presenting and contrasting the views of many various members within these groups, we shall examine intensively the analysis of only one or two leading representatives from each school. The writers selected for this detailed study are: Smith and Ricardo (the classical school); Marx; Marshall, Wicksell, and Cassel (the neo-classical school); Schumpeter; and Domar and Harrod (post-Keynesian school). This procedure enables us to analyze various models of economic development without becoming bogged down in many usually minor differences among the numerous writers within each school. The essential theoretical contributions of each group are what we want.

Having examined how these representatives investigate the problem, we shall then synthesize their various analyses of development. Thus, the final objective of this Part is to bring together in a systematic and integrated fashion the major theoretical conclusions about the nature and causes of development.

We may now begin our study of the theories of development by considering the views of the classical economists—in particular, the ideas of Smith and Ricardo.

Chapter 1

Classical

Analysis

Classical economists approach the study of economics with a bold and expansive outlook. They wish primarily to discover the causes of long-run growth in national income and the process by which this growth occurs. Problems such as how a nation allocates a given supply of productive resources among alternative uses or how individual consumers and business firms reach economic decisions—problems which neo-classical economists later studied in detail—are not of much interest to classical economists. For them, these are secondary matters; their main topic is economic development.

The causal importance of component parts of the economy in the development process seems to determine the degree of disaggregation in the classical model. For example, classical writers divide the national income into only three parts (wages, rent, and profits) because they believe that the relations among these shares significantly affect development. They consider a finer breakdown to be unnecessary for adequately understanding the development process. On similar grounds they separate the national output into agricultural and manufactured commodities. In addition, they not only discuss mainly those policy issues which they believe particularly affect development, but also they judge these policies by the criterion of whether they help or hinder development.

The classical analysis of development may be best understood by studying the thought of Adam Smith and David Ricardo. In terms of fashioning an ordered and elegant model of economic activity, the most outstanding figure among classical writers is Ricardo, whose brilliant analysis long dominated English economics. However, although Ricardo is the most analytically accomplished of these writers, undoubtedly Smith is the most famous.

1. Adam Smith

Smith's *An Inquiry into the Nature and Causes of the Wealth of Nations* (1776)[1] ranks as one of the best-known books on economics. In popular discussion, he is identified with the policy of "laissez-faire." Moreover, his influence in economic theory is tremendous. In a sense, even much of Ricardo's theory of development can be regarded as merely an attempt to formulate in a rigorous fashion relationships that Smith saw but failed (perhaps intentionally) to state explicitly.

Because Smith's work is more of a rough summary of economic ideas than a well-reasoned piece of economic analysis, he is not examined in as great detail as Ricardo. For the desired emphasis here is on theorists who present well-defined theories of development. Yet, this should not be interpreted to mean that Smith does not contribute greatly to a better understanding of the development process.[2] Some of his major contributions will be studied presently.

Although his formal analysis is confusing and rambling, a strong and recurring policy theme runs throughout the work—a condemnation of governmental or private actions tending to hinder free, atomistic competition within the economy. In this view, Smith is influenced by the widely held, eighteenth-century doctrine of natural law. In brief, this doctrine asserts that "there is a set of rules of right or justice, and perhaps even of morality in general, which are, or may be, known by all men by the help either of 'reason' or of a moral sense, and which possess an authority superior to that of such commands of human sovereigns, and such customary legal and moral regulations, as may contravene them."[3] Smith extends this concept to economics. In

---

[1] Adam Smith, *An Inquiry into the Nature and Causes of the Wealth of Nations*, ed. Edwin Cannan, The Modern Library, Random House, New York, 1937.

[2] See especially his historical analysis, *ibid.*, Book III.

[3] O. H. Taylor, *Economics and Liberalism, Collected Papers*, Harvard University Press, Cambridge, 1955, 73.

effect he argues that "Nature" arranges matters so that the just legal system which she prescribes is also the best means of promoting development. For Smith, the just legal system, which Nature prescribes, involves in essence the protection of every man's right to pursue his own interests free from oppression by other members, yet within the limits imposed by the necessity of giving similar protection to every other member of society. Special advantages and restraints in the economic world, he contends, conflict with this system of natural liberty and tend to retard national growth. Instead, if each member of society is free to pursue his self-interests (subject to the controls of the "natural" legal system), a harmonious, beneficial economic order will result. Smith's famous "invisible hand"—the operation of a perfectly competitive market structure—ensures this goal.

But exactly how does economic progress take place in this world of enlightened self-interest? Smith gives credit to the principle of the "division of labor" for increases in the productive powers of labor. Greater division of labor and specialization lead (1) to an increase in dexterity among workers; (2) to a reduction in the time necessary to produce commodities; and (3) to the invention of better machines and equipment. The last source of greater efficiency stems both from those working directly with existing equipment and from those devoting their efforts to more abstract research—an occupation that in itself is the result of previous divisions of labor.

The principle that first occasions the division of labor is a natural propensity among men "to truck, barter, and exchange one thing for another."[4] This is Smith's rather awkward way of asserting that it is self-interest that leads to exchange and thus to the division of labor. Before, however, division of labor can occur (or, at any rate, proceed very far—Smith is not exactly clear on this point) capital accumulation is necessary. Consequently, he strongly emphasizes that saving is a necessary condition for economic development. "Every increase or diminution of capital, therefore, naturally tends to increase or diminish the real quantity of industry, the number of productive hands, and consequently the exchangeable value of the annual produce of the land and labour of the country, the real wealth and revenue of all its inhabitants."[5] Furthermore, "Capitals are increased by parsimony, and diminished by prodigality and misconduct."[5]

Smith stresses another limitation to the division of labor, namely, the "extent of the market." As he says, "When the market is very small, no person can have any encouragement to dedicate himself

[4] Smith, op. cit., 13.
[5] Ibid., 321.

entirely to one employment, for want of the power to exchange all that surplus part of the produce of his own labour, which is over and above his own consumption, for such parts of the produce of other men's labour as he has occasion for."[6]   He is making the obvious but important point that, although the division of labor can increase labor's productivity in a physical sense, this division may not be profitable unless market demand is sufficiently large.   The expansion of international trade is especially beneficial in this respect.   Speaking of the discovery of America, he notes, "By opening a new and inexhaustible market to all the commodities of Europe, it gave occasion to new divisions of labour and improvements of art, which, in the narrow circle of the ancient commerce, could never have taken place for want of a market to take off the greater part of their produce.   The productive powers of labour were improved, and its produce increased in all the different countries of Europe, and together with it the real revenue and wealth of the inhabitants."[7]   He clearly appreciates the role that trade was playing in the development of Britain—a point that is emphasized in Part 2.

According to Smith, once development starts, it tends to become cumulative.   First, given adequate market possibilities and the basis for capital accumulation, division of labor takes place and raises the level of productivity.   The resultant increase in national income and the probable growth of population associated with the rise in income not only increase the extent of the market but permit a larger saving out of the increased income stream.   Moreover, as labor becomes more specialized and markets expand, the ability and incentive to introduce "improvements of art" increase.   These improvements lead to still further specialization and productivity gains.

In this view of the development process, Smith recognizes in a general way the significance of external economies[8]—a concept stressed later by neo-classical writers.[9]   The concept of external economies refers to a situation in which the cost curves of individual firms shift downwards because of the historical development of their environments.[10]   For example, an increase in the size of an industry may attract a more efficient labor force and thereby bring benefits to all

[6] *Ibid.,* 17.

[7] *Ibid.,* 416.

[8] For example, see his discussion on "Effects of the Progress of Improvement upon the Real Price of Manufactures," *ibid.,* 242–247.

[9] Cf. Chapter 3, section 3.

[10] Of course, external diseconomies are also possible.   The term "external" is used because the factors causing the economies are beyond the direct control of an individual firm.

firms in the industry. Or the growth of transportation facilities in a particular area may lead to a lowering of costs for firms using the services of the transportation industry. The notion of external economies recognizes the interdependence and complementarity of various sectors of the economy. As one part grows, it stimulates other parts not only by increasing demands but also by decreasing costs. These repercussions, in turn, induce additional expansion in the sectors where the initial stimulation occurred.

Although Smith emphasizes the cumulative nature of development, he asserts that there are limits to expansion possibilities. The explanation of this conclusion requires a discussion of his theory of income distribution.

Consider first his theory of wage determination. There is unfortunately no one clear and consistent theory of wages in *The Wealth of Nations*. Smith first states that wages depend upon the relative bargaining strengths of the workers and capitalists. Since he believes that employers have all the advantage, he maintains that wages tend to be driven to the subsistence level for workers and their families. For periods when capital accumulation is proceeding at a rapid rate, however, he modifies this conclusion. During these periods capitalists compete more vigorously for employees, and wages tend to rise. But there is a check to upward movements in wages. "If this demand [for labor] is continually increasing, the reward of labour must necessarily encourage in such a manner the marriage and multiplication of labourers, as may enable them to supply that continually increasing demand by a continually increasing population. If the reward should at any time be less than what was requisite for this purpose, the deficiency of hands would soon raise it; and if it should at any time be more, their excessive multiplication would soon lower it to this necessary rate."[11] In other words, his view is that, under stationary conditions, wage rates fall to the subsistence level whereas, in periods of rapid capital accumulation, they rise above this level. The extent to which they rise depends both upon the rate of accumulation and upon the rate of population growth.

What happens to profits—the return to capital—during the development process? Like Ricardo (but for a different reason) Smith asserts, "The increase of stock, which raises wages, tends to lower profit."[12] But his reason is an unconvincing one. "When the stocks of many rich merchants are turned into the same trade, their mutual competition naturally tends to lower its profit; and when there is a

[11] Smith, *op. cit.*, 80.
[12] *Ibid.*, 87.

like increase of stock in all the different trades carried on in the same society, the same competition must produce the same effect in them all." As Ricardo observes, the last part of this statement need not follow from the first part.[13]

Starting from a recently settled region, rich in natural resources, Smith visualizes the relation between the profit rate and wage rates as behaving in the following manner as development proceeds. First, because the capital stock is small in relation to resource opportunities, the rate of profit is high. Furthermore, because the rate of capital accumulation is high, wage rates also are relatively high. But, as more and more capital is accumulated, the rate of profit falls. So long as the rate of accumulation is maintained, however, wage rates tend to remain high. Finally, as the population grows, and the capital stock becomes very large, the economy attains "that full complement of riches which the nature of its soil and climate, and its situation with respect to other countries, allowed it to acquire."[14] When the economy approaches this stage, the rate of accumulation slackens, and, therefore, wages decline. A stationary state is reached. At this point, the process of capital accumulation—and therefore development—ceases.

At the stationary state position, Smith contends that rents are much larger than when the economy is passing through its earlier, more vigorous stages. His analysis of rent, however, is unusually obscure. In general, he regards this return as due to a monopoly in land. Exactly why, however, rent increases as a society progresses is not clear in Smith. He more or less takes it as a self-evident proposition that, when the national product increases, the landlord is bound to benefit.

As the economy moves towards the stationary state, the sequence of development by industry which he believes to be "according to the natural course of things"[15] is first, agriculture, then manufactures, and finally, commerce.

Although Smith's reasoning concerning the pattern of development lacks the rigor of later writers, such as Ricardo, his conclusions about the process and prospects for development do have a profound influence on subsequent writers. His emphasis on the importance of capital accumulation in the development process is a fundamental element in later development theories. Moreover, his outline of the stationary state in which the rate of profit is low, in which wages per worker are near the subsistence level, and in which rents are high

[13] P. Sraffa (ed.), *The Works and Correspondence of David Ricardo,* Cambridge University Press, Cambridge, 1951, I, 289–290.

[14] Smith, *op. cit.,* 94.

[15] *Ibid.,* 360.

dominates the thinking of classical writers. Similarly, his view that the real prices of manufactured commodities tend to fall and the real prices of some types of agricultural products tend to rise during the process of development influences classical thinking for many years. And his condemnation of governmental interference in the development process also sets the pattern for much of the later discussion on the subject. Finally, his conception of economic development as a gradual, self-perpetuating (within limits) process is a view that is adopted by most of the later classical and neo-classical economists.

2. Ricardo's Framework

As mentioned, Ricardo, a one-time stockbroker, a gentleman farmer, and a member of Parliament, is the first economist to weave classical doctrine into a consistent body of economic analysis. Drawing heavily on Adam Smith's famous work, he refines and extends the classical theory of development. The rest of this chapter examines this system as an illustration of the major stream of classical thinking about the development process. But, unfortunately, Ricardo, like Smith, does not present his views in a very clear or orderly manner. Essential parts of the analysis are scattered rather haphazardly throughout his book, *The Principles of Political Economy and Taxation* (1817), and among his many letters to other economists. Consequently, to obtain a general view of his system, the rest of this chapter brings together the various parts of Ricardo's writings and interprets the manner in which they fit together. Before proceeding to details of Ricardo's analysis, it is useful to outline the main concepts and relationships in the Ricardian system.

It should first be noted that Ricardo considers agriculture the most important sector of the economy. The difficulty of providing food for an expanding population serves as the focal point for his entire analysis. Ricardo and even later classical writers, such as John Stuart Mill, do not appreciate fully the important role that technological progress can play in increasing productivity in agriculture, thereby lessening the difficulty of feeding a growing population.

In Ricardo's vision of economic society, there are three major groups of actors on the economic scene: capitalists, laborers, and landlords. The capitalists—those who direct the production of goods and services—play the key role in the economy. In undertaking production, they rent land from the landlords, provide the laborers with tools and other implements of production (fixed capital), and advance as wages the food, clothing, and other commodities (circulating capital) consumed by the workers during the production period. Capitalists perform two significant functions. First, by continually searching for the most profitable employment opportunities for their capital, they tend to equalize the rates of profit on capital among the various branches of manufacturing and agriculture (with due allowances for differences in risk and uncertainty among various businesses). This action tends to bring about an efficient allocation of resources at any particular period of time. The second function is even more important than the first: capitalists initiate the process of economic development. They reinvest their income—profits—and thus further the accumulation of capital. And capital accumulation is, as will be seen later, the spark setting off a series of reactions which result in the growth of national income.

Labor is numerically the largest of the three groups. This group is entirely dependent upon the capitalists for employment, since labor does not own any of the implements necessary for production. The wage rate for any year is simply the total amount of funds that capitalists advance to the workers for their maintenance during the year, i.e., the wages fund, divided by the number of workers (assuming, for simplicity, that the wages fund turns over only once annually, and that labor is measured in terms of a common level of skill).

The laboring population regulates its own numbers by the quantity of necessities and conveniences that the laborers can purchase with their wages. There is a certain real wage, fixed by custom and habit, at which the laborers just perpetuate themselves without either an increase or a diminution. Above this figure they multiply rapidly, and below it they decrease in numbers. Ricardo concedes that this "natural" real wage varies over time and among countries, but he does not present an explanation of its change. At the time at which he wrote he clearly believed that the "natural" real wage in England was at a level where the "moderate comforts"[16] that it afforded consisted almost entirely of basic foodstuffs and a minimum of clothing and shelter. For this law of population Ricardo is indebted to Malthus who sets it forth so effectively in his *Essay on the Principle of Population* (1798).

In the progress of society, by means of an expansion in population and an accumulation of capital, there arises, according to Ricardo, an increasing scarcity of the most fertile types of land. In meeting the larger demand for food, the successive employment of equal units of labor and capital on poorer grades of land (together with the more intensive use of labor and capital on better grades of land) brings diminishing returns in terms of agricultural output. As poorer lands are brought under cultivation, and diminishing returns occur, competi-

<hr />

[16] Sraffa (ed.), *op. cit.,* I, 94.

tion among the capitalists for the better grades of land causes a portion of the produce of the land to be transferred to the landlords—those who own the land. This return is "rent," or "that portion of the produce of the earth, which is paid to the landlord for the use of the original and indestructible powers of the soil."[17] It arises in the competitive process whereby the profit rates earned from a unit of labor and capital employed on the various qualities of land are equalized.

Such, in brief, is Ricardo's over-all view of the major groups in the economic system. Other classical economists view the economy in a similar manner. They divide the national income into three parts— wages, rent, and profits—and attempt to discover the way in which the relative income shares of labor, capitalists, and landlords vary in the development process. It should be noticed, however, that they study the *relative,* not the *absolute,* shares of these groups. Ricardo justifies this procedure in a letter to Malthus: "No law can be laid down respecting quantity, but a tolerably correct one can be laid down respecting proportions. Every day I am more satisfied that the former enquiry is vain and delusive, and the latter only the true objects of the science."[18] In other words, Ricardo contends that he can reach conclusions regarding the rate of growth in national income (or product) by studying the behavior of relative income shares. However, his analysis of the behavior of relative income shares or "proportions" relates to a rather special meaning of these terms. He does not set forth "laws" concerning the relation of total wages, total profits, and total rent to the nation's total income (or output); instead his "laws" apply to the behavior of the rent, the wages, and the profits (in real or money terms) earned from any unit of labor and capital in relation to the output or income produced by this unit of labor and capital, as national income grows.

The most useful way of looking at Ricardo's (and the other classical writers') vision of the development process might be to consider their distinction between gross and net revenue. Ricardo defines "gross revenue" as the market value of the final commodities produced during a particular time period. The difference between this and the value of the commodities needed to just sustain the labor force that produces this output (and, presumably, the value of commodities necessary to maintain the fixed capital stock) is termed the "net revenue" of the society. This is the highly important concept of the economic surplus which is available for the further growth of output. Unless it exists, no progress is possible. According to the classical vision, because labor in

[17] *Ibid.,* 67.
[18] *Ibid.,* VIII, 278–279.

conjunction with natural resources and fixed capital does produce a surplus over and above what is required to maintain the labor force, economic development is feasible. Profits, rents, and even wages, to the extent that they exceed subsistence, constitute the net revenue of the economy. But only if the net revenue is employed for further capital accumulation does development occur. This is why the capitalist class is so important, since neither the laborers nor the landlords save. By saving and increasing the wages fund, the capitalists set in motion the sequence of events that eventually raises the level of output. Yet, according to Ricardo, because of the niggardliness of nature, the process of development shifts the relative shares of the various economic groups in such a way that the portion of net revenue from which accumulation stems—profits—is eventually reduced to an insignificant level. Then further growth ceases.

Additional attention should be given to a more detailed investigation and appraisal of what Ricardo believed to be the principles of income distribution which characterize the development process. Before doing this, however, a few additional assumptions and analytical tools, which Ricardo uses, should be recognized.

3. Ricardian Assumptions and Analytical Tools

At the very beginning, before he can present an integrated theory, Ricardo faces a major obstacle. To James Mill he writes, "I know I shall soon be stopped by the word price, and then I must apply to you for advice and assistance."[19] At this point, Ricardo recognizes that for a complete analysis he must be able to compare exchange relationships among the many commodities in an economy. Accordingly, he employs the labor theory of value suggested earlier by Smith.[20] This theory states that the ratios at which reproducible commodities exchange for each other, in the long run and in a purely competitive market, depend upon the comparative quantities of labor expended in producing them. Ricardo recognizes that this theory is not completely satisfactory. First, there is the problem of comparing labor categories that differ in terms of skill, training, etc. Second, variations in the durability of fixed and circulating capital employed in different lines of production as well as different ratios of fixed to circulating capital in different

[19] *Ibid.*, VI, 348.

[20] One can, perhaps somewhat charitably, interpret Ricardo's theory of price determination to be a cost of production theory. See George J. Stigler, "The Ricardian Theory of Value and Distribution," *Journal of Political Economy, LX,* No. 3, 201 (June 1952); see, however, Sraffa (ed.), *op. cit.,* I, xxxvii–xl. Also see J. A. Schumpeter, *History of Economic Analysis,* Oxford University Press, New York, 1954, 594–595.

lines of production cause inescapable difficulties for the theory. Ricardo is fully aware of these difficulties, and he admits that the labor theory is "not rigidly true."[21] Yet, "I say that it is the nearest approximation to the truth, as a rule for measuring relative value, of any I have ever heard." Accordingly, except in the first chapter of his book, Ricardo seldom qualifies his analysis of price determination and reasons as though the labor theory of value is adequate to explain changes in relative prices during the development process.

Nevertheless, in spite of the difficulties associated with its use, the labor theory of value does provide Ricardo with a theory by which he can compare the exchange relationships among commodities that are physically dissimilar. Now, in practice each commodity is not compared directly with every other commodity; instead, the exchange relationships among commodities are related by comparing each commodity with some common standard of value, that is, money. Ricardo, of course, follows this procedure and uses money prices, gold being the standard of value. But, in examining long-run price variations, he wishes to emphasize those changes in commodity prices that are caused by changes in the real production conditions of the commodities themselves. If the quantity of money in circulation increases, but the output of all commodities remains the same, then the money prices of all these commodities will increase.[22] Yet, the real conditions of production, that is, the amounts of labor needed to produce each commodity, are unchanged for these commodities. To express the prices of commodities in money terms while avoiding as much as possible this type of money price change, Ricardo adopts the following convention. As the economy develops and national output grows, the money prices of those commodities whose labor requirements per unit of the commodity remain the same are assumed to remain constant. Money prices of items requiring more or less labor to produce a unit of the commodity are assumed to increase or decrease proportionately to the change in their labor requirements. The money supply is assumed to adjust itself to the flow of commodities in order to satisfy these conditions.

Another important assumption in the Ricardian theory of value and production is that there is no factor substitution. Fixed coefficients of production in each line of production are assumed. Within a given state of knowledge, there is only one ratio of labor to fixed capital that is technologically feasible for the production of any particular manufactured commodity. If wage rates rise relative to the prices of fixed capital goods, a capitalist cannot lower his production costs by substituting

[21] Sraffa (ed.), *op. cit.*, VIII, 279.
[22] Assuming, of course, that the additional money is not merely hoarded.

capital for labor; there is only one method of production possible. Furthermore, given a certain quantity of the correct proportion of labor to fixed capital, the classical theory of production assumes that a doubling or tripling of this quantity doubles or triples the output of the particular manufactured commodity. Ricardo does not discuss the determinants of the size of any particular firm. It must therefore be assumed that this information is given or is determined on non-economic grounds.

The situation is similar in agriculture. Only one proportion of labor and fixed capital can be used in producing a particular commodity. Unlike manufacturing, however, agriculture is not subject to constant returns as output expands, but rather diminishing returns. This is because both the total quantity of land and the quantities of land of various degrees of fertility are limited. Although this factor is not important for the manufacturing sector (Ricardo ignores the land requirements of manufacturing industries), it is extremely significant for agriculture. In the Ricardian system, when the total amount of labor and fixed capital employed in agriculture is doubled, it is impossible also to double the quantity of land of the same fertility as that already in use. To expand agricultural output, farmers either must utilize poorer grades of land or they must cultivate more intensively land already in use. In either case, diminishing returns are encountered. Moreover, in agricultural production as in manufacturing, the question of the size of any single farm is not studied by Ricardo, and it must be assumed as given.

It also should be noted that there is no problem of a general glut of commodities in the Ricardian model.[23] Income paid out in the productive process as wages, rent, and profits is completely respent by the income recipients in purchasing commodities. More specifically, in his formal model Ricardo visualizes both the workers and landlords as spending their entire income on consumption commodities. Only capitalists save. And what they save, they also invest. In modern terminology, intended saving always equals intended investment, and consequently, there is never a deficiency of effective demand.

4. The Landlord's Share and Agricultural Prices

Having met the question of price—if only to turn aside the difficulties inherent in the labor theory of value—Ricardo proceeds with a general theory of the behavior of rent, wages, and profits during the development process. As mentioned before, rent is the payment to the landlord which equalizes the profit rate among capitalists in the employ-

---

[23] Malthus did not agree with Ricardo's analysis of this question. See Sraffa (ed.), *op. cit.*, IX, 9–11 and the letters between Ricardo and Malthus which follow.

ment of equal units of labor and capital on lands of different qualities. Imagine that a certain amount of labor and capital used in cultivating an acre of a particular grade of land yields 100 bushels of wheat, whereas the same amount of labor and capital on a less fertile or less favorably situated acre produces only 90 bushels. If these are the only grades of land in use, perfect competition among the many capitalists and landlords creates a rent equal to 10 bushels of wheat for a unit of labor and capital employed on the better land. For, if the owners of this land do not charge any rent, capitalists working the poorer land offer to pay up to 10 bushels as rent in order to improve their position. No more than 10 bushels is paid as rent, however. This follows from the assumption that it is unnecessary to employ the entire supply of the second grade of land in order to furnish the food required by the community. No price, therefore, is paid for the use of this land; it is free. If an owner of the first grade of land charges any capitalist using his land more than 10 bushels per acre, the capitalist moves to the free, second-quality land. Therefore, there is a rent of 10 bushels per acre on the best land, and no rent on the poor land. The amount received by a unit of labor and capital on either land is 90 bushels.

If the population and capital of the nation expand, and a third grade of land, even poorer than the second, must be brought under cultivation, rent rises on the first grade of land and comes into existence on the second grade. A yield of 80 bushels per acre for a unit of labor and capital on the third grade of land increases rent on the best land to 20 bushels and gives rise to a rent of 10 bushels on the second grade of land.

With the increase in population and the accumulation of capital, capitalists also employ more units of labor and capital on the better grades of land. There are, however, diminishing returns in this activity too. Suppose a second and third unit of labor and capital on an acre of the first grade of land yields 90 and 80 bushels of wheat, respectively, and a second application of a unit of labor and capital on an acre of the second grade returns 80 bushels. If all the labor and capital is employed in this manner, rent on the first type of land is $(100 - 80) + (90 - 80)$ or 30 bushels, and on the second grade $(90 - 80)$ or 10 bushels. As explained before, there is no rent on the poorest grade of land, that is, the marginal land, since it is assumed that its supply is greater than the demand for its use.

Thus, growth in population and the capital stock causes an increase in the absolute amount of rent in terms of agricultural output. The proportion that this rent bears to the output of any unit of labor and capital previously employed increases. But the proportion of commodity rent to the total output of the community could increase or decrease, depending upon the manner in which diminishing returns occur.[24]

Because Ricardo assumes that successive applications of units of labor and capital each yield the same output in manufacturing, there is no differential surplus among units of labor and capital employed here, and hence no rent. As society progresses and the production of all goods increases, the prices of agricultural commodities rise in terms of manufactured commodities. A greater amount of labor is required to produce the additional units of agricultural commodities—that is, diminishing returns occur—whereas the production of the additional manufactured commodities still require only the same amount of labor.

Suppose, for example, that the least productive unit of labor and capital yields 50 bushels of wheat per acre. The price of this wheat in the long run must be sufficient to cover the wages of the labor and the profits on the capital that are employed in this production, or else the labor and capital would not have been employed here. Say the price is $2.00 per bushel. Since the output of this unit of labor and capital is 50 bushels, the value of the output is $100. Suppose, also, that an equal unit of labor and capital employed in shoe production, for example, yields 10 pairs of shoes at a price of $10 per pair. Since the outputs of equal amounts of labor and capital sell for identical sums (in this case, $100), 5 bushels of wheat will exchange for 1 pair of

[24] *Ibid.*, II, 193. For example, the output of a unit of labor and capital on the best grade of land in the above illustration is assumed to be 100 bushels. When only two grades of land are employed, the rent on this unit of labor and capital is 10 bushels or 10 per cent of its total product. When three grades of land are used, the rent rises to 20 or 20 per cent of its total product. Thus, the proportion that rent bears to the output of this unit of labor and capital increases. Now consider the relation between the total rent on all units of labor and capital and the total output of these units. In the stage where two grades of land and two units of labor and capital (one on each grade) are used, total rent is 10 bushels and total output is 100 + 90 or 190. The total rent at this stage is equal to $10\!/\!190$ or 5.3 per cent of total output. At the stage in which three grades of land and three units of labor and capital are employed, as was assumed, total rent becomes 20 + 10 or 30 and total output is 100 + 90 + 80 or 270. Rents, therefore, equal $30\!/\!270$ or 11.1 per cent of the total output. As a little experimentation will show, however, it would also be possible to pick the second set of numbers so that the proportion that total rent bears to total output declines. For example, assume that the units of labor and capital on the first and second grades of land still produce 100 and 90 bushels, respectively, but the unit of labor and capital on the third grade yields 89 bushels. Now, at this stage, total rent is 11 + 1 or 12 bushels. Total output is 100 + 90 + 89 or 279 bushels. Therefore, total rent equals only 4.3 per cent of total output. However, the proportion that the rent on the first unit of labor and capital bears to the output of this unit still increases in this second stage —from 10 per cent to 11 per cent.

shoes—that is, 50 bushels of wheat/10 pairs of shoes = 5 bushels of wheat for 1 pair of shoes.

With a growth in population and a further accumulation of capital more wheat and shoes are required. If, after the increase, the least productive unit of labor and capital produces only 40 bushels of wheat, whereas each of the additional units employed in shoe manufacturing still produces 10 pairs of shoes, the price of wheat in terms of shoes rises. Only 4 bushels of wheat (40 bushels of wheat/10 pairs of shoes) exchange for 1 pair of shoes. Ricardo expresses this relationship in money terms by keeping the price of shoes constant and increasing the money price of wheat. Formerly, shoes cost $10 per pair, and wheat $2.00 per bushel. After the expansion of production shoes still sell for $10 per pair, but the wheat sells for $2.50 per bushel, since 1¼ units of labor and capital (50 bushels/40 bushels) will now be necessary to produce the same amount of wheat as the formerly least productive unit.

Before the growth in population and capital accumulation, there is no rent on the last unit of labor and capital employed in agriculture. But, after the increase in population and the capital accumulation, a rent of 10 bushels—the difference between 50 and 40 bushels, or $25 in money terms (10 bushels × $2.50 per bushel)—arises on the unit of labor and capital that previously had been the least productive one. So, although the value of the output from the formerly least productive unit of labor and capital rises from $100 (50 bushels × $2.00 per bushel) to $125 (50 bushels × $2.50 per bushel), the increase in rent absorbs this increase in value.

As Ricardo points out, productive improvements in agriculture can thwart temporarily the rise of rent in both money and commodity terms—that is, before any population increase stimulated by the inventions. He distinguishes between two kinds of agricultural improvements. First, there are improvements that are land-saving in the sense that less land is necessary to produce the quantity of agricultural commodities consumed before the invention. But second, some inventions, although they increase labor's productivity as in the first case, i.e., are labor-saving, are not land-saving.[25] The same amount of land must be cultivated to

---

[25] Inventions can be classified in several ways. Mrs. Robinson's definition of labor, capital, and land-saving or using inventions turns on whether the invention reduces or increases the quantity of the factor required to produce a given rate of output. Joan Robinson, *The Rate of Interest and Other Essays,* Macmillan and Co., Ltd., London, 1952, 42, 50. A neutral invention under her classification is one that reduces labor, capital, and land per unit of output in the same proportion. Mr. Harrod defines a neutral invention as one that, at a constant rate of interest, does not change the ratio of the value of capital in use to income per period (the quantity of capital per unit of output, i.e., the capital coefficient, re-

produce the same volume of output. Ricardo contends that initially the first category of improvements lowers money rent and also rent in terms of agricultural produce. The second type, however, lowers money rent but it may not diminish rent measured in terms of agricultural output. Unfortunately, Ricardo's analysis of these effects is not very satisfactory. His conclusions regarding land-saving improvements depend on rather special assumptions,[26] whereas his statements concerning the other type of improvements, although theoretically possible, are not established by the arithmetic example he presents.[27] Nevertheless, he appreciates the significance of the factor-saving effect of innovations for the development process. J. S. Mill, who also uses Ricardo's twofold division of agricultural improvements, points in particular to the growth stimulus provided by the land-saving improvements of the late eighteenth century.[28] Ricardo contends, however, that in the long run the flow of improvements will not be sufficiently rapid to counteract the opposite tendency brought about by the growth of population and further accumulation of capital. Hence, in his system rents and the prices of agricultural commodities tend to increase over the long run.

5. Behavior of Rent, Wages, and Profits:
The Stationary State

This ingenious theory of rent enables Ricardo to concentrate attention on the remaining part of the national income, namely, that portion di-

---

mains constant). If the stream of inventions requires capital to increase at a rate greater than the rate of increase of income engendered by it (the capital coefficient increases), it is labor-saving; and if it requires capital to increase at a rate less than the rate of increase of income engendered by it (the capital coefficient falls), it is capital-saving. R. F. Harrod, *Towards a Dynamic Economics,* Macmillan and Co., Ltd., London, 1948, 26–27.

Hicks defines a neutral invention as one that raises the marginal productivity of labor and capital in the same proportion, a labor-saving invention as one that raises the marginal productivity of capital more than that of labor, and a capital-saving invention as one which raises the marginal productivity of capital less than that of labor, the amounts of the factors being unchanged. J. R. Hicks, *Theory of Wages,* Peter Smith, New York, 1948, 121–127.

[26] See the discussions by E. C. K. Gonner in his edition of Ricardo's *Principles,* George Bell and Sons, London, 1903, Appendix B, and by A. Marshall, *Principles of Economics,* eighth edition, Macmillan and Co., Ltd., London, 1930, Appendix L.

[27] E. Cannan, *A History of the Theories of Production and Distribution in English Political Economy from 1776 to 1848,* third edition, P. S. King and Sons, Ltd., London, 1924, 329.

[28] J. S. Mill, *Principles of Political Economy,* ed. by W. J. Ashley, Longmans, Green and Co., London, 1940, 183.

vided between wages and profits. In studying the income obtained by
workers and capitalists, Ricardo is concerned with the *relative* share
of the output produced by a unit of labor and capital which labor and
capital each receives. Consequently, whenever he refers to rising wages
and falling profits (without any qualifications) he simply means that
wages rise relatively to profits, not that absolute wages increase while
absolute profits fall. In determining the division of income between
labor and capital, wages play the active role. Profits "depend on high
or low wages, and on nothing else."[29] How are wages determined? As
previously mentioned, the "natural" price of labor is equal to the
money price that is necessary to enable the laborers to secure a subsistence real wage and thereby just perpetuate themselves. This implies
that, as the population grows, wage rates in money terms must rise. For
one of the principal items consumed by labor, namely, agricultural goods,
is subject to diminishing returns. The rate of profit therefore tends to
fall as population grows and capital accumulates.

This process takes place in the following manner. A rate of profit
above zero encourages capitalists to forgo consuming their entire income;
they save a portion of their income. They then use their savings to hire
additional workers in order to expand production. Capital accumulation is thus the fundamental force in the economy and sets in motion a
series of consequences. If the wage rate is assumed to be initially at its
"natural" price, the addition of the savings to the wages fund which
already exists for the purpose of hiring labor causes the wage rate to
be bid up above its "natural" price. For the wage rate is merely the
size of the wages fund divided by the number of workers. The laboring
groups spend their additional income partly on agricultural products
and partly on manufactured commodities. In any event, they spend
all of this additional income. Depending upon the former composition
of the national output, these expenditures by the workers may, through
price changes, stimulate the output of some commodities and curtail
the production of others.

Gradually, however, the population demon takes over. Since the
workers are receiving more than their "natural" wage, they increase in
numbers. In their budgets, parents substitute the food necessary to
feed their additional children for the comparative luxuries that they have
been enjoying. There is a shift in production towards more agricultural
commodities.

Assuming the wages fund does not become any larger through further

[29] Sraffa (ed.), *op. cit.,* II, 252.

capital accumulation, the eventual entrance of these children into the labor market decreases the wage rate.[30]

The population is unable, however, permanently to increase sufficiently to return the money wage rate to its former level. The enlarged demand for food can be supplied only at increased costs. Consequently, because the price of food rises, the workers are forced to spend more on food to secure their customary standard of living. The larger absolute wages of the laborers are exhausted on the necessities of life before they can increase their numbers proportionately to the initial increase in the wages fund.

What is the relation between wages and profits when the repercussions from the initial increase in the wages fund work themselves out? The real wage rate returns to its customary, near-subsistence level. But, in money terms, the wage rate is higher because the prices of agricultural commodities—the major component of the customary real wage—are higher. This implies that the rate of profit is lower. Why? First, recall that money price changes in the Ricardian analysis reflect changes in real production conditions. If the money price of a commodity rises, it means this commodity requires more labor to produce a unit of the commodity. A general increase in all prices caused by a greater money supply is excluded from the analysis, since in this case the exchange ratios among commodities would not change at all.

Thus, although more manufactured goods are produced after the population has increased, the money prices of these goods do not increase because each additional unit is produced with the same labor and fixed capital requirement. The money wage rate, however, is higher in manufacturing as in agriculture, since competition equalizes the wage rate in all industries. The profit earned on any unit of labor and capital—or the rate of profit on the total amount of fixed and variable

---

[30] The employment of these workers is no problem in the Ricardian system. As long as they can secure profits, capitalists attempt to increase output. They hire as many workers as they can obtain with their wages fund. Competition among the workers lowers wages sufficiently so that all become employed. An exception to the full employment rule, however, exists if wages are inflexible. For example, if wage rates are already at the subsistence level and workers refuse to accept any lower wages, an increase in the labor force will simply increase unemployment. This kind of reasoning seems to be behind Ricardo's famous discussion of the effects caused by the introduction of new machinery. Mechanization, he argues, may be so capital-using that it causes not only a permanent decrease in labor's relative and even absolute share in national income—a point which is not disputed—but also long-run unemployment. This, however, could occur in his system only if wages are rigid. Even then the "redundant" labor tends to be reemployed, as he notes, by means of additional capital accumulation. But a rigid wage assumption does not agree with his previous analysis of wages.

capital employed—therefore falls. But, since both the wage rate and agricultural prices rise, why should the profit rate be lower in agriculture? Do not profits remain the same in agriculture? This view, however, ignores rent. As poorer lands are cultivated, and better lands are used more intensively in order to supply the additional food, the rent from any unit of labor and capital already in use on the land rises. Although the rise in agricultural prices increases the sales value of the output from any unit of labor and capital already employed in agriculture, rent also rises and absorbs this increase in the value of the output. The capitalist, therefore, is left with the same money sum to distribute between the labor and capital. But, since wages increase, this means that the profit rate falls.

These relations can be seen more clearly by referring to the numerical example already given on pages 32 and 33. In this example, the least productive unit of labor and capital, initially, yields 50 bushels of wheat at $2.00 per bushel—a total revenue of $100. After additional development, it is assumed that the least productive unit of labor and capital yields only 40 bushels of wheat. As explained, the price of wheat, therefore, rises to $2.50. Consequently, the capitalist employing the unit of labor and capital that produces 50 bushels of wheat sells it for 50 × $2.50 or $125. But, originally this capitalist pays no rent; now he pays a rent of 10 bushels (the difference between 50 and 40) or $25 in money terms. Consequently, his revenue available for wages and profits is still $100.

Suppose that subsistence wages for the labor in a composite unit of labor and fixed capital are 10 bushels of wheat in real terms. It was previously assumed that, before the additional accumulation, wages were at the subsistence level, and it was explained how they return to this level after the accumulation. Before the accumulation, therefore, the capitalist producing the 50 bushels of wheat pays $20 in wages (10 bushels × $2.00 per bushel). His profit is $80 or 40 bushels.[31] After the accumulation, however, his rent rises to $25 or 10 bushels and his wages to $25 (10 bushels × $2.50 per bushel). His profit on the unit of labor and capital, therefore, falls to $75.

In manufacturing, both before and after the accumulation, each unit of labor and capital produces 10 pairs of shoes at $10 per pair or a total revenue of $100. However, since competition equalizes wage rates in all industries, this capitalist's wage bill per unit of labor and capital rises from $20 to $25 after the increase in national output. Therefore, profits per unit of labor and capital also drop from $80 to $75. There

---

[31] For simplicity such items as the cost of raw materials are ignored.

is no rent in manufacturing because of the assumption of constant returns to scale.

One further point should be noted: it might be thought that, even though everyone cannot raise his money prices (since this would not change the real situation), one capitalist, or one industry, might raise prices at the expense of someone else in the economy. But such action would create unequal rates of profit among industries. Competition among capitalists to obtain the greatest rate of profit and employ all their capital would then drive this price back to the point where it reflected the common wage costs and profit return in all industries.

From the point of view of the whole economy, the process of capital accumulation and population growth increases aggregate wages. It may or may not increase aggregate profits. The amount of circulating and fixed capital is increased but the profit rate declines. How rapidly the profit rate falls in relation to the increase of capital determines whether aggregate profits decline. The ratio of aggregate wages to aggregate profits rises, however, since the ratio of wages to profits rises on each unit of labor and capital.

The effects from the accumulation of capital need not, of course, operate precisely as just described. Capital accumulation takes place continuously as long as the rate of profit is above some minimal level, and population continues to grow as long as the workers receive a real wage above their customary minimum. Ricardo grants that it is quite possible for the accumulation of capital to occur at a more rapid pace than the increase in population for a long period. In this case, wages would remain above their "natural" price. This is most likely to happen in newly settled regions where rents are comparatively low because fertile land is abundant and the return to labor and capital is comparatively high.

As Ricardo shows, technological improvements also mitigate the downward pressure on the rate of profit. In agriculture, by diminishing the amount of labor needed to grow a given amount of food, inventions tend to reduce the prices of these commodities. This enables a given population increase to take place without as great an increase in money wage rates as would otherwise be necessary. The rate of profit, therefore, does not fall as much with the given population increase. Manufacturing inventions also lower the prices of manufactures. To the extent that the workers consume these goods in their customary budgets, money wage rates do not rise as much when population increases a given amount.

Even though such exceptions are recognized by Ricardo, he nevertheless maintains that they are not sufficiently powerful to vitiate his

general principles of distribution. He contends that in mature economies the real wage rate hovers about the customary subsistence level.
Capital accumulation tends to raise both the real and money wage
rate, but the rise in the real wage is only temporary because the rapid
growth in population stimulated by this increase drives the real wage
back to its customary minimum. The money wage, however, continues to rise. Additional food can be obtained only by cultivating
less productive lands, and the price of food increases. Since food is
the main component of the workers' budget, the greater cost of the
subsistence income causes the money wage rate to increase. This, in
turn, squeezes the profit rate in agriculture and manufacturing. But
the lower profit rate curtails the rate of capital accumulation, for the
rate of accumulation depends on the rate of profit. In turn, the rate
of growth in national income declines. Finally, when the rate of
profit falls so low that it does not afford adequate compensation for the
trouble and risk involved in additional capital accumulation, the
economy becomes stationary. No further expansion of capital or
population occurs. Rents are high, the real wage rate is at its minimum,
and the profit rate is near zero. The stationary state arrives: capital
accumulation and population growth cease.

Such is Ricardo's analysis of the development of the whole economy
over a long period of time—an analysis of development shared, at
least in its essentials, by most classical economists. Regardless of its
limitations (which are discussed below), the Ricardian system must
be deemed an outstanding accomplishment in economic thought.

First, it asks the fundamental question, how do relative income
shares (in the sense explained) behave as development occurs? Second,
it views the economy in dynamic—not static—terms: the economy
is not taken to be frozen in a once-for-all position, but rather is considered to be ever-changing as it passes through time until the stationary
state emerges. Third, it focuses on the major variables of capital
accumulation, population, profits, wages, and rent.

In summary, the Ricardian system formulates certain interrelations
among capital, population, and output; on the basis of these relations,
it traces the course of rent, wages, and profits over time; and, finally,
it concludes with the celebrated forecast of the eventual advent of a
stationary state.

6. Policy Implications

What did Ricardo propose to do about the gloomy picture that
emerges from his analysis? Ricardo is influenced in his policy outlook, although not in his analysis of the economy, by the Utilitarians

of his time. He wishes to promote the Utilitarian objective of "the greatest good for the greatest number."

Some government policies, Ricardo argues, are definitely detrimental to this general goal. One such policy is tariffs. Given the assumption of international factor immobility, he shows how trading partners can increase their real incomes by each specializing upon those commodities in which they possess a comparative cost advantage in real terms. Later, J. S. Mill elaborates upon the question of how the trading gains are distributed among the various nations. Using the concept of the terms of trade, he explains the manner in which demand and supply conditions determine the equilibrium ratio of the exchange of one country's commodities for another's.[32] For Ricardo and others of the classical school, free trade enables the benefits of specialization and the division of labor to be reaped on an international basis. World income is raised by a more efficient utilization of resources. Moreover, the expansion of import and export markets by increasing income permits additional domestic accumulation and stimulates invention. In particular, Ricardo argues that the free importation of grains into Britain (in exchange for manufactures) alleviates the pressure on profits by keeping the prices of agricultural commodities, and thus wages, down.

Classical writers make a notable exception to the free trade case, however. This is the so-called "infant industry" argument. J. S. Mill writes, "The only case in which, on mere principles of political economy, protecting duties can be defensible, is when they are imposed temporarily (especially in a young and rising nation) in hopes of naturalizing a foreign industry, in itself perfectly suitable to the circumstances of the country. The superiority of one country over another in a branch of production often arises only from having begun it sooner. There may be no inherent advantage on one part, or disadvantage on the other, but only a present superiority of acquired skill and experience. . . . A protecting duty, continued for a reasonable time, might sometimes be

[32] The classical writers refer to the terms on which a nation trades by comparing the number of units of productive services of a foreign country whose product exchanges for the product of one unit of the productive services of the home country. Viner calls this measure of the terms of trade the double factoral trading terms. See J. Viner, *Studies in the Theory of International Trade,* Harper and Brothers, New York, 1937, 561. However, since these early writers frequently assume constant and historically stable costs in their analysis of international trade, they often use the commodity terms of trade, i.e., the ratio of export to import prices, as a shorthand representation of changes in this more fundamental concept. For an extensive discussion of the terms of trade and their significance for British economic development, see Chapter 11.

the least inconvenient mode in which the nation can tax itself for the support of such an experiment. But it is essential that the protection should be confined to cases in which there is good ground of assurance that the industry which it fosters will after a time be able to dispense with it; nor should the domestic producers ever be allowed to expect that it will be continued to them beyond the time necessary for a fair trial of what they are capable of accomplishing."[33]

One other feature of the classical analysis of international trade should be noted. In their formal model, classical writers assume that labor and capital are internationally immobile. They do so not because they believe there are no international movements of labor and capital but because they think labor and capital are relatively less mobile internationally than domestically. Ricardo's position on this matter is as follows: "Experience, however, shows, that the fancied or real insecurity of capital, . . . together with the natural disinclination which every man has to quit the country of his birth and connections . . . check the emigration of capital. These feelings . . . induce most men of property to be satisfied with a low rate of profits in their own country, rather than seek a more advantageous employment for their wealth in foreign nations."[34] J. S. Mill takes essentially the same position, but he also maintains that the volume of international movements of labor and capital is increasing because of a lessening of international differences in manners and institutions.

Classical economists give separate consideration to colonial areas. J. S. Mill remarks, "These are hardly to be looked upon as countries, carrying on an exchange of commodities with other countries, but more properly as outlying agricultural or manufacturing establishments belonging to a larger community. Our West India colonies, for example, cannot be regarded as countries, with a productive capital of their own. . . . All the capital employed is English capital; almost all the industry is carried on for English uses; . . . . The trade with the West Indies is therefore hardly to be considered as external trade, but more resembles the traffic between town and country, and is amenable to the principles of the home trade."[35] The flow of capital and labor to new areas benefits the older communities by raising their rate of profit and by providing them with cheap food and raw materials. Those who emigrate also gain since they move ". . . from a place where their productive power is less to a place where it is greater. . . ."[36]

[33] J. S. Mill, *op. cit.*, 922.
[34] Sraffa (ed.), *op. cit.*, I, 136–137.
[35] J. S. Mill, *op. cit.*, 685–686.
[36] *Ibid.*, 970.

Mill believes, however, that in order to secure the greatest advantages the movement of labor and capital to the colonies should be regulated by the government. As he says, ". . . the planting of colonies should be conducted, not with an exclusive view to the private interests of the first founders, but with a deliberate regard to the permanent welfare of the nations afterwards to arise from these small beginnings; such regard can only be secured by placing the enterprise, from its commencement, under regulations constructed with the foresight and enlarged views of philosophical legislators; and the government alone has power either to frame such regulations, or to enforce their observance."[37]

Classical economists also discuss the effects of an outflow of capital on the balance of payments. Mill's explanation of the mechanism of adjustment associated with international transfers of capital is as follows.[38] Assuming the existence of a gold standard, the price of foreign exchange in the capital-exporting or lending country rises to the gold export point, and gold then flows from the lending to the borrowing nation. This causes the price level of the gold-losing country to fall and the price level of the gold-receiving or borrowing country to rise. The shift in relative price levels then causes exports of the capital-exporting country to increase and its imports to decrease. When this adjustment creates an export surplus on current account in the capital-exporting nation equal to the capital transfer, the exchange rate returns to par and the gold flow ceases. Besides altering the distribution of gold reserves, the capital transfer worsens the commodity terms of trade for the capital-exporting nation. The essential point, however, is that classical writers believe that the gold standard provides an automatic mechanism of adjustment. Balance of payments disequilibrium is not considered a problem that requires government action.

Ricardo also favors the gradual abolition of the Poor Laws—the system of unemployment relief that existed in England during the time he wrote. He contends that "by engaging to feed all who may require food you in some measure create an unlimited demand for human beings, ..."[39] "The population can only be repressed by diminishing the encouragement to its *excessive* increase,—by leaving contracts between the poor and their employers perfectly free, which would limit the quantity of labour in the market to the effective demand for it."[39] It should be noted in this connection that Ricardo does not believe that the "natural" real wage in England at that time is one of

---

[37] *Ibid.,* 970.
[38] *Ibid.,* 627–628.
[39] Sraffa (ed.), *op. cit.,* VII, 125.

extreme poverty or one that calls for radical reforms. Rather, he deplores the periodic tendency of the population to overshoot its bounds and thereby drive the wage rate below its "natural" rate temporarily. For some countries, however, he is alarmed at the low level of the "natural" wage, and he advocates government measures to raise the customary level in such nations.

Ricardo devotes most of his attention to taxation. He wishes to discover where the ultimate burdens of the various taxes fall. The expenditure side of government activity is mentioned only briefly since, like other classical economists, Ricardo terms governmental services "unproductive." This does not mean that unproductive labor is labor that is poorly allocated (although this connotation often creeps into the discussion), but rather labor that does not produce utilities embodied in material objects—that is, wealth. The labor of the army and navy, for example, is classified as unproductive because it performs only the service of protecting the nation and does not produce wealth. Closely associated with the terms productive and unproductive labor is the concept of "productive" and "unproductive" consumption. Those who in their work do not contribute either directly or indirectly to the production of wealth are called unproductive consumers. Even part of the consumption of productive workers, however, is termed unproductive consumption. For, to the extent that it consists of luxuries that do not help to maintain or improve the consumers' capabilities as workers or does not aid in rearing other productive laborers, the consumption is unproductive.

According to Ricardo, all taxes are ultimately paid either from the revenue of the country or from capital. In other words, unless there is greater production or diminished unproductive consumption when taxes are raised, taxation impairs the growth of the capital stock. For example, according to Ricardo, a specific tax on essential agricultural products raises the prices of these articles by the amount of the tax (assuming a completely inelastic demand) and therefore raises the general wage rate. This, in turn, diminishes the rate of profit and the rate of accumulation. Most other taxes, according to Ricardo, also fall on profits to some extent and thereby limit development. Taxes on rent and luxuries are least objectionable. In the case of rent, the tax falls entirely on the landlord, who is not regarded as an important saver by Ricardo. But, Ricardo argues, capital might still be impaired by such a tax because in practice rent usually includes a payment for the use of capital facilities. In the case of luxuries, the tax neither raises wages nor lowers the profit rate because luxuries are not included in the workers' customary budget.

As these illustrations show, classical economists believed in a minimum of government interference. The government only makes the situation worse. By levying high tariffs, it keeps the price of food high; by subsidizing the poor, it encourages overpopulation; and, by appropriating part of the national product for unproductive uses, it impairs the potential for the creation of wealth. Yet one should not take the view that classical economists merely formulated a theory of misery for the bulk of the population, making no recommendations to alleviate this condition. On the contrary, the non-intervention policies that they supported were regarded as liberal and even radical at the time. They strongly believed that, by removing the vestiges of the widespread governmental interference prominent in the earlier period of Mercantilism, economic development would be stimulated and excessive poverty eliminated.

7. Appraisal of Classical Analysis

Classical economics is an outstanding illustration of a dynamic, aggregative theory of development. It is essentially an analysis of the process by which a portion of the economic surplus available in the community is employed for the purpose of capital accumulation. To classical writers, in other words, the fundamental feature of economic development is capital formation. Although their analysis is oversimplified, it does bring out many important aspects of the accumulation process.

The pessimism of Ricardo and later classical economists regarding the prospects for continued capital formation and higher levels of per capita income rests on two assumptions: historical diminishing returns and the Malthusian principle of population. As subsequent history proves, classical economists seriously underestimate the possibility of technological progress countering the tendency towards diminishing returns. The existence of a rapid rate of technological progress nullifies their assertions concerning the declining rate of profit and rising rents. The Malthusian population principle also is inadequate to explain population changes in the Western world. If this theory is dropped, there need be no tendency towards subsistence wages. Their conclusions about the eventual cessation of economic development thus depend upon two unrealistic assumptions about economic behavior in the Western world.

Classical economists, moreover, fail to analyze adequately the problem of maintaining aggregate demand. According to them, depressions are caused only by such factors as overspeculation and sudden changes in the channels of trade. Although Malthus argues with Ricardo on this matter, Ricardo's logic prevails over Malthus' insight and becomes the accepted word. Now, however, most economists believe that the problem of maintaining full employment is by no means as simple as classical writers contend. The classical description of the balance of payments adjustment process must then be modified under conditions of less than full employment.

The analyses of most classical theorists also are based upon an economic environment in which development occurs gradually, in which perfect competition prevails, and—most important—in which institutions, attitudes, abilities, etc., favorable to development already exist. To the extent that these conditions do not prevail, their analyses and economic policy recommendations require modification.

Chapter 2

Marxian
Analysis

Few thinkers in history have had a more direct or pervasive influence than Karl Marx. Essentially, he is the author of a philosophy of history which predicts the inevitable downfall of capitalism and the advent of socialism. The Marxian system of thought is supported by his followers with a tenacity akin to religious zeal. For, to an orthodox Marxist, an "opponent is not merely in error but in sin."[1]

This chapter examines the Marxian analysis of the process of economic development. Consequently, the discussion covers only those portions of Marx's thought that are relevant to this topic. Although economics forms a large part of his general system, Marx is much more than an economist. Economics, sociology, political theory, history, and philosophy are all mixed into his sweeping analysis.[2]

[1] Joseph Schumpeter, *Capitalism, Socialism, and Democracy,* second edition, Harper and Brothers, New York, 1947, 1 (footnote).

[2] See, for example, *ibid.,* Chapters I–IV; Isaiah Berlin, *Karl Marx,* Oxford University Press, Oxford, 1948; E. O. Golob, *The "Isms": A History and Evaluation,* Harper and Brothers, New York, 1954; Sidney Hook, *Towards the Understanding of Karl Marx,* The John Day Co., New York, 1933; H. B. Mayo, *Democracy and Marxism,* Oxford University Press, New York, 1955; K. R. Popper, *The*

1. The Materialistic Interpretation of History

The general framework for Marx's analysis is a unique, materialistic interpretation of history that boldly attempts to explain the foundations and evolutionary cause of all social life. Marx rejects historical explanations which refer to metaphysics or psychological laws of human nature. The first type of exposition he denounces as meaningless mysticism; the second he dismisses with the remark that "it is not the consciousness of men that determines their existence, but, on the contrary, their social existence determines their consciousness."[3] For Marx, history is by no means merely an aggregate of chance events. It follows certain discoverable laws which produce ever-changing and ever-new forms of social organization.

The Marxian key to humanity's behavior is the "mode of production." This term refers to a particular social arrangement of production in a society which is uniquely characterized by the following components: "(1) the organization of labor in a scheme of division and cooperation, the skills of labor, and the status of labor in the social context with respect to degrees of freedom or servitude; (2) the geographical environment and the knowledge of the use of resources and materials; and (3) technical means and processes and the state of science generally."[4]

In the Marxian system, the mode of production in material life determines the general character of the social, political, and spiritual processes of life. More specifically, corresponding to a particular mode of production is an appropriate set of "relations of production." In legal terms, the relations of production are expressed as a certain set of property relations. These relations of production define the character of a society's class structure—a "class" being defined as a group of individuals who find themselves in a similar position both with respect to the degree of ownership of the property essential to the labor processes and to the degree of personal freedom which the group enjoys. According to Marx, the class structure in every society except the final classless society under socialism consists chiefly of a dominant, directing class and a toiling, oppressed class.

The mode of production and the relations of production breed a

Open Society and Its Enemies, George Routledge and Sons, Ltd., London, 1947, II; W. H. Walsh, *An Introduction to the Philosophy of History,* Hutchinson's University Library, London, 1951.

[3] Karl Marx, *A Contribution to the Critique of Political Economy,* tr. by N. I. Stone, The International Library Publishing Co., New York, 1904, Preface, 11–12.

[4] M. M. Bober, *Karl Marx's Interpretation of History,* Harvard University Press, Cambridge, 1950, 24.

superstructure of ideas and institutions. Marx does not insist that *all* ideas and institutions represent passive adaptations to the mode of production; some cultural expressions may arise quite independently. He contends, nevertheless, that such autonomous non-economic forces exert only a minor influence on historical development.

Evolution in society occurs because the material forces of production, i.e., the elements that constitute the mode of production, change. Alterations in these elements are the independent forces in the Marxian system. Different forms of society may accelerate or retard the development of these economic factors, but some change in the productive forces takes place under all economic conditions. In the early stages of a particular social system, the material forces of production are compatible with the relations of production and the superstructure of ideas and institutions. In this period the existing relations of production are "forms of development of the forces of production."[5] But changes in the relations of production and the cultural superstructure lag behind the development of the material forces of production. At a certain stage, the productive forces come into conflict with the relations of production. The existing property relations "turn into fetters" on the forces of production. "Then comes the period of social revolution."[5]

The class struggle is the mechanism that effects this change. As the relations of production mature and harden, while the forces of production continue to develop, the lines between the ruling and oppressed classes sharpen. The abused class, which stands to gain by a modification of the existing property relations that would permit the productive forces to expand, asserts itself and attempts to secure political control. Since this class is aligned with the all-powerful productive forces, its eventual success is guaranteed. A new set of property relations develops which is appropriate for the expansion of the new productive forces. With the change in the relations of production, the entire superstructure of ideas and institutions is more or less rapidly transformed. All history, according to Marx, follows this cycle of revolution, progressive evolution, the rise of and need for resistance to institutional change as a part of further progress, degeneration, and again, revolution. Marx and Engels discern four social systems in history: (1) primitive communism, (2) the ancient slave state, (3) feudalism, and (4) capitalism.

Although most Western observers agree that Marx's historical materialism is a highly suggestive philosophy of history, few concede that the scheme is the master key that unlocks all the secrets of social evolution. It is a much too simple and rigid theory. First,[6] his division of

---

[5] Marx, *op. cit.*, 12.

[6] The three following criticisms are from O. H. Taylor, *Economics and Liberalism, Collected Papers,* Harvard University Press, Cambridge, 1955, 270–271.

history into a series of discrete, self-contained, and dissimilar economic-social systems is an oversimplification. For this fails to take adequate account of the frequent, continuing influence of the traditions of older cultures on their successors.   Second, Marx's position that each economic-social system passes through the same general cycle, i.e., birth, progressive evolution, decline, and death, seems especially weak. Like most "stage" theories of economic development, it can be supported by a few historical examples but not by all.[7]   Third, the Marxian two-class view of society and his assumption that the class struggle is the only means by which economic changes produce social and cultural changes cannot be accepted.   The nature of society and the cultural shifts within society are much too complex to be understood adequately by such a simple formula.

In describing economic development as a process that occurs in definite stages, Marx generalizes unduly from the particular period of the transition from medieval feudalism to capitalism when his description is somewhat appropriate.   To recognize the importance of economic factors during this particular historical period, however, is quite different from accepting the Marxian interpretation of history.   Even this period cannot be understood by dwelling upon economic forces alone.   The effort by Marx and Engels to fit earlier history into their grand scheme is even less satisfactory.   In brief, like all single-factor theories, the Marxian interpretation of history has the appeal of simplicity and generality.   But this is a multifactor world, and truer though less spectacular explanations involve a recognition of complex interactions among many variables.   This may be why history has shown that the Marxian theory is too crude to pass the test of being able to predict accurately.

2. Theory of Surplus Value

The past is not Marx's prime interest. He is a revolutionary, passionately devoted to the immediate overthrow of the existing social order. Considerations of former periods merely furnish a background for his principal concern with the nature and causes of the imminent disintegration of capitalism.

Marx's theory of surplus value provides the framework on which he bases his analysis of economic development under capitalism. The essence of the capitalist system, in his view, is the division of the population into two classes. One group, the capitalists, owns all the means of production; the other class, the workers, have only their own labor power to sell. The available supply of labor power and

[7] Cf. Chapter 7, section 1.

the existing means of production (the equipment and natural resources owned by the capitalists) are capable of producing a flow of commodities that is greater than that needed to maintain the labor supply and the stock of equipment intact. The economy, in other words, is able to produce a surplus over and above the value of the subsistence needs of the workers and the value of the raw materials and equipment used up in production. Marx calls this "surplus value." The surplus is reaped by the capitalist class in the form of net profits, interest, and rent. In approaching the study of development by focusing upon this economic surplus, Marx follows much the same procedure that classical writers employ.[8]

How does the surplus arise and why are the capitalists able to obtain it? According to Marx, labor power, which the capitalists purchase in the market and consume in the productive process, possesses the unique characteristic of yielding more than its own value as it is used. This excess value created by labor power is the surplus value that capitalists gain. The value of the labor power "is determined, as in the case of every other commodity, by the labour-time necessary for the production, and consequently also the reproduction, of this special article. . . . in other words, the value of labour-power is the value of the means of subsistence necessary for the maintenance of the labourer."[9] How are actual wages made equal to the value of labor power? Marx's solution to this problem involves the concept of the "industrial reserve army." In Marx's model, aggregate employment is determined by the size of the capital stock and the state of technology. There is no possibility of substituting labor for capital equipment within a given state of technology. Furthermore, at any particular time, the supply of labor exceeds the volume of employment that capacity utilization of the existing stock of capital equipment can provide. The redundant labor,

---

[8] Marx himself carefully traces the development of the concept of surplus value in the writings of the classical economists. Cf. Karl Marx, *Theories of Surplus Value,* trans. by G. A. Bonner and Emile Burns, Lawrence and Wishart, London, 1951.

[9] Karl Marx, *Capital,* edited by Frederick Engels, Charles H. Kerr and Co., Chicago, 1926, I, 189–190. Hereinafter cited as Marx, *Capital.*

Marx, like Ricardo, adopts a labor theory of value. The difficulties in which he becomes involved in attempting to explain actual market prices with this theory are not discussed here. Cf. Joan Robinson, *An Essay on Marxian Economics,* Macmillan and Co., Ltd., London, 1949, Chapter III; P. M. Sweezy, *Theory of Capitalist Development,* Oxford University Press, New York, 1942, Chapter VII; J. S. Chipman, "The Consistency of the Marxian Economic System," *Economia Internazionale, V,* No. 3, 527–558 (Aug. 1952).

i.e., the industrial reserve army, competes with the employed labor force and tends to press wages down to the subsistence level.[10]

But might not surplus value originate from the raw materials and capital equipment utilized in production instead of from the labor power expended in production? According to the Marxian viewpoint, this is impossible. Nature without human assistance, such as land, water, and wind, transfers no value to the product. Raw materials, which have been prepared by previous labor, and capital equipment, which is used by labor, only transfer to the product their own value. The capitalists who sell these commodities to other capitalists for use in production gain the surplus value. As these commodities are used in production, purchasers get back merely the value they pay for them. Although Marx does not deny that better machines increase surplus value, he asserts that the labor working with the machines creates the surplus value—not the machinery.

The value of the total product produced in the economy during any period is the sum of three components: constant capital (c), the value of the plant and raw materials used up in production; variable capital (v), the value of the labor power expended during the period; and surplus value (s). Marx describes three ratios with these components of total value. The ratio, s/v, is the rate of exploitation. He expresses this as a division of the working time into the period that labor works for itself and into the time that it works for the capitalists. If s/v is 1 or 100 per cent, this means that labor takes only one-half its working period to produce the value of its means of subsistence; during the other half of the period, labor produces surplus value for the capitalists. Assuming for simplicity that the variable and constant capital each turn over once during the period, the ratio, $s/(c+v)$, is the "rate of profit" on the total capital invested. Finally, the relation between constant and variable capital, i.e., c/v or (as some writers express it) $c/(c+v)$, is what Marx terms the "organic composition of capital."

The goal of the capitalists is to increase the mass of surplus value which they receive. With a given employed labor force this can be achieved by raising the rate of exploitation. There are three ways of accomplishing this. First, the working day can be extended. If it takes only 4 hours for labor to produce the commodities necessary for a day's subsistence, then the longer labor works beyond this time, the greater becomes the surplus reaped by the capitalists. Second, the

---

[10] Marx's reasons for the excess laboring population arising in the first place will be explained in the next section.

wages paid to labor can be reduced below the subsistence level. This can be done only temporarily, however; labor must receive at least subsistence wages if the labor supply is to be maintained. Third, the economic surplus accruing to the capitalist class can be increased by raising the productiveness of labor. This involves a change in the state of technology. The improved technique increases the total output produced by a given labor force, and thus increases the difference between total output and subsistence output.

This method of technological progress brings out an important difference between the Marxian and Ricardian systems. Ricardo minimizes the significance of technological progress. Improvements in technology are not sufficiently powerful to prevent the ultimate arrival of the stationary state; they only delay temporarily its arrival. In the Marxian model, however, technological improvements take place at a rapid rate. Indeed, as will be seen, the enticement of ever-improving technology leads the capitalist class to its eventual doom.

Marx believes that on balance there is a strong tendency for technological progress to increase the quantity of machinery and other implements per worker, i.e., for capital-deepening to take place. Thus, to take advantage of new techniques which raise the productivity of labor, capitalists require a larger stock of capital. And, the only way they can increase the capital stock is to save. They must not consume all the economic surplus.

Moreover, Marx contends that, in the course of development under capitalism, an increase in the productivity of labor is the major way in which capitalists attempt to increase surplus value. The other methods of lengthening the working day and reducing wages have definite physical limits. Each capitalist discovers that he can temporarily gain on his competitors by introducing more productive instruments. By doing this, he immediately lowers his costs of production, whereas the price of the product falls only gradually as other capitalists follow. Those who are among the first to introduce a new technique, therefore, gain extra profits. Thus each capitalist tries to get the jump on his competitors or, failing this, introduces new machinery merely to hold his relative place in the industry.

Still another way in which an individual capitalist can increase his absolute profits is by expanding his output under existing methods of production. This requires an increase in his outlay for labor, raw materials, and capital equipment. In short, each capitalist discovers that to increase his profits he must accumulate capital by reinvesting his profits. This is the goal of capitalist activity. As Marx says, "Accumulate, accumulate! That is Moses and the prophets!"[11]

[11] Marx, *Capital*, I, 652.

3. Economic Development Under Capitalism

With the preceding background, the various parts of the Marxian theory of capitalist development can now be brought together. In a forceful statement about the path which lies before capitalism, Marx says, "That which is now to be expropriated is no longer the labourer working for himself, but the capitalist exploiting many labourers. This expropriation is accomplished by the action of the immanent laws of capitalistic production itself, by the centralisation of capital. One capitalist always kills many. Hand in hand with this centralisation, or this expropriation of many capitalists by few, develop, on an ever extending scale, the co-operative form of the labour-process, the conscious technical application of science, the methodical cultivation of the soil, the transformation of the instruments of labour into instruments of labour only usable in common, the economising of all means of production by their use as the means of production of combined, socialised labour, the entanglement of all peoples in the net of the world-market, and this, the international character of the capitalistic regime. Along with the constantly diminishing number of the magnates of capital, who usurp and monopolise all advantages of this process of transformation, grows the mass of misery, oppression, slavery, degradation, exploitation; but with this too grows the revolt of the working class, a class always increasing in numbers, and disciplined, united, organised by the very mechanism of the process of capitalist production itself. The monopoly of capital becomes a fetter upon the mode of production, which has sprung up and flourished along with, and under it. Centralisation of the means of production and socialisation of labour at last reach a point where they become incompatible with their capitalist integument. This integument is burst asunder. The knell of capitalist private property sounds. The expropriators are expropriated."[12]

While this gloomy forecast is being fulfilled, successively deeper and more disastrous commercial crises, which are manifestations of the weaknesses of capitalism, shake the foundations of this society. Indeed, it is during a crisis that the final revolution and overthrow of capitalism are likely to come.

For expository purposes, however, it is useful to separate Marx's short-run, or cyclical, analysis from the longer-run "laws" which he asserts are operating under capitalism. Most of this long-run analysis can be subsumed under three principles or theories: (1) the increasing misery of labor; (2) the concentration of capital; and (3) the falling rate of profit. Since all these are interrelated, they will be considered together.

[12] *Ibid.,* 836–837.

The capitalist class is at the center of the Marxian analysis. This group ushers in capitalism by forced expropriation of the means of production from the workers. Since these means are now possessed by the capitalists, all that a worker can contribute to production is his labor time. Naturally, all the efforts of the capitalists are designed to expand the flow of surplus value which accrues to them. For, in so doing, they are able not only to raise their standard of living by consuming a portion of the surplus value but also to increase their power and control in society. As indicated above, this surplus value is increased by accumulating more and more capital and enlarging the size of the labor force.· The funds for accumulation come from the surplus value itself, and the additional labor required is provided by an expanding population, since "ordinary wages suffice, not only for its [the working class's] maintenance, but for its increase."[13]

Strangely enough, according to Marx, the conditions most favorable to labor are accumulation within a given state of technology. For in the reinvestment process the demand for labor may well increase more rapidly than the natural increase of the population, and thus lead to a higher standard of living for the workers. But even with a given technology, the resultant increase in wages would engender some counteracting forces to halt the wage rise. If wages rise too rapidly, the rate of accumulation may diminish, since the rate of accumulation depends on the rate of profits; the rate of increase of the demand for labor then falls.[14] The higher wage rate also facilitates earlier marriages and thus increases the supply of labor more rapidly. Here Marx comes very close to the Malthusian principle of population.

If, however, this were all that Marx says about the process of accumulation, he could hardly lament the economic status of the working class. He does not wish to press the Malthusian principle too hard, and yet, without "an iron law of wages," wages are likely to be above the subsistence level. But Marx does have more to say. "Once given the general basis of the capitalistic system, then, in the course of accumulation, a point is reached at which the development of the productivity of social labour becomes the most powerful lever of accumulation."[15] In other words, Marx uses technological progress as the basis for his dire forecasts for capitalism.

---

[13] *Ibid.,* 636. Marx apparently believes that wages in the long run do not fall to an absolute subsistence level in the sense that real wages are just sufficient to maintain a constant number of workers. Instead, the laboring class receives a real income that is sufficient to enable this group to increase its size gradually.

[14] *Ibid.,* 679.

[15] *Ibid.,* 681.

Once technological progress is introduced, instead of just accumulating by duplicating old productive methods, capitalists now are able to expand their surplus value even more by introducing labor-saving inventions which raise the productivity of a given amount of labor-time.

When all capitalists in an industry introduce an invention, the price of the product declines to reflect the smaller amount of labor necessary to produce the commodity. But, if a capitalist can introduce these improvements before others in the industry, he can increase labor productivity (and his profits) without causing a lower price, since his output is only a small fraction of the total market production. When one capitalist introduces such an invention, however, his competitors follow—first in an effort to share those extra gains and, then, because of the price pressure from those who have already innovated. To stand still is to be forced to the wall. Indeed, this is the fate of many capitalists who cannot withstand the competitive struggle and are, consequently, thrown into the proletariat class. There is thus a growing tendency for the concentration of capital in fewer and fewer hands.

Another significant effect of accumulation through these new forms of constant capital is the creation of a surplus laboring population. "The instrument of labour, when it takes the form of a machine, immediately becomes a competitor of the workman himself. The self-expansion of capital by means of machinery is thenceforward directly proportional to the number of the work-people, whose means of livelihood have been destroyed by that machinery. . . . That portion of the working class, thus by machinery rendered superfluous, i.e., no longer immediately necessary for the self-expansion of capital, either goes to the wall in the unequal contest of the old handicrafts and manufactures with machinery, or else floods all the more easily accessible branches of industry, swamps the labour market, and sinks the price of labour-power below its value."[16]

Thus, capitalism is an unstable, explosive system: it discards workers at a faster rate than it hires them. If only technology would remain constant, the laboring class might have a chance as accumulation proceeds. But labor-saving inventions are too rapid, and so the industrial reserve army, expanding also by the increase in population, grows and grows. The larger capitalists absorb the businesses of the small capitalists; machines take the place of skilled labor; and those workers who are fortunate enough to find employment are nonetheless enslaved to a life of dull routine and monotony. It is even worse. Competition of the unemployed for jobs enables capitalists to reduce wages to a near-starvation level. Not only do they cut wages, but they also

[16] *Ibid.,* 470.

lengthen the working day and squeeze more and more surplus value from a given wage payment.   In competing among themselves the capitalists even resort to hiring and overworking women and children at still lower wages than the men.   More and more people are thrown into the proletariat and ground down to a state of abject misery.

The competitive struggle among the capitalists is made more vicious by the tendency for the rate of profit, $s/(c+v)$, to decline, although the absolute mass of surplus value expands through increased output. Marx contends that the introduction of new techniques tends to increase the organic composition of capital, $c/(c+v)$.   According to Marx, it follows that the rate of profit tends to decline.[17]

There are, however, some counteracting, though not dominating, factors to this general principle.   The nature of technological progress, for example, may "cheapen the elements of constant capital."   This merely means that inventions may reduce capital cost per unit of output as much as labor cost by improving the efficiency of labor in making machines as much as it improves it in working machines.   Furthermore, faced with a falling rate of profit, the capitalist class will make every effort to maintain the profit rate by lengthening the working day, by "speed ups," and by cutting wage rates—in other words, by increasing the rate of exploitation.   Moreover, as the rate of profit declines and the capitalists turn with intensified vigor to the task of expropriating weaker fellow-capitalists, the resultant concentration and centralization bring temporary solace.   This, however, leads to a general increase in the organic composition of capital and, therefore, a further decline in the rate of profit.   Eventually, the declining profit rate causes a decrease in the rate of accumulation.   And this tendency towards economic stagnation threatens the very foundations of capitalism.

Although Marx's long-run and cyclical analyses are separated here, it is important to understand that he views cyclical fluctuations as an integral part of capitalistic development.   His discussion of crises is only sketchy, but three separate causes of crises can be discerned from his writings: a failing rate of profit; disproportionality among the various lines of production; and underconsumption.

The connection between the long-run fall in the rate of profit and

---

[17] Let p stand for the rate of profit, $s/(c + v)$; s' for the rate of exploitation, s/v; and q for the organic composition of capital, $c/(c + v)$.   These three variables are related in the following way:

$$p \equiv \frac{s}{c + v} \equiv \frac{s}{v} \cdot \frac{v}{c + v} \equiv \frac{s}{v}\left(1 - \frac{c}{c + v}\right) \equiv s'(1 - q)$$

Therefore, if s' remains constant, p declines as q increases.

economic crises is not very clear in Marx. His case for the long-run decline in the profit rate rests on a secular increase in the organic composition of capital. But gradual changes in the profit rate do not have very much to do with a particular crisis.

A rise in the wages of labor is another reason, however, for a falling rate of profit, and Marx relates this in a general way to the problem of crises. For short periods, capital accumulation may draw down the pool of unemployed until full employment is reached. Up to the full employment level, labor is hired at a subsistence wage. But after this point the pressure of accumulation bids the wage rate up and thereby decreases the rate of profit.[18] This decline so slackens the rate of accumulation that a crisis ensues.

Another factor contributing to the downturn in economic activity is the frenzied attempt by capitalists to avoid the fall in the profit rate by speculative ventures. These endeavors are not based on solid economic grounds and invariably come to a disastrous conclusion. Marx summarizes this kind of crisis: "a fall in the intensity of exploitation below a certain point calls forth disturbances and stagnations in the process of capitalist production, crises, destruction of capital."[19]

Once a crisis develops (whatever its cause), there is a rush for liquidity; ". . . now the cry is everywhere: money alone is a commodity!"[20] This rush for liquidity paralyzes the function of money as a medium of exchange. "The chain of payments due at certain times is broken in a hundred places, and the disaster is intensified by the collapse of the credit system."[21] Workers are laid off in increasing numbers, and their wages are cut to a near-starvation level. The small capitalists are particularly hard hit. Their capital is either destroyed or absorbed by other more powerful capitalists. However, the cut in wages, destruction of capital, and elimination of speculative ventures tend to increase the profit rate, and another upward surge in investment eventually begins again.

The second cause of crises, disproportionality, refers to the possibility of errors and blunders on the part of capitalists in estimating their markets. Capitalistic production is so complex and individual capitalists are so poorly informed about the actions of their competitors and the market in general, that overproduction (in the sense of an inability to sell the output at remunerative prices) can easily occur in important sectors of the economy and precipitate a general crisis.

[18] In the identity $p \equiv s'(1 - q)$, s' falls.
[19] Marx, *Capital*, III, 300.
[20] *Ibid.*, I, 155.
[21] *Ibid.*, III, 298.

Perhaps Marx's most celebrated crisis theory is his underconsumption theory. He rejects the classical tenet that "supply creates its own demand": "Nothing can be more childish than the dogma, that because every sale is a purchase, and every purchase a sale, therefore the circulation of commodities necessarily implies an equilibrium of sales and purchases. . . . If the interval in time between the two complementary phases of the complete metamorphosis of a commodity becomes too great, if the split between the sale and the purchase becomes too pronounced, the intimate connection between them, their oneness, asserts itself by producing—a crisis."[22]

In explaining a crisis caused by underconsumption, Marx contends that the consuming power of the capitalist class is "restricted by the tendency to accumulate, the greed for an expansion of capital and a production of surplus-value on an enlarged scale. This is a law of capitalist production imposed by incessant revolutions in the methods of production themselves, the resulting depreciation of existing capital, the general competitive struggle and the necessity of improving the product and expanding the scale of production, for the sake of self-preservation and on penalty of failure."[23] As already mentioned, this accumulation drive, according to Marx, increases the size of the proletariat class, creates a relative surplus population, and drives the wages of the workers down near the subsistence level. Because of these antagonistic conditions of distribution, a contradiction results. As productive power develops, "it finds itself at variance with the narrow basis on which the condition of consumption rests."[24] The consumption power of the workers is limited by their poverty, whereas that of the capitalists is limited by their greed for accumulation. The resultant inability of the consumption-goods industries to absorb the output of capital goods causes a persistent tendency for general overproduction which manifests itself in periodic crises and economic stagnation.

4. Colonialism and Imperialism

Marx and especially his followers also emphasize what they consider to be the vicious nature of the international features of capitalist development. Marx argues that early colonial expansion played a major role in the establishment of capitalism. On the one hand, "the discovery of gold and silver in America, the extirpation, enslavement and entombment in mines of the aboriginal population, the beginning of the conquest and looting of the East Indies, the turning of Africa into a warren for

[22] *Ibid.*, I, 127–128.
[23] *Ibid.*, III, 286–287.
[24] *Ibid.*, 287.

the commercial hunting of black-skins"[25] served as major means of primitive accumulation. On the other, the expansion of world markets associated with colonialism created a demand for commodities that could not be satisfied in the old feudal society.

Moreover, according to Marxists, foreign trade continues to play an important role as capitalism develops. By means of this trade, older capitalistic countries can take advantage of both larger markets for their manufactures and cheaper sources of foodstuffs and raw materials. To regulate the terms of this trade, however, so that they can obtain the major benefits from trade, the mature capitalistic nations tighten and extend their control over poorer areas by building up colonial empires. In other words, Marxists maintain that colonialism is designed to increase the degree of exploitation in the poorer countries for the benefit of the advanced capitalistic nations.

Foreign markets become even more important as capitalism moves into what Marxists term its monopoly stage. This occurs when the concentration and centralization of capital gradually eliminate most areas of free competition in the economy. At this stage imperialism emerges. As Lenin says, "Imperialism is capitalism in that stage of development in which the dominance of monopolies and finance capital has established itself; . . . in which the division of the world among the international trusts has begun; in which the division of all territories of the globe among the great capitalist powers has been completed."[26]

At this point in capitalist development, so argue the Marxists, the forces of stagnation in the form of a low rate of profit and chronic overproduction are conditions that press ever harder upon the economy. The older capitalistic countries turn more and more to the foreign sector in order to postpone their final destruction. The export of capital to backward areas in which the rate of profit is higher becomes a major means of attempting to lessen the tendency towards stagnation. This also becomes a means for encouraging the export of commodities which relieves the pressures of overproduction at home.

According to the Marxist view, further domination of the poorer countries by the advanced capitalist countries accompanies this export of capital. There are resistances to be overcome within these areas, if foreigners are to find profitable outlets and exploit the people. Each capitalist power also desires to exclude competition from other capitalist nations who are in similar difficulties. Consequently, the governments

[25] *Ibid.*, I, 823.

[26] V. I. Lenin, *Imperialism, The Highest Stage of Capitalism* in *New Data for V. I. Lenin's Imperialism*, edited by E. Varga and L. Mendelsohn, International Publishers, New York, 1940, 194.

of the great powers step in and forcibly create conditions favorable to the process of exploitation. In all this, the people of the poorer regions benefit little, if any. Traditional habits and customs are destroyed; handicraft industries are wiped out by cheap manufacturing imports; and the masses are stripped of their means of production. In short, "Finance capital and the trusts are increasing instead of diminishing the differences in the rate of development of the various parts of world economy."[27]

However, even the gradual extension of domination by the advanced capitalist countries over the less developed areas of the world does not serve to prevent the emergence of the contradictions of capitalism. From a Marxist viewpoint, it merely postpones them. After the world is divided by the rich nations, they begin to turn on each other in an effort to solve their economic problems by extending their spheres of influence. This period is characterized by wars among the great imperialist powers for the purpose of redividing the world. At the same time, however, the weaknesses of capitalism become more apparent. Class conflicts grow sharper within the older countries and nationalism increases within the colonial empires. The final outcome in the Marxist vision is the destruction of capitalism and the emergence of socialism.

5. Appraisal of Marxian Analysis

It is easy to understand why Marx's outline of economic development under capitalism has had such a widespread appeal. For the theory is not a single indictment of capitalism on merely one or two grounds; instead, Marx claims that the whole capitalistic system by its very nature is an overwhelming contradiction which manifests itself in every form of economic activity. To the Marxist, the strongest forces on his side in his struggle for a new society are the laws of capitalism itself; nothing can hold back the final surge of self-destruction. The capitalistic economy has a "built-in" doom. And just as capitalism is inexorably doomed, so too is socialism bound to emerge. The Marxist does not have to wrestle with the principle of diminishing returns; nor does he have to convince the world that his aims are right. Accept the dialectic faith, and the desired goal must perforce appear in time.

But time has passed, and still the Marxists wait. Consider, for example, the theory of the increasing misery of labor. As a theory of wages, it must be deemed inadequate. Workers in capitalistic countries have clearly not been kept at a near-subsistence level. As will be noted in Part 2,[28] their real wages have continued to increase with capitalistic development. Marx vastly exaggerated the effects of technological un-

[27] *Ibid.,* 206.
[28] Chapter 9, section 1.

employment. Sometimes particular occupations have been hard hit by this phenomenon, but it has by no means been so general as to create any large, permanent pool of unemployed. On the contrary, the net effect of technological progress has been to increase the demand for labor rather than decrease it, since the investment associated with technological progress raises aggregate demand and income.

Some Marxists claim that Marx is describing labor's relative share of the national product instead of its absolute share. This position usually amounts to the assertion that labor's relative share would be higher under socialism than capitalism. Although occasional statements by Marx might support this interpretation, it is not consistent with the bulk of Marx's comments. Marx quite clearly believes that under capitalism the real wage of workers will not rise, but will instead hover around the subsistence level. Moreover, if this interpretation is abandoned, the Marxists are left without a theory explaining the division of the national product between labor and capital.

Regarding the matter of concentration, Marx perhaps made his most successful prediction. He did see that technological progress would lead to the establishment of large-scale business units. Nevertheless, he overestimated the rapidity and extent of this trend. His tools also are too blunt to deal with the monopoly and oligopoly problems which arise with a trend towards big business.

As to Marx's extensive discussion of the falling rate of profit, Mrs. Robinson summarizes this with the remark that "his explanation of the falling tendency of profits explains nothing at all."[29] As previously noted, Marx believes that the development of capitalism brings a rising organic composition of capital, i.e., $c/(c + v)$, increases. In other words, the capital employed per worker rises. Since he postulates a constant rate of exploitation, s/v, it can be seen in the identity

$$\frac{s}{c + v} \equiv \frac{s}{v}\left(1 - \frac{c}{c + v}\right)$$

that the rate of profit, $s/(c + v)$, falls as $c/(c + v)$ rises.[30]

Marx can maintain that the rate of profit falls, however, only at the cost of abandoning his claim that real wages remain at the subsistence level. As the capital employed per man rises, labor becomes more productive, and a given labor force produces a greater output. A constant rate of exploitation means that the output (net of depreciation) is divided between the capitalists as profits and labor as wages in a constant

[29] Joan Robinson, *An Essay on Marxian Economics*, Macmillan and Co., London, 1949, 42. Much of the following is based on this essay.

[30] See above, footnote 17.

manner. Thus, labor receives a constant share of a growing stream of output or a greater absolute real wage.

In discussing this principle, Marx does not appreciate the fact that, if real wages remain constant, the rate of exploitation rises quite independently of such factors as lengthening the working day. For total output increases, and, if the absolute amount going to labor stays the same, the amount of output going to the capitalists as profits must rise. And when productivity increases, there is no logical necessity for $c/(c + v)$ to increase in such a way compared with the rise in s/v that $s/(c + v)$ falls. In short, Marx cannot establish the necessity of a falling rate of profit. Apparently, he is misled by a desire to have such a law in order to follow the orthodox tradition of such a principle. But, as was seen in the last chapter, classical writers, such as Ricardo and J. S. Mill, argued their case on quite different grounds.

With regard to the problems of business cycles, Marx must be credited with a significant contribution to development thought. There is no question but that the importance of the cycle was underestimated in the orthodox literature of that time. Marx views crises as an integral part of capitalistic development, founded on the real nature of capitalistic production, rather than on monetary factors. Nevertheless, despite Marx's outpouring of lowly regard for the orthodox thinking on this subject, his analysis of cycles must be classed merely as highly suggestive rather than revolutionary. The trouble is that he does not have an adequate theory of effective demand. He seems to oscillate between rejecting and accepting the classical position. Consider, for example, his argument based on the short-run fall in the rate of profit. Under the stimulus of some special inducement to capital accumulation, such as the opening of new markets, the reserve army is depleted, and wages rise. This rise in wages, in turn, decreases the rate of profit and thus cuts off the supply of capital funds. Accumulation slackens, and the wage rate again falls as the reserve army expands.

This argument is in the classical vein. To Marx, the rate of accumulation does not decrease because of a lack of inducement to invest, but because the source of investment funds is smaller. Total output—consumption plus investment goods—remains the same; there is merely a different distribution of these commodities. In other words, except for oblique suggestions that he does not follow through, Marx does not emphasize the deficiency of effective aggregate demand. Instead, by stressing the relative decline in investible funds, he seems to follow the classical stagnation thesis. But a crisis theory must account for an absolute decline in total output. In short, if there is this type of cycle, it can hardly be used as an adequate explanation of what is usually regarded as the business cycle. Moreover, Marx in his argument asserts an important consequence that is not at all obvious. The increased demand for labor due to capital accumulation might raise money wages but it need not increase real wages. The price level may merely increase, with the relative shares received by labor and the capitalists remaining the same. Thus, he does not even establish that profits must fall relatively when accumulation is accelerated.

Marx's discussion of production errors as a cause of crises in a dynamic, uncertain world is likewise in the orthodox tradition. Most writers point to such errors as a complicating factor, but few regard this haphazard type of overproduction or underproduction in particular industries as sufficiently powerful to explain the general downturn in the typical business cycle.

With his underconsumption theory Marx does attempt to break sharply with classical thinking. Here he explicitly rejects the notion that there cannot be a chronic deficiency of effective demand. Here too, however, Marx's analysis of this problem is inadequate; it is suggestive but limited and vague.

As already mentioned, Marx contends that the basic cause of this type of crisis is a lack of consumption demand. He argues that the consuming power of the workers is limited by their poverty, and that of the capitalists is limited by their inordinate desire to accumulate. If, however, capitalists are willing to accumulate irrespective of the rate of profit, there should be no problem at all. For then the output of capital goods would fill the gap between total output and consumption. These commodities would be a form of consumption for the capitalists. But, if the inducement to invest does depend upon the rate of profit (as it must in order for a crisis to occur), Marx must explain how the profit rate changes so as to produce this underconsumption crisis. He does not do this. He fails to show the manner in which the rate of profit, and thus investment, depends upon consumption.

The Marxian theory of imperialism likewise is unconvincing. It depends upon the statements that Marx makes concerning the internal behavior of a capitalistic economy. If these are rejected, then this theory loses its foundations.

In summary, as a formal model, Marxian economics is weak. The "internal contradictions" are more those of the Marxian system itself than they are of capitalism, which the system purportedly analyzes. As has been noted, most of the reasoning about the so-called long-run and cyclical "laws" of capitalistic behavior does not stand up in the light of analytical scrutiny and historical experience. Furthermore, the materialistic interpretation of history is a grossly oversimplified framework within which to examine economic development.   Nevertheless, no anti-Marxist need deny that Mark contributes some important insights in his study of development.   For example, his view of the development process as occurring in an uneven, sometimes discontinuous fashion is appreciated by all modern economists.   And, in spite of all its fallacies and invalid conclusions, Marxism must be understood.   For it still remains an appealing political religion challenging the future of poor and rich countries alike.

Chapter 3

Neo-Classical

Analysis

About 1870 there is a definite shift in the main currents of economic thought, as a new approach gradually begins to replace the classical tradition. The reasons for the shift are not hard to discover. By this time, the significance of the great nineteenth-century technological and resource discoveries were apparent to all. Not only had a rapid rate of development, based upon these discoveries, already been achieved but also the possibilities for continued growth under existing and improved technology appeared to be reasonably bright. Real wages were considerably above the subsistence level, the rate of profit was high, and rents did not constitute an alarming share of the national income. In short, the fear of a stationary state with subsistence wages ceased to be a matter of general, current interest.

As a result of these circumstances, the neo-classical economists abandoned the magnificently bold approach of the classical writers.[1]

[1] Most of the neo-classical economists considered here are writers who were prominent before World War I. But even narrowing the group in this manner leaves a wide range of different views. Consequently, a short discussion of neo-classical development thought is bound to be rather selective.

In particular, the problem of economic development tended to subside into the background of economic discussion. The classical and Marxian economic visions, which focus upon the surplus of total output over the output required to maintain the population at a subsistence level and to keep the fixed capital stock intact, did not seem very relevant to these economists, who were living in countries where real wages were considerably above the subsistence level. And dropping a subsistence wage theory breaks the simple classical and Marxian connection between the distribution of income and the volume of saving in the economy.

It was apparent by then that in the Western world, at any rate, population changes no longer could be tied to changes in per capita income in any simple Malthusian manner. Furthermore, much of the capital accumulation seemed to be stimulated by the progress in technology and resource knowledge. And these improvements in technology could not be explained by any simple set of economic relations. Thus, changes in the so-called "heavy" variables, i.e., population, the capital stock, and technology, which affect the rate of change in national income, appeared to be determined to a large extent by forces generally considered outside the realm of economics. Classical writers believed it was legitimate to assume that the state of technology and natural resource conditions remain constant and that population changes depend upon the level of per capita income. Not only were they able, therefore, to analyze the mechanism of capital accumulation and population growth, but they also were able to formulate principles with regard to the long-run behavior of the rate of development. Once it is granted, however, that factor supplies may change in an autonomous and unpredictable fashion, then analyses of the development process tend to be restricted to a discussion of the consequences of certain changes in factor conditions. Although such analyses are extremely important, they lack the grandeur of classical development theory.

Neo-classical economists turned their attention to shorter-run problems. In studying the distribution of income, or value theory, or general equilibrium theory, these writers greatly shortened their time horizon. Most of them were primarily interested in the interrelations among the various parts of the economy at a particular moment of time rather than in how these parts behaved over long periods of time. The type of development that one visualizes with this approach is that achieved by a more efficient allocation of given resources. Neo-classical economists, for example, emphasized that with given factor supplies it is possible to produce a greater national income under competitive market conditions than under monopolistic conditions, since perfect competition results in a more efficient allocation of resources. There was, however, one significant exception to this general practice of concentrating upon the short run. One price they studied was the rate of interest, a price that connects the present with the future. Their discussion of the rate of interest opened up the subject of capital accumulation. And in this field the neo-classical economists made a major contribution to development theory.

1. Theory of Capital Accumulation

Although there are many differences among neo-classical writers concerning capital theory, their general approach is basically the same.[2] First, they abandon the classical assumption that fixed proportions of labor and capital are required in production within a given state of technology. They recognize the possibility of the substitution of capital for labor. This implies that an economy can accumulate capital without the necessity of increasing the labor force. Capital theory, therefore, is freed from population theory. And, as the capital stock grows in relation to a given population, national and per capita incomes increase. However, with a given state of technology, neo-classical economists assume that the marginal productivity of capital declines as this type of accumulation occurs.

According to neo-classical writers, the rate of interest and also the level of income determine the rate of saving. Because the future involves uncertainties and risks, a person generally prefers present income to future income; a dollar today is preferred to the promise of a dollar next year. Consequently, to generate a flow of saving in the economy, the rate of interest must be positive. The typical lender must be promised, say, $1.05 next year, or 5 per cent interest, to refrain from spending the dollar today on consumption goods. Furthermore, the more an individual saves out of a given income, the greater his preference for present income becomes; a higher interest rate is necessary to secure a greater rate of saving at a given income level. However, the higher the typical individual's level of income, the greater becomes the amount he is willing to save at a given interest rate.

In the neo-classical model, given the state of technique and the level of population, the interest rate also determines the rate of investment.

---

[2] Discussions of the differences among neo-classical economists on the matter of capital theory are contained in works on the history of economic doctrine. For example, see J. A. Schumpeter, *History of Economic Analysis*, Oxford University Press, New York, 1954, 898–909, 924–932; and G. J. Stigler, *Production and Distribution Theories*, The Macmillan Co., New York, 1946.

To maximize profits, an investor continues to purchase capital assets if the discounted marginal revenue productivity of the last asset added is greater than or equal to its cost. A lower rate of interest is needed to increase the rate of investment, i.e., the amount of net investment per unit of time, in the economy, first, because the yield on any given type of capital falls as the supply of that type of capital is increased and, secondly, because high rates of investment raise the relative prices of capital goods.

The process of capital formation in the neo-classical system with a given population takes place in the following way. Assume a sudden, once-for-all increase in investment opportunities brought about, for example, by an improvement in technology. The demand for investment goods then increases. The rate of interest is pushed up, and the rate of saving is increased. The relative prices of capital goods also rise as the rate of investment increases, because of limitations on the supply of factors specialized to the production of these goods. Both the higher rate of interest and the higher relative prices of investment goods act as rationing devices and restrict investment to the highest-yielding projects. As these projects reach completion, however, both the interest rate and the relative prices of capital goods fall. Consequently, as time passes, lower-and-lower-yielding projects become profitable. Finally, the rate of interest declines to such a low level that the community is unwilling to save. At this stage accumulation ends, and the economy reaches a stationary position. The rate of interest may be zero at this point, but this is not necessary. Neo-classical economists assume, it should be noted, that full employment is maintained throughout the entire accumulation process. They also generally assume that the money supply remains constant. Thus the expanding output rate decreases the general level of money prices.

The increase in the quantity of capital per unit of labor during this type of accumulation process is termed "capital-deepening" in contrast to the process of "capital-widening," where capital accumulation is proportionate to the increase in the labor force.

Consider next the effects of a given increase in population (more precisely, the labor force) within a given state of technology. According to neo-classical theory, an increase in the labor supply, by lowering money wage rates, leads to an increase in employment. The reason for this is that aggregate money demand is assumed to remain constant as money wage rates decline. Demand schedules, therefore, remain fixed in spite of the fall in wages. Hence producers find it profitable to expand output by employing more labor. However, the more intensive utilization of existing capital equipment raises the marginal productivity of capital and thus the demand for investment goods. The interest rate rises, and, to the extent that saving is responsive to the higher rate of interest, the rate of investment increases. Then the process of accumulation proceeds towards the stationary state in exactly the same manner as previously described. As before, the price level falls as output increases. At the new stationary state position, per capita income may be higher, lower, or the same as its initial level. If there is an abundant supply of natural resources and the resultant percentage increase in the capital stock is at least as large as the percentage increase in the labor supply, per capita income may rise.[3] However, the more limited the supplies of natural resources become, the greater is the likelihood that per capita income will fall as population grows.

Technological progress is another factor that stimulates the growth of national income. By lowering costs, improvements in productive methods encourage producers to expand output. One interesting aspect of the neo-classical view of technological change is the belief that the majority of inventions tend to save labor but use capital—or at least that they tend to be relatively more labor-saving than capital-saving.[4] J. B. Clark, an outstanding American economist in the neo-classical school, makes this point. "There is a common impression that whatever saves labor usually requires an increase of capital in the industry where the economy is secured, and this impression is justified by the experience of the century following the invention of the steam engine and the early textile machinery."[5] This view that the general stream of technology creates strong demands for capital goods illustrates how close these writers regard the connection between capital accumulation and the process of economic development. As to why the pattern of invention takes this form, the neo-classical authors have little to say. They do not seem to possess a theory of "induced" inventions—such as one that emphasizes the effect of changes in relative factor prices.[6]

2. Development As a Gradual Process

Although the analysis of the accumulation process that has been presented thus far illustrates many of the fundamental notions in the neo-classical development model, there is much more to the neo-

[3] In other words, increasing returns to scale may prevail.

[4] In stating that inventions tend to save labor but use capital, neo-classical economists seem to mean that inventions tend to raise the marginal productivity of capital more than the marginal productivity of labor.

[5] J. B. Clark, *Essentials of Economic Theory,* The Macmillan Company, New York, 1907, 301. He notes, however, that this tendency is not as strong as formerly. See also G. Cassel, *The Theory of Social Economy,* tr. by J. McCabe, T. Fisher Unwin, Ltd., London, 1923, I, 219.

[6] J. R. Hicks, *Theory of Wages,* Peter Smith, New York, 1948, 124–125.

classical conception of development than can be explained in aggregate terms. A more complete understanding of neo-classical thought can be gained by discussing three interrelated ideas in the economic vision of most writers in this group. First, neo-classical economists consider development to be a gradual and continuous process. Second, they emphasize the harmonious and cumulative nature of the process. Third, they are generally optimistic concerning the possibilities for continued economic progress.

The view that economic development takes place in a gradual and continuous manner is particularly evident in the writings of Alfred Marshall, probably the most famous of the English writers in the neo-classical school.[7] The evolution theories of Darwin and Spencer seem to influence greatly Marshall's economic views.[8] Being aware of the evolutionary and organic nature of an economic system, Marshall frequently uses biological analogies rather than rigidly static mechanical analogies. Marshall regards the economy as organic in fundamental nature: " 'Progress' or 'evolution', industrial and social, is not mere increase and decrease. It is organic growth."[9] Or again, "The Mecca of the economist lies in economic biology rather than in economic dynamics."[10]

A Darwinian view of economic life naturally leads to the position that economic development is a gradual and continuous process. According to Marshall, ". . . the maxim that 'Nature does not willingly make a jump' . . . is specially applicable to economic developments."[11] Because of this belief in slow, gradual progress, economists like Marshall feel justified in generally employing static partial equilibrium techniques to analyze the various components of total economic activity.

How do these writers reconcile the great technological innovations of the eighteenth and nineteenth centuries with their model of gradual change? As the next chapter explains, Schumpeter sees in these innovations the basis of a discontinuous and disharmonious view of eco-

---

[7] For analyses of Marshall's views on economic growth, see T. Parsons, *The Structure of Social Action,* McGraw-Hill Book Co., New York, 1937, Chapter 4; B. Glassburner, "Alfred Marshall on Economic History and Historical Development," *Quarterly Journal of Economics, LXIX,* No. 4, 577–595 (Nov. 1955); A. J. Youngson, "Marshall on Economic Growth," *Scottish Journal of Political Economy, III,* No. 1, 1–18 (Feb. 1956).

[8] Glassburner, *op. cit.,* 581.

[9] A. C. Pigou (ed.), *Memorials of Alfred Marshall,* Macmillan and Co., Ltd., London, 1925, 317.

[10] Alfred Marshall, *Principles of Economics,* eighth edition, Macmillan and Co., Ltd., London, 1930, xiv. Hereinafter cited as Marshall, *Principles.*

[11] Alfred Marshall, *Industry and Trade,* Macmillan and Co., Ltd., London, 1919, 6.

nomic growth. The answer is not that neo-classical writers minimize the importance of these discoveries. Marshall, for example, in explaining the rapid development of Britain after 1760, strongly emphasizes the significance of improvements in such industries as transportation, textiles, agriculture, iron, and coal. Rather, the neo-classical position is that both the act of invention and the adoption of new techniques are also gradual and continuous. As Marshall says, "And though an inventor, or an organizer, or a financier of genius may seem to have modified the economic structure of a people almost at a stroke; yet that part of his influence, which has not been merely superficial and transitory, is found on inquiry to have done little more than bring to a head a broad constructive movement which had long been in preparation."[12]

In short, the neo-classical writers seem to regard technological progress as stemming from the gradual "progress and diffusion of knowledge,"[13] a force that they regarded as autonomous in Western society. What looks to be a radical and sudden change in productive techniques is in fact generally the result of the collective efforts of many previous inventors and is the culmination of a continuous process of invention. And the new technique itself is likely to form one link in the chain of another series of invention. Furthermore, the introduction of the invention into the economic stream is viewed as generally occurring in a relatively smooth and continuous fashion.

3. Development As a Harmonious Process

Closely related to the idea of development as occurring gradually is the neo-classical view that it is also harmonious and reinforcing. The majority of economists in the neo-classical school maintain that development generally benefits all major income groups. They take particular care to explain the advantages reaped by labor. The economic system is assumed to have a strong tendency to produce full employment. Neo-classical writers admit that temporary unemployment caused by monetary factors, wars, and the introduction of new productive techniques is possible, but they think that long-run equilibrium unemployment is impossible. Similarly, they believe that de-

[12] Marshall, *Principles,* xiii. J. S. Nicholson expresses a similar view: "The law or tendency which . . . History reveals, is—I. That a radical change made in the methods of invention will be *gradually and continuously adopted;* and II. That these radical changes, these discontinuous leaps, tend to give place to advances by small *increments of invention.*" J. S. Nicholson, *The Effects of Machinery on Wages,* Swan Sonnenschein and Co., London, 1892, 33.

[13] Marshall, *Principles,* 222.

velopment tends to raise the real wages of labor as a whole. The introduction of labor-saving machinery first tends to cause a relative reduction of demand in the affected trades. But as Gustav Cassel, the famous Swedish economist, writes, simultaneously ". . . the prices of the products are generally much reduced, so that the demand for them, and therefore also the demand for the relevant labour, is absolutely increased; which, of course, means a tendency to raise wages. On the other hand, the assumed technical progress brings about an increase of the total production of the community, and consequently an increase of its total income. From this we get a general increase of the demand for labour. When this demand is spread over all the different kinds of labour, the working class as a whole derives an advantage from technical advances."[14]

The economists of this period also maintain that the absolute income shares received by landlords and capitalists rise during the process of economic development.[15] But, regarding relative shares, they are not very specific. Unlike Ricardo, who hints that class conflicts may arise in the growth process, and Marx, who explicitly states that these conflicts develop under capitalism, the neo-classical writers emphasize the beneficial effects of development upon all the major income groups.

Their analysis of production illustrates another aspect of the harmonious and cumulative view of the growth process. This is associated with the extremely important concept of external economies, a term introduced by Marshall. Although the notion has some applicability to static, partial equilibrium analysis, it is most useful for analyzing a developing economy.[16]

By the terms "internal" and "external" economies Marshall distinguishes between those economies arising from an increase in the scale of production which depend upon the resources and efficiency of the individual firm and those which depend upon general development of the firm's own industry or other industries that supply its needs. The former type of economies are those which result from the introduction of more complicated machinery, the better organization of marketing and research activities, the greater specialization of labor and management, etc., as the scale of a firm's operations increases. External economies, according to Marshall, "depend on the aggregate volume of production of the kind in the neighbourhood; while others

[14] Cassel, *op. cit.,* I, 319. Also, see Marshall, *Principles,* 542; Clark, *op. cit.,* 312–317.

[15] Marshall, *Principles,* 678–681.

[16] Stigler, *Production and Distribution Theories,* The Macmillan Co., New York, 1946, 68–76; T. Scitovsky, "Two Concepts of External Economies," *Journal of Political Economy,* LXII, No. 2, 143–151 (April 1954).

again, especially those connected with the growth of knowledge and the progress of the arts, depend chiefly on the aggregate volume of production in the whole civilized world."[17] In another place he speaks of external economies resulting from "the growth of correlated branches of industry which mutually assist one another, perhaps being concentrated in the same localities, but anyhow availing themselves of the modern facilities for communication offered by steam transport, by the telegraph and by the printing-press."[18]

Thus, Marshall emphasizes the interdependent and complementary nature of the economy. As an industry expands in a particular area, it attracts a well-trained labor force. The rate of technological progress in the industry is increased because of the better opportunities for the interchange of knowledge. The expansion also induces the growth of other industries to exploit by-products, to supply equipment, and to facilitate transportation and communication needs. These various repercussions improve profit prospects for the firms within the industry and thereby stimulate additional growth, which, in turn, has further expansionary effects on other sectors.

Allyn Young in his famous discussion of increasing returns extends and sharpens certain features of external economies that are only implied in Marshall's analysis.[19] "First, the mechanism of increasing returns is not to be discerned adequately by observing the effects of variations in the size of an individual firm or of a particular industry, for the progressive division and specialisation of industries is an essential part of the process by which increasing returns are realised."[20] In other words, the concept of a given set of industries is too static; an important aspect of historical increasing returns is qualitative changes in old industries and the creation of entirely new products and markets. "What is required is that industrial operations be seen as an integrated whole."[20]

Using this framework, Young points out that "the securing of increasing returns depends upon the progressive division of labour, and the principal economies of the division of labour, in its modern forms, are the economies which are to be had by using labour in roundabout or indirect ways,"[20] i.e., the use of capitalistic methods of production. And, although "the division of labour depends upon the extent of the market, . . . the extent of the market also depends upon the division

[17] Marshall, *Principles*, 265–266.
[18] *Ibid.*, 317.
[19] Allyn Young, "Increasing Returns and Economic Progress," *Economic Journal, XXXVIII*, No. 152, 527–542 (Dec. 1928).
[20] *Ibid.*, 539.

of labour."[20]   Thus there is a basis for growth to be progressive and to propagate itself in a cumulative way.

In Young's view of this development process, the rate of growth in any one industry is influenced by the rate of expansion of other industries.   A certain initial expansion in one sector tends to induce growth in another sector as the market for the products of this latter sector increases.   And, as the market for these products increases, the further division of labor becomes a vehicle for increasing returns. Although the division of labor permits a higher degree of specialization in management and a better geographical distribution of production operations, the main advantages stem from the introduction of more capitalistic techniques.   Given the state of scientific knowledge, some capitalistic methods of production that lower unit costs are not profitable unless the market is large.   Growth in one sector, by increasing the demand for the output of another sector, enables these methods to be utilized.

This process of the division of labor causes increasing industrial differentiation.   The firms in the industry of initial expansion can be viewed as engaged in a series of distinct operations: purchasing and storing materials; transforming materials into semi-finished products and semi-finished products into finished products; storing and selling the outputs, etc.[21]   Considering an individual firm, assume for simplicity that separate average cost curves can be drawn for each of these functions and that they can be summed to obtain the average cost curve for the final product.   Some of these average cost functions may fall continuously over the relevant range for the firm, even though the average cost curve for the final product is U-shaped.   The firms in the industry do not increase their exploitation of a process subject to increasing returns because an expansion of output encounters diminishing returns associated with the other processes necessary for producing the product.   On the other hand, the use of the process subject to increasing returns is too small to enable a firm to specialize in this process and thereby to take full advantage of the increasing returns.   As the output of the industry grows, however, the demand for this function increases and a new type of firm is created.   The new firm is a monopolist at first but, after it takes full advantage of the increasing returns to scale (which are assumed not to continue indefinitely as the output of the firm increases), further expansions in demand induce the entry of other firms.   The new industry becomes competitive and

[20] Ibid., 539.

[21] G. J. Stigler, "The Division of Labor Is Limited by the Extent of the Market," Journal of Political Economy, LIX, No. 3, 187 (June 1951).

in turn may lose parts of its productive processes to a new set of specialists.

The creation of the new industry tends to lower costs in the original industry and to stimulate additional growth. The expansion in the new industry also leads to further unsettling effects in the economy. Development in one sector of the economy induces growth in other sectors. According to Young, however, realization of increasing returns is a slow and (unlike the Marshallian view) an uneven process. It requires new skills and habits, new geographical distributions of population, and capital accumulation which can only occur gradually. After one step forward is made, the next important step "cannot be taken until a certain quantum of prospective advantages has accumulated."[22] On the other hand, the discovery of new natural resources, population growth, and the increase of scientific knowledge operate to hasten and reinforce the other factors that make for increasing returns. Nor are these factors entirely autonomous, in the sense of being determined by non-economic factors. In Young's view, the growth of scientific knowledge is a consequence as well as a cause of the growth of industry.

4. Optimism Concerning Development

From what has already been said, it is not surprising to find that neo-classical writers are generally optimistic about the future possibilities for continued development. Ricardo visualizes historical development as being limited by the scarcity of fertile lands. Productive improvements only mitigate temporarily the consequences of this obstacle. Historical diminishing returns tend to prevail in the sense that, given the fact of a fixed supply of land and taking into account expected technological progress, as labor and capital increase over time the ratio between the increment in national product and the increment of labor and capital tends to decline. Moreover, in Ricardo's view, Britain was not far from a stationary state position.

The neo-classical writers are more optimistic. "There seems to be no good reason for believing that we are anywhere near a stationary state . . . ."[23] They have greater faith in man's ability to overcome the limitations on growth imposed by his material environment; technological progress and improvements in the quality of labor produce a tendency towards historical increasing returns. In Marshall's words, "while the part which nature plays in production shows a tendency to diminishing return, the part which man plays shows a tendency to increasing re-

[22] Young, *op. cit.*, 535.
[23] Marshall, *Principles*, 223.

turn."[24]   Furthermore, for the economy as a whole "the tendencies to increasing and diminishing return appear pretty well balanced, sometimes the one, sometimes the other being the stronger."[25]   Under these conditions, a proportionate increase in labor and capital leaves output per dose of labor and capital the same.   Therefore, wages per worker and the interest rate need not change.   If, however, capital increases faster than labor, i.e., capital-deepening occurs, wages per worker tend to rise, and the interest rate tends to fall.   Thus, neo-classical economists strongly emphasize the importance of capital-deepening.   In a sense, they regard economic development as a race between capital accumulation and population growth.

They do not consider technological limitations on the possibility of raising income per unit of labor to be serious.   As their discussion of internal and external economies indicates, most neo-classical writers believe that even with a constant state of technological knowledge and a given labor supply the possibilities of increasing national income by capital accumulation are extremely favorable.   The marginal productivity of capital is assumed to decline very gradually as the capital stock grows over time.   As Cassel says, a slight drop in the interest rate "suffices, as a rule, to set free possibilities of the profitable use of durable goods to such an extent that the consequent demands for a disposal of capital completely exhaust the supply, and so prevent any further fall of the rate."[26]   Furthermore, these economists assume that there is a gradual and autonomous growth of technological knowledge and wants in the society.   This continually opens up new physical possibilities for increasing income per unit of labor.

Neo-classical writers focus particular attention on the willingness to save as a major requirement for development.   Thrift is the great virtue. For, unless society is prepared to save, the technological possibilities for raising per capita income by capital formation will remain unutilized. Fortunately, they believe the habit of thrift to be growing.   In Marshall's

---

[24] *Ibid.,* 318.   What Marshall seems to mean is that as the economy develops over time within a given state of technology the average productivity of equal doses of labor and capital tends to decline.   However, the efforts of man lead to technological progress and improvements in labor efficiency.   Historically, these tend to produce an increase in the average productivity of equal doses of labor and capital.

[25] *Ibid.,* 670.   Marshall thus appears to believe that constant returns to labor and capital tend to prevail in a historical sense, i.e., taking into account changes in technology, natural resource conditions, and the efficiency of the labor force.

[26] Cassel, *op. cit.,* I, 215.   Marshall, *Principles,* 223, also is very optimistic about the opportunities for capital-deepening with a given state of technology and population.

words, compared to earlier periods, man "is more unselfish, and therefore more inclined to work and save in order to secure a future provision for his family; and there are already faint signs of a brighter time to come, in which there will be a general willingness to work and save in order to increase the stores of public wealth and of public opportunities for leading a higher life."[27]

Nevertheless, neo-classical economists are not completely able to allay Malthusian fears. When they look far ahead, they are not so confident. Knut Wicksell, another leading Swedish economist, remarks, "The unprecedented growth of population recently witnessed in Europe, and still more in certain extra-European countries, will certainly, sooner or later—probably in the course of the present century—prepare the way for much slower progress and possibly for completely stationary conditions."[28] Even Marshall writes, "And yet, if the growth of population should continue for very long even at a quarter of its present rate, the aggregate rental values of land for all its uses (assumed to be as free as now from restraint by public authority) may again exceed the aggregate of incomes derived from all other forms of material property."[29]

These economists also express some concern over the opportunities for continued rapid progress in their discussions of the long-run course of international trade. Marshall warns that when only "a few small areas" of the world do not possess the population and capital to produce their own manufactures, "those who have surplus raw products to sell will have the upper hand in all international bargains. . . . It is this consideration, rather than the prospect of any immediate danger, which makes me regard the future of England with grave anxiety."[30] The old industrial countries, in other words, may be faced with a secular deterioration in their terms of trade, i.e., the ratio of export to import prices.

As the poorer nations grow by introducing industrial techniques developed in the older countries, these older industrial countries also must contend with increasing competition in their export markets. "That combination of liberty with order, and of individual responsibility with organised discipline, in which England excelled, was needed for pioneer work in manufactures; while little more than mere order and organised discipline will go a long way towards success, where the same tasks are

---

[27] Marshall, *Principles*, 680.

[28] K. Wicksell, *Lectures on Political Economy*, tr. by E. Classen, George Routledge and Sons, Ltd., London, 1934, I, 214.

[29] Marshall, *Principles*, xv–xvi.

[30] Alfred Marshall, "Memorandum on the Fiscal Policy of International Trade," *Official Papers*, Macmillan and Co., Ltd., London, 1926, 402.

performed by modern machinery 'which does most of the thinking itself.' Thus England is at a steadily increasing relative disadvantage in trading not merely with people like the Japanese, who can assimilate every part of the work of an advanced factory; but also with places where there are abundant supplies of low-grade labour, organised by a relatively small number of able and skilled men of a higher race. This is already largely done in America, and it certainly will be done on an ever-increasing scale in other continents."[31]

5. International Aspects of Development

The theory of international trade as formulated by neo-classical writers should also be examined in this survey of development theory. Even today this theory dominates thinking in the field of international economics in discussions both of rich and poor countries.

Neo-classical economists, following the classical theorists, continue to study international trade largely in static terms. They ask two main questions. First, what are the causes of trade among nations and what determines the composition of this trade? Secondly, what is the adjustment mechanism by which equilibrium in the balance of payments among trading partners is maintained?

In analyzing the first question, the neo-classical writers extend and refine the doctrine of comparative costs. Briefly, this theory states that if trade is left free each nation in the long run tends to specialize upon the production of those commodities in which it enjoys a comparative cost advantage in real terms. It exports these commodities, while importing those goods for which it possesses a comparative cost disadvantage. Following this principle, countries possessing an abundant stock of fertile land in relation to other factors tend to specialize upon land-requiring agricultural products; nations with a large stock of capital in relation to the other productive means tend to specialize upon manufactures, i.e., goods requiring relatively large amounts of capital.[32] A country thus exports commodities that embody intensively in their production the country's relatively abundant, and therefore cheap, factors of production. It imports commodities whose production requirements are better fulfilled by other countries that have a different factor endowment and different costs of production. Compared with a condition of no trade, this international specialization with given factor supplies achieves an optimum allocation of resources throughout the world economy, thereby enabling the world production of at least some com-

---

[31] *Ibid.,* 404.

[32] For a more detailed discussion of the theory, see Chapter 10, section 1.

modities to be increased without decreasing the world output of other goods.

Using this theory neo-classical writers, like classical economists, stress the advantages of international trade to a country in its efforts to raise real national income. By opening new markets, foreign trade allows the nation to reap the benefits of further specialization and division of labor. The resultant increase in income also permits a larger volume of saving and raises the rate of domestic capital formation.

These economists are more cautious, however, than the early classical writers in concluding that free trade is the best policy for each nation. They clearly recognize "that under conceivable circumstances advantage may result to the home country from a tax on exports or imports."[33] The gain is secured via an improvement in the terms of trade. Similarly, they recognize that a technological improvement in a country may actually worsen this country's real income position because of a sharp deterioration in its terms of trade.[34] The "infant industry" argument is also granted. "It may be admitted that there is some force in the claim that a Protective tariff is needed to aid giant businesses in establishing a complete standardization on the most advanced modern model."[35] Marshall also advances another interesting argument. The tax may be justified because "the energy developed in a few high-class progressive industries may spread over a great part of the industrial system of the country."[35] Finally, some neo-classical theorists also point out that it is possible for the earnings of a particular factor to decrease after the introduction of free trade.[36]

Although these writers admit such exceptions to the free trade argument, nonetheless they still favor a general policy of free trade. Edgeworth's remark expresses their feelings: "protection might procure economic advantage in certain cases, if there was a Government wise enough to discriminate those cases, and strong enough to confine itself to them; but this condition is very unlikely to be fulfilled."[37] Most

[33] F. Y. Edgeworth, *Papers Relating to Political Economy,* Macmillan and Co., Ltd., London, 1925, II, 16–17. Hereinafter cited as Edgeworth, *Papers.*

[34] See C. F. Bastable, *The Theory of International Trade,* fourth edition, Macmillan and Co., Ltd., London, 1903, Appendix C, 185–187, for a review of the controversy between Edgeworth and Nicholson on this point.

[35] A. Marshall, *Money, Credit, and Commerce,* Macmillan and Co., Ltd., London, 1929, 218. Hereinafter cited as Marshall, *Money, Credit, and Commerce.*

[36] See H. Sidgwick, *Principles of Political Economy,* Macmillan and Co., Ltd., London, 1883, 494–497; C. F. Bastable, *op. cit.,* 97–109, 187–191; F. Y. Edgeworth's review article on the third edition of Bastable's book, *Economic Journal, X,* No. 39, 389–393 (Sept. 1900).

[37] Edgeworth, *Papers,* II, 18.

neo-classical economists believe along with Nicholson that "Free trade, like honesty, still remains the best policy."[38]

The formal international trade model of the classical and neo-classical economists focuses upon those aspects of development which are related to a more efficient utilization of given factor supplies or which are associated with the stimuli to the domestic growth of productive factors that an increase in national income from trade generates. The model does not center attention upon the type of development connected with international flows of labor and capital. It has been sharply criticized for this reason.[39]

Yet the neo-classical writers are aware of the limited nature of their international trade theory. They realize that labor and capital are not completely immobile internationally. Like classical theorists, however, they believe that labor and capital are usually relatively more mobile within a country than among countries. As Marshall remarks, "first, a capitalist has, as a rule, a slight preference for an investment in his own country over one that holds out equal prospects of success and high profits in another; and secondly, a smaller expectation of an increase in earnings and other material advantages, in return for equally difficult and arduous work, will generally suffice to induce a man to migrate from one part to another of his own country, rather than to emigrate to another country."[40] This is their justification for a separate theory of international trade.

Furthermore, the neo-classical writers appreciate that their model is not very realistic in describing the trading relationships among "old" and "new" countries. Their arithmetical examples explaining the doctrine of comparative costs invariably deal with two advanced countries. In these cases, they maintain that, because of linguistic and cultural obstacles, the international movement of population and capital can be neglected. In analyzing the economic relations between the industrial countries and those countries that are developed by immigrants from advanced countries, they seem to think more in terms of their domestic theory of development.

They also give some explicit attention to how the international flow of labor and capital affects the development of new countries. Marshall states that "the expansion of a country's foreign trade depends largely

---

[38] Quoted in Edgeworth, *ibid.,* 17. For a discussion of some of the modern criticisms of the neo-classical theory of international trade, see Chapter 15, section 3, and Chapter 19, section 1.

[39] For example, J. H. Williams, *Postwar Monetary Plans and Other Essays,* Alfred A. Knopf, New York, 1945, 134–135.

[40] Marshall, *Money, Credit, and Commerce,* 10.

on her facilities for internal transport; and that these facilities, in so far as they do not proceed from natural waterways, are generally indications of a highly developed internal trade. The chief exceptions to this general rule are found when colonists from an advanced industrial country take up mineral, pastoral, or agricultural land in a new country; for then they obtain, chiefly from their own home, the capital required for building railways from the interior to convenient ports. This is one of many ways, in which developments of external trade anticipate varied industrial activities, and prepare the way for them."[41] The ensuing development "tends to increase the prosperity of both old and new countries."[42] The old countries gain by the expansion of the market and resultant division of labor, and the new countries "gain by the resources which their external trade supplies for making great truck roads and railroads, and for developing harbours."[42] Development, which is stimulated by factor movements, in other words, tends, like domestic development, to be a harmonious process, at least during its early stages.[43]

According to neo-classical writers, international capital transfers occur without creating serious balance of payments difficulties. There are, they contend, strong equilibrating forces in the balance of payments mechanism. By equilibrium in the balance of payments, they mean that exports and imports of goods and services differ only by the amount of long-term capital movements. If this condition does not exist, balancing gold or short-term capital movements must be taking place, since both sides of a balance of payments account always are equal in an accounting sense. However, gold or short-term capital movements in one direction usually can continue only for a short period; there are limits to a country's gold reserves and its ability to borrow short-term capital. But, neo-classical economists, like classical writers, maintain that long-term capital flows produce repercussions that prevent the necessity of gold or short-term capital movements from occurring for more than a short period.[44]

Neo-classical theorists distinguish at least five borrowing-lending stages through which a country may pass. First, in the early stages of its development, a country is likely to be a net long-term importer of capital. Net interest and dividend payments are less than the country's net long-term capital imports. The adjustment mechanism in the bal-

[41] *Ibid.,* 112.

[42] *Ibid.,* 203.

[43] As mentioned previously (pp. 77–78), Marshall is somewhat pessimistic about the long-run effects on the older countries.

[44] See Chapter 1, section 6, for the classical writers' description of this equilibrating mechanism. Neo-classical discussion of this process is essentially the same.

ance of payments therefore operates so that the country tends to have a net deficit on current account even excluding interest and dividend payments.[45]   The country is a young debtor.   Later, as interest and dividend charges on the country's debt mount and surpass net capital imports, the nation passes into a second stage.   Now the nation tends to have a net surplus on current account if interest and dividend payments are excluded.   However, since net payments on the interest and dividend account are so large, the current account as a whole shows a net deficit.

Next, the country begins to buy back and redeem its outstanding debt and also starts to lend to other countries.   These long-term capital exports exceed long-term capital imports.   Thus, the country shifts from being a net long-term capital importer to a net long-term capital exporter.   But interest and dividend payments still exceed interest and dividend receipts, i.e., the country remains a net international debtor. At this stage the country tends to have a net surplus on current account as a whole.   The country is a mature debtor.

In the fourth stage the country has net interest and dividend receipts. It becomes a young creditor.   Net receipts of interest and dividends, however, are less than net exports of long-term capital.   Therefore, the country tends to have a surplus on current account even excluding net interest and dividend receipts.

Finally, the nation reaches the position in which net interest and dividend receipts exceed net long-term capital exports.   The country tends to have a net deficit on current account if these net interest and dividends receipts are excluded but a surplus for the current account as a whole.   The country is a mature creditor.

6. Appraisal of Neo-Classical Analysis

As with all theories, the adequacy of neo-classical theory as an explanation of the development process depends upon the accuracy of its vision concerning the important causal variables in economic activity. In constructing models relevant for an analysis of development in Western capitalist countries, most neo-classical writers, like the classical economists, generally assume the existence of such conditions as political stability, a firm "will to develop" among the people, strong habits

---

[45] The current account includes merchandise transactions, interest and dividend receipts and payments, and such service items as transportation, insurance, and tourist receipts and payments.   A deficit on current account exists if the payments a country makes in connection with these transactions exceed its receipts from foreigners.   A current account surplus, on the other hand, means that the country's receipts from these transactions are greater than its payments.

of thrift, given tastes, an adequate supply of trained labor and managerial skill, atomistic competition, a high degree of domestic factor mobility, and a rapid flow of economic knowledge within and among nations. They especially emphasize quantitative changes in population, capital stock, natural resources, and improvements in techniques. In this area, they unquestionably make a significant contribution to the better understanding of the causes and processes of economic development.

Yet such an approach to the development problem is obviously open to the criticism of being too narrow. For it tends to minimize the significance for development of changes in such unmeasurable, non-economic elements as the degree of political stability and the attitudes of the population. A notable exception, however, is Marshall, who fully recognizes the limited nature of the theoretical analysis. Marshall never lets formal theory dominate his writing; he discusses these matters outside the traditional confines of economics and stresses their importance for understanding economic growth. But most neo-classical economists do not approach the study of economics with as broad a vision as does Marshall.

Another criticism of the neo-classical scheme might be offered on the grounds that neo-classical economists assume that the forces making for development operate in a gradual, continuous fashion. This implies the existence of an economic environment in which a high degree of certainty exists and in which careful rational calculation is feasible. Consequently, the price mechanism becomes an important device in determining the nature of an economy's production for both current and future needs. In particular, the rate of interest is considered an important determinant of investment. If, however, the neo-classical assumptions are modified to allow the forces of development to behave in a discontinuous fashion, the picture changes considerably. The degree of uncertainty about the future increases—so much, perhaps, that the interest rate ceases to be an important factor in the decision-making process of investors.

The neo-classical view of development as a process that is generally harmonious and beneficial to all sectors of the economy and to other countries is closely related to the concept of development as a gradual process. If the continuity of growth is not emphasized so strongly, the disruptive and harmful aspects of development acquire more significance. Neo-classical writers do not emphasize these aspects of economic change sufficiently.

Still another drawback of neo-classical theory is the assumption of full employment. Neo-classical writers do not analyze adequately the problem of maintaining aggregate demand at a full employment level. The international trade theory of the neo-classical writers is open to the same kind of criticisms. When full employment conditions do not exist and when governments are unwilling to play according to the "rules" of the gold standard, their analysis of the balance of payments adjustment mechanism must be modified. The price-specie-flow theory cannot then be the full explanation; other forces must also be operative.[46] Furthermore, if one accepts a discontinuous, volatile picture of dynamic economic change rather than the neo-classical framework, their free trade policy advice may be less relevant.

[46] See Chapter 11, section 3, below.

Chapter 4

Schumpeterian

Analysis

In studying development themes, one becomes increasingly concerned over the pessimism of many economists regarding capitalism's ability to promote continued and successful growth. In the Ricardian model the future (under all systems) holds only the promise of stagnation with subsistence wages; according to Marx, capitalism is doomed to explode and suffer a painful death. Stagnation theorists (as will be seen in Chapter 5) predict that mature capitalistic economies are in danger of sliding into a state of chronic unemployment. Schumpeter's approach, at first sight, offers the promise of a refreshing change from these disquieting forecasts.

In his analysis there is no immutable law of diminishing returns or Malthusian population principle to crush progress (Ricardo); nor is there an inherent tendency towards a maldistribution of income to produce successively more severe crises (Marx). There is, moreover, no persistent lack of investment opportunities coupled with institutional rigidities to cause under-full-employment equilibrium (the stagnationists). Quite the contrary, on narrow economic grounds alone, Schumpeter contends that capitalism can yield ever-higher levels of real income at the cost of nothing more than temporary interruptions in economic activity. His argument, however, has a Marxian twist. The very success of capitalism in the economic realm breeds changes in social attitudes and institutions that destroy the system. Thus, "In a way, Schumpeter is the most uncompromising stagnationist of them all."[1]

1. Schumpeter's Vision

Schumpeter rejects the neo-classical description of development as a gradual, harmonious process.[2] Instead, he argues that significant advances in national product occur by disharmonious leaps and spurts as entirely new investment horizons are exploited. Furthermore, this progress is invariably associated with alternating periods of short-run prosperity and depression. Bursts of economic activity, such as those led by the railroadization movement in the last century and by the expansion of the electrical and automotive industries in this century, illustrate the type of rapid development that interests Schumpeter. To him, this is not only the most interesting but also the most important (in a quantitative sense) type of economic development for industrial, capitalistic nations.

The only other major pre-Schumpeterian economist who attempts to interpret development in a dynamic, discontinuous fashion is Marx. And the influence of Marx on Schumpeter is strikingly apparent. But this influence is reflected more by Schumpeter's general sympathy with Marx's dynamic viewpoint towards economic activity than by his use of the specific Marxian tools of analysis. Furthermore, on ideological grounds, few are more opposed to Marxism than is Schumpeter. For the basic tools with which to analyze economic processes under stationary conditions, Schumpeter relies on the neo-classical writers, particularly Walras with his general equilibrium theory. It is a propitious combination—the elegant general equilibrium framework of the neo-classical theorists and the essentially dynamic vision of capitalism which Marx stresses.

---

[1] Arthur Smithies, "Joseph Alois Schumpeter," *American Economic Review,* XL, No. 4, 640 (Sept. 1950).

[2] Schumpeter's major works relating to the problem of economic development are: J. A. Schumpeter, *The Theory of Economic Development,* tr. by R. Opie, Harvard University Press, Cambridge, 1934; J. A. Schumpeter, *Business Cycles,* McGraw-Hill Book Co., New York, 1939; J. A. Schumpeter, *Capitalism, Socialism, and Democracy,* second edition, Harper and Brothers, New York, 1947; and J. A. Schumpeter, *Imperialism and Social Classes,* tr. by H. Norden, Augustus M. Kelley, Inc., New York, 1951. Hereinafter cited as Schumpeter, *The Theory of Economic Development;* Schumpeter, *Business Cycles;* Schumpeter, *Capitalism, Socialism, and Democracy;* and Schumpeter, *Imperialism and Social Classes.*

The central figure in Schumpeter's analysis of the development process is the entrepreneur. He is the innovator, the one who undertakes new combinations of the factors of production. Innovations may occur in the following forms: (1) the introduction of a new good; (2) the use of a new method of production; (3) the opening of a new market; (4) the conquest of a new source of raw material supply; or (5) the reorganization of any industry.

The nature of this entrepreneurial function reveals the dynamic nature of Schumpeter's conception of economic development. Entrepreneurship is not ordinary managerial activity. The latter type of performance consists merely in directing production under existing techniques, but the former function requires the introduction of something entirely new. Nor is the entrepreneur synonymous with the capitalist, although in some cases he may be the same person. The capitalist furnishes the funds, whereas the entrepreneur directs the use of these funds. "It is leadership rather than ownership that matters."[3] Furthermore, the entrepreneur may, but need not, be the inventor of the product or process that he introduces. In this regard, it should be noted that Schumpeter, like Marx, postulates the existence of a continuous stream of innovation possibilities.[4] The existence of innovation possibilities, according to Schumpeter, is a necessary but not sufficient condition for development; entrepreneurs are also needed for carrying out innovations.

Classical and neo-classical economists certainly are aware of the great importance of the role that exceptional business leaders play in the development process,[5] but in their theoretical formulations they do not stress entrepreneurship to the extent that Schumpeter does. The reason Schumpeter emphasizes entrepreneurship is connected with his view of development as occurring by discontinuous spurts in a dynamic world. In the neo-classical view of the economic world, development takes place gradually and smoothly. Consequently, investment decisions can be based on reasonably rational calculations. Rather than stress the difficulties involved in making investment decisions, the neo-classical writers concentrate upon the significance of the act of saving in the development process. But, in a Schumpeterian world, a high degree of risk and uncertainty exists. Under these circumstances, rational calculation is impossible, and the ordinary businessman hesitates to increase the size of his operations.

[3] Schumpeter, *Business Cycles*, I, 103.
[4] *Ibid.*, 130.
[5] For example, see A. Marshall, *Industry and Trade*, Macmillan and Co., Ltd., London, 1919, 47–49.

A specially motivated and talented type of individual—the entrepreneur—is therefore necessary in this environment both to see potentially profitable opportunities and to exploit them. The entrepreneur's motivation for profits (the measure of his success) is based, says Schumpeter, not merely on the desire to raise his consumption standard but also on such non-hedonistic goals as the desire to found a private dynasty, the will to conquer in the competitive battle, and the joy of creating.

Nevertheless, is not the role of the saver, the person who does not consume his entire income, vitally important in the development process? It is, but the act of saving enters the Schumpeterian system in a novel way. The entrepreneur secures the funds for his projects not from saving out of current income but from the credit-creating banking system. Here is a sharp and fundamental break from the classical and neo-classical traditions. Theorists in these traditions invariably analyze the "real" side of economics under the assumptions either of a given supply of money or a supply that passively responds to changes in the output of goods and services so that the general price level remains constant. They assume that money plays no significant, independent part in determining the real variables in the system. Money is merely a veil which tends to hide the behavior of the basic forces at work and consequently should be handled by one of the above assumptions. Only after discussing these fundamental forces do most neo-classical economists introduce variations in the supply of money. Then the analysis usually explains only how these changes affect the general level of prices over the business cycle, thus slighting their effects on the basic real variables. It is not until after the publication of Lord Keynes's *General Theory of Employment, Interest, and Money* (1936) that most economists agree on the misleading nature of this approach. But Schumpeter already sees its inappropriateness early in this century.

When credit creation is made an integral part of a development model, one is more likely to think of growth as an uneven process, since investment can be increased quickly through bank borrowing. Under conditions of full employment, when entrepreneurs expand their innovating activities by borrowing from the banks, they bid up the prices of the desired means of production. If these productive factors were previously employed in producing consumption goods, their movement into the investment channels of the entrepreneurs curtails the output of consumption commodities, "forcing" the economy to save more, i.e., consume less in real terms. Thus credit-creating facilities tend to free investors from the voluntary abstinence routine of savers. "Forced savings" become an important means of capital accumulation. Nevertheless, there are definite limits to the amount of capital accumulation that can occur by this inflationary method. As the price level rises and the money supply expands still more (because of borrowing by all groups), entrepreneurs find it increasingly difficult to secure real resources. However, in the Schumpeterian model, after entrepreneurs complete their projects, they repay the bank loans out of their profits. The net effect is a spurt in real investment which would have been impossible but for the expansion in credit.

Another feature of the dynamic Schumpeterian model, which increases the prominence of the entrepreneur in the development process, is the minimization of the role of consumer sovereignty. Specifically, Schumpeter assumes (as did Marx) that changes in consumer tastes are brought about by producer's actions. He does not deny that sometimes consumers initiate these changes, but he feels that such shifts are of negligible importance in accounting for rapid economic change. Unless this supposition is made, innovations would tend to be restricted to those types that reduce the costs of producing existing products—a much too narrow view of the total development process.

All these assumptions by Schumpeter are designed to emphasize the crucial role that entrepreneurship plays in the development process. Without the presence of this vital economic function, Schumpeter asserts that progress under capitalism would be much slower than it actually is.

2. Economics of Capitalist Development

Given a society in which entrepreneurship can flourish, how do entrepreneurs spark the process of economic development? The explanation is quite simple.[6] As a starting point, Schumpeter assumes a purely competitive economy in a stationary state; i.e., there is neither net investment nor population growth, and full employment prevails. There are, however, opportunities for new combinations of the means of production. Entrepreneurs recognize these profit opportunities and prepare to exploit them. To secure the requisite resources to undertake the innovations, entrepreneurs borrow from credit-creating banks and "raid the circular flow." The price they must pay for these funds is the interest rate which represents a portion of their potential profits.[7] With

[6] The best brief account of this theory of development is in Schumpeter, *Business Cycles,* I, Chapter 4.

[7] In his early work, *The Theory of Economic Development,* Chapter V, Schumpeter held that in the stationary state the rate of interest would be zero and that, therefore, in a dynamic economy entrepreneurial profit is the only source of interest payments. Unfortunately, much of the discussion of Schumpeter has centered around this unnecessary point and has tended to cloud his main argument. In *Business Cycles,* Schumpeter modified his position on this point or, more

a few leaders smoothing the path, the original innovators soon are followed by a "swarm-like" appearance of entrepreneurial activity. The boom then gathers speed. Prices and money incomes rise as entrepreneurial spending permeates the entire economy and productive factors are released from consumption-goods industries as a result of forced saving. This, in turn, induces a secondary economic wave, which is superimposed upon the innovational activity. Old firms, being encouraged by more consumer spending, expand their production. Speculation develops as businessmen attempt to anticipate additional rises in prices and money income. Now bank borrowing no longer finances only innovational activity but also finances a general expansion under existing methods of production. In quantitative terms, this imitative investment may be larger than the original innovational investment.

During the early stages of the upswing, the composition of total output shifts from consumer to producer goods. But gradually the innovations are completed, and the flow of goods from these activities increases. Then a process of "creative destruction" ensues. Old firms find their markets destroyed or curtailed by the advent of new, competing products or by new firms who can market products at much lower prices. Some of these established firms are forced into bankruptcy; others must accept positions of less prominence in their industry. In short, a painful process of readjustment is necessary to absorb the effects of the primary entrepreneurial activity.

Moreover, as innovational activity is brought to fruition the repayment of bank loans by entrepreneurs sets deflationary forces in action. And these deflationary forces are not offset by new entrepreneurial borrowing because the increasing stream of both new commodities and old commodities produced under new conditions creates a state of disequilibrium which makes it impossible for entrepreneurs to calculate costs and receipts in a satisfactory manner. Uncertainty and risk are so high that entrepreneurial activity declines and eventually stops. Innovation halts not because there is a lack of inventions, but because the economic environment is unfavorable to further innovation. As innovational activity declines, the deflationary effect of loan repayment by entrepreneurs forces prices and money incomes lower, thus intensifying the adjustment process. All of this is not sufficient, however, to

---

correctly, was willing to accept a more conventional theory of the interest rate (see pp. 123–129) in order to minimize this side issue. For an excellent criticism of Schumpeter's theory of the interest rate, see P. A. Samuelson, "Dynamics, Statics, and the Stationary State," *Review of Economic Statistics, XXV*, No. 1, 58–68 (Feb. 1943).

cause a full-scale depression. It causes a painful readjustment process or recession, but, before long, the climate again is ripe for further entrepreneurial activity.

However, the effects of the cessation of innovational activity on the secondary investment wave precipitate a full-scale depression. Secondary investments are based upon actual or expected price rises. In the early stages of the boom these price rises actually occur. But, once the process of creative destruction halts the primary wave, these secondary investments also collapse and cause a sharp cumulative downward movement in economic activity. This decline overshoots the position to which the economy would have declined with the existence of the primary wave alone and brings a typical depression. Although Schumpeter believes that it is theoretically possible that the system may never recover, he maintains that the usual case is a return to equilibrium and full employment before too long a period. The liquidation of weak enterprises gradually exhausts itself as the necessary adjustments to the innovations are completed. Once equilibrium is restored, the stage is then set for a new wave of innovations and a repetition of the cycle.

The new equilibrium, however, is higher than the one from which the growth began. National and per capita incomes in real terms continually rise via the cyclical mechanism. Furthermore, all the major income groups in the economy benefit. Unlike Ricardo or Marx, Schumpeter does not emphasize a conflict of distributional interests during the process of development. Labor, in particular, reaps large gains, since a major share of innovational efforts under capitalism are directed towards mass-produced consumer commodities.

To complete his model, Schumpeter assumes the existence of investment that is financed by saving from current income, population growth, and elements of imperfect competition. Furthermore, he notes, the process need not start from a stationary position nor need the innovations be introduced merely in the neighborhood of equilibrium. Although these various factors blur the detailed operation of the pure model, Schumpeter argues that they do not change its essential characteristics.

In summary the key individuals in Schumpeter's theory of development are the entrepreneurs. They are the initiators of significant advances in national product. And these increases do not occur through a smooth, continuous process; economic development is an uneven, disharmonious process. Cyclical swings are the cost of economic development under capitalism.

3. Sociology of Capitalist Development

So far as Schumpeter's argument has been discussed, there are no purely economic barriers under capitalism to the general upward move-ment in national product. There is, however, a catch. In Schumpeter's words, ". . . the actual and prospective performance of the capitalist system is such as to negative the idea of its breaking down under the weight of economic failure, but . . . its very success undermines the social institutions which protect it, and 'inevitably' creates conditions in which it will not be able to live and which strongly point to socialism as the heir apparent."[8]

Schumpeter begins his reasoning towards this conclusion by asserting that the cultural complement of the capitalist economy rests on rational-ism, as distinct from those cultures in which decisions are made by disregarding logic and in which beliefs are derived from non-empirical sources. A rationalistic civilization does not imply the absence of all non-rational criteria but merely the incessant widening of rational thought. Nor does Schumpeter say that capitalism is the only culture in which rationality exists. But he stresses that capitalism supports rationality and extends it. Capitalism exalts the monetary unit into a unit of account and adopts a cost-profit calculus, which facilitates the logic of business enterprise. This attitude of rational individualism, in turn, permeates every branch of thinking—art, science, religion, medicine. Capitalism also creates a new and conducive social en-vironment for individual achievement in the economic field. The attraction of the best brains in society into this area gives the rationalist engine additional force. Consequently, "Not only the modern mecha-nized plant and the volume of the output that pours forth from it, not only modern technology and economic organization, but all the features and achievements of modern civilization are, directly or indirectly, the products of the capitalist process."[9]

With this sweeping background, Schumpeter then argues that the economic and social foundations of capitalism are beginning to crumble. He bases his case on three points: (1) the obsolescence of the entre-preneurial function; (2) the destruction of the institutional framework of capitalist society; and (3) the destruction of the protecting political strata.

As was pointed out in the previous section, entrepreneurial activity consists of breaking through existing economic patterns and creating something entirely new. Obstacles are overcome, and economic change

[8] Schumpeter, *Capitalism, Socialism, and Democracy*, 61.
[9] *Ibid.*, 125.

results. This was the great contribution of the early captains of industry and commerce under capitalism. But their very success makes innovation routine. Technological progress is now the business of teams of specialists operating within large productive units; the marketing and the administering of new activities is a well-established automatic process; consumers are thoroughly conditioned to new commodities and accept them as a matter of course. Innovation thus degenerates into a depersonalized, routine activity carried on in big businesses through a bureaucracy of highly trained managers. Entrepreneurs, in the sense of unique, individual leaders, find their economic function usurped.

Without an economic role, the entrepreneur and the entire bourgeois class, which depends on present and past entrepreneurial activity for its existence, lose their social function. This in turn tends to reduce the industrial bourgeoisie from a group living, directly or indirectly, off profits to a wage class, which is paid merely for current administrative work.

Moving to the second point, Schumpeter contends that the entrepreneur tends to destroy not only his own economic and social functions by his very success but also the institutional framework within which he operates. The trend towards concentration and large business units destroys the vitality of such basic capitalistic institutions as private property and freedom of contract. The evils of bigness are not in the economic field, according to Schumpeter. Indeed he believes that bigness contributes to more rapid economic progress. The evil is that bigness weakens the concepts of private property and freedom of contract.

In the large corporation the figure of the proprietor and the specifically proprietary interest frequently disappear. The proprietor's role is performed by a group of professional, salaried managers; the specifically proprietary interest is replaced by large and small stockholders. These changes tend to weaken the concepts of private property and free individual contract. For the managerial group tends to acquire an employee attitude and does not identify itself merely with the stockholders' interests. The stockholders, on the other hand, are divorced from active management and lose the essential attitudes of an owner interest. "Dematerialized, defunctionalized and absentee ownership does not impress and call forth moral allegiance as the vital form of property did. Eventually there will be *nobody* left who really cares to stand for it—nobody within and nobody without the precincts of the big concerns."[10]

[10] *Ibid.,* 142.

The picture is even blacker. Not only do the functions of the entrepreneur and the institutional framework of capitalism crumble but also the group that protected early capitalism in the political sphere is destroyed. Along with capitalism, strong national states based on a monarchial type of government arose during the sixteenth–eighteenth centuries. Having subjugated the landed aristocracy, the royal power supported the rising industrialists and merchants politically and was in turn supported by the industrialists and merchants economically. But the very success of capitalism eventually destroyed the royal power. As industrialists and merchants became economically more powerful and their rationalistic attitudes spread into every field, they entered into the political arena where they secured power and instituted wide political reforms based on their rationalistic attitudes. But, according to Schumpeter, this group is ill-equipped to rule. "There is surely no trace of any mystic glamor about him [the industrialist or merchant] which is what counts in the ruling of men."[11] Rational, unheroic means are insufficient to handle successfully the domestic and international problems which inevitably face a ruling group.

Although the obsolescence of the entrepreneurial function, the destruction of such institutions as private property and freedom of contract, and the dissolution of the social class that protects the bourgeoisie politically weaken the economic and social foundations of capitalism, they are not enough to destroy capitalism. According to Schumpeter, active hostility against the social order is necessary. This hostility is furnished by the intellectual, who voices and leads the anti-capitalist interests. For the capitalist process itself gives the intellectual much greater freedom and more means to practice his profession. This profession, Schumpeter maintains, consists typically of criticism—criticism of persons, current events, classes, and institutions. Moreover, these intellectuals are swelled in numbers by an oversupply of educated, white-collar groups (another "fruit" of capitalism) who find employment opportunities insufficient in terms of their training and desires. This further aggravates the hostile attitude towards the social system. Still another feature of capitalism is the creation of a labor movement. Here the intellectual finds a ready-made class for which he can provide intellectual leadership and by means of which he can secure the anti-capitalist political reforms that he desires. The net result is a steady decomposition of the political framework upon which capitalism rests and a continual movement towards socialism.

Finally, Schumpeter emphasizes the disintegration of the bourgeois family. Rationalism even extends to family life. Parents begin to

[11] *Ibid.*, 137.

weigh the advantages of children on a kind of cost calculus, comparing the "joys of parenthood" with the alternatives of increased leisure, freedom, and real income. This attitude weakens the traditional idea of the home with all its social and economic implications. Along with this decline in the driving power supplied by the family motive, the businessman shortens his time horizon. No longer is there the desire to found a family dynasty. The accumulation drive weakens, and, with it, so does another vital aspect of the capitalist milieu.

4. Appraisal of Schumpeterian Analysis

Schumpeter's theory must be ranked as a major performance, one worthy of the tradition of such great economists as Smith, Ricardo, Mill, Marx, Marshall, and Keynes. But, even though it is replete with the brilliant reasoning and insights of a great theorist, it risks generality by emphasizing one particular set of relationships.

As was pointed out, the economic act upon which Schumpeter concentrates is the process of innovation as initiated by entrepreneurs. Clearly, his analysis of entrepreneurial innovation is highly useful in understanding better the historical development of capitalism. In this century, however, there has been a gradual change in the nature of the innovating process. Previously, most innovational activity was undertaken either by the inventors themselves or by entrepreneurs who purchased rights to the inventor's new product or process. Today, however, the acts of invention and innovation frequently are carried on by large corporations in a rather routine, calculable fashion and without the identification of a single entrepreneur. Under these conditions, one might suggest that it is best to regard innovation merely as a normal part of business activity.[12] Certainly, the nature of entrepreneurship in modern capitalism is markedly different from that described in Schumpeter's pure model. The functions of innovation in the large business unit typically are performed by a large and changing number of individuals. It is hard to identify the entrepreneurs of many actual innovations or to distinguish their performanace and motivation in this activity from their ordinary business activities. Research and development costs might be regarded as business expenses that yield a normal return in the form of new products and processes, just as other business costs do.

Of course, in a sense, Schumpeter makes this point himself in so far

[12] See C. Solo, "Innovation in the Capitalist Process: A Critique of the Schumpeterian Theory," *Quarterly Journal of Economics, LXV,* No. 3, 417–428 (Aug. 1951).

as he asserts that the entrepreneur is becoming obsolete. Realizing that his description of entrepreneurial activity does not agree with modern capitalistic practices, he concludes not that his theory is inadequate but that the lack of harmony between his theory and modern practices indicates capitalism is dying.

Schumpeter's discussion of the innovational process centers mainly on the truly great innovations of the last 200 years, such as the steam engine, the railroad, the electric motor, and the gasoline engine. Although there also have been quantitatively important innovations in more recent years, nonetheless it can be argued that the economic shocks produced by these innovations are considerably less severe than those associated with most of the important earlier inventions. The growth of big business is a major reason for this, since large diversified business units can better absorb and plan for the adjustments required by innovation.

If this is true, Schumpeter's cyclical theory may have to be modified for an analysis of business cycles in modern capitalistic economies. In his theory, the cause of the downturn is the maladjustments created by a wave of innovations. But, if a big-business environment softens the destructive powers of innovational waves, then this factor may not be significant in explaining economic crises. Again, Schumpeter recognizes this: ". . . they [the monopolistic practices of big business] may in the end produce not only steadier but also greater expansion of total output than could be secured by an entirely uncontrolled onward rush that cannot fail to be studded with catastrophes."[13] In other words, he does not argue that his cycle theory is inadequate but that the forces making for peace-time crises are less powerful as big business develops. Although most modern cycle theorists accept Schumpeter's explanation of the downturn as a contributory cause of peace-time depressions and thus grant this conclusion in part, they also contend that Schumpeter's cause is only one (and usually not the most important) reason for depressions.

Schumpeter in presenting his pure model assumes that innovations are financed by borrowing from credit-creating banks. It may be questioned whether this is a very realistic assumption. One case where this assumption is usually regarded as valid is the period of German industrialization. The extensive renewal of short-term loans by German bankers meant in effect that they did finance long-term investment. But this type of financing has not occurred in many other capitalistic countries (for example, Britain, as will be seen in Chapter 8). The banking system usually grants only short-term loans; most innovations

[13] Schumpeter, *Capitalism, Socialism, and Democracy*, 91.

requiring fixed capital are financed by retained earnings or by the issuing of corporate securities.

It is not entirely clear why Schumpeter regards the financing of innovation as the "logical" source of credit creation. One interpretation might be as follows. Beginning at a non-stationary state position, firms see investment opportunities and begin borrowing. To meet the short-term commitments involved in the investment programs, they go to the banking system; for long-term funds, they rely upon the current volume of saving in the economy. As the money supply increases because of the expansion of short-term credit, inflation occurs. This tends to redistribute income in favor of profit receivers. And, since the saving propensity of this group tends to be comparatively high, a relatively greater volume of real, long-term investment can be undertaken in the economy than would otherwise be possible. Thus, an increase in innovational activity and an expansion of credit are closely linked. If this is Schumpeter's point, then criticisms concerning the question of whether in fact banks directly financed long-term investment are not too relevant.[14] For, in his pure model, he wishes merely to emphasize the connection between monetary expansion and the increase in investment. Schumpeter does overemphasize, however, the possibilities of increasing real investment by the inflation method in a fully employed economy.

Schumpeter's broad socioeconomic analysis of the capitalist process is generally admired. Yet few seem prepared to accept its conclusions. His arguments are stimulating, but not completely convincing.

It will be recalled that Schumpeter maintains that rational thought and behavior are responsible both for the success and for the destruction of capitalism. Although capitalism did not create rationalism (economic necessity had long before forced it on the human mind), the Industrial Revolution, with its transformation of basic economic factors, furnished unprecedented opportunities for the expansion of rationalism. Rewards in the economic sphere were so fascinating that enlightened individuals were attracted to it. And the very success of these individuals meant that their systematic and purposeful way of thinking spread slowly to other spheres of social life. Entrepreneurial success depended, however, upon the coexistence of non-rational attitudes. For these attitudes supplied not only the sources of motivation for entrepreneurs and indeed the entire bourgeois stratum but also the basis for maintaining a favorable political environment in which entrepreneurship could flourish. Repeated successes in the economic sphere, however, caused rationalistic thinking to become more important. Furthermore, business success was

[14] Schumpeter, *Business Cycles*, I, 109 (footnote).

so pronounced that it created business units that both changed the underlying institutions upon which capitalism arose and made the entrepreneur obsolete.

The concept of rationalism that Schumpeter uses here is sufficiently general for most to agree that the gradual extension of this way of thinking is of great importance in explaining the cultural performance of capitalism. Most students of capitalist history would also agree that the development of rational thinking in the field of business gave impetus to the spreading of this attitude into other fields of endeavor. Not many writers, however, go as far as Schumpeter and formulate a one-way link between rationalism in economic matters and rationalism in other fields. Like Marx, Schumpeter appears to overemphasize the determining power of economic factors in explaining the development of modern Western culture.

Moreover, most observers question Schumpeter's views that capitalism is crumbling and that socialism is likely to follow capitalism. Schumpeter's analysis does indicate that the nature of capitalism has changed since its early days—a conclusion everyone will grant. But it does not demonstrate convincingly that socialism (in Schumpeter's sense of "an institutional pattern in which control over means of production and over production itself is vested with a central authority") will emerge sooner or later from capitalism. Certainly, the change in attitudes towards government of which he speaks when discussing the destruction of the protecting political strata cannot be denied. Furthermore, one might accept his conclusions concerning the different status of the entrepreneurial function in modern capitalism, the changed nature of private property and freedom of contract, and even the different attitude towards family life. But to admit that capitalism has changed and is changing is a long way from concluding that socialism is on the way.

According to Schumpeter, it does not take much to upset capitalism. In economic matters he depicts the entrepreneur as a vigorous, adaptable individual who can overcome all sorts of obstacles. But, in the political and social field, he portrays the entrepreneurial group (and the bourgeois class in general) as weak and inept. The entrepreneur is incapable of adjusting to the political changes under modern capitalism. Nor can the bourgeoisie learn to govern effectively. Furthermore, Schumpeter argues that the people cannot be ruled on rational grounds alone. He never takes the final step and allows the spirit of rationalism to spread to the masses. Thus, he pictures a discontented intellectual class leading the laboring class down the road to socialism.

Although Schumpeter's analysis is provocative, it seems one-sided and overemphasized. To recognize that history involves perpetual change is quite different from concluding that "a socialist form of society will inevitably emerge from an equally inevitable decomposition of capitalist society."[15] Schumpeter clearly is influenced by Marx's life-cycle conception of history.[16] Seeing capitalism change, Schumpeter deduces that it is declining and inevitably will die. Such a view depends upon a special interpretation of history. Just how will capitalism die? And why will it be replaced by socialism? Here, he is vague—". . . we know nothing as yet about the precise way by which socialism may be expected to come except that there must be a great many possibilities ranging from a gradual bureaucratization to the most picturesque revolution."[17] But, even accepting all that Schumpeter says about the changing conditions of capitalism, one may still see a great many possibilities for capitalism merely to keep on changing (still fitting his definition of capitalism) or for capitalism to be finally replaced by a system markedly different from socialism.

[15] Schumpeter, *Capitalism, Socialism, and Democracy*, xiii.
[16] See Chapter 2, section 1.
[17] Schumpeter, *Capitalism, Socialism, and Democracy*, 162–163.

Chapter 5

Post-Keynesian
Analysis

Those economists who are attempting to formulate a dynamic extension of the Keynesian system have provided the most recent contributions to the theory of development. Although Keynes's *General Theory* revolutionized the theory of business fluctuations, it was confined to short-period analysis. Keynes assumed the following elements as given and constant: ". . . the existing skill and quantity of available labour, the existing quality and quantity of available equipment, the existing technique, the degree of competition, the tastes and habits of the consumer . . . ."[1] Restricted to this static analytical framework, Keynes did not concentrate on the long-run problems that were of such concern to classical economists, Marx, and Schumpeter.

Post-Keynesians, however, are endeavoring to extend the Keynesian system into a more comprehensive long-period theory of output and employment which analyzes short-run fluctuations as being embedded in a long-run setting of economic growth. In this analysis the central questions are: What are the requirements to maintain a steady growth of full employment income without deflation or inflation? And will

[1] J. M. Keynes, *The General Theory of Employment Interest and Money*, Harcourt, Brace and Co., New York, 1936, 245; also 24, 28.

income actually grow at such a rate so as to prevent secular stagnation or secular inflation? It is clear that, if population is growing, per capita income cannot be maintained unless real income also increases. Moreover, if the labor force is expanding, then output must also expand to maintain full employment. And if there is net investment, then real income must also grow in order to avoid idle capacity. These points are rigorously analyzed in the models of growth as presented by Harrod and Domar.

1. The Harrod-Domar Analysis of Steady Growth

Both Harrod and Domar are concerned with determining the conditions required for smooth uninterrupted growth in real national income.[2] Although their models of steady growth differ in details, they are essentially similar in substance.

As did earlier writers, Harrod and Domar assign a crucial part in the process of growth to capital accumulation. But they emphasize that capital accumulation has a double role: on the one hand, investment generates income; on the other, it increases the productive capacity of the economy by enlarging its capital stock. Classical economists gave attention to the capacity side of capital accumulation, but took for granted adequate demand; in the earlier Keynesian literature attention was given to the problem of adequate demand, but the problem of capacity was ignored. Although Keynesian analysis improved on earlier analysis by considering the saving-investment problem, it nonetheless failed to consider the longer-run problem of the increasing productive capacity which results from investment. As represented by the Harrod-Domar analysis, the post-Keynesian growth models attempt to consider both sides of the investment process.

Stated simply, the major point of these models is this: assuming

---

[2] Evsey Domar, "Expansion and Employment," *American Economic Review, XXXVII*, 34–35 (March 1947); "The Problem of Capital Formation," *American Economic Review, XXXVIII*, 777–794 (Dec. 1948); "Economic Growth: An Econometric Approach," *American Economic Review, Papers and Proceedings, XLII*, 479–495 (May 1952); "Capital Expansion, Rate of Growth and Employment," *Econometrica, XIV*, 137–147 (April 1946); "Depreciation, Replacement, and Growth," *Economic Journal, LXIII*, 1–32 (March 1953); R. F. Harrod, "An Essay in Dynamic Theory," *Economic Journal, XLIX*, No. 193, 14–33 (March 1939); *Towards a Dynamic Economics*, Macmillan and Co. Ltd., London, 1948; "Supplement on Dynamic Theory," in *Economic Essays*, Macmillan and Co. Ltd., London, 1952.

For an elaboration of the Harrod-Domar analysis, see W. J. Baumol, *Economic Dynamics*, The Macmillan Co., New York, 1951, Chapter 4; W. Fellner, *Trends and Cycles in Economic Activity*, Henry Holt & Co., New York, 1956, Chapter 4; D. Hamberg, *Economic Growth and Instability*, W. W. Norton & Co., New York, 1956, Chapters 2, 3.

initially a full employment equilibrium level of income, the maintenance of this equilibrium year after year requires that the volume of spending generated by investment must be sufficient to absorb the increased output made possible by investment. But if the marginal propensity to save is given, then the more capital is accumulated, and the higher national income already is, the greater must be the absolute volume of net investment. Therefore, if full employment is to be maintained, the absolute amount of net investment must ever expand. This, in turn, requires continuous growth in real national income.

This point can also be recognized if one imagines a situation in which real income does not grow but remains constant, and then asks what will be the effects of net investment. Since net investment is the formation of capital, and since this increases the productive capacity of the economy, the creation of new capital equipment would have one or more of the following effects if real income simply remained constant: (1) the new capital would remain unused, (2) the new capital would be used at the expense of previously constructed capital, whose labor and/or markets the new capital has taken away; (3) the new capital would be substituted for labor. Thus, capital formation, if not accompanied by an increase in income, would result in unemployed capital and labor. Therefore, growth in income is required to avoid excess capital goods and unemployed labor.

The objective of a growth model, accordingly, is to find the conditions needed for maintaining full employment over the long run, that is, the rate of growth of income that the maintenance of full employment requires.

Domar constructs his model around the following question: since investment increases productive capacity and also creates income, what should be the rate of increase in investment in order to make the increase in income equal to that of productive capacity, so that full employment is maintained?

The main assumptions of the model are these: (1) an initial full-employment level of income has already been achieved;[3] (2) there is no government and no foreign trade; (3) there are no lags in adjustment;

[3] Two different growth rates should be recognized—the full-capacity growth rate and the full-employment growth rate. The first ensures the continuous utilization of capital at full capacity; the second ensures the full employment of a growing labor supply. Cf. D. Hamberg, *Economic Growth and Instability,* W. W. Norton & Co., New York, 1956, 157–172.

In Domar's model, however, it is assumed that an equilibrium of full employment of both labor and capital exists initially, and that the same rate of growth will ensure both full-capacity use of capital and full employment of labor when both are expanding.

(4) the average and marginal propensities to save are equal;[4] (5) the propensity to save and the capital coefficient (ratio of capital stock to output) are constant. Not all of these are necessary assumptions; some are made only for purposes of analytical simplicity and can be relaxed in a more complicated analysis. Income, investment, and saving are all defined in the net sense, that is, over and above depreciation.[5]

The solution of the problem follows.

Let investment be represented by I.

Let the annual productive capacity per dollar of newly created capital be equal on the average to s, where s denotes the increase in the annual amount of real income that can be produced by a dollar of newly created capital. That is, s stands for the ratio of increase in real income or output to an increase in capital; it is the reciprocal of the accelerator or the marginal capital coefficient.[6] For example, if $2 of additional capital is required to produce $1 of additional output, s will be $\frac{1}{2}$ or 50 per cent per year. Thus, the total increase in productive capacity of I dollars invested will be I times s dollars per year.

The operation of this new capital, however, will take place, to some extent, at the expense of previously constructed plants with which the new capital will compete for markets and factors of production. If the output of previously existing plants is then curtailed, the productive capacity of the whole economy will not increase by I times s dollars, but by a smaller amount that can be indicated as I times σ. The difference between s and σ is the difference between the increase in productive capacity per dollar invested only in new plants and the productive capacity of the whole economy (that is, considering the gain in capacity in new plants less the loss in capacity of previously existing plants). Accordingly, σ is less than s.

Now I times σ is the total net increase in output that the economy can produce. It represents the aggregate supply side of the economy. The

[4] That is, it is assumed that in the long run the saving function is linear and passes through the origin.

[5] This assumes that depreciation charges and replacement expenditures are identical. Actually, in a growing economy, replacement falls far short of depreciation. But since the logic of the analysis remains the same, output, investment, and saving will simply be defined as net of depreciation.

The reader may examine the more complex models in Domar, "Depreciation, Replacement, and Growth," *Economic Journal, LXIII*, 1–32 (March 1953).

[6] The accelerator usually refers to induced investment (that is, investment induced by a change in income), but since autonomous investment (that is, investment which is independent of income growth) also provides additional capital to produce output, the accelerator should in strict terms be regarded only as a component part of the marginal capital coefficient. As discussed in the next paragraph, some adjustment is made for this by considering σ instead of s.

aggregate demand side of the economy is the familiar Keynesian multiplier. Let investment increase at an absolute annual rate of ΔI, and let the absolute annual increase in income be denoted by ΔY, and the propensity to save by α. Then, the increase in income will equal the multiplier $(1/\alpha)$ times the increase in investment:

$$(1) \qquad \Delta Y = \frac{1}{\alpha}(\Delta I)$$

If the economy is initially in full employment equilibrium, so that national income equals productive capacity, national income and productive capacity should then increase at the same rate in order to maintain full employment. The annual increase in potential productive capacity is equal to I times σ; and the annual increase in actual income equals $(1/\alpha)$ (ΔI). It follows that, to maintain full employment equilibrium, $(1/\alpha)$ (ΔI) must be equal to $I\sigma$. This gives the fundamental equation of the model:

$$(2) \qquad \frac{1}{\alpha}(\Delta I) = I\sigma$$

The left part of equation 2 shows the annual increase in income, and is the demand side of the problem; the right part of the equation represents the annual increase in productive capacity, and is the supply side of the problem.

Solving this equation, by multiplying both sides by α and dividing by I, it follows that

$$(3) \qquad \frac{\Delta I}{I} = \alpha\sigma$$

The left side of equation 3 is the absolute annual increase in investment divided by the volume of investment itself; in other words, it is the annual percentage rate of growth of investment. It is thus seen that the maintenance of full employment requires that investment, and hence income, grow at the annual percentage rate of $\alpha\sigma$.[7] The answer to the problem of what rate of growth is necessary to maintain a continuous state of full employment is that investment and real income must grow at a constant annual percentage rate (or compound interest rate) equal to the product of the propensity to save and the average productivity of investment (the inverse of the capital coefficient or accelerator).

[7] Given that $\Delta Y = (1/\alpha)(\Delta I)$, then by integration $Y = (1/\alpha)(I)$, and by division it follows that $\Delta Y/Y = \Delta I/I$. Income thus grows at the same required rate as that indicated for investment in equation 3.

Domar also presents a numerical example which may elucidate the analysis. Let σ be 25 per cent per year; let α be 12 per cent per year, and let Y initially be $150 billion per year. If full employment is then to be maintained, investment must equal $150 \times 12/100$, or $18 billion; that is, investment must offset the amount of full employment savings. But this investment will raise productive capacity by the amount invested times σ; that is, by $150 \times 12/100 \times 25/100$, or $4.5 billion. If unused productive capacity is not to result, national income will have to rise by $4.5 billion. But the relative rise in income will equal the absolute increase divided by the income itself; that is,

$$\frac{150 \times \frac{12}{100} \times \frac{25}{100}}{150} = \frac{12}{100} \times \frac{25}{100} = \alpha\sigma = 3 \text{ per cent}$$

Thus, income must grow at a rate of 3 per cent per annum if full employment is to be maintained and there is not to be an excess of capital goods.

This long-run analysis may be contrasted with the usual short-period income analysis which neglects growth. In short-period analysis it is said that, to maintain a level of income, investment must offset saving, or the savings of "yesterday" (previous period) must be invested "today" (current period). To maintain full employment over a long period of time, however, the investment of "today" must always exceed the savings of "yesterday."[8] This requires that investment grow at an increasing absolute rate (or constant compound interest rate) equal to the propensity to save (α) times the inverse of the capital coefficient (σ).

As can be seen in equation 3, the larger α is, the larger must be the amount of investment if the level of income is to be maintained. Similarly, the larger σ is, the greater is the increase in productive capacity resulting from the investment, and therefore the larger must be the rise in income to avoid idle capacity. But, since rising income depends on a rising rate of investment, if income is to grow, investment must also grow. How much more investment must grow is given by the product $\alpha\sigma$.

Thus the economy faces a serious dilemma: if sufficient investment is not forthcoming today, unemployment will be here today; but, if enough is invested today, still more will be needed tomorrow in order to increase demand so that the expanded capacity can be utilized and excessive capital accumulation avoided tomorrow. Otherwise, the excessive capital accumulation will lead to a fall in investment, and hence a depression the day after tomorrow. The economy must, so to speak,

[8] If allowance is made for the government and foreign trade, growth would require that today's private investment plus government expenditure plus exports must exceed yesterday's savings plus taxes plus imports.

run faster and faster to stay in the same place; otherwise, it will slip downwards.

In contrast to the situation in which a depression occurs when investment is below the required rate, too rapid a rate of growth presses on existing capacity and encourages investment, which in turn accelerates the growth of output and increases the pressure on capacity all the more. Therefore, to eliminate idle capital, more capital should be built (assuming a given propensity to save or that the propensity to save does not decline sufficiently rapidly). To avoid a capital shortage, investment should be reduced. This paradoxical conclusion can be understood by recognizing the effect that an increase in output or investment has on demand. Too rapid an increase in output or investment will increase the quantity to be sold, but it will also raise demand even more, and so there will be underproduction and a capital shortage. To eliminate this capital shortage, investment should be reduced, thereby reducing demand and the pressure on capacity. The converse holds for too slow an increase in output: to eliminate idle capital, more investment is needed so that demand will rise.

After considering at what rate income should grow to maintain full employment equilibrium over time, Domar asks whether sufficient investment actually will be forthcoming to allow the required increase in income. Unlike the classical analysis which leads to the stationary state, or the Marxian analysis which leads to the inevitable downfall of capitalism, Domar's model shows that there is no inherent logical impossibility in conceiving a capitalist system enjoying continuous expansion: there is no inescapable necessity for the capitalist machine to run down. Nonetheless, Domar's model demonstrates that certain special conditions are necessary for continuous expansion; it contradicts any simple view that there is an automatic tendency for capitalism to keep moving "onwards and upwards."

Moreover, Domar suggests that the growth of monopoly may lead to increasing unemployment of capital and, by retarding innovation, may also cause unemployment of labor. If this inhibition to new investment which results when unused capacity develops in monopolistic industries is not offset by exogenous forces such as territorial, technological and population expansion, chronic depression and increasing underemployment may result. The discussion of secular stagnation in the next section explores this issue further.

Like Domar, Harrod also considers the conditions for a steady rate of progress, and indicates the nature of possible paths along which the economy might advance.

Harrod begins by stating the familiar truism that saving equals investment. He expresses this equation as follows:

(4) $GC = s$

G stands for the rate of growth of output and is defined as the ratio of the increase in income to total income in a given period; C represents the addition to capital, and is the ratio of investment to the increase in income; s is saving, expressed as a proportion of income. Since G can be expressed as $\Delta Y/Y$, C as $I/\Delta Y$, and s as S/Y, equation 4 becomes

(5) $$\frac{\Delta Y}{Y} \times \frac{I}{\Delta Y} = \frac{S}{Y}; \quad \frac{I}{Y} = \frac{S}{Y}; \quad I = S$$

This equation is simply the equation of saving and investment, where saving and investment are interpreted in the "actual," "realized," or "ex post" sense.

Two important behavior relations are then postulated: saving depends on the level of income, and investment depends on the rate of growth of income. The latter relation involves the acceleration principle, that is, investment is proportional to the rate of increase in income: the increase in the rate of output that is taking place "induces" the increase in the stock of capital that makes it possible.

To maintain full employment, the desired (or planned or intended or ex ante) savings out of a full employment income must be offset by an equal amount of desired (or planned or intended or ex ante) investment. But to induce this much investment, income must be growing. Harrod expresses the equation that denotes an equilibrium of a steady advance as

(6) $G_w C_r = s$

G_w is the "warranted rate of growth," interpreted as the rate of income growth required for the full utilization of a growing stock of capital so that entrepreneurs will be satisfied with the amount of investment actually made.[9] C_r is the required capital, that is, the capital coefficient required to sustain the output that will satisfy the demands for consumption arising out of consumers' marginal addition to income; in other words, C_r denotes the amount of capital required to maintain the rate of advance given by G_w. Harrod assumes that saving intentions are always realized, so that any discrepancy between desired saving and desired investment takes the form of unintended investment (inventory accumulation if desired saving exceeds desired investment).

Harrod's model can be readily translated into Domar's. Both models show that to maintain full employment, desired savings out of a full

---

[9] The warranted growth rate is the full-capacity rate of growth.

employment level of income must be offset by an equal amount of desired investment.

Let desired saving, denoted as S^*, be expressed by the marginal (or average) propensity to save times income, that is, $S^* = \alpha Y$. Let desired investment, denoted as I^*, be expressed by the capital coefficient, denoted by v, times the increase in income (output), that is, $I^* = v\Delta Y$.[10] Thus, if S^* is to equal I^* at a full employment level of income, it must be true that $\alpha Y = v\Delta Y$, or

$$(7) \qquad \frac{\Delta Y}{Y} = \frac{\alpha}{v}$$

This means that to ensure steady growth income must grow at a rate of $100 \times (\alpha/v)$ per cent per year. This rate of growth is the same as Domar's $\alpha\sigma$ and Harrod's G_w. That income must grow steadily to maintain full employment can be recognized if it is realized that, to induce sufficient investment to offset savings at full employment, income must grow, but growth of income means that I will be greater, and, in order to have entrepreneurs want this higher I, income will have to grow even faster than before. The equilibrium rate of growth thus depends on the size of the multiplier (determined by α) and the productivity of new investment (σ or $1/v$). This rate of growth will ensure that each year's income exceeds that of the previous year by just enough to permit absorption of the product of the additional capacity installed in the previous year.

Equation 6 assumes, however, that the economy is at all times in a state of Keynesian equilibrium with desired investment equal to desired saving. This means that equation 6 denotes only one possible path of development—that of steady advance. Actually the economy may follow some other line of advance.

Thus, if G (the actual rate of growth) is greater than G_w (the warranted rate of growth that would give steady advance), then the value of C (actual capital accumulation) must be less than C_r (required capital accumulation for steady advance). There will then be a deficiency of capital: the amount of desired capital goods will be greater than the actual amount of capital goods. This situation leads to a chronic inflationary gap: desired investment would be greater than desired saving, and production would be less than aggregate demand. Domar makes this same point when he considers the possibility of I growing at a rate greater than $\alpha\sigma$.

If, in contrast, real income grows more slowly than the warranted

---

[10] $v = 1/\sigma$ where σ is Domar's expression for the net increase in productive capacity resulting from a dollar of newly created capital.

rate of growth (G less than G_w), then the actual capital accumulation will tend to exceed the required capital accumulation (C greater than C_r), and a chronic deflationary gap will appear; desired saving would be greater than desired investment, and businessmen would not be able to sell all that they have produced. Domar's point is the same when he considers the possibility of I growing at a rate less than $\alpha\sigma$.

As in Domar's model, where it was shown that investment and income must grow at an increasing absolute rate to maintain full employment over the long run, it may seem paradoxical that, if the actual rate of growth is too high (G greater than G_w), the economy will actually produce too little, whereas, if the actual rate of growth is too low (G less than G_w), the economy will produce too much. Again, the paradox is resolved once the demand side of the problem is recognized. If G is greater than G_w, then output rises, but demand rises even more because of induced investment, and so the result is underproduction and inflationary tendencies.

Harrod also states that deviations of G from G_w are unstable: if G departs from G_w, then it will depart farther and farther from it. A departure from the path of steady advance is self-sustaining; it feeds on itself. Thus, if G is greater than G_w, then desired investment is greater than desired saving, and this stimulates further growth. In contrast, if G is less than G_w, then desired saving exceeds desired investment, unintended investment in inventories results, entrepreneurs become pessimistic to such an extent that they will keep the rate of increase in output below G_w, and this retards growth even more.

If it is assumed that there are no variations in the proportion of income saved, or in the capital coefficient, what then will stop income from shooting up or down without limit? Harrod points out that generally there is an upper limit to the expansion in output which is determined by such fundamental "natural" conditions as the size of the labor force, the nation's natural resources and capital equipment, and the state of technical knowledge. This limit is a "full employment ceiling," the maximum potential rate of growth which, in the presence of full employment, is permitted by the growth in labor force and the rate of technological progress.[11] Over time, this upper limit may change as the factors of production grow and technological progress occurs. Harrod calls the growth in this upper full employment ceiling the "natural rate of growth," denoted by G_n. But G_n may be less than G_w: the upper physical limit to the rate at which national output can grow may not be sufficient to allow the warranted rate of growth. If this is so, it means that, even if

[11] Hamberg, op. cit., 96; J. R. Hicks, A Contribution to the Theory of the Trade Cycle, Oxford University Press, Oxford, 1950, Chapters VII, X.

income does grow at the warranted rate for a while, and if nothing else causes it to stop, capacity output may eventually be reached. When that happens, income cannot grow any longer at the warranted rate; overproduction will result; and this will lead to a cumulative downswing. Thus, if G_w exceeds G and G_n, the economy will be depressed and tend towards secular stagnation: there will be chronic underemployment.

In actuality, business cycles are constrained and are not free to vary without limit. In the upward direction, G_n provides a limit in the form of a "full employment ceiling" beyond which real income cannot expand in the short run because of shortages of labor and capital. In the downward direction there is also a limit given by a "floor" of autonomous investment, the "break-even point" of the consumption function, the impossibility of gross investment being negative (disinvestment cannot exceed the rate of depreciation), and eventually replacement investment. Hicks has analyzed these constraints in some detail;[12] he has also refined the Harrod-Domar analysis by introducing lags, psychological elements, and monetary factors.

The main points of the Harrod-Domar analysis may now be summarized:

(1) Investment is at the center of the problem of steady growth, because the investment process has a dual character: it generates income, but also increases the productive capacity of the economy.

(2) The increased capacity can result in greater output or greater unemployment, depending on the behavior of income.

(3) Conditions can be stated for the behavior of income that will allow full employment to be maintained over time. These conditions specify a certain rate of growth of full employment income which is sufficient to absorb full employment savings and have full utilization of the capital stock.

According to Domar, this equilibrium rate of growth depends on the size of the multiplier and the productivity of new investment. It is equal to the propensity to save times the inverse of the accelerator. Income must increase, therefore, at a compound interest rate if full employment is to be maintained.

(4) These conditions, however, designate only a steady line of advance for the economy. The actual rate of growth may differ from this warranted rate of growth. If the actual rate of growth is greater than the warranted rate of growth, the economy will tend towards chronic inflation. If the actual rate of growth is less than the warranted rate of growth, the economy will tend towards chronic deflation.

    [12] *Ibid.*, Chapter 2; also Harrod, "Supplement on Dynamic Theory," in *Economic Essays,* Macmillan and Co. Ltd., London, 1952, 281, 290.

(5) The business cycle is viewed as a deviation from the path of steady advance. Deviations become self-aggravating and are limited in the upward direction by a full employment ceiling and in the downward direction by a floor of autonomous investment and consumption. Even if the actual rate of growth is greater than the warranted rate of growth, nonetheless the economy may become depressed if the natural rate of growth is less than the warranted rate of growth. For then output cannot actually expand sufficiently rapidly.[13]

Some of these conclusions, however, depend on crucial assumptions.[14] The models are particularly weak in assuming that such key parameters as the propensity to save and the capital-output ratio are constant; in reality the savings ratio and the capital-output ratio are likely to change over the long run. These changes would modify the requirements for steady growth, and, if the ratios change in a certain direction, the requirements may not be as severe as these models indicate. For instance, the less durable the additions to capital, the less investment increases capacity, and, the greater the marginal propensity to consume, then the less likely it is that the maintenance of full employment requires perpetual growth of investment.

Moreover, if the assumption of fixed proportions in production is abandoned, and labor can be substituted for capital, then the requirements for steady growth do not appear so rigid.[15] Adjustments within the economy are then more flexible, and the system can more easily approach a path of steady expansion. Unlike Harrod's model, this path is not so knife-edged or in such unstable balance as to make the system

---

[13] Other economists have also attempted to carry Keynesian analysis into the treatment of long-run factors. Perhaps the most notable among these are Robinson, Kalecki, Rostow, and Keirstead. None of the models of these authors is intended to constitute a general theory of development, but each model focuses on a number of important elements which might be included in a more general theory, and each model provides significant points of departure for further research. Cf. Joan Robinson, *The Accumulation of Capital,* Macmillan and Co. Ltd., London, 1956; M. Kalecki, *Theory of Economic Dynamics,* Rinehart, New York, 1954; W. W. Rostow, *Process of Economic Growth,* W. W. Norton & Co., New York, 1952; B. S. Keirstead, *The Theory of Economic Change,* The Macmillan Co., Toronto, 1948.

An illuminating graphical version of the Harrod-Domar-Hicks dynamic system is presented by K. E. Boulding, "In Defense of Statics," *Quarterly Journal of Economics, LXIX,* No. 4, 492–493 (Nov. 1955). And a model of long-run growth which accepts all the Harrod-Domar assumptions except that of fixed proportions is presented by R. M. Solow, "A Contribution to the Theory of Economic Growth," *ibid., LXX,* No. 1, 65–94 (Feb. 1956).

[14] For a criticism of these models, see L. B. Yeager, "Some Questions about Growth Economics," *American Economic Review, XLIV,* 53–63 (March 1954).

[15] Cf. Solow, *op. cit.,* 65–84.

experience either growing unemployment or prolonged inflation if the actual rate of growth does not coincide with the warranted rate of growth. The models also fail to consider whether price changes facilitate steady growth. A small degree of price flexibility may actually be sufficient to stabilize an otherwise highly unstable situation. For instance, if prices rise, they may halt a runaway movement in the rate of growth of income and stabilize it at a moderate rate of growth, since a given increase of expenditure then brings out less than a proportional increase in production and thus requires a correspondingly smaller amount of new investment.[16] If allowance is made for price changes and variable proportions in production, then the system may have much stronger stability than the Harrod model shows.

Although one may believe the analysis is unnecessarily rigid and should be refined, for example, by breaking down the aggregates into their components so as to examine the structural features of growth, nonetheless the Harrod-Domar analysis does raise fundamental questions. Even if the saving and capital ratios are not constant, it would indeed be fortuitous if they should adopt whatever values are required for steady growth. The issues considered in the Harrod-Domar analysis are an integral part of any examination of development problems in countries that have experienced considerable development in the past but now face the problem of maintaining development in the future.

2. Theory of Secular Stagnation

Although their reasons are different, it is striking that Ricardo, Marx, Schumpeter, Domar, and Harrod have all presented arguments that indicate that the capitalist economy may eventually reach a position of chronic underemployment and "economic stagnation." The bases for these pessimistic conclusions should now be examined in more detail. The arguments will then be subjected to empirical data and critical evaluation in Chapters 24 and 25, where consideration will be given to the future maintenance of development in rich countries.

"Secular stagnation" refers to a mature phase of capitalist development in which net saving at full employment tends to grow, whereas net investment at full employment tends to fall.[17] It denotes a long-term trend towards a relative contraction in economic activity and an increased

---

[16] Cf. S. Alexander, "Mr. Harrod's Dynamic Model," *Economic Journal, LX,* No. 240, 737 (Dec. 1950).

[17] The theory of secular stagnation may also be termed "economic maturity," "growing deflationary gap," or "increasing underemployment." Cf. B. Higgins, "The Theory of Increasing Under-Employment," *Economic Journal, LX,* 255 (June 1950).

intensity and prolongation of short-period depressions. Although the business cycle persists, the booms are weaker and shorter, and the slumps are deeper and longer. Over the long run, the economy is thus chronically depressed: the essence of secular stagnation is "sick recoveries which die in their infancy and depressions which feed on themselves and leave a hard and seemingly immovable core of unemployment."[18]

Under these conditions there is a growing gap between the trend of full employment income (without inflation) and the trend of actual income. Since it is this gap that is significant, the stagnation thesis can be consistent with a rising trend of actual per capita income, and even with a rising trend of actual gross investment. It is also the widening gap between potential employment and actual employment that matters, so that the stagnation thesis can also be consistent with an increase in actual employment if at the same time there is a progressive increase in unemployment. The concept of secular stagnation, therefore, is not necessarily confined to an economy without growth or to an economy with declining real income per capita; it may refer to an economy in which the rate of growth is slowing down, and underemployment is increasing. Broadly interpreted, it simply means that the economy is realizing less and less the attainable growth in output of which it is capable: the economy may be slipping down, or moving sidewise, or moving forward at too slow a rate.

These possibilities are illustrated in Figure 5.1.[19] The curve Y_p is potential gross national real income, showing the trend of income at full employment. The curve Y_a is the trend of actual gross national real income. According to the possible interpretations of stagnation, stagnation begins, therefore, at time S. From time S onward the gap widens between the trend of potential income and the trend of actual income. Aggregate demand lags behind aggregate supply. In Domar's terminology, $I < \alpha\sigma$; in Harrod's terminology, $G < G_w$ and $G_n < G_w$.

Secular stagnation may be contrasted with secular exhilaration or secular inflation in which situation aggregate demand tends to exceed aggregate supply. In Domar's terminology, $I > \alpha\sigma$. In Harrod's terminology, $G > G_w$, and $G_n > G_w$. If, in Figure 5.1, Y_a were measured not at constant prices but at current prices, then there would be a chronic inflationary gap when Y_a exceeds Y_p. Business cycles over the long run would have an upward trend, upswings being strong and extensive, and downswings weak and brief. Over the long period there would be

[18] A. H. Hansen, *Fiscal Policy and Business Cycles,* W. W. Norton & Co., New York, 1941, 353. Hereinafter cited as Hansen, *Fiscal Policy.*

[19] Cf. B. Higgins, "The Concept of Secular Stagnation," *American Economic Review, XL,* 160–167 (March 1950).

chronic overfull employment, an intensive use of capital, and a rising price trend. Until the government deficit became so important, many economists were more concerned with the problem of secular stagnation than with that of secular inflation. And, disregarding massive deficit spending, many economists believe the secular stagnation doctrine cannot be ignored.

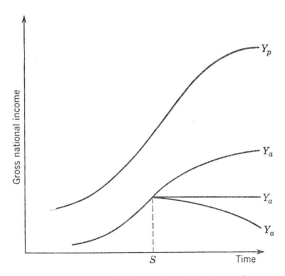

Figure 5.1. Possibilities of secular stagnation.

A variety of stagnation hypotheses have been formulated. Most of them, however, fit into one of the following categories:[20]

1. Hypotheses that emphasize primarily exogenous factors such as technology, population growth, and the opening up and development of new territory.

2. Hypotheses that are based primarily on fundamental changes in social institutions, such as increasing state control of business and growth of labor unions.

3. Hypotheses that mainly emphasize endogenous factors, such as

[20] A. H. Hansen, "Growth or Stagnation in the American Economy," *Review of Economics and Statistics, XXVI,* No. 4, 409 (Nov. 1954). Hereinafter cited as Hansen, "Growth or Stagnation." Mrs. Robinson also discusses various kinds of stagnation to which capitalist economies may be subject: stagnation due to (1) technical poverty, (2) satiety, (3) defects in the financial and monetary mechanism, and (4) consumption of profits. Joan Robinson, *The Accumulation of Capital,* Macmillan and Co. Ltd., London, 1956, 76, 92–94, 256–258, 371–374.

the development of monopolistic competition and the concentration of industry.

A leading exponent of the secular stagnation doctrine in terms of exogenous factors is Hansen. According to him, rapid population growth, the development of new territory and new resources, and rapid technological progress stimulate net investment and provide an offset to savings, so that income grows. If, however, population growth slows down, frontiers close, and technological progress slackens, then net investment will be unfavorably affected and may not be sufficient to offset savings. The trend in actual real income may then fall progressively below the trend in potential full employment real income, and increasing underemployment results.

In contrast to the classicists' pessimistic conclusions regarding the effects of population growth, the Keynesian view of population growth is that it stimulates the economy.[21] An increasing population supports aggregate demand, particularly investment. The Keynesian approach recognizes, of course, that a mere increase in population is not what is significant, but rather an increase in purchasing power: "an increase in the number of paupers does not broaden the market."[22] It is assumed, however, that there is sufficient technological progress to raise the productivity of labor and that the demand for labor keeps pace with the increase in population.

If population growth slows down, then there may be less stimulus to investment, and aggregate demand may fall. When population growth is retarded, capital accumulation is likely to slacken for several reasons. Entrepreneurs might then expect narrower markets, and, since the rate of profit is in part geared to the extent of the market, investment which is influenced by the rate of profit will appear riskier and will decline.

Investment may also decline because of a shift in demand as population growth slows down. When population grows rapidly, there is increasing pressure on housing facilities and public utilities. When the rate of population growth falls, the opportunities for investment in these areas contract. And, since the demand for housing and public utilities requires more investment of capital than most other kinds of consumer demand, the ratio of capital to output, as a whole, will tend to decline

[21] J. M. Keynes, "Some Economic Consequences of a Declining Population," *Eugenics Review, XXIX*, No. 1 (April 1937); Joan Robinson, "Economic Consequences of a Decline in the Population of Great Britain," in *Collected Economic Papers*, Basil Blackwell, Oxford, 1951, 115–132; A. H. Hansen, "Economic Progress and Declining Population Growth," *American Economic Review, XXIX*, No. 1, 1–15 (March 1939).

[22] Kalecki, *Theory of Economic Dynamics*, Rinehart, New York, 1954, 161.

when population growth declines and the composition of the final flow of consumption goods is altered.[23]

Moreover, a retardation in population growth may result in an over-accumulation of capital in the sense that capital becomes too abundant relative to labor. As the ratio of capital to labor rises, the marginal productivity of capital falls, and this will tend to inhibit further capital accumulation.

A closing of the frontier also retards capital accumulation. For when population moves into new territory, when land and natural resources are developed, and when new communities are built, a considerable amount of capital accumulation is needed. The removal of these stimuli will narrow investment opportunities.

Finally, institutional developments may retard innovation, thereby narrowing investment outlets, making replacement less necessary, and exerting less influence towards a lifting of the propensity to consume. The growing power of trade unions and trade associations, and the development of monopolistic competition in which market rivalry comes through advertising instead of through price competition may also retard innovations. If, in addition, the innovations that do occur are financed from the internal savings of business, rather than from external sources, then to that extent personal savings are not offset. And, lastly, if inventions are capital-saving, rather than capital-using, this will reduce the ratio of capital to output.

The Harrod-Domar analysis agrees with the emphasis on exogenous factors in stimulating development. The models do show, however, that, even if investment is not sufficiently high to maintain growth, some support could come from an increase in the level of consumption (a fall in α). Instead of being a high-investment economy, the economy may be a high-consumption economy and grow accordingly. But few growth theorists believe that the propensity to save will fall sufficiently to make this possibility realistic. The propensity to save has remained reasonably constant over long periods, and there is not sufficient proof to depend on a declining propensity to save. Technological progress, expansion of natural resources, and population growth must then provide the stimulus.[24] Otherwise, investment opportunities will not be sufficient to raise the actual trend of income towards the potential trend of full

[23] Hansen, *Fiscal Policy,* 35–38. This would lower Harrod's C_r and raise Domar's σ (reciprocal of capital coefficient), thereby making the maintenance of full employment growth more difficult.

[24] Or—now introducing foreign trade and the government—the stimulus may come from increasing exports, or deficit spending. There are always "four tricks in the deck": high investment, high consumption, high exports, high deficit spending.

employment income: the economy will tend to suffer increasing under-employment soon after the rate of growth falls off.

The secular stagnation doctrine, therefore, rests fundamentally on arguments based on the weakened stimulus of the exogenous factors. But changes in social institutions and endogenous factors inherent in the development of capitalism may also fortify the stagnation thesis.

In this connection, it will be recalled that Schumpeter emphasized that innovation is being reduced to routine; economic progress tends to become depersonalized and automatized; industrial concentration attacks the economic standing ground of the small producer and trader; the separation of ownership, management, and control in the modern corporation makes the figure of the proprietor and with it the specifically proprietary interest vanish from the picture; and public policies, particularly tax systems, public investment and trade unions, grow more and more hostile to capitalist interest.[25] Given proper political and social attitudes, the capitalist engine would continue to achieve spectacular increases in real income. But, according to Schumpeter, the capitalist system itself generates the political and social attitudes that ultimately destroy it.

The third view of stagnation refers to endogenous structural changes which increase the degree of monopoly and oligopoly in the economy. The essence of this argument is that the trend towards oligopoly in an advanced economy raises profit margins; this tends to produce excess capacity; and the existence of excess capacity leads, in turn, to a decline in the rate of growth of capital. If industries were competitive, excess capacity would be eliminated through price cutting, freedom of entry, and the withdrawal of submarginal firms from the competitive industry, thereby re-establishing a normal level of utilization of the capital stock. With monopoly or oligopoly, however, price cutting does not occur, so that the only way oligopolistic industry can respond to excess capacity is to slow up the process of expansion. Surplus capital is not squeezed out. Fears of excess capacity then constitute a drag on the inducement to invest.[26]

Domar also emphasizes that monopoly may retard innovation by hampering the application of new inventions. The fear of spoiling the market by excess capacity may restrict innovations. Further, an innovation is likely to cause losses to some existing interest, and, if these vested interests are protected by strong monopoly organizations, innovations will be delayed. This may cause unemployment of labor as well as unem-

25 Cf. Chapter 4, pp. 92–94.
26 Cf. Hansen, "Growth or Stagnation"; J. Steindl, *Maturity and Stagnation in American Capitalism*, Basil Blackwell, Oxford, 1952.

ployment of capital. "It is the ability of monopolies to protect themselves from capital losses that is injurious to the economy. They try to postpone investment until existing equipment is sufficiently depreciated, and thus new technical devices are financed from depreciation reserves, therefore failing to create investment opportunities for outside savings."[27]

Such in brief are the arguments in support of the view that a rich economy is likely to face stagnation as it matures. But for every proponent of the stagnation doctrine there is a critic. Critics of the doctrine do not deny that, if the exogenous factors, social institutions, and endogenous factors are such as suggested above, and other things are equal, then net investment will be retarded. But they argue that (a) these factors may not be such as suggested, and (b) other things are not equal.[28] To this extent, the stagnation doctrine is an overexaggeration. The arguments of the critics of the stagnation thesis will be considered in Part 4.

This chapter has simply pointed up the possibility of secular stagnation. The growth models show the rigorous requirements for smooth uninterrupted growth and indicate the possibilities of stagnation. They do not say that stagnation is inevitable. But they do indicate how precarious continued expansion may be, and that to forestall possible stagnation certain public policies may be necessary.

[27] Evsey D. Domar, "Investment, Losses and Monopolies," in *Essays in Honor of Hansen,* W. W. Norton & Co., New York, 1948, 39; Hamberg, *op. cit.,* 127–128; Robinson, *The Accumulation of Capital,* Macmillan and Co. Ltd., London, 1956, 407.

[28] Cf. G. Terborgh, *The Bogey of Economic Maturity,* Machinery & Allied Products Institute, Chicago, 1945; J. A. Schumpeter, *Capitalism, Socialism, and Democracy,* Harper and Brothers, New York, 1942, Chapter X.

Chapter 6

A Comparison of Development Theories

The major development theories from Smith to the post-Keynesians have been outlined in the five preceding chapters. As a background for analyzing the topics studied in Parts 2–4, this chapter summarizes the major differences and similarities among these diverse theories. Both their contributions and their limitations for understanding the development process are stressed.

1. Limits of an Economic Approach to Development

Someone once quipped that economic development is much too serious a topic to be left to economists. The point, of course, is that the subject soon runs far beyond the usual confines of economic analysis. As the economic historian well knows, a full account of a nation's economic development efforts embodies its entire cultural history. Consequently, to organize the maze of interrelationships affecting development into anything but a loosely woven story requires the utilization of extensive knowledge in many subjects.

Traditional economics (in the classical and neo-classical vein) usually dwells only upon the immediate determinants of an economy's potential output. These are: (1) the state of technique and knowledge in general; (2) the quantity and (in a broad sense) the "quality" of the labor force; (3) the quantity and composition of the capital stock; and (4) the nature of natural resource conditions. Within this framework, the rate of development depends upon the degree of utilization and the rate of increase of these various productive means. Even within this relatively narrow approach to the development topic, however, many difficulties arise. For example, it is impossible to express quantitatively many significant characteristics of these productive factors. But most important, when one attempts to trace the causes of changes among the productive factors, he becomes enmeshed in a myriad of social, political, and economic forces.[1] These forces, moreover, cannot be arranged in any neat hierarchy of cause and effect. All of them are interrelated.

In one way or another, all the economists studied in the previous chapters recognize these difficulties. Consequently, instead of attempting to formulate a "general" theory of development, they usually concentrate upon a relatively small number of variables that they believe to be especially important in determining the rate of development. In doing so, they assume as given (either explicitly or implicitly) certain conditions with respect to the nature of the many other complex forces affecting development. This implies that the generality of their analyses depends in part on the validity of these assumed conditions. To the extent that these conditions vary over time and from country to country, the theories of these writers must be modified and expanded.

Only one of the writers studied, Marx, attempts a truly general theory of the development process. He includes all cultural manifestations as variables in his system. The only "given" in his model is the development of the material forces of production; from this everything else follows. But this theory suffers not only by being a gross simplification of the behavior of social processes but also by being so general as to be almost useless in explaining specific historical cases of development. When he discusses capitalism, Marx, like the others, seems to make many specific assumptions about institutions and behavior patterns, assumptions that, in terms of historical comparisons,

---

[1] For a typical list of factors influencing development, see J. J. Spengler, "Theories of Socio-Economic Growth," *Problems in the Study of Economic Growth,* National Bureau of Economic Research, New York, 1949, 52–53. He lists nineteen "determinants" of growth. A more manageable group of determinants is suggested by W. W. Rostow, *The Process of Economic Growth,* W. W. Norton & Co., New York, 1952, Chapters 2 and 3. He defines six "propensities" that determine the rate of development.

do not seem to follow from his general description of the mode of production.

Another reasonably "general" writer among those examined is Schumpeter. He does not attempt to explain all economic development, only that under the capitalistic system. He adopts, however, a very broad vision of the economic process. According to him, the spirit of rationalism, operating within capitalism, accounts for all the achievements—economic, social, and political—of the system. As with Marx, however, it is hard to see how one can accurately deduce from any general rationalistic spirit many of the actual institutions and attitudes Schumpeter employs in his analysis of capitalism.

The other writers are content to begin immediately with a much more restrictive view of the development process than either Marx or Schumpeter. Except for occasional side references, they limit their analyses to the economic performance of Western capitalism. And, for this purpose, they make many assumptions about the general sociological, political, and economic nature of this society.

Such authors as Smith, Ricardo, Marshall, Keynes, and Hansen first assume that the population normally possesses a strong drive for material improvement. Although they do not deny the importance of other motives, they consider the desire to improve one's economic position to be dominant. Workers, capitalists, and landlords are assumed to seek the most favorable economic opportunities and to respond to economic incentives. To Ricardo, this attitude is particularly important among members of the capitalist group. Initially, they not only possess a level of income sufficiently high to cover more than subsistence needs but also are willing to forgo present consumption for the possibility of a higher future income. Among the other two groups in his system, the workers and the landlords, this futuristic outlook for material gain is not as strong. When workers receive an income above the subsistence level, they spend the extra income for immediate consumption purposes and eventually use it to support larger families. Landlords also tend to spend their entire income on consumption goods.

By the time of the neo-classical writers, a materialistic behavior assumption is even more firmly entrenched. These economists assume that every individual possesses a well-defined preference function for economic goods and that each person consciously seeks to maximize his total utility. Moreover, individuals are generally assumed to be highly responsive to marginal changes in the array of economic prices.

A second set of assumptions by these economists relates to the general political, economic, and social institutions present in the economies that they analyze. They accept as given, for example, a stable and effective government which maintains civil order and preserves the capitalistic institutions of private property and freedom of contract. Neither the government nor any other social or economic institution operates as a serious obstacle to the successful pursuit of economic gain. Instead, these writers assume as extant many institutional arrangements to facilitate further development. For example, the knowledge of economic opportunity quickly spreads throughout the economy; the degree of geographic and occupational mobility is high; the economy is market-oriented; the use of money as the main medium of exchange is general; and there is a well-established credit and banking system as well as organized capital markets.

An additional group of assumptions by these authors concerns the initial level of development and the physical potentials for further growth. On the first point, they generally accept as initially given a level and distribution of the national income that permit a significant volume of saving within the economy. The level and distribution of national income are also such as to create no serious market obstacles to the large-scale domestic production of most manufactured commodities. With regard to future possibilities of growth, these theorists assume that the degree of managerial and labor skills required for further development does not constitute a development obstacle. These skills are either high enough initially or respond without any serious difficulties. The supply of natural resources and the state of technological knowledge are also taken as sufficiently favorable initially to allow a significant degree of economic expansion.

These various assumptions enable this group of authors to treat the development problem on rather narrow economic grounds. In effect, the assumptions attach certain qualitative characteristics to the productive factors and consequently allow the writers to concentrate upon quantitative changes in the productive means.

The inappropriateness of many of these assumptions for studying poor countries will be emphasized in Part 3. But, even to the extent that these assumptions are (or were) applicable to Western capitalism, it must be stressed that a significant part of an explanation of the actual development in these nations must also consider why these assumed conditions came to be what they are (or were).

Theories of broad cultural change in which attempts are made to explain such factors do, of course, exist. The Marxian and Schumpeterian contributions to the subject have already been discussed. Other economists also adopt a much broader approach to the development topic.[2] An example[3] is Max Weber, who stresses the role of the Calvinist ethic in the development of the profit motive in Western capitalism. Sombart,[4] who emphasizes "the spirit of capitalism" as the creative force in the evolution of modern capitalism, and Pareto,[5] who develops a general cyclical theory of social change, are two other famous economists who study economic development within a general socioeconomic framework. Veblen[6] and more recently Ayres[7] are examples of Americans who break from the traditional approach to economic problems. Parsons[8] is still another who tries to integrate traditional economic theory with sociological theory. Among efforts by non-economists to study the causes of general cultural change, Toynbee's theory of "challenge and response,"[9] Sorokin's description of the three phases of cultural development[10] and Spengler's morphological view of the rise and fall of cultures[11] represent outstanding attempts to theorize about this complicated problem. And there are many other writers who have studied the causes of cultural change.

Clearly, for a more complete understanding of the problem of economic development, economists must draw upon these works.[12] The widening of the traditional boundaries of economics, so far, has proceeded only very slowly. Although one must be cautious about the

[2] For a general summary of these approaches, see J. J. Spengler, "Theories of Socio-Economic Growth," *Problems in the Study of Economic Growth,* National Bureau of Economic Research, New York, 1949.

[3] Max Weber, *The Protestant Ethic and the Spirit of Capitalism,* tr. by T. Parsons, Allen and Unwin, London, 1930. For a discussion of Weber's thesis, see Chapter 8, section 2.

[4] W. Sombart, *Der moderne Kapitalismus,* second edition, Duncker and Humblot, Leipzig, 1916.

[5] V. Pareto, *The Mind and Society,* tr. by A. Bongiorno and A. Livingston, Harcourt, Brace and Co., New York, 1935.

[6] T. Veblen, *The Instinct of Workmanship,* The Macmillan Co., New York, 1914.

[7] C. E. Ayres, *The Theory of Economic Progress,* University of North Carolina Press, Chapel Hill, 1944.

[8] T. Parsons, *The Structure of Social Action,* McGraw-Hill Book Co., New York, 1937, and *The Integration of Economic and Sociological Theory,* The Marshall Lectures, University of Cambridge, 1953.

[9] A. Toynbee, *A Study of History,* abridgement by D. C. Somervell, Oxford University Press, New York, 1947.

[10] P. A. Sorokin, *Social and Cultural Dynamics,* American Book Co., New York, 1937.

[11] O. Spengler, *The Decline of the West,* Alfred A. Knopf, New York, 1947.

[12] The drawback of using these theories alone is that their economic analysis generally is limited.

generality of the development theories previously examined, they nevertheless represent vital contributions to the understanding of development. For they do focus upon certain crucial economic factors that usually are relevant to the problem of development in any kind of society. And, in doing so, they yield insights upon the kind of forces that affects these factors. That other forces affect the crucial economic factors should not be interpreted to mean that these theories are irrelevant. They are limited, but they are extremely valuable within their limits as a foundation upon which to construct more elaborate and complete explanations of this complicated social problem. Most important, not only do they answer many economic questions in their own right but they also suggest many questions to ask of other subjects. Indeed, without these theories it would be much more difficult to know what contributions the other disciplines might make to a more adequate understanding of development.

The economic foundation of these theories is summarized in the next three sections. The first examines the different views of the theorists studied here concerning the causes and effects of population changes; the next section contrasts their analyses of the process of capital formation; and the last discusses their various theories about the international aspects of development.

2. Population Growth

In Ricardo's model of development, population changes appear most sharply as a dependent variable. According to him, the rate of population increase depends upon the rate of accumulation; i.e., an increase in the rate of accumulation raises wages, which then induces a more rapid growth in population. Although he admits it is possible for the rate of accumulation to outstrip the rate of population growth (and thus keep wages above the subsistence level) over fairly long periods, he emphasizes the powerful response of population to the accumulation process. Indeed, it is so powerful that, under his assumptions of relatively insignificant technological progress and diminishing returns in agriculture, the long-run tendency is towards subsistence wages.

Both Adam Smith and Marx postulate a less rigid connection between accumulation and population. Smith, for example, speaks of an increasing demand for labor (because of capital accumulation) as encouraging "the marriage and multiplication of labourers, as may enable them to supply that continually increasing demand by a continually increasing population."[13] But, on the basis of this population response,

---

[13] A. Smith, *An Inquiry into the Nature and Causes of the Wealth of Nations,* ed. Edwin Cannan, The Modern Library, Random House, New York, 1937, 80.

he does not formulate a long-run subsistence theory of wages. Marx is even less exact about the relation between the rate of accumulation and the rate of population increase. His view is that "ordinary wages suffice, not only for its [the working class's] maintenance, but for its increase."[14] Although he mentions the possibility of a rapid increase in population growth when the rate of accumulation increases,[15] he does not stress this relation too strongly, for obvious reasons.[16]

By the time of the neo-classical economists, it is evident that for the Western European countries, at any rate, no simple relationship between the rate of accumulation and the rate of population growth could be formulated. They recognize that many complex non-economic factors affect the rate of population growth.[17] Consequently, the rate of population increase tends to be accepted as an autonomously determined element in their models.

Unlike Ricardo, they are not currently concerned about the adverse effects of population increases on per capita income. They analyze rich industrial economies in which per capita income is already considerably above the subsistence level, in which the rate of technological progress is high, and in which the opportunities for trade with rich agricultural regions further mitigate the Ricardian difficulties associated with providing food for an expanding labor force. Marshall maintains that, in a historical sense, constant returns tend to prevail when population and the capital stock increase proportionately. Neo-classical writers, moreover, contend that opportunities for increasing the capital stock at a faster rate than population—and thereby contributing to a rise in per capita income—are very favorable. Nevertheless, when they look far into the future, their optimism begins to diminish.

Hansen, in his analysis of population growth,[18] almost completely inverts the Ricardian problem: Ricardo is concerned about excessive population growth; Hansen about inadequate growth. The particular problem that each studies is, however, quite different. Ricardo is concerned with the impact that rapid spurts in population have on wage rates. In his model, too large a response of population to accumulation can temporarily drive wages below the subsistence level. Hansen

[14] Karl Marx, *Capital*, ed. F. Engels, Charles H. Kerr and Co., Chicago, 1926, I, 636.

[15] *Ibid.*, III, 256.

[16] If population increases too rapidly when the rate of accumulation is high, wages may be driven to the subsistence level even under socialism.

[17] See, for example, Marshall's discussion in *Principles of Economics*, Macmillan and Co., London, 1930, eighth edition, Book IV, Chapter 4.

[18] A. H. Hansen, "Economic Progress and Declining Population Growth," *American Economic Review*, XXIX, No. 1, 1–15 (March 1939).

discusses a mature industrial country where this repercussion is not the prominent problem. Instead, he dwells upon the employment-generating effects of population growth through its stimulating effects on investment.

Hansen utilizes the Keynesian framework to analyze the consequences of population growth. In this system a less than full-employment equilibrium is possible. When unemployment prevails in the neo-classical system, wages fall but, because aggregate money demand does not, prices do not immediately fall.[19] Producers, therefore, find it profitable to expand output and absorb the unemployed labor.

In the Keynesian system (assuming prices and money wages are flexible), a cut in money wages lowers aggregate money demand and thus prices. A fall in prices proportional to the drop in wages leaves real consumption expenditures unchanged. Employment thus tends to remain the same. If prices do not fall proportionately, there will be an income redistribution in favor of profit receivers. This is likely to shift the consumption function downward and, according to Keynes, increase unemployment.

With regard to the other component of effective demand, namely investment, Keynes does point out that a cut in money income—the money supply remaining constant—tends to lower the rate of interest. Less money is needed for transactions purposes, and therefore the rate of interest tends to fall. The extent to which the interest rate falls depends upon the elasticity of the liquidity functions, and the extent to which investment increases depends upon the elasticity of the marginal efficiency of capital schedule. These functions may be so shaped that this repercussion is entirely ineffective in stimulating real investment expenditures and thus employment.[20] To avoid the conclusion that with flexible prices and wages the system would simply collapse if the labor force is not entirely employed, Keynes introduces the assumption of inflexible money wages.

Using this Keynesian framework, Hansen stresses that population growth stimulates investment by causing a shift in demand towards such high capital-requiring items as housing and public utilities. Population growth, moreover, tends to increase the short-run consumption

---

[19] In the neo-classical model aggregate money demand depends upon the quantity of money and the income velocity of money (the ratio of income to the money supply). Most neo-classical writers assume that the income velocity of money remains constant or changes only slowly over time. They assume, in particular, that a reduction of money wages does not change either the income velocity or the supply of money.

[20] See J. M. Keynes, *General Theory of Employment, Interest, and Money*, Harcourt, Brace and Co., New York, 1936, Chapter 19.

function. The existence of additional consumers, even though unemployed, is likely to bring about an increase in the economy's consumption level at the expense of saving that otherwise would be made. Both of these repercussions tend to increase employment. Consequently, Hansen argues that a decline in the rate of population growth may well result in large-scale unemployment and a lower rate of development. As Chapter 5 points out, however, other economists contend that the decline in investment expenditures associated with a decline in the rate of population growth is likely to be offset by investment expenditures for other purposes.

In Harrod's development model, the rate of population growth as well as the rate of technological progress determine the "natural rate of growth," i.e., the full-employment growth rate. The greater the rate of population growth, the greater is this upper limit to the average actual growth rate over a long period. As is noted in Chapter 5, if the natural rate of growth is less than the warranted rate of growth, i.e., the full-capital-capacity growth rate, the economy is prevailingly depressed and there is chronic underemployment.[21] An increase in the rate of population growth, therefore, tends to alleviate these stagnant conditions. On the other hand, if the natural rate is greater than the warranted rate, then the actual development rate may exceed the warranted rate most of the time. Under these conditions there may be a frequent tendency to approach full employment. If, however, the actual rate of development equals the warranted rate when the natural rate exceeds the warranted rate, a progressive increase in unemployment occurs.[22] Full-capacity growth is insufficient to absorb the growing labor supply into the production process. The resultant unemployment is similar to the kind that Marx describes. Consequently, a lower rate of population growth acts to decrease this unemployment. However, apart from changes in the rate of population growth, the arguments for a self-correction of these unemployment conditions through an appropriate change (an increase under these circumstances) in the propensity to save appears to be stronger than in the situation where the warranted growth rate exceeds the natural rate.[23]

Because of the nature of the employment problem, it seems most appropriate to base an analysis of population growth in rich, industrial countries on the Keynesian and post-Keynesian models rather than neoclassical and classical systems. An increase in the rate of population

---

[21] See Chapter 5, section 1.

[22] See D. Hamberg, *Economic Growth and Instability,* W. W. Norton & Co., New York, 1956, 167–172.

[23] *Ibid.,* 186.

growth not only tends to increase the actual rate of development but also increases the rate of development necessary to achieve full employment. But unfortunately, in industrial countries, there seems to be no necessary reason for the actual development rate to be the full employment rate. As Keynesians and post-Keynesians emphasize, whether the actual development rate and the full employment rate coincide depends upon such factors as the rate and nature of technological progress, the propensity to save, the magnitude of the accelerator, and the responsiveness of investment to any interest rate changes. The trend of per capita income, therefore, also depends upon these factors.

In many predominantly agricultural countries, on the other hand, an analysis of population growth based upon classical and neo-classical theory seems more relevant. The unemployment problem of industrial economies is not likely to arise. Additional labor is employed without difficulty on family-size agricultural units by utilizing the given supply of land and existing capital goods more intensively. Although output tends to expand as employment rises, per capita income tends to fall in accordance with the principle of variable proportions. At the same time, the more intensive use of the capital stock increases the marginal revenue productivity of capital and thereby the demand for investment goods.

Whether this will induce enough capital accumulation to counter the tendency for per capita income to decline depends upon the behavior of saving and the rate of technological progress. The increase in the demand for investment goods tends to increase the interest rate. Consequently, if saving is responsive to interest rate changes, the rate of saving tends to rise. The increase in total income associated with the greater employment likewise may increase saving, although this also· may operate to reduce saving if per capita income already is very low. If the rate of saving and the rate of technological progress are low, per capita income tends to fall as population growth occurs until finally the Malthusian positive checks begin to operate. The existence of imperfectly competitive market conditions and a low level of managerial efficiency would also cause per capita income to decline even more rapidly to the subsistence level. On the other hand, if an increase in the rate of population growth were to coincide with rapid technological progress, a high rate of saving, highly competitive market conditions, and a high degree of entrepreneurial ability, then the rate of development would more likely increase and the level of per capita income would rise.

3. Capital Accumulation

As Part 2 explains, remarkable advances in technology and rich discoveries of natural resources were the most powerful forces behind the rapid rate of capital accumulation in rich countries during the last two centuries. Although most of the writers studied here accept this position, there are considerable divergences among them in the manner in which they treat these forces in their theoretical models. Marx and Schumpeter, for instance, accept a rapid stream of new techniques and resource opportunities as "givens" under the capitalistic system. Their pessimism for the future of capitalism is not based upon fears that objective investment opportunities are deficient. Marx, instead, views technological progress as too labor-saving for the capitalist system to handle successfully. According to Schumpeter, capitalism performs successfully under the stimulus of technological improvements, but its very success undermines the proper social environment for capitalistic progress. Both writers further conclude in different ways that capitalism eventually is destroyed.

In contrast, neo-classical economists assume a more regular and harmonious increase of technological opportunities. If population growth is moderate, if habits of thrift are strengthened, and if the quality of the labor force is continuously improved, then, according to these writers, per capita income increases gradually.

Ricardo, Keynes, the stagnationists, and some of the post-Keynesian growth theorists treat the rate of technological progress not as something automatically given but as a factor subject to considerable autonomous variation. They tend to assume, moreover, that the outlook for rapid technological advances and new resource discoveries is not very favorable. Economic stagnation in the fairly near future is a distinct possibility in their view. For Ricardo, the stagnation takes the form of subsistence wages and no further capital accumulation. For the others, it appears as a growing gap between actual and full employment national income.

Apart from the differences among the various theorists on the rate of technological improvement, one may now ask what are the differences among them concerning the manner in which new techniques affect capital accumulation?

In the classical model the mechanism is reasonably simple. Each capitalist, operating within a purely competitive market structure, sees an opportunity to increase his profits by introducing a new technique before his competitors. But, of course, as all the firms introduce the innovation, the relative prices of the products affected fall to reflect the lower labor requirements per unit of output. But to the extent that these improvements influence agricultural and manufactured commodities consumed by workers, the rate of increase in money wage rates associated with accumulation diminishes. The fall in the prices of these commodities enables a larger expansion of population before the wages fund is exhausted by the workers on the necessities of life. Consequently, money wage rates tend to increase less rapidly than if these improvements do not occur (they could even decrease), and the rate of profit tends to fall less rapidly than otherwise (it might even rise). And, since capitalists save most of their income at any profit rate above the near zero level, the relatively larger share of national income consisting of profits increases the rate of capital accumulation. In other words, the pace of accumulation increases because a relative redistribution of income in favor of capitalists occurs. It should be noted, however, that Ricardo modified his views concerning the repercussion of such accumulation on the laboring class in the third edition of his work. In addition to decreasing money wages by reducing the cost of food, the introduction of new machinery may, he argues, cause unemployment. This creates further downward pressure on wages—a point that Marx uses in his theory of wage determination.

The neo-classical analysis is somewhat more elegant. As in the classical case, a purely competitive market structure is generally assumed. The introduction of improved productive techniques lowers the marginal cost of each firm's current output below the price, thereby encouraging expansion. This opportunity for larger profits increases investment demand and thereby the interest rate. To the extent that a larger flow of saving is forthcoming at the higher interest rate, the rate of investment rises, since resources are released from consumption uses.

The process continues in the familiar fashion. The increase in the interest rate and the relative prices of capital goods (because of limitations on the supply of factors specialized to the production of investment goods) limits investment to only the highest-yielding projects. As these projects are completed, however, the interest rate and the relative prices of capital goods gradually drop, and lower-yielding projects become feasible. Finally, the interest rate falls to such a low level that net saving is discouraged and capital formation halts. This is the stationary state without the disadvantage of subsistence wages.

The Marxian analysis in many respects is like the classical description of the accumulation process. Marx, however, visualizes the accumulation process under the stimuli of improved techniques or new resource discoveries to be much more destructive and disharmonious than either the classical or the neo-classical authors do. According to him, under this kind of accumulation the contradictions inherent in capitalism express themselves most sharply. In his description of capital formation, entire industries are wiped out, skills and crafts are made obsolete, and weaker firms are incorporated into ever-larger firms. But, worst of all, workers are so rapidly displaced by new machinery that a more or less permanent pool of unemployed arises. These unemployed workers keep the wage rate near the subsistence level and thus prevent the benefits of development from reaching the laboring class. Even the capitalists eventually lose out as periodic crises and a falling rate of profit weaken the vitality of capitalism.

In the writings of Schumpeter, there is a mixture of classical, neo-classical, and Marxian elements. Perhaps his most important contribution is to argue that the act of investment is far from the rather routine process described by the classical and neo-classical writers. Among the latter group, the decision of what specific new projects to undertake involves a reasonably simple comparison of the potential profitability of various projects with the current rate of interest. In other words, they seem to view this activity as requiring no extraordinary talents. What neo-classical writers emphasize is the act of saving. To them, the desire for current consumption is the greatest bottleneck to progress—given technological progress.

Schumpeter stresses that technological progress is merely a necessary and not a sufficient condition for development. Indeed, he says, sufficiently attractive opportunities from a technological point of view can be accepted as invariably given. But the ability to perceive these opportunities and the courage to undertake them are by no means present in every economy. A specially motivated entrepreneurial group is necessary to initiate progress. For, argues Schumpeter, the most important investment projects involve such tremendous risk that careful calculation is impossible. In particular, many new undertakings involve the creation of entirely new commodities and thus new wants on the part of consumers. In such an environment, the rate of interest becomes a minor consideration in the determination of investment. Neo-classical writers concentrate in their formal analyses upon cost-reducing inventions and reason about an economy in which uncertainty is at a minimum.

Regarding the nature of saving, Schumpeter is something of a classical or Marxian economist because only one group, the entrepreneurial, saves. Entrepreneurs undertake investment by securing from credit-creating banks the funds necessary to raid the circular flow for goods and services. Then, having undertaken their investment and forced the economy to save via inflation, the entrepreneurs voluntarily save out of their profits and repay the bank loans.

Like Marx, Schumpeter also emphasizes the destructive nature of accumulation under the drive of new knowledge, although to a lesser degree. The creation of new products destroys or weakens old activities, which causes a depression. But a new higher equilibrium, according to Schumpeter, is generally restored quickly, and the benefits of progress become available to all classes.

In the Keynesian model the mechanics of investment are similar to those in the neo-classical model. It is a comparison of the expected profitability of various capital projects with the interest rate that determines investment. However, the rate of interest is no longer a direct determinant of the rate of saving. According to Keynes, saving is a function of the level of income rather than of the rate of interest. Thus, once full employment is achieved in the Keynesian system, the rate of accumulation is limited by the volume of full employment saving.

It remained for the post-Keynesian growth theorists, however, to dynamize Keynes's general approach to national income determination. Unlike Keynes, who concentrates on the short-run employment problem, these writers study a progressive economy in which technological improvements and population growth occur. On the saving side, the post-Keynesian writers employ Keynes's relation that intended saving is a function of the level of real income. On the investment side, their assumptions are quite different. The post-Keynesian growth theorists resemble Schumpeter in minimizing the importance of the rate of interest as a determinant of investment. Specifically, in their simplified models, these economists assume a constant rate of interest and a completely elastic money supply. Under these conditions net investment is partly determined autonomously by technological progress, i.e., there is a flow of new inventions which lowers costs and encourages investment irrespective of the level of income or its rate of change; and it is partly dependent upon the rate of change of income or output, i.e., there is an increase in investment because the increase in output presses upon a firm's capital capacity. In other words, investment intentions depend partly upon the rate of technological progress and partly upon the rate of change of income. By combining the saving and investment relations these writers show that, to the extent that the saving and investment coefficients remain constant, an increasing absolute rate of growth in investment is necessary to prevent cyclical disturbances.

What generalizations emerge from these various analyses of capital accumulation in a progressive economy?

First, in analyzing capital accumulation in rich industrial nations, it appears more realistic (as when discussing population growth) to abandon the classical and neo-classical full employment assumptions. The Keynesian approach in which full employment is not automatically guaranteed seems much more relevant. Secondly, most modern economists agree that the topic of capital accumulation in a progressive industrial economy should be studied within a theoretical framework that considers cycles as being embedded in a setting of longer-run trends. In this respect, the Schumpeterian, Marxian, and post-Keynesian approaches are more appropriate than either the Keynesian or the crude neo-classical ones.

On the matter of the determinants of investment in rich capitalistic countries, only a rather rough unity among present economists exists. All agree that technological advances directly stimulate investment. Almost all the writers also agree that a developing economy induces, in some sense, a large amount of investment. But just how best to explain this type of investment is a matter of dispute.[24]

Post-Keynesian growth theorists utilize a simple acceleration principle: they assume that induced investment depends upon the rate of change of output. In addition these writers usually assume a constant accelerator coefficient. As mentioned in Chapter 5, explanations of investment behavior in these terms have been rather severely criticized. At least three conditions must prevail for a "pure" accelerator model to hold: (1) existing capacity is fully utilized; (2) finances are adequate to permit satisfaction of accelerator-generated demand; and (3) the change in output is thought to be non-temporary. Such requirements obviously limit the generality of the principle.

The incorporation of other determinants of induced investment into the basic acceleration analysis, however, removes most limitations of a "pure" accelerator model.[25] Induced investment, for example, can be made to depend not only upon the value of the accelerator coefficient but also upon the degree of existing capacity utilization. Finances can be accounted for by introducing a profits index into the basic accelerator model. Furthermore, allowance can be made for any pattern of expectational behavior. Economists, however, do not agree on the relative importance of these various factors in the actual investment process.

On one point there seems to be considerable agreement among modern economists. Most contend that the neo-classical theorists overemphasize the role of the interest rate as a determinant of investment. Because of the high degree of uncertainty in economic affairs, modern writers

[24] Cf. A. J. Youngson, "The Disaggregation of Investment in the Study of Economic Growth," *Economic Journal, LXVI*, No. 262, 236–243 (June 1956).

[25] Hamberg, *op. cit.*, 317–330.

tend to minimize the sensitivity of investment to interest rate changes, especially at low rates of interest.

Because a generally accepted theory of investment does not exist, there is also considerable divergence among economists as to why the rich capitalist nations do not exhibit a steady rate of development. Specifically, why is the upward trend in national income periodically interrupted by a general business depression? Explanations of the downward turning point in the cycle are almost as numerous as cycle writers. They range from theories that stress changes in various "real" factors in the system to purely monetary theories.[26] Probably no one explanation is correct because, in the actual world, the importance of the various causal elements varies from cycle to cycle. One might best use an eclectic approach to the problem.

Although important differences among modern cycle theorists exist, too much should not be made of them. When it comes to the question of policy recommendations to mitigate cyclical activity, there is surprising unanimity. And, although economists differ concerning the specific reasons for the upward and downward turning points in the cycle, they generally agree on the mechanism by which cyclical changes in income tend to be cumulative. Furthermore, there is general accordance on the conditions that are required if the rich nations are to prevent either widespread unemployment or inflation and still continue to develop. These aspects of harmony among economists represent significant advances in the understanding of development processes and of the ways to facilitate growth. This knowledge of the development process is highly useful in analyzing the problem of maintaining development in the rich countries.[27]

The capital theories formulated by the economists considered here also provide a valuable framework for explaining the historical process of development and for analyzing the problem of capital accumulation in the poor countries of the world today.[28] Of course, they cannot be expected to provide all the answers that one would like. Economists of the past were influenced (just as economists of today are) by the nature of their contemporary economic environment.

Most economists have analyzed the development problem with a vision derived from the experience of Western capitalistic countries where rapid growth was already under way. In studying the poor countries of today, however, economists must modify this vision. Keynesian theory, which emphasizes the problem of maintaining full employment,

---

[26] For a survey of busi. ess cycle theories, see R. A. Gordon, *Business Fluctuations,* Harper and Brothers, New York, 1952, Chapters 11 and 12.

[27] This subject is discussed in Part 4.

[28] These topics are discussed in Parts 2 and 3, respectively.

is not directly relevant. In poor countries, inefficient utilization of the existing labor supply in relation to the capital stock and natural resources is more of a problem than the kind of unemployment situation that Keynes analyzes. Similarly, the neo-classical model has some drawbacks. This model assumes the existence of conditions that enable the pricing system to operate so that an efficient allocation of resources is achieved. This assumption is not valid in poor countries, as Part 3 explains. Moreover, with regard to the problem of capital accumulation, there is obviously a very large pool of technical knowledge in the rich countries which the poorer nations might utilize. But how is this knowledge to be transferred to these economies? The point is hardly discussed by the authors examined here. Only Schumpeter puts any appreciable emphasis on the problems involved. It is, however, an even more complicated problem for these countries than he suggests. For Schumpeter, like the others, assumes the presence of many institutions and attitudes that facilitate the transfer and introduction of improved technology.

Nevertheless, in analyzing the subject of capital accumulation, the various economists do focus upon a factor that greatly affects the possibilities for rapid development regardless of the particular economic and non-economic milieu. They set forth fundamental economic requirements for capital formation which apply to any type of society. Moreover, they suggest a wide range of possible determinants of investment. As Part 3 will show, elements of their analyses are useful in answering the questions: What are the obstacles to capital formation in the poor countries? What are the requirements for an increase in the rate of accumulation? What type of policy measures may facilitate the accumulation process?

4. International Aspects of Development

Almost all the economists studied give considerable attention to the international aspects of development. Classical, neo-classical, and even Marxian economists point to the benefits that the rising industrial nations of the eighteenth and nineteenth centuries gained from foreign trade. The classical and neo-classical doctrine of comparative costs stresses the gains from trade that result from a better allocation of world resources. Foreign trade widens markets, promotes the division of labor, stimulates capital accumulation, yields external economies, and intensifies competition. All of this, according to classical and neo-classical economists, is conducive to evelopment.

Marx also cites the advan‘ ges of foreign trade to the early capitalist nations. Large profits derived from colonial trade permitted the original accumulation of capital that ushered in capitalism. Furthermore, according to Marx, the extension of world markets hastened the destruction of the feudal society which preceded capitalism. Marxists also argue that the international market is the last, but insufficient, prop for mature capitalist nations. The domestic rate of profit is so low that these countries are forced to turn towards less developed areas to avoid stagnation. The export of capital becomes the major method of preventing the profit rate from falling to a disastrous level. But even this outlet is limited. And, once the older capitalist countries complete the division of the world market, they turn on each other. Imperialistic wars break out for the purpose of re-dividing the world market.

By the time of the neo-classical writers, Germany and the United States were beginning to undermine Britain's previous position of dominance in the export of manufactured products. These economists, therefore, devote more attention to some of the possible unfavorable repercussions from the foreign sector on older industrial countries. English economists, in particular, are concerned about increasing competitive pressures in export markets, and they emphasize the need for flexibility and for continued technological improvement in the export industries. They also fear a long-run rise in import prices compared with export prices as industrialization spreads. But these apprehensions are not sufficient to shake their faith in the over-all advantages of free trade for Britain.

So far only the effects of international trade on the industrial nations have been considered. How do the various writers differ concerning the repercussions of trade on the non-industrial nations? Classical and neo-classical economists emphasize the mutually beneficial nature of trade. Both industrial and non-industrial nations gain by specialization according to the comparative cost principle. Furthermore, these writers recognize some features of the dynamic nature of comparative costs. They concede that a policy of protection based upon the infant industry argument is justified in some of the primary-producing countries. But they are skeptical about the ability of a country to limit protection to infant industries.

In so far as the classical and neo-classical economists consider international capital and labor movements, they regard the effects of these flows to be mutually beneficial. Wages rise (or are prevented from falling) in older countries; capitalists in these countries obtain higher returns on their funds; emigrants raise their income levels; and much needed capital goods generally are imported into the new regions. In short, these writers treat the topic in much the same way that they treat the problem of the efficient allocation of resources domestically.

The Marxist view of trading relations between the industrial and non-industrial countries differs radically from the classical tradition. To Marxists the poor countries are pawns in the game of survival among the rich capitalistic nations. The poor countries gain little if anything. For an extension of trade merely represents the extension of capitalistic exploitation and the ensnarement of these countries in the web of capitalistic contradictions.

A number of modern authors, although not accepting the Marxian position, argue that the classical and neo-classical theorists overemphasize the gains that poor countries derive from international trade and the inflow of capital. As will be analyzed in detail later,[29] these authors allege that there is a long-run deterioration in the commodity trading terms of many poor countries and that this represents an unfavorable distribution of the gains from trade. They also claim that foreign investment in many poor countries tends to develop natural resources rather than the population. Furthermore, they assert that protectionist arguments for these countries are much stronger than neo-classical writers admit. By stressing the existence of an inefficient allocation of resources in the poor countries and generalizing from the ideas supporting the infant industry argument, these economists build a case for extensive protection.

Another important subject relating to the international features of the development process is the balance of payments mechanism. Classical and neo-classical economists maintain that balance of payments adjustments to disequilibrating elements, such as capital movements, take place primarily through changes in the relative price levels of the countries concerned. Modern writers, however, criticize this theory for minimizing the changes in money income involved in capital movements and their effects on the balance of payments through the marginal propensity to import, i.e., the change in imports associated with a given change in real income. Even without any price level changes, it is possible for a part (and conceivably all) of a loan to be transferred through changes in imports induced by changes in income. With constant prices, a certain amount of borrowing during each period raises the level of income in the recipient country (via the multiplier process) by a multiple of the new borrowings in each period. Given a positive marginal propensity to import, the higher income level leads to an increase in the country's imports. The increase in income may also induce domestic investment via the acceleration principle. If this occurs, income and imports rise still further. In the lending country, the export of capital may reduce income and thus imports.

All these factors operating together may increase imports and de-

[29] Chapter 11, section 2; Chapter 15, section 3; Chapter 19, section 1.

crease exports in the borrowing country to a sufficient extent for the
real transfer of the entire loan to be accomplished without any price
changes in the two countries.[30]   If these conditions are not fulfilled,
then something akin to the classical price-specie-flow mechanism with
fixed exchange rates or a relative depreciation of the lender's currency
under flexible rates is required to transfer a portion of the loan.

The modern analysis, nevertheless, helps explain the ease of adjustment to capital flows in the nineteenth century.[31]   It further suggests
that in rich countries, where wage and price rigidities are extensive,
monetary and fiscal authorities must take appropriate actions to facilitate the adjustment process.   For poor countries, the modification of this
analysis to include the effects of changes in purchasing power suggests
that their task with capital loans is likely to be one of preventing excessive domestic inflation and dissipation of the loan on non-essential
imports.

[30] For simplicity, a two-country model is assumed.
[31] See Chapter 11, section 3.

PART 2

Historical

Outlines

of

Economic

Development

"*Thus the past is on top of us and with us all the time; and there is only one way of mastering it even remotely in any one sector: by knowing how these things have come to be, which helps to understand their nature, character, and their correlation, or lack of correlation, to the present realities of life.*"

—L. B. NAMIER

ECONOMIC DEVELOPMENT IS THE GRAND THEME of economic history. The historical approaches to development, however, are various, ranging from studies of individual countries to the realm of philosophy of history. By showing the wide diversity of conditions that exist in many countries at different times, the detailed case studies illustrate the uniqueness of history. In contrast, a philosophy of history, such as the Marxian, attempts to enunciate laws of historical development; by seeking large patterns or regularities in the procession of historical events, a philosophy of history emphasizes the recurrence in history rather than the uniqueness.

At any given time, countries display widely different economic features; a variety of economic systems exist in the world side by side. Similarly, over a long time period, every country is also likely to show widely varying economic features; an economic system can change from one period to another. Volumes would have to be written, however, to compare all these interspatial and intertemporal differences country by country.

To go to the other extreme, and approach the history of development from the viewpoint of the philosophy of history, would also entail disadvantages. Whether they are happy promises of progress or dire prophecies of doom, the Marxian notion of history or Toynbee's comparative study of "civilizations," philosophies of history take a view of the development process that is too Olympian and speculative for our purposes. Before any such broad interpretative position can be attained, we should first consider the development process in more detail and ground our interpretation on an empirical base.

Beginning and ending points in historical analysis are difficult to discover, and between the starting point and the conclusion the nature and scope of any particular historical topic may change radically. The past two centuries, however, provide the richest experience of economic development. Despite the difficulties involved in tracing issues over so long a time span, the student of development must draw on this historical experience. In interpreting some of this experience, we may select Great Britain as our best vantage point. For the British economy provides a classic example of industrial development. Moreover, Britain had unusually close connections overseas, which allow us to investigate the forces of development in an international setting.

The most striking economic features of British history in the eighteenth and nineteenth centuries are the Industrial Revolution and the growth of a British-centered world economy. In the following chapters we shall examine first the process of development in Britain, concentrating on the Industrial Revolution and the emergence of

Britain as the center of the world economy. Then we shall consider Britain's position during the transformation of the world economy into its modern shape, giving particular attention to the movement of capital and labor from Britain to other countries on the periphery of the world economy and to the connections between international trade and economic development.

Our objective is not a detailed history of the spread of development through the international economy; instead it is limited to a "structured history" of some of the more significant forces in international development. A historical review of these forces should serve several functions. First, it should give some check to our theoretical conclusions. Second, it should provide perspective; we should recognize temporal and spatial differences in the rates of development of different countries and realize how historical trends have resulted in the different levels of development currently attained by various countries. Third, it should furnish quantitative dimensions to our discussion of development. Although we must treat the statistics of long periods with reserve because of their narrow coverage and speculative nature, we may appreciate at least the relative magnitudes of many of the variables that we have discussed in preceding chapters. Fourth, a historical review should provide lessons: a knowledge of how some obstacles to development were overcome in the past can be of practical use in considering current problems of development.

Chapter 7

Emergence of the Center (1)

In a historical review of international development, the general pattern should stand out, but there should also be a clear unfolding of the main features of the development process. To achieve this, some broad classificatory system is desirable. Accordingly, this chapter first considers the possibility of classifying different economies according to various "stages" in historical development.[1] For several reasons, however, it rejects this, and then considers as an alternative the possibility of examining development in the world economy in terms of a center and a periphery. This appears more sensible, and the rest of the chapter then begins a review of Britain's emergence as the center of the world economy.

1. Stages in Economic Development?

Many economic historians have asserted that a country passes through different stages in the course of its development—a stage being

[1] N. S. B. Gras, "Stages in Economic History," *Journal of Economic and Business History, II,* 397 (May 1930).

defined as "a new condition competing with an old one."[1] Adam Smith, for example, used the sequence of hunting, pastoral, agricultural, commercial, and manufacturing. And Marx was a "stages-man" par excellence—Hegel's thesis, antithesis, and synthesis becoming in Marxian economics feudalism, capitalism, and socialism. The idea of stages has appealed most to the German writers. List (1844) thought each nation passes through five phases of economic growth: savagery; pastoral life; agriculture; agriculture and manufactures; agriculture, manufactures, and trade. Hildebrand (1864) concentrated on a particular sequence of exchange relations: barter, money economy, credit economy. Bücher (1893) took the area of economic transactions as a criterion of the stage of economic development: independent domestic economy (production for one's own use, absence of exchange), town economy (custom production, direct exchange of products by producers), and national economy (wholesale production, wide circulation of goods). Some English and American economic historians have also referred to a linear development in an economy's history. Ashley and Unwin used the sequence of household system, guild system, domestic system, factory system. And Gras followed a scheme based on the range of market: village, town, nation, world.

In surveying the world economy, others have tried to classify countries by the extent of industrialization or by the relative significance of capital goods. For instance, Hoffmann measures the growth of industrialization by the ratio between the net value of the output of consumer goods and that of capital goods. According to Hoffmann, the value of consumer goods is usually 4 to 5 times the value of capital goods at an early stage of industrialization; during industrialization the output of capital goods rises much faster than that of consumer goods; in highly developed industrial countries, the two types of goods are approximately equal and in some cases the output of capital goods may even exceed that of consumer goods.[2]

Studying economic development in relation to the economic structure of different countries, Colin Clark has also maintained that, as a country develops, the proportion of its working population engaged in primary production (agriculture, forestry, and fishing) declines, the proportion in tertiary production (commerce, transport, services) increases, and the proportion engaged in secondary production (manufacturing, mining, building) rises to a maximum and then begins falling—thereby indicating that each nation reaches a stage of maxi-

[2] W. G. Hoffmann, "The Growth of Industrial Production in Great Britain: A Quantitative Study," *Economic History Review, II,* No. 2, 169 (1949).

mum industrialization beyond which industry begins to decline relatively to tertiary production.[3]

But all these classifications are vulnerable. Although some may correspond broadly to the historical experience of certain economies, no single sequence fits the history of all countries. It cannot be maintained that every economy always follows the same sequence of development with a common past and the same future. A country may reach a so-called "later" stage of development without first having passed through an "earlier" stage: stages may be skipped, and different types of economy do not have to succeed or evolve from one another. Russian history, for instance, belies the Marxian sequence. It must also be recognized that the stages are not mutually exclusive and that there are hangovers from earlier periods; anything later than the stage of settled agriculture, and even that stage itself, is necessarily composite: agriculture-cum-trade, or agriculture-cum-trade-cum-industry.[4] In general, by postulating a one-way economic evolution, these classifications unnecessarily circumscribe the course of development. Almost all historians now recognize the limitations of such a linear conception of history and no longer attempt to classify countries according to stages of development.

If, however, the idea of stages is abandoned, can countries be grouped into any better working classification? It might be more suitable to view the most distinguishing characteristics of different countries in terms of their domestic economic organization and their external relations in the context of world markets. From the standpoint of the domestic market structure, all the sequences discussed above imply in essence two general types of domestic economic organization: the subsistence type of economy and the market type of economy.[5]

The subsistence type of economy denotes an economy in which different economic activities are not clearly differentiated, there is little division of labor, the extent of the market is narrow, the amount of capital investment is small, and each household meets most of its needs by its own production. Agriculture in the form of farming for home use predominates over all other forms of economic activities. Most poor countries would be in this category.

[3] For a general discussion of the classification of economic patterns and the use of stages in economic history, see W. S. Woytinsky and E. S. Woytinsky, *World Population and Production,* Twentieth Century Fund, New York, 1953, Chapter 13.

[4] C. R. Fay, *English Economic History,* W. Heffer & Sons Ltd., Cambridge, 1940, 45.

[5] Cf. Woytinsky and Woytinsky, *op. cit.,* 416–423.

The market type of economy, in contrast, is one in which specialized economic units perform different functions, the division of labor is extensive, the extent of the market is wide, the amount of capital investment is large, and each household exchanges or sells its products. The predominant form of economic activity may be either agricultural or industrial, or there may be a roughly balanced combination of agricultural and industrial production. The essential characteristic is that production, whether agricultural or industrial, is dominated by market-and-money relations rather than by local production for immediate home consumption. All rich countries are market-type economies.

This classification of subsistence-type and market-type economies is very general and can incorporate many of the particular characteristics that the various sequences of stages consider. This method does not say, however, that over the long swing of history countries inevitably pass from the subsistence type of economy to the market type. On the contrary, poor countries may retain a subsistence-type economy for centuries, unless certain forces begin operating to initiate the process of development. Countries may remain in a state of what can be termed "underdevelopment equilibrium"—the long-period analogue to Keynes's short-period "underemployment equilibrium."[6] Nor does this classification imply that to achieve a higher level of development a country must pass from a primarily agricultural to a primarily industrial economy. Further, the fact that countries with a high level of development have a market-type economy does not imply that all countries with a market-type economy have high levels of development. For there are, of course, many different levels of development, not just the two extremes of "high" and "low." Between there will be countries at a different level which can be called "middle" or "intermediate." Many countries with a market-type economy may have reached only this middle level of development.

Finally, within a given country there may exist a sector of subsistence agriculture alongside other sectors in which market-and-money relations are highly developed. Even though this mixture is possible, an economy is placed in the subsistence-type category or in the market-type category according to whether the one or the other type predominates in terms of the whole economy.

Other dimensions can be introduced into this classification. Turning to a consideration of countries from the viewpoint of their positions in the world economy, one can distinguish between countries at the

[6] R. Nurkse, *Problems of Capital Formation in Underdeveloped Countries,* Basil Blackwell, Oxford, 1953, 10.

center of the world economy and countries on the periphery. A country can be termed a center of the world economy if it plays a dominant, active role in world trade. Usually such a country is a rich market-type economy of the primarily industrial or agricultural-industrial varieties. Foreign trade revolves around it: it is a large exporter and importer, and the international movement of capital normally occurs from it to other countries. In contrast, a country can be considered on the periphery of the world economy if it plays a secondary or passive role in world trade. In terms of their domestic character-istics, peripheral countries may be market-type economies or subsistence-type economies. The common feature of a peripheral economy is its external dependence on the center as the source of a large proportion of imports, as the destination for a large proportion of exports, and as the lender of capital.

2. Center and Periphery

If the mid-nineteenth-century world economy is viewed as composed of a center and a periphery, it is clear that at the center was Britain, the leading industrial country and the dominant trading country in the world's economy. Compared with Britain's position, other countries were in a distinctly secondary position. They were peripheral. The extent of development in the peripheral economies varied, of course, among countries. Some had achieved a higher level of develop-ment than others, but none had achieved a level of development as high as Britain's. In foreign trade all played a secondary role relative to Britain. Many peripheral countries were actually still isolated from world trade at the middle of the nineteenth century and were not to become significant parts of world markets until later in the century.

About 1850, the periphery was subdivided between Empire coun-tries and non-Empire countries. The map of the British Empire was already visible in broad outline, and the rapid expansion of the second British Empire was well under way. But all the areas in the overseas Empire were still at a low level of development. Compared with Britain, all the non-Empire countries were also either at a low level or intermediate level of development. South America, the Middle and Near East, Southeast Asia, Japan, and China were all poor areas. Some European countries such as Belgium, France, and Germany were at an intermediate level of development by 1850, as was the United States.

The discussion in the rest of this chapter and the next chapter will consider—by way of a "flash-back"—the Industrial Revolution before

1850 and some development forces associated with Britain's emergence as the center of the world economy.

3. Industrial Revolution in Britain

The Industrial Revolution is commonly said to have transformed Britain between 1760 and 1830. But economic revolutions, unlike political revolutions, are difficult to date and cannot be confined within precise time limits. Instead of considering the Industrial Revolution as a definite series of events occurring only between 1760 and 1830, it is better to interpret it as a process that began long before 1760. For, in the course of historical revisions, many economic historians have come to question the adequacy of the word "industrial" and the overtones of the word "revolution."[7] Large-scale industry, owned by private capitalists, was common in mining and many branches of manufacture long before the middle of the eighteenth century. And the changes in industrial technique and organization between 1760 and 1830 were not unique phenomena without roots in the past; they had been preceded by considerable scientific thought and economic activity in the sixteenth and seventeenth centuries.

Nevertheless, regardless of how long the preparatory period was, there is still much justification in regarding the 1760's as a special historical boundary, in the sense that "it ushered in a fresh epoch," a period in which the pace of industrial development began to accelerate, and qualitative changes in social organization accompanied quantitative changes. The preceding period had certainly not been one of stagnation, but the rate of development had been slow.[8] About the middle of the eighteenth century, however, there began an "expansion of undeveloped forces, the sudden growth and blossoming of seeds

[7] Cf. H. S. Beales, "Historical Revisions: The Industrial Revolution," *History, XIV*, 16–18 (July 1929); D. C. Coleman, "Industrial Growth and Industrial Revolutions," *Economica, XXIII*, No. 89, 1–22 (Feb. 1956); J. U. Nef, "The Progress of Technology and the Growth of Large-Scale Industry in Great Britain, 1540–1640," *Economic History Review, V*, Nos. 1, 3; J. U. Nef, "The Industrial Revolution Reconsidered," *Journal of Economic History, III*, No. 1, 1–31 (May 1943).

[8] Contrary to this common view, it has been suggested on the basis of early national income estimates by contemporaries that real income definitely advanced up to about 1770, but then failed to keep pace with the growth of population from 1770 to 1820. See Phyllis Deane, "The Implications of Early National Income Estimates for the Measurement of Long-Term Economic Growth in the United Kingdom," *Economic Development and Cultural Change, IV*, No. 1, 3–38 (April 1955).

In view of the primitive nature of the national income estimates, however, this conclusion must be treated as a highly tentative hypothesis.

which had for many years lain hidden or asleep."[9]   The long sequence of technological change mounted to a climax, and after the middle of the century the British economy began to expand more rapidly.

The development that ensued between the mid-eighteenth and mid-nineteenth centuries was composed of several outstanding forces that transformed the British economy in a way which no country had ever before known.   Previous chapters discussed in theoretical terms how population growth, technological progress, and capital accumulation are all interwoven in the process of development.   These features may now be considered in the context of Britain's development as a modern industrial system.

4. Population Growth

The essential problem of economic development is how there can be a greater increase in real national income than in population, so that per capita real income rises.   At bottom, this is the success story of the Industrial Revolution in Britain.   Operating alone, population growth could not have produced a rising standard of living.   But an increasing population, when accompanied by "the industrial revolution, with the attendant changes in agriculture and transport, rendered the maintenance of a rapidly growing British population possible, without resort to the cabin-and-potato standard of life."[10]   In Britain's case, the Industrial Revolution comprised a high rate of development, and population and per capita real income were both able to increase.   Population growth forced Malthus and his generation to speculate on the causes and cure of overpopulation, but the Industrial Revolution demonstrated that the population problem was soluble in Britain.   History confirmed the neo-classical answer to the Malthusian problem.   Britain's development vindicated the Marshallian view that organization as well as invention would result in a "law of increasing return" and in the emergence of external economies that would offset any tendency for diminishing returns to set in.

During the last half of the eighteenth century and the nineteenth century, Britain's population grew rapidly.   The increase in the entire previous century from 1650 to 1750 had been only about 1 million, but in the next 50 years the increase in the United Kingdom was almost 5 million, and from 1800 to 1850 over 10 million.   If 1913 represents a base of 100, the index number of population in 1750 was

[9] Paul Mantoux, *The Industrial Revolution in the Eighteenth Century*, Jonathan Cape, London, 1928, 489.

[10] J. H. Clapham, *An Economic History of Modern Britain*, I, 2nd ed., Cambridge University Press, Cambridge, 1930, 54.

approximately 18; in 1800, 26; and in 1850, 50.[11] And, whereas the number of persons per square mile in England and Wales was approximately 106 in 1750, it was 162 in 1800, and 278 in 1846.[12]

This large increase in population occurred when production was also expanding at a rapid rate. How is this parallel movement of population and production to be interpreted? Is the population growth explained better in Malthusian or Keynesian terms?[13] Did the growth of industry influence the growth of population, or did the increase in population stimulate the expansion of industry? Important as these questions are, students of demography are still uncertain as to what have been the determinants of population, and how population growth and development have been causally interrelated.

The view is commonly accepted that population expansion during the last half of the eighteenth century is attributable to a marked fall in the death rate caused primarily by improvements in medicine and public health.[14] Opposing this interpretation is the belief that the development of industry could have stimulated a rise in population by providing more economic opportunities, increasing the demand for labor, and allowing a rise in real wages, thereby making possible earlier marriages and a higher frequency of marriages. To this extent, growth of production would stimulate a higher birth rate. As noted in Chapter 1, Smith and Malthus related the rapid increase in population to "a great and continued demand for labor." In his classic work on the Industrial Revolution, Mantoux presents a similar view, stating that the causal connection runs from industrial growth to growth of population through an increasing birth rate.[15] Most recently, Habakkuk also argues in favor of the hypothesis that the acceleration of population growth in the later eighteenth century was to a large extent the

---

[11] W. G. Hoffmann, *British Industry 1700–1950* (tr. by W. O. Henderson and W. H. Chalmer), Basil Blackwell, Oxford, 1955, 331–332.

For Britain's population in the eighteenth century, see G. Talbot Griffith, *Population Problems of the Age of Malthus,* Cambridge University Press, Cambridge, 1926; M. C. Buer, *Health, Wealth and Population in the Early Days of the Industrial Revolution,* G. Routledge & Sons, London, 1926; T. H. Marshall, "The Population Problem during the Industrial Revolution," *Economic History, I,* 429–456 (Jan. 1929).

[12] W. Bowden, M. Karpovich, and A. P. Usher, *An Economic History of Europe Since 1750,* American Book Co., New York, 1937, 3.

[13] Cf. Chapters 5, 6.

[14] See, for example, J. R. Hicks, *The Social Framework,* 2nd ed., Oxford University Press, Oxford, 1955, 41; G. Talbot Griffith, *Population Problems of the Age of Malthus,* Cambridge University Press, Cambridge, 1926.

[15] Mantoux, *op. cit.,* 354–364.

result of a high birth rate.[16]   Habakkuk believes that this view accords
better with what is known about the mechanism of the population
change in comparable preindustrial societies than does the explanation
based on a falling death rate, and that it recognizes how expansion of
economic opportunities might stimulate a population increase by
lowering the age of marriage, influencing general social attitudes
towards marriage, and making it easier to support more children.

This discussion of population is not intended to determine in any
definitive way whether one or the other of the opposing views on population growth is correct.   That remains an open question.   Although
there may well be no conclusive answers to the question of population
determinants, it is clear that in the eighteenth century the birth rate
and death rate were both high; that economic development itself
supported a high birth rate; that medical measures, better nutrition,
and improved living conditions all contributed to a decline in the
death rate; and that in the nineteenth century improvements in medical
science and practice were very important in lowering the death rate.

If a falling death rate, due to improvements in medicine and sanitation, was the primary cause of the population growth, then population might be considered to be an exogenous factor in economic
development, and the Industrial Revolution might be interpreted as
being largely induced by the unparalleled rise in population.   If, however, the increase in population resulted mainly from a rising birth
rate which was stimulated by an increased demand for labor, then the
population growth might be interpreted as an effect of the economic
expansion.   One must then look elsewhere for other initiating factors
of the Industrial Revolution, even though population growth might have
sustained and magnified economic expansion after it had begun.

As another mainspring of development during this period, the role
of technological progress should now be examined.

[16] H. J. Habakkuk, "English Population in the Eighteenth Century," *Economic
History Review, VI*, No. 2, 117–133.   High birth rates associated with economic
expansion are also emphasized by T. H. Marshall, "The Population Problem
during the Industrial Revolution," *Economic History, I*, 429–456 (Jan. 1929).
Regarding Habakkuk's thesis, it has been argued that medical evidence supports
the conclusion that specific medical measures introduced during the eighteenth
century are unlikely to have contributed substantially to a reduction in the death
rate; but a decline in mortality, due to improved living conditions, is, nevertheless,
a more plausible explanation of the increase in population than a rise in birth rate.
See T. McKeown and R. G. Brown, "Medical Evidence Related to English Population Changes in the Eighteenth Century," *Population Studies, IX*, No. 2, 119–
141 (Nov. 1955).

5. Technological Progress

Technological progress was most rapid in the manufacture of cotton textiles. In the 1760's, Hargreaves devised a simple hand machine, called the "jenny," by means of which many spindles could be used simultaneously. In 1768, Arkwright produced the "frame" which made use of rollers to draw out the thick coarse threads and twist them into yarn. Since the jenny's operation did not require great strength, an artisan could work the new device in his own cottage, and it was thereby compatible with the retention of the domestic system of industry. The artisan alone, however, could not manipulate the frame; the process was therefore carried on in mills and factories where the power was first provided by horses, then by water. The adoption of the water frame thus became the starting point of a trend away from the domestic system towards the establishment of a factory system, illustrating how the technological form of production may condition institutional organization.

During the 1780's came the third important invention in textile machinery, Crompton's "mule," so named because the machine was a cross between the jenny and the water frame. The mule produced finer thread than either the jenny or the water frame, and this made possible the production of higher-quality cotton fabrics. At the same time, as one aspect of the larger innovation of steam-powered rotary motion, Watt's steam engine was first applied to spinning by rollers, and, after 1790, steam power was increasingly used to drive the mules. It then became possible to establish large factories in towns.

In the mid-1780's appeared Cartwright's power loom which could be operated by horses, water wheels, or steam engines. Before the power loom could become an effective instrument of factory production, many additional improvements were necessary. But by 1820 there were about 14,000, and by 1833 about 100,000 power looms in Britain.[17] At this time, however, there were still twice as many hand looms as power looms. Technological progress was not limited to only the processes of brushing, spinning, and weaving. At the later stages of production machine methods were also introduced for the finishing processes of bleaching, dyeing, and printing. The rise of industrial chemistry was closely associated with the discovery of new methods of bleaching and the production of new bleaching materials.

The history of these inventions in the textile industry has been presented in great detail by economic historians. It is sufficient here

[17] T. S. Ashton, *The Industrial Revolution,* Oxford University Press, London, 1948, 75.

merely to emphasize the main features of technological progress in the manufacture of textiles: the new forms of power, new machinery replacing hand labor, and new applications of chemistry to industry. By 1850, the cotton industry stood forth as the prime example of the completely mechanized factory industry, but it had only recently attained that position after a long period of technological change.

If the invention of machinery was one major feature of technological progress, the production of iron (and after the mid-1850's steel) was another, for it provided the metal used for making the machines. And, although the beginnings of machine industry belong to the history of the textile trades, its expansion was made possible only by the development of the metal industries.

The problem of smelting iron ore with coal challenged inventors for two centuries before Darby succeeded in 1709 in substituting coke for charcoal in the production of pig iron. The next advance was to utilize mineral fuel instead of wood charcoal for making bar iron. In the early 1780's, Cort combined the two processes of puddling and rolling. Coal then became used for both the smelting and the forging of iron. A third major development in the iron industry was the application of Watt's steam engine, first to the blast furnace, then to the forge hammers, and finally to the rolling and slitting mills. The next major improvement was Neilson's invention in 1828 of the hot air blast which allowed a large reduction in the consumption of coal in the furnaces.

Development of coal mining, with which the iron industry became so closely related, was also gradual. The problem of pumping water out of the pits was not adequately solved until Newcomen invented, in 1708, a new form of atmospheric engine. As this engine was perfected and its use became more widespread, the working of seams in and below the watery layers became possible, and the output of mines correspondingly increased. But steam was initially used only for pumping; not until the end of the eighteenth century was it possible to apply steam to raise the coal from the pit by using Watt's double-acting steam engine.

The increased output of iron, itself based on coal, had, in turn, significant effects on mining practice. The use of cast-iron tubing in the shaft made it possible to sink to greater depths. Then the replacement of wooden rails by iron rails after 1767 facilitated transportation of the coal from the pits to canals. The introduction of cast-iron rails into the pits also furthered economy in underground transport. And the use of iron wire rope for winding up the coal made it possible to abandon the miserable practice of carrying the coal up ladders.

These developments in mining permitted a great increase in iron production, a fall in production costs, and the introduction of iron for new purposes. Especially significant was the resultant expansion in engineering products. So long as the only materials available were the softer and more expensive metals, wood, and handwrought iron, the production of machinery was necessarily limited. But with the perfection of the production of cast iron, advances in mechanical engineering and the metal-working trades then became possible.

The discussion so far has considered two major features of technological progress, the invention of machinery and the development of metals for making the machines. But if there had not been a third feature, the introduction of a motive force with which to drive the machines, the other two developments would not have been so influential. In the same year in which Arkwright patented his water frame, Watt also patented his steam engine. When Watt began his investigations, however, the basic principles of the steam engine, the piston and the cylinder, were already known. Newcomen's engine had been in use for a quarter of a century before Watt was born. But Watt conceived the idea of a separate condenser, thereby eliminating the waste of fuel that had been a serious defect of Newcomen's engine. Nevertheless, many years had to pass between the conception of the idea of a separate condenser and its commercial application. One serious handicap was the lack of competent mechanics who could execute the designs. To make parts of the engine Watt had to acquire the support of Boulton and use the craftsmen in Boulton's workshops. He also profited from the experience of the great ironmaster, Wilkinson, whose patent for boring cannon could be adapted to boring cylinders with an accuracy previously impossible. As Ashton has remarked, "Watt was fortunate in his associates . . . . It was Watt's merit, not only that he was among the first to apply to industry the methods of systematic experiment used in pure science, but that he was able to synthesize the ideas of others and bring together the varied skills required for the creation of a complex mechanism."[18]

Not until a dozen years after his first patent was Watt able to take out a second patent for a steam engine that could be used for driving machinery. Because of its rotary movement, this new steam engine then became a major source of motive power and was capable of many additional uses. At the end of the eighteenth century the steam engines constructed by Boulton and Watt were beginning to supersede water power in textile mills, coal and copper mines, the iron industry, breweries, and corn mills. Applied to the blast furnace in 1776, the

[18] Ashton, *op. cit.,* 69.

steam engine was successively introduced to Wedgewood's pottery works in 1782, a cotton mill in 1785, the printing press in 1814, river navigation in the 1820's, and railway locomotives in the 1830's. "It thus passed through three stages of development—draining water from mines, driving machinery, propulsion in traction. From being a 'giant with one idea,' as Coleridge called it in reference to its original purpose, it became the pivot of modern industry and transport."[19]

After the steam engine, there was considerably more technological progress in transportation, as improvements were made in roads, canals, and railroads. From the middle of the eighteenth century the road-making movement was active. Hundreds of private turnpike trusts appeared, and the system of turnpike roads spread over the whole country. In the last half of the eighteenth century, the two engineers Telford and Macadam did much to revolutionize travel. Telford laid stress on solid foundations, and Macadam introduced the durable surface of broken stone or flint. As a result, the carrying capacity of the highways increased substantially.

Turnpike roads alone, however, were inadequate for the growing traffic. Accordingly, after 1760 there began the era of canal building which lasted until around 1830. Private individuals were responsible for the building of the canals, and canal construction reached a peak during the period of low interest rates in the early 1790's. By 1830, almost 2000 miles of canals and over 1300 miles of improved rivers formed a network of interconnecting waterways throughout the country.

After 1830, canal building declined as the iron railroad and the steam locomotive began to reveal the vast potentialities of steam transport. In the eighteenth century, rails had been used in coal mines and iron works to facilitate the movement of the wagons, but these rails were imperfect until Birkinshaw patented in 1820 a method of making improved rails by rolling wrought iron. Then, in 1829, Stephenson's "Rocket" dramatically demonstrated the superiority of steam locomotion over horse traction in railway work. Railway development, undertaken by individuals without State aid, then began on a large scale. In the mid-1840's, a number of amalgamations transformed many disconnected lines into a relatively small number of main lines, forming the framework of the English railway system as it now exists. By mid-century approximately 7000 miles of railroad were open, and the railways were carrying more passengers and goods than were the roads and canals.

Technological progress also had significant effects on English agri-

[19] E. Lipson, *The Growth of English Society*, Adam and Charles Black, London, 1949, 208.

culture and rural life. Although the introduction of simple machinery might at first have promoted certain kinds of household industry, the further extension of machinery gradually eliminated the spinning and other part-time employments of agricultural families and the full-time employment of villagers in such trades as tanning, milling, brewing, cobbling, cloth weaving, and carriage and wagon building. As production became concentrated in factories and urban districts, these industries gradually moved to the towns. Not that the migration was even nearly finished by mid-nineteenth century; but it was well under way. The changing industrial structure was attracting new workers to the textile areas and the mining districts. As is usually true of labor migration, both attractive and repellent forces were operating. Higher and steadier wages in factories and mines provided some "pull"; and the attractions of a higher standard of living in industrial towns also motivated labor to migrate from agricultural areas to the towns.[20] The loss or inadequacy of small land holdings, coupled with the natural increase of the peasant population, gave some "push."[21] Nevertheless, even by mid-century, the typical Englishman was not yet a townsman: the census of 1851 still placed nearly half of the English population in rural areas, and agriculture was still the largest single industry, employing one-fifth of the total occupied population.

The enclosure movement during the latter half of the eighteenth century and early part of the nineteenth century was to remove the remaining vestiges of the early medieval system of open-field cultivation. As late as 1760, however, at least a third of the cultivated land of the country was still being farmed on the open-field system. This system made agricultural improvements difficult: it prevented individual control of the use of land; all the cultivators were bound by inflexible customary rules; efficient drainage was impossible; the scattered strips of arable land were too narrow for cross-plowing; and many leases were of only a year of even shorter duration, so that tenants were unwilling to make capital improvements.

From the 1770's onward, the pressure of a growing population and the extension of manufacturing industries which created new markets

[20] Cf. A. Redford, *Labour Migration in England,* Longmans, Green & Co., London, 1926, 60.

[21] It is commonly believed that, by dispossessing the peasantry, the enclosure movement acted as an expulsive force and increased the supply of industrial labor. Research, however, has cast considerable doubt on this view. The migration from agriculture to urban districts can be attributed more to the inducements of an expanding economy and the natural growth in the peasant population than to the effects of enclosures. See J. D. Chambers, "Enclosure and Labour Supply in the Industrial Revolution," *Economic History Review, V,* No. 3, 319–343 (1953).

for foodstuffs made it imperative to increase the food supply. Under the pressure of a growing population, and the strain of the Napoleonic wars (1793–1815), agricultural prices rose. This need for increased supplies of foodstuffs accelerated the enclosure of the common pastures and open-field arable land and also altered the leasehold system in the direction of long leases. The result was a substitution of large tenant farms for small tenancies and small copyholds and freeholds. With compact holdings in place of scattered strips in the open village field, farmers after the middle of the nineteenth century were then able to increase output by utilizing on a general scale the improved agricultural methods which had become known earlier.

A considerable increase in agricultural production did occur during the latter eighteenth and early nineteenth centuries, as the result of both a departure from traditional agricultural practices and the use of more land and more labor. Until almost the mid-nineteenth century, however, the increase in factor supply associated with a larger population and an extension of acreage of land under cultivation may have been more important in expanding output than was the increase in productivity.

There had been agricultural improvements during the eighteenth century—adoption of new crop rotations, greater use of root crops, the practice of hoeing and drilling, drainage of heavy soils, and attempts at scientific stockbreeding. The eighteenth century has been termed the age of "improving landlords" in acknowledgment of those landlords who put their capital into the land, and who studied, practised, and preached scientific agriculture and stockbreeding. Tull and Townshend, for example, had demonstrated that productivity could be increased by skillful rotation of crops and careful fertilizing; Arthur Young, as Secretary of the Board of Agriculture, which was established in 1793, popularized technical literature on farming; Bakewell had shown considerable success in his experiments in improving stockbreeding. But these improvements were not general. The existence of small holdings and commons was a serious obstacle to the spread of agricultural innovations. Knowledge and acceptance of agricultural innovations came only gradually towards the middle of the nineteenth century after large landholdings became typical and large-scale capitalistic farming became common.

Until the mid-nineteenth century, then, technological progress had not exercised its full influence on agriculture; the impact was still only indirect via industrial progress which was destroying the rural crafts and cottage industries of village life. For the most part, the progress was an organizational one: new units of administration were created by the parceling out and enclosure of the common fields, or the breaking up of the rough pasture and waste which had previously contributed little to the agricultural output of the village. The average unit of cultivation had increased in size as a result of the consolidation of ancient small holdings and the creation of new large holdings. This ended communal control over farming practice and allowed the individual more scope for experiment. Production was now able to be directed towards the market rather than simply for subsistence. Proprietors were more willing to undertake improvements, and the tenants were encouraged to work the land more efficiently. After the mid-nineteenth century a more substantial increase in productivity resulted from major technical advances in agricultural implements and machines and from the application of chemistry to agriculture. Reforms in property relations and rights of land use allowed reforms in agricultural methods and made individualized use of the land possible, thereby providing the basis for the increase in productivity that was to come during the latter half of the nineteenth century as steam and mechanical invention allowed intensive cultivation of the land.

Chapter 8

Emergence of the Center (2)

An attempt should now be made to determine the conditions that brought forth the inventions discussed in the previous chapter. Then attention will be given to the importance of industrial innovations and capital accumulation in Britain's development before 1850.

1. The Process of Industrial Invention

Much has been written about the evolution of industrial techniques and the work of individual inventors.[1] But because the process of invention is so much a mixture of psychology, sociology, and economic dynamics, a completely satisfactory analysis of the process is still lacking. Is necessity the only parent of invention? Are the determinants of inventions to be found only in individual genius, or are they

[1] Cf. G. N. Clark, *Science and Social Welfare in the Age of Newton,* Oxford University Press, Oxford, 1937; R. C. Epstein, "Industrial Inventions: Heroic or Systematic?", *Quarterly Journal of Economics, XL,* 232–272 (1926); S. C. Gilfillan, *The Sociology of Invention,* Follett Publishing Co., Chicago, 1935; W. F. Ogburn and Dorothy Thomas, "Are Inventions Inevitable?", *Quarterly Journal of Economics, XXXVII,* No. 1, 83–98; A. P. Usher, *A History of Mechanical Inventions* (rev. ed.), Harvard University Press, Cambridge, 1954.

part of the broader socioeconomic environment? Just what is the process by which previously unknown methods of production are discovered?

There are essentially two different theories of the process of invention: the "heroic theory" and the "systematic theory." According to the heroic theory, the credit for a particular invention belongs completely or mainly to one individual, who has the unique inspiration. Necessity and the stimulus of economic needs may play a part, but advocates of the heroic theory assert that without the one man a particular invention could not, or would not, have been readily forthcoming. Thus, the invention of the spinning mule is attributed to Crompton, the steam engine to Watt, and so forth.

One must wonder, however, whether the spinning mule or the steam engine would not have been discovered if Crompton or Watt had not lived. The fact that in many cases two or more inventors have independently made the same invention deflates the role of individual genius. These duplicate inventions constitute strong evidence in support of the social or systematic theory.

Not only are inventions duplicated about the same time by identical solutions but also there are equivalent inventions—that is, the use of unlike means for achieving the same objective.[2] This fact of equivalent inventions also supports the systematic theory of invention. If inventions are called forth by social forces, then it is not surprising, as it would be if inventions depended only on individuals, to find a number of independent solutions by different inventions about the same time, some identical and others unlike, yet filling the same need.

Moreover, since an invention can be decomposed into separate constituent elements, it may be argued that an invention depends upon these constituent elements which, in turn, are dependent upon other constituent elements *ad infinitum*. It has been stated, for example, that, at the beginning of the eighteenth century, every element of the modern steam engine had been separately invented and practically applied.[3] The existence of all the constituent elements of an invention makes one wonder whether the invention is not inevitable. Was not the final invention of the steam engine merely the culmination of a train of efforts reaching far back into the past, so that the invention is to be attributed more to a process of successive development than to Watt?

From a consideration of such questions, most historians, psycholo-

---

[2] Gilfillan, *op. cit.,* 137–139; also Gilfillan, "The Prediction of Technical Change," *Review of Economics and Statistics, XXIV,* No. 4, 378–380 (Nov. 1952).

[3] R. H. Thurston, *A History of the Growth of the Steam Engine,* D. Appleton & Co., New York, 1878, 55.

gists, and economists now believe that the great inventions were not the creations of individual geniuses but rather the culmination of successive increments of discovery. "Nowhere do we find evidence of such *a nihilo* creations, bursting forth like miracles, which only the mysterious power of individual inspiration could explain. The history of inventions is not only that of inventors, but that of collective experience, which gradually solves the problems set by collective needs."[4]

This theory of systematic invention—the invention being the culmination of successive increments—has been elaborated in considerable detail by Usher. According to his analysis, technological progress is not an exogenous force but a social process which is influenced by the values of society and by cultural traits. Moreover, the process of mechanical invention can be viewed as a continuous flow consisting of a sequence of acts of insight which leads to a cumulative synthesis of individually small elements.[5] The process begins with the recognition of a new or an incompletely gratified want; the second element in the establishment of a new configuration consists in the total experience of the individual inventor—his interests, experience, and knowledge. But a mere putting-together of the want and the experience of the individual is alone not sufficient. A third element, the special setting of the stage, is also necessary; the constituent materials must be appropriately arranged and sufficiently brought together to facilitate their organization into a new circuit or configuration. Finally, there is the act of proceeding from the constituent elements to the achievement of a single new concept, design, pattern, or configuration which becomes the invention. This final act of invention is not an isolated item, but forms "part of an orderly sequence, which embraces in its entirety the full record of the steps by which we achieve the complete realization of our ends."[5] Instead of appearing full-blown from the mind of an individual genius, the invention is the culmination of a long process of analysis and synthesis. And even after its appearance, the invention usually undergoes a period of critical revision during which refinements of construction and design are introduced to improve its practical use.

But what, it may be asked, determines when the invention will appear? Why did the great inventions of the industrial revolution appear when they did? If inventions are accidental or if the process of invention involves merely abstract speculation on the part of an individual inventor, inventions would appear haphazardly: they would be spontaneous or autonomous. If, however, they are related to the

---

[4] Mantoux, *The Industrial Revolution in the Eighteenth Century*, Jonathan Cape, London, 1928, 201–211; also, Thurston, *op. cit.*, 2–3.

[5] Usher, *op. cit.*, 16–19.

circumstances of time and place, then their appearance is not purely random, and they may be, at least in part, a function of the economic environment. Systematic thought lies behind them; they are achieved only after repeated trial and error; and many involve two or more previously independent ideas or processes which are brought together in the inventor's mind. The part played by chance is diminished when one realizes that the process of invention involves the bringing together of mental ability and constituent cultural elements. "Inherent ability may exist but it must receive the necessary cultural training and it must be applied. The problem has to be seen, its solution socially desired and the ability must be trained and stimulated to attack the problem."[6] To this extent, inventions may be said to be induced by the operation of the social process instead of being simply spontaneous.

Spontaneous inventions can be explained only in terms of chance happenings, the curiosity of the individual inventor, or what Taussig called the "instinct of contrivance." For such inventions, necessity is not the mother of invention; the act of inventing is its own justification.[7]

If, however, an invention is induced, then its appearance is connected with what may be termed "inducements to invention" and "permissive conditions." The great inventions of the Industrial Revolution may then be best explained by the variety of economic necessities calling forth the inventions, and by the fact that environmental conditions were becoming more favorable for invention.

The economic inducements to invention can be classified as follows: (a) the desire to share in widening markets; (b) the desire to solve practical production problems; (c) the desire to take advantage of changes in relative factor prices.

In the latter half of the eighteenth century, markets were widening, not only physically through the opening of overseas territories and improvements in transportation and communication but also economically through an increase in demand associated with growth in population, changing consumption standards, rising real income, and an extension of warfare.[8]

[6] Ogburn and Thomas, op. cit., 92.

[7] Cf. Arnold Plant, "The Economic Theory Concerning Patents for Inventions," Economica, N.S. I, 33–34 (Feb. 1934).

[8] Cf. E. W. Gilboy, "Demand as a Factor in the Industrial Revolution," in Facts and Factors in Economic History, Harvard University Press, Cambridge, 1932, 620–629. Habakkuk also concludes that most of the important inventions of the Industrial Revolution period can more plausibly be ascribed to the pressure of increasing demand rather than to the random operation of the human instinct of contrivance, changes in factor prices, or the Schumpeterian innovator (who became an important agent of advance only at a relatively later stage). See H. J.

Population was able to increase without a fall in per capita real income.[9] The Malthusian situation did not hold. Instead population growth acted more in accordance with the Keynesian view: it was favorable to investment and thereby to income generation and employment. To meet the rising demand associated with population growth, an expansion in output was necessary. Moreover, changing consumption standards stimulated output, especially in the cotton industry. The expanded scale of warfare also increased the government's demand for industrial and military products. The fact that so many inventions during this period allowed the adoption of mass-production techniques generally shows the need of meeting the pressure of increasing demands as markets widened. In particular, the growing demand for textile products is reflected by the many inventions in the textile industry, an industry especially well suited for the production of standardized finished products. Thus, changes in production technique frequently were in response to an increase in demand and changes in the pattern of demand, and industry increasingly sought methods of production that would allow greater output.

Many inventions were also answers to practical production problems. An insufficient supply of a raw material, for example, might direct attention towards the discovery of some other method for producing the product without using the scarce raw material, or it might shift demand to some other product that did not rely on the scarce raw material. Thus, Cort's introduction of puddling and rolling was designed to counter the shortage of charcoal; and the timber famine during the latter half of the eighteenth century increased the demand for coal as a domestic fuel, thereby stimulating coal mining and technical progress in mining engineering. The timber shortage also stimulated the invention of new methods in the iron industry.

Further, one invention may necessitate another invention. Invention

---

Habakkuk, "The Historical Experience on the Basic Conditions of Economic Progress" in L. H. Dupriez (ed.), *Economic Progress,* Institut de recherches economiques et sociales, Louvain, 1955, 150–151.

[9] Statistical evidence of an increase in real wages by the end of the eighteenth century may be found in E. W. Gilboy, "Wages in Eighteenth Century England," *Journal of Economic and Business History, II,* No. 4, 603–629 (Aug. 1930); A. P. Wadsworth and J. de L. Mann, *The Cotton Trade of Industrial Lancashire, 1600–1780,* Manchester University Press, Manchester, 1931, Bk. IV; M. D. George, *London Life in the Eighteenth Century,* A. A. Knopf, New York, 1925; A. D. Gayer, W. W. Rostow, and A. J. Schwartz, *The Growth and Fluctuation of the British Economy,* Clarendon Press, Oxford, 1953, II, Chapter XI. These statistics are not, however, of wide coverage; and generalizations drawn from them can only be tentative.

may be the mother of necessity; an improvement in one process frequently puts pressure on those concerned with an earlier, parallel, or later process in the same industry.[10] For example, the use of machines in spinning created a surplus of yarn, and a weaving machine was gradually adopted to use up the yarn. As the output of piece goods increased, the bleaching and dyeing processes had to be accelerated, and this stimulated improvements in industrial chemistry.

Finally, changes in relative factor prices constitute a third group of economic inducements to invention. A change in relative factor prices stimulates invention in so far as efforts are made to economize on the use of a relatively expensive factor. If capital is increasing more rapidly than the supply of labor, there should be a stimulus to labor-saving inventions.[11]

Considering changes in relative prices of factors, Ashton states, "From the 'thirties and 'forties, when capital was relatively abundant, and industrial workers still relatively scarce, attention was centered on labour-saving mechanisms, such as those of Kay and Paul in the textile industries; and the search continued until, in the 'sixties and 'seventies, it culminated in the appliances of Hargreaves, Arkwright, and Crompton. . . . Towards the end of the century and later, when rates of interest were moving up, some (though by no means all) of the inventors turned their minds to capital-saving ends. The newer types of engine of Bull and Trevithick, and the newer ways of transmitting power, dispensed with much costly equipment; the newer methods of bleaching were economical of time; and the improved means of transport, with their greater speeds, released capital that had hitherto been locked up in goods on their way from producer to manufacturer, or manufacturer to consumer."[12]

It may be concluded that there were economic inducements to invention: widening markets, production problems, and changes in relative

---

[10] T. S. Ashton, *The Industrial Revolution,* Oxford University Press, London, 1948, 89. In general it may be said that the inventions of the Industrial Revolution were interdependent, and much of their spread during the nineteenth century may be explained by the fact that they all reached a point in the eighteenth century where they could be utilized together so that they reacted on and stimulated each other. Cf. L. C. A. Knowles, *The Industrial and Commercial Revolutions in Great Britain during the Nineteenth Century,* George Routledge & Sons, London, 1941, 20–23.

[11] Cf. Chapter 1, section 5.

[12] Ashton, *op. cit.,* 91–92. Strictly, what matters is the relative prices of factors which rule at the time that the invention is put into use. If there is a long lag between the time of an invention and its application, factor prices may have changed so that an invention that was formerly profitable, may have become no longer profitable.

factor prices. The inventions involved more than flashes of inspiration. Inventors became aware of what was desired or required. And they responded to economic inducements. Even if there were exceptions, the general conclusion remains that accidental inventions were of no importance in the great social processes by which technology has grown.[13] Instead of relying on the heroic theory of inventions, most students of the problem realize that the inventions of the Industrial Revolution had a systematic character and that many of the proximate causes of inventions were within the economic process.

If inducements to inventions represent half the picture, the other half is to be seen in the set of permissive conditions that made the environment more favorable for invention. These permissive conditions can be summed up as the extension of specialization, the scientific movement, and the cumulative nature of inventions.[14]

The very extension of specialization which technological progress made possible was also a cause of additional technological improvements. As Smith observed, the subdivision of labor facilitates inventions through concentrating the attention of the worker upon a narrow field. When the division of labor increased, and the production process became more and more differentiated into various steps, it became easier to recognize just where an improvement in technology might increase output or save the use of some input. The field for invention thus broadened.

But without the advance in science during the sixteenth and seventeenth centuries, the inventions of the eighteenth century could not have been forthcoming. Achievements in pure science did not come about because the scientist was trying to solve practical problems of industry, commerce, and transport. The social background of the scientific movement contained some stimulus from economic life, but there were other influences—from medicine, from the arts, from religion, and (not least) the disinterested desire to know.[15] These impulses, however, set the scientific movement going, and some of the results of pure science percolated into practice, being applied in the form of inventions. In

[13] Clark, *op. cit.*, 4–8. Rostow also emphasizes that "as for the direction which industrial inventiveness takes and the directions in which it is applied, we can look in substantial part, to recognizable economic inducements." See W. W. Rostow, "Some Notes on Mr. Hicks and History," *American Economic Review, XLI,* No. 3, 318 (June 1951).

[14] It is an open question whether the patent system affected the total amount of inventive activity. It may be maintained that but for the existence of a patent system there would have been very little inventing; on the other hand, it may be argued that the guarantee of a monopoly position blocked the way to additional inventive activity and that other inducements to invention were more important than the monopoly grant. Cf. Plant, *loc. cit.*, 38–43; Ashton, *op. cit.*, 12–13.

[15] Clark, *op. cit.*, 86.

general, the progress of pure science—both in its range of subjects and its methods—was the *sine qua non* of many inventions: the stream of technology was able to broaden and deepen as it drew upon scientific advances.

Finally, technological progress became easier as a discovery in one field of activity was able to be used in another activity. A cross-mutation of inventions became possible. For example, Wilkinson's method of boring cannon was turned to the making of steam-engine cylinders, and the development of coke ovens enabled the extraction of tar.

2. Industrial Innovations and Entrepreneurship

If the industrial inventions had not been adopted commercially, they would have had no economic significance. Not the scientific discovery of new technology, but the utilization of technological advances is what matters for development. The invention itself is only a scientific fact; the innovation, as Schumpeter emphasized, is the economic fact. What then determined whether the many inventions were to be put into operation as innovations? More generally, why was there the creative response involved in an innovation?

To a large extent entrepreneurs were motivated to innovate if by so doing they thought they could increase their profits. An innovation was either cost-reducing or demand-creating. It lowered the unit cost of producing an article of the same quality as before, or enabled an article of superior quality to be produced for the same cost, or allowed the production of a new commodity that could replace some old product.

The economic inducements to invention also carried over as inducements to innovations. Changes in factor prices, widening markets, and growing demand called forth inventions that could be utilized to save the use of a factor that had become relatively expensive, or expand output to meet a greater demand. The point is that economic data changed—supply conditions or demand conditions altered—so that the old way of doing things was no longer the best way: a change was necessary. The need to reduce costs, or expand output, or alter the pattern of demand then made the entrepreneur look for new technical devices or some method of reorganizing production to meet the requirements of the new situation.

In broad terms, changing demand and supply conditions were the basic features of the Industrial Revolution. If the pattern of demand, composition of output, and methods of production had remained immutable, there would have been no stimulus to innovation. Innovations were actually prompted because cost difficulties were encountered in some fields and opportunities for profit making were possible in others.

After the innovation appeared, it also created additional changes with repercussions elsewhere in the economy.

A rough index of innovation can be obtained from the record of the number of patents taken out. The annual number of patents shows a strong rising trend,[16] but the peak years correspond with peak years of the business cycle. The fact that so many patents were taken out in years of prosperity, and so few in years of depression, suggests that it was the hope of profits, rather than that of avoiding losses, that gave the impulse to innovation.

Although the hope of profits was a major stimulant to innovation, there were also other prerequisites: first, technical knowledge which could be utilized; second, entrepreneurs who recognized the opportunities, and responded to them; third, the ability to respond by having adequate finance for the introduction of new techniques. The increasing amount of inventive activity has already been considered, but the role of entrepreneurs and the role of finance now require amplification.

Schumpeter's hero, the "innovating entrepreneur," played a central part in the rise of modern capitalism. The "enterprising spirit" of the entrepreneur is also emphasized by Sombart, who interprets this spirit as a mental attitude that is dominated by the principles of acquisition, competition, and economic rationality.[17] Even though the natural environment of the eighteenth century was favorable to growth, there must also have been individuals who were willing to undertake the risks of innovating and who were prompted to do so by an attraction to money-making. Otherwise the potential advantages bestowed by technological progress would not have been realized in practice in a private enterprise economy.

Psychologists and sociologists should be as concerned as economists with the question of why there was an increase in the number of entrepreneurs. What are the origins of the business-like type of personality? Why are some individuals motivated by risk-taking and money-making?

Max Weber contended that the origin of this business-like type is to be found in the rise of Protestantism.[18] Weber maintained that the

---

[16] For a statistical series of patents in Britain, see Ashton, "Some Statistics of the Industrial Revolution in Britain," *Manchester School of Economic and Social Studies*, May 1948, 229.

A detailed list of technological innovations in England by county, parish, and date is available in M. T. Hodgen, *Change and History*, Viking Fund Publications in Anthropology, New York, 1952, Table 5.

[17] W. Sombart, "Economic Theory and Economic History," *Economic History Review*, *II*, No. 1, 1–19 (Jan. 1929).

[18] Cf. Chapter 6, section 1; also Max Weber, *General Economic History*, The Free Press, Glencoe, 1950, 366–369.

religious outlook of Protestantism, especially Calvinism, was more favorable to the progress of capitalism than some other great creeds, and that the advance of capitalism in England during the seventeenth century was related to Puritanism. The Protestant ethic regarded as the supreme duty of man the glorification of God by good works on earth. The pursuit of wealth became more than a matter of economic self-interest: it was a duty, consistent with man's "calling." Production, enterprise, mastery over nature, and frugality were high moral virtues. To the Calvinist, business was an ally of religion, for the calling is not a condition in which the individual is born, but an exacting enterprise chosen by himself, and to be pursued with a sense of religious responsibility and piety. The Calvinistic doctrine of predestination led psychologically to a religious sanctification of diligent business activity, inasmuch as it was by their works and the methodical organization of their life that the elect could be distinguished from the damned.

Other writers have also emphasized the close affinity between capitalist enterprise and religious non-conformity.[19] Such groups as the Dissenters, the Scots, and the Jews played significant parts in Britain's industrialization. A notable example of Quaker industrialism is provided by the iron-making industry from 1700 to 1825. Several alternative explanations might be offered for this, but the essential fact is that entrepreneurs frequently come from a minority group in which the spirit of dissent is strong.

The list of entrepreneurs who were instrumental in introducing new production methods, new products, or new types of industrial organization is a long one. Although drawn from all strata and classes of the population, these individuals formed a sociological and psychological type with certain common characteristics. They were individuals who appreciated the possibilities of an innovation; they were determined to overcome the resistances that stood in the way of doing new things; they valued business as a means and sign of achievement. The motive or result of entrepreneurial activity was an increase in profit or efficiency, an accession or shift of personal power, or the growth or survival of the business as a unit.[20] The great figures of the Industrial Revolution made

[19] W. Sombart, *The Quintessence of Capitalism*, T. F. Unwin Ltd., London, 1915, 287–290; T. S. Ashton, *Iron and Steel in the Industrial Revolution*, Longmans, Green and Co., London, 1924, 211–226; E. D. Bebb, *Nonconformity and Social and Economic Life 1660–1800*, The Epworth Press, London, 1935; W. J. Warner, *The Wesleyan Movement in the Industrial Revolution*, Longmans, Green and Co., London, 1930; A. Raistrick, *Quakers in Science and Industry*, Bannisdale Press, London, 1950.

[20] Charles Wilson, "The Entrepreneur in the Industrial Revolution in Britain," *Explorations in Entrepreneurial History, VII*, No. 3, 132 (Feb. 1955).

their reputations as organizers: their distinctive characteristic was that they fulfilled in one person the functions of capitalist, financier, manager, merchant, and salesman, "a new pattern of the complete business man."[21] More generally, all these individuals had the common characteristic of a sense of market opportunity combined with the capacity needed to exploit it.[22] As an organizer, the entrepreneur's aim is efficiency, and his means are system and forethought. This may seem but platitudinous now, but, in the perspective of history, individuals with these business-like traits have been rare.[23]

From the standpoint of development, it was a major accomplishment during the eighteenth century that such individuals became more numerous, more class-conscious, and more closely organized for the defence of their common interests. This class was soon to compete with the landed aristocracy for political as well as economic importance. And the social environment became more congenial for entrepreneurship, as the rigidity of agricultural custom diminished and business became increasingly a source of achieved status in society.

Thus much of the history of Britain's Industrial Revolution may be written in terms of innovating entrepreneurs. Yet even though there were entrepreneurs who were willing to innovate, and even though technological progress made such innovations possible, there was also another necessary condition for innovation—the ability to finance the innovations. As will be discussed in the next section, this was facilitated by the increase in the supply of finance: "If Science is the mother of invention, Finance is its father."[24]

The effects of the innovations were significant. An immediate effect was to change the combination of factors used in production. If the innovation was capital-saving, it resulted in a greater proportion of labor to capital per unit of final product. If it was capital-using, it resulted in a greater proportion of capital to labor per unit of final product. There was some tendency for capital-using innovations to be bunched during the upswing of the business cycle, since attempts were made to save on the use of labor which usually became relatively expensive. In the depression phase, there was a tendency to adopt more capital-saving innovations, since labor usually became relatively cheap. But over the long run, innovations tended to be capital-using, since labor became the relatively expensive factor, and attempts were made to

[21] Mantoux, *op. cit.*, 382.
[22] Wilson, *op. cit.*, 132.
[23] E. H. Phelps Brown, *Economic Growth and Human Welfare,* Ranjit Printers & Publishers, Delhi, 1953, 12.
[24] T. H. Marshall, *James Watt,* Small, Maynard & Co., Boston, 1925, 84.

economize on its use. In one industry after another the capital co-efficient increased. This increase in capital, in turn, raised the productivity of labor. Had this not been so, the pressure of population would have set a limit to growth, as postulated in the Ricardian model.

The increase in productivity from the application of technical advances was thus a second important, and a very important, effect of innovations. This is readily understandable in so far as entrepreneurs innovated if they believed that the new combination of factors would allow costs of production to fall. By enabling the production of the same output with a smaller amount of resources, innovations set free resources that could then be used to increase the supply of the commodity in the production of which the innovation occurred, or to increase the supply of other commodities.[25] In either case, the innovation increased real income by allowing a given supply of resources to be used more efficiently.

The industrial innovations also gave rise to external economies. Technical advances in an industry led to an expansion of its capacity and thereby frequently lowered prices of its products. These price reductions benefited other industries that used the products of the first industries in which innovations had occurred.

Another major consequence of changes in technique of production was the transformation in industrial organization. Mass production of standardized commodities gradually displaced small-scale handicraft production, and factory organization superseded the domestic system. For economic and technological advantages, production was increasingly carried on in large units, with a larger proportion of the work done by power-driven machinery, and the power itself generated and applied by mechanical means. All this involved the complementary changes of a greater degree of integration of processes and a further increase in the division of labor. These developments are frequently summarized rather loosely as the "rise of the factory system."

The large-scale transition to modern factory labor began in the latter part of the eighteenth century. Increasing urbanization and a greater degree of labor mobility accompanied the growth of factories. The mechanization and organization of the factory also weakened the per-

---

[25] In the extreme case, there would be no increase in production of final products in the industry where the innovation occurs if the elasticity of demand for the product is zero. The volume of production in other industries will expand if the elasticity of demand for the product of the industry in which the innovation occurs is less than 1. If it is greater than 1, output in other industries may increase or diminish, depending on the degree to which increasing returns are operating in the industry in which the innovation occurs and diminishing returns in other industries. Cf. N. Kaldor, "A Case Against Technical Progress?" *Economica, XII,* No. 36, 186–189 (May 1932).

sonal relations that had traditionally prevailed between employers and workers. A major obstacle, however, was labor's resistance to the introduction of machinery and labor's reluctance to accept the new factory discipline. Although wages in the newer industrial centers were higher than on the farms and in older centers, many workers opposed the spread of the factory—even to the point of violent riots against machinery. The orthodoxy of nineteenth-century social and economic history calls for a somber picture of social disorganization and cruel hardships on labor as the factory system spread.[26] However, a more critical examination of the facts has led some historians to believe that the common picture is distorted and exaggerated.[27] Nevertheless, it remains clear that there was at first no strong desire on the part of the workers themselves to enter factories; that the early manufacturers frequently had real difficulty in recruiting a labor force; and that the transformation of the English agricultural laborer or craftsman into a factory worker was prolonged and gradual. Nor can it be denied that sharp political and social tensions arose from the economic changes. But it is significant that the British social and political system was able to contain these tensions.[28] Resistance was gradually diminished as the worker's position improved with collective self-help by the workers, the Factory Acts beginning in 1802, the spread of trade unions, and the extension of social services.

It should not be thought, however, that the factory system and large-scale production units completely dominated British industry even by the mid-nineteenth century. Some of the inventions were tools that could be worked by hand and hence were compatible with the retention of the domestic system of production. The factory became essential only when the invention involved the use of a machine worked by power. The new methods affected to a significant extent only the iron, cotton, beer, pottery, and coal industries. Even as late as 1830 in the cotton industry, there were still four times as many hand looms as power looms, and only after the 1830's was the hand-loom weaver driven out of the industry by economic pressure. By 1850, the cotton industry was the main example of the completely mechanized factory industry, but it had only recently attained that position. In general, by the mid-nineteenth

[26] For example, J. L. Hammond and Barbara Hammond, *The Town Labourer,* Longmans, Green and Co., London, 1917; J. L. Hammond, "The Industrial Revolution and Discontent," *Economic History Review, II,* No. 2, 215–228 (Jan. 1930); Mantoux, *op. cit.,* 409–450.

[27] See F. A. Hayek (ed.), *Capitalism and the Historians,* University of Chicago Press, Chicago, 1954.

[28] Cf. W. Woodruff, "Capitalism and the Historians," *Journal of Economic History, XVI,* No. 1, 1–17 (March 1956).

century, there were still many industries operating on a handicraft basis. Less than 1 per cent of the employers who made a census return in 1851 employed more than 100 workers. Innovations in manufacturing industries had begun the transition from handicraft or water power to steam power and metal machinery, but the transition was not to be completed until after the mid-nineteenth century.

3. Capital Accumulation

Although adequate estimates of the rate of capital accumulation are not available, indirect evidence indicates that such components of private domestic investment as residential construction, business construction, and producers' durable equipment all increased substantially. This is reflected in the expansion of industrial output, the spread of transportation facilities, and the increasing degree of concentration in manufacturing centers with the attendant expansion of housing and public utilities.

As most theories of development emphasize, capital accumulation is a fundamental part of the development process. What then were the conditions that permitted and stimulated expansion in Britain's capital stock during the Industrial Revolution? There must have been real resources and financial resources to allow capital accumulation, and there must also have been incentives to investment. Together these factors constituted the supply and demand sides of capital accumulation.

Once an economy rises above the subsistence level, all production need not be devoted to consumption. The British economy had certainly risen above the subsistence level long before the mid-eighteenth century. Real resources were thus increasingly available for the production of capital equipment.

There was also an expansion in the supply of finance. Hamilton has suggested that the financing of investment during the second half of the eighteenth century was facilitated by a profit inflation.[29] From his interpretation of price and wage movements during the period 1750–1800, Hamilton concludes that forced savings through the lag of money wages behind rising prices facilitated the accumulation of funds for investment in new enterprises and widened the margin of earnings to be plowed back into the extension of the factory system. Moreover, Hamilton believes that an absolute scarcity of financial capital was avoided by the wider margin of earnings.

Hamilton may have overstated his position, however. For there have been similar cases of profit inflations in other countries, and yet industrial

[29] Earl J. Hamilton, "Profit Inflation and the Industrial Revolution, 1751–1800," *Quarterly Journal of Economics, LVI,* No. 2, 256–273 (Feb. 1942); "Prices and Progress," *Journal of Economic History, XII,* No. 4, 325–349 (Fall 1952).

development was not stimulated. Moreover, other data may be interpreted as showing that real wages did not fall so strikingly as Hamilton maintains.[30] There are also gaps in the logic of the argument. Hamilton's attribution of the rise in prices to increased production of specie may be queried. And the problem of how there could have been adequate effective demand in spite of falling real wages is not explained: a supply of finance does not guarantee that investment will be forthcoming unless market demand is adequate. Hamilton's analysis is indeed difficult to reconcile with modern economic theory.

Internal financing, rather than external financing through the banking system or stock exchange, appears to have been the main method of financing industrial enterprises during the eighteenth century and early part of the nineteenth century. Those with savings were mostly landlords whose wealth came from rents and merchants who had prospered in the home or overseas trade. There was no general capital market, but the landed proprietors, merchants, and industrialists who were the leading investors found it relatively easy to start a project with their own private savings and the savings of friends and relatives. The financing of industry thus depended mainly on the resources of a single man, or a partnership.[31] Not until the middle of the nineteenth century did external financing through the issuance of securities become frequent. In 1855, the Companies Acts incorporated the principle of limited liability, and after this the spread of the joint stock company (corporation), itself a much earlier device, facilitated industrial expansion.[32] But the expansion had begun when there was no national capital market, and reliance was initially placed on individual financing and the plowing back of profits.

Nor did external financing through the banking system become significant until almost the middle of the nineteenth century. During the eighteenth century, the London money market was associated more with government finance and the needs of commerce than with industrial finance. Landowners, however, were significant borrowers from the banks during the late seventeenth and eighteenth centuries. And they used part of their borrowings for financing enclosures, building better

---

[30] See references in footnote 9, p. 163.

[31] Cf. T. S. Ashton, *An Eighteenth Century Industrialist,* University of Manchester Press, Manchester, 1939, 116; *Iron and Steel, op. cit.,* 46–48; L. H. Jenks, *The Migration of British Capital to 1875,* A. A. Knopf, New York, 1927, 15; B. F. Hoselitz, "Entrepreneurship and Capital Formation in France and Britain since 1700," in National Bureau of Economic Research, *Capital Formation and Economic Growth,* Princeton University Press, Princeton, 1955, 320–325.

[32] Cf. G. Todd, "Some Aspects of Joint Stock Companies, 1844–1900," *Economic History Review, IV,* No. 1, 46–71 (Oct. 1932).

roads, and cutting new canals. Through such improvements in agricultural efficiency and in transportation, the landowning groups contributed to the progress of industrialization.[33]

Towards the end of the eighteenth century there was a rapid growth in private banking. It is estimated that the number of private banking firms in London rose from about 32 in 1760 to 52 in 1786;[34] and, whereas in 1750 there were only 12 banks outside London, by 1800 there were at least 400 country banks issuing notes.[35] After the Act of 1826, joint stock banks were able to be formed with note-issuing powers. This facilitated the transfer of surplus funds from agricultural areas to expanding industrial areas, and bank credit became more and more a substitute for currency. Although bank credit played an increasingly important role in Britain, nevertheless it was used chiefly for working capital, and most of the fixed capital in British industry was supplied out of the savings of private individuals and from reinvested profits. Clapham summarizes the situation by saying that the London money market "was important mainly as a furnisher and economiser of circulating capital . . . . It was of more immediate importance to the merchant than to the manufacturer, because the circulating element dominates commerce . . . . The provincial banker gave every assistance to men he trusted, allowing them ample overdrafts at all times; but even he regarded plant, machinery or 'works of any description' as ideally bad security for loans. Almost all the fixed capital of manufacturing industry, as it existed in 1850, and the overwhelmingly greater part of the additions and renewals made during the next thirty-six years, came from what the economists of the age called—with more reason than their critics have sometimes allowed—the abstinence of those steady manufacturers whom the provincial bankers trusted."[36]

The funds required for innovations thus came from a variety of sources. In many enterprises personal saving played a great part. The

[33] Cf. H. J. Habakkuk, "Economic Functions of English Landowners in the Seventeenth and Eighteenth Centuries," *Explorations in Entrepreneurial History, VI*, No. 2, 92–101 (Dec. 1953).

[34] D. M. Joslin, "London Private Bankers, 1720–1785," *Economic History Review, VII*, No. 1, 173 (Aug. 1954).

[35] A. Andréadès, *History of the Bank of England*, P. S. King and Son, London, 1909, 171. For more details of the banking system, see A. E. Feavearyear, *The Pound Sterling*, Oxford University Press, Oxford, 1931; W. F. Crick and J. E. Wadsworth, *A 100 Years of Joint Stock Banking*, Hodder and Stoughton, London, 1936; W. T. C. King, *History of the London Discount Market*, George Routledge & Sons, London, 1936; L. S. Pressnell, *Country Banking in the Industrial Revolution*, Oxford University Press, Oxford, 1956.

[36] J. H. Clapham, *An Economic History of Modern Britain*, II, Cambridge University Press, Cambridge, 1932, 355–356.

large iron business of Walkers at Rotherham rose in the 1740's largely on capital amassed from retained profits. In the 1880's, Lever was making £50,000 a year, living mostly on £400 a year, and with the remainder creating and purchasing his own ordinary shares. In yet other instances, funds were raised by means of partnership deeds and mortgages, whereas short-term funds came from the banks. Only the large public enterprises—turnpikes, canals, docks, and the like—were public companies drawing on a national capital market. For the rest, investment was local.[37]

The demand side of capital accumulation—the incentives to invest-ment—have already been discussed in connection with the factors deter-mining population growth and the adoption of innovations. As a stim-ulus to capital accumulation, population growth was important. Keynes estimated that over the period 1860–1913 something like half of all the capital accumulation that occurred was required merely to maintain capital per head.[38] Similarly, technical progress extended the scope for profitable investment. Fluctuations in patents were closely related to general fluctuations in long-term investment, with the peaks in patents corresponding to expansion phases of long-term investment.[39]

The preceding discussion of innovations certainly points to an increase in capital equipment. It may be suggested that the factors on the demand side, rather than the supply side of the capital market, provided the stimulus to capital accumulation. In the historical development of rich countries, the lack of finance has not been a serious bottleneck: there has been a general tendency for the supply of finance to move with the demand for it, once monetary institutions are established. As Mrs. Robinson has stated, "It seems to be the case that where enterprise leads finance follows. The same impulses within an economy which set enterprise on foot make owners of wealth venturesome, and when a strong impulse to invest is fettered by lack of finance devices are invented to release it (the invention of the joint stock company was a technical revolution comparable to the invention of the steam-engine), and habits and institutions are developed accordingly (it was possible for the prej-udice against banks participating in industry to take root in England, where other sources of finance were forthcoming, but not in Germany, where they were not)."[40] Credit expansion was important in permit-

[37] Wilson, op. cit., 139.

[38] J. M. Keynes, "Some Economic Consequences of a Declining Population," Eugenics Review, XXIX, No. 1 (April 1937).

[39] A. D. Gayer, W. W. Rostow, and A. J. Schwartz, The Growth and Fluctuation of the British Economy 1790–1850, Clarendon Press, Oxford, 1953, I, xi.

[40] Joan Robinson, "The Generalization of the General Theory," in The Rate of Interest and Other Essays, Macmillan and Co., Ltd., London, 1952, 86–87.

ting capital accumulation to proceed without encountering a barrier of scarcity of finance.

4. The Great Exhibition

By the middle of the nineteenth century, the forces of population growth, technological progress, innovations, and capital accumulation had combined to give Britain commercial and industrial supremacy. Limited and speculative as the data are, it might be roughly estimated that between 1800 and 1850 real per capita income rose by over 25 per cent.[41] The rates of growth per decade in per capita real income have been estimated as follows: 1800–1822, 8 per cent; 1812–1831, 33 per cent; 1822–1846, 13 per cent; and 1800–1846, 11 per cent.[41]

As a mid-century monument to Britain's emergence as the center of the world economy, and as a testimonial to the belief in future progress, the Great Exhibition of 1851 was held in London's Hyde Park. Its unprecedented display of raw materials, machinery, and manufactures from Britain and foreign countries was at once a symbol of the past and a portent of the future.

For this festival of industry Sir Joseph Paxton designed an architectural masterpiece, the Crystal Palace. Its huge canopy of glass covering 22 acres was in itself an artistic triumph. Its more prosaic features, however, have a special significance for economic historians:

"It was one of the first great examples of standardized production. All the material used on the Palace was interchangeable; girders, columns, gutters, sash-bars were identical throughout. This, of course, enormously simplified the actual building operations and made it possible to run up the structure at a rate that amazed both the technical and the lay public . . . . Fifty years earlier such a technique of construction would have been impossible. In 1851 you could multiply in the engineering field; in 1801, you could not. Interchangeability was the harvest yielded by the great machine-tool makers of the earlier industrial revolution, Boulton, Maudsaly, Whitworth. This made possible uniform mass output, except of the master machines which guided the uniformity."[42]

Notable as the Crystal Palace was in inaugurating a new era in building, its significance was even greater in terms of the actual exhibits dis-

---

[41] This is based on six different contemporary estimates of national income, as given by Phyllis Deane, "Contemporary Estimates of National Income in the First Half of the Nineteenth Century," *Economic History Review, VIII*, No. 3, 353 (April 1956).

[42] C. R. Fay, *Palace of Industry, 1851,* Cambridge University Press, Cambridge, 1951, 15–16.

played. Here was visible evidence of the industrial progress that Britain had already made, and here was a measure of Britain's achievement as the "workshop of the world." Some of the spirit of this achievement can be recaptured by taking a brief tour through the Crystal Palace.

We enter the building to see the largest sheet of plate glass ever made and a miscellany of mineral ores and foodstuffs; also a model of the Liverpool Docks (Britain the great metropolitan consumer). Machinery, headed by locomotives and other railway equipment: James Watt of Soho: the hydraulic press which lifted the Britannia tubular bridge: . . . . Manufacturing and tools—James Nasmyth's steam-hammer easily first, being so big and so gentle. Bridges and lighthouses. Ship models and life-belts. A prodigious assemblage of sporting arms . . . . Agricultural implements . . . . Among philosophic [scientific] instruments the great Ross telescope and some photographic apparatus; balloons of course, for it was the age of balloon flights . . . .
Here inevitably the textiles took first place. England had made its money in cotton, though it was now eagerly investing it in railways. There were fabrics, and clothing made from them. After that came boots and shoes made of leather, which introduces us to skins and furs and the exhibits of the Hudson's Bay Company. The hardware displayed was a real miscellany—grates and a gas cooker, cast-iron railings and the locks and safes of Chubb and Milner . . . .
Inevitably it is the machinery exhibited in the Crystal Palace that interests us most, as it did the contemporary visitor . . . . Machinery was in two sections, moving machinery and machinery at rest. Whitworth's stand of engine-tools—Appold's centrifugal pump—four-cylindered marine engines—the great hydraulic press from the Britannia Bridge; but of such enumeration there would be no end . . .
Regarding the imperial and colonial exhibits . . . let us only note here that seven whole sections were devoted to them.
Do we not see how nonsensical it is to talk of the "Little Englandism" of the 1850's and 1860's? It was anything but this—call it insular megalomania, if you will, to suppose that an island without a preferential tariff could focus on itself the trade of its colonies and overseas posses- sions without losing their allegiance. It was because Britain believed she had things to offer to them as to the rest of the world, which whether the world wanted them or not was destined to enter into its consumption, that she bestrode with such nonchalance the free-trade horse. For she was herself the supply side of the Industrial Revolution.[43]

Taking leave of the Crystal Palace, the visitor must have been im- pressed by the solid evidence of Britain's industrial supremacy and over- seas expansion. He had seen the fruits of the Industrial Revolution which had come earlier and with greater impact to Britain than to any other country. In contrast to the British exhibits, the foreign exhibits offered relatively little from the standpoint of industrial achievement.

[43] *Ibid.,* **80–89.**

The marked contrast between the wide variety of British industrial products and the limited range of foreign products at the Great Exhibition illustrates the different degrees to which various countries of the world economy had developed by the mid-nineteenth century. And for the future, the Great Exhibition portended remarkable accomplishments in manufacture, mining, and metallurgy. During the century after the Great Exhibition the earlier trends already noted in connection with the Industrial Revolution continued, and the British economy proceeded to develop intensively. The next chapter investigates the course of this intensive development.

Chapter 9

Intensive Development

at the Center

Much of the record of Britain's development in the century after the Great Exhibition can be written in terms of the spread of mechanization and increasing productivity in both manufacturing and agriculture. This chapter summarizes four salient features of the intensive development in Britain after 1850: (*a*) the rise in real income, (*b*) the increase in manpower and the accumulation of capital, (*c*) the gains in productivity, and (*d*) the shifts in the industrial structure.

1. Trends in Real Income

Available statistics of real income since 1870 provide a comprehensive measure of Britain's development.[1] As Figure 9.1 shows, the increase in

[1] In his pioneer attempt to construct an index of total industrial output of Britain, Hoffmann calculated that industrial output grew at an annual rate between 2 per cent and 3 per cent from 1856 to 1876, and at a rate below 2 per cent after 1876. In 1931, the actual volume of production was more than 30 times as large as it had been in 1851. See W. Hoffmann, *British Industry 1700–1950*, Basil Blackwell, Oxford, 1955, 33, 50.

The reliability of Hoffmann's index of total industrial production may be strongly questioned, however. Although the index may be significant for the late nineteenth century, it is extremely narrow and highly speculative for the eighteenth century and early nineteenth century.

real national income and the rise in per capita real income are striking. Real national income almost quadrupled between 1870 and 1939, increasing from approximately £769 million (calculated at 1900 prices) in 1870 to approximately £2,725 million (also at 1900 prices) in

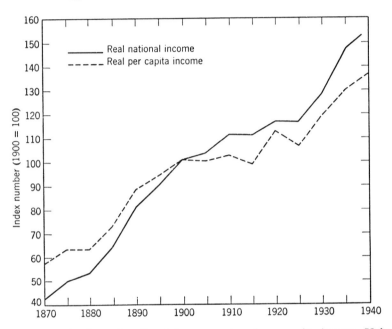

Figure 9.1. Rise in real national income and real per capita income, United Kingdom, 1870–1938. (Based on calculations by Prest, *Economic Journal*, *LVIII*, 58–59.)

1938.[2] And even though population rose during this period by about 50 per cent, real income per capita more than doubled, rising from approximately £25 (at 1900 prices) in 1870 to approximately £58 (at 1900 prices) in 1938.[2] According to Table 9.1, net national income per capita at 1912–1913 prices increased from an average of £30.4 during the decade 1870–1879 to an average of £74.0 for the period 1948–1952. And from 1870–1879 to 1940–1949 the percentage change per decade in net national income per capita was over 13 per cent.

With an increase in the working population, however, it is natural to expect that real national income should rise: more workers should pro-

[2] A. R. Prest, "National Income of the United Kingdom, 1870–1946," *Economic Journal, LVIII*, 58–59 (March 1948).

TABLE 9.1. POPULATION AND NET NATIONAL INCOME
PER CAPITA, AT CONSTANT 1912–1913 PRICES,
UNITED KINGDOM, 1870–1952

Period	Population (decade avgs.) (millions)	Percentage Change per Decade (per cent)	Net National Income per Capita (£) (decade avgs.)	Percentage Change per Decade (per cent)
1870–1879	32.7	—	30.4	—
1875–1884	34.4	—	32.0	—
1880–1889	35.9	9.9	35.6	17.0
1885–1894	37.4	8.8	40.1	25.3
1890–1899	39.1	8.9	44.4	25.0
1895–1904	41.0	9.6	46.9	16.8
1900–1909	42.9	9.7	48.0	8.0
1905–1914	44.6	8.9	50.0	6.6
1910–1919	46.0	7.3	49.7	3.5
1915–1924	45.4	1.8	49.3	−1.3
1920–1929	44.9	−2.5	52.7	6.1
1925–1934	45.8	0.9	56.4	14.5
1930–1939	46.8	4.3	62.0	17.7
1935–1944	47.9	4.5	70.2	24.3
1940–1949	49.1	4.9	73.5	18.6
1948–1952	50.0	—	74.0	—
1870/79–1940/49	—	6.1	—	13.7

Source: J. B. Jefferys and D. Walters, "National Income and Expenditure of the United Kingdom, 1870–1952," in S. Kuznets (ed.), *Income and Wealth*, Series V, Bowes and Bowes, London, 1955, 14.

duce more goods. It is more exacting, therefore, to consider real income per head of the working population, instead of real income per head of the total population. Phelps Brown has calculated the real income per head of the working population for the period 1862–1938, as shown in Figure 9.2. Even this narrower measurement indicates the marked expansion of the British economy: real income per head of the working population more than doubled between 1862 and 1938.

Closer examination of Figures 9.1 and 9.2 discloses a significant phenomenon. Although over the entire period there is a strong upward trend in real income, the rate of increase slackens considerably during the late 1890's. There is a definite contrast between the sustained advance before 1900 and the slower increase after 1900. This clearly discloses the fact of intertemporal differences in the rate of development, some periods being more rapid than others, with no guarantee of continuous development.

Indeed, the break in Britain's rate of development around 1900 raises the possibility of stagnation in modern industrial economies.[3] It suggests that as an economy becomes more advanced it may encounter forces that tend to retard its future rate of development. Considering Britain's development, one should therefore examine both the positive forces, which promoted development during the last half of the nine-

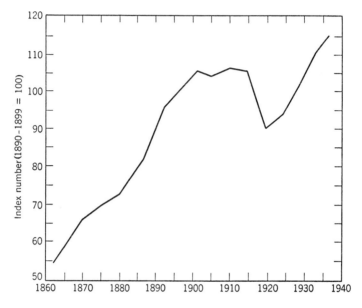

Figure 9.2.   Rise in real income per head of working population, United Kingdom, 1862–1938. [Based on calculations by E. H. Phelps Brown and S. V. Hopkins, "The Course of Wage Rates in Five Countries, 1860–1939," *Oxford Economic Papers, II,* No. 2, 276 (June 1950).]

teenth century and after World War I, and the negative forces, which tended to check the rate of development at the turn of the century.

As classical economists emphasized, it is to be expected that income per capita will rise with an increase, per capita, in the amount of economic resources put into production and with an increase in productive efficiency. An increase in exports should also be stimulating. The next two sections examine the trends in factor supply and productivity, and the following chapter will consider the role of exports.

[3] For a quantitative analysis of the question of long-term retardation, constancy, or acceleration in the rate of growth in 10 countries, including the United Kingdom, see S. Kuznets, "Quantitative Aspects of the Economic Growth of Nations," *Economic Development and Cultural Change, V,* No. 1, 35–43 (Oct. 1956).

2. Trends in Factor Supply

Since the services of labor and capital are the major resources put into production, the trends of these inputs should have greatly influenced the trend of Britain's output. Figure 9.3 shows a substantial increase in the number of people gainfully occupied. Until 1913, there is virtually a constant growth curve. The growth between 1924 and 1938 remains rapid and is greater than that of population as a whole.[4]

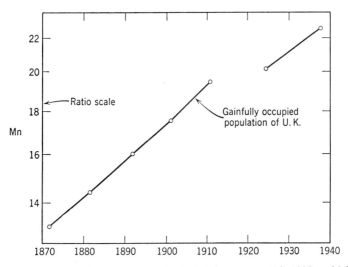

Figure 9.3. Growth of labor force, United Kingdom, 1870–1938. (Adapted from Phelps Brown and Weber, *Economic Journal, LXIII,* No. 250, 265.)

The growing proportion of the population that entered the labor force tended to increase the amount of work done per capita. Hours of work fell, however, especially after World War I. Although data are inadequate for a definite conclusion, the net result of these opposing trends would seem to have been a modest increase in annual hours of work per head of the population in the last half of the nineteenth century, followed by a decline during this century. But the exact course of labor input per capita is not so significant because increase in capital per head has been much greater than any change in labor input per capita.

The amount of capital accumulation was most impressive. The stock of capital goods, excluding buildings, increased from approximately

[4] War casualties and the withdrawal of Southern Ireland account for the difference between 1913 and 1924.

£1.5 billion in 1870 to approximately £5.5 billion in 1938 (both valued at 1912–1913 £).[5]   Figure 9.4 shows the growth in real capital (excluding buildings) per occupied person, and also compares this increase with the expansion in home-produced real income (excluding rent on buildings) per occupied person.[6]   Over the entire period,

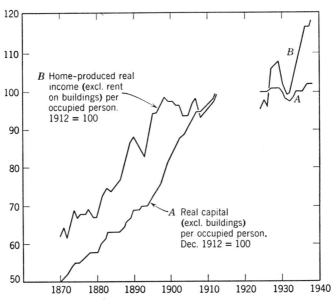

Figure 9.4.   Growth of real capital and real income, per occupied person, United Kingdom, 1870–1940.   (Adapted from Phelps Brown and Weber, *Economic Journal, LXIII,* No. 250, 269.)

capital grew at about the same rate as income: both real capital per head and real income per head nearly doubled.   There are, however, some interesting movements within subperiods.   It appears that, during the years of Victorian expansion from 1870 to near 1900, real income and the stock of capital moved together: expressed as amounts per occupied person, they both rose by almost 50 per cent.   Then, from 1900 to 1913, real income per head scarcely increased, even though capital accumulation continued.   During the interwar years, income

[5] E. H. Phelps Brown and B. Weber, "Accumulation, Productivity and Distribution in the British Economy, 1870–1938," *Economic Journal, LXIII,* No. 250, 286–287 (June 1953).

[6] By home-produced real income is meant total net national real income minus property income from overseas.   Curve *B* in Figure 9.4 is therefore lower than the curve of real income in Figure 9.2, which includes property income from overseas.

again rose, but, from 1924 to 1938, the quantity of capital per person did not rise on balance at all.

This course of capital accumulation and real income raises two important questions: (1) What driving forces lay behind the capital accumulation? (2) Why was the increase in real income checked during the decade of the 1900's even though capital accumulation was increasing?

Technological progress continued to be a major determinant of the increase in capital, just as it had been during the Industrial Revolution. The diffusion of new methods, materials, and products required more capital. One striking feature of technical advance was the wider use of the steam engine as a source of power. With the use of steam, the coal industry grew in relative importance, and the expansion in coal production (almost threefold between 1860 and 1900) required considerable investment. The great innovation, however, was the introduction of cheap methods of making steel. The Bessemer process and the Siemens open-hearth process made possible a large expansion in steel production (from one-half million tons in 1870 to almost 5 millions in 1900). The repercussions of cheap and abundant steel extended throughout the economy: from a transformation of the engineering industries, to a spread of mechanized mass production in a wide range of commodities. Advances in the application of chemistry to industry were also significant: new products of many kinds, including synthetic dyestuffs, fertilizers, and explosives, began to be produced in large quantities. The electrical, rubber, paper, glass, and many other industries also have their stories of technical progress.

In transportation, although nearly all the main railway lines were completed by the 1870's, many improvements in railway equipment were introduced during the last quarter of the century. In the 1870's, urban transport facilities were supplemented by the introduction of tramways, and towards the end of the century underground railways were also introduced. The most striking progress in transport between 1870 and 1914, however, was in shipping.

The coming of the steamship had effects similar to the earlier railroad. Considerable investment entered into the eightfold expansion between 1850 and 1900 in the carrying power of British tonnage and in the introduction of new types of ships such as the tanker and refrigerating ship. In addition, the extension of shipping facilities allowed the opening of new outlets for British products and also made it possible to realize the economies of cheap food and raw materials from overseas—a result that stimulated investment in other industries.

In the interwar period such fundamental changes as the perfecting of the internal-combustion engine, ball bearings, new alloy metallurgy, welding, new chemical processes, and precision control led to an expansion in the new industries of electrical apparatus, motor vehicles, cycles, aircraft, electrical engineering, and silk and rayon.[7] Paced by technological progress in transportation, commerce, and industry, the British economy continued to accumulate large amounts of capital. Table 9.2 shows the substantial amounts of net capital formation from 1870 to 1952.

TABLE 9.2. NET CAPITAL FORMATION AT CURRENT PRICES, UNITED KINGDOM, 1870–1952

Period	Net Domestic Capital Formation Including Stock Changes and Net Overseas Lending	
	Yearly Averages (£ million)	Percentage
1870–1874	152	12.8
1875–1879	82	7.0
1880–1884	123	9.7
1885–1889	133	10.3
1890–1894	120	8.5
1895–1899	159	10.0
1900–1904	175	9.5
1905–1909	225	11.3
1910–1913	245	11.2
1924–1928	342	8.1
1929–1933	181	4.5
1934–1938	325	7.2
1948–1952	1209	10.8

Source: Jefferys and Walters, "National Income and Expenditure of the United Kingdom, 1870–1952," in S. Kuznets (ed.), Income and Wealth, Series V, Bowes and Bowes, London, 1955, 18.

Capital accumulation was, however, more than simply a response to the stimulus of technical advance. More fundamentally, it involved a process that might be termed "the beneficent spiral of accumulation." As the theories of development show, once an economy begins to develop, its advance can gain momentum. For once investment becomes sufficiently high to increase productivity, then the rising income will increase the capacity of the economy to provide savings for further investment, and the rate of development can, in turn, be greater. As

[7] R. S. Sayers, "The Springs of Technical Progress in Britain, 1919–39," Economic Journal, LX, No. 238, 275–291 (June 1950).

productivity rises and real income increases, capital accumulation can, so to speak, feed upon itself.

During the period 1870–1913, most of Britain's capital accumulation came from the growing middle class: little from those worth £1000 or less; 40 per cent or so from those worth between £1000 and £25,000.[8] Moreover, while the organized capital markets financed mainly the transport industries and public utilities, at least half of industrial investment came from undistributed profits. Reinvested profits were a more important source of accumulation than either the borrowings of old or new companies on the stock exchange.[9]

Besides technical advance and the beneficent spiral of accumulation, which mainly had the effect of increasing capital per unit of output, there was also a need to widen capital as the economy expanded. Capital accumulation increased income, but the increase in income also facilitated the growth in capital. As output expanded, there was an increase of stocks and work in progress to keep pace with output: investment was induced via the acceleration principle. There was also a considerable amount of investment geared to the growth in population. An increase in residential building, shopping facilities, schools, and public utilities accompanied an increase in population. Housing, transport, and other public utilities actually absorbed far more capital than industry.[10]

In the period 1924–1938, however, the growth in capital was interrupted. The virtual failure to make any increase for 14 years in industrial equipment per head of the occupied population was serious and illustrates, as post-Keynesian analysis suggests, that the maintenance of sustained growth is a precarious problem.

Changes between 1913 and 1924 have been likened to a geological fault in the economy.[11] There was an unusually large shift in the distribution of income: rents and profits were squeezed, as earned income rose from about 55 per cent to over 65 per cent of home-produced national income.[12] As a source of savings, profits were not only relatively reduced but also taxed more heavily, and this also diminished the incentive to save. At the same time, there was a fall in the rate of return on investment in industrial capital: the average rate of return, which was between 10 per cent and 13 per cent from 1870 to 1914,

---

[8] A. K. Cairncross, *Home and Foreign Investment 1870–1913*, Cambridge University Press, Cambridge, 1953, 86.

[9] *Ibid.*, 99.

[10] *Ibid.*, 6, 102.

[11] Phelps Brown and Weber, *op. cit.*, 280–281.

[12] For an explanation, see Phelps Brown and Hart, "The Share of Wages in National Income," *Economic Journal, LXII*, 246 (June 1952).

fell to around 7 per cent in 1924–1926, and was still under 9 per cent when at its highest in 1937–1938. As a result of these changes, total industrial investment was negligible during the interwar period. This tended to restrain the rise in real income. Fortunately, however, other forces tended to maintain the rise, namely, an increase in industrial productivity and a favorable movement in the terms of trade. Nonetheless, the cessation in the growth of industrial capital in Britain during the interwar period points up the problem of maintaining sufficient investment to sustain smooth development in a rich industrial country.

3. Trends in Productivity

The improved efficiency in production, as shown by an increase in output per unit of resources, was another major driving force in Britain's economic advance. With a given "dose" of labor and capital, the economy was able to produce an ever-larger volume of goods.

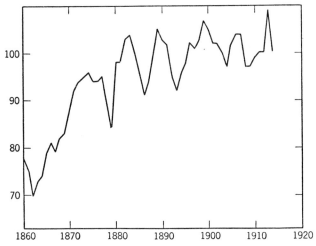

Figure 9.5. Output per worker in mining and manufacture, Great Britain, 1860–1914 (1890–1899 = 100). (Adapted from Phelps Brown and Handfield-Jones, *Oxford Economic Papers, IV,* No. 3, 271.)

The upward trend in industrial productivity closely parallels the trend in real income per occupied person, as is evident from a comparison of Figure 9.2 with Figure 9.5, which shows output per worker in mining and manufacturing.[13]

[13] This measure of industrial productivity has been obtained by dividing Hoffmann's index of output (covering a wide range of industries and accounting for about 70 per cent of the value added by all industry) by the number of workers in the industries covered. The fluctuations in Figure 9.5 are those of the trade cycle, since the numbers of workers have not been adjusted for unemployment.

According to these calculations by Phelps Brown,[14] the rate of growth in industrial productivity shows, however, a substantial slowing down after 1885. The change is so marked that the trend can be closely approximated by a linear rise from 1860 to 1885, in which output per worker rose by nearly a third, and after that a barely rising course until 1914. After World War I, productivity shows another increase: output per wage earner in British industry rose over one-third between 1924 and 1937.[15]

The trends in real income per worker and output per worker are thus seen to be parallel: rising real income per worker and rising output per worker until around 1900; then very little advance in real income or productivity from 1900 to 1914; and then a rise in real income and a rise in productivity from the mid-twenties to the late-thirties.[16]

This parallel movement is more than mere chance. Phelps Brown attributes the slowing down in the rise in real income during the 1900's mainly to the slackening in growth of productivity. And he believes the reason for this slackening is found in the process of innovation. Phelps Brown's hypothesis is that, whereas the rise before 1900 had been carried forward by the massive application of techniques of power, transport, and machinery during the "Age of Steam and Steel," the rapid and general extension of these techniques was coming to an end in the 1890's. "The supersession of sail by steam at sea is a striking example. . . . The replacement of each sailing-ship by a steamship makes a big advance in the productivity of transport, but once the sailing-ships have been replaced, such rapid improvements are no longer possible: only those annual advances remain which can be brought about by gradual improvements in the performance of the steamship itself."[17] At the same time, the new techniques of electricity,

[14] E. H. Phelps Brown and S. J. Handfield-Jones, "The Climacteric of the 1890's; A Study in the Expanding Economy," *Oxford Economic Papers, IV*, No. 3, 266–307 (Oct. 1952).

[15] L. Rostas, "Comparative Productivity in British and American Industry," *National Institute of Economic and Social Research, Occasional Papers, XIII*, Cambridge University Press, Cambridge, 1948, 42–43. Rostas' calculations cover manufacturing, mining, building, and public utilities.

[16] Output per unit of labor and capital combined, that is, "total productivity," probably rose somewhat less rapidly than is indicated by output per worker, that is, "labor productivity," alone.

A study of productivity in British manufacturing between 1907 and 1948 shows that output per employee hour in manufacturing more than doubled between 1907 and 1948 (1907 = 100; 1924 = 142; 1935 = 171; 1948 = 203). A. Maddison, "Output, Employment, and Productivity in British Manufacturing in the Last Half Century," *Bulletin of the Oxford University Institute of Statistics, XVII*, No. 4, 380 (Nov. 1955).

[17] Phelps Brown and Handfield-Jones, *op. cit.*, 282–283.

the internal-combustion engine, and the new chemical processes did not attain massive application until during and after World War I. They were as yet big only in promise, not achievement.

Alternative hypotheses are rejected by Phelps Brown. Many contemporaries believed that diminished efforts by management and some enforcement of restrictive practices by labor were reducing the efficiency of management and labor in Britain, thereby holding back the increase in productivity. But in view of the fact that great advances in British productivity have been achieved in later years when similar inefficient practices by management and labor existed, Phelps Brown concludes that these had but minor influence on the check to productivity.[18]

Nor can the check to the growth of productivity and real income be explained by a lower rate of capital accumulation. For the physical amount of equipment per head rose by more than a sixth. A weakening of the "innovation effect," however, did matter: "the tonnage of steamships, so to speak, might continue to increase faster than the occupied population, but adding one steamship to others would not make so much difference as substituting a steamship for a sailing-ship had done."[19]

Finally, the course of output per worker in British agriculture shows no setback such as occurred in industrial productivity: agriculture was not responsible for the check in rise of real income.[20]

The weakening of the innovation effect of steam and steel was all the more serious for Britain because it also affected adversely the terms of trade. Steam and steel had been instrumental in opening up new overseas sources of food and raw materials. But by the 1890's this process was almost at an end, and the supplies of food and raw materials were no longer rising as rapidly as previously. At the same time, the growth in population continued. The terms of trade between Britain's exports (mainly manufactures and coal) and Britain's imports (mainly foodstuffs and raw materials) deteriorated for Britain: import prices rose relatively to export prices.[21] This deterioration in Britain's terms of trade from 1900 to 1913 also played a part in dampening the rise in real income. But it can be concluded that the slow increase in productivity within Britain itself was a greater check to real income than the deterioration in the terms of trade.[22]

[18] *Ibid.*, 280–281.
[19] *Ibid.*, 286.
[20] *Ibid.*, 276–278.
[21] Movements in the terms of trade are considered more fully in Chapter 11.
[22] Phelps Brown and Handfield-Jones, *op. cit.*, 269–270. It might also be

Phelps Brown's argument may, however, be challenged on several counts. Some would give more importance to the reduced efficiency of entrepreneurial activity than does Phelps Brown. For, although other factors may account for the later rise in productivity, it can still be said that, if at the same time entrepreneurship had also been more active, the rise in productivity would have been all the greater.[23] Further, it is difficult to reconcile the continued accumulation of capital at a time when the massive innovations had supposedly ceased. Most significantly, however, if the effects of short-run fluctuations are removed from Phelps Brown's series of industrial productivity, then the break in trend appears in the 1870's rather than the 1890's.[24]   A diminution in the "innovation effect" may still account in part for this check to productivity, since the 1870's mark the end of the general application of steam power and iron machinery to Britain's staple industries, and the subsequent effects of steel were less powerful than those of iron.[25]   But if the decline in productivity is placed in the 1870's, then it may more reasonably be associated with the parallel decline in growth of industrial production and exports which also occurred after the 1870's. This issue will be discussed further in Chapter 11, where the decline in growth of exports will be examined.

4. Shifts in Industrial Structure

Changes in productivity can also be explored by considering indexes of output per head in particular industries. From Figures 9.6 and 9.7, it can be seen that in the coal mines and in rail transport output per worker reaches earlier turning points than in the other industries. Iron and steel manufactures and wool show no slackening. This leaves four important industries in which productivity was checked around the turn of the century: cotton, beer, the mining of iron ore, and iron and steel smelting.

In agriculture, productivity also rose, but the increase was less than

---

argued that the building cycle and a shift from wages to profits also contributed to the check in real income. Cf. W. A. Lewis and P. J. O'Leary, "Secular Swings in Production and Trade, 1870–1913," *Manchester School of Economic and Social Studies, XXIII*, No. 2, 125 (May 1955).

[23] Thus, Landes places much emphasis on entrepreneurial factors in Britain's loss of industrial preeminence, especially in contrast to Germany. See David S. Landes, "Entrepreneurship in Advanced Industrial Countries: The Anglo-German Rivalry," in *Entrepreneurship and Economic Growth*, Harvard University Research Center in Entrepreneurial History, Nov. 1954.

[24] D. J. Coppock, "The Climacteric of the 1890's: A Critical Note," *Manchester School of Economic and Social Studies, XXIV*, No. 1, 3–8 (Jan. 1956).

[25] *Ibid.*, 22.

in manufacture and mining, and there was no restraint on agricultural productivity in the 1900's as there was in industrial productivity. From an index of 100 in 1867–1869, output per worker in agriculture rose steadily to 126 in 1904–1910, then fell during the next decade to a low of 116 in 1920–1922, and rose again to a level of 140 in 1930–1934.[26]

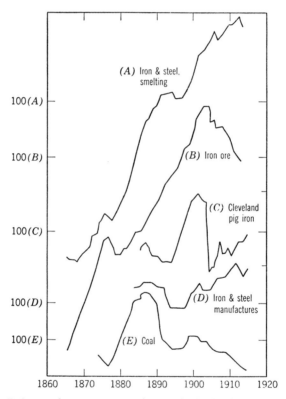

Figure 9.6. Indexes of output per worker, United Kingdom, 1860–1914 (5- or 7-year moving averages; 1890–1899 = 100). (Adapted from Phelps Brown and Handfield-Jones, *Oxford Economic Papers, IV,* No. 3, 273.)

To explain adequately the causes of these differential rates of productivity in individual industries, one would have to undertake detailed studies of the specific factors shaping productivity in each industry. Some general influences may be considered, however.

The most immediate factor affecting output per worker is the amount of machinery available. It is to be expected that the worker helped

[26] E. M. Ojala, *Agriculture and Economic Progress,* Oxford University Press, Oxford, 1952, 153.

by machines will produce more than the worker operating with little or no machinery. But this does not mean that output per worker can be automatically increased simply by adding to the available equipment per worker employed. This will also depend on the size of the firm,

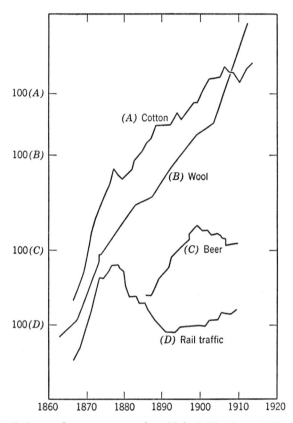

Figure 9.7. Indexes of output per worker, United Kingdom, 1860–1914 (5-, 7-, or 10-year moving averages; 1890–1899 = 100). (Adapted from Phelps Brown and Handfield-Jones, *Oxford Economic Papers, IV*, No. 3, 274.)

which, in turn, is determined by the size and the character of the market. Moreover, the installation of machinery will not in itself procure high output per worker, unless the production is sufficiently standardized to allow the economical use of this machinery. It must also be remembered that output per unit of real resources (total productivity) is a more basic measure of productivity than is output per worker (labor productivity).

These refinements notwithstanding, there is considerable evidence that the output per worker in different industries is affected by the amount of machinery, its quality, its rate of replacement, and such factors as the size of market, standardization, and size of plant, which determine the use of machinery. Besides the degree of mechanization or technique of production, "organizational" factors associated with the skill of management in achieving and operating the best factory organization are also important. Lastly, a host of circumstances that influence the willingness and ability of labor to make an effort are significant: the number of hours worked, the system of wage payments, methods of work simplification, labor turnover, and all the intangibles which come under the rubric of "workers' psychology" and "industrial relations."

Considering agriculture, one may note that the increase in productivity was made possible by continued technical improvement, the contraction of tillage to the best soils, and a general pressure to save labor as product prices fell relatively to money wage rates. On the other hand, the slower rate of increase in agricultural productivity than in industrial productivity is explained primarily by the relative immobility of agricultural labor which keeps redundant workers in relatively inefficient production, the relative inflexibility of economic organization in agriculture which results in farms below optimum size, the diminishing returns in agricultural production, the lack of capital accumulation in agriculture, and finally the inelasticity of demand for food.

Besides the range of different rates of growth of productivity in various industries within a given period, one may also observe a tendency for older industries to shift downward in the distribution from one period of time to another. Retardation generally characterizes the rate of growth of output of individual industries and outputs.[27]

An analysis of the statistics of several British industries supports the commonly held notion that the percentage rate of growth in an individual industry tends to decline as its age increases. Thus, Kuznets found that a logistic curve applies quite well to production in the British coal, pig iron, steel, and cotton industries.[28] Hoffmann's work also reveals striking differences in the rates of growth of various British industries over similar periods. Industries for which figures are avail-

[27] Cf. Solomon Fabricant, *Economic Progress and Economic Change,* National Bureau of Economic Research, New York, May 1954, 14.

[28] S. Kuznets, *Secular Movements in Production and Prices,* Houghton Mifflin Co., New York, 1930, 124, 126, 129, 133. The shape of a logistic curve is such that it shows more rapid growth in the beginning of the period and then slower relative increase during the latter part of the period, that is, a declining rate of percentage increase.

able for at least a century show three typical phases of development: (a) a phase of industrial expansion, characterized by a rising rate of growth of output, (b) a phase of industrial development when the rate of growth of output is declining, and (c) a phase of industrial development when there is an absolute decline in output.[29] As a summary of the "life history" of many British industries, Table 9.3 shows the different phases of growth in detail.

In considering this phenomenon of retardation in the growth of individual industries, some writers have referred to a "law of growth" which might be expressed mathematically by "growth curves" such as are used in population studies or biological studies of an organism's life history. But the precision of such curves does not have general applicability: the rates of growth differ in duration and intensity from industry to industry. At most, the only general rule of uniformity that can be established is that an industry tends to grow at a declining rate.[30]

How is this retardation to be explained? The diverse rates of growth in different British industries can be adequately explained only in terms of each industry's position in the total British economy and the various changes that occurred in the economy. Hoffmann concludes that the following factors are significant in determining changes in an industry's rate of growth:[31] (a) the general structure of the economy: the development of the consumer goods industries influences the rate of growth of the producer goods industries, and particularly the investment goods industries; (b) the extent of the industry's market which depends upon the proportion of home demand that is satisfied by home output and upon the possibility of opening up overseas markets; (c) the character of the industry's market: the rate of growth of an industry will be stimulated if the demand for its products is a new one, and if the demand is capable of long-term expansion; and (d) the industry's capacity for attracting capital and labor: if a shortage of capital and labor occurs, the growth in output will slow down.

Similar reasons for the retardation in growth of different industries are given by Kuznets who summarizes his findings as follows: (a) technical progress slackens; (b) resources are exhausted; (c) the slower growing industries exercise a retarding influence upon the faster growing complementary branches, while the rapidly growing industries exercise a similar influence upon competitive branches; (d) an industry in one

[29] Hoffmann, op. cit., 180.
[30] For a more adequate critique of laws of industrial growth, see A. F. Burns, Production Trends in the United States Since 1870, National Bureau of Economic Research, New York, 1934, 169–173.
[31] Hoffmann, op. cit., 111.

TABLE 9.3.   CHANGES IN PATTERN OF DEVELOPMENT OF
INDUSTRIAL OUTPUT OF THE UNITED KINGDOM,
1701–1913

	Growth of Output		
Industries	Rising Rate of Growth	Declining Rate of Growth	Absolute Decline in Output
Producer Goods	1701–1847	1847–1913	
Coal	1701–1860	1860–1913	
Tin ore		1854–1871	1872–1913
Iron ore		1851–1880	1880–1913
Copper ore	1728–1798	1798–1856	1856–1913
Lead ore		1849–1863	1863–1913
Zinc ore	1854–1875	1875–1883	1883–1913
Iron and steel	1803–1847	1847–1913	
Iron goods, machinery	1787–1847	1847–1913	
Copper	1772–1883	1883–1892	1893–1913
Lead		1849–1864	1864–1913
Aluminium		1890–1913	
Copper goods		1821–1913	
Shipbuilding	1790–1853	1853–1906	1906–1935
Railway construction		1831–1902	1902–1913
Timber and woodworking industries	1832–1865	1865–1903	1903–1913
Hemp goods	1791–1835	1835–1913	
Building	1786–1861	1861–1902	1902–1913
Consumer Goods	1701–1830	1830–1913	
Cotton yarn	1699–1800	1800–1913	
Cotton piece goods	1699–1800	1800–1913	
Wool yarn	1780–1865	1865–1913	
Woollen goods	1740–1866	1866–1913	
Silk thread		1788–1857	1857–1913
Silk goods		1788–1855	1855–1913
Linen yarn		1762–1873	1873–1903
Linens		1787–1908	
Beer	1788–1864	1865–1902	1902–1913
Malt	1703–1864	1864–1898	1898–1913
Spirits	1801–1870	1870–1900	1901–1913
Leather goods	1803–1866	1868–1913	
Paper	1714–1895	1895–1913	
Total of all industries	1701–1830	1830–1913	

Source: W. G. Hoffmann, *British Industry 1700–1950*, Basil Blackwell,
Oxford, 1955, 184.

country may be retarded by the competition of the same industry in an
industrializing country.[32]

[32] Kuznets, *op. cit.*, 10–58.

Perhaps the most inclusive answer is to be found in the somewhat paradoxical statement that retardation in the growth of individual industries is but an expression of the progressiveness of the economy: a rapid growth in general production and a decline in the rate of growth in individual industries go together.[33] As the history of the British economy illustrates, the innovational forces in a developing economy affect the markets for goods. In one direction, the incessant introduction of new commodities restricts the increase in demand for old commodities: every new product involves an absolute or relative shift of purchasing power from an old product. The faster these new industries expand at first, the greater is this restrictive influence, and the more difficult it is to sustain their own rates of growth for long, since a sustained increase for a long period would eventually mean the marketing of impossibly large quantities. In another direction, changes in methods of production have stimulated the development of some industries, but at the same time have tended to restrict the development of others. For example, the increasing use of steel instead of wood in ship building tended to retard the growth of the lumber industry; in general, every improvement in industrial technique making possible a more effective utilization of a raw material has tended to retard the growth in production of the material. Finally, because resources are scarce, when new industries compete with old industries for capital, labor, and materials, the rise of new industries will also tend to have a retarding influence on older industries.

These differential rates of development among various industries are also reflected in changes in the occupational distribution. The outstanding transformation in Britain was the unbroken decline in the proportion of the total working population engaged in agriculture: from about 22 per cent in 1851 to 12 per cent in 1881, 8 per cent in 1911, and down to little more than 6 per cent in 1931. The proportion engaged in manufacture remained relatively constant, being approximately 39 per cent in 1851, 33 per cent in 1881, 34 per cent in 1911, and 33 per cent in 1931. The proportion of the working population engaged in providing services, however, increased substantially—from about 30 per cent in 1851, to over 33 per cent in 1881, 46 per cent in 1911, and to almost 50 per cent in 1931.[34]

It is commonly observed that this diversion of labor from primary production to the service industries, so-called tertiary production, is both a consequence and an indication of the rising standard of living. Thus, according to Colin Clark,

"Low real income per head is always associated with a low proportion

[33] Burns, *op. cit.,* xvi, 122.
[34] Ojala, *op. cit.,* 84.

of the working population engaged in tertiary production and a high percentage in primary production. High average real income per head compels a large proportion of producers to engage in tertiary production. The reasons for this growth of the relative number of tertiary producers must largely be sought on the demand side. As incomes rise the demand for such services increases, and being non-transportable they must be supplied by workers within the country concerned."[35]

The trend in the distribution of Britain's labor force away from agriculture is explainable mainly by the combination of a high rate of growth of productivity per worker in agriculture and a lower rate of growth in the per capita use of agricultural products. The difference between growth of agricultural productivity and growth in the per capita use of agricultural products made possible a reduction in the ratio of agricultural workers to total working population. It should be recalled that the increase in productivity was largely the result of changes in agricultural organization and technology. The lower rate of growth in demand for agricultural products is explained by some substitution of products of non-agricultural labor for products of agricultural labor, by the changing pattern of consumption which shows that satiation of the need for agricultural products is reached sooner than is the need for non-agricultural products, and by such changes in social organization as urbanization.[36] Improvements in agriculture increased agricultural output, and, in accordance with the theory of economic surplus discussed in Chapter 3, this provided a margin for urbanization and industrialization. The technological revolution in agriculture was indeed an essential foundation for Britain's industrial growth. As will be seen in Part 3, the importance of a technological revolution in agriculture as a prerequisite for industrial change is one of the most important historical lessons for poor countries.

The trends of occupational distribution within Britain appear consistent with this hypothesis. But a word of warning is needed.[37] Statistical

[35] Colin Clark, *Conditions of Economic Progress,* Macmillan and Co. Ltd., London, 1940, 6–7. Also, A. G. B. Fisher, *Economic Progress and Social Security,* Macmillan and Co. Ltd., London, 1945, 5–6.

[36] Cf. S. Kuznets, "Toward a Theory of Economic Growth," in R. Leckachman (ed.), *National Policy for Economic Welfare at Home and Abroad,* Doubleday & Co., New York, 1955, 99.

[37] This is advisable in the light of a recent critique of both the analytical and statistical foundations of Clark's generalization, made by Bauer and Yamey. Their criticisms may be summarized as follows: "The analytical basis of the generalization of Mr. Clark . . . is open to criticism on several independent grounds. . . . First, a substantial proportion of tertiary products are not luxuries with a relatively high income elasticity of demand; conversely, some products of primary and secondary production, possibly on a large scale in their aggregate, are such

correspondence does not necessarily prove that the hypothesis is true, and the generalization has not been established as a conclusive economic law. Moreover, even if it were true for Britain, it need not follow that it has general applicability to all countries. In many poor countries tertiary activities are significant, and, in many cases where there may be an observed correlation between economic progress and occupational distribution, this may be more accurately regarded as a statistical accident rather than as the result of consistent underlying forces which always operate uniformly in different developing economies. It is best, therefore, to interpret Clark's proposition simply as a broad tendency, although the general idea of a "hierarchy" of occupations is important to recognize.[38]

There is no doubt, however, that the fundamental structural change in the British economy was the decline in agriculture. As a percentage of national income, agricultural incomes fell from a little over 20 per cent in 1867–1869, to about 7 per cent in 1911–1913, and to only 4 per cent in 1935–1939.[39] It is clear that after the "golden age of English farming" in the 1860's and early 1870's, agriculture became increasingly subordinate to industry.

A striking feature of this expanding industrialization was the large migration from the countryside to the towns. In 1841, the population of rural districts formed 39 per cent of the total for the country; by 1911 it formed no more than 19 per cent. Over the same period, the population of the colliery districts rose from 8 per cent to almost 15 per cent, and that of the towns from 53 per cent to 66 per cent.[40]

In his study of internal migration in Victorian England, Cairncross concluded that a major cause of this redistribution of population was

---

luxuries. Secondly, there may be large-scale substitution of capital for labor in tertiary production in the course of economic progress. Thirdly, the concept of the income elasticity of demand applied to a whole economy raises problems of aggregation which render doubtful any universal proposition about changes in its average value in conditions of change and economic growth; and this is particularly doubtful when relative factor prices and the distribution of income change." See P. T. Bauer and B. S. Yamey, "Economic Progress and Occupational Distribution," *Economic Journal*, LXI, No. 244, 748–754 (Dec. 1951).

[38] Cf. Fisher, "A Note on Tertiary Production," *ibid.*, LXII, No. 248, 820–835 (Dec. 1953); Fisher, "Marketing Structure and Economic Development," *Quarterly Journal of Economics*, LXVII, No. 1, 151–154 (Feb. 1954); S. G. Triantis, "Economic Progress, Occupational Redistribution, and International Terms of Trade," *Economic Journal*, LXIII, No. 251, 627–637 (Sept. 1953); A. L. Minkes, "Statistical Evidence and the Concept of Tertiary Industry," *Economic Development and Cultural Change*, III, No. 4, 366–373 (July 1955).

[39] Ojala, *op. cit.*, 129.

[40] Cairncross, *op. cit.*, 77, 79.

the building of railways and the consequent revolution in transportation. "Railway-building provided employment, and stimulated employment; it put the towns in need of more metal workers, engineers, and so on. Railway-building also increased mobility, both by taking men long distances to assist in the work of construction, and by making journeys to town easier and cheaper. It provided a vent for the surplus population of the countryside. Finally, the railways, by improving communications, immensely reinforced the competitive power of large-scale, urban enterprise and brought about the displacement of rural crafts and small country industries to the towns."[41]

Although British agriculture had earlier led the world, its position declined rapidly from the 1870's onward. Britain became ever more dependent on foreign supplies of foodstuffs and raw materials. During the 1860's, Britain had imported less than a quarter of its total consumption of grain; during the 1880's, imports rose to 45 per cent of the total consumption of grain, and to 65 per cent of wheat.[42] The area of cultivation contracted, and the agricultural population continued to decline.

The decline of English wheat growing after the 1870's was particularly striking. Between 1870 and 1910 the wheat-producing area fell by over one-half, as English wheat could no longer compete with wheat from the vast new producing areas opened up by railroad expansion in the American West and the Canadian prairies. Moreover, an abundance of cheap ocean-going steamer transport contributed to a fall in transportation costs: for example, in 1884, the cost of sending grain from Chicago to Liverpool was only about a third of what it had been a decade earlier—transport costs were not much higher between continents than they once had been between counties.[43]

The decline in British agriculture indicates the general proposition that land was no longer the limitational factor it once was. As the economy became technically advanced, new and better production possibilities emerged, and the economy freed itself from the severe restrictions formerly imposed by land. The limits which had been of so much concern to classical economists were overthrown; the classical law of secular diminishing returns lost its hold. The forces underlying this declining economic importance of land can be summarized as follows:

(1) A declining proportion of the aggregate inputs of the community is required to produce farm products.

(2) Of the inputs employed to produce farm products, the proportion

---

[41] *Ibid.,* 75.

[42] R. C. K. Ensor, *England 1870–1914,* The Clarendon Press, Oxford, 1936, 116.

[43] J. H. Clapham, *An Economic History of Modern Britain,* III, Cambridge University Press, Cambridge, 1951, 72–73.

represented by land is not an increasing one, despite the recombination of inputs in farming to use less human effort relative to other inputs, including land.

(3) International trade makes possible the exchange of the output of an industrial worker for a larger amount of agricultural produce than the same worker could produce if employed in domestic agriculture.[44]

When these forces are operative, the value added by all agricultural land as an input must necessarily decline relatively to the value productivity of all inputs of the community. The downward drift in the proportion of Britain's national income imputed to agriculture reflects the first force. It is also supported by the fact that, whereas just prior to 1800, worker families in England spent about 75 per cent of their income for food, in 1948 only 27 per cent of the expenditures of consumers in the United Kingdom appear to have been for food.[45] The proportion of income required to obtain food has certainly fallen remarkably. It also appears to be empirically valid that land as an input in agricultural production has not increased relatively to all other inputs used in farming.[46]

In the course of its development, the British economy had at its disposal an ever-increasing effective supply of aggregate inputs. And it found it both possible and desirable to produce or acquire its farm products with a smaller proportion of its productive resources. In part, this was made possible through the increase in agricultural productivity, as has already been discussed. More importantly, since the value of net output per worker in agriculture was generally less than in manufacturing industry,[47] Britain realized that it was possible to gain by importing agricultural products and employing people in producing manufactured goods for export instead of in agriculture (with lower output). In addition, as new production possibilities emerged, the community demanded more non-farm products and services; in accordance with Engel's law, the preferred consumption pattern became one in which farm products constituted a decreasing proportion of all products and services.

So it was that agriculture lost its importance in the developing British economy. After the 1890's, England was practically dependent on for-

[44] Points (1) and (2) are elaborated, both analytically and empirically, in T. W. Schultz, *Economic Organization of Agriculture*, McGraw-Hill Book Co., New York, 1953, Chapter VIII.

Different measures of the importance of land are possible; the measure used here is that of "value added" by all land relative to all other inputs.

[45] *Ibid.*, 129.

[46] *Ibid.*, 134–139.

[47] Rostas, *op. cit.*, 79–80, 90–91.

eign trade for essential foodstuffs and raw materials. By the turn of the century agriculture had been relegated to insignificance. England had become the most highly industrialized and urbanized country, and it staked its future upon this industrial specialization.

5. Intensive Development: Summary

It has now been seen that the process of industrial development in Britain involved an interweaving of many influences and forces. The result was a conjuncture of changes in population, technology, productivity, finance, market structure, and social relations. As a summary, some dominant features of this classic case of intensive development may be recalled:

(1) Between 1870 and 1939, real national income almost quadrupled, and per capita real income more than doubled.

(2) An important proximate cause of the increase in real income was the increase in productivity.[48] The increase in productivity was associated mainly with the massive application of technical advances. Most conspicuous of the earlier innovations were the extended use of the steam engine, the making of machine tools, the application of machines to manufacturing and agriculture, and the use of railroads and steel ships.

(3) Another important proximate cause of the increase in real income was the increase in factor supply connected with population growth and capital accumulation. Capital formation was of an impressive magnitude and was linked in large part to technological progress.

(4) Significant organizational changes occurred with the rise of the factory system, integration of market structures, and expansion of the banking system.

(5) In spite of population growth, the shadow of Malthus which hovered over the economy during the early nineteenth century was dispelled: land was not a limitational factor, as the productive basis of society was transformed from one in which land predominated to one in which industry and commerce became most important.

(6) The extension of manufacturing, as well as population growth, required increases in agricultural production which were met by changes in the agricultural system, the application of science to agriculture, and the extension of the area of cultivation.

(7) Different sectors of the economy had different rates of growth, but individual industries commonly experienced a decline in their percentage rates of growth. Differential rates of growth among industries also produced changes in the relative positions of industries, thereby

---

[48] Subsequent chapters discuss the international forces that contributed to the rise in real income.

necessitating continual structural shifts in the industrial and regional distribution of resources.

(8) Without social and intellectual change, the extent of economic change would not have been so remarkable. Changes in motives, values, and ideas were essential to the entire process of development.

(9) The institutional and ideological setting within which Britain's development occurred was that of liberal capitalism. The operation of effective incentives allowed the innovating entrepreneur to play a key role. The government contributed to development not so much through direct action as through the creation of a congenial framework of law, order, and freedom for the rising commercial and industrial groups. The mobilization of capital for industrial expansion was directed through private—not public—channels.

(10) The progress of productivity and real income, however, was unstable. As the check to real income around the turn of this century illustrates, the maintenance of sustained development cannot be automatically relied upon.

Chapter 10

International Movement

of Factors

During the last half of the nineteenth century the history of Britain's development lies in the larger history of extensive development through the world economy. As mechanization spread, as other countries developed, as international migration of labor and capital increased, as more countries were brought into world markets, and as the network of world trade became more integrated—as these extensive developments occurred, each country's own expansion became ever more linked with development in other countries. The intensive development of one country was extensive development from the viewpoint of another country, and the development of each country influenced the development of other countries. The domestic development of each country also influenced international trade, and international trade became significant in its own right as a means of development.

As part of this general picture, this chapter considers the international movements of capital and labor; the next two chapters examine other features of the interaction between intensive and extensive development.

1. Factor Endowments and International Trade

Basic to an understanding of the international process of development is the simple fact of great heterogeneity in the distribution of resources among countries of the world economy. Countries differ in their natural wealth: land, minerals, climate; in their possession of capital goods; and in the size and quality of their populations. In short, the factors of production are unequally distributed among countries.

Given unequal supplies of the different factors and a different structure of demand for the factors,[1] there will be different relative factor prices in various countries. Thus, about 1870 the supply of capital in England was large relative to the supplies of land and labor, so that the price of capital was low relative to the price of labor or the price of land; in the United States, however, the price of land was low relative to the price of labor or the price of capital; in India the price of labor was cheap relative to the price of land or the price of capital.

As discussed in Chapter 3, differences in the proportions of various productive factors between countries form a basis for international trade. This point can be expressed schematically as shown in the accompanying table.[2]   In this situation, A will tend to export labor-intensive goods

Relative Factor Supply	Relative Factor Price	Country A	Country B	Country C
"Most abundant"	Cheap	Labor	Land	Capital
"Less abundant"	Moderate	Land	Capital	Labor
"Least abundant"	Expensive	Capital	Labor	Land

(such as coffee, sugar, rubber) to B; B will tend to export land-intensive goods (such as grains, wool) to C; and C will tend to export capital-intensive goods (such as textiles) to A.   Through multilateral trade, a deficit in one direction may then be neutralized by a surplus in another direction: A's import surplus from C is offset by an export surplus to B; B's import surplus from A is offset by an export surplus to C; and C's import surplus from B is offset by an export surplus to A.

---

[1] What is important is the relative, not absolute, supply of the factors.   Thus a country (like Belgium) may have a small population in absolute size, but its labor supply relative to the country's land and capital may be the most abundant factor. Or, a country (like India) may have a large amount of land, but, relative to the demand of its large population for foodstuffs, land is a scarce factor and capital is relatively even more scarce.

[2] The following section is adapted from Karl-Erik Hansson, "A General Theory of the System of Multilateral Trade," *American Economic Review, XLII,* No. 3, 59–68 (March 1952).   Unlike Hansson's discussion, however, comparative advantage, not absolute advantage, is emphasized as the explanation of trade.

Over time, however, changes occur in the distribution of resources. Shifts take place in the relative factor supply as labor and capital migrate from one country to another, as technological progress occurs, as domestic capital is accumulated, as population changes, and as the economic extent of land is modified. Such changes in factor endowments will then alter the comparative cost structure and modify the pattern of world trade. The pattern of trade is not frozen once-for-all, but rather is fluid as comparative costs change over time.

About 1850, the structure of the relative supply of factors was in broad outline roughly as shown.

Relative Factor Supply	Tropics	Continental Europe	United Kingdom
"Most abundant"	Labor	Labor	Capital
"Less abundant"	Land	Land	Labor
"Least abundant"	Capital	Capital	Land

After the Civil War and the invention of steamships and new steel-making processes, and the extension of railroads, the Middle West of the United States was developed and became an important source of land-intensive products for the United Kingdom. From the 1850's to the 1870's, there was also an increase in the relative supply of capital through domestic savings in continental Europe (particularly Germany and France), whereas the tropics experienced an increase in population. In the early 1870's, the relative factor supply structure had thus become as shown.

Relative Factor Supply	Tropics	United States	Continental Europe	United Kingdom
"Most abundant"	Labor	Land	Labor	Capital
"Less abundant"	Land	Labor	Capital	Land
"Least abundant"	Capital	Capital	Land	Labor

From the 1870's to the 1890's, domestic saving and capital accumulation continued in continental Europe, and capital accumulation became especially rapid in the United States. The relative factor supply structure then took a new form.

Relative Factor Supply	Tropics	United States	Continental Europe	United Kingdom
"Most abundant"	Labor	Land	Capital	Capital
"Less abundant"	Land	Capital	Labor	Labor
"Least abundant"	Capital	Labor	Land	Land

After the closing of the Western frontier in the 1890's, land became relatively less abundant in the United States, while capital grew more abundant. Indeed, after World War I, the United States became the major capital market of the world. The result of this change was to give a relative factor supply structure which is now as the accompanying table indicates.

Relative Factor Supply	Tropics	United States	Continental Europe	United Kingdom
"Most abundant"	Labor	Capital	Capital	Capital
"Less abundant"	Land	Land	Labor	Labor
"Least abundant"	Capital	Labor	Land	Land

Changes in the supply of land and labor come primarily from domestic sources associated with intensive development. An important source of capital, however, has been foreign investment. This is associated with extensive development through the world economy. From the standpoint of development, the importance of foreign investment lies only incidentally in its effect on monetary demand. More significant is its contribution to real capital accumulation. When a country borrows from abroad, it can consume and/or invest more than before. The borrowing appears in the form of an increase in imports which is equivalent to an increase in the resources available for consumption and/or investment in the receiving country. The real productive power of the borrowing country increases. Saving performed in one country thus serves to build up real capital elsewhere.

2. Foreign Investment from the Center

No other period has involved such a large amount of private foreign investment as that which occurred during the four decades before World War I. The principal lender was Britain. As may be noted in Table 10.1, by 1914 other countries—France, Germany, Belgium, the Netherlands, Switzerland—had foreign investments that should not be overlooked, but these sums were small compared with British foreign investment. The second most important creditor country, France, had only half the value of Britain's foreign investments in 1913, and the United States had little more than one-fifth.

During the middle of the nineteenth century almost all of Britain's savings were directed to the building of British railways and towns. Only a small amount of foreign investment, about £200 million, had occurred, mainly in railway building and commercial and banking ventures in Europe and in speculative loans to foreign governments, generally in the Near East or in South America. After the early 1870's, however, the character of the investment changed, and its magnitude swelled. Before then European governments were the principal re-

TABLE 10.1.   LONG–TERM FOREIGN
INVESTMENTS, 1913–1914

Investing Countries:	Amount ($ million)
United Kingdom	18,000
France	9,000
Germany	5,800
United States	3,500
Belgium, Netherlands, Switzerland	5,500
Other countries	2,200
Total	44,000
Foreign Long-Term Investments in:	
Africa	4,700
Asia	6,000
Europe	12,000
United States	6,800
Rest of North America	3,700
Latin America	8,500
Oceania	2,300
Total	44,000

Source: United Nations, Department of Economic Affairs, International Capital Movements during the Inter-war Period, Lake Success, Oct. 1949, 2.

cipients of British capital; afterwards the main flow of capital was towards the less-developed, primary producing countries of North and South America, Asia, Australia, and South Africa.   During the four decades before 1914, British investments in Europe fell by about one-half in absolute value while elsewhere they increased about five times. In the 1870's, investment was directed mainly to Australia, India, South America, and the United States; during the late 1880's, to Argentina, Australia, South Africa, and the United States; and, in the decade before World War I, to Argentina, Canada, and South Africa.

In 1870, only one-third of Britain's foreign investments were within the British Empire, but by 1885 the proportion had risen to about one-half and was maintained at this level until 1913.   The main borrowers within the Empire were, in order, Canada, India, South Africa, Australia, and New Zealand.   Outside the Empire, the principal borrowers were the United States and Latin America, with Argentina and Brazil receiving over one-half of the investment in Latin America. Thus, although British capital was dispersed widely over many countries, actually the greater part was concentrated in a relatively few countries: by 1913, over three-quarters of the investment had gone to Argentina,

Australia, New Zealand, Brazil, Canada, India, South Africa, and the United States.

Between 1875 and 1913, Britain's foreign investments increased approximately 250 per cent, and amounted to approximately £4 billion in 1913. At its peak in 1913, foreign investment took more than half the total of British savings.[3] During the 40 to 50 years before 1913, Britain had invested overseas about as much as her entire industrial and commercial capital, excluding land. As a percentage of net national income, Britain's overseas investments averaged 4 per cent over the entire period 1870–1913; from 1905–1913 the ratio was about 7 per cent, and in 1913 was 9 per cent.

How was Britain able to invest such large sums abroad? An explanation is to be found in the fact that Britain was itself a rapidly growing economy and in the fact that certain characteristics of the international investment process allowed the process to be self-maintaining.

As has been seen, Britain's real national income increased almost threefold between 1870 and 1913. Such an extensive rise in national income, together with an unequal distribution of income, should have contributed to an increase in national savings. Without such an increase in savings, the supply of investible funds would have been, of course, substantially less.

Superimposed on the secular expansion in national income, however, were cyclical fluctuations. There is a high positive correlation between the years of high foreign investment and the years of prosperity. The years of maximum capital exports (as measured by the ratio of foreign investment to net national income), 1872, 1881, 1890, 1907, and 1913, corresponded closely to the peaks of the British business cycle, 1873, 1883, 1890, 1907, and 1913.[4] During each peak in the business cycle there was also a maximum in the absolute share of profits, rent, and interest in the national income.[5] This positive correlation of high foreign investment, boom years in the trade cycle, and maximum profits is consistent with the view that a large proportion of Britain's foreign investment was made out of high profits realized during a trade boom.

If, however, the investment process itself had not possessed certain properties that made it self-sustaining, it is doubtful if the amount of

[3] A. K. Cairncross, *Home and Foreign Investment 1870–1913*, Cambridge University Press, Cambridge, 1953, 2.

[4] W. W. Rostow, *British Economy of the Nineteenth Century*, Oxford University Press, Oxford, 1948, 33.

[5] A. R. Prest, "National Income of the United Kingdom, 1870–1946," *Economic Journal, LVIII*, 58–59 (March 1948).

foreign investment would have reached such an impressive magnitude. Once foreign investment had begun to stimulate development overseas, there occurred a multiplier effect in Britain as the demand rose for British exports to these developing economies overseas. If the United States or Argentina built more railways, Britain exported more steel rails and railroad equipment, or more textiles, or other export commodities. The expanding exports also contributed to the increase in national savings via the expansion in national income resulting from the exports. Important as were the multiplier effects of this expansion in exports, even more significant was the continuous growth in the income that Britain received from abroad. In the period 1870–1913, interest and dividends on foreign investments gave an average income from overseas of almost £100 million a year, and about 10 per cent of Britain's national income was in the form of interest on foreign investments.[6] During the 40 years before 1913, Britain was able to invest large sums abroad, but these amounted to only about 40 per cent of the income that Britain was receiving from past foreign investments made during the same period. As a rapidly developing economy, Britain had initially generated a sufficient supply of investible funds to allow a considerable amount of foreign investment. Then the investment process itself produced a continuous increase in income receipts which subsequently allowed additional capital to be exported.

Granted that Britain had the means of investing abroad, there arises the additional question of why Britain was willing to direct its investible funds overseas. Why should foreign investment have been preferred to home investment? What were the determinants of foreign investment?

British investors were not directed by any government program for the conscious development of the peripheral countries. There was no control of investments; there was but little governmental suasion to invest overseas. True, after the mid-90's when Joseph Chamberlain, as Colonial Secretary, referred to the colonies as "undeveloped estates," the public became more aware of the implications of foreign investment, and the government's support became more active.[7] But the record of Britain's overseas investment was still written for the most part by individual promoters, numerous enterprises, and many shareholders, not by a governmentally directed program. And contrary to what

---

[6] Cairncross, *op. cit.*, 3, 23.

[7] Chamberlain established the Imperial Department of Agriculture in the West Indies and West Africa; the Colonial Loans Act of 1899 granted loans to the Crown colonies for transport development; and the School of Tropical Medicine was also established in London in 1899.

might be expected from the hypothesis of imperialism, a large part of Britain's foreign investment was outside the Empire in 1913.[8]

The foreign investor recognized many opportunities for speculation and the possibilities of profit. New territories were being opened, new resources were being discovered, and new products were being introduced. There is no need to catalogue here all these opportunities and possibilities; many writers have already told the stories of gold and diamonds in South Africa, grain in North America, and coffee, tea, and rubber in the tropics.[9]

The fact that many of the recipients of British capital were poor countries makes the character of foreign investment in these countries more understandable. Most of Britain's foreign investment from 1870 to 1913 was employed in the construction of railways and the development of natural resources. Throughout the period, these fields of investment expanded most rapidly. By 1913, slightly more than 40 per cent of Britain's investment had been used directly in railways, and approximately another 15 per cent had been directed to the development of mines and raw materials. A large proportion of an additional 30 per cent in government loans was also used for these two major purposes.

Although discoveries of valuable natural resources stimulated investment overseas, a more fundamental basis for foreign investment was the intensive development of the British economy itself. This too contradicts the allegation, such as Hobson made, that the "tap root of imperialism" is underconsumption in the country which seeks outlets in foreign investment. On the contrary, high demand at home facilitated British foreign investment. Without substantial imports of raw materials, Britain would have been unable to sustain its expanding industrial output and meet the requirements of its growing population. Investors were aware of this need and recognized that in many respects overseas investments were complementary to home investment, or in some cases actually indispensable. Knowing that the exports of primary products from the borrowing countries would not lack overseas markets, and hence that they would be able to earn foreign exchange, investors directed their capital in large part to the primary

[8] For a more thorough discussion of the issue of imperialism, see W. K. Hancock, *Survey of British Commonwealth Affairs,* II, Oxford University Press, London, 1940; R. Koebner, "The Concept of Economic Imperialism," *Economic History Review, II,* No. 1, 1–29 (1949); R. Pares, "The Economic Factors in the History of the Empire," *Economic History Review, VII,* No. 2, 119–144 (May 1937); J. A. Schumpeter, *Imperialism and Social Classes,* Meridian Books, New York, 1955, 7–22, 64–98.

[9] See Appendix C.

producing export sectors of these countries. In this sense, Britain's own demand for imports induced much of the investment overseas.[10]

Thus, in the peripheral and underdeveloped areas, Britain's overseas capital was used principally for the development of primary products for export. Investments in the primary producing export sectors and in railways from the supply sources to seaports were favored, almost to the exclusion of any conscious development of domestic markets in the borrowing countries; commercial and industrial enterprises received scarcely 4 per cent of Britain's total investment.

Investment in public utilities was not an exception to the dominant influence of exports, since the existence of public utilities was generally necessary before the production of exports could be expanded. Directly in the agricultural and mineral regions, and indirectly in public utilities, British capital facilitated the production of primary product exports— palm oil in Nigeria, rubber and copra in Malaya and Ceylon, gold in South Africa, tin ore in Malaya and Nigeria, graphite in Ceylon, copper in Northern Rhodesia, cocoa in the Gold Coast and Nigeria, tea in Ceylon, cane sugar in the West Indies, grain and meat in Argentina. As of 1913, over 88 per cent of British foreign investment was in countries active in the export of primary materials.

Where a country such as Canada had already demonstrated its ability to produce for world markets, or where, as in many tropical areas, there were possibilities of developing products for export, to these areas capital flowed. Any development that foretold an increase in the value of a country's exports was viewed favorably. An increase in the price of a country's export commodity, bumper harvests, or a fall in transportation costs, any of these might stimulate investment.

Besides the strong demand for imports from the borrowing countries, other factors combined to create a congenial environment for foreign investment. A general atmosphere of optimism characterized the Victorian era. There was confidence in the progress of the British economy, and there was security in the imperial aspects of Britain's foreign policy. The Colonial Stock Act of 1900 placed the securities of colonial governments on the list of "trustee securities," thereby enabling trust funds to be invested in them. The operations of the Crown Agents for the colonies were also significant. These agents furnished information to investors, acted as issuers for the bulk of the loans raised by the colonies, and secured many of the loans upon the revenues of the colonies. Since they also served as purchasing agents

[10] Cf. R. Nurkse, "Some International Aspects of the Problem of Economic Development," *American Economic Review, Papers and Proceedings, XLII,* No. 2, 575 (May 1952).

for the larger public works contracts, the Crown Agents were influential in having the export of British goods follow British investments.

Further, the governments of many of the borrowing countries, both colonial and foreign, guaranteed returns on British loans. For example, by 1875 the profits or interest on 80 per cent of British investments in Argentina were payable either directly by governmental authorities or were guaranteed by them. Without this government guarantee system, long-term loans at low rates of interest would not have been so readily forthcoming.

Foreign investment was also facilitated by Britain's ability to perform the ancillary services associated with overseas investment. Great mercantile establishments, issuing houses of high repute, and well-established banking and insurance agencies were intimately connected with foreign investment. Moreover, if foreign investment led to an increased demand for British exports, the British economy had the capacity to meet this demand. Finally, as will be discussed in Chapter 11, the international mechanism of adjustment operated smoothly; had there been balance of payments crises, foreign investment would have been seriously curtailed.

Thus, there was a favorable structural environment for foreign investment. But another simple, yet indispensable, factor was even more influential—foreign investment was more profitable to the individual investor than was home investment, and sufficiently more profitable to compensate for the extra risks involved. Between 1870 and 1880, the yield on British Consols was significantly lower than the average yield on foreign government bonds; an investor who wanted to hold government securities would have done better to buy the government bonds of Turkey, Egypt, India, or South American countries. After 1880, yields on colonial and foreign investments, especially the latter, continued to be generally more attractive than those at home. Between 1900 and 1904, the return promised on foreign investments was 2.2 per cent higher than the return on home investments; between 1905 and 1909, the return was 1.3 per cent greater.[11] Investments in the development of raw materials were most profitable: in 1907–1908, investment in coal and iron ore mines yielded 13.2 per cent, copper mines 30.5 per cent, diamonds 9.3 per cent, gold 8.0 per cent, tin 15.0 per cent, oil 8.2 per cent, rubber 8.2 per cent, tea and coffee 8.4 per cent.[12] Finally, for the period 1900–1910, it is estimated that foreign

[11] Sir Arthur Salter, *Foreign Investments,* Princeton University, International Finance Section, Feb. 1951, 5; Cairncross, *op. cit.,* 226–230.

[12] Sir George Paish, "Great Britain's Capital Investments in Other Lands," *Journal of Royal Statistical Society, LXXII,* 465–480 (Sept. 1909).

investments gave an average yield of 5.2 per cent compared with about 3 per cent on Consols, and 3.5 per cent on home securities generally.[13]

If the flow of capital from Britain constitutes a remarkable chapter in the history of international development, so too does the migration of labor that accompanied the migration of capital. In the nineteenth century much of Britain's foreign investment was directed to the relatively sparsely settled areas where labor was scarce: roughly two-thirds of British overseas investment went to the so-called "regions of recent settlement"—the spacious, fertile and virtually empty plains of Canada, the United States, Argentina, Australia and other "new" countries in the world's temperate latitudes.[14] To these regions also went millions of emigrants from Britain. As entrepreneurs and workers, these emigrants complemented the capital that was flowing to these new countries. The complementary nature of these movements of labor and capital should now be examined.

3. Foreign Investment, Migration, and Home Investment

The principal British overseas possessions by the middle of the nineteenth century were Canada, Australia, New Zealand, territories in Africa, Ceylon, and the West Indies. In 1825 restrictions on the emigration of artisans were removed; a parliamentary committee in the following year recommended colonization as a remedy for the redundancy of population, and the government appropriated money for the purpose. In 1840 the Colonial Land and Emigration Commission was established to advise settlers and direct them on the outward voyage. Individual colonial reformers, such as Gibbon Wakefield, also promoted the planned settlement of Australia and New Zealand.[15]

This public interest in the overseas possessions as outlets for Britain's growing population is also reflected in the writings of the classical economists.[16] The classical economists in general viewed emigration as a means of defeating the tendency of diminishing returns from land. They also saw it as a means of stimulating the flow of capital overseas, which in turn would arrest the decline of profits in England. The classical theory of colonization thus gave support to governmental policies designed to promote areas of settlement in the overseas possessions.

[13] Salter, op. cit., 5.

[14] R. Nurkse, "International Investment Today in the Light of Nineteenth Century Experience," Economic Journal, LXIV, No. 256, 745 (Dec. 1954).

[15] For a critical discussion of the Wakefield theory of colonization and a general review of problems of colonization, see Herman Merivale, Lectures on Colonization and Colonies, Oxford University Press, London, 1928.

[16] See Chapter 1, section 7; Brinley Thomas, Migration and Economic Growth, Cambridge University Press, Cambridge, 1954, Chapter I.

But until the mid-nineteenth century emigration from the United Kingdom remained relatively small: in the 1820's, 50,000; in the 1840's (the decade of the Irish famine), 120,000. The great wave of emigration to the colonies was to come after the mid-point of the century. At mid-century, the colonies still remained sparsely populated. The population growth at the center of the world economy was not being matched by any similar population growth either in the colonies or other peripheral countries. Such regions as Burma, India, and Ceylon did not confront problems of population pressure at the middle of the last century as they do now. Rapid population growth and population pressures were not to appear in these countries until later in the century.

By the middle of the nineteenth century there were four dominant features in the picture of world population: (1) the population of Western Europe, particularly Britain, had increased rapidly; (2) there were colonies of British settlers overseas, but still sparse populations in the British overseas possessions; (3) migration from Western Europe, especially Britain, to the United States and British overseas areas had begun, but the outflow was still relatively small compared with the emigration later in the century; (4) in general, the peripheral economies outside of Europe had not yet experienced rates of growth in population comparable with that of Europe.

The sources of migration and its destinations are summarized in Figures 10.1 and 10.2. The greatest international movements during the half century before 1914 were from Europe and Asia into the United States, Canada, Argentina, and Brazil. These migrations served to redistribute some of the world's agricultural population to new primary producing regions; later in the century, it also provided part of the labor supply for American and Canadian industrialization.

The major waves of emigration from Britain came in the 1880's and the 1900's. During the 1880's there was a heavy exodus from rural areas, associated with agricultural depression. During the 1900's, the previous rise of real wages in Britain came to a halt; conditions of distress may therefore have played some part in providing a "push" to emigration. But most of the emigration is better explained in terms of the "pull" offered by opportunities in the new countries abroad. By 1913, the majority of British emigrants had gone to the sparsely populated Dominions and the United States, where they could find employment opportunities in the newly developing economies.[17] Although

---

[17] For a detailed treatment of this subject, see C. E. Carrington, *The British Overseas,* Cambridge University Press, Cambridge, 1950, 503 *ff.*; Thomas, *op. cit.,* Chapter VII; R. T. Berthoff, *British Immigrants in Industrial America,* Harvard University Press, Cambridge, 1954; G. F. Plant, *Oversea Settlement. Migration*

tropical areas received only a small flow of British settlers, the quality of this labor influx was high—administrators, traders, engineers, and planters whose skills were essential for development of the tropical economies.

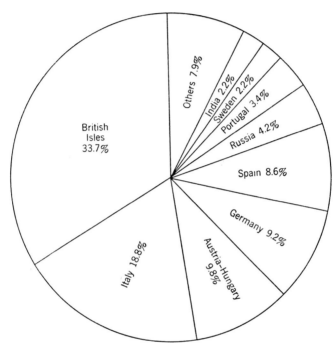

Figure 10.1. Sources of intercontinental emigration, 1846–1932. (Based on A. M. Carr-Saunders, *World Population*, Oxford University Press, Oxford, 1936.)

A striking feature of the outflow of labor from Britain was its parallel movement with the outflow of capital. The peak periods of labor migration coincided closely with the peak periods of capital migration. Britain's capital exports rose from £266 million in the period 1871–1880 to £561 million in 1881–1890, and the net loss of population by migration from Britain increased from 257,000 in 1871–1880 to 819,000 in 1881–1890; the capital outflow then increased from £286 million in 1891–1900 to £721 million in 1900–1910, and net emigra-

from the United Kingdom to the Dominions, Oxford University Press, London, 1951; W. S. Shepperson, "Industrial Emigration in Early Victorian Britain," *Journal of Economic History, XIII,* No. 2, 179–192 (Spring 1953); W. F. Wilcox (ed.), *International Migrations,* National Bureau of Economic Research, New York, 1929.

tion increased from 122,000 in 1891–1900 to 756,000 in 1900–1910.[18] It is also significant that, whereas foreign investment and emigration moved together, Britain's foreign investment and home investment moved in opposite directions over the long period. The three periods

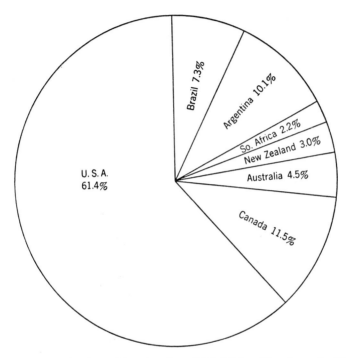

Figure 10.2. Destination of immigration, 1820–1930. (Based on A. M. Carr-Saunders, *World Population*, Oxford University Press, Oxford, 1936.)

of large overseas investment, 1870–1873, 1886–1890, and 1905–1913, were not accompanied by any substantial increase in home investment. The most prominent increases in home investment occurred between 1873 and 1884 and between 1895 and 1905, periods during which foreign investment was low.

Was there some connection between foreign investment, emigration, and home investment? According to Cairncross' study there was an interrelated pattern which can explain why home and foreign investment moved in opposite directions, whereas foreign investment and emigration moved together. Cairncross first establishes that the attractiveness of British foreign investment generally varied with Britain's terms of

[18] Cairncross, *op. cit.*, 209.

trade—increasing when the terms of trade worsened. This conforms with the previous discussion of how an increase in the export prices from the primary producing countries (Britain's import prices) would make investment opportunities in these countries more attractive. The boom in foreign investment after the mid-1880's was finally brought to an end by a sharp break in prices of foodstuffs and raw materials in the early 1890's. After 1903, when the terms of trade had ceased to move in Britain's favor, foreign investment revived. The greatest burst of foreign investment after 1905 coincided with a period of rising import prices and practically stationary terms of trade.

Changes in the terms of trade would also affect real wages: a movement in the terms of trade unfavorable to Britain lowered real wages, since the cost of living of the working class closely followed import prices, imports forming about half the total supply of foodstuffs. Consequently, at the same time that it would stimulate an outflow of capital, a deterioration in the terms of trade would also exert some push on emigration. And the inflow of capital in the overseas countries also made settlement more attractive through the employment opportunities that it created. Thus, there was general consistency between a worsening of Britain's terms of trade, falling real wages, rising emigration, and rising foreign investment.[19]

Finally, the relation between foreign and home investment becomes clear when it is realized that building activity and public utility services constituted a major proportion of home investment,[20] and that these components of home investment moved inversely with foreign investment. The major building booms were during periods of low foreign investment, such as in the late 1870's and 1890's. In periods of high foreign investment, emigration was high, and building activity was low. The connecting link is a simple one: emigration left houses empty, and the decline in demand naturally curtailed building activity as well as public utility services and public works which are closely dependent upon the rate of growth of population and urbanization. This, in turn, is reflected in a fall in home investment. The accompanying pattern may therefore be suggested:[21]

[19] The period of the 1880's is an exception for a variety of specific reasons. See *ibid.*, 190–193, 215–216.

[20] Gross investment in housing fluctuated between 25 per cent and 45 per cent of the total amount of gross home investment between 1870 and 1913. J. H. Lenfant, "Investment in the United Kingdom, 1865–1914," *Economica, XVIII,* No. 70, 163 (May 1951).

[21] Strong statistical evidence supporting this hypothesis is presented in Thomas, *op. cit.,* Chapters VII, XI, Appendix 4.

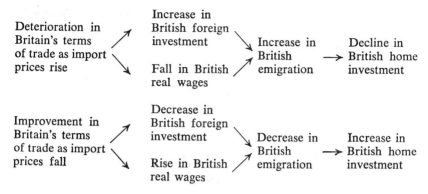

This schematic pattern illustrates that the flow of capital from one country to another is but part of a larger picture. At bottom, it reflects an unequal distribution of productive resources throughout the world and the fact that capital, labor, and land are used in unequal proportions in production in different parts of the world. In the period before 1914, the movement of capital from Britain was large and important. The movement of capital, however, must also be associated with the migration of people: both capital and labor moved from the center towards the new opportunities overseas. The natural resources of South America could not go to Britain, but British capital and British engineers and technicians could and did go to South America. This movement of capital and labor from the center to developing economies overseas remains unique in its magnitude and impact.

4. American Foreign Investment

After World War I, the United States replaced Britain as the major lending country. During the war, Britain liquidated some $4 billion worth of its foreign investments, and during the 1920's the annual average net capital export from Britain was little more than a third of the amount just before the war. The United States began to invest capital in foreign countries to an increasing extent after 1890, and in 1913–1914 American long-term foreign investments amounted to about $3.5 billion (Table 10.1). Investments by foreigners in the United States amounted to some $6.8 billion so that the United States was still on balance a debtor at the start of the war. But it emerged from the war as the principal creditor country on private account, and was to remain the chief source for international loans after the war.

The American experience with foreign investment, however, is quite different from the British experience. American foreign investment has been neither as large nor as significant in influencing international development.

The major period of American foreign investment was the 1920's. In this decade the par value of United States holdings of foreign dollar bonds rose from about $2 billion to $7.3 billion; the annual rate of portfolio lending (purchase of foreign securities) expanded from $418 million in 1920 to $1.1 billion in 1927; and private direct investment (investment in foreign branches and subsidiaries of American companies) amounted to about $3 billion in the 1920's.

During the 1930's, foreign investment practically vanished, as the Great Depression, memories of previous defaults, political instability, and exchange controls all combined to make foreign investment unattractive. American investors became extremely pessimistic regarding the whole conception of foreign lending. During the 1930's, the United States was, on balance, actually an importer of long-term capital, owing partly to regular amortization receipts and partly to an excess of foreign purchases of American securities over sales of foreign securities to Americans. From 1932 to 1939, new portfolio investment amounted to only $194 million, and new additions to United States direct investments abroad were small after 1932.

The total of all American foreign investments amounted to about $17 billion in 1930, and $11 billion in 1939. In 1930, approximately half of America's foreign investments were direct investments; in 1939, this had risen to about 65 per cent.

Relatively little of the portfolio investment went to poor countries. The geographical distribution of portfolio investment between 1920 and 1931 was as follows: 40 per cent to Europe; 29 per cent, Canada; 22 per cent, Latin America; and about 9 per cent, Far East. Four-fifths of these loans were to governments or were government-guaranteed. A larger proportion of direct investments, almost half, went to poor countries. But most of this was in Latin America.

After World War II, foreign investment revived somewhat, but was still negligible compared with foreign investment in the nineteenth century. Most of the United States' foreign private investment consisted of direct investment, and a large part of this was concentrated in the petroleum industry, distributed mainly among the few countries possessing exploitable petroleum resources. In the decade after the war, the total amount of American direct investments outstanding abroad was about evenly divided between rich and poor countries. In the richer countries, only a small portion was directed to extractive industries, and the major part went to manufacturing and distribution. In the poor countries, however, the major portion of the investment was directed to extractive industries, and only a small percentage went to manufacturing and distribution. The long-established pattern of foreign investment flowing into primary production for export has persisted in the poor areas.

Since World War II, private foreign investment has been much less than during the 1920's. The annual average of total private investment during 1946–1952 was approximately $788 million, whereas from 1919–1929 the annual average was over $1.6 billion (adjusted to the price level of 1948)—more than twice the rate for the years of 1946–1952. Table 10.2 summarizes the international investment position of

TABLE 10.2. INTERNATIONAL INVESTMENT POSITION OF THE UNITED STATES IN SELECTED YEARS, 1914–1955
($ billions)

	1914*	1919	1930	1939	1946	1955§
U. S. investments abroad	3.5	7.0	17.2	11.4	18.7	44.9
Private	3.5	7.0	17.2	11.4	13.5	29.0
Long-term	3.5	6.5	15.2	10.8	12.3	26.6
Direct	2.6	3.9	8.0	7.0	7.2	19.2
Portfolio	.9	2.6	7.2	3.8	5.1	7.4
Short-term	†	0.5	2.0	0.6	1.3	2.4
U. S. Government‡	—	—	—	—	5.2	15.9
Foreign investments in the U. S.	7.2	4.0	8.4	9.6	15.9	29.6
U. S. net creditor position	−3.7	3.0	8.8	1.8	2.8	15.3

* At June 30.
† Not available.
‡ Excludes World War I loans.
§ Preliminary.

Source: U. S. Department of Commerce, *Survey of Current Business,* 15, Aug. 1956.

the United States in selected years from 1914 to 1955, and Table 10.3 shows direct investments abroad, by selected countries and major industries in 1955.

In 1955, United States private investments abroad rose by $2.4 billion, to a year-end total outstanding of $29 billion. Of this increase, direct investments amounted to about $1.5 billion, and the total value of the United States direct foreign investments abroad at the end of 1955 was over $19 billion. In 1955, Canada continued as the major recipient of direct foreign investments, attracting almost 40 per cent of the total increase. Direct investments in Latin America increased by some $300 million in 1955. Of the $6.5 billion in United States direct investments in Latin America at the end of 1955, about 42 per cent was in mining

TABLE 10.3. VALUE OF UNITED STATES DIRECT INVESTMENTS
ABROAD, BY SELECTED COUNTRIES AND MAJOR
INDUSTRIES, 1955
($ millions)

Countries	Total	Mining and Smelting	Petroleum	Manufacturing	Public Utilities	Trade
All areas, total	19,185	2,195	5,792	6.322	1,588	1,289
Canada	6,464	862	1,329	2,834	318	384
Latin America, total	6,556	1,022	1,779	1,366	1,132	440
Brazil	1,107	na*	186	563	158	137
Venezuela	1,424	na	1,056	59	18	55
Western Europe, total	2,986	40	761	1,630	35	292
Africa:						
Egypt	72	—	49	13	na	4
Liberia	261	na	205	—	9	na
Union of South Africa	257	73	60	87	na	29
Other countries	62	43	na	—	na	na
India	96	na	na	30	2	10
Indonesia	86	—	na	21	na	3

* na = not available; all estimates are preliminary.

Source: U. S. Department of Commerce, Survey of Current Business, 19, Aug. 1956.

and petroleum. Aside from some Latin American countries, the only other poor countries that received any sizable increase in direct investments from the United States were Indonesia and some Middle East countries in which petroleum investments continued to expand.[22]

The record of American foreign investment is certainly far different from that of British foreign investment before 1914. As already noted, Britain's role as the center of the world economy and the leading creditor nation was based on higher yields abroad than at home, so that foreign investment was attractive; no tied loans; complementary foreign trade; a rapidly expanding network of world trade, conducted under essentially multilateral and free-trade conditions; reinvestment abroad of any balance of payments surplus resulting from dividends on earlier investments. Foreign investment was sufficiently large in magnitude and sufficiently consistent with other factors to operate as a vital constructive force in international trade. Overseas investment, the migration of population, and the growth of international trade were all integrated together in the process of international expansion before 1914.

In contrast, American foreign investment in the post-1914 era has

[22] U. S. Department of Commerce, Survey of Current Business, 19, Aug. 1956.

been relatively insignificant. From 1905 to 1913, Britain invested overseas an amount equal to about 7 per cent of her national income. If, in the early 1950's, the United States had invested abroad a similar percentage of her national income, she would have had to invest some $20 billion each year. Compared with this, the actual amount of private foreign investment was trivial, representing less than one-third of 1 per cent of national income. Although particular impediments to foreign investment will be examined in detail in Chapter 20, it can be recognized here in a general way that the breakdown of the system of international investment is merely symptomatic of the broader problem of the disintegration of the world economy after World War I. With the trend towards economic nationalism, free multilateral trade was restricted, political uncertainties heightened, and a complementary flow of labor with capital became impossible. Transfer difficulties also increased as the Great Depression brought with it international monetary and financial crises. The result has been that the United States government has had to assume a much larger role as a foreign investor than has the private investor.

In summarizing the record of American private foreign investment, one may note four outstanding features: (1) the small magnitude, (2) the concentration in the 1920's, (3) the considerable extent to which investment has been direct investment in rich countries rather than poor countries, and (4), in general, the minor influence of American private foreign investment since 1914, compared with the highly important role of British foreign investment before 1914.

Chapter 11

International Trade

and Economic Development

The international migration of factors is one connecting link between intensive and extensive development. Other links, as already noted in theoretical terms in Chapter 3, are the volume and composition of foreign trade, the terms of trade, and the system of international payments. These are important in affecting the nature and extent of a country's development after it becomes a part of the network of world trade. Such elements of international trade are not given once-and-for-all, however. They change over the long period, and the manner in which they change may influence the course of development in various countries differently. This chapter and the next examine some of these long-run changes.

1. The Export Sector

All sectors of an economy do not grow at the same time at the same rate. Instead, as implied in the Schumpeterian analysis, some sectors are key propulsive sectors. Expansion in one industry may induce growth in another, and this, in turn, may stimulate another sector of the economy. This is partly because of the action of the accelerator working back from an increase in final demand to the supporting industries, and partly because of the external economies that Marshall discussed.

A country's export sector may be very important in serving as a propulsive sector. First, overseas markets widen the market for particular commodities. As classical economists emphasized, an industry may grow much more rapidly if it can sell overseas rather than in only the narrower home market. This allows the producers in an industry to take advantage of the economies associated with expansion within the industry, and to increase to such an extent that there may be a sizable induced effect on the growth of other industries. The long-run trends in manufacturing output, investments, and exports are all likely to be closely correlated.[1]

Second, expansion of the export trade also facilitates development when a particular export industry can grow without requiring as much investment in social capital as would otherwise be necessary if the commodities were to be sold internally. Domestic markets are limited not only by the level of real income but also by the physical connections among internal market areas. To tap the different market areas within the country, large expenditures may be necessary to provide adequate transportation and distribution facilities. If, however, the country enters the international market, it can by-pass this bottleneck.

Third, exports create new effective demand, thereby increasing the demand for commodities in the domestic market. By competing with home industries for resources, the export industries may also stimulate the home industries into innovations designed to increase their productivity.[2]

The quantitative importance of exports in Britain's development is impressive. During the period 1870–1913, exports were larger than home investment, amounting to about one-fifth of the national income and probably one-third of industrial production.[3] Many individual industries were highly dependent on overseas markets. In the cotton industry the proportion of output exported rose from an average of 57 per cent in 1841–1845 to 74 per cent in 1871–1875; the proportion of output exported in the pig iron and steel industry was 27 per cent in 1841–1845, 45 per cent in 1871–1875, and about 24 per cent in

[1] Some confirmation of this is given for many European countries during 1913–1937. See I. Svennilson, *Growth and Stagnation in the European Economy,* United Nations, Economic Commission for Europe, Geneva, 1954, 224–226.

[2] Cf. W. A. Lewis, *The Theory of Economic Growth,* Allen & Unwin, London, 1955, 280.

[3] W. A. Lewis and P. J. O'Leary, "Secular Swings in Production and Trade, 1870–1913," *Manchester School of Economic and Social Studies, XXIII,* No. 2, 120–122 (May 1955).

1901–1905; in the woolen industry the percentage exported was about one-third of total output in the 1840's, and one-half in the 1870's; in the 1870's, 30 per cent of British jute products was exported; and the proportion of coal output exported rose from an average of 10 per cent in the 1870's to 22 per cent in 1901–1910.[4]

Exports from these industries had not only direct effects in expanding the output of these industries but also indirect effects in so far as every increase in demand from overseas buyers gave the industry an opportunity to increase its capital and adopt cheaper methods of production, which in turn would lead to increased sales in the home market.

In Britain's development, the textile export trade played a prominent role. By 1850, textile exports constituted about 80 per cent of Britain's total exports (by value in 1913 prices). Quite clearly, Britain would never have been able to absorb domestically this great output of textiles. By utilizing foreign markets, however, the industry had a much greater potential for expansion. It was not limited by the requirement of balanced expansion of supporting industries to the extent that would have been true had the domestic market been the only source of expansion. As this major industry grew, led by Schumpeterian-type entrepreneurs, it drew on the surplus agricultural population and the growing total population for its labor force. Since labor productivity was higher in the textile industry than in agriculture, Britain's specialization in textiles increased the national product by a greater amount than would have been the case if the additional labor had been absorbed in agriculture.

Through the operation of a multiplier-accelerator process the increased income earned in the textile industry induced expansion in other industries. Part of the growing total income earned in the textile trade was spent on consumption commodities, and this induced an expansion of output in other industries whose factors of production spent, in turn, part of their greater income on consumption goods and thus induced further production—and so on, as the multiplier process gradually worked itself out.

A rising national income created investment opportunities in other industries. Capital expenditures were induced in the iron, coal, machinery, transportation, and building industries. These, in turn, produced further multiplier effects, as the multiplier and acceleration process interacted.

In the last quarter of the nineteenth century, however, Britain's exports ceased to grow as rapidly as they had in the earlier part of the century. One estimate is that the rate of growth of exports of manufactures

[4] W. G. Hoffmann, *British Industry 1700–1950*, Basil Blackwell, Oxford, 1955, 83–84.

dropped from 5.6 per cent per annum in the period 1820–1860 to
2.1 per cent per annum in the period 1870–1913; another estimate is
that the rate of export market expansion declined from 4.5 per cent per
annum in the 1840–1860 period to a rate of 1.5 per cent in the period
1900–1913; a third estimate is that British manufactured exports grew
at about a 4.8 per cent rate from 1854 to 1872 and then slowed to an
approximate 2.1 per cent average rate from 1876 to 1910.[5]   Table 11.1

TABLE 11.1.   RATE OF GROWTH OF VOLUME
OF BRITISH EXPORTS, 1780–1900

Periods	Annual Average Percentage Increase in the Rate of Growth of Exports
1780–1800	6.1
1800–1825	1.2
1825–1840	4.0
1840–1860	5.3
1860–1870	4.4
1870–1890	2.1
1890–1900	0.7

Source: W. Schlöte, *British Overseas Trade from 1700 to the 1930's* (tr.
by W. H. Chaloner and W. O. Henderson), Basil Blackwell, Oxford, 1952,
42.

presents Schlöte's calculations of the rates of growth in the volume
of British exports from 1780–1900, and shows how the rate of increase
fell after 1860.   Although these estimates vary somewhat in magnitude,
they all indicate a decline in the rate of growth of Britain's exports during
the last quarter of the nineteenth century.   At the same time that the
growth in exports was declining, there was also a decline in the rate of
industrial expansion in Britain.   Table 11.2 shows the parallel movements between production and exports for some leading industries.

Was there a causal connection between the decline in exports and
the decline in industrial output?   It is commonly suggested that the
general decline in the growth of exports after the 1870's may account
for the check to the rate of growth of industrial production.   An empirical examination of this question concludes that "if exports had continued to grow in the last quarter of the century as in the third, English
industrial output would have more than maintained the rapid pace of

[5] Lewis and O'Leary, *op. cit.*, 122; J. R. Meyer, "An Input-Output Approach to
Evaluating the Influence of Exports on British Industrial Production in the Late
19th Century," *Explorations in Entrepreneurial History, VIII*, No. 1, 12, 21
(Oct. 1955).

TABLE 11.2. PERCENTAGE AVERAGE ANNUAL GROWTH
RATES, UNITED KINGDOM INDUSTRIES AND EXPORTS

Industry	1827/36 to 1866/74		1866/74 to 1908/13	
	Production	Exports	Production	Exports
Coal	4.0	8.3	2.1	4.4
Iron and steel	5.4	4.8	2.4	2.3
Machinery	5.1	8.1	2.8	5.1
Cotton	3.9	4.3	1.5	1.7
Wool	2.1	4.4	1.6	−0.2

Source: D. J. Coppock, "The Climacteric of the 1890's: A Critical Note," *Manchester School of Economic and Social Studies, XXIV,* No. 1, 28 (Jan. 1956). Based on Hoffmann's production series and Schlöte's exports series.

the earlier years."[6]   This conclusion is derived by considering in an input-output table of the British economy what the level of industrial output would have been in Britain in 1907 if the rate of export growth from 1854 to 1872 had continued from 1872 to 1907. According to Hoffmann, the actual growth rate of industrial output was only 1.75 per cent from 1872 to 1907. If, however, exports had continued to grow from 1872 to 1907 at the same rate as they had from 1854 to 1872, the growth rate of industrial output would have been 4.1 per cent.[7]

This result is consistent with the hypothesis that the total effects, indirect as well as direct, of the retardation in expansion of exports were sufficient to account for the slower rate of British industrial growth in the last quarter of the nineteenth century.   It does not mean, however, that it is the sole explanation. All the factors that were mentioned earlier in the discussion of secular stagnation might also have had some influence: a decline in entrepreneurial vigor, more monopolistic market structures, an unfavorable alteration in the distribution of income, and a slowing down in the rate of innovations. But even though these may have had some influence, the export trade was of such quantitative significance that the decline in export expansion must be given considerable emphasis in the total explanation of the slower growth in the British economy after 1870.

The British case thus demonstrates how influential an expansion in exports may be in stimulating an economy's development, but at the same time it illustrates that, unless additional home investment, consumption, or government expenditures are forthcoming, retardation in the growth of exports will have repercussions that slow down the rate

[6] Meyer, *op. cit.,* 12.
[7] *Ibid.,* 17.

of intensive development for the whole economy.   Lest this occur, a country that bases its development on exports must always maintain its competitive position in the world economy.

2. The Terms of Trade

The terms of trade also affect the nature and extent of a country's development, and the course of development, in turn, affects the terms of trade.[8]   An improvement in the terms of trade (that is, an increase in the ratio of export prices to import prices) promotes a country's development by increasing the country's purchasing power on international markets.   With a given amount of exports, the country can now import more, and this provides a greater capacity for development in so far as resources are released from export or import-competing production.   An improvement in the terms of trade brought about by a rise in export prices also stimulates an inflow of foreign capital.

In contrast, a deterioration in the terms of trade caused by a fall in export prices reduces the country's purchasing power on international markets, decreases the capacity for development in so far as more resources must now be absorbed in exports to gain the same amount of imports (unless the decline in export prices is due to increased productivity), inhibits the inflow of foreign investments, and may cause a redirection in the allocation of resources away from exports.

On the other side of the picture, the course of development affects the terms of trade.   As development proceeds, there are likely to be changes in consumption patterns, technology, factor supply, factor prices, and the competitive and monopolistic elements in market structures.   All these will affect commodity prices, and hence the terms of trade.

An interesting question is how have the historical trends in the terms of trade affected the real income position of trading nations.   Care must, of course, be taken to avoid the fallacy of equating changes in the terms of trade with variations in the amount of the gains from trade.   It is necessary to determine how the changes in the terms of trade have

[8] Unless otherwise specified, the following discussion refers to the "net barter" or "commodity terms of trade," defined as the ratio between the prices of exports and imports.   Other concepts of the terms of trade are the "gross barter terms of trade," expressed as the ratio between volume of exports and imports; "income terms of trade," which equal the net barter terms of trade multiplied by the quantity of exports; and the "double factoral terms of trade," which are the net barter terms of trade divided by the relative change in productivity in the exports of a given country and in the foreign industries producing its imports.   For a full discussion, see J. Viner, *Studies in the Theory of International Trade,* Harper and Brothers, New York, 1937, 558–564.

originated, and to connect the terms of trade, relating to a unit of trade, with the total gains from trade, relating to the total volume of trade.

Classical and neo-classical literature on international trade clearly recognized this problem by attempting to go behind the quantity of exports to consider the amounts of resources used in producing exports. It may then be that, although the commodity terms of trade (which show the terms on which commodities exchange) deteriorate when the production costs of exports fall, the factoral terms of trade (which show the terms on which factors of production exchange) may nevertheless improve, so that the country may now receive more imports than previously for the productive services embodied in its exports.

The contention that movement in the terms of trade denotes a change in the gains from trade must also be qualified when the change is due to an alteration in demand. If there is a shift in demand away from import commodities, stemming from a change in tastes, the consequent improvement in the terms of trade is not an unambiguous gain. For the situations being compared involve trade in different commodities. Alternatively, if the terms deteriorate because demand increases for imports, it may not be true from the criterion of "utility" that a loss is incurred. For it is necessary to consider not only the utility of the import but also the relative utilities of the import and the domestic commodities whose domestic consumption is precluded by allocation of resources to production for export. Were it measurable, the "utility terms of trade" index would be relevant for this type of problem.[9]

The British statistics, as given in Table 11.3, show an improvement in Britain's terms of trade until the turn of this century, then a slight deterioration in the decade before World War I, followed by an improvement after 1918. For the whole period between the 1870's and the 1930's, the general trend is one of improvement.

One way of viewing the gain from improved terms of trade is to consider the difference between what the balance of payments is after prices vary and what it would have been without the price changes, assuming the quantities traded are the same in both situations. Or one might determine the value of the quantity of goods that would have been just enough to offset the effect of price changes so that the balance of payments remained unchanged. For example, on the basis of Taussig's computations of the quantity of exports given by Britain in exchange for a given quantity of imports from 1880–1884 to 1895–1899, it can be said that, if the terms of trade had not improved, Britain

---

[9] The utility terms of trade reflect changes in tastes, or the relative average utility per unit of imported commodities and of domestic commodities whose domestic consumption is precluded by allocation of resources to production for export. *Ibid.,* 560.

TABLE 11.3. TERMS OF TRADE OF THE
UNITED KINGDOM, 1850–1938

Year	(1) Export Price Index of U. K. Produce and Manufactures (1800 = 100)	(2) Import Price Index (1880 = 100)	(3)* Terms of Trade (Imlah) (1880 = 100)	(4) Terms of Trade (Kindleberger) (1913 = 100)
1850	100.8	90.7	111.1	
1851	99.1	90.1	110.0	
1852	98.1	93.5	104.9	
1853	108.1	107.2	100.8	
1854	108.7	114.9	94.6	
1855	106.1	118.7	89.4	
1856	108.4	118.4	91.6	
1857	111.7	128.3	87.1	
1858	109.1	111.3	98.0	
1859	111.5	113.5	98.2	
1860	110.6	116.5	94.9	
1861	111.1	113.3	98.1	
1862	116.9	110.5	105.8	
1863	128.8	120.1	107.2	
1864	141.3	134.9	104.7	
1865	134.6	125.8	107.0	
1866	139.1	126.5	110.0	
1867	130.9	121.4	107.8	
1868	122.2	121.8	100.3	
1869	121.4	117.7	103.1	
1870	118.5	115.8	102.3	
1871	118.0	107.9	109.4	
1872	130.6	115.6	113.0	
1873	135.2	115.4	117.2	
1874	127.7	112.8	113.2	
1875	120.0	107.5	111.6	
1876	110.5	104.8	105.4	
1877	106.2	107.8	98.5	
1878	102.3	99.9	102.4	
1879	96.4	94.8	101.7	
1880	100.0	100.0	100.0	
1881	95.8	99.1	96.7	
1882	97.7	98.1	99.6	
1883	94.4	95.8	98.5	
1884	90.9	91.0	99.9	
1885	87.4	85.3	102.5	
1886	83.6	80.1	104.4	
1887	83.4	78.4	106.4	
1888	82.9	81.0	102.3	
1889	84.6	82.1	103.0	
1890	88.3	80.9	109.1	

TABLE 11.3. TERMS OF TRADE OF THE UNITED KINGDOM, 1850–1938 (Continued)

Year	(1) Export Price Index of U. K. Produce and Manufactures (1800 = 100)	(2) Import Price Index (1880 = 100)	(3)* Terms of Trade (Imlah) (1880 = 100)	(4) Terms of Trade (Kindleberger) (1913 = 100)
1891	87.5	81.5	107.4	
1892	83.6	78.1	107.0	
1893	83.4	76.3	109.3	
1894	79.2	71.1	111.4	
1895	76.2	68.8	110.8	
1896	76.9	69.4	110.8	
1897	76.0	69.1	110.0	
1898	76.2	69.7	109.3	
1899	79.8	71.1	112.2	
1900	91.7	76.4	120.0	
1901	87.3	73.9	118.1	
1902	83.3	73.0	114.1	
1903	83.2	74.0	112.4	
1904	84.2	74.3	113.3	
1905	84.0	74.6	112.6	
1906	89.0	77.8	114.4	
1907	93.4	81.3	114.9	
1908	89.8	78.3	114.7	
1909	86.5	79.1	109.4	
1910	90.2	83.6	107.9	
1911	91.8	81.5	112.6	
1912	93.4	83.0	112.5	
1913	96.9	83.4	116.2	100
1920				126
1921				141
1922				132
1923				129
1924				123
1925				119
1926				122
1927				121
1928				118
1929				119
1930				129
1931				143
1932				142
1933				149
1934				142
1935				140
1936				138
1937				131
1938				143

* Column (1) divided by column (2).

Source: Columns (1), (2), (3): A. H. Imlah, unpublished revised series. Column (4): C. P. Kindleberger, The Terms of Trade, John Wiley & Sons, New York, 1956, 13, 322–326.

would have had to export 14 per cent more goods than she actually did to pay for imports: that is, additional exports to the value of £35–40 millions.[10]   In currency units this was the British gain from improved terms of trade during this period.   Again, however, without knowledge of real costs and the specifications of some national indicators of preference, or utility assumptions, the gain in real units is inexpressible.

Notwithstanding these qualifications, economic historians generally agree that a substantial part of the increase in Britain's real income can be attributed to a secular improvement in its terms of trade.   During the latter part of the nineteenth century, Britain was literally reaping the harvests of earlier foreign investment.   This increased supply of primary product imports is reflected in the fall in Britain's import prices.   The index of import prices for "food, drink, and tobacco" from the United States fell from 100 in 1872 to 77 in 1900, and from "areas of recent settlement" it fell from 100 in 1872 to 69 in 1900. The index of import prices for "raw materials" from the United States declined from 100 in 1872 to 55 in 1900, and from "areas of recent settlement" it fell from 100 in 1872 to 71 in 1900.[11]

A large part of this fall in the price of imported foodstuffs and raw materials between 1880 and 1900 resulted from railway building facilitated by British capital in the United States, Argentina, India, Canada, and Australia.   In 1870, there were less than 62,000 miles of track in these countries; by 1900, there were 262,000 miles of track.[12]

During the last quarter of the nineteenth century, as Britain depended more and more on agricultural imports, and the population continued to increase rapidly, the course of real wages in Britain was strongly influenced by Britain's terms of trade.   To the extent that British foreign investment facilitated the importation of foodstuffs at lower prices, it contributed to a rising standard of living in Britain itself.

The improvement in Britain's terms of trade raises the broader questions of whether there has been a long-run deterioration in the terms of trade of primary producing nations, and whether this has been an important factor inhibiting their development.   Some writers and several United Nations reports have maintained that there has been a deterioration, over a long period, of the relation between prices of raw materials and those of manufactured goods, and that this has resulted

---

[10] Bertil Ohlin, *Interregional and International Trade,* Harvard University Press, Cambridge, 1935, 470.

[11] Kindleberger, *op. cit.,* 34.

[12] A. K. Cairncross, *Home and Foreign Investment 1870–1913,* Cambridge University Press, Cambridge, 1953, 233.

in a constant decrease in purchasing power and capacity for development in the countries producing raw materials.[13]

Prebisch, for instance, argues that the evidence on prices of exports and imports in the period between the 1870's and 1930's indicates that industrial centers kept the whole benefit of their technical progress, whereas primary producing countries on the periphery of the world economy transferred to industrial nations a share of the fruits from their own technical progress. Prebisch contends that money incomes and hence prices have risen more rapidly than productivity in industrial countries, whereas in primary producing countries the gains in productivity, although smaller, have been distributed in the form of price reductions or in only proportional increases in money income. Prebisch attributes the contrasting behavior of prices in industrial and primary producing countries to the different movements of primary product prices and industrial prices over successive business cycles and to the greater number of monopoly elements in industrial markets. He asserts that in prosperous periods primary products have risen sharply, but have subsequently lost this gain in the downswing of the business cycle. In contrast, although manufacturing prices have risen less in the upswing of the cycle, these prices have not fallen so far in depression as they have risen in prosperity, because of the rigidity of industrial wages and price inflexibility in the more monopolistic industrial markets. It is therefore asserted that over successive cycles the gap between the prices of the two groups of commodities has widened, and the primary producing areas have suffered an unfavorable movement in their terms of trade.

This is a provocative hypothesis, but it may be criticized on both factual and analytical grounds. Price data on the exports and imports of primary producing countries are not directly available for a thorough examination of Prebisch's hypothesis. And Britain's terms of trade cannot simply be used in reverse as a measure of the terms of trade of countries exporting to Britain, for these countries exported to other countries besides Britain, and they imported from other countries.[14] Resort must therefore be had to only indirect evidence, such as a gen-

[13] United Nations, Department of Economic Affairs (Raul Prebisch), *The Economic Development of Latin America and its Principal Problems,* Lake Success, 1950; H. W. Singer, "The Distribution of Gains between Investing and Borrowing Countries," *American Economic Review, Papers and Proceedings,* May 1950, 473–485; United Nations, Department of Economic Affairs, *Relative Prices of Exports and Imports of Under-Developed Countries,* New York, 1949; Lewis, *op. cit.,* 281–283.

[14] Thus, according to Kindleberger, although Britain's terms of trade improved from 1872 to 1900, the terms of trade of Industrial Europe actually worsened. See Kindleberger, *op. cit.,* 233.

eral index of prices of primary commodities relative to prices of manufactures in world trade.

From Table 11.4, it appears that the terms of trade between primary
production and manufactured products did deteriorate between the
1870's and 1930's; the index fell from 111 in 1870 to 75 in 1938
(1913 = 100). Similarly, a United Nations study concludes that the
secular trend in prices of primary commodities relative to prices of
manfactured goods was downward from the latter part of the nineteenth
century to the eve of World War II: at the end of this period, a given
volume of exports of primary commodities would pay, on the average,
for only 60 per cent of the quantity of manufactured goods that it could
buy at the beginning of the period.[15]

TABLE 11.4. TERMS OF TRADE, PRIMARY PRODUCTS
AND MANUFACTURED PRODUCTS, 1870–1950
(1913 = 100)

Year	(1) Price Index of Primary Products	(2) Price Index of Manufactured Products	(3) Index of Terms of Trade: (1)/(2)
1870	118	106	111
1880	102	102	100
1890	86	90	95
1900	86	88	98
1913	100	100	100
1921	131	186	70
1938	53	72	75
1950	124	122	102

Source: Lewis, "World Production, Prices and Trade, 1870–1960," *Manchester School of Economic and Social Studies, XX*, No. 2, 118 (May 1952).

These statistics, however, are subject to many reservations, and they
should be interpreted with caution. Commodity terms of trade between raw materials and manufactured products are, of course, not the
same as the terms of trade between poor and rich countries. Moreover, many statistical problems are associated with the methods of
compiling the price series from which these trends are computed. Some
of these reservations are the adequacy of the samples used, the relative
weights assigned to different commodities, the absence of provision
for changes in quality, shifting coverage due to the appearance of new
and disappearance of old commodities in foreign trade, and the treatment of transportation costs.

[15] United Nations, *op. cit.,* **7, 23.**

Although it cannot be proved quantitatively, nevertheless most writers agree that quality improvements have been greater in manufactured commodities than in primary goods. If this is true, then the statistics have a systematic bias which makes changes appear less favorable to the primary producing countries than they actually were.

During the past century there has also been a large decline in ocean freights relative to the prices of the commodities transported. Since the United Kingdom values its exports at the port of exit, the recorded prices of these commodities do not include shipping charges. Import values, in contrast, include shipping costs, since they are valued at the port of importation. The primary producing countries, however, usually bear these costs for both their imports and exports because the commodities are generally carried on foreign ships. Therefore, if British data are used to indicate even indirectly the terms of trade of primary producing countries, the recorded terms of trade should be corrected for shipping charges. These costs should be excluded from British import values and included as an export item. If it is recognized that much of the decline in British import prices was caused by the fall in transport costs,[16] and that export prices actually fell more because of the decrease in the price of the exported shipping services, then the statistics in Table 11.3 overemphasize the improvement in Britain's terms of trade.

Thus, imperfections in the statistical measures cast doubt on the thesis that the terms of trade have deteriorated for primary producing countries over the long period. There is no conclusive evidence that these countries actually have suffered a deterioration in their terms of trade over the past 75 years or so. It might even be argued, in contrast, that their terms of trade have improved because of quality changes and the fall in transport costs.

A complete appraisal of Prebisch's thesis requires not only more adequate data on the terms of trade but also more evidence on the relative trends in monopoly elements and technological progress for manufactured products and primary products. Has there been a more rapid trend towards monopoly in the export trade in manufactures than in the export trade in primary products? Has technological progress in manufactures been more rapid than in primary production? Has monopoly prevented reductions in real costs from being reflected in price reductions? Affirmative answers are needed to support Prebisch's argument that the existence of monopoly in industrial countries has prevented buyers in non-industrial countries from sharing in the benefits

---

[16] Statistical evidence of this is given in C. M. Wright, "Convertibility and Triangular Trade as Safeguards against Economic Depression," *Economic Journal,* LXV, No. 259, 424 (Sept. 1955).

of technological progress. But before such conclusions can be reached, detailed analysis must be made of various influences on the terms of trade, such as shifts in consumption patterns, technological advances, changes in factor supply, and modifications in market structure. Even if there is agreement on why a country's terms of trade have changed, there may still be disagreement regarding the effects of this change on the country's gains from trade. For these gains cannot be quantified unambiguously, and final judgments on the relevance of changes in the terms of trade to economic welfare must be inconclusive.

Of more fundamental importance than any movement in the terms of trade is the fact that income statistics do indicate broad gains for both industrial and non-industrial areas over the past century. Primary producing countries have supplied essential raw materials for the industrialization process in exchange for consumer goods and capital goods from the industrial countries. The technology and capital goods supplied by industrial regions have also provided an important basis for further expansion within non-industrial countries. This broad dynamic relation between imports and increased production possibilities in primary producing regions and the more general interrelations between intensive and extensive development must always be remembered in assessing the history of world trade and economic development.

3. Balance of Payments Equilibrium

Additional aspects of international trade and development are revealed in the balance of payments. In Chapter 3 it was seen that a country's balance of payments may indicate various stages of international borrowing and lending. Certain relationships between domestic saving and domestic investment govern the behavior of the balance of payments at these different phases. According to national income analysis, exports plus domestic investment are equal in equilibrium to domestic savings plus imports (leaving the government out of account).

When a country is a young debtor, imports are greater than exports, and domestic investment exceeds domestic savings. Foreign capital fills the gap. In some cases, the domestic investment must await foreign capital, and the import surplus then follows after the foreign funds are available to finance it. In other cases, there may be a tendency for domestic investment to exceed savings; then the import surplus develops in advance of the availability of long-term capital from abroad, and the foreign capital is induced by the passive balance on current account. Later when the country is a mature debtor, or a young creditor, exports exceed imports, and domestic savings exceed domestic investment.

Poor countries of the world are thus normally in the position of borrowing long-term capital and having domestic investment in excess of domestic savings by the amount of the foreign borrowing or import surplus. Rich countries, in contrast, normally have an excess of domestic savings over domestic investment opportunities and increase their investment by investing overseas.

This flow of international capital raises the problem of the "transfer mechanism"—the mechanism by which the balance of payments is adjusted to the international flow of capital. In young debtors, an import surplus has to be created, and the import surplus has to be confined to the limits of the capital inflow. In mature debtor countries, the payments for interest and amortization become larger than the amount of new capital imported, and they have to create an export surplus. The neo-classical theory of international trade gave considerable attention to this problem.[17] The fact that balance of payments equilibrium was maintained by such a large creditor as Britain and by the borrowing countries indicates that there was a mechanism of adjustment of international balances which did operate smoothly and rapidly in the nineteenth century.[18]

In the young debtor nations the forces of development in themselves promoted balance of payments equilibrium. To the extent that loans from Britain were spent in Britain, there was no transfer problem. Only a portion of the loans, however, were so directly tied.[19] Yet the remainder was successfully transferred in the form of an import surplus.

For primary producing countries that were borrowing countries it is difficult to explain the expansion in imports in classical terms of price variations among domestic, export, and import-competing commodities. In countries such as Malaya, the West Indies, Burma, Ceylon, or India there was nothing equivalent to changes in central bank policy. And their export and import prices were largely determined by world con-

[17] See Chapter 3, section 6.

[18] A definition of "balance of payments equilibrium" applicable to all cases is difficult to formulate. Several different definitions are possible according to the extent to which one admits normative considerations. For present purposes, the balance of payments is interpreted as being in equilibrium if there are no net movements of gold or "equilibrating" (induced) capital movements, provided that the country is not suppressing a potential deficit by suffering excessive unemployment relative to other countries, controlling imports to restrict the demand for foreign currencies, or being the recipient of "distress borrowing" which is acceptable to neither the lender nor the borrower.

[19] In the case of British colonies, this portion was generally high, and the process of adjustment was thereby eased. Cf. H. J. Habakkuk, "Free Trade and Commercial Expansion," in *Cambridge History of the British Empire,* II, Cambridge University Press, Cambridge, 1940, 800.

ditions which they could not influence. Even more significantly, the unavailability of commodities that were substitutes for imports must have meant that the elasticity of substitution between domestic and foreign commodities was low for these countries: there was not the "variety and resourcefulness of a rich and energetic country's supply causing her demand for imports to be elastic."[20]

The achievement of an import surplus into these countries may be more reasonably explained by the inflation that came with the monetary expansion as foreign borrowings were received. The monetary systems of these countries varied in structural details, but in all of them the money supply was sensitive to changes in the balance of payments. Cash formed the greater part of the money supply, and, in so far as currency reserves were maintained in gold or sterling securities, the money supply reflected the country's external trading position. This external dependence was naturally most complete for those countries on a gold exchange standard or a sterling exchange standard. When borrowings were made in England, the banks commonly held the excess funds in London. On the basis of these funds a credit expansion ensued at home. Within such an environment of strong inflationary forces, imports increased. And, with a high marginal propensity to import, high income elasticity of demand for imports, and low propensity to save, the increase in imports would be considerable.

The situation was somewhat different for other young debtors such as Canada, New Zealand, and Australia before they became mature debtors. In these countries there were more opportunities for the sectional price changes to be effective. But the full explanation cannot depend only on price changes. It must also be recognized that the capital borrowings stimulated development and thereby increased output, employment, and real income. In these economies there also ensued a degree of inflation greater than that in Britain, even though it was due less to monetary expansion than in the more underdeveloped areas. Both the price and income effects of this inflationary process contributed to increased imports. In a fundamental manner this was owing to the development process associated with foreign borrowings.

The record of debt servicing and repayment by the mature debtors before World War I is impressive. Although there were many defaults during the period, the amounts were not excessively large relative to the total investment involved. Indeed, as far as government bonds were concerned, the average annual amount in default between 1882 and

[20] Alfred Marshall, *Money Credit and Commerce,* Macmillan and Co. Ltd., London, 1923, 172.

1911 was only about $0.39 per $100 of such bonds outstanding.[21] And the defaults, particularly during the 1870's and 1890's, were due more to political disorders and financial maladministration than to unproductive expenditures or balance of payments difficulties.

Some broad observations can be made of how the majority of mature debtor countries were able to create an export surplus. Normally the export surplus materialized with both exports and imports increasing, but with exports increasing more rapidly. Certainly the longer-period movements in the mature debtor's trade balances were dominated by a strong upward-rising trend in exports. Foreign investment had been directed to the export sectors of these countries; productivity had increased most rapidly in export industries; and there was a readily available overseas market for the primary products of the debtor countries. For example, Britain's demand for raw materials and foodstuffs increased absolutely throughout the period before 1914.[22] And even though, with the exception of the 1890's, the rate of increase in Britain's consumption of raw materials was declining, the rate of growth in German imports of primary products increased and helped to sustain the strong demand for exports from the mature debtor countries. . Concentration on export production may have limited home development in other directions, but from the viewpoint of servicing the foreign debt this distribution of investment was best calculated to accomplish a net export surplus. Moreover, the existence of a well-defined system of multilateral clearings made it possible for the debtors to settle their balances with Britain multilaterally rather than through narrower and more difficult bilateral channels. If the data were available, it would also be worth investigating whether money wage rates lagged behind productivity in the mature debtor countries. For, if they did, the resultant price decline would be an additional stimulus to exports.

The slower growth in imports is more difficult to explain. According to the "demonstration effect,"[23] that is, a poor country's attempt to emulate a rich country's consumption pattern, and hence import consumer goods, it might have been expected that imports would have risen more rapidly. It could be argued, however, that the demonstration effect was weak internationally during the pre-1914 period when

[21] Cf. Council of the Corporation of Foreign Bondholders, *Annual Reports,* London, annually.

[22] See the statistics in W. Schlöte, *British Overseas Trade,* Basil Blackwell, Oxford, 1952, 42, 139–143; C. T. Saunders, "Consumption of Raw Materials in the United Kingdom, 1851–1950," *Journal of the Royal Statistical Society, CXV,* Part III, 313–346 (1952).

[23] The "demonstration effect" is discussed more fully in Chapter 15, section 3.

differences in levels of living were neither so large nor so widely known as they now are. Further, the growth of local manufactures also caused the imports of consumer goods to become a smaller proportion of total imports in some countries; for example, in New Zealand the ratio fell from 54 per cent in 1880 to 39 per cent in 1892 and to 32 per cent in 1906.[24] For a general explanation of the restrained increase in imports it is necessary to look to the weak demonstration effect and to the extension of local manufactures. In some countries, however, internal adjustments might be part of the particular explanation. Brazil and Argentina, for example, experienced considerable depreciation of their currencies, and this may have retarded imports and promoted exports. But there is little, if any, evidence of deliberate deflation or measures designed to worsen the debtor country's terms of trade in order to create an export surplus.

Finally, there is the problem of how Britain was able to maintain balance of payments equilibrium in the face of ever-increasing commercial rivalry from Germany, the United States, and Japan. Fundamentally, the answer lies in a great increase in the volume of multilateral transactions during the pre-World War I period. An expanding world economy was much more conducive to equilibrium than a contracting or stationary world economy would have been; it allowed Britain to retain at least its absolute position, if not its relative position, in world markets and made compensating adjustments in the composition of trade easier. When economies grow at different rates, the more slowly growing economy need not suffer disequilibrium in its balance of payments if the direction of growth in the more rapidly growing economies leads to a greater expansion in imports than it does in exports and import-competing commodities. With increasing productivity there comes a higher real income and a greater demand for a variety of products which may on balance increase imports by a greater amount than the new production of import-competing goods diminishes imports.

As Germany, the United States, and Japan industrialized, there was no diminution in British exports to these countries. On the contrary, exports increased.[25] A considerable part of this expansion can be attributed to the exchange of manufactures against manufactures and to the increasing importance of invisibles in trade. It is true, however, that, although the absolute amount of Britain's exports of manufactures to Germany and the United States increased, the ratio of manu-

[24] C. G. F. Simkin, *The Instability of a Dependent Economy,* Oxford University Press, Oxford, 1951, 62, 64.

[25] Cf. Schlöte, *op. cit.,* 84.

factured exports to total exports to these countries declined. But this fall was compensated by the increase in Britain's exports to these countries of raw materials, mainly coal, wool, and metals. And concerning third markets, even though Britain's exports did not grow as rapidly as German and American exports, nonetheless they did continue to grow absolutely. More to the point, however, is the increase in Britain's exports of "invisibles." Although merchandise exports lagged, an ever larger share in Britain's balance of payments was assumed by shipping, financial, and insurance services.

In addition to the "market-creating" effects of development, there were two other major factors conducive to Britain's maintenance of balance of payments equilibrium: improvement in the terms of trade and the multilateral trading system. The fact that Britain did not have to export so much as formerly to realize the same amount of imports was an important offset to foreign competition, especially during the 1880's and 1890's. More significantly, however, the adjustment process was eased by the existence of a flexible world-wide pattern of trade which allowed settlements on a multilateral basis rather than bilaterally or even within a region.[26]

Differential rates of development certainly called for adjustments in the pattern of foreign trade. During the four or five decades before World War I, British exports to industrial nations formed a smaller proportion of total British exports, and primary producing regions became better export markets. Whereas almost 48 per cent of Britain's exports and re-exports by value went to industrial nations in 1877–1879, only 38 per cent did so in 1909–1913; the percentage to agricultural countries, however, rose from approximately 55 per cent in 1877–1899 to 62 per cent in 1909–1913.[27] The greater competitive power of Germany and the United States accounts for much of this diminution in trade to industrial nations. But the expansion of the multilateral trading system during the half century before 1914 allowed the greater competitive power to be neutralized through triangular transactions. To a considerable extent the very growth in British exports to primary producing areas resulted from the increased purchasing power in these areas as they exported industrial raw materials to rapidly industrializing countries such as Germany and the United States. Industrial countries, other than the United Kingdom, generally had an import surplus from the primary producing countries which they financed by an export

---

[26] Details of the pre-1914 network of world trading settlements are given by S. B. Saul, "Britain and World Trade, 1870–1914," *Economic History Review, VII,* No. 1, 49–66 (Aug. 1954).

[27] Schlöte, *op. cit.,* 82.

surplus to the United Kingdom. The latter, in turn, generally had an export surplus to the new primary producing countries. By 1900, Britain relied more and more upon building up her export surpluses with the newly expanding countries of Asia and Africa to offset her import surpluses from America, Europe, Argentina, and Canada. India had a key position in the whole payments pattern: from 1900 to 1913 Britain's export surplus to India financed more than two-fifths of Britain's total deficits.[28]

Such triangular transactions were especially important for the process of development and the transfer of capital which it involved. Capital exports and returns on foreign investments outstanding did not simply offset one another without affecting trade. Capital exports from Britain were normally transferred in bilateral trade with the borrowing countries, but interest and dividends owed to Britain were transferred in multilateral trade by import surpluses from countries other than the major borrowing countries.[29]

During the 1880's Germany emerged as a separate link in the transfer chain leading to the United Kingdom. With its rapid growth in industry, Germany became increasingly dependent upon net imports of primary goods from continents other than Europe which it financed by export surpluses with the United Kingdom. From the late 1890's, the United States became a net exporter of manufactured goods and a net importer of industrial raw materials. About the same time, the "regions of recent settlement in the temperate belts", emerged as a separate group occupying a place between the United States and Continental Europe in the system of multilateral trade. These areas, especially the Argentine, Australia, New Zealand, and Canada, rapidly acquired import surpluses with the United States and offset them with export surpluses to Europe. And the United States' export balance with the countries of recent settlement became largely offset by import balances with the tropics, particularly India, British Malaya, and the Netherlands Indies.

Thus, the existence of a well-defined system of multilateral settlement helped to promote balance of payments equilibrium. It furthered specialization according to comparative advantages, and, as the comparative cost structure evolved, the transitional problems of adjustment were made less difficult than they otherwise would have been. It promoted exchange stability and uniformity of exchange rates in different

[28] Saul, *op. cit.*, 64.
[29] Cf. League of Nations, *Network of World Trade*, Geneva, 1942, 82–87; Folke Hilgerdt, "The Case for Multilateral Trade," *American Economic Review, Papers and Proceedings, XXXIII*, No. 1, 397–401 (March 1943).

markets, making discriminatory exchange rates unnecessary. It also made the servicing of foreign investments considerably easier than it would have been had the transfer of capital been limited to bilateral transactions between debtor and creditor countries. The entire process was highly integrated. Without British capital, the primary producing areas would have been unable to expand their exports sufficiently to meet the demand from industrial countries which were developing rapidly. And were it not for multilateral clearings, the transfer of interest and dividend payments to Britain would have been limited. A unique combination of circumstances had favored the acceleration of development in eighteenth century Britain, and in the nineteenth century favorable forces combined to facilitate the growth of international trade in a multilateral network.

Chapter *12*

Extensive Spread

of Development

In the last half of the nineteenth century, many countries followed Britain in the industrialization process. As the pattern of development changed in the world economy, so too did the structure of international trade. After World War I, however, the world economy had little resemblance to its nineteenth-century pattern. The United States assumed the role formerly held by Britain as the center of the international economy. The nineteenth-century international order disintegrated during the interwar period, and after World War II international organizations were established in an attempt to recreate through institutional methods the stability of the pre-1914 international environment. A conscious demand for active development has arisen in the poor countries of the world, and there has been greater recognition of the need for the maintenance of development in the rich countries. This chapter considers these aspects of the extensive spread of development.

1. Differential Rates of Development

It is impossible to generalize about the extensive development that occurred throughout the world economy during the past century. The

245

diversity of countries is too great, and the phases of development in various countries are too disparate. On the other hand, it would be too involved and detailed a task to present here individual case histories of countries; numerous country studies are available elsewhere.[1]

These individual country studies are of extreme interest for a comparative study of development. Within the total complex of development, they reveal different productive and organizational structures of industry, a variety of institutions through which the development process operated, differences in "spirit" or ideology, different degrees to which development relied on foreign capital, different roles of the government in the development process, different emphases on industry and agriculture, and different degrees to which international trade fostered development.

For present purposes, it is sufficient simply to recognize the broad distinction between some countries in which development proceeded fairly rapidly and other countries that developed very slowly, if at all. The former group of countries may be termed the "progressive economies," and the latter group the "quasi-stationary economies." The first group contains the countries that are now rich. Some of them were poor countries in 1850, but they subsequently developed until they are now rich nations. In contrast, the quasi-stationary economies were poor countries at mid-nineteenth century, and they still are so. These countries constitute the hard core of the world's development problem.

Considering the progressive economies, one should recognize that, although Britain maintained the most rapid rate of development until the middle of the century, other countries developed during the latter half of the nineteenth century, and in some the rate of development soon surpassed that of Britain. There was some imitation of Britain's earlier development, especially in the industrialization of Western Europe until the 1870's.[2] New machines, methods, and ideas were introduced on the Continent from Britain. The spread of technical knowledge from Britain was particularly significant. So too was the part played by British entrepreneurs, managers, and skilled workmen in promoting the expansion of textiles, engineering, and transport in France, Germany, Belgium, and Switzerland. British capital also established several important industrial enterprises on the Continent.

---

[1] See Appendix C.

[2] W. O. Henderson, *Britain and Industrial Europe, 1750–1879*, University Press of Liverpool, Liverpool, 1954; Henderson, "The Genesis of the Industrial Revolution in France and Germany in the Eighteenth Century," *Kyklos, IX,* No. 2, 190–207 (1956).

In other countries, for example, Sweden and Russia, development was not influenced so much by Britain but was more self-generated. In all the industrializing countries, however, there appear the fundamental forces of population growth, technological progress, capital accumulation, and expanding home and overseas markets.

Particularly impressive was the rise of Germany and the United States as rivals to Britain's industrial supremacy after the 1890's. By the end of the century, Japan had also become a modern industrial power, and in recent decades Russia has joined the ranks of leading industrial nations. Australia, New Zealand, and Canada must also be included among the progressive economies that have developed during the past century although their development has not been so rapid and has not been concentrated so much in industry.

A general indication of the differential rates of growth in various parts of the world economy may be seen in the changed distribution of national income throughout the world. Although data are scarce and of questionable reliability, it has been estimated that in 1850 the real income of the world was between a fifth and a quarter of what it was in 1937. In the world-wide process of development, the real income of the world has also come to be differently distributed. Of the world income of 1850, the largest share went to the Far East, which appears to have had over 40 per cent of the whole; North America had a real income comparable with that of Africa today, and accounted for only about 10 per cent of world income, with Central and South America representing another 3 per cent; Western Europe had a slightly smaller share than now, with about 29 per cent; Eastern Europe had about 14 per cent; the Middle East had about the same share as today; the shares of Australia and Africa were negligible. Of the world income of 1937, however, it is estimated that about 29 per cent was that of the North American countries, and 4 per cent that of Central and South America; Western Europe accounted for about 31 per cent, and Eastern Europe for about 11 per cent; the Far East for only 20 per cent; all other areas, including Africa, Australia, and the Middle East for about 5 per cent.[3]

Table 12.1 indicates more directly the spread among the rates of development in different countries. The challenge to Britain's industrial supremacy may also be seen in Tables 12.2 and 12.3. Although in the middle of the nineteenth century Britain's share of world manufacturing was as yet unchallenged, the extensive spread of development overseas made it impossible to retain this share indefinitely. Towards

[3] E. A. G. Robinson, "The Changing Structure of the British Economy," *Economic Journal, LXIV,* No. 255, 447–448 (Sept. 1954).

TABLE 12.1. GROWTH RATES OF REAL NATIONAL PRODUCT OF "PROGRESSIVE" ECONOMIES, 1860–1950

(Per cent per Year)

Aggregate Real National Product

	U.S.	Can-ada	Aus-tralia	New Zea-land	U.K.	France	Ger-many	Nether-lands	Bel-gium	Switzer-land	Swe-den	Nor-way	Den-mark
1. 1860–1913*	4.3	—	3.7	—	2.4	1.1	3.0	2.3	2.2	2.6	2.0	2.3	2.8
2. 1913–1938	2.0	1.7†	2.1	—	1.0	1.1	1.3	2.1	1.0	1.6	1.9	1.9	2.1
3. 1938–1950	5.7	5.9	2.6	3.3‡	1.6	0.2	2.3§	1.8	0.6	2.1	2.5	3.0	2.2
4. 1860–1950	3.8	—	3.2	—	1.8	1.1	2.4	2.2	1.7	2.1	2.0	2.3	2.5
5. 1913–1950	3.0	2.8	2.3	—	1.2	0.9	1.7	1.7	0.9	1.8	2.1	2.3	2.1

Real National Product per Head

	U.S.	Can-ada	Aus-tralia	New Zea-land	U.K.	France	Ger-many	Nether-lands	Bel-gium	Switzer-land	Swe-den	Nor-way	Den-mark
6. 1860–1913*	2.3	—	1.7	—	1.5	0.9	2.0	0.8	1.4	1.4	1.3	1.6	1.8
7. 1913–1938	0.9	0.2	0.4	—	0.8	0.9	0.7	0.6	0.6	1.2	1.4	1.2	0.8
8. 1938–1950	4.2	4.0	1.1	2.4	1.2	0.0	0.7§	0.6	0.3	1.1	1.7	2.1	1.2
9. 1860–1950	2.2	—	1.3	—	1.2	0.9	1.4	0.7	1.1	1.3	1.4	1.6	1.4
10. 1913–1950	2.0	1.4	0.6	—	0.9	0.7	0.7	0.6	0.5	1.2	1.5	1.5	0.9

* First period starts with following years other than 1860; U.S., 1869/78; Australia, 1886; U.K., 1870; Netherlands, 1900; Belgium, 1846; Switzerland, 1890; Sweden, 1870; Norway, 1891; Denmark, 1870.
† 1911 instead of 1913.
‡ 1938/39 to 1947/48.
§ From 1936 to 1952.

Source: R. W. Goldsmith, "Financial Structure and Economic Growth in Advanced Countries," in *Capital Formation and Economic Growth,* National Bureau of Economic Research Special Conference Series, Princeton University Press, Princeton, 1955, 115.

TABLE 12.2. PERCENTAGE DISTRIBUTION
OF THE WORLD'S MANUFACTURING PRODUCTION
BY COUNTRY, 1870–1938

Period	World	U.S.A.	United Kingdom	Germany	France	Russia	Others
1870	100.0	23.3	31.8	13.2	10.3	3.7	17.7
1881–1885	100.0	28.6	26.6	13.9	8.6	3.4	18.9
1896–1900	100.0	30.1	19.5	16.6	7.1	5.0	21.7
1906–1910	100.0	35.3	14.7	15.9	6.4	5.0	22.7
1913	100.0	35.8	14.0	15.7	6.4	5.5	22.6
1926–1929	100.0	42.2	9.4	11.6	6.6	4.3	25.9
1936–1938	100.0	32.2	9.2	10.7	4.5	18.5	24.9

Source: League of Nations, *Industrialization and Foreign Trade*, Geneva, 1945, 13.

TABLE 12.3. ECONOMIC INDICATORS;
UNITED KINGDOM, GERMANY, UNITED STATES
1893–1913

	Per Cent Increases		
	United Kingdom	Germany	United States
Population	20	32	46
Coal production	75	159	210
Pig iron	50	287	337
Crude steel	136	522	715
Exports of raw materials	238	243	196
Exports of manufactures	121	239	563

Source: R.C.K. Ensor, *England 1870–1914*, Clarendon Press, Oxford, 1936, 503.

the end of the century, Britain was unable to maintain her rate of growth in output of such industries as coal, iron, and steel as compared with the rates of growth in the United States, Belgium, Germany, and France. It will be noted in Table 12.2 that by 1881–1885 the United States already had a greater share of the world's manufacturing production than the United Kingdom; after 1900 manufacturing production in the United States increased extremely rapidly, the percentage of the world's manufacturing production attributable to the United States reaching over 35 per cent in 1908–1910, whereas the United Kingdom's proportion fell to less than 15 per cent. By 1906–1910, Germany had achieved a proportion higher than the United Kingdom. Over the period 1870–1913, the rate of growth of manufacturing production in the United States and Germany was more than double that of the United Kingdom. During the interwar period, the output of the U.S.S.R. rose markedly. And by the end of the interwar period, Britain was producing less than

10 per cent of the world's manufacturing output as compared with nearly one-third in 1870.

Because it now occupies a focal position in the world economy comparable to that of Britain in the nineteenth century, the United States may be singled out among the progressive economies for more attention. Since the 1870's the development of the American economy has been remarkable. Table 12.4 gives some measures of this development.

TABLE 12.4.   MEASURES OF U. S. ECONOMIC GROWTH,
1869–1878 TO 1944–1953

	Relatives for 1944–1953 (1869–1878 = 100)
(1) Net national product	1325
(2) Population	334
(3) Net national product per capita	397
(4) Labor force	423
(5) Ratio of labor force to population	127
(6) Employment	427
(7) Ratio of employment to population	128
(8) Capital	993
(9) Capital per capita	297
(10) Index of total input of resources	381
(11) Index of input per capita	114
(12) Net national product per employed worker	310
(13) Net national product per man hour	426
(14) Net national product per capital unit	134
(15) Index of net national product per unit of total input	348

Source: M. Abramovitz, "Resource and Output Trends in the United States since 1870," *American Economic Review, Papers and Proceedings, XLVI,* No. 2, 8 (May 1956).

Between the decade 1869–1878 and the decade 1944–1953, net national product in constant prices rose more than 13 times.[4]   This increase implies an average rate of growth of 3.5 per cent per annum.   During the same period, population more than tripled, so that net national product per capita almost quadrupled, implying an average rate of growth of 1.9 per cent per annum.[4]   The magnitude of this increase might be better appreciated if it is realized that, whereas in 1953 the average American family had an income somewhat over $5000, if the rate of growth continues at as high and as constant a rate for the next eight decades as it has in the last, the average family income will then be

[4] M. Abramovitz, "Resource and Output Trends in the United States Since 1870," *American Economic Review, Papers and Proceedings, XLVI,* No. 2, 7 (May 1956).

about $25,000 of 1953 purchasing power, a level now attained only by approximately the top 1 per cent of the nation's families.[5]

Part of this development is attributable to the increase in factor supply, especially capital accumulation. Although the percentage of net national product going into capital formation actually declined from a level between 14 per cent and 16 per cent in the 1880's and 1890's to around 11 per cent in the 1920's,[6] the absolute amount of new investment has risen significantly. Between the 1870's and the 1920's, capital per person rose at a fairly constant average rate of about 2½ per cent. During the depression of the 1930's and World War II, however, this growth was checked; since the war, although capital per person has grown rapidly, this acceleration has done little more than offset the decline during the preceding 15 years; and on net balance, capital per person in 1952 was only moderately above the predepression high.[7]

It may also be observed that, although the hours of work fell, a growing proportion of the population entered the labor force. The net result was a modest increase, about 10 per cent, in the annual hours of work per head of population from the 1870's to the 1900's, followed by an equal or perhaps somewhat larger decline during the next four decades. Labor input per capita has thus changed little during the past eight decades. Total input, that is, labor and capital inputs together, rose moderately in relation to population during the first four decades and fell slightly during the last four decades. Over the eight decades, there appears to have been a net rise of no more than a fifth or a sixth in the amount of input per capita used in production. Since there was only a small increase in total input per capita, whereas national income per capita increased about fourfold, it follows that most of the increase in income resulted from an increase in productivity.[8] A given amount of labor and capital was able to produce a larger output. Indeed, output per man hour nearly tripled between the decade of the 1890's and the 1940's,[9] and output per unit of input rose about 1.7 per cent a year on the average.

This increase in productivity is due to the very rapid rate of techno-

[5] S. Fabricant, *Economic Progress and Economic Change,* National Bureau of Economic Research, New York, 1954, 5.

[6] S. Kuznets, *National Income: A Summary of Findings,* National Bureau of Economic Research, New York, 1946, 32.

[7] Fabricant, *op. cit.,* 7.

[8] Income from foreign investment was negligible as a contribution to national income, and changes in the terms of trade were of minor significance since foreign trade contributed only a small proportion to national income.

[9] F. C. Mills, *Productivity and Economic Progress,* National Bureau of Economic Research, New York, 1952, 2.

logical and organizational progress.[10]   Along with impressive technological advance, there has been a broadening of research activities in
business and government and a spread of the "scientific spirit" in industrial practice.   This investment of resources in research and education
and the growth of applied knowledge have contributed to much greater
efficiency in production.   The aggregate increase in productivity is also
reflected in trends of output per head in major sectors of the economy.
The "productivity histories" of agriculture, manufacturing, mining, transport, and communications all show remarkable progress trendwise.

   In the distribution of the labor force there has been a relative shift
away from agriculture towards manufacturing, trade, and services.   If
output per head in each of the major sectors of the economy had
remained throughout the period 1900–1930 at the level of 1900, the
increase in real income per head by 1930 would have been 30 per cent
as a result of only the changing distribution of the labor force.[11]   Thus
the transformation in the distribution of the labor force accounts for
some of the increase in real income per head, but the over-all increase
in productivity in different sectors remains the most significant feature
of American development.

   As in Britain, the pattern of technical progress helps to explain these
fluctuations in growth.   Although there was gradual continuous improvement in many unrelated inventions and innovations, the major basic
innovations affecting large groups of industries or even whole areas of
productive activity were discontinuous.   The period 1870–1882 was
associated with the wide application of innovations of steam power to
industry and transport.   The application of steam to transport was
particularly important in the opening of the West and the resultant development of new resources.   The faster rate of growth in 1894–1907
was related to the massive extension of steam now combined with steel,
and to innovation by the discovery and development of new resources.
Steel in the form of machinery, rails, ships, and buildings had especially
widespread repercussions.   The third period of rapid advance during
the 1920's was linked to electricity, the internal-combustion engine, and
industrial chemicals.   The intervening periods of slower growth were
characterized by gradual exhaustion of the scope for further widespread
application of the innovations which were carried out on a broad scale
during the periods of faster advance.

   [10] Cf. W. Fellner, *Trends and Cycles in Economic Activity*, Henry Holt & Co.,
New York, 1956, 62, 66–67.
   [11] B. Weber and S. J. Handfield-Jones, "Variations in the Rate of Economic
Growth in the U.S.A., 1869–1939," *Oxford Economic Papers*, *VI*, No. 2, 104
(June 1954).

Much of the historical record of American development can therefore be interpreted in terms of widespread innovations, capital accumulation, and rising productivity. All these elements, however, were interwoven in a dynamic process which may best be summarized as basically a multiplier-accelerator process. This process operated on an interplay of forces between the East and the newly settled West. The opening of the West and the movement of population westward provided new investment opportunities with attendant multiplier effects. As agricultural output expanded in the West, income rose, and the demand for Eastern manufactures increased, thereby inducing further investment in the East.[12]

In sharp contrast to the United States and other progressive economies, there has remained on the periphery of the world economy a group of countries that have experienced little development. It is not too much of an exaggeration to say that areas of Africa and Asia have remained economically stagnant. There have been relatively insignificant changes in productive techniques, in the structure of the economy, in the standard of living. Although the economies do not exactly duplicate the characteristics of the classical "stationary state," they approximate them in several respects, and may at least be termed "quasi-stationary."

Initially the indigenous peoples of these countries raised only subsistence crops. Total output was low and not easily expandable, so that, after consumption needs were fulfilled, there remained little, if any, surplus for capital accumulation and a subsequent increase in output. Without foreign capital from richer countries, these quasi-stationary economies had made little progress by 1850, and some areas in the African and Asian tropics were not yet opened to world markets.

Tropical and subtropical regions received only about a quarter of total British capital exports. The greatest achievements of international investment in the nineteenth century were in Canada, the United States, Argentina, Australia, and other "new countries" in the world's temperate latitudes, not in the tropical regions. The foreign capital that came to the tropical areas was not in response to development already in progress, but rather in anticipation of future development of export products. Foreign investments, enterprises, and administrators did have an impact on these countries, but their impact was confined mainly to the export sector of the economy where transportation facilities, new production units, and efficient resource utilization were introduced.

[12] For a fuller discussion of this process, see J. S. Duesenberry, "Some Aspects of the Theory of Development," *Explorations in Entrepreneurial History, III,* No. 2, Dec. 15, 1950, 96–102.

Accordingly, after a period of gestation, the fruits of the foreign investment appeared in the form of an increased supply of exportable primary products.
Nevertheless, even though the exports of these poor countries in-

TABLE 12.5. COUNTRIES CLASSIFIED BY
SIZE OF PER CAPITA INCOME, 1949
(U.S. $ of 1949 Purchasing Power)

Per Capita Income	Country	Per Capita Income	Country
$1440	U.S.A.	100–200	Brazil
			Bulgaria
600–900	Australia		Chile
	Canada		Columbia
	Denmark		Egypt
	New Zealand		Greece
	Sweden		Japan
	Switzerland		Mexico
	United Kingdom		Peru
			Southern Rhodesia
450–600	Belgium		Spain
	France		Syria
	Iceland		Turkey
	Luxembourg		Yugoslavia
	Netherlands		
	Norway	Under $100	Burma
	Venezuela		Ceylon
			China
300–450	Argentina		Dominican Republic
	Czechoslovakia		Ecuador
	Finland		India
	Germany (West)		Indonesia
	Ireland		Iran
	Israel		Kenya
	Poland		Malaya
	Uruguay		Northern Rhodesia
	U.S.S.R.		Pakistan
			Paraguay
200–300	Austria		Philippines
	Cuba		Thailand
	Hungary		
	Italy		
	Puerto Rico		
	Union of South Africa		

Source: United Nations, Economic and Social Council, "Volume and Distribution of National Income in Under-Developed Countries," June 28, 1951, E/2041, Tables 1, 2. Also see U. S. Department of State, Point Four, Economic Cooperation Series No. 24, Jan. 1950, 113–114.

creased remarkably, development of the export sector did not carry over to the rest of the economy. Many countries that were poor a century ago are still so—in contrast to other progressive economies which, although possibly poor a century ago, have now become rich countries. Part 3 will discuss in detail the reasons for this limited development of the quasi-stationary economies.

A variety of indexes show the contrast between the progressive and the quasi-stationary economies. Table 12.5 indicates how wide is the gap between per capita real income in the progressive economies and in the poor countries which are at the bottom of the list. Although these estimates are subject to many reservations, and their statistical precision is illusory, nevertheless they do indicate the general picture of the extreme differences in the levels of living in different countries.[13]

More specific indexes may also be noted. Table 12.6 shows comparative indicators in communications, fuel and power, and industry for India, Pakistan, Ceylon, and Malaya on the one hand, and the United Kingdom and the United States on the other.

TABLE 12.6. LEVELS OF ECONOMIC DEVELOPMENT
IN 1949; COMPARATIVE INDICATORS

	Units per 1000 Population	India	Pakis- tan	Ceylon	Malaya	U.K.	U.S.A.
Electricity production	1000 kwh	13	1.9	9.6	117	1033	2296
Coal consumption	tons	80	18	28	85	3884	3473
Petroleum consumption	tons	7.8	11	23	99	327	1638
Steel consumption	tons	3.8	1.3	6	16	194	364
Cement consumption	tons	7.2	3.6	19	25	148	229
Locomotives	nos.*	22	16	32	31	410	309
Rail freight	1000 ton miles	65	—	—	32	446	4568
Load-carrying vehicles	nos.	0.18	0.17	1.41	3	16	43
All-weather roads	miles	0.32	0.1	0.87	0.93	3.7	2.2
Telephones	nos.	0.37	0.21	2.2	7.7	98	261

* Per million population.
Source: Report by the Commonwealth Consultative Committee, *The Colombo Plan,* H.M.S.O., London, Cmd. 8080, Nov. 1950, 10.

[13] The limitations to these statistics are fully discussed in United Nations, Economic and Social Council, "Volume and Distribution of National Income in Under-Developed Countries," June 28, 1951, E/2041. Also, A. R. Burns, *Comparative Economic Organization,* Prentice-Hall, New York, 1955, 6–9.

Finally, a fairly inclusive comparison of countries is given in Table 12.7, which scores countries with respect to their national consumption levels in the period 1934–1938. The basis is a variety of statistical

TABLE 12.7. NON-MONETARY INDICATORS OF
RELATIVE NATIONAL CONSUMPTION LEVELS,
31 COUNTRIES, TYPICALLY 1934–1938

	Non-monetary Indicators	
	Absolute	Relative Data
Country	Data	(U.S. = 100)
United States	1707	100.0
Canada	1375	80.6
Australia	1365	80.0
United Kingdom	1290	75.6
Germany	1058	62.0
France	984	57.6
Argentina	916	53.7
Czechoslovakia	803	47.0
Cuba	708	41.5
Japan	685	40.1
Italy	676	39.6
Union So. Africa	660	38.7
Spain	628	36.8
U.S.S.R.	573	33.6
Brazil	540	31.6
Mexico	495	29.0
Poland	492	28.8
Yugoslavia	468	27.4
Philippines	439	25.7
Rumania	434	25.4
Turkey	413	24.2
Egypt	378	22.2
Thailand	365	21.4
India	355	20.8
Korea	331	19.4
Persia	310	18.2
China	307	18.0
Nigeria	306	17.9
Fr. Indo-China	302	17.7
Neth. Indies	291	17.0
Fr. W. Africa	269	15.8

Source: M. K. Bennett, "International Disparities in Consumption Levels," American Economic Review, XLI, No. 4, 648 (Sept. 1951).

series all of which are non-monetary in character, and hence more dependable than monetary series. The final index incorporates 19 different series which reflect national consumption levels with respect to food and tobacco, medical and sanitary services, education and recreation, and transportation and communication.[14] The highest ranking country receives 100 for each indicator, so that the maximum total would be 1900 points if the country ranked highest for each of the 19 different indicators. The table gives the absolute number of total points scored by each country, as well as the relative score. The high position of the United States is outstanding, and it is interesting to observe that only six countries scored more than half as many points as the United States, and 13 countries scored from a fourth to a half as many, and 11 countries scored less than a fourth as many as the United States.

2. Changing Structure of International Trade

It has been seen that during the nineteenth century many of the springs of development in the progressive economies lay outside the country. The migration of capital and labor from Britain was important in the development of Australia, Argentina, Canada, New Zealand, South Africa, the United States. Other progressive economies, however, were not so dependent on foreign capital—for example, France, Germany, and Japan. Nonetheless, all the progressive economies became integrated into the world economy, and to this extent international trade contributed to the development of these countries. International trade became a substitute for domestic production. Factors moved in the guise of commodities, and imports constituted indirect production. At least until the turn of the century, the international economy became increasingly characterized by a greater degree of international specialization, a widening of overseas markets, and a general expansion in production.

At the same time as its export sector was highly important in propelling the British economy forward, the very process of development both in Britain and in other countries overseas altered the character of Britain's foreign trade. Some broad changes in the structure of Britain's foreign trade may be seen in Tables 12.8, 12.9, and 12.10. Between 1850 and 1870 Britain was rapidly adjusting her economy to a world market. This is apparent in such features as high specialization, a high ratio of imports to national income, great dependence on manufactured exports, and diminishing dependence on domestic raw materials and home food supplies. By 1850, the ratio of imports to net national income had risen to about 18 per cent; over 90 per cent of exports were manufactures; imports were still largely composed of raw materials for

---

[14] For details of construction, see M. K. Bennett, "International Disparities in Consumption Levels," *American Economic Review, XLI,* No. 4, 638–640 (Sept. 1951). Also see Table C, p. 11.

TABLE 12.8. DEPENDENCE OF THE BRITISH
ECONOMY ON IMPORTS

Year	Approximate Ratio of Retained Imports to Net National Income at Factor Cost (per cent)
1820	12
1850	18
1870	28
1880	33
1900	26
1913	28
1937	21
1953	26

Source: E. A. G. Robinson, "The Changing Structure of the British Economy," *Economic Journal, LXIV,* No. 255, 458 (Sept. 1954).

TABLE 12.9. COMPOSITION OF THE
UNITED KINGDOM'S EXPORTS

Year	Manufactured Exports As Per Cent of Total Exports	Textile Exports As Per Cent of Total Exports	Metal and Engineering Exports As Per Cent of Total Exports
1830	91	67	11
1850	93	63	18
1870	91	56	21
1890	86	43	25
1913	79	34	27
1937	78	24	35
1951	88	19	49

Source: E. A. G. Robinson, "The Changing Structure of the British Economy," *Economic Journal, LXIV,* No. 255, 460 (Sept. 1954).

TABLE 12.10. COMPOSITION OF
UNITED KINGDOM IMPORTS

	1820	1850	1870	1900	1913	1929	1953
Food and livestock	31	34	35	42	37	40.5	46
Raw materials	60	59	50	39	43	39.5	41
Finished manufactured goods	9	7	15	19	20	20.0	13
Total	100	100	100	100	100	100	100

Source: E. A. G. Robinson, "The Changing Structure of the British Economy," *Economic Journal, LXIV,* No. 255, 460 (Sept. 1954).

the textile industries, accounting for about 32 per cent of the total; but food imports were increasing, and amounted to about 34 per cent of the whole.[15] Between 1870 and 1913 the over-all ratio of retained imports to net national income remained relatively steady, rising from 28 per cent in 1870 to a peak of 33 per cent in the 1880's and then falling back to slightly lower figures in the 1890's. By the turn of the century, food imports had risen to about 42 per cent of the whole and were for the first time larger than raw material imports. At the outbreak of World War I, Britain had a high degree of specialization in manufacturing, and a high degree of dependence on imported raw materials and foodstuffs.

In 1913, Britain was still the world's leading importer and exporter, but from the 1890's onwards her relative position had been declining. As Britain's share of world manufacturing fell, so too did her share of world trade in manufactures—from about 40 per cent in 1870 to 27 per cent in 1913. This drastic decline is attributable not only to Britain's failure to concentrate on industries that were of increasing importance in world trade but also by her failure to maintain her relative share of world trade in industries that were of stable and declining importance in international trade. Britain could not keep pace with the manufactured products of the expanding industrial nations, and was also unable to retain her competitive position with respect to these countries in the stable and declining industries. The problem of adapting to the changing pattern of world trade was especially difficult in so far as almost two-thirds of Britain's exports at the turn of the century were in industries that were of declining importance in world trade.[16] As world demand shifted towards industries in which British exports were relatively unimportant, Britain's international position became competitively weaker, and structural readjustments were required.

Changes in the composition of Britain's trade also reflected changes in the world economy as new industrial powers emerged. This may be noted in Table 12.11. Until 1873, two-thirds of Britain's trade was of the type usually associated with a great imperial power—the exchange of manufactured goods for raw materials and foodstuffs. By the end of the century, however, this type of interchange had become only one-third. With the rise of the industrial powers of the United States and Germany, more of Britain's trade took the form of the interchange of manufactures for manufactures.

[15] E. A. G. Robinson, "The Changing Structure of the British Economy," *Economic Journal, LXIV,* No. 255, 448 (Sept. 1954).

[16] J. M. Letiche, "Differential Rates of Productivity Growth and International Imbalance," *Quarterly Journal of Economics, LXIX,* No. 3, 389 (Aug. 1955).

TABLE 12.11. PERCENTAGE DISTRIBUTION OF
THE FOREIGN TRADE OF THE UNITED KINGDOM,
BY TYPES OF INTERCHANGE, 1854–1929

Period	Commodities against Invisible Items	Raw Materials and Food against Raw Materials and Food	Manufactures against Manufactures	Manufactures against Raw Materials and Food
1854–1863	14.2	11.1	8.8	65.9
1864–1873	12.1	10.9	13.2	63.8
1874–1883	20.1	12.1	17.2	50.4
1884–1893	18.2	14.3	20.1	47.4
1894–1903	23.9	16.3	25.3	34.5
1904–1913	15.1	20.0	22.7	42.2
1925–1929	23.1	15.8	25.7	35.4

Source: A. O. Hirschman, *National Power and the Structure of Foreign Trade,* University of California Press, Berkeley, 1945, 145.

As will be discussed more fully below, the absolute growth in this type of trade illustrates the principle that industrial nations need not fear industrialization abroad in so far as the rising incomes of industrial nations allow them to be the best customers of one another, and the increasing degree of specialization within manufacturing permits a broad base for international trade. Thus, at the turn of the century, Germany and the United States were Britain's two best customers even though they were rapidly industrializing.

For the world as a whole the value of international trade expanded considerably from 1870 to 1913, as may be seen in Table 12.12. The

TABLE 12.12. VALUE OF WORLD TRADE, 1870–1913

Year	(1) 1907 = 100	(2) (£ million, at current rate of exchange)	(3) (£ million, at 1929 prices)
1870	31	2,297	2,795
1876	39	3,000	3,925
1880	44	3,024	4,230
1885	44	3,056	4,980
1890	53	—	—
1895	52	—	—
1900	68	4,025	6,610
1905	86	4,955	7,960
1910	111	6,430	9,050
1913	137	7,840	10,710

Sources: (1) J. Tinbergen, *Business Cycles in the United Kingdom, 1870–1914,* North-Holland Publishing Co., Amsterdam, 1951, 141.
(2) and (3) Clark, *The Conditions of Economic Progress,* London, 1940, 461.

value, according to Tinbergen, increased more than fourfold between 1870 and 1913. The trade of leading countries also reflects this over-all increase.

How can this growth in international trade be explained? It might be thought that migration, population growth, and foreign investment had the net effect of reducing disparities in the ratios of factor supplies among countries, and that technical skills and technical knowledge became ever more diffused throughout the world, so that there was a narrowing of the gaps in comparative costs on the side of production. And, regarding the demand side, one might contend that with the spread of industrialization, improvement in communications, and extension of international advertising, expenditure patterns became more similar. Moreover, trade restrictions also increased throughout the period. In view of these changes, all of which would operate to reduce trade, it might appear surprising that trade actually expanded.

The answer to why trade did expand must lie in the introduction of new commodities, the emergence of increasing physical returns to scale, the course of the absolute level of demand, and the reduction in transportation costs. Throughout the period new commodities were introduced, and there was a finer gradation in qualities of what appear to be the same commodities. Innovations were occurring in international markets as well as in domestic markets. More and more the different countries in the world economy produced different kinds of goods for specialized kinds of markets. Such progress in the production of new goods and progress in quality meant a greater differentiation of products, and this broadened the scope for international exchange, particularly in manufactured articles.

Moreover, as manufacturing production expanded internally, decreasing costs were realized in the production of some commodities, and as technology improved there was an increase in the optimum size of plant in many industries. These developments created the need for a wider market which was frequently sought in foreign outlets. Even more significantly, they meant that the international economy was becoming increasingly characterized by complete specialization rather than partial specialization.

Further, with the secular increase in income, there was an absolute increase in the demand for commodities entering into foreign commerce. As incomes rose in industrial countries, there emerged a demand for a greater variety of imported commodities. Improved transportation facilities made it possible to ship a greater range of products, and freight costs were less of a trade barrier as they became smaller in proportion to the value of the quality goods towards which demand tended to shift when income rose. Moreover, with the secular increase in income and population growth, the demand for foodstuffs rose absolutely. And the spread of industrialization led to an expansion in the imports of industrial raw materials.

Instead of confirming the fears of those who thought that international commerce must be based merely on the exchange of manufactures for primary products, and hence believed that the spread of industrialization would diminish the volume of trade, the continued spread of industrialization actually increased the volume of world trade. Although development in overseas countries reduced some markets for the previously industrialized countries, nonetheless the industrialization process also yielded at the same time an income effect that, on balance, increased imports by a greater amount than the new production of import substitutes diminished them. Imports of all kinds rose with increasing per capita income. And what was most significant from the viewpoint of the advanced industrial nations was the fact that imports of manufactures generally showed the greatest relative expansion in those countries that were industrializing most rapidly. Exports of industrialized countries to each other became almost as great as their exports to non-industrial countries. New industrialization led to shifts in the type of manufactured products exported by the older industrial countries, but greater specialization among countries was possible as technical progress created new products and improved methods of production. Instead of leading to a decrease in imports of manufactured goods, the industrialization process has generally had the opposite result. In the absence of restrictive commercial policies and currency disorders, imports of manufactures tend to be stimulated by the industrial growth of the less developed countries. This relationship is evident in Table 12.13.[17]

Although the over-all effects of development are normally to expand trade through the rise in real income and finer degree of specialization, the particular pattern of development in an industrializing country may act to limit this expansion. If through undue protection or subsidizing of local industry, the developing country diverts resources away from export industries to such an extent that exports decline, or if a cost inflation is generated by development expenditures so that the competi-

---

[17] For a fuller discussion of this issue, see A. O. Hirschman, "Effects of Industrialization on the Markets of Industrial Countries," in B. F. Hoselitz (ed.), *The Progress of Underdeveloped Areas,* University of Chicago Press, Chicago, 1952, 270–283; N. S. Buchanan and F. R. Lutz, *Rebuilding the World Economy,* Twentieth Century Fund, New York, 1947, 49–56; A. G. B. Fisher, "Some Essential Factors in the Evolution of International Trade," *Manchester School of Economic and Social Studies, XIII,* No. 1, 1–23 (Oct. 1943); A. J. Brown, "Economic Development and World Trade," *Journal of International Affairs,* Spring 1950.

TABLE 12.13. MOVEMENT OF MANUFACTURING
PRODUCTION AND TRADE IN MANUFACTURED ARTICLES

Country	Manufacturing Production (1926–1929 as percentage of 1891–1895)	Imports of Manufactures
Japan	1932	628
Finland	583	473
United States	436	230
Sweden	405	480
Italy	394	189
Germany	279	185
France	260	127
United Kingdom and Ireland	143	195

Source: League of Nations, *Industrialization and Foreign Trade*, Geneva, 1945, 93.

tive position of exports is impaired, then the import capacity will be reduced, and the volume of world trade will to that extent decline.

Moreover, even though the market-creating effects of industrialization usually more than offset the market-destroying effects, so that the advanced country's trade in manufactures increases in absolute amounts, nonetheless the relative share need not also increase. Thus, while the more recently developed countries such as the United States, Japan, and Canada increased their percentage shares in the value of world trade in manufactures from 1899 to 1937 by 8.4 per cent, 5.7 per cent, and 4.7 per cent, respectively, the United Kingdom's share declined by 10.1 per cent.[18] Only to a small extent can this decline be attributed to the fact that the United Kingdom was exporting goods that were declining in relative importance in world trade. On the contrary, the fall in the United Kingdom's share was due mainly to the decrease in the United Kingdom's share in the iron and steel and engineering trades which were actually becoming of greater importance in the international market.

The process of extensive development has now been seen to have affected the volume of trade and the relative shares of world trade of different countries. Changes in the composition of trade have also resulted. The composition of trade changes most rapidly and markedly for those countries that are proceeding through the industrialization process. The changes may be expected to differ according to the pro-

[18] H. Tyszynski, "World Trade in Manufactured Commodities, 1899–1950," *Manchester School of Economic and Social Studies, XIX,* No. 3, 286 (Sept. 1951).

ductive structure of each country, types of innovations, changes in tastes, and governmental policies. It is difficult to formulate any general "laws" which would be applicable to the trade of all countries in the course of their economic development. Nonetheless, a review of the trade statistics of countries that have industrialized reveals some significant tendencies.

As poor countries develop they may at first have to concentrate on importing capital to be used with their raw materials and labor. But as industrialization proceeds, the developing country tends to import more of all the major categories of commodities. Imports of raw materials, semi-finished goods, and fuels tend, however, to increase in relative importance, while manufactured consumer goods become a smaller proportion of total imports. The general increase in imports is attributable to the rising level of income. The increasing importance of raw material imports is related to the greater demand for industrial raw materials and to the transfer of resources from primary production to secondary and tertiary production, thereby reducing the home supply of primary products.

Transformations in America's trade constitute one of the clearest examples of how a country, in the course of development, may change from being a net exporter of primary products to being a net exporter of manufactures and a net importer of primary products. In the middle of the nineteenth century, the United States was chiefly an exporter of cotton and tobacco and an importer of manufactured goods from Europe. In the 1870's and 1880's, as the interior of the country was developed, foodstuffs became the principal exports. From the mid-1890's, however, the growth in manufacturing industry began to exercise a predominant influence, and the former import surplus of manufactures was transformed into a steadily rising export surplus. From 1898 onwards, raw material imports exceeded imports of finished manufactures, and the country became a net importer of primary products. The increase of population and the rise of income created a greater home demand for foodstuffs and limited their exportation, and more raw materials were required for the expanding home industries. With the growth of the home market, accumulation of capital, and progress in technology, the comparative cost structure had changed to such an extent that the country's original comparative disadvantage in manufacturing had been transformed into a comparative advantage.

Certain variations in the composition of trade for the world as a whole also emerge clearly. Throughout the period 1870–1913, the average percentage rate of increase in the volume of trade of both manufactured articles and primary products was well above 2 per cent per annum.

The ratio of trade in primary products to that in manufactured articles, however, increased by more than 25 per cent from 1876–1880 to 1896–1900.[19] This relative increase in the importance of trade in primary products was associated with the deterioration in the terms of trade for primary products and with the sharp increase in tariffs on manufactures after 1890. From 1900–1913, however, the ratio of trade in primary products to manufactured articles declined from an index of 112 to 100.[19] In these years the terms of trade were improving for primary producing countries. Moreover, the *ad valorem* equivalent of specific tariff rates on manufactures declined as the prices of manufactures increased; as prices rose, the incidence of the tariff rates (when unchanged) decreased, and commercial restrictions on manufactures became less effective.

Further, over the period 1870–1913, the exchange of "foodstuffs and raw materials against manufactures" amounted to a relatively smaller proportion of world trade, while the exchange of "commodities against invisible items" and the exchange of "manufactures against manufactures" became more extensive. By 1913 the two latter types of exchange accounted for the same percentage of total trade as did the exchange of "foodstuffs and raw materials against manufactures."[20]

This development is understandable in so far as world production in secondary and tertiary industries grew during the period, and demand increased relatively for secondary and tertiary products as income rose. Furthermore, instead of being competitive with the secondary industries already established in the older industrialized countries, the secondary industries of newly industrialized countries were frequently complementary and produced different goods or goods of different quality. The wide range of varying qualities of manufactured products permitted the expansion in the interchange of manufactures. The fact that countries with a relatively high proportion of international trade per head of population exported and imported what were apparently the same commodities was chiefly due to the different qualities of the imported goods suited to different classes of the population.[21] If the dynamic changes and innovations associated with domestic development diversified the composition of home production, they naturally did the same on international markets.

[19] Calculated from League of Nations, *Industrialization and Foreign Trade*, Geneva, 1945, 157.

[20] A. O. Hirschman, *National Power and the Structure of Foreign Trade*, University of California Press, Berkeley, 1945, 151.

[21] S. H. Frankel, "Industrialization of Agricultural Countries and the Possibility of a New International Division of Labour," *Economic Journal*, LIII, No. 210–211 (June–Sept. 1943).

Finally, within the broad category of manufactures, it is also possible to distinguish changes in the relative importance of various groups of manufactured commodities entering into world trade. A statistical study[22] has shown the following: (1) considering the total manufactured exports of leading manufacturing countries, it is observed that from 1899 to 1950 the commodities that constituted a higher proportion of the total trade were iron and steel, motor vehicles, industrial equipment, electrical goods, and agricultural equipment; (2) chemicals and non-ferrous metals maintained constant shares in the total; (3) textiles and apparel show the greatest rate of decline. All the trends are remarkably steady and continue throughout the period with considerable strength.

It is thus apparent that the volume and composition of world trade changed over the long run. These changes are related fundamentally to the emergence of different comparative cost structures as extensive development occurred and the levels of production and income altered in various countries. Any analysis of international trade and development must recognize the basic features of a continuously evolving comparative cost structure, the extent to which international markets may promote a country's development, and the manner in which intensive development within a country will influence the extensive development of the world economy in general.

3. The New Pattern of International Development

After World War I, the international economy lost its stable framework. General progress and a harmony of national interests were no longer characteristic of the international economy. Structural changes of the war, the relative decline of the British economy, the abandonment of the gold standard, the impact of the Great Depression in the 1930's, the control of international trade, and the extension of domestic planning for national objectives—all these contributed to mark the international economy of the interwar period as a period of disintegration. External stability was sacrificed for internal stability, and a series of short-period crises destroyed the productive long-run smoothness of the pre-1914 international economy. In such an environment the external springs of development practically dried up. "Beggar-my-neighbor" trading policies and the negligible international movement of factors prevented international trade from expanding and acting as an engine of growth.

Since World War II, the most notable feature of the international economy has been the attempt to fill the vacuum of the interwar

[22] H. Tyszynski, *op. cit.*, 283.

period with international organizations that would recreate by institutional methods the desirable features of the pre-1914 international setting. After the international disintegration of the interwar period, the establishment of the United Nations in 1945 was hailed as a recognition that the well-being of mankind is an international responsibility. Among the stated objectives of the world organization was the desire "to promote social progress and better standards of living in larger freedom" and "to employ international machinery for the promotion of the economic and social advancement of all peoples."[23] The Economic and Social Council, under the authority of the General Assembly and supported by the Specialized Agencies of the United Nations, became the arm of the world organization to promote "higher standards of living, full employment, and conditions of economic and social progress and development." Several of the Specialized Agencies of the United Nations have particular interests in international development. Most important economically are the International Monetary Fund (I.M.F.) and the International Bank for Reconstruction and Development (I.B.R.D. or World Bank).

The United States government also strongly endorsed the particular objectives of development in the poor countries. In 1949, President Truman launched the Point Four program of technical assistance as a "bold, new program for making the benefits of our scientific advances and industrial progress available for the improvement and growth of underdeveloped areas."

Through its Colombo Plan, adopted in 1950, the British Commonwealth has undertaken to promote the development of countries in South and Southeast Asia. The plan states that the "improvement in the welfare of the South and South-East Asian peoples is a vast human endeavour, and the community of free nations stands to gain immensely by it. . . . The conception of the Commonwealth countries' approach to the problem is that a fresh impetus should be given to economic development in South and South-East Asia in order to increase production, raise standards of living, and thus enlarge the volume of trade around the world from which all countries may benefit."[24]

The establishment of international organizations that are specifically designed to aid international development, and the enunciation of the Point Four program and the Colombo Plan all symbolize the present concern with economic development. Whereas nineteenth-century development proceeded almost spontaneously without design or plan,

[23] United Nations Charter, Article 55.
[24] Report by the Commonwealth Consultative Committee, *The Colombo Plan*, H.M.S.O., London, Cmd. 8080, Nov. 1950, 3.

there is now a conscious and active demand for development by both poor countries and rich countries.

The poor countries are no longer content with being quasi-stationary economies. Instead of playing a passive role, as so many countries did during the nineteenth century, the poor countries now wish development to be purposively accelerated. Many of their leaders believe that national and international government policies to introduce economic change are both necessary and possible. Against a background of poverty and hunger, and the realization of self-government in an increasing number of formerly colonial countries, the poor countries seek a new approach to the problem of raising their living standards through determined vigorous development. Indeed, there is a development ferment, and economic independence as well as political independence is widely sought. The question now is not whether change is to be allowed, but rather what will be the degree and speed of change.

Rich countries now also have a conscious interest in maintaining the development of their economies. The Great Depression focused attention on achieving full employment in the short run. But it is now recognized that the more fundamental problem is maintaining development so that full employment may be achieved over the long run without chronic deflation or inflation. Although the expansion that followed World War II allayed the fears of secular stagnation which were prominent in the 1930's, these fears are still latent, and it is recognized that retardation in the rate of development in rich capitalist economies may have serious consequences. So may the opposite situation of secular inflation.

Thus problems of development are now of major concern throughout the world economy. Poor countries wish to accelerate their development, and rich countries wish to maintain stable growth. The following chapters will consider in detail the nature of these problems and their policy implications.

As a comparison of the discussion in this Part with that in Part 3 will reveal, there are several notable differences between the setting of the development problem at the mid-twentieth century and the setting at the mid-nineteenth century. Some of these particular differences can be interpreted as being more favorable to present development, but other differences are less favorable. From the discussion in the next chapter, it may be seen, for example, that the poor countries now generally have a less favorable ratio of population to resources than did England or the other progressive economies in the nineteenth century. An additional limiting difference in the poor countries is their failure to have had previous agricultural and commercial revolutions, such as occurred in England during the seventeenth and eighteenth centuries to facilitate subsequent industrial development. It will also be noted that all the conditions that are included under the general characteristic of "backwardness" are differences that make the present problem of development more difficult than it was during the nineteenth century for the progressive economies. Further, the positions of the poor countries in the international economy differ from the nineteenth-century positions of the progressive economies, particularly with respect to the pattern of international trade, the freedom of international trade, and the relative importance of the international migration of factors.

Some favorable differences, however, will be recognized from the discussion of the general requirements for development in Chapter 16 and policy issues in Chapters 17–20. It will be apparent that in having "a late start" the poor countries can advantageously avoid some of the costs and mistakes of nineteenth-century development and can borrow some of the achievements of the rich countries without having to repeat for themselves the whole course of development of the already developed countries. Another favorable difference is the intense determination and eagerness that governments of the poor countries have for development. Not only was the deliberate objective of development unknown in the nineteenth century, but so too were the various policy measures that might achieve them. Now the challenging question is whether the possibilities of deriving development from the rich countries and having the government exercise a more active role in promoting development will allow the poor countries to telescope the sequence of their development and shorten its time span.

PART 3

Accelerating

Development

in

Poor

Countries

"I sell here, Sir, what all the world desires to have—Power."

— JAMES WATT

AGAINST THE BACKGROUND OF THE MAJOR THEORIES of economic development and some features of the historical course of international development, we may now focus directly on the contemporary problem of accelerating development in the poor countries.

This problem raises five major questions: (1) What are the characteristics of the poor countries? (2) What obstacles have limited their development? (3) What are the general requirements for their development? (4) What domestic policies might fulfill these requirements? (5) What international policies might fulfill these requirements? The chapters in this Part consider each of these questions in turn.

Answers to these questions are vitally important. For the stakes of development are high. If the efforts to accelerate development are well-conceived and successfully executed, the benefits will be great, embodying not only economic gains but also social and political achievements.

The answers offered in this Part, however, are not intended to be definitive. They should be interpreted as being simply suggestive rather than conclusive. For our objective is the relatively limited one of providing a general framework within which more detailed studies of specific developmental problems and policies can be incorporated. In seeking generality, our discussion cannot say as much as more specific studies would say about the sociocultural aspects of development, the particular problems of individual countries, and the exact programs and policies that have been proposed or adopted in individual countries. Discussion of these topics calls for case studies on a country-by-country basis. Case studies can also provide the remedy to whatever errors of overgeneralization we shall commit. But to be meaningful these specific studies should first be set within a general framework such as will be provided in this Part.

Chapter 13

Basic Characteristics

of Poor Countries (1)

In examining the problems of poor countries it is useful at the outset to have in mind a general portrait of what constitutes a poor country. What are the general economic characteristics of poor countries? To ask this question may seem illegitimate in view of so many case studies that demonstrate a wide variety of differences among poor countries. It would certainly be difficult to locate a representative poor country on the map. Nevertheless, it is possible to focus on some fundamental characteristics common to many poor countries. For it may be said that a poor country has in essence six basic economic characteristics: (1) it is primary-producing, (2) it faces population pressures, (3) it has underdeveloped natural resources, (4) it has an economically backward population, (5) it is capital-deficient, and (6) it is foreign trade-oriented.

All these characteristics are not found to the same degree in all poor countries; nor are these the only characteristics of a poor country. But in broad terms these characteristics can be interpreted as typical, and in combination they portray a type.

This chapter elaborates the first two characteristics, primary production and population pressures, and the next chapter considers the other four characteristics.

1. Primary Production

Raw materials and foodstuffs dominate the structure of production in a poor country.   The high percentage of the labor force in agriculture and the large percentage contribution of agriculture to national income

TABLE 13.1.   ECONOMICALLY ACTIVE POPULATION IN
AGRICULTURE AND MANUFACTURING

Country	Total Economically Active Male Population (thousands)	Agriculture (thousands)	Manufacturing (thousands)
Rich Countries:			
Australia (1947)	2,479	474	617
Canada (1951)	4,131	970	1,086
Denmark (1953)	1,389	381	391
Netherlands (1947)	2,923	578	5,813
New Zealand (1951)	569	126	136
United Kingdom (1951)	15,662	998	5,813
United States (1950)	43,542	6,720	12,215
Poor Countries:			
Bolivia (1950)	512	275	65
Ceylon (1946)	2,042	1,032	201
Chile (1952)	1,551	595	247
Costa Rica (1950)	230	144	23
Egypt (1947)	7,058	3,656	609
El Salvador (1950)	545	399	50
Haiti (1950)	873	771	37
India (1951)	85,461	59,313	8,078
Malaya (1947)	1,463	889	125
Mexico (1950)	7,208	4,824	973
Nicaragua (1950)	284	218	27
Pakistan (1951)	21,100	16,096	1,306
Puerto Rico (1950)	459	216	49
Thailand (1947)	1,463	889	125
Venezuela (1950)	1,403	669	124

Source: United Nations, Statistical Yearbook 1955, New York, 1955, Table 6.

indicate the concentration in primary production.   Tables 13.1 and 13.2 illustrate the general pattern of the great relative importance of primary production in poor countries.   In Asia, Africa, and the Middle East, from two-thirds to more than four-fifths of the population earn their living in agriculture, and, in most Latin American countries, from two-

TABLE 13.2. INDUSTRIAL ORIGIN OF NET DOMESTIC
PRODUCT, PERCENTAGE DISTRIBUTION

Country	Agriculture, Forestry, Fishing	Manufacturing
Rich Countries:		
Canada (1954)	9	29
Denmark (1954)	19	29
Germany, Western (1954)	11	49
Netherlands (1954)	13	36
United Kingdom (1954)	5	38
United States (1954)	6	30
Poor Countries:		
Belgian Congo (1953)	34	6
Burma (1954)	44	10
China (1953)	38	16
Chile (1952)	17	21
Colombia (1953)	40	17
Ecuador (1950)	39	16
El Salvador (1950)	53	8
Egypt (1953)	32	8
Greece (1953)	38	19
Guatemala (1949)	46	20
Honduras (1952)	54	10
Indonesia (1952)	56	8
Kenya (1953)	41	12
Nicaragua (1950)	40	14
Nigeria (1952–1953)	66	2
Pakistan (1953)	59	8
Paraguay (1953)	50	19
Thailand (1952)	49	11
Turkey (1953)	52	10

Source: United Nations, *Statistical Yearbook 1955*, New York, 1955, Table 158; United Nations, *Monthly Bulletin of Statistics*, March 1956, xvii–xxi.

thirds to three-fourths of the population work in agriculture. Of the total population of the world, some 60 per cent, or approximately 1.3 billion people, depend upon agriculture; of these, over 1 billion live in Asia, Africa, Central and South America, and only some 160 million in Europe and North America.

Some poor countries are also highly dependent on non-agricultural primary production, that is, minerals. Poor countries account for a very high proportion of the world's production of tin, aluminum, copper, nitrates, manganese, diamonds, chromium, tungsten, and petroleum. In most mineral industries, although the smaller mines are domestically owned, many of the larger mining companies are organized and controlled by industrial countries. The large amount of capital needed, the financial risk involved, and the managerial and technical skills required hamper the establishment of domestic enterprises. The main markets for the mineral output lie in industrial countries, and, because of the limited degree of industrialization in the poor countries, only a small fraction of the output, unlike foodstuffs, can be used domestically. From the standpoint of the country's development, the direct physical effect of the minerals industry is therefore less significant than the benefits derived from its role as an earner of foreign exchange.

Concentration on primary production is understandable in so far as the relative factor supply in poor countries normally favors specialization in labor-intensive or land-intensive primary products. This specialization frequently concentrates on only two or three commodities: for example, in Ceylon, tea, rubber, and coconut products; Indonesia, rubber, tin, and oil; Malaya, rubber, tin, and palm oil; Pakistan, jute and cotton. In a few extreme cases, monoculture, the production of a single product, may exist.

Although there is generally some industry, this consists mainly of the processing of agricultural products, the production of agricultural implements, or the simple manufacture of textiles, and light industries of minor importance. Traditional handicraft industries account for most of the manufacturing employment. In a few poor countries, industry may be more prominent; but generally only a small percentage of the economically active population is engaged in manufacturing, as may be noted in Table 13.1. And, for all the poor countries, there has not been the relative decline in the economic importance of land such as has occurred in the richest countries.

Since the economies of poor countries are based so much on the land, the conditions of land tenure are significant. These systems vary considerably. The ownership unit may be the tribe, village, family, or individual. Different types of ownership may also exist in combination, as in the Middle East; or, as in Greece, Turkey, and Cyprus, arable land may be mostly individually owned, and grazing land village-owned. In many sections of the world the land is in the hands of a few owners, often absentee owners. In some cases peasant proprietorship is established, but in many countries tenancy is an outstanding feature of systems of land ownership. In Syria, for example, it is estimated that about half the land is owned by large landowners, and cultivated by small share tenants; in southern Iraq, large landowners own most of the land, letting it to share tenants through a series of intermediary lessees.[1] Where

[1] United Nations, Department of Economic Affairs, *Land Reform,* New York, 1951, 14.

tenancy exists, the land is often fragmented into strip parcels and scattered holdings. Systems of inheritance according to which every son receives a parcel of land, or every daughter receives land as dowry, also make for a continual division of fields and the scattering of arable land of a farmer over a wide area. Moreover, many tenure systems are custom-bound and semi-feudal, without well-defined rights and obligations between landlords and tenants.

The extremes of very large and very small landholdings are also reflected in the contrasting types of plantation and peasant farming. Cultivation by peasants on farms of extremely small size is a salient feature of the agrarian structure in many poor countries—particularly in India, Southeast Asia, the Caribbean, and Egypt. Peasant cultivation has been generally maintained and even increased in the cultivation of those products which are either marketed without processing, or which require only the application of simple processes within the financial and technical capacity of the native smallholders. Subsistence crops for the personal use of the grower are under peasant cultivation. The greater part of agricultural production in the tropics is still of this character, being intended for direct consumption by the family or the village. Cash crops, however, are grown for sale under a variety of systems: plantation, peasant, and mixed. Some cash crops that are mainly for export are rubber, sisal, cotton, tea, coffee, cacao, sugar, palm oil and kernels, coconuts, rice, groundnuts (peanuts), jute, and bananas. Of these, tea, coffee, sugar, and sisal are mainly plantation crops, whereas groundnuts, rice, and jute are usually peasant crops. Most agricultural products, however, are grown under mixed conditions of both peasant and plantation type of cultivation. When peasants cultivate the crops the scale of operation is small, and the quality of production may be low because of the limited amount of capital, inadequate cash reserves, lack of storage facilities, and the narrow markets confronting the peasant.

Plantations or large estates involve large centrally managed and operated units of production employing hundreds or thousands of low-paid workers. The plantation system of cultivation usually prevails if a single crop must be planted over an extensive area to obtain a marketable bulk; if the returns from the investment are long deferred and large amounts of financing are required; or if equipment is needed to prepare the product for the market—in short, where high standards of cultivation, superior techniques of production, wide knowledge of market conditions, and extensive distributing and servicing organizations are necessary.

Whether plantation or peasant cultivation is followed depends generally on the relative density of population, the relative cheapness of production in large and small units, capital requirements, and the degree to which factory equipment is required for processing. In some cases, plantation owners may sublet part of their land to be cultivated by peasants under the supervision of the plantation management, and the factory then obtains the produce by contract from peasant growers.

Not only does the type of land utilization vary among crops, but it may also differ among countries for the same crop. For example, oil palms have been planted by plantations in Malaya and Sumatra, but in Nigeria peasant cultivation dominates; cacao is produced by peasants in West Africa, but by plantations in Ceylon and Ecuador, and under both forms in Trinidad. Such diversity is to be expected in so far as the countries differ according to technical conditions, labor supply, and governmental policies regarding land tenure.

The extent of plantation production has generally declined, but it still survives in nearly all the tropical and subtropical cultivated areas of the world. Sugar is plantation-cultivated in Cuba, Puerto Rico, Jamaica, Mexico, Brazil, British and Portuguese Africa; tobacco in Mexico and British and Portuguese Africa; bananas in Central America; coffee in Brazil, Colombia, Indonesia, Kenya, and Tanganyika; cacao in Brazil; coconuts in British and Portuguese Africa; pineapples and rubber in India, Malaya, and the Dutch East Indies; citrus fruits in Southern Rhodesia; and tea in India, Ceylon, and East Africa.

A final point associated with primary production should be emphasized—the low agricultural productivity in poor countries. The level of output per acre is generally lower than it is in the rich countries; the level of output per person in agriculture is even much lower, as the density of the farm population per acre is generally greater, and the average yield per acre is less. In general, production per head of the farm population in North America and Northwest Europe appears to be 10 to 20 times greater than in the Far East, Near East, and Latin America.[2] When the output per person in agriculture averages approximately 2½ tons, as it does in North America, the standard of living of the farm population will obviously be higher than where it is less than one-quarter of a ton, as in Asia, or one-seventh of a ton, as in Africa.[3]

There are several reasons for the low agricultural productivity in

[2] United Nations, Department of Economic and Social Affairs, *Proceedings of the World Population Conference 1954*, New York, 1955, 107.

[3] United Nations, *Monthly Bulletin of Food and Agricultural Statistics*, II, No. 9, Washington, D. C.

poor countries: low ratio of land to worker, inferior soils, inefficient land-use patterns, low quality of the worker, small amount of capital in use, inefficient techniques of production, inadequate knowledge of better methods of production, and inefficient methods of organizing agricultural production.

A major limitation on productivity is the low amount of land per worker.[4] There is normally a high positive correlation between a large amount of land per worker and high output per worker. But as Table 13.3 shows, the ratio of land resources to population is lowest in the

TABLE 13.3. RELATION OF LAND TO POPULATION

Country	Year	Cultivated Land per Capita (net acres)
Afghanistan	1947	0.10
Brazil	1947	0.37
Burma	1947	0.47
Ceylon	1950	0.17
Chile	1946	1.01
Colombia	1946	0.19
Cuba	1946	0.37
Egypt	1948	0.12
El Salvador	1947	0.20
Haiti	1947	0.12
India	1947	0.29
Indonesia	1947	0.15
Kenya	1948	0.29
Korea	1948	0.15
Lebanon	1949	0.17
Malaya	1948	0.42
Nigeria	1947	0.21
Pakistan	1948	0.28
Peru	1948	0.19

Source: United Nations, Department of Economic Affairs, *Land Reform,* New York, 1951, 96–100.

poor countries. Whereas cultivated land per worker is high in such sparsely settled countries as Canada and Australia, it is less than 1 acre per person in Egypt, Haiti, Korea, Indonesia, Lebanon, Ceylon, India. The low ratio of land to worker could possibly be overcome by greater use of capital, better techniques of production, or more efficient

[4] The "amount of land per worker," however, is not an exact concept in so far as "land" differs in quality, and physical units of land do not reveal these qualitative differences.

organization. But poor countries also suffer on these counts. Since capital is deficient in supply, agriculture as a field for investment must compete with other uses of capital, and these alternatives may be much more attractive for whatever capital is available. And in so far as labor is the relatively abundant factor, and wages are low, there is little inducement to substitute capital for labor.

Another major limitation to higher agricultural productivity is the use of inefficient production techniques. In many poor countries production methods have changed but little over the centuries. Where peasant cultivation prevails, the knowledge of better production methods has increased only slowly, if at all. Knowledge of plant nutrition remains rudimentary. In some cases a crop rotation that would reduce the waste of land in fallow and increase output has not yet been introduced. The use of chemical fertilizers is still largely confined to countries with high agricultural yields: in 1954–1955, Europe accounted for 45 per cent of the total world use of commercial nitrogenous fertilizers; North America, 32 per cent; Latin America, 4 per cent; Near East, 3 per cent; Far East, 16 per cent; Africa, less than 1 per cent.[5] Except in specialized plantations, knowledge of the adaptation of plant and animal strains is also extremely limited in countries of low productivity.

Manual labor and animal draft power also still predominate. In 1954, North America had 68 per cent of the world's tractors; Europe, about 23 per cent; Latin America, 3 per cent; the Near and Far East, 1 per cent; and Africa, 2 per cent.[6] And whereas the number of acres of arable land per tractor in 1951 was only 119 in the United States and 247 in Canada, it was 24,710 in Guatemala, 20,398 in India, and as high as 271,810 in Indonesia.[7]

The type of land tenure may also be incompatible with the most effective methods of production. Many of the land tenure systems impair productive efficiency in two general ways: through excessive subdivision of the land into numerous small uneconomic holdings, and by limiting the incentive to make productive improvements. Extremely small farm holdings may result from the subdivision of farms because of the pressure of population on the land, from inequality in the distribution of land ownership, or from the practice of subdividing inherited land among all the male heirs. When the holdings consist of widely scattered and fragmented parcels of land it is difficult to use draft

[5] Food and Agriculture Organization of the United Nations, *Yearbook of Food and Agricultural Statistics,* Rome, 1956, 213.

[6] *Ibid.,* 222.

[7] W. S. Woytinsky and E. S. Woytinsky, *World Population and Production,* Twentieth Century Fund, New York, 1953, 515–517.

animals or agricultural machinery, crop rotation is limited, considerable effort is wasted in moving from one plot to another, and irrigation projects are restricted. The incentive to make permanent improvements is also discouraged by periodic reallocation of land, uncertainty as to ownership and control, short leases, rack-renting, arbitrary evictions, absentee landlords, excessive rentals, and chronic indebtedness of the tenants.

2. Population Pressures

The emphasis on primary production leads to the next characteristic, population pressures. These pressures take three principal forms: (1) many poor countries have rural underemployment, (2) high birth rates create a large number of dependent children per adult, and (3) falling death rates with high birth rates bring about a rapid increase in population. It is better to concentrate directly on these specific features of the population structure, rather than attempting to compare the population of a poor country with some notion of an "optimum population." For when the supply of factors and technology are changing over time the concept of an optimum population becomes too elusive.[8]

From the standpoint of development, what really matters about the population structure in many poor countries is that labor is the relatively abundant factor, per capita output is low, and the supply of labor remains larger than the demand for labor. Unlike the situation that generally prevails in a rich industrial country, the marginal product of labor in a poor country is negligible, zero, or even negative. When one sector of the economy expands, such as the export sector, it can then

---

[8] "Overpopulation" usually refers to a population larger than the "optimum population"—an optimum population being defined as one that maximizes per capita output, given the other inputs and state of technology. In this sense, so long as there are increasing returns to scale in the economy, population may be less than optimum. But, after a point, as population increases, the rate of rise of output per head slows down, until eventually in conformity with the classical and neo-classical principle of diminishing returns output per head declines as population grows. The market will have reached a size that has enabled a large part of all potential economies of large-scale production to have been realized, so that the disadvantages of having to employ additional labor with only a constant amount of land and capital will begin to outweigh the advantages of production on a larger scale. Beyond this point, a larger than optimum population will be reached. This interpretation of an optimum population, however, has no precise meaning in a dynamic context.

Cf. H. Leibenstein, *Theory of Economic-Demographic Development,* Princeton University Press, Princeton, 1954, Chapter IX; E. F. Penrose, *Population Theories and Their Application,* Stanford University, Food Research Institute, 1934, 47–91.

draw on a pool of labor from the subsistence sector of the economy without causing a rise in real wages.[9]

This phenomenon of "disguised" or "concealed unemployment" frequently appears in agriculture and services.[10]   If there are three persons trying to till an amount of land that could be tilled as well by only two persons, then only two of these are really fully employed, and the other one represents disguised unemployment.   Disguised unemployment is usually associated with family employment where the unit of production and the supply of labor is the family who work on their own account, not for wages.   A large number of children in the family provides not only additional workers but may also be a source of status in the community.   The disguised unemployment exists because the resources of the family are too small to keep all working members of the family fully employed throughout the year and because there exist no alternative opportunities for redirecting a part of the excess labor supply away into other occupations at appropriate times.   If such rural underemployment exists, labor can be withdrawn from agriculture without reducing agricultural output, even though no significant reorganization of production or substitution of capital occurred in this sector.

Quantitative measurement of this underemployment is difficult, and observers differ in their estimates of its extent.   A United Nations report states that for many regions of India and Pakistan, parts of the Philippines, and Indonesia the surplus agricultural population is between 20 per cent and 25 per cent.[11]   Unemployment and underemployment in India may annually waste as many gross man-years of labor as is contributed by the entire labor force of the United States.[12]   A general estimate is that in densely populated areas perhaps as much as 25 per cent of the agricultural labor force could be withdrawn without diminishing agricultural output.[13]   However, a few economists have questioned

[9] Cf. W. A. Lewis, "Economic Development with Unlimited Supplies of Labour," *Manchester School of Economic and Social Studies, XXII,* No. 2, 141–144 (May 1954).

[10] Cf. P. T. Bauer and B. S. Yamey, "Economic Progress and Occupational Distribution," *Economic Journal, LXI,* No. 244, 742–744 (Dec. 1951); United Nations, Department of Economic Affairs, *Measures for the Economic Development of Under-Developed Countries,* New York, 1951, 7–8; R. L. Meier, *Science and Economic Development,* Technology Press and John Wiley & Sons, New York, 1956, 171.

[11] United Nations, *Measures for the Economic Development of Under-Developed Countries,* New York, 1951, 9.

[12] C. Wolf, Jr., and S. C. Sufrin, *Capital Formation and Foreign Investment in Underdeveloped Areas,* Syracuse University Press, Syracuse, 1955, 13–14.

[13] N. S. Buchanan and H. S. Ellis, *Approaches to Economic Development,* Twentieth Century Fund, New York, 1955, 45; R. Nurkse, *Problems of Capital Formation in Underdeveloped Countries,* Basil Blackwell, Oxford, 1953, 35.

whether there actually is any disguised unemployment in agriculture.[14] Although there is certainly a need for more and better empirical evidence, most observers do believe that labor is usually the most wasted resource in most poor countries.

The second striking contrast between the demographic patterns of rich and poor countries is the fact that a much higher proportion of the total population in poor countries is in younger age groups, and life expectancy is much lower than in rich countries. For example, the percentage of the population below 15 years of age is about 40 per cent in Asia, Africa, and Latin America, but only about 25 per cent in the United States and 23 per cent in the United Kingdom. And, whereas the average expectation of life of a newborn male child is about 66 years in the United States and Canada, 69 years in Norway, and 67 years in England, it is less than 40 years in parts of Asia and the Far East, the Middle East, and Latin America, and as low as 35 years in Egypt and 32 years in India.[15] In poor countries the mortality rates in the younger age groups are appreciably higher than in rich countries, and the productive years remaining to those who do not die in childhood are much fewer. If the economically productive age bracket is taken as 15 to 64 years, the proportion of population in this category is considerably less in poor countries than in rich countries.[16] The "bottom heavy" age structure of population results in a large number of dependents and in a relative deficiency of adult manpower. This reduces the differentiation and productive power of the labor force, and it also entails a greater burden of consumption since a larger proportion of children means a larger proportion of non-producers to producers. The

[14]Although Schultz was a member of the committee that issued the United Nations report referred to in footnote 11, above, he now questions the actual existence of this underemployment and states that he knows "of no evidence for any poor country anywhere that would even suggest that a transfer of some small fraction, say, 5 per cent, of the existing labor force out of agriculture, with other things equal, could be made without reducing its production." See T. W. Schultz, "The Role of Government in Promoting Economic Growth," in L. D. White (ed.), *The State of the Social Sciences,* University of Chicago Press, Chicago, 1956, 375.

[15] United Nations, *Demographic Yearbook 1955,* Statistical Office of the United Nations, New York, 1955, Table 32.

[16] In Africa, the percentage of total population between ages 15 and 64 in 1947 was approximately 56 per cent; in Asia, 57 per cent; in Latin America, 55 per cent. Although a fall in death rates will lengthen the average span of economically active life of each successive generation, this will not improve the balance between the productive and dependent parts of the population unless there is also a corresponding fall in birth rates. It is primarily the birth rate that determines the age structure. If death rates fall while birth rates remain constant, each successive generation will be larger in size but the average number of dependent children per adult will be practically unchanged.

unfavorable age structure of the population, due primarily to high birth rates and high mortality rates, requires the economy to devote a considerable part of its resources to the maintenance of children who die before reaching a productive age.

The Malthusian fear of population growth has relevance to many poor countries. In the densely populated rural areas of Egypt, India, Java, and most of the Caribbean there is a constant struggle against the law of diminishing returns. In 1954, the average population density per square kilometer in India was 115 persons; Ceylon, 128; Puerto Rico, 251; Trinidad, 136. A high population density, however, does not characterize all poor countries: in 1954, the density per square kilometer in Chile was only 9; Kenya, 10; Thailand, 39; Nigeria, 34; Guatemala, 29; Cuba, 51; Mexico, 15; Colombia, 11; Iraq, 11; Turkey, 30; Gold Coast, 20.[17]

Nonetheless, even though not all the poor countries are now densely populated, the rate of population growth is, or gives indications of becoming, a serious problem for most poor countries. Three types of demographic development can be recognized: those of "high growth potential" (high fertility rate and high but declining mortality rate), "transitional" (declining fertility and mortality rates), and "low growth potential" (low and declining fertility and mortality rates).[18]

Some poor countries have high birth rates but also high death rates, and there is a rough balance so that population growth is small. Included among countries in this phase are Afghanistan, China, Indonesia, some African countries, and parts of South America. Many poor countries, however, are in the high growth potential phase and have high birth rates which show no clear indication of downward trend—Egypt, Central Africa, much of the Near East, almost all of Asia, islands of the Pacific and Caribbean, and much of Central and South America.[19] The populations are designated as high growth potential because the birth rates are very high and sufficiently resistant to change for population growth to be large whenever the mortality rate falls. The contrast between birth rates in the rich and poor countries is especially striking, as Table 13.4 shows.

[17] United Nations, *op. cit.,* Table 1. The density in rich countries varies considerably: in 1954, the density per square kilometer in the United States was 21; Canada, 2; Denmark, 103; Netherlands, 328; United Kingdom, 245.

[18] Cf. F. W. Notestein, "The Population of the World in the Year 2000," *Journal of the American Statistical Association, XLV,* No. 251, 335–345 (Sept. 1950); W. S. Thompson, "Population," *American Journal of Sociology, XXXIV,* No. 6, 959–975 (May 1929).

[19] F. W. Notestein, "Population—The Long View," in T. W. Schultz (ed.), *Food for the World,* University of Chicago Press, Chicago, 1945, 48.

Even though all poor countries do not now confront a Malthusian problem, nonetheless many certainly do, and many others will face the problem in the future if present trends continue. As Table 13.5 indicates, the populations of most poor countries are of the high-growth-potential type. Fertility rates and mortality rates are high, and neither

TABLE 13.4. CRUDE BIRTH AND DEATH RATES,
SELECTED COUNTRIES, 1955

	Birth Rate (per 1000 population)	Death Rate (per 1000 population)
Rich Countries:		
Belgium	16.7	12.6
Canada	28.3	8.1
Denmark	17.3	8.8
France	18.4	12.0
Norway	18.7	8.3
Sweden	14.8	9.4
United Kingdom	15.4	11.7
United States	24.6	9.3
Poor Countries:		
Ceylon	37.9	11.0
Chile	35.0	12.8
Costa Rica	51.4	10.5
Dominican Republic	43.6	9.5
Ecuador	44.0	16.1
El Salvador	47.0	13.9
Guatemala	51.7	18.5
Honduras	41.9	11.2
India	30.5	12.7
Malaya	43.8	12.2
Mexico	46.4	13.1
Peru	30.0	9.1
Puerto Rico	34.8	7.1
Trinidad	41.6	10.2
Venezuela	47.1	10.2

Source: United Nations, Statistical Office of the United Nations, Monthly Bulletin of Statistics, X, No. 7, 6–10 (July 1956).

natality nor mortality has passed under any reasonably secure control in these countries. As modern medicine becomes more widely applied in these countries, the fall in the death rate, without a corresponding fall in the birth rate, will result in rapid population growth. And, unlike during the nineteenth century, the possibilities for population outlets through international migration are now limited by economic, cultural, and political obstacles.

Progress in controlling disease-bearing insects and the discovery of modern drugs now make it possible to control and diminish death rates much more rapidly and at lower per capita cost than was ever possible in the cases of development in Western Europe. For example, the change in mortality that took place in the few years between 1940 and the early 1950's in British Guiana, Chile, and Malaya is equivalent to the change that occurred in Scandinavia between 1850 and 1912, and

TABLE 13.5. WORLD POPULATION, GROWTH RATES, BIRTH
RATES, AND DEATH RATES

Area	Annual Increase 1920–1950 (per thousand)	Annual Rates, 1946–1948 (per thousand)		
		Birth	Death	Natural Increase
World	9	35–37	22–25	11–14
Low-growth-potential type				
N.W. Central Europe	6	19	12	7
North America	13	25	10	15
South America*	9	23	12	11
Oceania	14	28	12	16
High-growth-potential type				
Far East	5	40–45	30–38	7–13
South Central Asia	11	40–45	25–30	12–18
Africa	13	40–45	25–30	12–18
Near East	10	40–45	30–35	7–13
Transitional†				
Soviet Union and E. Europe	7	28	18	10
Latin America*	19	40	17	23
Japan	14	31	15	16

* On the basis of more recent data, much of Central and South America should be classified under "high growth potential."

† Transitional populations are in transition from a high-growth-potential state to one of low growth potential.

Source: J. J. Spengler, "Demographic Patterns," in H. F. Williamson and J. A. Buttrick (eds.), Economic Development, Prentice-Hall, New York, 1954, 88.

in Belgium between 1890 and 1920. The death rate in Puerto Rico fell from 30 per 1000 in 1900, to 18 in 1940, and to 7.6 in 1955. The Mexican death rate fell from approximately 27 in 1930 to 13 in 1954. In Trinidad, a two-year campaign against tuberculosis cut the death rate from this disease from 100 per 100,000 to 64 per 100,000. Ceylon provides one of the most striking examples of a reduction in mortality: at a cost of only about 22 cents per person in the area treated, the use of D.D.T. to control malaria allowed the death rate to fall from 20.2 per 1000 in 1946 to 14.3 in 1947; in 1954, the death rate was only one-half of what it was in 1946; and, whereas life expectancy was only 32 years in 1920, it rose to 60 years in 1954. On the basis of data for 15 poor countries, Table 13.6 shows that the crude death rate dropped by 53 per cent during the 30 years from 1920–1924 to 1950–1954. The table also indicates that the diminution has been accelerating.

TABLE 13.6. PERCENTAGE DECLINE OF CRUDE DEATH RATES IN POOR COUNTRIES

Periods	Number of Countries Compared*	Average Per Cent Decline from Previous Period
Half-decade changes		
1920–1924	—	—
1925–1929	15	6.0
1930–1934	16	4.6
1935–1939	18	6.3
1940–1944	16	8.5
1945–1949	16	15.2
1950–1954	18	20.1
30-Year change		
1920–1924	—	—
1950–1954	15	53.1

* Eighteen countries were used, but in some cases data were missing for one or both periods compared. The countries used were: Barbados, Costa Rica, Ceylon, Cyprus, Egypt, El Salvador, Fiji, Formosa, Jamaica, Malaya, Mauritius, Mexico, Panama, Philippines, Puerto Rico, Surinam, Thailand, and Trinidad and Tobago.

Source: K. Davis, "The Unpredicted Pattern of Population Change," The Annals, 56, May 1956. Computed from death rates as reported in the United Nations Demographic Yearbook, 1953, 1954, and Population and Vital Statistics Reports, Oct. 1955.

Unless fertility rates also fall sharply, the expected decline in mortality rates will cause many poor countries to experience within two or three generations much greater increases in population than occurred in Western Europe during the nineteenth century. For example, although Latin America is still relatively sparsely populated, its rate of population growth is among the highest in the world: if the present rate of growth continues, the population will double itself every 40 years. Between the censuses of 1926 and 1951, the African population of Southern Rhodesia doubled, and it is now probably doubling itself in 20 years rather than 25 years. In view of the growth of the Egyptian population, it has been estimated that, even if the amount of arable land in Egypt could be doubled, it would be only 50 years before the population would again overtake the land expansion, and the problem of population pressure would again have to be faced. The annual rate of population growth in Malaya is nearly 4 per cent, which will double the population in about 18 years. And in India the population is increasing at the rate of 4,500,000 to 5,000,000 a year, and it is estimated that annually there are about 2,000,000 new entrants into the labor market. Table 13.7 summarizes the population growth in 38 poor countries from 1935

TABLE 13.7. POPULATION GROWTH IN POOR AND RICH
COUNTRIES, 1935–1955

		Per Cent Gain, 1935–1955	
		Unweighted	Weighted
Types of Countries	Number of Countries	Average	Average*
Poor†	38	51.2	37.4
Rich:			
European‡	10	15.6	11.6
New World§	6	38.8	32.6

* Weighted by population of each country.
† Angola, Brazil, Burma, Ceylon, Chile, Colombia, Costa Rica, Cuba, Cyprus, Egypt, El Salvador, Fiji, Formosa, Gold Coast, Greece, Guatemala, Honduras, India, Jamaica, Malaya and Singapore, Mauritius, Mexico, Nicaragua, North Borneo, Northern Rhodesia, Nyasaland, Panama, Philippines, Puerto Rico, Ruanda-Urundi, Southern Rhodesia, Tanganyika, Thailand, Trinidad and Tobago, Turkey, Uganda, Venezuela, Yugoslavia.
‡ Belgium, Denmark, Finland, France, Italy, Netherlands, Norway, Sweden, Switzerland, United Kingdom.
§ Argentina, Australia, Canada, New Zealand, Union of South Africa, United States.

Source: Davis, *op. cit.,* 54.

to 1955 and contrasts this growth with the much lower rate of growth in rich countries. If the rates of growth are continued, more than half of the 38 countries will double their populations in less than 40 years, and the combined population of all of them in less than 50 years.

Instead of comparing rates of population growth in poor and rich countries, it is more meaningful to compare the growth in poor countries with the growth rates that occurred in the now rich industrial nations when they were in earlier phases of their development. Table 13.8 shows that the countries of Northwestern Europe grew during previous periods at a rate less than half that shown by the poor countries. Moreover, in the past the decline of the death rate in industrializing countries was mainly due to the development process itself—improved diets, better

TABLE 13.8.   POPULATION GROWTH IN
RICH COUNTRIES, 1800–1940

(Per Cent Gain during Previous Twenty Years)

1820	1840	1860	1880	1900	1920	1940
23.1	17.2	19.7	18.1	19.9	18.0	14.1

Source: Davis, op. cit., 55.
Countries included: Denmark, Finland, France, Great Britain, Netherlands, Norway, Sweden, Switzerland.

housing, sanitation. Now, however, mortality rates are falling in poor
countries not because of development but because the modern medical
knowledge and scientific techniques of death control can be readily
transferred from the rich countries and applied in non-industrial areas.
Modern medical and public health advances have tended to make the
decline in death rates independent trends in economic development and
social change.   And, whereas European industrial countries began
lowering their birth rates before their sharpest declines in mortality, the

TABLE 13.9.   ESTIMATES OF POSSIBLE GROWTH RATES,
1950–1980, BY CONTINENTS

Estimated Population (millions) 1980

Continent	1950	"High" Estimate	"Medium" Estimate	"Low" Estimate
World	2454	3990	3628	3295
Africa	198	327	289	255
America	330	577	535	487
North America	168	240	223	207
Latin America	162	337	312	280
Asia	1320	2227	2011	1816
Europe	593	840	776	721
Oceania	13.0	19.2	17.5	16.1

Source: United Nations, Department of Economic and Social Affairs,
Proceedings of the World Population Conference 1954, New York, 1955, 77.

poor countries now will not do so until long after their mortality has
reached a modern low level.[20]

Table 13.9 presents some projections of future populations in 1980
for various regions, based on "high," "medium," and "low" expectations
of growth rates.   On the medium assumption, the increase in population
between 1950 and 1980 will be 46 per cent for Africa, 52 per cent for

[20] Cf. Davis, "The Unpredicted Pattern of Population Change," The Annals,
56–57, May 1956.

Asia, and 92 per cent for Latin America, in contrast with 33 per cent for North America and 31 per cent for Europe. Although population forecasts are frequently very wide of the mark, most demographers agree that poor countries will experience rapid population growth in the future. These countries will therefore confront the problem of having to accelerate their rates of development in order to outstrip their rates of population increase. Otherwise, there will simply be more people at the subsistence level. Thus, many poor countries are already experiencing population pressures, and other poor countries may face a population problem in a relatively short time, unless their rates of development are accelerated. In this respect the classical analysis has considerable relevance: potential increases in population threaten to absorb increases in production.

Chapter 14

Basic Characteristics
of Poor Countries (2)

1. Underdevelopment

The economy of a poor country can also be said to be under-developed in the sense that there are natural resources that are underdeveloped. Without using complementary natural resources, labor and capital can make only a limited contribution to national income. It might, accordingly, be thought that, besides capital deficiency, another characteristic of poor countries is a deficiency of natural resources. Yet it is difficult to maintain that any country has an absolute deficiency of resources. At most, this might perhaps be said of such areas as Antarctica and some large desert tracts in Asia and Africa. But even in these cases it is highly questionable whether the areas are poor in resources in any absolute sense, since the usefulness of resources depends on technical knowledge, demand conditions, and new discoveries. The discussion of the Industrial Revolution should have shown that the concept of an economic resource is always relative to the given state of technology, and that there are innumerable examples of how the relative scarcity of some irreproducible natural resource has been overcome by a change in technology or the substitution of a new resource. Although a country may now be poor in resources, it is entirely possible that in

the future it may become rich in resources as a result of the discovery
of presently unknown resources or because new uses may be found for
the known resources. Instead of saying that poor countries are inexorably deficient in natural resources, it is more reasonable to say that
they are poor because they have not succeeded in overcoming the
scarcity of natural resources by appropriate changes in technology and
social and economic organization.

A detailed survey of the natural resources in poor countries cannot
be undertaken here.[1] A few examples, however, may dispel the belief
that these countries are absolutely deficient in resources. As for land
resources, the great areas of underdeveloped soil are in the poor countries of Latin America, Africa, and Asia. India still has about 90 million
acres of "cultivable wasteland," and the vast irrigation projects undertaken in India during the last five or six decades demonstrate how
millions of arable acres can be added. The wasteland in Burma that
can be converted to farm land is estimated at 19 million acres, almost
as much as the present cultivated area. Irrigation could increase the
arable land in Iraq from 6 million acres to 20 million; in Syria, from
4 million to 10 million acres; and Turkey could enlarge its crop area
from 25 to 40 million acres.[2] Considering that land resources can be
expanded in the poor countries, one might conclude that the "core of
the problem of the carrying capacity of the earth is not the scarcity
of fertile land in comparison with the number of mouths that must be
fed but the insufficient ability of men to make full use of their available
resources."[3]

Considerable reserves of minerals also exist—copper, bauxite, and
tin in Africa; petroleum, iron, bauxite, and tin in Asia; petroleum, iron,
copper, and zinc in South America. Even though the poor countries are
generally deficient in coal reserves, many might utilize oil and gas as
major sources of energy. Furthermore, the unused reserves of water

---

[1] See the various reports of the I.B.R.D. survey missions, books on economic
geography, and such specific studies as L. Dudley Stamp, *Land for Tomorrow;
the Underdeveloped World*, Indiana University Press, Bloomington, 1953; W. S.
Woytinsky and E. S. Woytinsky, *World Population and Production*, Twentieth
Century Fund, New York, 1953, Chapters 10, 15, 19, 21, 24, 25; United States,
Department of State, *Energy Resources of the World*, Washington, 1949; E. W.
Zimmerman, *World Resources and Industries* (revised edition), Harper and Bros.,
New York, 1951; United Nations, Department of Economic and Social Affairs,
Non-Ferrous Metals in Under-Developed Countries, New York, 1956; United
Nations, Statistical Office of the United Nations, *World Energy Supplies 1929–
1950*, New York, 1952; *Oxford Economic Atlas of the World*, Oxford University
Press, Oxford, 1956.

[2] Woytinsky and Woytinsky, *op. cit.*, 533–534.

[3] *Ibid.*, 324.

power are heavily concentrated in poor regions. The rate of utilization of available water power is about 60 per cent in Europe, but only 3 per cent in South America, 5 per cent in Middle America, 13 per cent in Asia, and little more than 0.1 per cent in Africa.[4] It is a striking fact that Africa possesses 44 per cent of the world's potential hydroelectric power.[5]

If, however, it cannot be maintained that the poor countries are absolutely deficient in land, water, mineral, forest, or energy resources, it must be concluded that their natural resources are still largely in the potential stage. Generally the poor countries possess resources, but the resources are unutilized, underutilized, or misutilized. The fuller utilization of these resources depends on conditions of accessibility to the supplies, availability of technical knowledge, accumulation of capital, and extent of the market. Until now the full potential has generally not been approached to any significant extent, and the resources remain underdeveloped.

2. Backwardness

Proceeding from a consideration of natural resources to human resources, one may say that the poor countries also have economically backward populations in the sense that the quality of the people as productive agents is low.[6] Instead of acquiring the greatest possible control over their physical environment, the people have struck a balance with nature at an elementary level. They have been relatively unsuccessful in solving the economic problem of man's conquest of his material environment. Particular manifestations of this are low labor efficiency, factor immobility, limited specialization in occupations and in trade, lack of entrepreneurship, economic ignorance, and a value structure and social structure that minimize the incentives for economic change.

At a basic level, the backwardness is evident in low labor efficiency. Although comparative data are scarce on the relative efficiency of labor in poor and rich countries, what evidence is available indicates that for manufacturing as a whole the level of productivity prevailing in poor areas is 20 per cent and less of that in the United States.[7] In a typically

---

[4] *Ibid.*, 345.

[5] A. L. Banks (ed.), *The Development of Tropical and Sub-Tropical Countries,* Edward Arnold Ltd., London, 1954, xiv, 70.

[6] This characteristic is particularly emphasized by H. Myint, "An Interpretation of Economic Backwardness," *Oxford Economic Papers, VI,* No. 2, 132–163 (June 1954).

[7] W. Galenson and H. Leibenstein, "Investment Criteria, Productivity, and Economic Development," *Quarterly Journal of Economics, LXIX,* No. 3, 355 (Aug. 1955).

poor area, it will require at least 5, and perhaps 10 or more, workers to produce the same amount of goods that a single American worker can produce.

The low labor efficiency generally stems from malnutrition, low standards of health, illiteracy, lack of training, obstacles to occupational mobility, and low value placed on work. Some notion of the wide

TABLE 14.1. PER CAPITA CALORIE INTAKE,
SELECTED COUNTRIES, 1954–1955

Country	Calories per Day	Total Protein (grams per day)
Rich Countries		
Australia*	3040	91
Canada	3120	98
Denmark	3330	89
France	2785	96
Germany, Western	2945	77
New Zealand*	3290	99
Norway	3140	91
Sweden	2975	87
United Kingdom	3230	86
United States	3090	92
Poor Countries		
Brazil†	2340	57
Chile†	2490	77
Egypt*	2390	69
Greece	2540	80
India*	1840	50
Pakistan*	2025	50
Peru†	2080	54
Rhodesia and Nyasaland*	2630	81
Turkey*	2670	86
Venezuela‡	2280	59

* 1953–1954.
† 1952.
‡ 1951.

Source: F.A.O., Yearbook of Food and Agricultural Statistics 1955, Rome, 1956, Table 80.

disparity in nutrition levels between rich and poor countries is evident in Table 14.1. In all the poor countries there are gross qualitative and quantitative deficiencies in the per capita diet. The level of calories is low, and the diet is unbalanced, being especially deficient in proteins.

The efficiency of labor is also impaired by endemic disease and the lack of adequate medical and hospital care. For instance, it is estimated that in Southern Rhodesia the loss of manpower due to malaria amounts to 5 per cent–10 per cent of the total labor force; for Egypt, it is estimated that bilharziasis decreases productivity by 33 per cent.[8] High rates of illiteracy also prevent the people from acquiring certain skills and performing various types of services. The disparities in conditions of health and education can be observed in Table 14.2.

Labor is also immobile among occupations. Caste systems, for example, inhibit occupational mobility and make vertical mobility difficult, thereby narrowing the choice of occupations. A characteristic trait of a caste system is social inheritance of occupation. Some of the Hindu castes are also forbidden to engage in business activity. In general, business may be derogated, and the upper social and income groups may be disdainful of practical and mechanical work. Thus, occupational mobility may have little meaning in societies where production is organized on a family basis, and occupations are tied to family status and kinship roles.

Moreover, labor mobility is low when workers do not respond to income incentives. Wage increases may have relatively little appeal to people whose economic organization has previously been of a non-monetary nature and who find their major satisfactions chiefly in traditional rewards and customary types of consumption. The barriers and antipathies in the problem of labor recruitment and the establishment of industrial practices have been summarized as follows: "ignorance of alternatives and of the skills for their adoption; the security system, both emotional and economic, provided by the social structure of non-industrial societies; the status system of non-industrial societies, which generally depends largely upon inherited position, rewards the performance of duties according to traditional expectations, and minimizes impersonal, functionally specific types of economic relations and division of labor; the 'freedom' and socially recognized skill of the independent producer in primitive and peasant societies."[9]

It is frequently maintained that a small rise in the wage rate may actually induce a worker to work less and instead enjoy more leisure. Similarly, it is asserted that an increase in the relative wages of some trades may not cause workers to transfer to the higher wage trades. For example, one observer of West Indian workers has said, "Many workers [do] not want to work for wages regularly five or six days a week all the year round . . . . They prefer to have a lower standard

---

[8] C. E. A. Winslow, *The Cost of Sickness and the Price of Health,* World Health Organization, Geneva, 1951, 15.

[9] W. E. Moore, *Industrialization and Labor,* Cornell University Press, Ithaca, 1951, 302.

TABLE 14.2.   INDICATORS OF HEALTH AND EDUCATION,
SELECTED COUNTRIES

Country	(1) Tuberculosis	(2) Per Cent of Population, Age 10 and Over, Illiterate (1945–1954)	(3) Number of Inhabitants per Physician (1951–1953)	(4) Elementary School Teachers per 1000 Population
Rich Countries:				
Australia	40	below 5	1,000	3.78
Canada	53	below 5	950	5.43
New Zealand	60	below 5	1,250	4.58
Norway	86	below 5	920	3.80
Sweden	75	below 5	1,400	4.03
United Kingdom	62	below 5	1,200	4.11
United States	47	below 5	770	4.29
Poor Countries:				
Bolivia	medium	69	4,700	1.62
Brazil	250	51	3,000	1.97
Ceylon	62	36	5,300	—
Chile	264	24	1,800	2.54
China	400–500	85	2,800	1.73
Colombia	102	44	2,800	1.41
Costa Rica	172	21	2,800	4.74
Ecuador	high	44	3,700	1.03
Egypt	52	75	3,600	1.58
El Salvador	high	58	6,000	1.81
Greece	128	41	1,000	2.17
Guatemala	medium	70	5,800	1.24
Haiti	high	89	10,000	0.63
Honduras	low	66	6,500	1.45
India	283	82	5,700	1.27
Indonesia	high	92	71,000	—
Mexico	56	62	2,400	2.40
Nicaragua	medium	57	2,200	2.15
Paraguay	102	32	2,500	3.34
Peru	high	90	4,500	1.93
Venezuela	233	51	1,900	0.94

Source: (1) and (4) United States, Department of State, *Point Four, Publication 3719*, Jan. 1950, 115–116, 122–123; (2) United Nations, *Demographic Yearbook 1955*, New York, 1955, Table 13; (3) United Nations, *Statistical Yearbook 1955*, New York, 1955, Table 172.

of living and more leisure; they are not educated to appreciate a higher standard of living, and would rather take life more easily than add to their material comforts."[10]

It may be questioned, however, whether the facts of a short work week or rejection of higher earning employments should be interpreted as evidence of a strong desire for leisure and a weak desire for income. In terms of the supply curve of labor, this would mean that the supply curve does not slope upward to the right throughout, but instead after a point turns backwards and slopes to the left; after a point of maximum aspiration is reached, small increases in wages will result in less labor being supplied. But such a "backward-bending supply curve" is subject to different interpretations. In particular, it may be argued that the supply of labor in poor countries is determined much more by the value system of the community and by cultural influences than by merely the price of labor in different trades. If this is so, the backward-bending supply curve cannot be explained simply as revealing a strong desire for leisure.

Thus, in the particular case of West Indian workers, Rottenberg concluded that the fact that workers sometimes rejected classes of employment cannot be taken as clear evidence that they are satisfied with little income and prefer leisure to work. Instead, the refusal of employment ought rather to be interpreted as evidence of occupational immobility created by compartmentalization of the labor force and by custom, tradition, and community values.[11]

This conclusion may also be applied generally. Cultural and psychological factors operative in poor countries may be more influential than wage rates in determining the supply of labor, either in the form of additional workers or in the form of additional hours of work from the individual laborer. The presence of institutions and attitudes associated with the family system, caste system, or village system may account for occupational immobilities. "The 'irrationality' of native laborers unresponsive to wage offers often turns out to be the 'rationality' of potential workers in a situation where goods and services have traditionally been secured through familial production, barter, and mutual aid, and where there is a limited development of a community market. Money is no incentive if there is nothing within the effective range of demand that money will buy."[12]

---

[10] T. S. Simey, *Welfare and Planning in the West Indies,* The Clarendon Press, Oxford, 1946, 133–134.

[11] S. Rottenberg, "Income and Leisure in an Underdeveloped Economy," *Journal of Political Economy, LX,* No. 2, 101 (April 1952).

[12] Moore, *op. cit.,* 306.

Another element of the backwardness appears in the form of economic ignorance. Knowledge is scarce. The people are ignorant of what natural resources are available, what alternative production possibilities exist, what the necessary skills are, and what the market conditions are. Not only has there been little growth in knowledge of how to improve production in the technical sense, but the knowledge of social relations has also been extremely limited. Social knowledge is just as important as technological knowledge, since development depends as much upon learning how to administer large-scale organizations, or how to create institutions that favor economizing effort and economic rationality, as it does upon the knowledge of how to breed new seeds or learning how to build bigger dams.[13]

The economic backwardness of a poor country also appears in its social structure and value structure. Frequently the structure of social relations is hierarchical, and social cleavages are pronounced. The emphasis is not on the individual but rather upon the family or class as the special unit. Social organization tends to be rigidly stratified, with mobility among groups almost impossible. An individual's status is ascribed in terms of who he is or who his antecedents were, rather than being achieved by his own efforts. An ascribed status, in contrast with an achieved status, means that people are evaluated not according to what they can do but according to their position in a system of social classification—by age, sex, kin, clan, caste, etc.

The value system minimizes the importance of economic incentives, material rewards, independence, and rational calculation. Such a value system may be criticized from an economic viewpoint, even though possibly commended on non-economic grounds, in so far as it inhibits the development and acceptance of new ideas and objectives and fails to compare the costs and advantages of alternative methods to achieve objectives. There is little belief in man's power over nature. Instead nature is commonly accepted as more powerful than man, something to be adjusted to, rather than overcome.

In many poor countries the operations of an exchange and market economy are scarcely understood, and instead of attaching significance to the practice of economic individualism which was so important for western development, the societies are custom-bound and non-individualistic. Values and motivations remain "tradition-directed," the emphasis being on an established pattern of economic life, family life, and religious life.

Further, religious attitudes may make secular affairs inseparable from

13 W. A. Lewis, *Theory of Economic Growth,* Allen & Unwin Ltd., London, 1955, 164.

non-secular affairs. Being more than a system of private belief, religion may have a communal character and actually be a social system which completely dominates the way of life. Material welfare may be subordinated to other-worldly ends. In the Hindu and Buddhist views, for example, desire may be considered evil, and austerity and resignation are ideals that will improve one's fortune in this life and in reincarnation. Religious belief may place the possibility of changing one's status in the next life, not in this one. Cultures in many parts of the world adhere in different forms to the belief that man has no causal effect upon his own future; God, not man, can improve man's lot. In many groups there is the attitude of accepting what happens to exist, rather than attempting to change it—an attitude of resignation rather than innovation. Indeed, the adjustment may be so traditional and automatic that the inadequacy may not even be noticed.

All these attitudes are related to the positive value which the traditional way of life holds for many of the people. Where tradition is paramount, there may be no future orientation, and change is either resisted or, if accepted, is restricted to fringe areas. Even though they may have latent abilities, the peoples lack the motivations and stimulations to introduce change. In so far as the social structure and value structure assign little importance to material accomplishments and change, community and personal relationships generate a stable and tradition-dominated environment in which the individual resigns himself to accepting group loyalties and group relationships which remain in a fixed pattern. These group relationships are generally associated with an extended family system or a village community which prevent the emergence of impersonal relations and the recognition of specific rights and obligations such as exist in the market economy. In short, the cultural value system within many poor countries is not favorable to economic achievement, and the people remain economically backward.

Even if a country has resources, labor supply, technological knowledge, and capital, its potential productivity still cannot be effectively realized unless there are also active entrepreneurs who have the ability to organize the other factors of production for the creation of economic goods and who are economically motivated. For development does not occur spontaneously as a natural consequence when economic conditions are in some sense "right": a catalyst or agent is needed, and this requires entrepreneurial activity.

By "economically motivated" is meant being motivated to maximize gains, with money as a measure of the degree of successful achievement. But the culture of a poor country may inhibit entrepreneurship. In many of these countries, there is little motivation to produce wealth since the social prestige that people desire may be more easily acquired in other non-economic ways, and the production of wealth may actually be held in contempt. If technological and business activity are not valued, entrepreneurs will be few in number. Moreover, if there is an ascribed status system, entrepreneurs will be few because they thrive on accomplishments and the possibilities of achieving status through a demonstration of capabilities for particular functions. Furthermore, the social system may deny opportunity to those creative qualities that distinguish entrepreneurship. Entrepreneurship is especially handicapped where the society is stratified by caste, color, or creed, and where custom or law restricts the activities of large sections of the population and makes the introduction of change difficult. Moreover, when private property, freedom of contract, and public order do not exist, the environment will not be conducive to entrepreneurship. Nor can entrepreneurial activity flourish if markets are narrow and knowledge is limited. In these societies there may well be many potential entrepreneurs, but the obstacles to the successful exercise of entrepreneurship are generally so formidable as to limit the number of individuals who are willing and able to recognize market opportunities and make effective decisions to exploit these opportunities. Instead of having a large class that is interested in long-term productive achievements, the poor countries have only a small class of businessmen, and these are typically merchants and traders who confine their activities to distribution, real estate speculation, and moneylending. In some cases the business class consists mainly of foreigners, for example, the Chinese in Indonesia, or the Hindus in Burma. Often the most active entrepreneurs come from relatively recent immigrant groups.

Whereas in a rich country the supply of entrepreneurs is always tending to be renewed, and the level of experience is increasing, the poor countries have continued to have a shortage of entrepreneurs. To a considerable extent, the diversity of activities that characterizes rich countries can be attributed to the supply of entrepreneurs. In a poor country, however, the shortage of entrepreneurs commonly restricts the extension of activities and frequently results in the monopolization of those activities that do exist. Multiple centers of entrepreneurial initiative do not exist.

If entrepreneurship is not forthcoming from private individuals, it might be thought the government can assume this function. But for the most part the governments have also remained backward: political leadership and the government's capacity to control have remained weak. After all, the government is composed of individuals, and there is no obvious reason why these individuals should necessarily be more entrepreneurial in spirit than private individuals. There is inadequate ability to recognize, introduce, and administer monetary, fiscal, and other public policies.[14] Statistical records are rudimentary, and such activities as effective budgetary control are handicapped by deficient statistical information. The practice of public administration is generally of low quality. There are few competent civil servants, government salaries are unattractive, the civil service system is inadequate for selecting and training personnel, and corruption may exist. Excessive centralization commonly causes ministers and high officials to be overburdened with detail to the neglect of policy formulation and planning. Parts of the government also make inadequate use of such talent and knowledge as are available elsewhere in the government, including local administrations. In general, the detailed administrative and technical preparation of development projects and their coordination are frequently beyond the capacity of the existing government services.

It is normally characteristic of a poor country's fiscal system that a high proportion of revenues is derived from indirect taxes and customs duties which are regressive. Taxes on land or the income from it are low and provide only a small proportion of all government income. And progressive income taxes are non-existent or low in yields; for example, in the Asian countries in the Colombo Plan, less than 1 per cent of adults pay income tax at all, and only a few pay large amounts.[15] These features in the tax systems of several poor countries can be recognized in Table 14.3. Not only are the tax systems generally arbitrary and regressive in character, but in addition there are problems of considerable tax evasion and inefficient tax collection. All this handicaps effective fiscal policy.

Monetary policy is also restricted in so far as money markets are not developed, deposit banking plays a much smaller role in poor countries than in the rich countries, and central banking may be non-existent or of recent origin with only limited powers. The capacity of the money market in a poor country is extremely limited, and there is not the large variety of submarkets that constitute an important characteristic of developed money markets. Most of them lack an organized, highly liquid call-loans market, and few possess a commercial bill market of any significance. There is often only a loose connection among different parts of the money markets, and there is little integration in the structure of money rates.

[14] The Indian government is a notable exception, and has been placed among the dozen or so most advanced governments; Paul H. Appleby, *Public Administration in India,* Report of a Survey, Cabinet Secretariat, New Delhi, 1953, 8.
[15] F. Benham, "The Colombo Plan," *Economica, XXI,* No. 82, 95 (May 1954).

TABLE 14.3.   MAJOR COMPONENTS OF GOVERNMENT
TAX REVENUE IN SELECTED COUNTRIES

Government Tax Revenue in Local
Currency Derived from:

Country	Total Receipts (million)	Direct Taxes on Incomes and Property (million)	Customs Duties (million)	Other Indirect Taxes (million)
Rich Countries:				
Canada (1954)	4,285	2,472	407	1,124
New Zealand (1954)	224	140	32	13
Norway (1955)	4,188	1,340	310	2,208
United States (1955)	69,369	57,070	606	9,194
Poor Countries:				
Brazil (1954)	46,539	17,798	2,738	22,455
Burma (1954)	979	332	255	112
Ceylon (1954)	909	238	503	81
Costa Rica (1954)	216	41	104	42
Egypt (1953)	177	38	15	78
El Salvador (1953)	140	17	84	26
Haiti (1954)	161	12	121	11
Honduras (1953)	51	7	23	5
India (1954)	5,568	1,228	1,587	974
Iran (1950)	7,785	1,160	1,679	2,667
Iraq (1953)	51	7	12	4
Lebanon (1952)	125	18	37	43
Malaya (1953)	660	164	311	68
Mexico (1953)	5,023	1,145	1,311	1,581
Pakistan (1954)	1,318	146	441	170
Syria (1954)	272	80	64	60
Thailand (1952)	3,055	174	1,118	596
Turkey (1953)	16,534	397	192	622

Source: United Nations, Statistical Yearbook 1955, New York, 1955, Table 166.

In many poor countries deposit banking is an uncommon practice. For instance, whereas in the United States and the United Kingdom demand deposits are normally three to four times the size of the currency issue, in Nigeria demand deposits are less than half the currency issue, and Nigerian commercial interests and individuals probably use currency ten times as much as demand deposits. Moreover, in Nigeria at the end of 1953 cash at hand covered almost 70 per cent of all deposits and was nearly equal to the level of demand deposits.[16]

[16] I.B.R.D., The Economic Development of Nigeria, Johns Hopkins University Press, Baltimore, 1955, 153. Even this comparison of deposits with currency over-

To hold a very high proportion of bank assets in the form of cash at hand and with banks abroad is a common practice in these countries. A corollary of this high liquidity of banks is the very low level of loans and advances, and even these loans are usually seasonal and confined to the import and export trade. In some countries where subsistence agriculture prevails, large segments of the indigenous population remain completely outside the money economy. In general the banks are few in number, frequently of foreign origin, and concerned mainly with foreign trade.[17]

The functions of a central bank are severely restricted when the money markets are undeveloped. The absence of a call-loans market and a bill market makes it difficult for the central bank to secure control over the activities of the commercial banks. Even more significantly, open market operations may not be possible in these money markets. There is no broad and active security market. And, since the banks do not generally maintain fixed ratios between their cash reserves and deposits, but instead are accustomed to allowing considerable fluctuations in their cash ratios, the banks are not likely to react to the small changes in their cash balances which are brought about by whatever open market operations are possible in these narrow security markets.[18] There are thus special difficulties connected with introducing the instruments of monetary control into the poor countries.

Finally, it should be recognized that in some poor countries the government is controlled by wealthy landed groups who oppose agricultural reform and any domestic growth of manufacturing. Groups with vested interests in the *status quo* tend to view development as threatening their own economic or political interests, for development is likely to lead to land reforms, higher wages in agriculture, demands for the elimination of very high incomes, and a loss of political power. Unless the government is willing to give greater freedom and support to those who wish to change the existing situation, the *status quo* may merely become more and more entrenched. The backwardness of the government may thus reinforce the other features of backwardness in the poor country.

3. Capital Deficiency

Capital deficiency is another general characteristic of poor countries. One indication of this deficiency is the low amount of capital per head

states the use of banking facilities by the private sector, since nearly half the deposits are made by the government or semi-government organizations, and an overwhelming part of the demand deposits is held by foreigners.

[17] Cf. S. N. Sen, *Central Banking in Underdeveloped Money Markets,* Bookland Ltd., Calcutta, 1952, 28.

[18] *Ibid.,* 58.

of population and the fact that even this small amount of capital is not diversified in type. Data on this subject are extremely limited, but it has been estimated that in the most developed British colonies the national capital per head of population is not more than 10 per cent of that in the United Kingdom, and in Africa it is less than 2 per cent.[19] It has also been estimated that in 1939 real capital per worker in Asia and the Far East outside Japan was only about 10 per cent of that in the United States.[20] ˋ The consumption of commercially produced energy provides one indirect measure of the gulf between rich and poor countries: in 1954, the per capita energy consumption (in coal equivalents) was 7.62 metric tons in the United States, 6.88 in Canada, 5.02 in Norway, and 4.78 in the United Kingdom, but averaged only 0.24 in Africa, 0.52 in South America, and 0.20 in Asia.[21] The total installed capacity of electric energy in 1953 was only 51,000 kilowatt-hours in Nigeria, 1,701,000 in Mexico, 2,104,000 in Brazil, 412,000 in Venezuela, 41,000 in Ceylon, 3,097,000 in India, 209,000 in Indonesia, 217,000 in Malaya, and 505,000 in Turkey, but 19,837,000 in the United Kingdom, and 107,354,000 in the United States.[22]

Not only is the capital stock extremely small, but the current rate of capital accumulation is also very low. In India and Pakistan, for example, gross investment is only 6 per cent or 7 per cent of gross national product, and in Indonesia only about 5 per cent,[23] whereas in the United States, Canada, and Western Europe it is about 15 per cent to 18 per cent. Compared with Southeast Asia and the Middle East, Latin American countries in general have recently had a much higher rate of gross investment—about 14 per cent of gross national product. But a considerable portion of this is foreign capital. Moreover, since the population growth in Latin America is high, about 2½ per cent a year, a large part of the capital is offset by population growth, so that capital per person is probably not rising any more significantly than in most of the Middle East and Southeast Asia.

Table 14.4 shows net saving as a percentage of national income in poor areas of the world in 1949. The average was only about 5 per cent.[24] Such a low rate of saving does not allow much investment in

[19] Colonial Development Corporation, *Report for 1948,* H.M.S.O. 188, London, June 1949, 6.

[20] United Nations, Department of Economic Affairs, *Economic Survey of Asia and the Far East in 1949,* New York, 1950, 296.

[21] United Nations, *Statistical Yearbook 1955,* New York, 1955, Table 124.

[22] *Ibid.,* Table 119.

[23] Department of State, Office of Intelligence Research, Report No. 6672, 3 (Aug. 25, 1954), quoted in W. W. Rostow, "The Take-Off into Self-Sustained Growth," *Economic Journal, LXVI,* No. 261, 36 (March 1956).

[24] Even though the statistics of savings in poor countries take insufficient account

new industrial enterprise. Indeed, in many poor areas the amount of net capital formation is scarcely sufficient to provide the growing population with a constant per capita endowment of capital assets. For instance, assuming a capital-output ratio of 4 to 1, a population increase of 1 per cent per year requires an annual investment of 4 per cent of the national income merely to maintain a constant amount of capital per person. With a population growth of 2 per cent a year, the amount of investment needed would be 8 per cent of national income. With a population growth of 3 per cent a year, approximately the rate in Ceylon, Mexico, Venezuela, and Puerto Rico in recent years, the required investment would be as high as 12 per cent of the national income. But, since

TABLE 14.4. NET DOMESTIC SAVING AS PER CENT OF NATIONAL INCOME, 1949

Region	Per Cent
Latin America	8
Middle East, including Egypt	6
Africa, excluding Egypt	5
South Central Asia	5
Far East, excluding Japan	3

Source: Calculated from United Nations, Department of Economic Affairs, *Measures for the Economic Development of Under-Developed Countries,* New York, 1951, 76.

few poor countries have a rate of *gross* capital formation as high as 15 per cent, it is apparent that these countries do not have sufficient capital to cover capital depreciation and maintain the amount of equipment available per worker, let alone increase the amount per worker.

Moreover, since real income is low, there is little demand for the products of manufacturing industry and the services of public utilities which tend to use a greater amount of capital per unit of labor and land than do agriculture or light consumer goods industries. Except for agriculture, demand is confined mainly to light consumer goods. In producing these products there is a natural pressure on producers to select from the available techniques those which have the lowest capital intensity. The poor countries have therefore tended to invest in light, labor-intensive, consumer goods industries rather than in the heavier, capital-intensive, producer goods industries. Basic producer goods industries are practically non-existent, and, although there are some local handicraft industries and small light industries, these industries are

of savings in non-monetary forms for investment in small-scale trade and agriculture, the ratio of saving to income in poor countries is clearly substantially smaller than in rich countries.

mainly labor-intensive. Public overhead capital is also deficient in amount and character.

One other interpretation of capital deficiency is important. If by capital formation is meant the use of any current resource that adds to future output, then the capital stock will consist not only of physical equipment but also the body of knowledge possessed by the population and the capacity and training of the population to use this knowledge effectively. According to this broad interpretation of capital, many of the categories now treated under flow of goods to ultimate consumers should be included under capital: for example, outlays on education and training, improvement of health, and research. If these expenditures are considered as capital expenditures, then the proportion of capital formation in national income in the rich countries would be much larger. But since poor countries do not make many such investments in the knowledge, training, and health of their populations, this broad interpretation of capital would not increase the proportion of their national incomes devoted to capital formation. Accordingly, it may well be, as Kuznets suggests, that instead of a difference in net capital formation proportions between 10 per cent in rich and, say, 3 per cent in poor countries, the true difference is more likely to be between 30 per cent or over and 3 per cent.[25]

Thus, the capital deficiency in poor countries is reflected in the small amount of physical equipment per worker and, more broadly, in limited knowledge, training, and scientific advance. It is in this sense, rather than a small capital-output ratio, that capital deficiency appears in poor countries. Indeed, the capital-output ratios in poor countries might actually be higher than in richer countries. For, if output grows only very slowly, then even if capital formation is only a small proportion of national income it would give a large capital-output ratio. For example, if a poor country's total output grows at the low rate of, say, 0.5 per cent per year, then a net capital-formation proportion of only 3 per cent of current product would, in the long run, yield a high capital-output ratio of 6 to 1.[26] It is from the standpoint of the small absolute amount of total physical capital, limited capacities and skills in the country's population, and low ratio of net investment that the poor country is said to be capital deficient.

At the root of this capital deficiency is the shortage of savings and the

[25] S. Kuznets, "Toward a Theory of Economic Growth," in R. Leckachman (ed.), *National Policy for Economic Welfare at Home and Abroad,* Doubleday & Co., New York, 1955, 39–40.

[26] Cf. *ibid.,* 38. Problems associated with the use and measurement of capital-output ratios are discussed in Chapter 16, section 3.

fact that much of the savings tends to go into prodigal consumption or short-term speculative investment rather than productive investment. The distribution of income in many of the poor countries aggravates this difficulty. Extreme inequalities in the distribution of income characterize many of these countries. Considering distributions of family income for India in 1949–1950, for Ceylon in 1950, and for Puerto Rico in 1948, Kuznets concluded that the data show that income distribution in these poor countries is somewhat more unequal than in the United States or United Kingdom. Usually the rich are relatively richer, and the poor relatively poorer, in the poor countries than in the rich countries. Thus the percentage of total income received by the poorest 60 per cent of the people is 28 per cent in India, 30 per cent in Ceylon, and 24 per cent in Puerto Rico—compared with 34 per cent in the United States and 36 per cent in the United Kingdom. The percentage of total income received by the richest 20 per cent is 55 per cent in India, 50 per cent in Ceylon, and 56 per cent in Puerto Rico—compared with 44 per cent in the United States and 45 per cent in the United Kingdom.[27]

It might be thought that, since the rate of saving should rise with income, these gross inequalities should foster capital formation. There are, however, two general reasons why such inequality in the distribution of income does not contribute as much to productive investment as might be expected. First, since the wider inequality in the income structure of poor countries is associated with a much lower level of average per capita income than in rich countries, positive savings are obviously possible only at much higher relative income levels in the poor countries: if in the richer countries some savings are possible in the fourth quintile, in the poor countries savings could be realized only at the very peak of the income pyramid by the top 5 per cent or 3 per cent.[28] The concentration of savings is then even more pronounced than in rich countries. Second, the group at the top of the income

[27] S. Kuznets, "Economic Growth and Income Inequality," *American Economic Review*, XLV, No. 1, 20–21 (March 1955). Hereinafter cited as Kuznets, "Economic Growth and Income Inequality." The comparison is for income before direct taxes and excluding free benefits from governments. A comparison in terms of income net of taxes and including government benefits would accentuate the wider inequality of income distribution in the poor countries.

Morgan also states that income distribution in underdeveloped economies, by size, by occupations and by national groups, is more unequal than in developed economies. See T. Morgan, "Distribution of Income in Ceylon, Puerto Rico, the United States and the United Kingdom," *Economic Journal*, LXIII, No. 252, 833 (Dec. 1953). See, however, H. T. Oshima, "A Note on Income Distribution in Developed and Underdeveloped Countries," *ibid.*, LXVI, No. 261, 156–160 (March 1956).

[28] Kuznets, "Economic Growth and Income Inequality," 23.

pyramid is composed of landowners and traders who tend to invest in more land, real estate speculation, capital flights, or inventory accumulation rather than long-term industrial investments or public utilities.

This is explained by several factors: the greater desire for quick gains than for longer-term gains; the high rates of return which the moneylender or landlord can get by short-term lending to small cultivators; the inability to recruit trained labor and to acquire machinery and other factory equipment; the investor's desire to have liquid assets as a hedge against currency devaluation and price inflation; the general uncertainty concerning the government's economic policies which may suddenly increase costs or reduce the domestic market or invite foreign competition; the fact that in many poor countries land ownership is a means of social and political power; and all the social, legal, and political institutions which restrict initiative and enterprise, inhibit the mobilization of savings, and prevent an effective channeling of these savings into more productive outlets.   As long as the entrepreneurial and capitalist groups remain small, entrepreneurial profits constitute only a small proportion of national income, and reinvestment of profits within the capitalist sector is negligible.   It was seen in Part 2 that historically much of the capital accumulation in the United States and Britain was based on the reinvestment of profits.   This has not occurred to any important extent in poor countries.   Finally, the culture of a poor country may place value on the construction of ornate temples, shrines, monuments, or public buildings.   These require savings, but they do not fulfill productive economic purposes.   From the standpoint of development, capital accumulation requires not only an excess of production over consumption, but also the investment of those savings in productive capital goods.

Turning now from a consideration of the short-run distribution of income to an examination of the secular increases in income levels, one finds that over the long run the volume of savings as a percentage of national income has been less than what might be expected from the absolute increase in the level of income that has occurred.   The failure of the saving ratio to rise over the long period has been explained by Nurkse in terms of the "demonstration effect," a concept originally devised by Duesenberry.[29]

Briefly, the concept is this.   At any particular time, a family's savings are positively correlated with its income.   The low-income families save little or nothing, while high-income families save a much larger per cent of their income.   But, if over time all family incomes rise in absolute

[29] R. Nurkse, *Problems of Capital Formation in Underdeveloped Countries,* Basil Blackwell, Oxford, 1953, Chapter III.

terms, then saving over time seems to depend on the family's relative, not absolute, position in the income scale. For example, if at one period the lowest 10 per cent of the families were receiving an average income of $400 per year, but now the lowest 10 per cent receive an average of $800 per year, it is possible that when these families received $400˙ a year they saved nothing, and those who were receiving $800 saved, say, 5 per cent. But today the lowest group who receive $800 now save nothing. If a family is at the bottom of the relative income scale, it saves a negligible amount regardless of the absolute size of its income. This is because the demonstration effect of the consumption patterns of higher income groups encourages higher consumption when poor families gain higher incomes.

The demonstration effect may also be relevant to countries. Although the incomes of the poor countries have risen in absolute terms, they are still at the bottom in relative terms, and their savings are roughly the same proportion as previously. The new and better commodities being produced in the richer countries with which the people of the poor countries have come into contact create new consumption wants in the poor countries. Thus, as their incomes rise, they satisfy these additional wants by holding the percentage of consumption to income about the same, rather than by consuming a lower percentage of their income as they would do if their tastes had remained static instead of being altered by the demonstration effect of more diversified and higher-quality commodities.

Although this interpretation is highly suggestive, it may be questioned in some respects. It remains an untested hypothesis, not having been subjected to extensive empirical evidence. The imports of some poor countries have been composed mainly of foodstuffs or raw materials, for which the demonstration effect is relatively negligible. Furthermore, in some countries where the transition to an exchange economy has not been completed, the demonstration effect, if operative, might actually stimulate more effort to create a surplus of agricultural products for the market. This promotes an exchange economy, since the ability to purchase new types of consumer goods depends on money incomes. The extension of the exchange economy involves greater specialization and increased production, and hence eventually additional saving. The more general point is that the demonstration effect tends to increase the "aspiration to consume" as well as the "propensity to consume." As long as it affects the aspiration to consume, it may actually lead to greater effort or to an inflow of producers from the subsistence sector into the exchange sector of the economy, thereby increasing production, and eventually the volume of savings.[30]　In Britain's development, for example, it may be suggested that the desire to share in the higher consumption standards of the industrial towns operated as a motivating force impelling agricultural labor to migrate to the towns.[31]

4. Foreign Trade Orientation

Finally, the economies of the poor countries may also be characterized as being foreign trade-oriented.　This orientation is indicated in several ways.

In one form it appears in the considerable extent to which the market-type sectors of the economy rely on the production of a few primary

TABLE 14.5.　IMPORTANCE OF EXPORTS, SELECTED
COUNTRIES

Country	Exports As Percentage of Gross National Product
Nicaragua	27
Guatemala	15
Cuba	34
Mexico	17
Colombia	12
Jamaica	17*
Surinam	36
Iraq	13†
Turkey	10*
Ceylon	42

* Based on national income, not GNP.
† Oil exports excluded.

Source: J. J. Spengler, "I.B.R.D. Mission Growth Theory," *American Economic Review, Papers and Proceedings, XLIV,* No. 2, 585 (May 1954). Data based on I.B.R.D. reports during the early 1950's.

products which usually are almost completely exported.　The ratio of this export production to total output is normally high; the share of the national income generated by exports normally exceeds the shares generated by private domestic investment or government expenditures.　Tables 14.5 and 14.6 indicate this dependence on exports in several poor

[30] It is unreasonable to maintain on the one hand the operation of the demonstration effect, and on the other, a backward-sloping supply curve of labor. For if new wants develop, it is difficult to believe that the supply curve of labor would be backward-sloping over the long period. Cf. H. Myint, "The Gains from International Trade and the Backward Countries," *Review of Economic Studies,* *XVII* (2), No. 58,　135 (1954–1955).

[31] Cf. Chapter 7, section 5.

countries. For poor countries as a whole, the ratio of exports to the national income appears to be not much less than 20 per cent.[32] In some cases, the export of only one or two staple commodities may account for a large part of foreign exchange receipts. For instance, in Venezuela,

TABLE 14.6. PRINCIPAL EXPORTS, AS PERCENTAGES OF
TOTAL EXPORTS, SELECTED COUNTRIES, 1949

Country	Export	Percentage of Total Exports
Belgian Congo	copper	25
French West Africa	groundnut products	42
French Equatorial Africa	cotton	35
Puerto Rico	sugar and molasses	60
Gold Coast	cocoa	73
Jamaica	sugar	39
Kenya	sisal	26
Malaya	rubber	50
	tin	25
Nigeria	palm oil	33
	cocoa	22
Northern Rhodesia	copper	81
Uganda	copper	74
El Salvador (1950)*	coffee	89
Iran†	oil	90
Ceylon‡	tea	42
	rubber	31
Indonesia (1951)§	rubber	42
	oil	20
Thailand||	rice	63

* I.M.F., *International Financial Statistics,* Oct. 1952, 46.
† *Ibid.,* 66.
‡ *Ibid.,* 139.
§ *Ibid.,* 151.
\|\| *Ibid.,* 161.

Source: United Nations, *Special Study on Economic Conditions and Development,* June 1952, 36–37.

exports of petroleum accounted in 1950 for 97 per cent of the credit side of the balance of payments; in Chile, copper accounts for almost 50 per cent and nitrates 25 per cent of foreign exchange; in Egypt, cotton contributes almost 90 per cent of foreign exchange receipts; in El Salvador, coffee accounts for almost 90 per cent of export receipts; in Bolivia,

[32] United Nations, *Measures for the Economic Development of Under-Developed Countries,* New York, 1951, 71.

approximately 70 per cent of foreign exchange receipts are obtained from tin ore exports; and in Cuba in 1949 exports of sugar and sugar products made up nearly 90 per cent of total exports.[33]

A major problem connected with this heavy reliance on exports, especially the export of only one or two commodities, is that the country is particularly susceptible to the transmission of the trade cycle from overseas. A depression abroad reduces the demand for the poor country's exports, and, being primary products, these exports suffer large price and value declines. Conversely, overseas prosperity raises the demand for the poor country's exports, and total export proceeds increase. According to a United Nations study, the cyclical fluctuations in export proceeds from 18 major primary commodities exported by poor countries amounted during 1901–1950 to about 37 per cent in amplitude; that is, on the whole, export proceeds fell from 100 to 63 and subsequently rose again to 100, during the average cycle of four years' duration.[34] Another study of fluctuations in the mineral exports of 25 poor countries revealed that the average year-to-year fluctuation in export proceeds was no less than 27 per cent during the period 1928 to 1950.[35] In other words, the average annual change in the foreign exchange yield of the ores and minerals exported by these countries was, on the average, from an index of 100 in any one year to an index of 73 or 127 in the next. These fluctuations in export proceeds disrupt, in turn, the domestic economy.

The foreign trade orientation is also revealed through foreign borrowings. The secular expansion in exports that has occurred in many poor countries is attributable largely to direct foreign investments in these countries. Such investments have concentrated typically on developing and processing primary products for export markets. Even the foreign investment in public overhead capital has been mainly in sectors ancillary to the export sector. Expanding the supply for overseas markets rather than for domestic markets has been the objective of foreign investment because the domestic markets have been narrow, there has been a demand for these export products in foreign markets, and foreign investors are interested in foreign exchange receipts.

The flow of capital to the poor countries is, however, unstable. In fact, capital inflow tends to fluctuate even more than earnings from

[33] Loc. cit.; International Monetary Fund, International Financial Statistics, Oct. 1952, 140.

[34] United Nations, Department of Economic Affairs, Instability in Export Markets of Under-Developed Countries, New York, 1952, 6.

[35] United Nations, Department of Economic Affairs, Non-Ferrous Metals in Under-Developed Countries, New York, 1952, 93–94.

export proceeds.[36]   Years of declining capital inflow also tend to coincide with years of decreasing export proceeds.   Fluctuations in foreign investment thereby intensify the instability of the domestic economy.

Another significant feature of the inflow of foreign capital is that it has brought with it foreign-owned plantation and mining enterprises and foreign trading firms.   In some extreme cases the non-indigenous enterprises account for almost the total product: in Northern Rhodesia, Southern Rhodesia, Kenya, and the Belgian Congo, the contribution of non-indigenous enterprise to the geographical product in these territories is between 90 per cent and 95 per cent, 85 per cent and 90 per cent, 80 per cent and 85 per cent, and 75 per cent and 80 per cent, respectively.[37]   In Ceylon, the tea industry is 80 per cent foreign-owned, the rubber industry is 40 per cent foreign-owned, and more than 80 per cent of the export-import trade and shipping is in foreign hands.

These foreign enterprises frequently have monopolistic positions or high concentration of economic power.   And in some cases even though the agricultural export goods are produced chiefly by numerous small landholders, the purchase of these crops is highly concentrated in a small number of foreign companies.   In Nigeria, for example, Nigerian and foreign companies operate as licensed buying agents of the governmental Marketing Boards.   One foreign company purchased in 1949 almost 45 per cent of all Nigerian non-mineral exports.[38]   The situation is similar for imports: the same few firms dominate the import trade.   Oligopoly is thus a characteristic of Nigerian trade: a small number of foreign firms handle a large proportion of the import trade as well as the purchase of produce for export.[39]

Along with the foreign firms has also come the introduction of the middlemen system.[40]   Under this system there is a multiplicity of traders who distribute the imports from the initial importing firm to the final buyers.   There are also many middlemen to whom advances are made by exporting firms for the purchase of export produce from native producers.   It has been estimated that in the Gold Coast there are 1500 brokers in touch with European trading firms, and some 37,000 sub-

[36] United Nations, Department of Economic Affairs, *Instability in Export Markets of Under-Developed Countries,* New York, 1952, 7.

[37] United Nations, Department of Economic and Social Affairs, *Scope and Structure of Money Economies in Tropical Africa,* New York, 1955, 15.

[38] P. T. Bauer, "Concentration in Tropical Trade," *Economica, XX,* No. 79, 22 (Aug. 1953).

[39] P. T. Bauer, *West African Trade,* Cambridge University Press, Cambridge, 1955, Chapter 5, 99–101.

[40] Cf. *ibid.,* Chapter 2, 15–16.

brokers,[41] and there are more than 14,000 traders in the three largest trading towns in Nigeria.[42]

The most important feature of the foreign enterprises is that they operate under efficient management with advanced production techniques, possess knowledge of market conditions, and have adequate capital. Such enterprises are in marked contrast with the native producers who lack capital, efficient techniques, and knowledge of market conditions.

As already noted in Table 14.3, poor countries are also dependent on international trade for a large percentage of government revenue. In some cases, like Malaya, customs revenue may account for as much as 80 per cent of government revenue. And in Chile, the Treasury receives or loses approximately $4 million in tax revenues for each American cent by which the price of a pound of copper varies.[32]

Finally, poor countries are also highly dependent on imports. Imports are generally manufactured products, textiles, light consumer goods, and in some cases food products. Not only is there a high marginal propensity to import, but the average propensity to import also tends to rise over the long period to the extent that the demonstration effect operates internationally.

Six important characteristics of poor countries have now been examined. Taking all these characteristics together, they may be summarized by saying that there is a wide gap between the potential output and actual output of a poor country's economy. Thus, the problem now becomes one of examining why this gap has persisted. Why have the poor countries remained poor?

---

[41] Nowell Commission, *Report of the Commission on the Marketing of West African Cocoa,* Cmd. 5845, 1938, Chapter IV, App. D.

[42] Bauer, *West African Trade,* 29.

Chapter 15

Obstacles

to Development

The more important obstacles to development are implicit in the general characteristics discussed in the preceding chapters. Even though the broad answers to the question of why poor countries have remained poor will not apply to all countries with equal force, there are sufficient common aspects in the answers to this question to allow some generalization. When, however, it comes to the ultimate level of case studies of individual countries, these general answers will have to be interpreted in the light of the particular circumstances of the individual country, and appropriate modification of emphasis made.

The characteristics of primary production and population pressures are best considered as only associative with poverty, but the other characteristics of poor countries have been causative—they have inhibited development.

Primary production in itself is not a cause of poverty: the cause is the low productivity in agriculture. The high ratio of agricultural population to total population is best viewed as a consequence, rather than a cause, of poverty. Where the agricultural population is poor, the non-agricultural population serving the agricultural population will be small and also poor. Where farmers are prosperous, the non-farm population will be large and probably also prosperous.[1]

To say a poor country has population pressures is equivalent to saying it has a low level of development. Rather than being the cause of the problem, population pressures may be considered as the problem: a higher rate of development is needed. Where population growth is or will be high, the need for accelerated development is intensified. Moreover, many countries that now have population pressures did not, of course, always have them; for instance, the population of Southeast Asia 50 or 60 years ago was only about half of what it now is, and there was no rural overpopulation. Yet, even though these countries were once sparsely populated relative to their resources, they too did not develop. In contrast, a country such as Japan has developed in spite of population pressures.

The other characteristics, however, are causative from the viewpoint of limitations to development. This can be seen more directly if these characteristics are now regrouped into three categories: (1) "market imperfections," (2) "vicious circles," and (3) "international forces." This chapter examines how the interrelations within and among these categories have impeded development.

1. Market Imperfections

The characteristics of underdevelopment and backwardness fall into place under market imperfections. Such market imperfections as factor immobility, price rigidity, ignorance of market conditions, rigid social structure, and lack of specialization have acted as frictions and impediments, preventing the achievement of an optimum allocation of resources. Efficiency of production has remained low, resources have been underemployed, and employment has been misdirected.

In a world of perfect factor mobility similar factors of production will flow from one industry to another until differences in their returns are narrowed. In the poor countries, there are apparently large numbers of workers whose productivity is near zero. Yet they do not migrate to industries where their returns could be much higher. Nor is capital efficiently allocated. As the characteristic of backwardness reveals, custom, habit, and attitudes towards alternative employment are powerful deterrents to the easy flow of capital and labor. Another limitation to labor mobility is simply the poverty of the worker. Financing the costs of movement and re-employment requires funds

---

[1] Cf. J. Viner, *International Trade and Economic Development,* The Clarendon Press, Oxford, 1953, 50; S. Kuznets, *Economic Change,* W. W. Norton & Co., New York, 1953, 222–225.

which many workers do not have. They are tied to their present employments by their very inefficiency and poverty. Still another imperfection is the lack of knowledge of market opportunities. Workers are unaware of better employment opportunities elsewhere, and producers are unaware of existing domestic and international market possibilities. Monopolistic practices create another set of imperfections that cause malallocation.

To the extent that resources have remained undeveloped because of underutilization or misutilization of resources, it follows that fuller utilization and a more efficient allocation of resources might allow a poor country to approach its productive potential more closely. A different combination of factors could increase real income.

This can be illustrated by the concept of the production possibility curve or "production frontier," as in Figure 15.1. Assume that a country is engaged in producing only two commodities, X and Y.

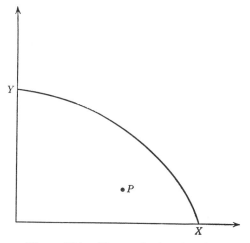

Figure 15.1. The production frontier.

The production frontier denotes the maximum amounts of the various combinations of X and Y that the country could produce with its given resources and given techniques by allocating its resources in the best manner in the production of these commodities. In Figure 15.1, the possible production frontier is XY. The production functions that are actually being used in poor countries, however, are very much "inferior" or "pseudo" production functions. Market imperfections and rigidities obstruct the movement of factors and prices, the best combination of factors is not used, and resources are not allocated most efficiently. The result is that the economy is producing at a point P which is far within the possible production frontier XY. Every country at any time is within its maximum possible production frontier, but the poor countries are unusually far below their potential.[2] This means that without any change in the poor country's capital stock, natural resources, and population, it is technologically feasible for the country to increase its national income through more efficient resource allocation.

Not only is the economy within its production frontier, but all the elements of backwardness also combine to make the poor country's economy highly inflexible. The composition of total output and the productive structure of the economy remain much more fixed over time than does that of a rich country. Various forms of immobility, social, geographical, and occupational, make the elasticities of supply low: output does not change much in response to price and income stimuli. By reducing the mobility of resources, these elements of rigidity and inflexibility make it difficult to achieve an optimum allocation of resources. And the pattern of production tends to persist in so far as there is an absence of entrepreneurs who undertake innovations.

As discussed in Chapter 3, neo-classical economists were not primarily interested in changes in factor supply but rather in the conditions necessary for achieving the best possibilities with a given supply of resources. Their accomplishment was to demonstrate that a completely free market economy under the conditions of perfect competition automatically brought a country to its maximum production frontier. This optimum allocation of resources is represented analytically by the fulfillment of "marginal conditions." Upon this analysis the neo-classicists based their policy attacks on monopolistic practices and other actions that impeded the mobility of resources and the perfection of the market.

In the poor countries, however, the widespread existence of market imperfections has prevented the achievement of the neo-classical objective. There has been a continual use of inferior production frontiers and a failure to achieve an optimum allocation of resources. The market imperfections which have persisted might thus be considered obstacles to development, although they are only a part of the explanation of why the poor countries have had such low rates of development.

[2] Cf. R. S. Eckaus, "The Factor Proportions Problem in Underdeveloped Areas," *American Economic Review, XLV,* No. 4, 561–565 (Sept. 1955).

2. Vicious Circles

More important than the market imperfections are those domestic obstacles that can be subsumed under the general heading "vicious circles." Many obstacles to development are both a cause and consequence of poverty. As such there are circular relationships that perpetuate the low level of development.

Including the characteristic of capital deficiency along with the market imperfections, the basic vicious circle is this:

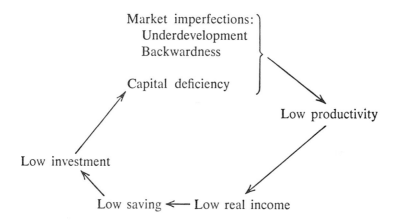

This circle emphasizes that total output is low, and that, after consumption needs are fulfilled, little remains as a surplus for capital accumulation. Because of the low level of real income in the poor countries the flow of saving is small. The low level of real income is, in turn, primarily due to the lack of an adequate capital stock and secondarily to market imperfections. And the low level of capital stock is, in turn, a result of the low level of real income. Thus, deficiency of real resources and low productivity constitute the basis for saying, "a poor country is poor because it is poor."

Other vicious circles overlap this basic circle. The low level of real income is both a cause and consequence of the low level of demand: low real income leads to a low level of demand which, in turn, leads to low investment and hence back to capital deficiency. The low level of real income thus accounts for the shortage of saving and the lack of investment incentives: it is a common point for vicious circles on both the supply and demand sides.[3]

[3] R. Nurkse, *Problems of Capital Formation in Underdeveloped Countries,* Basil Blackwell, Oxford, 1953, 5.

Another vicious circle encompasses the underdeveloped resources and the backward people. For the development of natural resources depends upon the character of human productive resources. The more economically backward are the people, the less developed will be the natural resources. Through illiteracy, lack of skills, deficient knowledge, and factor immobility, the resources will remain unutilized, underutilized, or misutilized. Underdeveloped resources are, therefore, both a consequence and cause of the backward population.

Thus the three major vicious circles appear as follows:

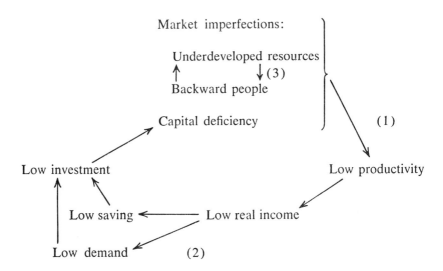

Different aspects of these circles may be examined in more detail. First, consider the economic life of the masses of low-income agricultural peoples in the poor countries. They are generally uneducated and unskilled individuals whose economic life is governed by habit and custom. The capital equipment they use is extremely small and crude, and their methods of cultivation have not changed for years. They consume most of the agricultural output that they produce. They buy little on the market, but instead remain in a subsistence-type economy with little division of labor. Their marginal productivity is very low. Net saving within this subsistence sector is negligible, and their effective market demand for consumption commodities is very small. Yet, although these people are at the subsistence level, many do not want to migrate to other areas even if opportunities are present, nor do they have the funds to migrate. In short, there is little impetus within this group for any economic improvement.

Now consider the other end of the income scale—the high-income group. The budget pattern of this group is such that a large proportion of their consumption expenditures is for durable consumer goods. Many of these cannot possibly be produced domestically—the market is simply too narrow. There are not enough of these wealthy people to support such industries as the automobile industry or electrical appliances industries where economies of large-scale production are significant. Furthermore, some of these commodities, although not requiring large-scale production, do require a high degree of labor skill which is absent domestically. In addition, conspicuous consumption plays an important role in their consumption patterns. They would prefer a foreign article for its prestige effect, rather than an equally adequate domestic commodity. It is common for these people to meet the problem of the limited market which they present for goods and services by their collective movement to a few centrally located cities: they move to the goods and services rather than vice versa. For example, in Latin American countries many large landowners have apartments in the central city in addition to their homes in the hinterland. Only if they all come together can shops and recreational facilities suitable to their income levels be supported.

This is the group, however, that does most of the saving. It may be asked why these savings do not flow into capital projects that will raise the level of national product. The answer relates to the fact that capital accumulation depends not only on the supply of savings but also on the demand for investment funds, and the incentive to invest is low when markets are narrow.

As far as tapping internal markets for simple consumer durables is concerned, potential investors are hampered by the lack of adequate transportation and marketing facilities to these areas as well as by the low incomes of the potential customers. In addition to securing capital, there is also the problem of recruiting and training a labor force for a manufacturing activity. The real transfer price of underemployed labor in agriculture may be near zero, but this does not mean a business can secure these workers for this rate. To overcome their reluctance to migrate, workers must be offered a considerably higher sum. Then one must entail large expenditures in training and holding the labor force.

What, then, do the people do with their savings—into what kind of investments do they flow? One set of capital items which the wealthy purchase, and which cannot be imported, are residential dwellings and buildings. There is an important market for the services of these capital items based on the consumption patterns of the higher-income groups. But the output of this capital can be consumed only by the wealthy members of the community, and it might be more realistic to consider the construction industry as essentially a consumption industry rather than an investment industry. In terms of its capacity-creating effects, these capital expenditures are negligible in raising the income levels of the masses.

Secondly, some of the savings flow back into the export industry and the marketing facilities that are closely allied to it. The demand side of this market lies abroad, and investors commonly believe that the risks involved are less in additional investments here than in industries based on potential domestic demand. Further, the "know-how" barrier and the problem of securing and training the larger labor force are not so serious in this kind of investment.

Finally, some of the savings go abroad into foreign securities. Latin Americans, for instance, invested $9 million and $8 million in United States long-term securities in 1951 and 1952, respectively. Here again it is partly a matter of less risk; the investors can count on a relatively certain return from this investment. Another factor that appeals is that this type of investment may give better balance to an investor's total portfolio. Returns from investment in the export sector vary greatly over the trade cycle—falling very low in depression and rising in prosperity. Since the economy is so closely tied to the export industry, investments in other domestic ventures follow the same profit pattern. But the income of foreign investments tends to fluctuate less and gives a greater degree of stability in the profit incomes of these wealthy individuals. The foreign investments also are generally highly liquid and permit the investors to avoid the danger of radical political changes at home. The basic point is that those with savings are frequently not interested in undertaking entrepreneurial activities: instead of being investors and entrepreneurs in productive activities at home, they simply prefer the income that can come from foreign investments.

Domestic investment cannot be discussed without emphasizing again the problem of entrepreneurship in these countries. Risks are high in domestic investment, but so too are the profit rewards. A venturesome entrepreneurial attitude is necessary to exploit these possibilities. A wealthy landed class, however, is not likely to supply such a group of entrepreneurs. The environment and attitudes of this group are such as to make them disdain manufacturing and industrial activities. The sons of large landowners would rather remain in agriculture, even though profit possibilities might be less than those in manufacturing. Yet this high-income group is a major group from which entrepreneurs might appear.

Although the middle-income group is another possible source, the productive structures of the poor countries are such that there is not a very large middle-income group. Whatever entrepreneurial endeavor there is in this group tends to be used in marketing and other service industries where market demands are more established. The reasons are fairly obvious. There is first the limitation imposed by the difficulties of securing funds for investment purposes. The joint stock concept is not yet familiar, and industrial credit is difficult to obtain. The individuals themselves can save only enough to start a business with low capital requirements. Yet many manufacturing activities require sizable capital outlays to reach efficient productive levels, for technological progress has tended to create significant economies of large-scale production in manufacturing. No longer can one build small factories and hope to compete with foreign products. Further, the degree of technical and managerial skills required is high. Potential entrepreneurs cannot secure this type of labor within their countries. In general these countries do not have the specialized financial, technical, and marketing institutions and services which support entrepreneurship in the richer countries. Therefore, the risks and responsibilities involved in establishing at the outset a large-scale operation are formidable. Because of this, banks and higher-income individuals are reluctant to provide the necessary funds. Thus entrepreneurs, even if they exist, are, on the one hand, prevented from starting on a modest level and gradually reinvesting profits because of the technological barriers; on the other hand, they are prevented from starting on a large scale because of the inability to secure the necessary capital and the trained labor and management.

The discussion so far has concerned only the private domestic sector of the poor countries. What about the governments of these countries? Why have their governments not long ago provided a basic groundwork of social capital? This would have fostered development at least to some extent. In some poor countries that were ruled by foreign powers, the governments may have had no particular concern with domestic development. They were more interested in investments that facilitated the economy as an exporter of raw materials rather than as a producer of manufactured articles. This is, however, only part of the answer, and it does not apply at all to those poor countries that have long had political independence. The real problem has been that the governments, like the private sectors, have been politically backward, unstable, and uncooperative in furthering development. In other words, the vicious circles have extended to the government as well as to the private sector.

Market imperfections make a tightening up of the economy difficult, but the vicious circles obstruct a widening of the economy. The widening of the economy involves the introduction of new factors, new commodities, new production techniques, and organizational changes, sizable structural changes, which push the production frontier outward. But the failure to break the vicious circles has limited this outward movement. And, since the vicious circles are coexistent and mutually aggravating, they are difficult to break. To accelerate development in poor countries, it is necessary to surmount the obstacles presented by the vicious circles of poverty.

3. International Forces

The remaining characteristic, foreign trade orientation, is connected with the third group of obstacles, "international forces." This refers to the role of poor countries in the world economy.[4]

The classical theory of international trade would interpret the foreign trade orientation of poor countries as being consistent with comparative costs. In following the dictates of comparative advantage, all trading countries benefit, real income for the world is maximized, and the poor countries are "better off" than they would be without trade. Indeed, there is some indication that classical writers, on the whole, tended to believe that the largest share of the gains from international trade would accrue to the economically small countries.[5]

Many economists, however, question whether the classical theory of trade is realistic for poor countries and whether it is relevant under dynamic conditions.[6] It is maintained that the classical theory of

---

[4] Additional aspects of this topic will be considered in Chapters 19 and 20.

[5] Cf. F. D. Graham, *The Theory of International Values*, Princeton University Press, Princeton, 1938, 236–237.

[6] Cf. T. Balogh, "Welfare and Freer Trade—A Reply," *Economic Journal*, LXI, No. 241, 72–82 (March 1951); W. A. Lewis, *Theory of Economic Growth*, Allen & Unwin Ltd., London, 1955, 176–189; E. S. Mason, "Raw Materials, Rearmament, and Economic Development," *Quarterly Journal of Economics, LXVI*, No. 3, 334 (Aug. 1952); H. Myint, "The Gains from International Trade and the Backward Countries," *Review of Economic Studies, XVII* (2), No. 58, 129–142 (1954–1955); G. Myrdal, *An International Economy*, Harper & Brothers, New York, 1956, Chapters VIII, XIII; Joan Robinson, "The Pure Theory of International Trade," *Review of Economic Studies, XIV*, No. 36, 98–112, (1946–1947); H. W. Singer, "Distribution of Gains between Investing and Borrowing Countries," *American Economic Review, Papers and Proceedings, XL*, No. 2, 472–492 (May 1950); J. Viner, "International Trade Theory and Its Present Day Relevance," in *Economics and Public Policy,* Brookings Lectures, 1954, 110; J. H. Williams, "The Theory of International Trade Reconsidered," *Economic Journal, XXIX*, 195–209 (June 1929); United Nations Economic Commission for Latin

comparative costs assumes that factors are mobile internally but are immobile internationally,[7] the production functions are known, private marginal product equals social marginal product, full employment and optimum allocation of resources exist internally before trade, and the balance of payments is in equilibrium. `It is argued that these "ideal conditions" are unrealistic for poor nations. Moreover, it is maintained that classical trade theory is essentially a static theory in so far as it assumes given tastes, given resources, and given technical knowledge, and is concerned with determining a once-for-all optimum allocation of given resources. These assumptions preclude an analysis of the long-run dynamic evolution of international trade and miss the essence of development, which is not so much that of achieving an optimum allocation of resources through the fulfillment of marginal conditions under static conditions as it is that of increasing the supply of resources through big structural changes and allocating resources under dynamic conditions.

Similarly, the classical theory of foreign investment states that, when capital flows from areas where it is relatively abundant and has a low marginal product to areas where it is relatively scarce and has a high marginal product, the flow will contribute to the achievement of an optimum distribution of resources in the world economy and will mean an increase in the combined national income of the countries involved. This conclusion, however, depends on the adoption of a cosmopolitan frame of reference, an implicit assumption that private marginal net product and social marginal net product are equal, and that the terms of trade do not change. If these assumptions do not hold, then the traditional conclusion can be contradicted.

There always have been dissenters who, by questioning the classical assumptions, have denied the validity of the classical conclusions for poor countries. It is certainly true that classical trade theory must be rethought in terms of developmental problems and the peculiar characteristics of poor countries. This has not yet been done adequately. But it does not necessarily follow that the extension of classical theory to long-run dynamic problems will prove the classical conclusions invalid: the theory of comparative costs and classical view of the gains

---

America (R. Prebisch), *The Economic Development of Latin America and Its Principal Problems,* New York, 1950.

For an earlier criticism of the classical theory which now merits reinterpretation in terms of the development of poor countries, see M. Manoïlesco, *Theory of Protection and International Trade,* P. S. King & Son, London, 1931.

[7] If factors are not assumed to be freely mobile internally, then it must be assumed that factor prices are freely flexible.

from trade may also prove valid under dynamic conditions. Never-theless, until this is demonstrated more adequately, there will be critics who question the relevance of the classical free-trade argument and who maintain that international forces have operated in the past to limit the development of poor countries.

Some of these critics, as noted in Chapter 2, have raised the issues of imperialism and colonialism. They oppose the Ricardian concept of mutual gains from trade with the Marxian concept of exploitation: they allege that the gains from trade have been withheld from poor countries. Historical fact is the simple refutation of this argument. It can scarcely be questioned that after entering international markets the poor countries have gained relative to their positions before trade.

A more sophisticated modern version of the exploitation argument, however, has been presented by such writers as Prebisch, Singer, Myint, Lewis, and Myrdal.[6] They do not charge deliberate exploitation, but they maintain that there were "disequalizing forces" operating in the world economy. These disequalizing forces made the gains from trade go mainly to the more developed countries, even though foreign in-vestors and foreign governments did not consciously exploit the poor areas. This argument has not been spelled out in any detail, but it appears to have essentially three main strands.

First, it is maintained that, after being opened up to world markets, many poor countries became "dual economies": the export sector be-came an island of development, but the rest of the economy made little advance, and the export sector remained surrounded by subsistence conditions and inferior methods of production. This contrast is part of a system that Boeke terms a "dual society." "Without doubt the most frequent form of social dualism is to be found where an imported western capitalism has penetrated into a precapitalistic agrarian com-munity and where the original social system—be it not undamaged—has been able to hold its own or, expressed in opposite terms, has not been able to adopt the capitalistic principles and put them into full practice. When stated in these general terms the case of social dualism is widespread."[8]

An outstanding result of foreign borrowings by poor countries has been a substantial increase in their exports. Production for export has grown generally at an increasing rate, and at a rate greater than population growth. Examples are many: rubber output in Malaya was only 200 tons in 1905, but by 1920 exports of rubber amounted to 196,000 tons; cocoa production in the Gold Coast and Nigeria in-

---

[8] J. H. Boeke, *Economics and Economic Policy of Dual Societies,* Institute of Pacific Relations, New York, 1953, 4.

creased over 40 times from 1905 to 1939; the total value of Burma's exports, covering years of high and low prices, rose at a rate of 5 per cent per annum from 1870 to the 1930's; palm oil exports from the Netherlands East Indies, Malaya, and Belgium Congo were only 23,000 tons in 1923, but 305,000 tons in 1937; coffee exports from French West Africa amounted to 6300 tons in 1936, but to 40,000 tons in 1948; cotton exports from French Equatorial Africa rose from 93 tons in 1926 to 27,000 tons in 1948; and so on for copper from Northern Rhodesia, cane sugar from the West Indies, tea from Ceylon, etc.[9]

Although exports increased, it is argued that this did not contribute much to the development of the rest of the economy; the economy merely became biased towards export production to the neglect of other requirements for development. On the one hand, it is contended that the export sector short-circuited the rest of the economy. On the other, it is argued that the poor countries' high foreign trade ratio is not a healthy sign of their exploiting the economic advantage of an international division of labor, but is rather one of the indications of their underdeveloped status and poverty.[10] Only a small part of the raw materials that were exported were also consumed at home; in the rest of the economy, there was not much imitation of techniques used in the export sector; the increase in exports had little educative effect elsewhere in the economy; and there was not much contribution to the domestic supply of entrepreneurship. Moreover, it is claimed that international trade has not tended to equalize factor prices, but rather has tended to set up a cumulative process away from equilibrium in factor proportions and factor prices. The export sector uses factor proportions that yield relative marginal products different from those in the subsistence sector, with large differentials resulting in factor returns in the different sectors and persistent underemployment.[11]

As for the shorter period, it is maintained that the dependence on exports exposes the economy to the buffetings of fluctuating world market demand and prices. The economy becomes unstable through the transmission of cyclical instability in foreign exchange receipts. The terms of trade also tend to worsen in a depression, and the inflow of capital is likely to diminish. As a result the poor country experiences balance of payments pressures.

The second major strand in the argument is that the effects of in-

[9] Cf. Myint, *op. cit.,* 129.

[10] Myrdal, *op. cit.,* 225–226.

[11] Cf. E. Despres and C. P. Kindleberger, "The Mechanism for Adjustment in International Payments," *American Economic Review, Papers and Proceedings, XLII,* No. 2, 338–343 (May 1952); Eckaus, *op. cit.;* Myrdal, *loc. cit.,* 224–228.

ternational factor movements have not been entirely beneficial. Foreign investment has merely developed the natural resources for export, not the domestic sector or the people. And, as for immigration, it is argued that this contributed to a "cheap labor policy": immigrant labor during the latter half of the nineteenth century from India and China to countries in Southeast Asia, the West Indies, and parts of East and South Africa pulled wages down in the "semi-empty countries receiving labour to the low level of the densely populated countries from which immigrant labour came, instead of allowing wages to rise closer to the level in the empty continents of North America and Australia."[12]

The third major element of the argument involves the contention that there has been a secular deterioration in the terms of trade for poor countries. Singer and Prebisch, for instance, argue that the benefits of technological progress have gone disproportionately to the advanced industrial nations, and Lewis suggests that an unlimited supply of labor at subsistence wages has kept prices low for tropical commercial produce.

These are challenging assertions, but their affirmation or denial must await detailed empirical investigations which cannot be undertaken here. Of immediate interest, however, is the simple observation that, in spite of foreign investment and the introduction of foreign enterprises in poor countries, the development of these countries has remained limited. Whether this has been due to imperialism, or to the factors just enumerated, or to other forces unconnected with international trade may remain for the time being an open question.[13] There are, however, some other international forces which are more clear cut and which may now be briefly noted.

Regarding the increase in exports that has occurred, one might have expected this increase to have had effects analogous to a rise in autonomous investment. And the expansion in exports at an increasing rate might have been expected to induce additional investment. There might thus have been a basis for a multiplier-accelerator process, and this process might have caught hold and become an engine of growth. After all, it was the export trade that played such a vital role in Britain's development. Why has not the international sector which is so important in the poor countries similarly given them the necessary power to break the vicious circles? Why has the export trade not stimulated the rest of the economy? Some answers to these questions may come from a study of movements in the terms of trade, the nature of the production function in the exports of these countries, and the repercussions of foreign investment.

[12] Myint, *op. cit.,* 135; Myrdal, *loc. cit.,* 225, 340.
[13] This issue will be discussed more fully in Chapter 19.

As already discussed in Chapter 11, the argument that the terms of trade have deteriorated for poor countries over the long run is subject to many reservations. At this point it should be recalled that movements in the terms of trade do not unambiguously indicate real income effects; that the statistics upon which the argument rests are biased; and that within the broad category of primary products there have been differences in price behavior in the subcategories of raw materials and foodstuffs, and also differences among commodities in each subcategory. A general conclusion on the secular movement of the terms of trade is thus unwarranted: it is necessary to assess in detail what the forces were that influenced the actual movements in the terms of trade of each country, giving special attention to the flexibility and adaptability of resource use on the one hand and the elasticity of demand facing the particular country on the other.[14] As it stands, the terms of trade argument is not very convincing, and it is doubtful if the terms of trade have turned against the poor countries as a whole over the last century. Even if they had it would not follow from this alone that the countries suffered a loss of real income.

Moreover, what matters now is the future trend of the terms of trade. Some experts believe that, with the limited possibilities for extending primary production in new areas of settlement, the continued growth of industry in rich countries, and the movement of labor out of agriculture, there will be a greater relative scarcity of the world supply of primary products. If this is so, the primary producing countries may experience improved terms of trade.

Cyclical movements in the terms of trade as distinct from long-run movements have been more of a handicap to poor countries. In periods of world prosperity or inflation the prices of primary products rise more rapidly than the prices of manufactured commodities. The terms of trade of most of the poor countries then improve. In prosperity with plentiful supplies of foreign exchange, however, the people are not so concerned with economic development—the country is relatively well off, and the foreign exchange proceeds are spent to a large extent on consumption of imports.

Furthermore, during these periods when foreign exchange earnings are high, there is usually considerable domestic inflation which leads to malallocation of domestic investment expenditures and severe balance of payments problems. The expansion in exports is, of course, not the only source of inflation: budget deficits, perverse monetary policies, and the effects of foreign borrowings also cause inflation, but

[14] Cf. C. P. Kindleberger, *The Terms of Trade,* John Wiley & Sons, New York, 1956, 253–257.

the export sector is a major source of inflation. Export production cannot be quickly increased in most lines, and the larger money income earned in the export industries and the larger reserves of the banks usually feed a sharp inflation.

Once inflation occurs, investment funds tend to be diverted to speculative ventures where profits are high although they are not very productive in a development sense. Inventory investment to catch the next rise in prices also diverts investment funds from fixed capital investments. Investment in real estate becomes another favorite avenue in most of the poor countries, as individuals try to protect themselves from being wiped out by a fall in the purchasing power of money. Still another way to seek protection is to send capital abroad, and flights of capital frequently accompany the inflation.

Moreover, the rise in domestic prices relative to foreign prices discourages the import-competing industries. And, of course, the rise in domestic incomes and prices also causes much of the income to spill over into the import market where the foreign exchange earnings may be quickly dissipated.

In depressions, primary prices fall more rapidly than manufactures, and the terms of trade of the poor countries then worsen. The parallel movement of the terms of trade with the business cycle tends to accentuate the effects of the cycle. This sharp fluctuation in export prices is accompanied by sizable swings in the foreign exchange earning capacity of the export industry. In depression, the inflow of foreign capital also tends to fall. Thus in the depressed periods when export prices and foreign exchange earnings are low, the countries do not have the funds for much importation of needed capital equipment.

It may be suggested that another obstacle to development in some poor countries with a plantation system has been the unfavorable technological nature of the production functions in their export industries.[15] The engineering constraints with respect to the factor combinations that can be used in the export sector might have had important effects in determining subsequent development by influencing both the type of labor that migrates into a region and the early distribution of national income. For example, a plantation-type crop such as sugar, tea, or cotton may be unfavorable for subsequent domestic development because its production requires the importation of large numbers of cheap unskilled laborers who become enmeshed in a vicious circle which is difficult to break. There was something of this element in the

[15] For an elaboration, see R. E. Baldwin, "Patterns of Development in Newly Settled Regions," *Manchester School of Economic and Social Studies, XXIV*, No. 2, 161–179 (May 1956).

importation of Indians and Chinese into Malaya, and of Indians into Ceylon. In contrast, the production function for a commodity like wheat seems to be much more favorable to development, and a country that initially specializes in this commodity has a much greater development potential. The high quality of the labor supply that migrates into this region, the better possibilities for expansion to optimum size units of production, and the less unequal distribution of income are more favorable to further growth. Even if the plantation economy possesses other natural resources, the domestic development of the country's full potential will be limited by the lack of adequate market demand based on the highly unequal distribution of income in the country, the great difficulties in training the uneducated and unskilled plantation workers and small farmers, and the deficiency of entrepreneurial activity. Instead, what is likely to happen is that these resources will be developed as an export industry, and the materials will be exported in their raw form. Most extractive industries are, however, capital-intensive and require only small amounts of highly skilled labor. Oil and iron ore are examples. Both the large capital requirements and skilled labor are likely to come from abroad with the result that the employment and income impact on the domestic economy tends to be relatively small.

In the non-plantation economy, however, the better distribution of income, the more favorable entrepreneurial activity, and the less difficult labor problems are more likely to facilitate the use of the natural resources for domestic purposes as well as for export. Processing and refining industries as well as consumer durable industries using the product are more likely to arise in this type of economy. In these industries additional favorable effects on raising per capita income occur.

A final international obstacle has been the repercussions of foreign investment. The direction of foreign investment has been mainly confined to furthering the production of exports. Exports have certainly risen, but the market imperfections have prevented the expansion of exports from having much of an impact on the rest of the economy. Moreover, although the plantation system promoted production in the export sector, the contribution of the foreign enterprises has been very small per person after deducting capital charges, profits, and wages of foreign personnel. And so far as the plantations have been able to draw upon a surplus supply of unskilled labor with low marginal products, there has been little increase in real wages.

The outflow of profits to foreigners has in some cases absorbed a large part of the potential real saving of the poor countries. In Latin America, for example, the annual average of investment income earned by foreigners from 1925 to 1929 was $660 million, but the net inflow of long-term capital was only $230 million; in 1950, the outflow was $755 million, and the inflow was only $33 million. Of course, this problem cuts both ways: although the country loses funds to foreigners through the profit outflow, there might well be no capital inflow and subsequent increase in exports if the country should restrict the profit outflow. Nevertheless, this outflow of profits in the form of straight withdrawals, rather than in the form of imports, does limit the potential real savings of the economy.

The position of foreign enterprise may also restrain the pace of development even if the plantation system does not exist. Where population density has been too high, or technical conditions are unsuitable for the plantation system, peasant production of commercial crops has continued to prevail. But in this case the peasant producers have frequently had to face a small group of exporting and processing firms who have monopsonistic powers in buying the crop. And as consumers of imported commodities, the peasants have confronted the same group of firms who are the monopolistic sellers or distributors of these commodities. Thus, in their roles as producers, consumers, and laborers facing large foreign mining and plantation concerns which have monopsonistic power over labor, the backward peoples have contended with monopolistic and monopsonistic forces. To this extent, it may be said that the native's real income has not risen as much as it would have if he had sold and bought in more competitive markets.

It should, however, be recognized that the foreign firms have also played an important role in promoting whatever development has occurred. Their distribution of imported goods into the interior has been among the most potent forces in furthering an increase in production for sale by demonstrating to the native the benefits he can derive from market production. In addition, many firms have reinvested some of their profits within the country. The point being made here is not that foreign enterprises have on balance limited development, but simply that some of the results have been limiting, and that, even though there have been absolute gains, the relative gains might have been greater.

Even more significantly, from the standpoint of the income effects to be expected from a multiplier-accelerator process, it can be said that the income-generating forces were considerably dampened by leakages abroad. Not only has there been the outflow of profits and interest to the lending country, but the poor country has also had to import any machinery associated with any induced investment that has occurred as its exports rose. The high marginal propensity to import and high income elasticity of demand for imports have also operated in the same direction of dampening a rise in income. The result has been that a given amount of investment in the poor country has generated a much smaller amount of income than an equivalent amount of investment would have generated in a less dependent country.

Thus, although the poor countries have followed the broad dictates of comparative advantage and have received foreign investment, the full potential of the gains from foreign trade and foreign investment have not been realized. To this extent, their development has been constrained.

In some cases the patterns of foreign investment and foreign trade may have been at fault in limiting the possible gains from trade, but it must also be emphasized that market imperfections—all the rigidities and inflexibilities previously discussed—have also made it difficult for the full benefits of foreign trade to be diffused throughout the economy. The progress in the export sector has not been able to carry over to the rest of the economy. And to this extent it has been more difficult to break the vicious circles.

Thus, a comprehensive view of the obstacles to development should recognize not only the three different categories of obstacles—market imperfections, vicious circles, and international forces—but also how the three are interrelated and mutually reinforcing. Fundamentally, the market imperfections have obstructed the realization of an optimum allocation of resources; the vicious circles have prevented the introduction of structural changes; and the international forces have not been optimal from the poor country's viewpoint. In so far as these obstacles overlap and intensify one another, it has been difficult to tighten and widen the poor country's economy, and poverty has persisted.

Chapter 16

General Requirements
for Development

With a profile of a poor country in mind and some reasons why it has remained poor, it is now possible to consider what are the general requirements for its development. An answer to this question involves more than merely saying "remove the obstacles to development" or "release the inhibitors." Such a "trigger approach" to the problems of development does not carry one very far. Nor does such a general answer as "stimulate innovation, capital accumulation, and cultural change." These answers are too mechanical and oversimplified; it is necessary to spell out what is involved in these requirements and what are their interrelations.

To do this, the aid of all disciplines is needed, especially history, psychology, sociology, and political science. This chapter considers in broad terms certain requirements for the acceleration of development. Subsequent chapters will then examine in more specific terms some domestic and international policies that might help to achieve these requirements.

1. Indigenous Forces

A major requirement is that the development process be established on an indigenous base within the society of the poor country. The fundamental desire for economic betterment and the initiative in carrying out material achievements must arise within the poor country; it cannot simply be implanted from outside. Forces outside the economy can stimulate and facilitate the indigenous forces, but they can only complement sustained development; they cannot serve as a substitute for it.

The importance of an indigenous base will be appreciated if it is recognized that there is a vast difference between initiating development and maintaining development. Some projects might be initiated with foreign aid, but this will not ensure the maintenance of development. Many spectacular short-run results can be achieved with a relatively small amount of external help: for example, the use of better fertilizers and disease-resistant seeds can raise agricultural output markedly. But other measures are needed to follow through and move forward from these innovations. Development will falter if incomes are increased through external aid, without sufficient internal motivation. If the process is to become cumulative and long-lasting, the development forces must be fundamentally based within the developing country. Unless the stimuli that initiate development catch hold elsewhere in the economy, and unless there are feedbacks within the economy—in short, unless development forces are created within the poor country—the initial stimuli will be dissipated, and the development will be only short-lived and artificial.

Another disadvantage in expecting the major part of the development drive to come from external aid is that foreign investors generally are more interested in developing the natural resources than the peoples of these regions. It therefore becomes all the more important that the initiative and institutional arrangements for development rest firmly on a domestic base. The attitudes of the domestic leaders must be such that they will resist the temptation of quick spectacular projects in favor of more substantial ultimate objectives. For rapid, but short-lived, development can conflict with slower, but sustained, long-run development. Unless the process of development becomes institutionalized within the poor country, there is little likelihood that the "islands of development" will merge into pervasive development throughout the economy, and that the propulsive forces of development will be able to prevail over longer periods.

2. Perfecting the Market

Another requirement is that market imperfections be removed. These restrict the transference of factors from less productive to more productive forms of employment, handicap the expansion and development of markets, and limit the impact on one sector of expansion in another sector. Alternative forms of social and economic organizations are required to remove the market imperfections.[1]   The opportunities for greater productivity within the existent state of knowledge and with the same resources must be more widely exploited, but the knowledge of market opportunities must also be increased.   Monopolistic practices throughout the domestic production and marketing sectors must be diminished.   The capital market must be widened, and credit facilities must be made more readily available to peasant producers, small traders, and small businessmen.   In brief, the economy must move towards a more efficient use of its existent resources.

A removal of market imperfections in order to achieve an optimum allocation of resources is, however, only part of the task of accelerating development.[2]   The problem is much more one of the dynamic utilization of resources and structural changes rather than the fine adjustment of existent resources at the margin.   In other words, the major requirement is to push the production frontier outwards rather than merely reach a given production frontier.   As Schultz observes, "In most poor countries there is not much economic growth to be had by merely taking up whatever slack may exist in the way the available resources are being utilized.   To achieve economic growth of major importance in such countries, it is necessary to allocate effort and capital to do three things: increase the *quantity* of reproducible goods; improve the *quality* of the people as productive agents; and raise the *level* of the productive arts."[3]

The type of development that some of the neo-classicists envisaged was an increase in national product as a result of a more efficient allocation of given resources—the movement to a maximum given production frontier.   In contrast, a shift in the maximum production frontier involves an increase in labor, capital, land, or improvement in technology.   The neo-classical view of the fulfillment of marginal conditions

---

[1] Some illuminating general propositions about economic organization are made by T. W. Schultz, *Economic Organization of Agriculture,* McGraw-Hill Book Co., New York, 1953, Chapters XV, XVI.   The necessary changes in values and social institutions are discussed in section 6, below.

[2] An interesting example of this is provided by Sol Tax, *Penny Capitalism: A Guatemalan Indian Economy,* United States Government Printing Office, Washington, 1953.   Tax describes the economic system of a particular Guatemalan village as "very strongly a market economy . . . which tends to be perfectly competitive." Yet, the economy is essentially static, and economic development remains at a low level.   Rational acquisitiveness and the most productive use of existent resources are alone insufficient for sustained development.

[3] T. W. Schultz, "The Role of Government in Promoting Economic Growth," in L. D. White (ed.), *The State of the Social Sciences,* University of Chicago Press, Chicago, 1956, 372.   Also see B. Higgins, "Development Planning and the Economic Calculus," *Social Research, XXIII,* No. 1, 45 (Spring 1956).

is alone not particularly useful in understanding development problems of poor countries. For what has been required in these countries has not been so much the small marginal type of adjustments, but rather sizable, discrete changes. The production of a new commodity or the introduction of a railway which may alter the entire productive structure of an area is a structural change which can scarcely be interpreted as a marginal adjustment; it is a structural change involving "total conditions" rather than "marginal conditions."

The removal of market imperfections may, however, also help to widen the economy and push the production frontier outwards. Taking a dynamic view of the nature of the development process, one may recognize that movements within a given supply of resources and changes in these resources actually blend together. One cannot then consider improving the allocation of given resources without also considering changes in the supply of these resources. For a gradual outward movement of the production frontier will help create the necessary fluidity to achieve the maximum potential from the given resources.

The removal of market imperfections is especially necessary if capital accumulation is to catch hold and if development in one sector is to spill over to other sectors. In particular, if rigidities and inflexibilities were reduced, foreign trade would have much more of an impact throughout the economy. The carry-over from the export sector to the rest of the economy would be greater in such forms as more advanced techniques and entrepreneurial activities, and the potential gains from trade would be able to be diffused more widely through the economy. A reduction in market rigidities and compartmentalized sectors would also help to divert what savings there now are away from presently unproductive outlets to more productive investment. Development involves an extension of the market, and artificial barriers can be just as restrictive in preventing this extension as can the real deficiency of effective demand. The less is the degree of market imperfection, the more efficient will be the allocation of resources, and the more rapidly and widely will an advance in foreign trade carry over to the rest of the economy, thereby making it easier to break the vicious circles.

3. Capital Accumulation

Most observers of the problem agree that a major requirement for development is the accumulation of real capital. This involves three interdependent activities: (1) an increase in the volume of real savings, so that resources that would have been used for consumption purposes can be released for other purposes; (2) a finance and credit mechanism, so that the resources may be claimed by investors; and (3) the act of investment itself, so that resources are used for the production of capital goods.

The requirement of capital accumulation cannot be met simply by creating financial institutions and by monetary expansion. A strong financial structure is important in influencing the mobility and allocation of capital and in channeling savings into productive investment. But the mere existence of channels of finance does not guarantee an increase in the level of capital formation.[4] Nor would the problem of capital accumulation in real terms be solved even if there were a perfectly elastic supply of money. Without additional real savings, monetary expansion may merely generate inflation.

The basic point is that the cost of development must be measured in real terms, not monetary terms. The real costs are those of the resources that must be mobilized to carry out the development program; the foreign and domestic services, materials, and equipment directly required for its execution; and the additional goods and services for which more demand will indirectly be created through development expenditures.

The problem is thus not one of simply increasing monetary demand, but rather that of raising the supply of real output. Physical deficiencies and absence of necessary technical factors cannot be overcome merely by expanding the money supply. Real capital accumulation is required. And this, in turn, comes down to the need for additional savings and productive investment. For, as has already been noted, much, and in some cases all, of the present savings in poor countries where population is growing is used merely to maintain the present amount of capital per worker. If this ratio is to be increased, if more efficient methods of production are to be introduced, if public overhead capital is to be extended, if industrial activities are to expand—if production in general is to increase—then more savings and greater capital accumulation are required.

The method of measuring capital requirements for the development of poor countries is broadly as follows. First, an estimate is made of the rate of population growth. Next, some target is established for the desired rate of increase in per capita real income. Then, some figure for the "marginal capital-output ratio," the ratio between investment and

---

[4] It is difficult to specify what type of financial structure is most conducive to a high rate of development. One study concludes that there is no clear connection between the financial structure and rate of development in advanced capitalist countries during the past century, and that it cannot be proved that differences in financial structure have been responsible for differences in rates of development. R. W. Goldsmith, *A Study of Saving in the United States,* Princeton University Press, Princeton, 1955, 115–117.

the resulting increase in production, must be applied, allowances being made for the movement of excess workers out of agriculture and for a certain increase in the capital equipment available for all workers.

Estimates of the required real savings or capital formation necessary to maintain per capita income for a 1 per cent increase of population vary between 2 per cent and 5 per cent of the national income. Assuming a required saving ratio of 4 per cent of the national income, and a population increase of 2 per cent a year, as is now true in many poor countries, then a saving rate of 8 per cent a year would be required merely to maintain per capita income constant. Even if population were to remain constant, but per capita income were to increase by 2 per cent a year, then a saving rate of 8 per cent would again be required. If population were to increase by 2 per cent and per capita income were also to rise by 2 per cent, then a saving rate of 16 per cent would be required.[5] In most of the high-population-growth-potential countries, however, the actual saving rate is in fact much lower than this, averaging only about 5 per cent.

Any such estimate of capital requirements is necessarily rough. Data on past experiences are extremely scarce, and forecasts are likely to be wide of the mark with respect to the marginal capital-output ratio, the amount of disguised unemployment, the amount of capital required for each non-agricultural worker, and the extent to which there will be other changes in productivity and techniques not associated with investment.

The marginal capital-output ratio is especially difficult to estimate. Some estimates of this ratio are very high, based on the arguments that in the poor countries there is a great waste in the use of capital, technical knowledge grows very slowly, public overhead capital is needed, certain kinds of investment are bound to be initially underutilized, limited natural resources require more substitution of capital, and as development proceeds the pattern of demand will shift towards more capital-intensive industries. In contrast, other estimates of the marginal capital-output ratio are quite low, based on the arguments that capital will be used to open up new natural resources that will increase output considerably, the pattern of development will emphasize the less capital-intensive sectors of the economy such as agriculture and cottage industry, capital-saving inventions can be introduced, there will be fuller use of previously unutilized capacity, a large part of the investment

[5] This method for measuring capital requirements is an alternative to that discussed in the Harrod-Domar analysis, Chapter 5. This method is more relevant when development is being governmentally planned, whereas the Harrod-Domar approach applies more to cases where growth is left undirected and the saving ratio is taken as given.

will remove bottlenecks, and a small increase in capital may result in a relatively large gain in labor productivity.

Various estimates have been made of capital-output ratios in poor countries. A group of experts appointed by the United Nations used a ratio ranging from 2:1 to 5:1, whereas two reports of the World Bank (Ceylon and Surinam) estimated the average ratio of reproducible capital to output characteristic of poor countries as 3.5–4.0:1. The first Indian five-year plan suggested an average capital-output ratio of 3:1; Kurihara has assumed a ratio for most poor countries in the order of 5:1; Singer, in his model for economic development, assumes a ratio of 6:1 in the non-agricultural sector and 4:1 in the agricultural sector; and Rosenstein-Rodan estimates that the ratio is at least 3:1 or 4:1.[6]

Even though attempts to estimate capital requirements may be futile, nonetheless the general conclusion is clear: if per capita real income in the poor countries is to increase, considerably more net capital accumulation will be needed than is currently taking place in these countries. If the economies of these countries are to be propelled forward, if there is to be anything approaching an Industrial Revolution, then the level of net investment must rise from its current low level of 5 per cent or so of national income to a level approaching more nearly the 10 per cent to 15 per cent figure of richer countries.[7]

How can this increase in the investment rate be achieved? There are several possibilities. First, an obvious way to increase savings is to restrict domestic consumption. This can be accomplished in various ways. Increased taxation, involving both more rigorous enforcement of already existing taxes and the introduction of new taxes, allows the government to force savings and reduce disposable incomes. A difficulty with this method, however, is that, while involuntary saving is increased, voluntary saving may be diminished since individuals may reduce their voluntary saving in order to maintain their former consumption levels.

Another drawback of taxation might be the negative effects which it

---

[6] United Nations, *Measures for the Economic Development of Under-Developed Areas,* New York, 1951, 47; K. Kurihara, "Growth Analysis and the Problem of Capital Accumulation in Underdeveloped Countries," *Metroeconomica, VI,* No. III, 110 (Dec. 1954); H. W. Singer, "The Mechanics of Economic Development: A Quantitative Model Approach," *Indian Economic Review, I,* No. 2, 1–18 (Aug. 1952); P. N. Rosenstein-Rodan, "Capital Needs in Underdeveloped Countries," *Économique Appliquée, I–II,* 1954.

[7] Cf. W. A. Lewis, *Theory of Economic Growth,* Allen & Unwin Ltd., London, 1955, 208, 226; also, W. W. Rostow, "The Take-Off into Self-Sustained Growth," *Economic Journal, LXVI,* No. 261, 33 (March 1956).

supposedly has on incentives. If taxes on wage earners diminish their incentive to work harder, if taxes on profits of the higher income groups reduce their incentive to save and to make investments in new enterprises, and if taxes on the output or income of farmers diminish the incentive to improve agricultural techniques, then the forced savings extracted through these taxes will not be an unmixed gain. Thus, it is necessary to devise a tax system that, while being within the administrative capacity of the poor country, will at one and the same time counteract the inflationary effects of development spending, not destroy incentives, and not violate the accepted notion of equity.

Second, as an alternative or supplement to financing development through taxes, the government may again force the people to save more through a system of compulsory lending to the government or some development corporation. Or, if there are potential savers, the government may attempt to borrow from these individuals by selling them government securities. Such voluntary saving, however, will not be anti-inflationary unless the buyers of government securities reduce their spending in order tp buy the securities; if they merely divert their savings from other liquid assets to the government securities, there is no anti-inflationary effect. For this reason lending to the government must be made attractive to potential savers and to groups as far down the income scale as possible; the securities would then be more likely to be bought with income that would otherwise be spent.

A third method of accumulating capital is through the restriction of consumption imports. If these imports are reduced, then domestic savings might increase, or essential capital equipment might be imported instead of the consumer goods. To achieve the desired results, however, it is necessary that voluntary saving not be reduced in order to raise domestic consumption when the consumption imports are restricted.

Fourth, consumption might also be curtailed through the inflation method described by Schumpeter. This is another form of forced saving since prices rise more rapidly than the incomes of some groups in the community, and their consumption in real terms is diminished. It is easy, however, for inflation to begin spiraling in a poor economy, and excessive inflation can play havoc with the development process, particularly by leading to a breakdown in the normal money market mechanism, misdirecting investment into speculative channels, and creating balance of payments difficulties.[8]

A fifth method of increasing capital formation is to remove the disguised unemployment from the land and service industries. If there

[8] This is discussed in more detail in section 5.

are agricultural workers with a zero marginal product, they can be transferred from the agricultural sector to the non-agricultural sector without diminishing agricultural output. The objective is to mobilize these unproductive workers and employ them on various capital-creating projects such as roads, irrigation systems, and simple construction work where they do not require much more capital with which to work. In general, to the extent that labor productivity is higher in manufacturing than in agriculture, a shift of labor from agriculture to manufacturing employment would make possible a higher rate of development. But how will the non-agricultural workers be fed? Previously they were subsidized by the productive workers. This must continue. In other words, average productivity in the agricultural sector must increase, and the consumption of the remaining productive workers must be kept at its former level; that is, they must still make available the surplus, which they did not formerly consume, to the workers who have been withdrawn. In this way there can be an increase in investment goods without any alternative cost.

This removal of disguised unemployment is, of course, simply the familiar point of achieving a more efficient allocation of a given supply of resources, that is, moving towards the maximum production frontier. This achievement, however, may be difficult. Those left on the farm are likely to want to consume most of the additional food left to them; their income elasticity for food is probably about unity since their incomes are so low. Those who are withdrawn from agriculture will probably have to be offered more than the income they have been receiving in order to induce them to move. The people withdrawn will need training for their new jobs, some additional capital equipment with which to work, plus houses and other types of overhead capital. All these problems hamper the transfer.

Foreign borrowings constitute a sixth way of securing the saving necessary for investment. The foreigner does the saving, and the foreign borrowings allow the accumulation of additional capital either directly through importation or indirectly by releasing resources from the domestic production of import-competing commodities or exports. If commodities are imported, rather than produced at home, the resources saved can be diverted to the production of investment goods.

Finally, the foreign trade sector may provide some potential for capital accumulation through an improvement in the income terms of trade. If export prices rise and export proceeds increase, then the country's import capacity increases. But if this capacity is dissipated on the importation of consumption goods which do not replace the domestic production of competitive goods, there is no increase in investment. Or if the extra income from exports goes into increased consumer spending on domestic goods, there is no rise in investment. To be a source of capital formation, the additional import capacity which results from an improvement in the terms of trade must be channeled into additional saving. If the increase in export proceeds is to bring about a corresponding growth in the volume of imports of capital goods, it is necessary to prevent consumption from rising: the increment in income resulting from the greater value of exports must be saved. To the extent that this saving does not occur voluntarily, it will have to be extracted through taxation, exchange control, or other protective measures.

Important as capital formation is, the mere objective of accumulation may be overstressed. For to gain the most from capital formation, a country must also have adequate capital-absorption capacity, as discussed below in section 5, and must also experience technological and organizational progress so that the capital may be used most productively. As British and American development show,[9] the saved proportion of output and the proportionate rate of growth of output have not moved together historically. This is because the growth rate of output depends on how much capital is needed per unit increase in output (the capital-output ratio) as well as on the amount of capital. A low capital-output ratio is thus as significant as capital accumulation, and a low ratio requires, in turn, technological and organizational progress so that capital becomes more productive.

4. Investment Criteria

When one proceeds from the general requirements of capital accumulation to the more specific requirements of allocating the additional investment expenditures, it becomes necessary to establish some investment criteria. For the character of investment expenditures, with respect to both industry selection and choice of production techniques, will be decisive in determining whether a given volume of investment contributes as much to development as is possible.

It is difficult, however, to establish criteria for the best allocation of investment. Alternative criteria will affect total output differently: a certain investment criterion may maximize total output over a given period of time, but another criterion may be more relevant for maximizing output over a different time period. Moreover, the allocation

[9] Cf. Chapters 8 and 9, above; W. Fellner, *Trends and Cycles in Economic Activity*, Henry Holt & Co., New York, 1956, 62–67; A. K. Cairncross, "The Place of Capital in Economic Progress," in L. H. Dupriez (ed.), *Economic Progress*, Institut de recherches économiques et sociales, Louvain, 1955, 235–248.

of investment will affect not only total output but also the supply and distribution of the labor force, social and cultural conditions, growth and quality of the population, tastes, and technological progress. If the problem of investment criteria is interpreted only in static terms, with a *ceteris paribus* assumption, then such significant aspects of the total problem will be overlooked.[10] The criterion under static conditions may then be completely inappropriate for the total dynamic situation. But when the dynamic situation is recognized, considerable disagreement over investment criteria is possible since there will be various judgments regarding which objectives should be given priority and how these objectives might be best fulfilled.

The most general criterion of investment should be that of productivity. The investment must be of a productive character if it is to be conducive to further development. But specifically, what does this over-all criterion mean?

The general rule of productivity is clear in a formal sense: those investments should be made in which the social marginal productivity is the highest. Those who advocate social marginal productivity as the main investment criterion have also deduced three corollaries which are frequently advanced as practical guides to policy: (1) a given volume of investment should be allocated in a manner that maximizes the ratio of current output to investment; (2) those investment projects should be selected that will maximize the ratio of labor to investment; and (3) to reduce pressures on the balance of payments, investment should be allocated in a manner that will maximize the ratio of export goods to investment.[11]

The use of these principles in specific situations is, however, likely to be difficult. For development is a dynamic process which involves change in the size and quality of population, tastes, technological knowledge, and social and institutional factors. The criterion of social marginal product must therefore be interpreted within the total dynamic complex.

To do this, one must make value judgments regarding various social objectives, some of which can be conflicting. Consider, by way of illustration, this example. Imagine the most productive type of invest-

---

[10] This has been emphasized by Galenson and Leibenstein, among others. Cf. W. Galenson and H. Leibenstein, "Investment Criteria, Productivity, and Economic Development," *Quarterly Journal of Economics, LXIX,* No. 3, 343–345, 363–367 (Aug. 1955).

[11] Cf. Galenson and Leibenstein, *loc. cit.,* 346; A. E. Kahn, "Investment Criteria in Development," *Quarterly Journal of Economics, LXV,* No. 1, 38–61 (Feb. 1951); H. B. Chenery, "The Application of Investment Criteria," *ibid., LXVII,* No. 1, 76–96 (Feb. 1953).

ment is in agricultural projects that require a large amount of labor. This raises income in agriculture, but, if this is a sector where population grows fairly rapidly in response to increases in income, then per capita income might fall back to its initial level. This result can be contrasted with another type of project that increased national product less, but because of the nature of the investment did not lead to an increase in population. This might happen because the wages of only a relatively few workers rose, and the aggregate rise in income was sufficiently large not to be offset by increased population with a consequent fall in per capita income. In the second case, national income might be raised less than in the first case, but per capita income would nevertheless be larger than in the first case. Thus, the question is whether national income or per capita income should be maximized.

Furthermore, different projects are likely to result in different distributions of income. If a project maximizes per capita income, but at the same time involves a more unequal distribution of income than would another project, should it be preferred? Answers to these questions involve value judgments, and different individuals may reach various conclusions. Even if the social marginal productivity of each investment project were known, this would still not resolve the issue of whether national output or per capita output should be maximized, and it would not be a sufficient guide to investment from the viewpoint of the most desirable distribution of income.

The simple criterion of social marginal productivity is also ambiguous as a guide to investment decisions when the shape of the income stream over time is considered. To determine the most productive investment projects, future yields of capital assets must be discounted to their present values, and these discounted values compared with their present costs. Investment decisions will differ according to the future shape of the income stream which is desired. For instance, from the standpoint of having a maximum increase in national output during the next 5 years, one type of investment, say, sugar production, might be the best. From the standpoint of having the highest national output 15 years from now, however, this might be a misdirection of investment, and some other direction, say, in manufacturing, might be better.

Similarly, there may be some conflict between maximizing the per capita level of consumption immediately or later. Investment project *A* may contribute more to per capita consumption in the short run than does investment project *B*. Over a longer period, however, project *B* may allow a higher level of consumption than would project *A*.

These questions, and other similar questions which can be readily asked, mean that specific decisions regarding the direction of investment cannot be made without first deciding on a set of social objectives. Some general remarks on the direction of investment may, however, be offered.

In what areas may investment be most productive? The relevant concept of productivity is, of course, a value concept and not simply a physical one. It may, for instance, be possible to produce a large output of shoes with a relatively small investment, but if there is no market for the shoes the economy will not benefit. Obviously, the shoe workers will spend only a small fraction of their income on shoes, and a market must be found for the remainder. When considering particular industries, one cannot assume that supply will create its own demand. There must be markets for the commodities produced.

Where then are the potential markets in the poor country? Domestic industries that are consumer-oriented but are presently operating inefficiently will provide some basis of market demand. The demand for building and construction is also likely to be high, since the poor country is deficient in roads, railways, houses, and public utilities. Investment in export industries for which there is a foreign demand is another attractive area, and import-competing industries provide still another potential market.

From the standpoint of supply, a requirement of the investment should be that it creates additional external economies. If investment can be directed so as to further the horizontal and vertical integration of the process of production, permit a better division of labor, and allow industry to make use jointly of such facilities as a pool of technical skill, a common source of raw materials, or better utilization of social overhead capital, then external economies are likely to emerge,[12] and the economy will more closely approach an optimum increase in total output.

These considerations of available market demand and the creation of external economies may be summarized by saying that investment should be directed to "growing points" in the economy. It is necessary to concentrate on certain focal areas which seem to have the promise of more rapid growth: those projects are favored that in themselves do not require a great deal of additional investment to succeed but will have a readily available demand, will provide significant external economies to other existing firms and industries, or will generate demand for supple-

[12] Cf. J. H. Adler, "The Fiscal and Monetary Implementation of Development Programs," *American Economic Review, Papers and Proceedings, XLII,* No. 2, 586–588 (May 1952).

mentary products and services. From these focal areas a chain reaction may then be started that will gradually spread change throughout the economy.[13]

This general conclusion of directing investment to "growing points" should be supplemented by two additional considerations. First, investment should be allocated according to a balance of payments criterion as well as a productivity criterion. Alternative types of investment expenditures will have different effects on the country's export capacity and import requirements. One investment project may be more export-creating than another, and one project may be more import-requiring than another. Recognizing that the poor country is particularly prone to balance of payments difficulties, one may favor investment projects that will reduce imports or increase exports, all other things being equal. Such projects are also desirable, even aside from the balance of payments problem, in so far as they increase the amount of foreign exchange available for the importation of essential capital equipment.

Second, one should take an over-all view of the pattern of investment and realize that the various sectors of the economy are interdependent. The concept of "growing points" then merges into the broader requirement of "balanced growth." This idea is implicit in the point that social rather than private productivity is the relevant investment criterion, and that attention be given to the creation of external economies. It is not enough to focus only on particular "growing points" in the economy because investment in one part of the economy will have effects on other parts. If the economy is viewed as a unit made up of interrelated parts, then it becomes apparent that investment must be made on a broad front in order that the various parts of the economy can move forward in balance. There must be some internal consistency in the pattern of production. If investment occurs over a wide range of industries, there is an over-all enlargement of the market as one industry provides a market for another industry's output. Whereas an individual investment, occurring in isolation, may be discouraged by the narrowness of the pre-existing market, a wave of investments on a broad front

[13] The same idea has been expressed by Rostow in terms of "primary" or "leading" growth sectors. Rostow suggests that the sectors of a developing economy can be classified into three groups: the "primary" sectors which lead the growth process, "supplementary" sectors, and "derived" growth sectors (such as food production) where growth is induced by the growth of such aggregates as population or national income. Rostow, "Trends in the Allocation of Resources in Secular Growth," Center for International Studies, M.I.T., unpublished paper, Cambridge, 1953.

will widen the market for each investment.[14]   A complementary system of different industries reduces each industry's risk that it will not be able to sell its product.   To insure that increased production in one sector is met by increased demand from another sector, a wide range of investments in a number of different industries is needed.

From the requirement of balanced growth it is apparent that an increase in non-agricultural production will also require an expansion in agricultural production, unless the country can expand its non-agricultural exports and import more foodstuffs and raw materials.   Instead of being competitive, agricultural development and industrial development are complementary: the rate of industrial development is largely dependent on parallel agricultural development.   If employment is increased in non-agricultural sectors, there will be a greater demand for foodstuffs from these additional workers.   Also the agricultural workers themselves will tend to consume part of any increase in agricultural output.   Supplies of food must therefore rise.

Urban communities also depend for their expansion on adequate supplies of raw materials.   And at the outset of any industrialization program, the chief market for light industrial products is in the agricultural population, so that an increase in the income of the peasantry is a prerequisite for the expansion of manufacturing.   Moreover, a failure to develop agriculture at the same time as non-agricultural sectors are expanding will very likely lead to inflation.   A balance is therefore needed between investment in the agricultural and industrial sectors of the economy.

A balance is also necessary between domestic trade and foreign trade.   Export revenue is an important source for financing development; imports rise as production and employment expand; and domestic trade itself requires increasing imports of necessary materials and equipment.   To pay for these rising imports, and to allow exports to finance development as much as possible, the country cannot expand its domestic trade at the expense of its foreign trade.   The domestic sector must grow in balance with the foreign sector.

More detailed aspects of interdependence must also be recognized.   If, for example, a steel mill is to be built, there must be a sufficient supply of all the inputs of raw material, capital, and labor that are directly and indirectly needed to sustain the operation of the mill.   Moreover, atten-

---

[14] Cf. R. Nurkse, *Problems of Capital Formation in Underdeveloped Countries,* Basil Blackwell, Oxford, 1953, 11–14; P. N. Rosenstein-Rodan, "Problems of Industrialization of Eastern and South-Eastern Europe," *Economic Journal, LIII,* No. 210–211, 205–206 (June–Sept. 1943); Allyn Young, "Increasing Returns and Economic Progress," *Economic Journal, XXXVIII,* No. 152, 527–542 (Dec. 1928).

tion must be given not only to the input side but also to the output side, that is, the existence of a market that is able to absorb the output. Such projects as steel mills, power plants, railways, or large manufacturing industries must be operated close to full capacity if the investment is to be most productive. This requires complementary industries to demand the output. Thus investment in one sector must always be considered with respect to the degree of complementarity among various sectors. Without sufficient complementarity, the large-scale investment project will not be economical: it will merely be an example of "conspicuous production."

One final problem associated with investment criteria should be discussed: the choice of production techniques.[15] Assuming that there will be a market for the output that results from investment, the question arises as to whether the poor country should make investments of a capital-intensive or a labor-intensive kind. There is considerable disagreement on this issue; some writers maintain that the best combination of factors involves a high ratio of capital to labor, whereas others maintain that a low ratio is desirable, and still others believe that this is not even a particularly relevant criterion. In a sense, all are correct, in so far as they consider different aspects of the problem.

If the production function for a certain product requires a higher ratio of capital to labor, and because of technological constraints labor cannot be substituted for capital, then it would be useless to employ much labor. In this case additional labor would not add anything to total output, and there would merely be a loss in what the additional workers had been producing previously. The relevant consideration is again the social marginal product. If the criterion of a high ratio of labor to capital is followed arbitrarily, this project would not be undertaken because it was technologically not feasible to use the labor. Clearly, any simple rule regarding the combination of factors cannot be followed without qualification and without consideration of its particular relevance in each case.

If, however, the production function permits wide substitution possibilities between labor and capital, what then is the best way to produce any given output of the product? Obviously, in the cheapest manner from a social point of view. And since in the poor country the social price of labor is likely to be low or even zero compared with the price of capital, a relatively high ratio of labor to capital will be favored. In general, where market opportunities exist, and where technological

[15] This problem is discussed further in Chapter 19, section 2. Also see V. V. Bhatt, "Capital Intensity of Industries," *Bulletin of the Oxford University Institute of Statistics, XVIII*, No. 2, 179–194 (May 1956).

restraints are not a problem, the most efficient use of resources in the poor country will tend to favor labor-intensive methods. With respect to innovations, it would also follow that land-saving and capital-saving innovations should be favored over labor-saving and capital-using innovations.

If, however, the employment of much cheap labor relative to capital raises the wages of the employed, consideration should also be given to the distribution of income and the effects on per capita income. Again, consider the two types of investment, one using much capital relative to labor and another using much labor relative to capital, and assume that each of the two methods would increase national product by the same amount. The capital-intensive project, however, may employ fewer individuals who would be paid a relatively high income; the other project would employ more labor with only a slightly higher wage than they originally received. From the standpoint of income distribution, the labor-intensive project may then be preferred since it would raise somewhat the income level of a relatively large number of low-income workers.

A labor-intensive project, however, is most likely to be an agricultural project, since for technological reasons many of the labor-intensive possibilities are in agriculture rather than in manufacturing. But manufacturing projects usually promote urbanization, and in an urban industrial environment the birth rate may tend to fall.[16] From the viewpoint of per capita income, therefore, the labor-intensive project in agriculture may be less desirable than the capital-intensive manufacturing project. For the agricultural project may stimulate population growth with the result that per capita income remains the same or is even reduced below its initial level.

Finally, to strengthen its balance of payments, the country may have to direct some of the new investment into export production. If the export industries are capital-intensive, such as mining and mineral refining, then, even though there is a surplus of labor, investment may have to be directed to these capital-intensive industries for the sake of earning necessary foreign exchange.

Thus, it may be concluded that there are no simple criteria for deciding on capital-intensive versus labor-intensive projects. The criteria depend ultimately on broad economic and social objectives. It is necessary to consider not only the existing amounts and quality of factor supply but also various repercussions of the project—the effects on na-

---

[16] Although this has been generally true in Western economies, it need not be true in other countries. Even recent experience in the United States contradicts this tendency.

tional income over different time periods, conditions of market demand, ability to realize economies of scale, length of gestation periods, the effects on the distribution of income and level of per capita income, and balance of payments requirements.

5. Capital Absorption and Stability

Although the preceding discussion has emphasized capital accumulation and investment criteria, one should not think that a poor country can absorb capital without limit and at any rate. Each country has a limited capital absorption capacity. This capacity is in general determined, on one side, by the availability of complementary factors of production with which capital is to cooperate, and on the other side, by the requirements of avoiding inflation and maintaining balance of payments equilibrium.

Usually the most important limitations on a poor country's capacity to absorb capital are the lack of technology, the shortage of skilled personnel, and the low geographic mobility of labor. The country is likely to be particularly deficient in managerial, technical, supervisory, and skilled manpower. Such limitations on the supply of factors other than capital, especially managerial capacity and labor skills, result in a sharp decline in the marginal productivity of capital as capital accumulates. The marginal productivity of capital in poor countries may well be larger than in rich countries; however, if the amount of investment is increased greatly, the marginal productivity may decline rapidly, because of bottlenecks in production, and may even become negative. If capital accumulation is to proceed rapidly, then it will be necessary to try to increase the supply of other factors cooperant with capital. Until these bottlenecks are surmounted, it is all the more essential to select investments carefully in accordance with rational investment criteria.

Once development becomes accelerated, then the absorptive capacity will increase. Since bottlenecks are fairly widespread in the poor country and result in unused capacities elsewhere in the economy, it should be expected that the removal of these bottlenecks will increase total productivity considerably.

Besides the shortage of skills and the existence of bottlenecks, the absorption of capital is also limited by the necessity of restraining the tempo of development so as to avoid inflation and balance of payments disequilibrium.

There are some reasons for believing that poor countries are more prone to inflation than are the richer countries. A major inflationary trend in the richer countries is likely to be a cost-price push type of inflation, but in the poor countries, although there is also some cost pressure, the chief influence is monetary expansion, and this may be a stronger and more pervasive force. Investment is more likely to be financed by credit creation in poor countries, whereas in more developed countries a considerable part of investment may be financed out of retained earnings. In richer countries there are also more entrepreneurs who prefer long-term investments in productive enterprise rather than speculative short-term ventures. Furthermore, the governments of poor countries are limited in their capacity to control inflation, especially in applying fiscal and monetary policies, while at the same time they are in a weak position to resist the increasing demands for more government services, especially of a social welfare character. All the market imperfections also intensify inflation.

Development is likely to be hindered when there is an increase in the general price level. True, by driving up the prices of scarce resources, inflation can achieve forced saving,[17] and it may be argued that a moderate amount of inflation is desirable "when inducements are necessary for large-scale movements of labor and for increased supplies of foodstuffs and raw materials to be made available by the village for the towns."[18] But even though unused resources do exist, there may be so many market imperfections and so much inflexibility in the economy that even inflation will not be effective in enticing these resources into the market. Furthermore, there will have to be sufficient complementary resources to use the newly liberated factors of production; but higher prices will be necessary to transfer these other resources from consumption to investment uses. And even if resources are transferred away from consumption, the inflationary forces are still likely to cause a misdirection of capital formation as judged by investment criteria. Moreover, in practice, once inflation begins, it becomes difficult to limit it to a moderate amount. Instead of allowing only a mild inflation, the government is more likely to be tempted into deliberately using inflation as an easy way of financing increased expenditures. The process becomes cumulative, and it becomes extremely difficult to halt it because of vested interests who rely on its continuation. Experiences in Chile and Brazil, for example, show the difficulty of stopping inflation in practice.

Most significantly, inflation is a wasteful means of increasing invest-

[17] This is relatively ineffective, however, if the economy is not very dependent on the use of money and if the mass of the population is so close to the subsistence level that it can contribute little even in forced saving.

[18] Maurice Dobb, *Some Aspects of Economic Development,* Ranjit Printers & Publishers, Delhi, 1951, 48.

ment. The fall in consumption is some multiple of the amount of investment produced through forced saving.[19] And this method is not selective: people who can least afford to save are usually the very ones who are forced to save. Voluntary saving is discouraged, and, although forced saving may be effected in the short run, it becomes progressively more difficult over the longer run. Indeed, in a country where there has been considerable inflation for a long time, such as in Chile, it may be argued that, if inflation were halted, increased investment might be financed from voluntary savings. Furthermore, long-term lending is discouraged because the price rise wipes out the benefits of the fixed interest income. The inflationary conditions also cause a misdirection of savings away from more productive outlets towards short-term projects because of the uncertainty about price rises, and towards the holding of stocks of goods, gold, foreign currency, and real estate where the speculative element predominates over the productive. Moreover, the pressure for efficiency in production is reduced when inflationary profits are easy to come by. The resource malallocations which result from inflation can be sizable: it has been estimated, for example, that Chile is forgoing between a fifth and a fourth of its normal output as a result of inflation.[20]

If capital accumulation exceeds the country's absorptive capacity, it is also likely to cause balance of payments difficulties. The process of development inevitably involves a need for foreign exchange as imports increase. The rate of development must therefore be geared to the export capacity and import capacity of the country. Otherwise, an import surplus will cause much of the scarce supply of foreign exchange needed for capital imports to be dissipated on luxury imports to the disadvantage of the development program. Moreover, if too rapid a rate of development spills over into inflation, then export industries are confronted with constantly rising costs, and balance of payments difficulties are aggravated. The situation is also likely to deter foreign investments in the country and to encourage capital flight. If such balance of payments difficulties emerge, then the country's development will be handicapped because it will be impossible to import the necessary raw materials and equipment; or, if the country must service previous foreign investment, it will experience a transfer problem that may require for

[19] Cf. E. M. Bernstein and I. G. Patel, "Inflation in Relation to Economic Development," *International Monetary Fund Staff Papers, II,* No. 3, 363–382 (Nov. 1952).

[20] T. W. Schultz, "Latin American Economic Policy Lessons," *American Economic Review, Papers and Proceedings, XLVI,* No. 2, 428 (May 1956).

its solution a reduction in domestic consumption and investment. The amount of foreign borrowing that a country can properly undertake must be restrained by the condition that the borrowing should add more to the country's output in the long run than it costs, taking into account not only the direct service of the debt but also the adjustments that the borrowings cause in the country's economic structure and its terms of trade.[21]

The rate of development must therefore be influenced by considerations of maintaining a balanced relationship between the creation of exports plus the receipt of foreign investments and the requirements of imports plus the servicing of foreign investments. In general, it can be said that the country will tend to encounter balance of payments problems the more the development program diverts resources from export industries, the more capital goods must be imported for the development program, the more the terms of trade deteriorate, the more the distribution of income changes in favor of groups with a high marginal propensity to import, the stronger is the demonstration effect internationally, and the less is the propensity to save.

Rich countries can also ease the maintenance of balance of payments equilibrium in the poor countries if they reduce their trade barriers against imports from the poor countries, and if they adopt measures to stimulate a capital flow to these countries. Balance of payments problems of poor countries will also be mitigated to the extent that full employment is maintained overseas, fluctuations in primary product prices are reduced, and a high rate of development is maintained in industrialized nations.

It may be thought that the government could resort to inflationary financing of development if the government were responsible for the major part of the development program and if by suitable controls it were able to suppress the inflation and prevent it from breaking out into an open inflation. The government may then forestall balance of payments disequilibrium by resorting to direct import controls, exchange restrictions, taxation to shift down the consumption function, limitation of investment elsewhere in the economy, and price and wage controls. But, as will be discussed in Chapter 19, the merits of controls on foreign trade are debatable, and the rudimentary credit and banking system and the elementary taxation machinery of the poor country make the imposition of domestic controls quite problematical. Without the powers to suppress the inflation, the country will confront a situation of balance

[21] Cf. D. Finch, "Investment Service in Underdeveloped Countries," *International Monetary Fund Staff Papers, II,* No. 1, 60–85 (Sept. 1951).

of payments disequilibrium which will require the receipt of "distress borrowing," or else the country will have to depreciate its currency continuously as inflation becomes cumulative, as has happened in the past in many poor countries.

6. Values and Institutions

All the foregoing requirements for development have been of an economic character. Although they have been isolated for analytical purposes, economic matters are, of course, interwoven in practice with the rest of the social system. The pattern of investment, for example, is a function of political, cultural, and religious, as well as economic, values and motivations. The economic requirements thus have repercussions throughout the culture, and an economic change will require other changes in the society. Indeed, the psychological and sociological requirements for development are as important as the economic requirements. They deserve full consideration in their own right. Only a few general observations, however, can be offered here.[22]

It is obvious that some institutional changes which are not merely economic must accompany successful development efforts. Economic development of sufficient rapidity has not taken place within the present cultural framework. New wants, new motivations, new ways of production, new institutions need to be created if national income is to rise more rapidly. Where there are religious obstacles to modern economic progress, the religion may have to be taken less seriously or its character altered. Fundamentally the backward peoples must recognize that men can master nature; they must be motivated towards economic achievement; they must acquire the means of accomplishing these objectives; and these objectives must become part of the society's value structure.

In considering the social and cultural requirements for development, a Western student should not make the mistake of ethnocentrism, that is, assuming that, because the West is developed, Western values and institutions are therefore necessary for development, and that Western cultural patterns must be imported into the poor countries. Many values and institutions of the West may be only accidentally associated with Western development, and many values and institutions in poor countries may not be obstacles to development. It would appear that what is needed is a combination of existing and borrowed ideas and institutions. In this connection, psychologists and sociologists can make sub-

---

[22] For a more thorough discussion of this topic, the reader is referred to Appendix *A*, which lists selected readings of a more specialized nature.

stantial contributions by assessing to what extent the economic requirements can be achieved in the context of existing institutions and to what
extent institutional changes are needed.

To avoid human discontent, changes should be introduced in ways
that will disrupt the existing culture as little as possible: the cultural
change should be selective,[23] and wherever possible the disruption that
occurs should be compensated for, or channeled into constructive developments for the future. Once it is determined what habits and practices
must be changed, it becomes necessary to determine how they can be
altered. It is necessary to know to what extent required institutional
changes can be realized directly through education, demonstration,
and conversion, and to what extent they can be achieved indirectly
by economic changes that undermine the inhibiting institutions and
values.

It should be recognized, however, that cultural change which is too
rapid or too pervasive will bring resistance and leave a vacuum which
will only slowly be filled. The price of cultural change in terms of
unrest, discontent, and frustration must be fully appreciated. Caution
should be exercised, lest existing institutional patterns be upset too
rapidly, and the social costs in non-economic terms exceed the gains
in economic terms. For economic welfare is only a small part of general
social welfare, and it is the latter which should have prime consideration.
An increase in national income will not entail an increase in social
welfare, if the increase is accompanied by deep cultural adjustments.
Clearly, development goals must include judgments about these more
general aspects of welfare.

It can be suggested that more rapid progress will come by utilizing
as much as possible existing attitudes and institutions rather than by
attempting a frontal breakdown of the culture. This principle is recognized, for example, in a report of an International Bank survey mission
to Nigeria. "Though there is much in Nigerian attitudes which may
curb economic growth, there is much in the social organization which
can serve its cause. Nigerians have strong local loyalties. They are
closely tied to their immediate family or clan, they support local 'unions'
(clubs) and they take pride in local achievements. The banding together
of families, clans and village communities in producers' cooperatives, in
the savings clubs . . . and in thrift societies . . . are practical and promis-
ing illustrations of self-help. We think full support should be given
to the cooperative movement as a vehicle for economic development,

---

[23] Cf. M. E. Opler, "The Problem of Selective Cultural Change," in B. F.
Hoselitz (ed.), *The Progress of Underdeveloped Areas,* University of Chicago
Press, Chicago, 1952, 126–134.

for it is a form of economic organization fully compatible with Nigerian tradition and social sentiment."[24]

Although principles of cultural change are usually stated in very broad terms,[25] it is possible to be more specific. Every specific principle of economic change should be considered alongside a specific principle of cultural change. For instance, the economic criteria of investment are alone not a sufficient guide for investment policy: they must be supplemented by non-economic criteria.[26] For illustrative purposes, some non-economic criteria of investment might be as follows: invest in industries that require prolonged and high level training so as to justify sending children at an early age to training schools where they can get not only skills but also new values; invest in capital-intensive projects so that complex machines requiring maintenance are used because servicing the more complicated machines develops more desired character traits—impulse control, initiative, and general know-how; invest in projects that break up village life by drawing people to centers of employment away from the village because, by preventing impersonal relations, village life is a major source of opposition to change. Such non-economic considerations may reinforce or contradict economic considerations, but they constitute an essential part in any assessment of the requirements for development.

Perhaps the basic sociocultural problem is to increase the supply of entrepreneurship. On what does this supply depend? What values and motivations favor entrepreneurship? A broad approach to these questions might consider the motives and abilities of entrepreneurship and the extent to which the social environment is congenial for entrepreneurship.

An entrepreneur might be motivated by one or a combination of several objectives. The attraction might be higher monetary rewards, especially when this is a sign of occupation success or when money provides the means of buying status in an "achieved status" society. Or one might undertake an innovation to increase his economic power; or to advance the growth or protect the survival of his business as a unit. The activity of innovating might also appear to some as simply enjoyable in itself: some might just like "getting things done." Business might even be viewed as a game, and some might get a greater psychic return if they "win" in a risky situation than in a non-risky situation. Or there might be some larger end, possibly a community orientation, or

[24] I.B.R.D., *Report on the Economic Development of Nigeria,* Johns Hopkins University Press, Baltimore, 1955, 21.

[25] Cf. UNESCO (Margaret Mead, ed.), *Cultural Patterns and Technical Change,* Paris, 1953, 288–289.

[26] David McClelland has been helpful on this point.

the achievement of nationalistic aspirations, or—following Weber's interpretation of the influence of Calvinism—the performance of one's "calling" in accordance with God's plan.

Not only must there be individuals who are willing to engage in entrepreneurial activity; they must also be able to do so. Certain abilities characterize entrepreneurs: the ability to recognize market opportunities, the ability to recognize alternative possibilities of action, the ability to combine elements of rational decision making with some elements of irrational risk taking—in short, the entrepreneur must be willing to behave in an independent manner, overcome resistances to change, and assume personal responsibility for the outcome of his actions.

The social and economic environment may be more or less conducive to the exercise of these entrepreneurial abilities. If a man's status can be achieved by his own action, rather than being traditionally ascribed, and if business is not derogated, then entrepreneurs will not be so restricted. A framework of public order, stability, and legal rights will also enhance the opportunities for entrepreneurship. So will public policies designed to provide overhead capital and favorable monetary and fiscal incentives. Such policies might make people more willing to forgo short-run speculative gains for more long-run gains: there might be more of the "future orientation" that contributes to entrepreneurship. The more freedom there is for individual rewards and individual responsibilities, the more entrepreneurship will be favored. Technological advance will also extend the possibilities for innovations, and the easier it is to finance innovations, the more likely they are to be forthcoming. Also, when there is a greater degree of mobility of resources, and markets are wider, there are more possibilities for entrepreneurship. These environmental factors are favorable not only for large-scale innovations but also for the existence of multiple centers of initiative which enable a large number of innovations to occur, even if each innovation is only on a small scale.

Motives, abilities, and a congenial environment all combine to promote entrepreneurship. The stronger are the motives and abilities, the less necessary it is to have a congenial environment. If, however, as is true for the people of a poor country, the motives and abilities are weak, then it becomes all the more essential to have a more congenial environment. Efforts should be made to stimulate entrepreneurial motivations and entrepreneurial abilities. But this is a complicated long-run sociological problem. In the shorter run a more direct attack on the problem might take the form of making the economic and social environment more favorable.

In general, the economic problems of development are relatively simple compared with the broader and deeper sociological problems of respecting the general cultural patterns and institutions of the poor countries at the same time that they acquire new wants and the means of attaining them. Not only must economic organization be transformed, but social organization—as represented by such major institutions as caste, the joint family, the rural village, the church, and the school—must also be modified so that the basic complex of values and motivations may be more favorable for development. Thus, the requirements for development involve both economic change and cultural change. The fundamental problem is likely to be not how much economic change the economy can absorb, but rather how much cultural change the backward people can accept and how quickly.

Chapter 17

Domestic
Policy Issues (1)

Attention should now be given to specific policy measures which can implement the general requirements for development. It has already been seen in Part 1 how the various theories of development have certain policy implications. According to their own value judgments, however, different individuals will recommend different policies. Moreover, policy decisions involve a choice among alternatives, and these alternatives differ from country to country. No single development program will do for all poor countries: what may be suitable and effective in one case will not be so in another. Each country needs particular policies suited to its specific characteristics, problems, and goals. Accordingly, instead of attempting to formulate a definite set of policy recommendations for a particular country, the present discussion will simply suggest various possible lines of action of general relevance and attempt to assess some of their relative merits and demerits in broad terms.

1. Role of the Government

In countries that have had considerable development there have been various degrees of governmental participation in the initiation and direction of the development process. As will be discussed in Chapter 22, the government has played a large initiating and active entrepreneurial role in some countries: for example, in Japan after 1870, in Imperial Germany, and in the U.S.S.R. since World War I. In contrast, the development of England and the United States occurred with much less deliberate governmental action. In England, the rise of the new industrial and commercial bourgeoisie actually led to a freeing of economic enterprise from old government restrictions, and rapid development was associated with a laissez-faire environment. In the United States, governmental promotion of development was restricted mainly to providing settlers and railroads with land, establishing land-grant colleges, developing roads and harbors, and fostering some industries through protective tariffs and subsidies.

Most students of the problem now agree, however, that more vigorous governmental action is necessary to accelerate development in the poor countries. Since these countries have remained for so long almost stationary, many believe that positive governmental intervention is essential to get these countries off dead center. It is recognized that these countries are now in far different situations from those of countries that developed during the past century. As a comparison of the discussion in the last two chapters with Part 2 shows, some of the obstacles to development in the poor countries are now much greater than they ever were in England or the United States. Development cannot now be as spontaneous as it was under nineteenth-century conditions. Instead it is widely believed that only governmental action may have sufficient power and scope to break through some of the obstacles that have limited the development of poor countries.

Various general areas for government action are suggested. First, the government may have to establish markets by promoting suitable institutional arrangements. Second, government enterprise is needed in those fields where profits are too low or the risks are too large to attract private enterprise. Third, government enterprise is justified in those activities in which, even though they might be performed by private enterprise, the results of private performance would be less satisfactory than those of government performance. Fourth, government direction is needed to promote external economies and, more generally, "balanced growth."

Although such areas of governmental activity may have common acceptance, especially since they are really only abstract generalities, differences of opinion will arise when it comes to instituting specific policies in these areas. Given the case of developing a particular country, some observers would restrict the government's role to framework planning whereby governmental decisions are general in scope and few in number; others would extend the role to direct interference with the market mechanism and to some specific controls over private enterprise; still others would completely supplant the market mechanism with central planning and control and have the State replace the private entrepreneur.

These differences are bound to arise in so far as there are different views on what the sequence and tempo of development should be. In broadest outline, there are two different schools of thought. One group believes that the obstacles to development are so formidable and pervasive that they can be overcome only by having the State attempt to industrialize deliberately and immediately: the government should engage in comprehensive programming and planning, assume most of the entrepreneurial activities and attempt to achieve a high rate of capital formation as soon as possible. A complete development plan is advocated. Such a plan would have at least four main components: first, specific production "targets" representing increases in the quantitative production of desired commodities; second, a capital budget, comprising public investment projects; third, a "human investment budget" covering government expenditures that represent investment in the people—education, manpower training, health; and fourth, regulatory measures governing the activities of private individuals, enterprises, and institutions intended to redirect and guide these activities in a manner contributing to the achievement of the objectives included in the plan.[1]

The second group shies away from this "all or nothing" approach. Instead, it advocates a more gradual approach which places little if any emphasis on deliberate industrialization, limits the degree of specific planning, relies mainly on the market mechanism and private efforts, and approaches development problems in a step-by-step fashion.

Those who oppose the gradualist approach do so on several counts. In general they believe that, if a development program is to gather sufficient momentum to be successful, it must operate rapidly and extensively throughout the economy: "insistence on 'slow' evolution . . . is defeatist, and indeed dangerous, because it is precisely slow evolution that cannot succeed in the face of all the obstacles."[2] Unless the program involves big changes, it is believed that the development

[1] B. Higgins, "Development Planning and the Economic Calculus," *Social Research, XXIII,* No. 1, 36, 47 (Spring 1956).

[2] B. Higgins, "The 'Dualistic Theory' of Underdeveloped Areas," *Economic Development and Cultural Change, IV,* No. 2, 114 (Jan. 1956). Hereinafter cited as Higgins, "The 'Dualistic Theory'."

process will never be able to become self-generating and cumulative: if the race is to bé run at all, a certain minimum speed is necessary. This view has been expressed more precisely in terms of a "critical minimum effort" thesis of development.[3] According to this theory, a development program must be at least of a certain size, a "critical minimum," to reduce indivisibilities and discontinuities in the economy, overcome diseconomies of scale, have an impact on values, and offset certain other forces that arise to depress development once development begins (for example, possibly an increase in population). Thus, regarding capital accumulation, it is argued that "development requires primarily large amounts of capital investment, especially in the underdeveloped sector. This investment must be made in a sizable lump, and not through marginal increments that result from a set of unrelated individual decisions. In other words, it needs capital investment on a scale, and of a type, that will only be possible through joint efforts of the underdeveloped countries, and of those advanced countries able to provide large-scale capital investment."[4] Regarding technical assistance, it is believed that "The trouble is not so much that assistance is of the wrong kind, but that it is on far too small a scale."[5] And regarding the sociocultural obstacles, advocates of comprehensive development programs believe that large economic changes may in themselves weaken these obstacles: "If truly ambitious programs of capital and technical assistance are undertaken, with the full, wholehearted and sympathetic cooperation of the underdeveloped countries themselves, . . . there is a good chance that the social and cultural obstacles may disappear without being attacked directly. However, this result will be attained only if the scale of such assistance is big enough both to provide a 'shock treatment' and to turn the present large-scale disguised unemployment into an asset."[5]

Development programs of several countries do involve a considerable degree of central planning and control in an attempt to telescope the process by which an agrarian economy may become an industrial economy. But the more gradual and decentralized approach has gained increasing favor. Instead of seeking deliberate industrialization through direct governmental intervention, many development programs now concentrate only on agricultural improvements, the promotion of social services, the extension of public overhead capital, and the establishment of small-scale dispersed light industry.

[3] H. Leibenstein, *A Theory of Economic-Demographic Development,* Princeton University Press, Princeton, 1954, Chapter IV.
[4] Higgins, "The 'Dualistic Theory'," 113.
[5] *Ibid.,* 114.

The rationale behind these more moderate programs is this. First of all the agricultural sector of the economy is predominant, and there is extreme poverty in this section, but the possibilities for a large and rapid increase in agricultural output appear highly favorable. Agriculture also provides the most important link with world markets. As regards welfare projects such as schools, hospitals, and disease control, a relatively small investment is likely to give high returns in reducing human misery. The heavier projects of public overhead capital are to be undertaken by the State, since private investors are reluctant to venture into these areas, yet these public facilities are necessary to remove production bottlenecks. Concentrated heavy industry; however, is not immediately emphasized for several reasons. Inadequate market opportunities, lack of capital, scarcity of skills and administrative capacity, and an insufficient supply of entrepreneurship are major obstacles to large-scale industrialization. Moreover, in some countries resources may not be sufficient in amount or diversity to allow growth in the manufacturing sector, and, although in some cases immediate extension of the manufacturing sector might be possible, it would result in a future scarcity of raw materials. Small-scale light industry may, however, be more readily extended from local handicrafts. Small rural industry can do without a large part of urban services, and can thereby save for productive purposes capital expenditures that would otherwise be involved in the cost of urbanization.[6] Possibilities also exist for the processing of agricultural products. Sugar factories, rice mills, vegetable oil factories, and similar processing plants may be promoted. Not only does this recognize the extent to which the economy is presently committed to the land, but it also has the advantage of moving industry to the labor supply which is immobile.[7]

More fundamentally, the advocacy of a gradual approach to development is based on a belief that the growth of industry is ultimately to be induced by expansion in other sectors of the economy, rather than by deliberate governmental efforts in the industrial sector. Income is to be initially raised in the agricultural sector, partly by more efficient methods of production, and partly by such projects as dams, irrigation systems, and farm-to-market roads. These projects are designed not only to increase agricultural production but also to facilitate the flow of commodities between rural and growing urban areas.

At first the industrial development may simply complement agricul-

[6] H. Aubrey, "Small Industry in Economic Development," *Social Research,* *XVIII*, No. 3, 297 (Sept. 1951).

[7] On the general subject of raw material processing, see Charlotte Lebuscher, *The Processing of Colonial Raw Materials,* H.M.S.O., London, 1951.

ture. This is illustrated, for example, by the proposals of the International Bank survey mission to Iraq. The mission proposed a chemical plant which would provide cheap fertilizers needed to raise the productivity of agriculture, and also a modern machine shop which would cater to agriculture by reducing the cost of irrigation pumps. It also expected an expansion of cotton textile production and vegetable oil extraction capacity to follow from an increase in cotton output.

Industrial development which complements agriculture is, however, only the beginning. The ultimate desire in many poor countries goes far beyond this to a general extension of manufacturing activity. As the level of agricultural income increases, agricultural workers will have a higher effective demand for non-agricultural products, in particular for manufactured consumption goods. This will, in turn, increase the derived demand for capital goods to make the manufactured commodities.

From the readings suggested in Appendix *B* one can note the wide range of programs and policies that are now being followed or proposed in particular countries. The gradual approach to development is characteristic of development plans in Latin America, most of the Near East, parts of Africa, and parts of Southeast Asia. The fact that the proportion of total investment set aside for manufacturing industry in official development plans is still relatively small can be seen more specifically in the investment programs of several countries. Thus, in Ceylon, of the investment projected in the government's six-year plan (1951 to 1957), only about 6 per cent was intended for secondary industry, with priority given to those industries that use domestic raw materials or are likely to raise agricultural productivity. In India's first five-year plan (1951 to 1956), only about 8 per cent of the public investment was to go into secondary industry, and almost half of this sum was for a new iron and steel industry. India's second five-year plan, however, allocates some 25 per cent of total investment expenditures to industry and mining. Among the official development plans for Asian countries, that of Pakistan allocated the greatest share, almost 20 per cent, of gross proposed expenditure under its six-year development plan (1951 to 1957) to manufacturing industry. In the non-self-governing territories of Africa, post-war development plans have been based mainly on the assumption that secondary industry was a field for private rather than public investment. The same is largely true for British dependencies in Africa. In Turkey, government policy has moved towards the encouragement of private investment in industry; of the increase in the gross national product between 1948 and 1952, agriculture contributed 57 per cent, as against only

9 per cent by manufacturing.[8]   In general, development plans place much more emphasis on agriculture, transport, power, and social services than upon manufacturing.

Whether these plans will succeed cannot yet be foreseen. Compared, however, with the comprehensive programs advocated by those who would rely on central planning and detailed controls, the more gradual approach appears to have some definite advantages. By concentrating on agriculture it does promise to increase national income and to distribute the increase to those people who need it most. This approach is also less inflationary, since efforts to achieve full-scale industrialization are likely to encounter problems of capital absorption and scarcity of raw materials or even foodstuffs. Moreover, it is not as disruptive of the entire culture as grand-scale industrialization would be. There is not, for example, the need for rapid urbanization with its attendant social problems. And even if this approach should not achieve its ultimate goal, the cost of failure will not be too onerous. At worst, agricultural income might increase but fail to induce industrial development, so that population pressure drives per capita income back to where it was initially. In contrast, if the larger-scale industrial development program fails, it will have dislocated many lives and caused much greater hardship; in terms of human discontent, the costs of abortive development plans would then be much greater. Furthermore, the smaller step approach to industrial investment is more likely to avoid the wastes of "conspicuous production" and those unproductive public symbols which frequently result from the more grandiose projects. In general, the program of deliberate industrialization is likely to have an artificial character, sacrificing the more solidly established smaller industrial undertaking for the more spectacular and larger project which becomes difficult to maintain over the longer run. More significantly, a program that focuses on agriculture is more consistent with the dictates of comparative costs, and through the gradual inducement of industrial enterprises it allows the comparative cost structure to evolve more naturally.

Finally, the form of state intervention required by the gradual approach has advantages over that required by a thoroughgoing industrialization program. The latter implies centralized planning, and, instead of relying on the market mechanism and private entrepreneurial activities, the government would institute comprehensive specific controls and would directly own and operate industries. The administra-

[8] United Nations, Department of Economic and Social Affairs, *Processes and Problems of Industrialization in Under-Developed Countries,* New York, 1955, 71–72.

tive model might be that of the Soviet economy or of a war-time economy, and the slogan of the program could be "nationalize, modernize, protect, and inflate."

The gradual program, in contrast, involves relatively mild measures of government intervention. In confining its activities to framework planning and to establishing a congenial atmosphere for private entrepreneurs, the government avoids the administrative problems, irreversible decisions, cumulative errors, and undemocratic controls which are likely to be associated with central planning. Errors in governmental decisions are especially costly in a poor country. Whereas a rich economy can afford the wastes involved in central planning, the diseconomies of large-scale governmental organization would in themselves intensify the problems of development in a poor country. Moreover, although the more intensive program of forced development may be more successful in initiating development, the gradual approach is likely to be more successful in maintaining development over the longer run. For it is more likely to nurture and promote the indigenous forces that are necessary to sustain economic advance and allow the development process to become self-generating and cumulative.

In practice, each country will have to decide where to draw the line between its public sector and its private sector on the basis of its own objectives regarding the sequence and tempo of development, its particular economic circumstances, its institutions, and the administrative strength of its government. Thus, whereas India's development program is based on the objective of moving towards "a socialized pattern of society" and reserves 17 basic industries for exclusive further development by the government, Pakistan's recent five-year plan emphasizes the aim of encouraging individual initiative and of confining official industrial enterprises to schemes that private owners cannot undertake, returning even these to private owners as soon as possible.

2. Education and Health

The support of social services is an undisputed area of governmental activity. In poor countries this is especially important, since an expansion of educational facilities and public health measures can weaken the obstacles to development by lessening the backwardness of the people, increasing their geographic and occupational mobility, raising their productivity, and facilitating innovations. Measures to improve education and health amount in effect to investment in human resources—the quality of the people as productive agents is raised.

All development programs recognize the urgency for more public education. The International Bank's mission to Iraq, for instance, calls for a great broadening of the educational effort, the gradual introduction over the next 15 years of compulsory primary education, and the launching of a vigorous campaign for the education of adults. Another mission states that for Nigeria the educational expansion already begun must be accelerated to gain an adequate supply of skilled manpower. It also observes that a changed emphasis in technical schools is required, and it suggests an expansion of higher education which should be allied with research programs in agriculture, veterinary science, and forestry.

The general case for public education is obvious, but it raises complex questions regarding specific objectives and procedures. Educational efforts must go beyond attempts to increase the degree of literacy, for literacy is only a means to education in all areas of life. From the viewpoint of accelerating development, the general objective of education must be that of spreading change throughout the society. Education must be related to modifications of the sociocultural environment so that new knowledge and skills may be taught, the desirability of change recognized, and the incentive for new ways stimulated.

Although poor countries confront a complex of educational problems, they do not have sufficient means to solve the entire array of problems at every level from primary education to administration and research. Priorities have to be established for the most urgent educational requirements. An over-all criterion for deciding whether expenditures on particular educational efforts should be made is whether it contributes directly to raising productivity. Education increases the human capital, but resources devoted to education may be at the expense of material investment—the formation of non-human capital. In deciding whether there should be investment in people or investment in material capital, the question becomes one of comparing the alternative increases in productivity. Many would share the view of a United Nations group that "most under-developed countries are in the situation that investment in people is likely to prove as productive, in the purely material sense, as any investment in material resources, and in many cases investment in people would lead to a greater increase of the flow of goods and services than would follow upon any comparable investment in material capital."[9]

Three particular areas may be suggested as deserving top priority for educational expenditures: the provision of agricultural extension services, training in industrial skills, and training in supervisory and administrative skills. Since agriculture is so important in poor countries,

[9] United Nations, *Measures for the Economic Development of Under-Developed Countries,* New York, 1951, 52.

many observers believe that expenditure on agricultural research and the spread of agricultural extension services which would teach modern techniques to farmers would probably yield bigger returns in the immediate future than any other form of investment. The United Nations has proposed for agricultural extension services that "something approaching a total of 1 per cent of the national income should be spent annually."[10] If this were done, it was believed that an increase of 50 per cent in two decades or less would be possible even without any substantial increase in capital or any widespread reorganization of the agricultural system.[10]

Training part of the labor force in the use of industrial skills is also necessary in so far as industrial activities become relatively more prominent in the course of a country's development. At the outset skilled personnel are required for some of the projects involved in the initial development program, and it may be necessary to train skilled personnel at various levels—from manual workers to engineers. As development proceeds, and the structure of production is transformed, there will be an increase in the number of "economically displaced persons" who must acquire new skills for the expanding occupations. In particular, to the extent that agriculture declines in importance as development progresses, the underemployed labor in the agricultural sector will have to be trained in industrial skills for the expanding industries. Unless the government reforms and extends the educational system so that it becomes more closely related to national economic needs, it will be difficult to remove rural underemployment, allow labor to move from low-wage jobs to higher-wage jobs, and increase the degree of vertical mobility from unskilled work to more skilled work.

The transfer of workers from agricultural and other traditional occupations to the highly rationalized enterprises of modern production entails, however, much more than the comparatively simple requirement of training more skilled workers. It is a qualitative problem involving a complex social process which penetrates the psychology of the worker and reorders his cultural norms and social relations.[11] In this connection, one student of the problem of recruiting wage labor in peasant societies has summarized the requirements for successful adaptation to wage work as follows:

[10] *Ibid.*, 53.

[11] Cf. M. Nash, "The Recruitment of Wage Labor and Development of New Skills," *The Annals,* May 1956, 23; M. J. Herskovits, "Motivation and Culture-Pattern in Technological Change," *International Social Science Bulletin, VI,* 388–400 (1954); W. E. Moore, *Industrialization and Labor,* Cornell University Press, Ithaca, 1951.

A wage labor force which is regular, efficient, and willing to learn new skills will be recruited from peasant societies and maintained at wage work if: (1) the economic returns of wage labor are significantly greater than alternative opportunity in an impoverished rural area; (2) the income is translatable into customary channels of expenditure; (3) the training for wage work, the exercise of authority on the job, and the standards of output allow the recruit to adjust occupationally at his own pace; (4) new relations emerge in the context of wage work, and if these new social relations involve personal bonds; (5) a workers' organization evolves which gives wage workers some command over the job and conditions of work; (6) the institutional structure beyond the wage work situation is relatively intact so that a set of cultural norms and social relations continue to give content and meaning to work effort and coherence to personality; (7) the wage worker is not significantly differentiated socially or isolated culturally from those with whom he has the greatest frequency and depth of social interaction; (8) there are new wants tied to money wages and some social and medical services contingent to staying at wage work.[12]

An increase in the general level of literacy and the extension of a basic general education would obviously do much to facilitate the training of skilled workers. The abolition of illiteracy and the institution of nation-wide compulsory free education are, however, long-run objectives for which the immediate requirements of development cannot wait. In the shorter run, major efforts have to be directed to vocational education and specialized training in the most essential specific activities. After surmounting the immediate bottlenecks of scarce personnel in specific key areas, the educational system should then be devised to meet the broader problem of a proper relation between general education, prevocational preparation, and vocational education and training.

In many poor countries there is a tendency for those who have attained certain educational standards to be so strongly attracted towards the white-collar "prestige occupations," such as law, that an excess supply rapidly results in these occupations. These unemployed "intellectuals" then have to accept "inferior" occupations, and they constitute a source of social and political discontent. Care must therefore be taken to avoid, on the one side, undue emphasis on education which would only increase the number of unemployed intellectuals, and, on the other, too extreme a specialization on only vocational training.

The third major educational requirement is to increase the number of people who have administrative knowledge and ability. If development programs and policies are to be intelligently framed and efficiently executed there must be government officials with administrative skills and businessmen with skills of organization and management. In so far

[12] Nash, *loc. cit.*, 29–30.

as development tends to increase the scale of organization both in government and business, there is a need for executive and administrative personnel who are capable of making decisions on matters requiring coordination, continuity, and unity of operation.[13] If such individuals are not available, it is practically impossible to give concreteness to the general objectives of a development program. To instill the ability of management is probably the most important, and at the same time the most difficult, task of the educational system. Much of this ability to make constructive decisions depends on individual psychology and experience, but public administration institutes, business schools, and in-job training may make some contributions. Particular efforts may be made to attract into entrepreneurial activity those individuals who would otherwise merely join the ranks of the disgruntled intellectuals.

If education is one obvious sphere in which the government can undertake positive policies, another is that of public health. To increase the productive power and efficiency of labor, the incidence of debilitating diseases must be reduced, and diets must be improved. Among the typical health measures recommended by many International Bank missions are an increase in the number of village dispensaries, training of midwives, organization of a corps of sanitarians, elimination of stagnant and polluted water, provision of safe water supplies and sewage disposals, slum clearance, and better housing.

From the standpoint of raising per capita real income, however, public health measures cut two ways: they facilitate development by improving the qualitative composition of the labor force, but they also make the need for development all the more urgent by increasing the size of the population. For with health improvements there will be a drop in the mortality rate, and unless the natality rate should fall proportionately, there will then be an increase in the rate of population growth. And this growth can be very large: such is the power of compound interest that even as low a per annum growth in population as 1 per cent would increase the population by almost two-thirds in 50 years, and a 3 per cent per annum rate of growth would double the population in about 23 years.

This population growth could be interpreted as merely emphasizing all the more the need for accelerated development. Alternatively, however, if population growth could be restrained, a given rate of development would permit a higher level of per capita income, and to this extent would lighten the task of development. There is some

---

[13] Cf. F. Harbison, "Entrepreneurial Organization as a Factor in Economic Development," *Quarterly Journal of Economics, LXX,* No. 3, 364–379 (Aug. 1956).

consolation from historical experience which suggests that over the long run a rising standard of living and an urban-industrial environment generally exercise a steadying influence on population growth, since sociocultural changes that accompany the rising living standard may bring about a declining birth rate.[14] But this is a slow process, and birth rates are already so high and the age distribution is so favorable to high fecundity that only a comparatively small fall in fertility might be expected from the social and cultural changes accompanying development. Furthermore, if historical experience is any indication, development will still be accompanied by a short-term trend towards a larger population. Nor is emigration now a feasible solution: few countries welcome immigrants, emigration is costly, and usually the more enterprising of the population, the element most needed in the poor country, emigrate. Population control therefore requires deliberate efforts to reduce fertility, so that the gap between birth and death rates will not become so large, and the potential "population explosion" will be avoided.

Public health measures are needed for the deliberate reduction of fertility rates. Methods of contraception have to be adapted for use in the kind of living conditions that exist in the poor countries. Public health authorities might assume the burden of cost involved in undertaking applied medical research necessary to provide effective and simple methods of fertility control and might establish birth control clinics to make the contraceptive techniques readily available for use. But the technical medical problem is minor compared with the legal, moral, and social problems connected with introducing these techniques and gaining their acceptance and widespread use among the backward peoples. Although inexpensive and effective means of limiting conception may be found, it is quite another matter to change the outlook of the people and create a strong motivation in favor of family planning. These problems may best be overcome more directly through public education, the establishment of birth control clinics, and official recognition by the government that population control can facilitate their development programs.

In this respect, India may become a leader among the poor nations in bringing fertility control to peasant-agricultural populations.[15] The Indian government already has taken the initiative and requested the

[14] Although this view is maintained by Notestein, Kingsley Davis has cast considerable doubts on it. See the readings in Appendix A, below; also p. 350, note, above.

[15] Kingsley Davis, "Social and Demographic Aspects of Economic Development in India," in Economic Growth: Brazil, India, Japan, Duke University Press, Durham, 1955, 291.

World Health Organization for assistance in solving India's population problem. The following general statement by the Indian government on this matter is noteworthy:

Family planning is thus a vital step in economic and social planning . . . . The State should provide facilities for sterilization or giving advice on contraception on medical grounds . . . . The State should also, through financial aid and otherwise, assist in the establishment of Research and Information Centers organized for the following purposes: (1) Collection, study and dissemination of information based on scientifically tested experience in our country and abroad in respect of all aspects of family limitation; and the countering of ill-effects of incorrect information; and (2) Research necessary for the development of inexpensive, safe and efficacious methods of birth control suitable for all classes of people; and methods of preparation of necessary appliances and materials based on raw materials available in the country.[16]

3. Public Utilities

The government's agenda must also give high priority to the extension of transportation, communication, power facilities, water supplies, and conservation works. Roads, railways, ports, and telecommunications are necessary to provide a basic transport and communication network within which the future development of the economy can proceed. Individual projects usually await the provision of public overhead capital. As the Colonial Development Corporation, which is concerned with development in British colonies, has stated, "In many cases the Corporation has not only to send heavy equipment to a Colony, but it must construct the wharf to land it, the road to take it to its destination, the workshops to maintain it, and the houses and services for those who will work it . . . . As a general statement, it may be said that the expense of providing housing and communications, and the minimum of necessary services, amounts in typical cases to a doubling of the normal capital cost of an undertaking."[17]

Much as investment in overhead capital would furnish a base for the expansion of the economy, the provision of such capital does not appeal to the private investor. The large-scale projects that are involved are beyond the scope of the domestic capital market in a poor country, the short-term risks are large, and the benefits are of an indirect and diffused character which accrue only over the longer period. Governments must therefore normally provide this public overhead capital.

[16] *The First Five Year Plan—A Draft Outline,* Government of India Planning Commission, Delhi, 1951, 206–207.

[17] Colonial Development Corporation, *Report and Accounts for 1948,* H.M.S.O., London, June 21, 1949, 10.

In doing so, the government should not absorb capital in public works if the capital would be more productive in agriculture or manufacturing or other activities. Nor should the government be tempted by public works that are unnecessary or done on too costly a scale. For instance, although farm-to-market roads are especially needed in many rural areas, it would be wasteful to improve roads beyond essential standards at the expense of providing farmers with better equipment. Nor would it be economical (although perhaps psychologically a valuable public symbol) to concentrate on a grand project for controlling a single river, if the same expenditures would yield more when devoted to many smaller streams.

It should also be realized that governmental responsibility for the provision of public overhead capital need not involve government ownership and operation. In theory, the role of government in this area can take various forms. For example, the State may finance the project, but private contracting firms may undertake the actual construction. Or the government could construct the project and then lease or sell it to private individuals. Still another possibility is for the State to make the funds easily available to private entrepreneurs who would construct, own, and operate the undertaking while the government merely regulated the operation. In practice, however, most development programs provide not only for the government financing of transportation and communication projects, but also for their construction and operation.

These projects usually constitute a major part of the development program. Thus, an International Bank survey mission to Guatemala states that the inadequacy of the transportation system is probably the greatest single barrier to development, and recommends the adoption of a basic national plan for highway development and maintenance, the expansion of domestic airlines to serve isolated areas, and the establishment of a non-political public utilities commission to regulate rates and services for all forms of transport. And in the Colombo Plan transport and communications account for 34 per cent of the total cost covered by the program from 1951 to 1957. This is a larger share than any other phase of the program; agriculture comes next with 32 per cent; then social services, 18 per cent; industry and mining, 10 per cent; and fuel and power, 6 per cent.

Chapter 18

Domestic

Policy Issues (2)

Although most development programs assign the government an important role in the areas of education and health and public utilities, there is much more disagreement about the government's activities in agriculture and about the uses of fiscal and monetary policies. Objectives and procedures in these areas are much less definite and are subject to a greater variety of interpretations. This chapter considers some of the many possible objectives and procedures.

1. Agricultural Improvements

A large number of policies are possible to promote the expansion of agricultural output, but specific measures can only be formulated after it is determined what are the particular causes of low agricultural productivity in the country being considered.

To raise agricultural output it is, of course, necessary to increase the yield per acre or the effective area of arable land. Greater yields, in turn, require technical improvements in the methods of cultivation and increased efficiency of workers. These requirements may be fulfilled through technical education, new tools and equipment, and land reform.

And to increase the area of arable land, land improvements and reclamation are necessary.

Technical education is needed, first, to make the people recognize what it is possible to accomplish with improved techniques of cultivation, and second, to give the workers the skills required for the use of these improved agricultural methods. Such education might include scientific research to provide improved plant varieties, seed, and livestock breeds; extension services, which are highly important, to make the results of this research available; instruction in the practice of soil management and soil conservation, including reforestation and contour ploughing, pest control, land improvement; and establishment of mechanization centers with training facilities for machinery operators. The essentials of all technical education are to discover the specific needs of a locality, to teach the people to recognize them, and to instill in the people the desirability of improvement.

Increased crop yields may also be obtained by the introduction of new and better agricultural implements. In this connection, the discussion of investment criteria in Chapter 16 should be recalled. Mechanical cultivation tends to increase output per worker, but it is usually less productive per acre than hand cultivation which permits more intensive and more careful cultivation. When labor is abundant relative to capital, the objective should be to increase output per acre, not output per worker; this requires that land be used intensively, and that hand cultivation be favored over mechanical cultivation. For, when there already is disguised unemployment on the land, the effect of introducing mechanization would simply be to create a larger surplus of labor in agriculture.

Thus, where labor is the cheap factor, there is a dilemma between perpetuating, on the one hand, labor-intensive methods of cultivation which are the most economical, and, on the other hand, introducing labor-saving machinery which would expose the disguised unemployment on the land and raise wages even though it displaced agricultural workers. Besides facing the problem of unemployment relief, the answer to how rapidly labor-saving innovations can be introduced must depend on the availability of alternative employment opportunities for the displaced workers. To absorb the displaced workers from the agricultural sector, the opportunities of alternative employment must be available on public works projects or industrial projects, and there must be educational and health measures designed to increase the geographical and occupational mobility of labor. This is but another illustration of the general principle that agricultural improvements and industrialization must be considered as complementary in the light of the requirement for balanced growth.

If, however, labor is scarce relative to land, then the objective should be to maximize output per worker. Mechanization would contribute to this by enabling each worker to cultivate more acres. But this does not mean that the most modern techniques should be imported from the rich countries. It is useless to demonstrate agricultural machinery to farmers who are too poor to afford its purchase and upkeep, or who have farms that are too small or topographically unsuitable for the effective operation of farm machinery, or who do not have access to adequate maintenance services. Actually, the need may simply be an improved hoe or plough, and such a change, for example, from a wooden to an iron plough or the introduction of the scythe, can raise productivity substantially. More advanced agricultural machinery may have to await the availability of fuel, less expensive spare parts, and the existence of technical skills. In the meanwhile the improvement of small farm machines, such as small bullock-drawn ploughs or small seed drills, may be the most feasible approach to mechanization.

Finally, higher agricultural productivity may result from reform of the land tenure systems. This involves decisions on the redistribution of land ownership, conditions of tenancy, and control of rents. Where agriculture is the main industry, such action is very important. India's first five-year plan, for example, maintained that the "future of land ownership and cultivation is perhaps the most fundamental issue of national development. The pattern of economic and social organization will depend upon the manner in which the land problem is solved."[1]

Land reform should be designed to attain more efficient land use by allowing farm units to approximate more closely the optimal size, and by instilling the cultivators with incentives to make productive improvements. To accomplish this, the abolition of tenancy may be desirable in some cases. A United Nations report condemned the tenancy system on three counts: (1) the tenant has little incentive to increase his output, since a large share in any such increase will accrue to the landowner, who has incurred no part of its cost; (2) the high share of the produce taken by the landowner may leave the peasant with a bare subsistence minimum, with no margin for investment; (3) it means that wealth is held in the form of land, and that the accumulation of capital does not lead to productive investment.[2]

Abolition of the tenancy system, however, is not required in all poor countries, for the institution of tenancy in itself need not handicap agri-

---

[1] India, Planning Commission, *First Five Year Plan,* People's Edition, Delhi, 1953, 88.
[2] United Nations, Department of Economic Affairs, *Land Reform,* New York, 1951, 18.

cultural output, as is apparent from the fact that tenancy rates are even higher in some countries with high agricultural productivity than they are in poor countries with low agricultural productivity.[3] Security of tenure, however, is essential: without it, the cultivator has no incentive to conserve land resources, improve the land with long-term investments, and raise productivity. Similarly, proportional rents—payment by a tenant to his landlord of some fixed proportion of output in kind or money—may lessen the farmer's incentive to make improvements. Furthermore, in many poor countries the landlords merely collect rents, without improving in return the productive capacity of the land.

These conditions have led in some cases to one type of land reform in which governments take possession of large landholdings and redistribute them in small tracts mainly to present tenant cultivators who then become freehold owners. The Egyptian land reform in 1952 limited the amount of acreage that could be owned, allowed the government to requisition and redistribute land, and fixed a ceiling on the rent to tenants. In many Indian states, laws have been enacted for the gradual abolition of large estates and the transfer of ownership of land to the peasant cultivators. Legislation enacted by Guatemala in 1952 provided that land not under "direct cultivation" may be expropriated by the State and redistributed.

Aside from the problems of outright expropriation of the land by the government or the provision of "fair compensation," there are other difficulties involved in comparing tenancy and ownership. Many would argue that peasant ownership is inefficient, that ownership makes land less mobile because landlords can then no longer change tenants and thereby alter the use or size of the farming unit, that excessive indebtedness occurs under peasant ownership, that marketable output may fall after land reform as farmers consume more on the farm, and that an increase of subdivision may result in holdings that are too small.[4]

Various degrees of redistribution of land ownership are, of course, possible. And, if Soviet experience provides any lesson, the redistribution may wisely stop short of a full farm collectivization program. Instead emphasis may be placed on reforms within a basically private enterprise system and on an extension of cooperative schemes. It is clear, however, that, if agricultural advance is to occur on a peasant basis, security of tenure must be established, and some government control may be necessary to guard against the possible harmful conse-

---

[3] Cf. N. S. Buchanan and H. S. Ellis, *Approaches to Economic Development,* Twentieth Century Fund, New York, 1955, 245–246.

[4] *Ibid.,* 124–125; Sir Alan Pim, *Colonial Agricultural Production,* Oxford University Press, London, 1946, 174.

quences of unrestricted individual tenure. Even at the level of relatively mild land reforms, the government must adopt measures governing landlord-tenant relations and leasing arrangements, measures for the provision of agricultural credit facilities, and land settlement programs.[5]

Large-scale agricultural operations are favored if there is economy in mechanical cultivation, uniform quality of product is desired, processing is necessary, large amounts of capital are required, or large-scale control of irrigation, seeds, disease precautions, or marketing is needed. The advantages of large-scale operation also explain why in some countries small farmers are being compelled to merge their lands into collectives. If a large landholding is operated as an integrated production unit, it may allow higher yields per acre than the alternative of many small individual holdings. In this case, the demand for a reform of the plantation system must be based more on social than on economic considerations: the need for more equal distribution of income and greater possibilities of social advance.[6]

Consolidation of fragmented and uneconomic units involves the problems of developing an administration that is financially and organizationally capable of carrying out an equitable exchange of hundreds of small plots per village, of obtaining legal sanction and political support for the compulsion required, and of providing alternative employment opportunities for the displaced cultivators.

Small-scale farming, however, may be more efficient than large-scale agriculture under certain conditions. Small farmers cultivate the land more intensively than large farmers, and this may yield a higher output per acre than on the larger farm. The farmer on the family-size farm also tends to work harder and more carefully than the hired agricultural worker on the large farm. Moreover, small-scale farming need not be concerned with the availability of a managerial and supervisory staff. There are also social reasons for preferring the family-size farm to the larger farm with its concentration of political and social power. For these various reasons, the land reform movements in many countries, especially in Latin America and Asia, emphasize the more intensive use of land that would result if some of the large estates were divided into small family farms.[7]

No definite policies with respect to land reform can be advocated here. They must vary from country to country, depending on the particular

---

[5] Cf. R. Barlowe, "Land Reform and Economic Development," *Journal of Farm Economics, XXXV,* No. 2, 177 (May 1953).

[6] United Nations, *op. cit.,* 21–23.

[7] Cf. W. A. Lewis, *Theory of Economic Growth,* Allen & Unwin Ltd., London, 1955, 133–134.

social and political structure of each country, on whether there are over-cultivated small holdings or extremely large holdings, on whether the large holdings are used to perpetuate an inefficient tenancy system or are centrally managed productive units, and on the specific effects of different types of land reforms on the total level of agricultural production and on the distribution of this output. By way of a general summary, however, the following measures may be listed as ways to meet certain aspects of the land tenure problem: (1) the consolidation into efficient-sized units of strip parcels and scattered holdings; (2) the reduction of excess rents, the regulation of rental rates and practices, and the enactment of lease protection laws; (3) the subdivision of large holdings if these are not efficiently integrated production units; (4) the control of land inheritance to prevent excessive subdivision of holdings, or to discourage the accumulation of large holdings; (5) the improvement of land surveys and systems of title registration; (6) the promotion of ownership by the cultivator and the reduction of absentee landlordship.[8]

In addition to the foregoing measures designed to raise agricultural productivity, the government may also expand agricultural production by increasing the effective area of arable land through drainage and irrigation projects. These projects not only increase the capacity of agricultural production but also have the advantage of providing employment for workers displaced from the land through labor-saving innovations. Land reclamation may also be a major objective of the large multipurpose development projects which combine irrigation, flood control, and the production of hydroelectric power. These projects can be very significant: in India, for example, three multipurpose projects were expected to bring about 6 million acres of new land under irrigation by 1956–1957, and in Pakistan two irrigation projects were to make an additional 4,800,000 acres available for cultivation. This extension of irrigated acreage may be one of the most important means of raising agricultural output and may be necessary before other techniques of agricultural improvement can be fully utilized.

In many poor countries there is considerable opportunity to extend the area of cultivation. The greatest areas of uncultivated soil are in Latin America, Africa, and Asia. Large parts of these areas are potentially arable, and could be brought under cultivation if irrigation and campaigns against erosion were undertaken.[9] In Malaya, for instance, a half million acres of swamps and sea-spoiled coastal land are already

---

[8] Cf. P. M. Raup, "Agricultural Taxation and Land Tenure Reform in Under-developed Countries," in *Conference on Agricultural Taxation and Economic Development,* Harvard Law School, Cambridge, 1954, 246.

[9] See Chapter 14, section 1.

being cleared and rehabilitated, and the International Bank mission to Malaya recommended the development of new land amounting to almost half the usable land in the country. The introduction of new farming areas may prove particularly helpful in facilitating a movement of farmers from densely populated zones, thereby providing a better location of the agricultural labor force.

Improvements in the marketing process should also be emphasized. The marketing process must be made more efficient so that the product loss and the waste of human and material resources in marketing channels may be reduced. Storage facilities and better handling facilities must be provided. The excessively long and complex channels of distribution, which result in a proliferation of middlemen and conceal considerable unemployment, might be simplified by licensing requirements, marketing cooperatives, or government distribution of part of the output.[10] The government may also provide basic public marketing services—market and price information, standardization, and transport facilities adapted to marketing needs.[11]

It should now be obvious that the government may do much to promote an increase in agricultural output—from providing agricultural extension services to instituting changes in land tenure. But these improvements cannot occur in isolation: the entire complex of agricultural improvements depends on other related measures throughout the economy. For instance, if the small-scale farmer is to escape excessive indebtedness to the moneylender, there must be action in the currency and credit sphere so that the high rates of interest and high burden of farm debt are reduced. If agricultural products are to be profitably processed and marketed, adequate transportation facilities and basic public utilities are necessary. If farmers are to be induced to take the risks of introducing new techniques, it may be necessary to use fiscal measures such as tax or rent remission to guarantee them against any possible loss resulting from the adoption of techniques recommended by the government. Above all, if the redundant labor on farms is to be a major source of capital formation, it is necessary not only to provide employment opportunities for such surplus labor outside of agriculture but also to ensure that the agricultural sector still provides the food that the surplus labor formerly consumed as members of the agricultural sector. As expansion of agricultural output continues, it becomes increasingly necessary to have a complementary expansion of industry

[10] Cf. R. H. Holton, "Marketing Structure and Economic Development," Quarterly Journal of Economics, LXVII, No. 3, 344–361 (Aug. 1953).

[11] Cf. W. H. Nicholls, "Domestic Trade in an Underdeveloped Country—Turkey," Journal of Political Economy, LIX, No. 6, 479 (Dec. 1951).

so that the rural surplus population can be absorbed and there can be expanding internal markets for the increasing agricultural output.

To conclude this discussion of agricultural improvements, attention may be given to the nature and extent of agricultural improvements in the development programs of some countries. Of the total outlay in India's first five-year plan, agriculture claimed about one-third. In the second five-year plan, the Indian Planning Commission proposed that by the end of the plan in 1960–1961, food production would be increased by 15 per cent, cotton by 34 per cent, and sugar by 29 per cent. And nearly 21 million acres of new land would have been brought under cultivation. In Pakistan's first six-year program, agriculture claimed 32 per cent of the total outlay, and by 1956–1957 an over-all increase of 33 per cent in agricultural production was expected.

India and Pakistan are also meeting the particular problems of agriculture through village development programs known as the Community Development Program in India and the Village Agricultural and Industrial Development Program in Pakistan. These programs involve comprehensive action at the village level, ranging from expanded agricultural extension services to the provision of rural credit facilities. The Community Development Program in India embraces some 55 areas containing about 11 million people.

Agriculture was to claim 37 per cent of the total cost of Ceylon's development program from 1954–1955 to 1959–1960. The major projects were devoted to land development in the sparsely inhabited dry zone in the eastern and north central parts of the country to which people are expected to migrate from the densely inhabited western part of the island. Acreage potentially available for cultivation is equivalent to the total acreage now being cultivated. Of the present acreage, however, approximately two-thirds is devoted to the production of tea, rubber, and coconut, leaving inadequate acreage for food production. By 1957, it was planned to have a 20 per cent increase in the acreage devoted to food production, without interfering with the production of export crops. The largest of the multipurpose projects was to provide yearly about 700,000 acre-feet of water for irrigation, with which it is hoped to irrigate 100,000 acres now under jungle, and to improve the irrigation of 30,000 acres already cultivated. The new land will be leased to peasant cultivators, who will each get in the area on which paddy is to be grown 4 acres of irrigated land and 3 acres of unirrigated land. In the area that is to be devoted to sugar-cane cultivation the proportion of irrigated land will be higher. It is hoped to provide 21,000 peasant holdings in the new area; and, in the area already cultivated, two crops a year instead of one may be possible on 30,000 acres.

For Malaya, the International Bank mission recommended a public investment program for 1955–1959 totalling Malay $775 million, of which 25 per cent is allotted to agriculture. The mission to Dutch Guiana stated that the major emphasis should be placed on the development of the country's three principal productive resources—agricultural land, tropical forests, and mineral deposits. Recommendations were made for increasing the productivity of agricultural workers, largely through the improvement of small farms. For Jamaica, a ten-year program was proposed to increase production and reduce chronic underemployment, largely through development of agriculture. Chief recommendations were programs of soil conservation, irrigation, reclamation of swampland, pasture improvement, land surveys for proper planning of land use, and changes in the system of land taxation. The report for Guatemala also places primary emphasis on agricultural improvements, particularly in coffee and low-cost food crops. The mission to Uruguay recommended measures to increase and improve agricultural and livestock production, to reduce costs, and to improve marketing methods. It also recommended a program of increased afforestation to protect agricultural and grazing land, and indicated numerous opportunities for improvements in the transportation, storage, and marketing of agricultural products. The mission to Iraq proposed that almost 40 per cent of the total expenditures in the development program for 1952–1957 be devoted to flood control, irrigation, draining, crop storage facilities, agricultural machinery administration, and an agricultural bank. And for Nigeria, a mission stated that research, surveys, extension, and demonstration are the priority needs in agriculture. Facilities for research into soils, plant nutrition, and plant varieties and disease must be promptly expanded so that efforts to stimulate production will rest on a firmer scientific base than they do now. Large-scale expansion in output of most products must await the results of survey and fundamental research, but increased production of some crops can be achieved soon if extension and demonstration services are more adequately organized to spread techniques already known.

2. Fiscal Policy

Extensive and effective use of fiscal policy is indispensable to the acceleration of development in poor countries. Policies connected with governmental revenues and expenditures can have four significant effects upon the rate of development. They can (1) affect the allocation of resources, (2) alter the distribution of income, (3) promote capital accumulation, and (4) restrain inflation.

Government expenditure in a particular sector of the economy tends to attract resources to that sector, whereas taxation of a particular sector tends to repel resources from that sector. In this general sense, by affecting factor mobility among industries and occupations, the pattern of revenues and expenditures will affect the allocation of resources. More particularly from the standpoint of development, land and property taxes can affect the system of land tenure, tax exemptions and tax discrimination can influence the direction of investment to particular sectors, taxes can limit industries with social costs, and subsidies can encourage industries with social benefits.

Fiscal measures modify the distribution of income by altering the institutional environment through which the distribution comes about, or by changing the resultant distribution. For instance, government expenditures on health and education may increase occupational mobility and allow an upgrading of workers; land taxes can affect the distribution of land ownership; and a system of taxes and subsidies can alter the degree of competition in various sectors of the economy. Or the resultant distribution can be made more equal through a greater degree of progressivity in the tax structure, and through governmental expenditures directed towards the benefit of lower-income groups.

The uses of fiscal policy for promoting capital formation and restraining inflation are, however, far more important than those of affecting resource allocation and income distribution. For, as has been stressed previously, the problem of development is much more that of insufficient resources, especially capital deficiency, than it is that of inefficient use of resources. And it is not the unequal distribution of the national income that causes the low per capita income in poor countries, but rather it is basically the low national income in the first place. Arguments for a modification of income distribution depend more directly on social and ethical considerations than on technical considerations of the economic requirements for development.

Capital can be formed through private investment financed either by a parallel increase in voluntary savings or by credit creation, by an inflow of foreign investment, or by public investment financed by taxation revenue and by borrowing. Obstacles to an increase in private investment have already been noted. The major limitation, that of the low level of private voluntary savings, cannot be overcome to any significant extent in the short run; an increase in private savings is only likely to occur over the longer run after national output rises substantially. Nor, as will be discussed in the next chapter, can foreign investment be expected to bear more than a relatively small part of the costs of capital accumulation. The government must therefore be responsible, at least in the short run, for most of the domestic capital accumulation that is necessary. To accomplish this, the government must increase tax revenues or engage in deficit financing.

Barring external sources of finance, the government will have to engage in deficit financing to the extent that taxes (and other minor sources of revenue such as surplus of state-owned enterprises) do not cover governmental expenditures. For instance, India's second five-year plan prescribes a total investment in the public and private sectors of £4,575,000,000. Of this amount, £1,725,000,000, or about two-fifths, is expected to come from the private sector. Taxes are to amount to £337,500,000. The balance must come from foreign exchange earnings, foreign investment in India, and deficit financing. Thus, the plan relies on deficit financing in the amount of £900,000,000, an amount equal to no less than one-quarter of the finance necessary for the public sector of the plan.

Capital accumulation through deficit financing, however, is likely to generate inflation, since the propensity to consume is high, there are many market imperfections, there is little excess capacity in plant and equipment, and the elasticities of food supplies are low. Since the poor country is so prone to inflation, a given amount of deficit-financed investment is likely to induce a smaller increase in output in a poor country than it would in a more developed economy. Inflation can, however, be a method of extracting forced savings, as has already been indicated. One must therefore weigh this result against the other disadvantageous results of inflation.[12]

To avoid the deleterious effects of inflation, the government should attempt to finance its expenditures by raising taxation revenue. In this sense, the size and tempo of the government's development program must be conditioned by the capacity of the tax system to mobilize the necessary resources. By enforcing collective saving in the community, taxation permits a redirection of resources towards capital formation. By raising taxes so as to reduce consumption, or to restrain consumption from rising to the full extent of any increase in output, the government releases resources for productive investment. Depending on how active a role is assigned to the government, the investment can be done by the State or left to private enterprises. The funds raised by taxes may be loaned to private investors by specialized government corporations or commissions for development such as have been established in Bolivia, Brazil, Chile, Colombia, India, Mexico, Peru, and other countries. Or, by retiring government debt held by the banking system, the government can place tax-generated savings at the disposal of private individuals through an expansion in deposits. The important consequence

[12] Cf. Chapter 16, section 5.

of taxation is that the State enforces an act of saving, whereas the act of investment can be public, private, or a mixed institutional arrangement. As Nurkse remarks, "The two components of capital formation, saving and investment, depend on thrift and enterprise; there is nothing to prevent collective thrift from being combined with individual enterprise."[13] The over-all concern of the government's fiscal policy should be directed towards maximizing savings, mobilizing them for productive investment, and canalizing them into directions that will best serve the objectives of a balanced development program.

Even with a balanced government budget, however, there can be inflationary forces in the economy: when private investment plus exports exceed private saving plus imports, and there is not a parallel increase in output, the situation will be inflationary. In this case, fiscal policy should be used, in combination with monetary policy, to offset the inflationary pressures: a budget surplus is required.

Although fiscal policy may have a large role in promoting a country's development, its actual efficacy will depend on improvements in the country's tax system and on an extension of the government security market. Desirable as an increase in taxation may be, the task of tax collecting is exceedingly difficult and is of such a magnitude that it may be unrealistic to expect a development program to be financed to any large extent from taxation. Again, this will depend on each country's taxable capacity and the various types of taxes that it can use.

The taxable capacity of a country will be delimited by the desire to avoid undesirable social effects and by administrative limits of efficient methods of tax collection. It has been suggested that to maximize efficiency of tax collection and minimize the burdens of taxation, efforts to increase the tax bill of a country must take into account these considerations: (1) What effect will increasing the tax bill have on the political structure of the country concerned? (2) What levels of government should impose the new or higher taxes? (3) How will the new taxes affect the equity desires of the country? and (4) Is it administratively feasible to collect the taxes at the new rates?[14]

In choosing among the various possible types and kinds of taxes, the governments of different countries have to consider such matters as their particular legal systems, the balance of political and social power within the country, the administrative ability to enforce the tax comprehensively and justly, the effects of different taxes on incentives,

---

[13] R. Nurkse, *Problems of Capital Formation in Underdeveloped Countries,* Basil Blackwell, Oxford, 1953, 151.

[14] *Conference on Agricultural Taxation and Economic Development,* Harvard Law School, Cambridge, 1954, 17.

and the objective of a proper balance between short-term revenue raising measures for financing urgent development projects and long-term tax reforms which will give steady encouragement to economic development over the longer pull.[15]

Although there are differences in the taxable capacity and types of taxes that can be used in different countries, it can generally be said that the present tax systems of poor countries leave much to be desired from the standpoint of such criteria as yield, equity, simplicity and certainty of enforcement, and minimum negative effects on incentives. A major problem of fiscal policy is to find a sufficient number of taxes that will satisfy these criteria. There are formidable difficulties in accomplishing this, but there are some possibilities. Although a poor country cannot be expected to take as high a proportion of its national income in taxation as can a richer country, nonetheless the total yield of taxation in many poor countries is very small, and most poor countries could readily secure an additional 3 per cent or 4 per cent of national income from taxation. Morever, direct taxation of wealth and income accounts for only a small part of tax revenue. A revision of the tax structure could provide a more equitable apportionment of the tax burden. In particular, some decrease in the burden of indirect taxes appears especially desirable, and the tax structure might be made more progressive. In many poor countries some tax reforms might have substantial results, even though the taxation base is narrow and too high a rate of taxation might possibly discourage the incentives to save and work.

It is impossible to enter here into the complex details of the specific fiscal policies that might be adopted by any one particular country. Some general observations, however, may be briefly offered on various taxes that can be used to raise savings and channel resources to productive investment in the interests of a balanced development program.

Personal income taxation may play some part, but it cannot be expected to be a major source of revenue in many poor countries. The scope of personal income taxes is limited for several reasons: the majority of people are so close to the subsistence level that they cannot be taxed; much income does not accrue through commercial channels but is directly consumed by the producer; there is a general lack of literacy and a failure to maintain adequate records so that assessment and collection are difficult; and there may not be the high degree of honesty, efficiency, and technical competence required for administering the tax. Although personal income taxes may not yield large amounts

[15] Cf. *ibid.,* 23.

of revenue, they do provide an element of equity in the tax system. Because of extreme inequality in the distribution of income and strong feelings for social justice, many poor countries might therefore use personal income taxes as a means of strengthening equity, if not as an important source of revenue.

In this connection, consideration should be given to the effects of the taxation on the incentive to save. If the high-income recipients are individuals who engage in luxury consumption, hoarding, capital flight, or unproductive speculative investment, the program of balanced development will not suffer if their incomes are taxed. If, however, the high-income recipients also have a high propensity to save, and these savings are directed to productive investment, then care must be taken not to destroy this source of savings. There may then be a conflict between the desire for equity and the desire to raise the level of savings. Some have argued that, for the sake of the incentive to save, taxation should not be on personal income, but rather on expenditure through excise and other indirect taxes.[16]

Even though income taxation cannot be used extensively, it may be desirable to tax selected forms of income, for example, the sizable incomes derived from land rents and interest. Land rents may constitute a large part of the community's income, and, if the rents accrue to inactive landlords who are contributing little to the productivity of land, an effective income tax might raise funds for developmental capital formation without impairing essential economic activity. Progressive income taxes on landlords may also stimulate disposal, or at least discourage further accumulation, of large landholdings. Reform of the tax system may also reduce the tax burden on small farmers and tenants who commonly bear a high burden of taxation: small producers may be exempted from land and produce taxes, and they may be granted remission of consumption taxes. Moneylenders may also be subjected to a steeply progressive income tax on the usurious interest payments that they receive for private credit. Such a tax could divert these usurious gains into productive investment.

It may also be desirable to introduce a greater degree of progressivity into the tax system through inheritance taxes. Not only would this increase taxation revenue but it would also tend to counteract the highly unequal distribution of incomes and wealth by not allowing huge concentrations of wealth to be passed on from one generation to another. Such a tax would also contribute to the equalization of landholdings in so far as any land was sold to satisfy liability incurred under the inheritance tax. Though easier to administer than an income tax, the in-

[16] Nurkse, *op. cit.,* 146.

heritance tax may arouse strong social opposition, and in the face of such opposition many governments may be unwilling to adopt such a measure.

From the standpoint of encouraging development, inheritance or estates taxes may be a better method of taxation than would heavy taxes on business profits. For taxes on profits may reduce the incentive to invest and may also reduce the ability to finance new investment from undistributed earnings. In the interests of having as high a level of private savings as is possible and maintaining an incentive for private enterprise, it would be desirable not to tax business profits heavily, unless the profits are very high. Although this sacrifices equity for the sake of incentives, some redress of the balance can be achieved by high inheritance taxes.

There is, however, more of a case for taxing profits when these profits are made by foreign companies. Frequently the profits of a foreign company are very large because it has acquired rights to some natural resource or has a monopoly of some public utility. In these cases, the government of the poor country should receive an adequate royalty or rental in return. A standard income tax may be applied to foreign investors, but royalties may be asked in special contracts, as a means of tapping excess profits. It is, however, essential to strike a balance between the necessity of preventing the profits of foreign enterprises from being exported without benefit to the poor country and the necessity of maintaining sufficient fiscal incentives to attract foreign capital. As in domestic enterprises, foreign companies can also be granted taxation immunity for a certain period of time if they are embarking upon new and necessary industries, and they can be given liberal tax allowances when there is a reinvestment of their business profits. These measures, however, are liable to be inequitable and to encourage vested interests who prevent the eventual removal of these discriminatory benefits. On this account, subsidies might be better, since they make the benefits explicit.

A case can also be made for property taxes rather than income taxes.[17] Since the distribution of real property in most poor countries is more uneven than the distribution of income, a proportional property tax with a relatively high level of basic exemptions would be more progressive than an income tax, and would also be easier to administer. It might also discourage the habit of devoting private savings to the acquisition or construction of real property, thereby allowing savings to

[17] J. H. Adler, "The Fiscal and Monetary Implementation of Development Programs," *American Economic Review, Papers and Proceedings, XLII*, No. 2, 594 (May 1952).

be directed into more productive investment. A capital gains tax can also be used as a supplementary measure to combat excessive speculation, especially in real estate during inflation. As a substitute for a capital gains tax on speculative sales of buildings, a transfer tax could be levied on the sale of buildings, applying high rates in cases where the interval between two sales was short and lower rates in those cases where it was long.[18]

Even though improvements can be made to increase the revenue from income taxes and business taxes, the major reliance will still have to be placed on agricultural and indirect taxes. Land taxes can be a form of property tax levied on the value of land, or it can be levied on the annual production, or on the rent from the land. Japanese development during the latter part of the nineteenth century is a classic case in which the government imposed high land taxes so that a large part of the increase in agricultural productivity was taken away from farmers and used for capital formation. Agricultural taxes can be used to tax large landowners on a progressive basis, but this is likely to encounter political opposition in many countries. If, however, the success of development depends on the full productive use of land, it is necessary to use land taxes to prevent the uneconomic use of land or even the keeping of land idle for prestige reasons or for purposes of speculation. Such practices may be discouraged by introducing a heavy capital gains tax on the sale of land with rates rising steeply, as the period during which land was held between two sales decreases. It may also be desirable to tax land at its potential market value, that is, at the value that it would have if it were effectively cultivated. Another argument in favor of a land tax is that as development leads to an appreciation of real estate values land taxes could make available to the government part of the windfall.[19] Large landowners and even medium-sized farmers might be subjected to such taxation, but small farmers and tenants should be excluded from taxation on the basis of their very low levels of income.

Indirect taxes such as excise and sales taxes have the advantage of falling on consumption rather than on saving, but they have the disadvantage of raising prices and the cost of living, and the sales tax tends to make the tax structure regressive within particular income brackets. To minimize these disadvantages, it is desirable to use excise and sales taxes selectively—discriminating in favor of necessary commodities and against luxuries. Governments must also avoid adding new taxes and

[18] United Nations, Technical Assistance Administration, *Taxes and Fiscal Policy in Under-Developed Countries*, New York, 1954, 36.

[19] *Ibid.*, 37.

supplementary rates on top of old ones to such an extent as to complicate the tax system and reduce its efficiency.[20]

Finally, it should be noted that, if the government is to be able to mobilize savings more effectively, a broader and better organized government securities market is needed. Even if taxation revenue is less than government expenditures, inflation can still be avoided if the government can tap sufficient public savings through voluntary loans to the government. If the public buys government securities with income that would otherwise be spent, the government borrowing is anti-inflationary. But in most poor countries the government securities market is now either non-existent or else too thin to be effective. An extended market may help in absorbing public savings, and a broader market would also allow more effective open market operations by the central bank, an indispensable part of monetary policy. The means of improving the government securities market might be through a wider variety of issues which would provide better marketability and competitive rates with private issues, and through such special features as ready convertibility to cash, acceptance of government securities at par for tax payments, and gold clauses.[21] Basically, however, a receptive market for government securities requires confidence in the stability of the government and no threat of inflation. Thus, the ability of the public to place its savings in government securities to any significant extent will have to await further development of the economy and a rising level of income.

3. Monetary Policy

Monetary policy may also play some part in accelerating development by influencing the supply and uses of credit, combating inflation, and maintaining balance of payments equilibrium. After development ·gains momentum, effective monetary policy is also necessary to provide an elastic credit supply which can parallel the expansion in trade and population.

To allow the use of monetary policy, the poor countries must first improve their currency and credit systems. There is a need for banks and financial institutions that will increase credit facilities and channel actual and potential voluntary savings into productive uses. At present the credit system is too narrowly restricted to providing credit for large estates, plantations, and foreign traders; credit facilities are not readily available for peasants, small industry, and small traders. Extension of commercial banks, and the introduction of savings banks, cooperative sav-

[20] Import and export duties are considered in Chapter 19.
[21] Cf. B. Higgins and W. Malenbaum, "Financing Economic Development," *International Conciliation,* No. 502, 334 (March 1955).

ings societies, and mutual societies may remedy this. Such efforts are especially needed in rural areas. In some countries, flexible monetary and credit institutions must be created; in others, they must be extended; in all, the imperfections of the money and credit markets must be reduced.

To control effectively the supply and uses of money, the art of central banking must be acquired. Central banks now exist in almost all poor countries, but they are still generally in a rudimentary stage as far as being able to fulfill the functions of central banks. To promote capital accumulation, combat inflation, and maintain equilibrium in the balance of payments, central banks must make more effective use of such weapons as open market operations, control over the availability and cost of rediscounting, and the power to vary reserve requirements for commercial banks. Selective credit controls may also be used more effectively to influence the allocation of resources by directing savings away from land speculation, urban real estate, and capital flights into more productive outlets.

Perhaps monetary policy can be most useful in shaping the character of investment. This will depend on the range of credit institutions that exist and the types of credit controls that are adopted. In most poor countries the commercial banks provide only short-term credit which is used mainly for carrying inventories, purchasing land and real estate, or financing the production of export crops. The banks are reluctant to supply many medium-term or long-term loans, and as a consequence credit for public authorities, credit for the purchase of raw materials, and credit for manufacturing production in general may be severely limited. To induce banks to make more medium-term and long-term loans of a productive character, the government may make appropriate guarantees or provide rediscount facilities. Joint loans by commercial banks and state-managed development finance institutes is another possibility.

Existing credit facilities are also deficient with respect to the highly important requirement of adequate and suitable rural credit. Small cultivators have no financial reserves of their own and are heavily dependent on loans, but the loans come from village moneylenders and traders who are frequently in monopolistic positions. The unequal conditions of lending and borrowing classes result in interest rates that are frequently "out of all proportion to the risk involved in the business and constitute an exploitation of the helplessness, ignorance and the necessity of the borrower."[22] Moreover, loans are commonly unrelated to productive purpose, many being for wasteful expenditure.

[22] All-India Rural Credit Survey, Report of the Committee of Direction, The General Report, II, Reserve Bank of India, Bombay, 1954, Chapter 14.

To equalize the position of the rural debtor and creditor, the government must reform the system of rural credit. Existing credit agencies are generally extremely inadequate for the needs of the peasant cultivator who must obtain credit from one of three sources—the village shopkeeper who may give credit on day-to-day purchases at rates of 100 per cent to 250 per cent per annum, the landlord who lends against the security of the crop, or the moneylender who may charge up to 300 per cent on unsecured loans. New institutional arrangements are clearly needed to make both short-term and long-term credit more readily available at lower interest rates to small cultivators and to guarantee effective use of credit. A system of cooperative credit societies, financed by the banks and the government, could contribute to this. So would the establishment of agricultural banks. In Cuba, for example, the government-sponsored Agricultural and Industrial Development Bank has become a most important factor in promoting cooperatives through which small farmers obtain financing for crops and improvements in equipment. Not only does the bank make loans to the cooperatives, but technicians of the bank attached to each cooperative also advise farmers on methods of cultivation, choice of crops, and ways to increase productivity. Being based in the village society with its local knowledge and joint responsibility, and thereby better able to reach the level of the small farmer and tenant, cooperative farm credit societies have shown notable expansion in several countries, Ceylon, Egypt, Turkey, and the Caribbean countries. And in Thailand a farmers' bank has been proposed by the government to assist all farmers who are not members of cooperatives, with land as a guarantee: farmers would receive loans with interest at 6½ per cent a year, compared with interest of over 44 per cent a year charged by many moneylenders.[23]

More use can also be made of selective credit controls to influence the pattern of investment and production. By differentiating between the cost and availability of credit to different sectors, selective credit controls can influence the allocation of credit and thereby the pattern of development. This selectivity can be introduced in credit policy by directly stipulating the loans that can be made, the amounts, the rates of interest, the duration, the type that is not desirable, the amount of collateral, and other provisions. Alternatively, if the central bank has sufficient power to control the commercial banks, such controls may be exercised selectively, so as to influence indirectly the behavior of the banks; for example, rediscount rates may vary according to the type of loan, or some selective exceptions may be made on reserve require-

[23] International Monetary Fund, *International Financial News Survey*, VIII, No. 5, 39 (July 29, 1955).

ments.[24]   According to a certain order of priorities required by the development program, the banking system can vary the cost and availability of credit to different sectors.

The potential effectiveness of monetary policy should not, however, be overestimated. As a means of promoting capital formation, monetary policy is of secondary importance compared to fiscal policy. An easy money policy makes credit more readily available, but this credit will not be utilized unless profit expectations are sufficiently high. Moreover, such a policy will feed inflation which, considering the costs of inflation, is an undesirable means of forcing saving. As has been emphasized previously, an increase in the community's saving is necessary for capital accumulation, but an inflation based on credit creation may increase saving only slightly if at all. The experiences of several countries demonstrate that the mere expansion of bank credit does not necessarily promote investment if inflation ensues; besides the wastes and disruption of inflation, there might even have been more private investment if there had been less inflation.

In their present state, many central banks function "not so much as a mechanism for monetary regulation, but as an engine for credit creation."[25]   And even if they do desire to combat inflation, the central banks are severely handicapped by the lack of a broad government securities market so that they cannot engage in open market sales, the most potent monetary weapon against inflation. Instead of expecting central banks to achieve immediately the objective of actively combating inflation, it may be more realistic to hope that they will simply stop compounding inflation. If monetary controls are not yet sufficiently strong to complement an anti-inflationary fiscal policy, the banking system may at least exercise sufficient restraint so as not to counteract fiscal policy.

Finally, as is true of so many development problems, the mere creation of new institutions guarantees no remedy. Although banks and financial institutions now exist only in limited form, the problem of inadequate saving cannot be solved merely by creating new institutions. The growth in savings depends basically on an increase in productive power and a rise in national income, so that the proportion of the national income that can be saved will grow. As this occurs, it may be expected that financial institutions through which saving is stimulated will establish themselves. Governments may foster their growth, but at present little, if anything, is to be gained by creating new institutions faster than the

[24] I. G. Patel, "Selective Credit Controls in Underdeveloped Economies," *International Monetary Fund Staff Papers*, IV, No. 1, 76–77 (Sept. 1954).

[25] Henry Wallich, *Monetary Problems of an Export Economy*, Harvard University Press, Cambridge, 1950, 284.

cumulative process will allow. The currency and credit system must be responsive to the stimuli of development, but monetary and financial institutions in themselves cannot be expected to be the primary and active movers of development in a direct sense. Given the fundamental stimulus which comes from enterprise and entrepreneurship, the monetary system must then be sufficiently responsive to the stimuli that arise as development gains momentum. The money supply should then increase roughly in proportion to the growth of population and to the rate at which resources are shifted from the non-monetary to the monetary sector of the economy. Without the vital factor of entrepreneurship, however, the mere creation of credit is ineffectual.

4. Supply of Entrepreneurship

On the crucial problem of promoting the supply of entrepreneurship, the government confronts its most difficult challenge. Measures must be taken to promote the domestic supply of entrepreneurship, foreign entrepreneurs must be attracted to the country, or the government itself must assume an active entrepreneurial role and thus be a substitute for private entrepreneurship. A substantial increase in the number of foreign entrepreneurs cannot be expected because many of the obstacles that face domestic entrepreneurs would also confront foreign entrepreneurs, and the government of the poor country is unlikely to take a favorable view of relying on foreign entrepreneurs in view of historical experience and the dislike of anything that has the tinge of "colonialism" or "foreign influence."

As for the government being the entrepreneur, it has been suggested that the direct role of the government be restricted essentially to the provision of public overhead capital and land reclamation and improvement. To maintain development and allow the process to become self-sustaining, private entrepreneurs must become more active. Although governmental development boards or corporations may stimulate, plan, and coordinate development activities at the state level, and mobilize financial resources, the shortage of private entrepreneurs must be overcome in order that private entrepreneurs will ultimately carry out many individual undertakings.

It has been repeatedly seen how a variety of obstacles inhibit entrepreneurship: an unwillingness to devote organizational abilities to business purposes, restrictive effects of custom and tradition, lack of response to monetary incentives, low status of businessmen, high risks involved in new enterprise, absence of vertical mobility in the social structure, market imperfections which deny potential entrepreneurs the resources they need for organizing new production units, and arbitrary changes in the administration of laws by the government which make the environment too uncertain for entrepreneurs.

These obstacles were interpreted in Chapter 16 in terms of the entrepreneur's motives and abilities and a congenial environment for entrepreneurship. The motives and abilities are positive inducements to entrepreneurship, and a more congenial environment means a diminution in the pressures that negate entrepreneurship. Ideally, measures should be undertaken that will intensify the motives, increase the abilities, and make the environment more congenial. To change the motives and abilities, however, involves difficult long-term cultural changes in values and institutions. Many of these changes may come only after development gains momentum. A more immediate contribution to the supply of entrepreneurship may come from measures directed towards making the social and economic atmosphere more conducive to the emergence of entrepreneurship. It is especially important to induce more people to be long-term entrepreneurs interested in permanent businesses, rather than short-term speculators or venturers interested merely in quick short-term gains which are now the concern of the merchants and traders.

The government itself may bear the initial risks of starting enterprises, and then dispose of them to private individuals after the initial "growing pains" are over. Various "pilot projects" may also be undertaken by the government to demonstrate what can be accomplished by certain technical innovations, and to give local technical people and administrators an opportunity to learn the skill and art of applying more modern production methods. The government may also indirectly stimulate entrepreneurship by establishing secure property rights, avoiding arbitrary changes in administration of laws and regulations, providing the necessary framework of public overhead capital, maintaining economic stability, and introducing favorable tax and monetary policies. In the short run, the basis for an expansion in entrepreneurial activities may be immediately laid through the promotion of cooperatives, emphasis on small-scale village-rural industry, and government construction of larger-scale industrial projects which will later be leased or sold to private entrepreneurs. In the longer run, governmental activities can improve the financial, fiscal, and technical structure within which private enterprise can develop industries suited to the economy. Public investment may thus ease the way for private investment. As the government projects make progress, as new lands are brought into cultivation, and as larger quantities of power are generated, the scope for private investment in agriculture and small industry will vastly increase.

At bottom, an increase in the supply of entrepreneurship depends on social and cultural changes in institutions and on changes in the society's value structure. Although efforts can be made to encourage this necessary spirit, it must come for the most part from within the poor country itself. It cannot be forced from without. The requirement is not so much that of devising ways of creating or superimposing entrepreneurship as it is that of trying to elicit what latent leadership there is and aiding it in directing the development efforts in the best manner. In particular, it is necessary to channel into more productive economic activities those entrepreneurial energies that are now devoted to commercial trading, speculation, and moneylending.

Thus, difficult as the problem is, there are two favorable possibilities. First, in so far as the government is willing to undertake innovations, the role of private individuals may simply be one of imitation. Technological innovations, for example, can be derived from richer countries, and if the knowledge of these innovations is made available, and if individuals are instructed in their use, then there may well be a sufficient supply of individuals who are willing to make use of the innovation in an imitative sense. Even though the government is the innovator, individuals may be responsible for the "swarm effect" which Schumpeter discussed as following the innovation. Second, as the development process becomes cumulative, it will generate a larger supply of entrepreneurs. For, if entrepreneurship contributes to development, so does development in turn contribute to entrepreneurship. As the economy loses its characteristic of backwardness, as markets widen, as the capacity to save increases, in short, as development proceeds, individuals will acquire more of the motives and abilities for entrepreneurship, and the environment will become more congenial.

Chapter 19

International

Policy Issues (1)

A variety of international measures can also help to accelerate development in poor countries. Some of these may enable the poor country to draw upon the technical knowledge and capital available in richer countries, others may give the country a greater share of the "gains from trade," and some may be utilized to complement the country's domestic policies. Although poor countries by themselves can undertake some of these measures, particularly in their commercial policy, others of the measures depend on action by foreign countries or international organizations. This chapter and the next chapter outline these various international policy measures.

1. Commercial Policy

Many poor countries are attempting to control their foreign trade as a means of accelerating their development. Although the traditional case for free trade is difficult to contradict for highly developed countries, the poor countries generally believe that many exceptions to free trade are legitimate when the objective is accelerated development. It has already been noted in Chapter 15 that some economists argue that the traditional theory of international trade is not realistic for poor countries and is not relevant under dynamic conditions. Moreover, it is maintained that, even within its static framework, classical trade theory only proves rigorously that some foreign trade is better than no foreign trade, but it does not prove unambiguously that free trade is necessarily the best form of trade from the standpoint of national interests. From the questioning of traditional theory it is a short step to advocating protection. Several types of arguments have been presented in support of controlling the trade of poor countries.

One particular argument rests on the alleged "inferiority of agriculture" thesis. According to this view, poor countries suffer because they are agricultural countries, and they should use commercial policy to reduce their dependence on agriculture. At the end of the 1920's, Mihäil Manoïlesco, Rumanian Minister of Industry and Trade, contended that agricultural production is inferior to industrial production, and that the free trade policy implications of the theory of comparative costs do not apply to countries with low agricultural productivity. Since he supposed that capital and labor were more productive in industry than in agriculture, Manoïlesco argued that industry should be protected by tariffs and that this would raise per capita income. Friedrich List had earlier extolled the advantages of industry and had urged protective tariffs for German industry. The Prebisch-Singer argument regarding the secular deterioration in the terms of trade for agricultural countries is also part of this argument.

The superiority of industry has also been emphasized in terms of the external economies that arise from industrial production and the contribution that industrialization can make in promoting social as well as economic change. It is maintained that an important indirect contribution of industry is "its effect on the general level of education, skill, way of life, inventiveness, habits, store of technology, creation of new demand, etc."[1] The expansion of output in one industry may thereby allow other industries to produce more efficiently. Through such external economies the extension of industry would then involve a social product that exceeds the private product. It may further be argued, as Singer does, that these external economies have been denied the poor countries because they have been preoccupied with exporting raw materials, and that protection may thus help to realize external economies by switching resources from agriculture to potentially productive enterprise in other fields.

The weakness of the inferiority of agriculture argument is that it

[1] H. W. Singer, "Distribution of Gains between Investing and Borrowing Countries," *American Economic Review, Papers and Proceedings, XL,* No. 2, 476 (May 1950).

would explain the poverty of poor countries in terms of their agricultural production. As has been repeatedly stressed, however, the trouble is not agriculture *per se,* but inefficient agricultural production. It is certainly question begging to compare efficient manufacturing with the inefficient agriculture of a poor country. One need only look at a wealthy agricultural country such as New Zealand to realize that there is no inferiority natural to agriculture, and that agriculture cannot be equated with poverty. As already discussed in Chapter 15, primary production is an associative characteristic of a poor country, but not a causative characteristic.

Moreover, even though the productivity of labor may be higher in industry than in agriculture, the productivity of capital must also be considered. The social returns from capital in agriculture are frequently underestimated; they may actually be very high, and even higher than in an import-competing industry.

Most importantly, however, a poor country simply cannot afford to minimize agriculture. The previous consideration of "balanced growth" emphasized how vital it is for a developing country to maintain a strong agricultural base. And as the historical discussion illustrated, an agricultural revolution is a precondition for an industrial revolution.

Closely allied with the inferiority of agriculture argument is a generalized modern version of the infant industry argument. By protection of an industry that has possibilities of future expansion and an eventual reduction in costs, a tariff might allow the country to enter a line of production in which it might eventually acquire a comparative advantage. The rationale is that, even though cheaper or better imports are excluded in the short run, the country will in the longer run be able to produce the former import. If the country is willing to undergo the short-run sacrifice, there may be a long-run gain: the protected infant may grow into self-reliant adulthood.

This type of protection has increased considerably since World War II. For example, in 1953 and 1954, Colombia prohibited the import of certain iron and steel products in bulk, El Salvador began to control the import of all metal articles, and Mexico prohibited the import of various bottled and canned foods.

It must be recognized, however, that infant industry protection overlooks the problem of capital supply.[2] Before an industry can be protected, it must first be created. Tariff protection of industries in poor countries commonly fails because it does little to create the capital needed for new industrial development. Although it might make a contribution

[2] R. Nurkse, *Problems of Capital Formation in Underdeveloped Countries,* Basil Blackwell, Oxford, 1953, 105.

on the demand side by increasing profit prospects, it does not meet the requirement of an increase in the supply of capital.

There are other difficulties with the infant industry tariff: it must be shown that the selection of industries to be protected is not arbitrary or misguided economically, that the industry would not expand except with a tariff, that the industry will eventually reach a position where the protection can be removed, and that vested interests in the perpetuation of the tariff will not arise.

The modern version of the infant industry argument applies to the over-all structure of the economy. It is contended that a poor country's economy can be considered as an "infant economy," and that changes in the structure of production can be effected through commercial policy. In particular, it is maintained that protection can promote the movement of excess labor out of agriculture into industry. When workers are withdrawn from their previous underemployed status in agriculture, the decrease in agricultural production will be zero or negligible; therefore, the import-competing commodities which they now produce is a clear gain, measured in terms of the prices of the imports excluded by trade barriers. To remove the disguised unemployment and stimulate the industrial sector, a country may impose a flat *ad valorem* tariff on a range of manufactures. By amounting in effect to a devaluation of the exchange rate, but only in respect to these manufactures, this policy may encourage industry in preference to agriculture.

Provided the required supply of capital in the new industries were forthcoming, protection could undoubtedly contribute to such shifts of factors from one sector of the economy to another. The question, however, is whether such shifts are desirable. Should the economy be diversified? Should industrialization be emphasized? Some reasons for a negative answer have already been considered, but, even if the answer is on balance affirmative, there is still the issue of whether protection is the only or the best possible policy for achieving this transfer of factors. The "infant economy" argument is somewhat analogous to the argument that protection is needed to maintain full employment. But just as it may be better to achieve full employment through domestic policies rather than through protection, so it can be submitted that it is better to achieve a movement of factors from one sector to another by domestic measures rather than through commercial policies that may achieve the objective, but at the expense of the gains from trade. A subsidy, for instance, is a more obvious and calculable method of promoting a new industry than is protection. Moreover, it may be better to stimulate labor mobility by direct investments in the public sector that will result in external economies for private industry; or land tenure reforms may encourage mobility; or an extension of the cash crop system may reduce the rural underemployment.

Some spokesmen for protection also advocate trade controls in order to diversify the economy and reduce its "exposure" to fluctuating world demand and to counteract the "bias" of the economy towards export production. This view stems from the argument, already discussed in Chapter 15, that as a result of being opened to foreign trade the poor country has a "dual economy" and international forces have operated in a "disequalizing" manner so that the gains from trade go mainly to the more developed countries.

Although many countries do display features of a "dual economy," it does not follow that these countries should reduce their export production and diversify production. Little is to be gained from diversification just for the sake of diversification. The extent to which an economy should be diversified must depend ultimately on comparative costs. Against this, however, it may be argued that, even though it would be costlier to develop import substitutes in the short run, it would still be safer over the long run to do this instead of trying to increase exports and then import if there is a question about the future existence of markets for exports, or if exports consist of exhaustible resources. Nonetheless, even if diversification is desired and is a sensible policy on the basis of non-economic considerations, an expansion in exports may still first be necessary to help speed the process of diversification. Moreover, diversification might better be directed towards expanding the range of exports, rather than withdrawing resources from exports. Indeed, by allowing more imports, an expansion of exports makes possible a higher rate of development without inflation and balance of payments problems than would be possible if foreign exchange receipts were less. The International Bank's recommendations for Cuba, for example, emphasize diversification of the Cuban economy, but the dependence on sugar is to be reduced not by curtailing sugar production but by promoting new enterprises using sugar by-products or using sugar as a raw material, and by promoting the export of non-sugar products such as minerals and foodstuffs. Instead of trying to isolate the economy or reduce the volume of foreign trade, it is far better to gain as much as possible from needed imports in exchange for exports, and from foreign investment directed so as to aid development.

In general, all the arguments based on "disequalizing forces" in trade suffer from misplaced emphasis. Instead of questioning the worth of international trade, one should recognize that the lack of carry-over of export production to the rest of the economy is basically an internal problem involving the obstacles of market imperfections and vicious circles. At most, the protection arguments are "second-best" arguments:[3] since there are divergences between marginal values and costs elsewhere in the economy, it can be argued that protection is better than no policy whatsoever. But it is still better to attack the divergences directly through domestic action. Instead of protection, it is better to focus on removing the market imperfections and allowing foreign trade to help break the vicious circles. Instead of attempting to solve the problem of a dual economy by restricting trade, it would be more appropriate to pursue domestic policies designed to create alternative forms of social and economic organization, increase the knowledge of market conditions, expand credit facilities, widen the capital market, create greater opportunities for technical substitutability of factors, and reduce monopolistic practices. If the internal limitations to development were removed or reduced, then adjustments could more readily be made to changing conditions in international trade, advances in the export sector could have more repercussions throughout the economy, and the export sector could even be the leading propulsive sector in the economy. Some of the richest countries are export economies, and many have also relied on exports of primary products. To lose the potential for development that can come from expanding export markets would be to run the risks of distorting development and losing the gains from trade.

Although the foregoing arguments for protection cannot be considered seriously, there are other arguments, more closely related to specific development objectives, which deserve more sympathetic attention. One of the strongest arguments is that through its commercial policy a poor country could increase its savings ratio and foster capital accumulation. This may be done in three ways: by improving the terms of trade, attracting direct foreign investment, and increasing the amount of compulsory saving.

To improve its terms of trade, a country may impose an "optimum tariff." This is a tariff that will result in either an increase in the country's export price level or a decrease in the country's import price level. If such a tariff can be imposed, then the country will in effect "make the foreigner pay the duty": it will have to give up less of its own real resources for the same real amount of imports that it received before the tariff, or for the same amount of real resources embodied in exports it will be able to receive a larger volume of imports. The hitch here, though, is that few, if any, of the poor countries have sufficient monopoly or monopsony power to "make the foreigner pay the duty." Only if they could act cooperatively as a group, and only if the elasticities of demand

[3] Cf. J. E. Meade, *Trade and Welfare,* Oxford University Press, New York, 1955, Chapter XIV.

and supply were within a critical range of values,[4] would they be able to impose an optimum tariff. And even if they were able to do so, it is likely that the gain would be only a short-term gain which would be eliminated quickly by retaliatory measures, changes in the values of the elasticities, or by changes in the government's expenditures of customs revenue.

A more practicable method of saving domestic resources is by imposing tariffs designed to attract direct foreign investment. So-called "tariff factories" may be established in the tariff-imposing country in order to get behind the tariff wall or to escape import controls which prohibit the importation of the finished product but permit imports of necessary machinery and raw materials. Canadian industrial development, for example, was aided by tariffs that stimulated American branch plants in Canada. Some of the foreign industrial investment in Mexico has also been of this type. But as long as domestic markets remain narrow in poor countries, tariff protection will still not give much of an inducement to foreign business capital.

Finally, the savings ratio might be increased by imposing selective import controls to reduce the consumption of certain commodities. Import tariffs, import licenses, quotas, exchange controls, and multiple exchange rates can be used to reduce the consumption of imported luxuries or other imported commodities. The decrease in consumption of imports is equivalent to an increase in disposable income, and this increase may then be channeled into capital formation. There are, however, disadvantages to selective import controls. The controls immobilize the full efficiency of the price system. If consumption merely shifts from imports to import-competing domestic consumption, no increase in disposable income will result, and there will be no increase in savings. In this event, since there is an increase in home consumption, inflationary pressures will result. The domestic consumption may also occur at the expense of domestic capital formation in so far as the greater consumption draws resources away from capital construction or maintenance. Moreover, the import controls also require complex administration and are subject to evasion and the practice of favoritism among would-be importers. And, as far as reducing the consumption of luxuries is concerned, domestic sumptuary or luxury taxes can accomplish the same objective; in addition, such taxes can include all consumption expenditures, not just imports, but domestic luxury items as well.

---

[4] In this connection, there is a similarity between the theory of tariffs and the theory of monopoly. See T. de Scitovsky, "A Reconsideration of the Theory of Tariffs," *Review of Economic Studies,* IX (2), 89–110 (1941–1942); J. de V. Graaff, *Theoretical Welfare Economics,* Cambridge University Press, Cambridge, 1957, 122–128.

Besides tariffs and quantitative restrictions, a system of multiple exchange rates may also be used to complement a development program. By setting the rates according to the priorities of the program, the government can influence the composition and pattern of foreign trade according to the essentiality of the imports and the availability of foreign exchange.[5] Multiple rates permit a kind of partial devaluation and are also a substitute for differential trade restrictions. They may also provide a source of government revenue. Multiple rates are especially appealing to poor countries where the exchange-rate machinery may be the most effective means of economic policy: in countries where effective fiscal and administrative machinery is limited, it may be necessary to achieve through the exchange-rate mechanism those measures that would be taken through monetary, fiscal, and price policies in the more developed countries.

By having the exchange rates vary according to categories of commodities, the government may encourage to different degrees the exportation of various commodities and can achieve a social rationing of foreign exchange for different types of imports. An overvalued rate for a particular commodity will encourage the importation of that commodity. In this case, the favorable exchange rate provides a "subsidy effect." Such a practice may be used for capital equipment, essential raw materials, and necessary consumer goods. If there is, however, an undervalued rate on a commodity, then the commodity is expensive to import, and domestic production of an import-competing commodity may be stimulated. In this case, the exchange rate provides a "shelter effect."

Multiple exchange rates, however, interfere with the efficient operation of the price system by directing foreign trade in accordance with currency criteria instead of price criteria. They also have the disadvantage of most forms of control: they involve complex and arbitrary administration; they have adverse disincentive effects on private capital inflows; they may increase internal inflationary pressure; and by being subject to frequent alteration, they are unsettling to the expectations and plans of private traders and producers.

Another major argument in support of restrictive commercial policies is that they may be used to promote balance of payments equilibrium. Poor countries are especially prone to balance of payments disequilibrium

---

[5] For an analysis and evaluation of the effects of multiple exchange rates see E. R. Schlesinger, *Multiple Exchange Rates and Economic Development,* International Finance Section, Princeton University Press, 1952; E. M. Bernstein, "Some Economic Aspects of Multiple Exchange Rates," *International Monetary Fund Staff Papers,* I, No. 2, 224–237 (Sept. 1950).

from three directions: the servicing of foreign investment, the international trade cycle, and excessive domestic inflation.

To service foreign investment, the borrowing country needs foreign exchange. Unless the rate of borrowing is continually increased, a return flow of capital from the borrowing country to the lending country will eventually occur; just when it will occur depends on the rate of investment, the amortization rate, and the interest rate.[6] A transfer problem may then accompany the development process: exports must rise, or imports must fall, in order to service the foreign borrowings. This is a question of the country's absorptive capacity for foreign investment. The absorptive capacity is generally greater for direct investment than portfolio investment in so far as complementary factors of production accompany the direct investment, and the direct investment is related to export markets. The absorptive capacity is also greater from the viewpoint of the whole economy than from any one sector, and the absorptive capacity increases over time as the educative effects and external economies of investment are realized. If the investment is directed productively, and with attention to its future servicing, it may contribute to exports or reduce the need for imports—either directly or indirectly. To this extent the problem of paying interest and amortizing the debt will not be a burden. If, however, the foreign exchange position is weak, then the country may have to use commercial policy to strengthen it.

The foreign exchange position can also be weakened by the spread of depression internationally. Since they export primary products, the poor countries are likely to experience substantial reductions in the value of their exports during a depression and encounter a deficit in their balance of payments. In this situation, trade restrictions may have to be used to limit imports, or commercial policy may have to be directed to the encouragement of exports. Wide fluctuations in the prices of staples over the business cycle may be better met, however, by stabilizing domestic income through international commodity agreements, international buffer stock arrangements, or the operation of marketing boards.

Commodity control agreements have frequently been considered for the purposes of limiting production, controlling exports and imports of primary products, or regulating prices.[7] Some multilateral agreements

[6] Cf. E. D. Domar, "Foreign Investment and Balance of Payments," *American Economic Review, XL,* No. 5, 805–826 (Dec. 1950).

[7] An excellent summary of the problems and prospects of commodity agreements and buffer stock arrangements is provided by G. Myrdal, *An International Economy,* Harper and Brothers, New York, 1956, 245–253; also, United Nations, *Measures for International Economic Stability,* New York, 1951; United Nations, *Commodity Trade and Economic Development,* New York, 1954.

have been concluded to stabilize the trade in particular commodities, such as wheat and sugar. The International Wheat Agreement of 1953 did not include provisions for qualitative control of production or export quotas, but it did provide that each exporter would sell specified qualities of wheat within a given price range and that each importer would purchase specified quantities within the same price range. In 1955, the United Nations Economic and Social Council established the Commission on International Commodity Trade to examine measures designed to avoid excessive fluctuations in the prices and volume of trade in primary products, including measures aiming at the maintenance of just and equitable relationships between the prices of primary commodities and the prices of industrial goods in international trade.

In several countries, for example, Nigeria, the Gold Coast, Burma, and Thailand, the governments operate marketing boards which purchase crops from domestic farmers at a fixed price and export these crops. These boards may be an especially appropriate means of stabilizing the flow of funds to producers by distributing subsidies to growers in depression years and accumulating funds during prosperous years. Some of the profits accumulated by the boards may also be used for other purposes than price stabilization: in West Africa and Uganda, for instance, some of the accumulated revenue has been used by regional development boards as grants for transportation and education. The financial resources of the West African marketing boards, established between 1947 and 1949, already exceed those of the West African governments; the disposal of these large reserves will have considerable influence on the political and economic situation in these territories.[8]

It is also suggested by some that the establishment of marketing boards reduces the likelihood of exploitation of producers by intermediaries, and enables farmers to borrow on more favorable terms from intermediaries. In some cases the price-fixing policies of the marketing boards may provide an incentive to higher quality production: for instance, by widening the difference between the prices of different grades of palm oil, the Nigerian marketing board has stimulated an improvement in quality and has penalized low quality.

To stabilize the domestic price, the board would have to choose a price that is the average of expected future prices; it would then make high profits during a boom, and suffer equal losses during a slump. In practice it is, of course, extremely difficult to select a price that would equate future profits and losses. There has been some tendency to set

[8] For a detailed description and analysis of the boards' activities see P. T. Bauer, *West African Trade,* Cambridge University Press, Cambridge, 1955, Part 5. Hereinafter cited as Bauer, *West African Trade.*

too low a price and to prolong the retention from producers of perhaps an excessively large part of the proceeds of their crops.[9] This may have a depressing effect on the long-run trend of output by reducing the wherewithal and the incentive to extend agricultural holdings.

Moreover, the idea of stabilization is ambiguous in so far as it may refer to prices, money incomes, or real incomes; stabilization of any one of these may destabilize the others.[10] It is also contended by some observers of the operation of marketing boards that, although they are an important instrument of compulsory social saving, they have made almost impossible private saving and investment by important classes of producers, and, by underpayment of producers, have retarded the spread of the exchange sector of the economy since there is not so much incentive to leave the subsistence sector and produce cash crops. Further, the operation of a marketing board involves the government in risks and responsibilities that the governments of some poor countries might be neither willing nor able to undertake.

Aside from the short-term fluctuations over the business cycle, a poor country is also likely to experience strong inflationary pressure as the development process gains momentum over the long run. If investment exceeds domestic saving and capital inflow, then there will be pressure on the balance of payments. Again, commercial policy may help to prevent a potential deficit from materializing, or may aid in removing an existing deficit. Exchange control may also be used to prevent a flight of capital into foreign currencies.

Of course, the commercial policy in itself will not lessen the inflationary pressure. Internal monetary and fiscal policies are required for this. It should also be recognized that, if a country can increase its exports, and hence have a greater import capacity, it can generate a higher rate of development without inflation and without encountering balance of payments difficulties than it could if its exports did not expand. But commercial policy, when inflation exists, may mitigate some of the socially undesirable effects of the inflation: for example, since the inflation tends to transfer incomes from wage earners to profit recipients, thereby altering the pattern of demand, commercial policy may be used to control imports of commodities to which demand has shifted. Here again partial selective devaluation through multiple exchange rates may

---

[9] P. T. Bauer and F. W. Paish, "The Reduction of Fluctuations in the Incomes of Primary Producers Further Considered," *Economic Journal, LXIV,* No. 256, 722 (Dec. 1954); Bauer, "Marketing Monopoly in British Africa," *Kyklos, IX,* No. 2, 164–178 (1956). For a more favorable assessment, however, see P. Ady, "Fluctuations in Incomes of Primary Producers: A Comment," *Economic Journal, LXIII,* No. 251, 594–607 (Sept. 1953).

[10] Bauer, *West African Trade,* 271–272.

have an advantage over the indiscriminate effects of a general devaluation which would increase the local price of every import and thus intensify the inflation and the cost of development.

The foregoing discussion shows that commercial policy may be used to achieve certain national objectives associated with a development program. It underscores the basic dilemma confronting those who, on the one hand, wish to see international trade conducted according to free trade principles of a minimum amount of restrictions, multilateralism, and currency convertibility, and, on the other hand, wish the poor countries to accelerate their development. For it emphasizes that development, free trade, and balance of payments equilibrium may be difficult to achieve simultaneously. If a poor country has to sacrifice one of these objectives, it will most likely be that of free trade. This is simply because commercial policy appears as the easiest solution to the problems of achieving the priorities of a development program and maintaining balance of payments equilibrium. Alternative measures of monetary and fiscal policies are difficult to follow in the poor countries, and the administrative apparatus is much more readily geared to controlling foreign trade than domestic trade.

Although it is true that a skillful use of export and import taxes or multiple exchange rates may reduce the exposure of the primary producers to fluctuations on world markets and may promote diversification of the economy, nonetheless at the same time it will interfere with the optimum pattern of world trade, may lead to uneconomic productive practices, and may inhibit the inflow of foreign capital. The costs of departures from a liberal trade policy must always be recognized. For, as nineteenth-century experience demonstrates, foreign trade can be a vital force in determining the rate at which a country develops. There are strong advantages to free trade and to an expansion in trade for poor countries as well as for the more developed countries. Each departure from free trade must therefore be carefully examined, and the merits of the exception must be established. Unless the exceptions are kept to a minimum, the poor country may only be perpetuating its poverty by denying itself the gains that are possible from international trade. A poor country cannot afford the luxury of forgoing international trade: it must take advantage of world markets as an indispensable means of accelerating its own development.

2. Technical Assistance

The discussion of commercial policy has concentrated on policies of poor countries and has assumed commercial policy of more developed countries as fixed. If, however, it is believed that poor countries can benefit from expanding foreign trade, then the rich countries can also contribute to the development of poor countries by maintaining free trade and not restricting imports from poor countries. Rich countries can contribute even more directly through technical assistance and foreign investment.

Technical assistance is an important area of international development policy. If foreign capital is actually to be incorporated into new patterns of activity, there must be educational investment in individuals as well as investment in plant and equipment. For, as Marshall said, "Ideas, whether those of art and science or those embodied in practical appliances, are the most 'real' of the gifts that each generation receives from its predecessors. The world's material wealth would quickly be replaced, if it were destroyed but the ideas by which it was made were retained. If, however, the ideas were lost, but not the material wealth, then that would dwindle and the world would go back to poverty."[11]

Beyond providing capital, the rich countries must also make available to the peoples of the poor countries the knowledge and technical experience which they have accumulated. It was seen in Part 2 that the flow of capital during the nineteenth century was accompanied by parallel migrations of people and technology. Although the migration of labor is necessarily insignificant today, the transfer of technical knowledge can be highly important. To transfer technical knowledge and help overcome the shortage of skills and organizational abilities in the poor areas, several technical assistance programs are in operation. Some of these programs are organized bilaterally between countries, while others are internationally organized.

An early technical assistance program was a feature of the United Kingdom Colonial Development and Welfare Act of 1929. Assistance under this Act has been directed mainly to education, medical services, agricultural services, roads, and water supply. The Colonial Development Corporation has also been instrumental in making available to the British colonies technical knowledge along with the provision of grants and loans.

Although the earlier British program made technical assistance subsidiary to the provision of capital, the more recent American activities have focused directly on technical assistance. To implement President Truman's "Fourth Point," the United States Technical Cooperation Administration was established in 1950; in 1953 it was incorporated in the Foreign Operations Administration which was formed to have responsibility for all types of foreign aid, except for loans which remained

[11] Alfred Marshall, *Principles of Economics,* eighth edition, Macmillan and Co. Ltd., London, 1930, 780.

under the jurisdiction of the Export-Import Bank and the International Bank; foreign aid activities are now under the International Cooperation Administration.

Table 19.1 shows the distribution of expenditures in the United States technical assistance programs during the fiscal years 1952 and 1953. In fiscal years 1954 and 1955, the appropriations for the program declined to approximately $116,900,000 and $116,400,000 respectively.

TABLE 19.1. UNITED STATES TECHNICAL ASSISTANCE, DISTRIBUTION OF EXPENDITURES, FISCAL YEARS 1952 AND 1953

	1952		1953	
Area	Total (million $)	Industrial Projects As Per Cent of Total	Total (million $)	Industrial Projects As Per Cent of Total
Middle East and Africa	37.8	11.7	51.4	8.2
Southern and Southeast Asia	85.7	17.7	68.4	19.9
Latin America	17.8	1.4	21.6	7.1
Total:	141.3	14.0	141.4	13.6

Source: Technical Cooperation Administration, Proposed Program, Fiscal Year 1954, Parts I and II, Washington, D.C., May 1954.

It will be noted that direct attention to industrial projects has been only a minor part of the program. The major fields have been health, agriculture, and education. Assistance schemes have taken a wide variety of forms. Some involve lending American engineers, technicians, and other expert personnel to poor countries; others involve the offering of training facilities in the United States; and others consist of pilot projects to demonstrate more efficient means of production. As of June 1954, some 3000 American technicians were at work in various countries: approximately 850 in Latin America, 1100 in the Near East and Africa, and 1100 in South and Southeast Asia.

A few specific examples of various activities follow. In Liberia, American technicians directed some 30 projects designed to provide public works and mineral and agricultural development to diversify Liberia's one-crop economy based on rubber cultivation. In Indonesia, in 1953, 13 American technicians were employed in providing assistance in connection with production, trade, and labor problems in chemical, mechanical engineering, and other industries. In Pakistan, not only technical advice but also financial assistance to the extent of $7 million was provided for the construction of an ammonium sulphate fertilizer factory which has been linked to schemes for increasing the yield of rice, the staple of East Pakistan. In Colombia, an industrial survey carried out with American assistance in 1951 resulted in the establishment of a *servicio,* or joint Colombia-United States agency within the appropriate government department, to aid both in improving methods in existing small factories and in initiating new industries. In several Latin American countries, Colombia, the Dominican Republic, and Panama, for example, assistance has been requested for the establishment of small-scale industries; in others, such as Brazil, Chile, and El Salvador, productivity centers have been established to deal chiefly with engineering techniques, production planning and control, plant layout, matériel handling, personnel practices, and other matters associated with the attempt to reduce costs and improve utilization of resources. One of the most notable forms of technical assistance has been the community development projects in India. In 1952 and 1953, the United States committed some $11 million for a large community development program. The funds are used to provide technicians, project supplies, and equipment.

The major internationally organized technical assistance program is that of the United Nations Technical Assistance Administration. In 1949, provision was made for an expanded program of technical aid in which all the specialized agencies of the United Nations might participate. The program is financed from voluntary annual contributions of governments that are members of the United Nations or of one of its specialized agencies. In 1954, the amount budgeted for the United Nations' and specialized agencies' programs of technical assistance was about $70,000,000 for the world, including $25,000,000 for the Expanded Technical Assistance Program.

Some principles that guide the United Nations and its specialized agencies in extending technical assistance have been formulated by the Economic and Social Council as follows: (*a*) to arrange for international teams to advise governments in connection with their economic development programs; (*b*) to arrange for facilities for the training abroad of experts of underdeveloped countries; (*c*) to arrange for the training of local technicians within the underdeveloped countries; and (*d*) to provide facilities designed to assist governments to obtain technical personnel, equipment and supplies, and to arrange for the organization of such services as may be appropriate in the promotion of economic development.[12]

---

[12] The guiding principles are elaborated in detail in United Nations, Economic and Social Council, E/1553, *Resolution 222A (IX), Annex I.* This resolution

Technical assistance by the United Nations can take several different forms. Individual experts or groups of experts and joint missions provide advice and practical assistance. At the end of 1955, some 1440 experts were working to promote better living conditions through improved agricultural and industrial production, health, education, and public administration. A small sample may illustrate the diversity of skilled personnel required for this activity: "a general expert on social and labor questions" for Indonesia; "experts on employment services and experts on vocational training" for Pakistan; "experts in the fields of technical training in general, craft training and training in machine-shop work" for Ecuador; "an expert to organize geodetical work with precision gravimetric equipment" for Pakistan; "a specialist in the teaching of science: to advise on science teaching and on the best methods for the popularization of science" in Thailand; "an irrigation engineer qualified to advise and instruct on the design of wells and pumping equipment" for Saudi Arabia; "a statistician to help in the organization of a modern statistical department" for Burma; and many other specialists.

To assist in training a domestic corps of technical and specialized personnel another type of technical aid takes the form of fellowships and scholarships made available by the United Nations and the specialized agencies to government-approved candidates from various countries, as well as local seminars and training courses given within the country. These fellows or scholars study such problems as power development, use and control of water, mining techniques, industrial processes, modern fiscal methods, and transport and communication techniques.

An important phase of technical assistance has been that of demonstration projects which spread knowledge among the population about the nature and application of advanced techniques. The projects are designed to increase productivity and to improve quality of production. These pilot schemes also provide technical training and offer local personnel opportunities for practical experience. Technical equipment and supplies needed for carrying out technical assistance projects are also furnished by the United Nations organizations rendering technical assistance. Table 19.2 shows the distribution of costs in various fields of activity sponsored by the United Nations Program of Technical Assistance.

Finally, the Public Administration Division in the United Nations Technical Assistance Administration attempts to improve the quality of native administrators. The success of many of the substantive assistance schemes depends on the availability of a trained civil service. Accordingly, the Public Administration Division not only gives governments

discusses standards of work and personnel, participation of requesting governments, coordination of effort, and selection of projects.

advice on administrative matters but also makes available practical assistance in the training of administrators who will be capable of accepting that advice and acting on it. The most important way in which this is done is through the establishment, in collaboration with the governments concerned, of Institutes of Public Administration which teach such subjects as principles of public administration, organization and methods, personnel management, and budgeting and accounting. It is hoped that after technical assistance is withdrawn complete operational responsibility can be assumed by qualified people within the country.

TABLE 19.2.   UNITED NATIONS EXPANDED PROGRAM OF
TECHNICAL ASSISTANCE: DISTRIBUTION OF DIRECT
PROJECT COSTS, 1954
(Thousands of U. S. $)

Field of Activity	Africa	Far East	Europe	Latin America	Middle East	Inter- regional	Total
Manufacturing, processing, mining	—	151.2	161.9	121.4	145.1	243.8	823.4
Cottage industries & handicrafts	9.7	253.0	—	35.6	19.2	—	317.5
Productivity centers, etc.	30.8	100.4	4.3	—	29.9	37.6	203.0
Industrial relations, labor legislation	11.2	66.1	11.1	92.0	9.4	—	189.8
Technical education & training	22.1	—	—	97.0	81.1	—	200.2
Vocational training	176.7	165.2	224.9	174.3	53.1	—	794.2
Total, above items	250.5	735.8	402.2	520.3	337.8	281.4	2,528.1
Total, direct project costs	1957.5	6020.7	1438.9	4368.0	3085.7	710.8	17,581.5

Source: U.N., Economic and Social Council, *Official Records:* 18th Session, *Supplement No. 4, Sixth Report of The Technical Assistance Committee,* 1954. Statistics relate to the approved program for 1954.

The Colombo Plan is another internationally organized arrangement for technical assistance. Besides most of the countries in Southeast Asia, other members of the organization are Australia, Canada, New Zealand, the United Kingdom, and Japan. In its first 3 years of operation the Commonwealth governments agreed to contribute an amount up to £8 million for technical assistance schemes to be administered by a Council for Technical Cooperation. The main functions of the Council include provision of such assistance as (*a*) training of personnel from countries in the area in countries where suitable instruction is available, and the despatch of missions abroad to study the latest techniques; (*b*) experts, instructors, and advisory missions to assist in planning, development, or reconstruction, or for use in public administration, health services, scientific research, or in industrial and other productive activities, and in the training of personnel; and (c) equipment required for training or use by technical experts in the region.[13]

As of June 1953, almost 200 overseas experts had been sent to Southeast Asian countries under the Colombo Plan, and almost 1150 trainees had been exchanged. The keenest demand for technical experts has been for engineers, experts in soil science and management, agronomists and ecologists, and medical and educational personnel. Many specific projects have also been undertaken, ranging from the supplying of equipment by the United Kingdom for new technical schools in Karachi, to the establishment of a printing trade school by Australia in Indonesia, and the construction of two cement plants and a pipe factory by Canada in Pakistan.

Although experience with technical assistance programs is still limited, some questions can be raised regarding how to derive the maximum advantage from a continuing program of technical aid. A basic issue is whether the program should operate on a bilateral basis, such as in the United States program, or on a multilateral basis such as in the Colombo Plan and the United Nations program. So far the United States program has been the most important quantitatively: in terms of personnel, the United States program is about twice as extensive as the United Nations program; in terms of expenditures, it is approximately ten times as large. There are, however, certain advantages to having technical assistance administered under international auspices. First, it may be politically more acceptable since receiving countries do not wish to be tied too closely to the grantor nation and may prefer to receive help from a multilateral organization to which they belong. In many countries "the exploitation and abuses often associated with development in the past have left a legacy of distrust, which in some cases hampers the introduction of new techniques into the less advanced countries. . . . Their confidence and cooperation is likely to be given most freely to a program under international auspices, in the direction of which the underdeveloped countries can take as full a part as the economically advanced countries."[14] Second, the contribution of one country to the international agency may set an example for other countries, thereby stimulating the contributions of funds and making more available than would otherwise be forthcoming under bilateral programs. A third advantage of the multilateral approach is that it generates a spirit of mutuality and cooper-

[13] Report by the Commonwealth Consultative Committee, *The Colombo Plan,* H.M.S.O., London, Cmd. 8080, 1950, 53.

[14] United Nations, *Technical Assistance for Economic Development,* New York, May 1949, E/1327, *Add. I,* 12–13.

ation which allows experts to be drawn from many countries, regardless of their country of origin. Fourth, the international approach avoids the limitations of tied loans which make technical assistance conditional upon purchases from the grantor nation. Fifth, it is likely to provide greater continuity in aid in so far as the necessity of receiving annual approval of a national legislature is avoided. Finally, the nature of many of the problems requires international action: transportation, communication, and health programs frequently transcend national borders.

Another important lesson from the experience of technical assistance programs is that the more advanced technologies of Western industrialized nations cannot be transplanted without considerable modification and adaptation to the particular economic, technical, and social needs of the poor countries. Extremely primitive conditions may rule out the use of modern machinery or modern methods. For example, in Haiti where, in the interior, the principle of the wheel is still unknown and where a plough has not been seen, technical aid might be better devoted simply to bringing the farmer from the hoe to the animal-drawn plough rather than from the hoe to the gasoline-driven tractor. Moreover, much of the technological research in industrialized countries is directed towards capital-using innovations, but in poor areas the relative factor supply commonly calls for labor-intensive technology. Modern technology which is capital-intensive also requires complementary supplies of skilled labor and managerial and technical skills which are scarce in the poor countries. Furthermore, the effective life of modern equipment is much shorter in poor countries than in industrialized countries because operation is less careful, standards of maintenance are lower, and repair facilities are inadequate. Modern technology also tends to be designed for large-scale production units, whereas the narrower market in poor countries dictates small-scale operations; this may require that the large-scale production process be broken down into smaller scale and simpler procedures which involve a reduction in the degree of mechanization.

These conditions do not mean that the poor country should utilize the technology of a bygone century and retrace the technological evolution of the West, but it does raise the question of whether technological research which would conform to the needs of poor countries should not be directed towards a technology that is somewhere between the outdated technology of a previous era and the most modern technology now used in the technologically advanced countries.[15] The full range of tech-

---

[15] Cf. Yale Brozen, "Invention, Innovation, and Imitation," *American Economic Review, Papers and Proceedings,* XLI, No. 2, 255–256 (May 1951); H. De Graff, "Some Problems Involved in Transferring Technology to Underdeveloped Areas,"

nological alternatives and their possible modifications and combinations must be evaluated in terms of relative factor prices, and the particular socioeconomic conditions of the country concerned. If the technology of industrial countries is transferred to poor countries without suitable modification, the results may simply be repeated breakdowns in the equipment, waste of capital, a low coefficient of utilization, and high unit costs of production.

This problem of appropriate technology cannot be settled in any general manner: the exact technologies required for different uses in different countries have to be decided upon within the framework of technical conditions, economic relationships, and sociocultural characteristics peculiar to each country. By and large, however, it may be said that "the most suitable technologies are likely to be those which yield the maximum social return per unit of capital, reckoning labor at its social cost rather than market cost. In many instances this means that the answer probably lies in the direction of choosing the simplest of alternative techniques, the sturdiest of available capital equipment, the smallest type of plant consistent with technical efficiency, the technology that makes the best use of the most plentiful factors of production."[16]

To these broad conclusions might be added the following: (1) it is preferable to introduce techniques that require less time to learn than those that require a longer time; (2) techniques that reduce the gestation period of investment are more suitable to poor countries; (3) techniques that save raw materials or other scarce resources do not meet with so much resistance as those that save labor; (4) techniques that enable the poor countries to expand their stocks of factors of production, such as an increase in minerals or land or electricity, are generally most welcome in these countries.[17]

Above all, the major problem of technical aid is that of succeeding in getting the new knowledge and new techniques actually applied on an extensive scale in the receiving country. The gap between the known techniques of the rich industrial country and the application of more advanced production techniques in the poor country must be reduced. In part this is a problem of recruiting additional personnel, improving

---

Journal of Farm Economics, XXXIII, No. 4, 697–704 (Nov. 1951); R. L. Meier, *Science and Economic Development,* John Wiley & Sons & The Technology Press, New York, 1956, Appendix.

[16] United Nations, *Processes and Problems of Industrialization in Underdeveloped Countries,* New York, 1955, 48.

[17] C. N. Vakil and P. R. Brahmanand, "Technical Knowledge and Managerial Capacity as Limiting Factors in Industrial Expansion in Underdeveloped Countries," in L. H. Dupriez (ed.), *Economic Progress,* Institut de recherches économiques et sociales, Louvain, 1955, 280–281.

the field organization, and establishing more demonstration projects. More significantly, it is a problem of incentives: without the incentive, the innovation may never be applied in practice. Relatively simple measures may help here: for example, the provision of low credit rates may be made conditional upon the acceptance of improved technical methods, and land reform may furnish a new security of tenure which will allow a former share tenant to have now an interest in land improvement. Moreover, much more progress may still be made in introducing techniques that, although more advanced than those that now exist, are nonetheless still in conformity with existing values and institutions in the poor country. Ultimately, however, changes in the value structure and character structure of the poor country's society will be necessary if technological progress is to occur extensively throughout the economy. As with all the requirements for accelerating development, technical aid is but one of the elements in the total problem. To achieve its full power as a catalyst, a technical assistance program must be accompanied by other complementary changes in the rest of the poor country's society— extending from an improved educational and administrative structure through which the producers can learn the new technology to social and economic changes which will provide an inducement to adopt the new technology.

Chapter 20

International

Policy Issues (2)

1. Private Foreign Investment

To the extent that domestic saving and taxation fall short of the amount of investment needed for its desired rate of development, the poor country must rely on foreign capital. The inflow of foreign capital serves important functions: it provides the recipient country with the means for acquiring local resources for domestic investment, it supplies foreign exchange for importing necessary materials and equipment directly needed for developing projects, and it also allows the importation of other commodities which will be demanded indirectly as development proceeds and national income rises. Without the use of external resources, the pace of development will have to be much slower than that desired by the governments of many poor countries, or else domestic resources will have to be diverted to development work by cutting down the standard of living, or inflation will have to be endured. As the Colombo Plan emphasizes,

> None of these courses is practicable. Curtailment of the development programs, while populations are increasing, would condemn the people of the area to continuing poverty; direct reduction of living standards could not be achieved without authoritarian government; the political,

social, and economic consequences of inflation are unpredictable, but the social fabric could hardly be expected to withstand the strain which it would impose.

In the absence of any effective means of making further progress with their economic development by their own unaided efforts, these countries need a large initial stimulus in the form of foreign investment.[1]

Table 20.1 indicates the extent to which individual national plans under the Colombo Plan rely on external capital during the first six-year period of the plans. As the table shows, domestic finance accounts for about 60 per cent of total expenditures in Ceylon, but for less than half in India, Pakistan, and Malaya. The second Indian Plan projects a foreign exchange deficit of about $1.6 billion over the next 5 years, and a similar projection for Pakistan would give a figure of $500 million to $600 million.[2]

TABLE 20.1. SOURCES OF FUNDS FOR DEVELOPMENT
PROGRAMS, SELECTED COUNTRIES, 1951–1957

	India	Pakistan	Ceylon	Malaya
	(millions of pounds sterling)			
	(six-year development program)			
Sources of Funds				
Total expenditure	1379	280	102	107
Domestic finance	561	135	62	46
Sterling balances	211	16	19	—
Other external sources	607	129	41	61

Source: Report by the Commonwealth Consultative Committee, *The Colombo Plan,* Cmd. 8080, H.M.S.O., London, 1950, 58.

External capital may come from private or public sources. Private foreign investment may take the form of "direct investment," in which the foreign investor owns physical assets abroad, or the form of "portfolio investment" which involves the purchase of securities. Public foreign investment comprises public loans and grants from foreign governments or international agencies.

Some special advantages are connected with private foreign investment. To the extent that it reduces the need for foreign public investment, private investment lightens the burden on the taxpayer of the lending country. And being subject to business calculation of private profit, it is likely to be employed productively. When it takes the form of entre-

[1] Government of Pakistan, Ministry of Economic Affairs, *The Colombo Plan for Co-operative Economic Development in South and South-East Asia,* 55.

[2] E. S. Mason, "Emerging Requirements for an Expanding World Economy," in *The Changing Environment of International Relations,* Brookings Lectures 1956, Brookings Institution, Washington, 1956, 89.

preneurial or direct business investment, private foreign investment may bring with itself new techniques of production, entrepreneurial skill, and new ideas. By setting an example, and through the training that it sponsors, private direct investments may constitute a "private Point Four" program and be effective in transferring technology to the poor countries and in encouraging the growth of skills. Direct investment also has some advantages over portfolio investment in so far as part of the earnings from direct investment are generally reinvested in expansion or modernization or invested in some related field within the borrowing country, whereas this is not generally true for portfolio investment. Furthermore, since direct investment is serviced by dividends which are related to profits instead of by fixed interest charges on bonds, it places less of a burden on the borrowing country's balance of payments during depressions. The flexible return on direct business investments is also an advantage over the rigid interest and amortization requirements attached to public foreign loans, even though some steps have been taken to lessen the rigidities. In many instances, direct private foreign investment may also help to induce more domestic investment, either in partnership with foreign capital or into local ancillary industries which the foreign enterprise has indirectly established. Finally, direct business investment creates a real addition to the productive capacity of the capital-importing country, whereas other types of foreign borrowings may be more readily diverted to unproductive uses.

Private foreign investment is now, however, extremely limited. As a result of two world wars, the United Kingdom has not been able to restore its balance of payments to sufficient strength to make possible any significant export of capital. Whereas in 1913, British capital exports were the equivalent of about £800 million in 1956 prices, they averaged only some £60 million a year from 1953 to 1956. The main source of private foreign investment is from the United States, but, as was observed in Chapter 10, private capital from the United States has declined markedly since World War II relative to the more active period of the 1920's. Compared with the 1920's, the investment in the post-war decade has been considerably less in real terms and has amounted to a smaller fraction of American national income than in the 1920's. Moreover, the poor countries have received only a minor part of this investment—for example, from 1947 to 1950 the Asian countries received only $250 million a year. Between 1950 and 1955 the value of American direct investments abroad increased by $7397 million, but of this increase $4151 million was in Canada and Western Europe.[3] Most of

[3] U. S. Department of Commerce, "Growth of Foreign Investments in the United States and Abroad," *Survey of Current Business*, Aug. 1956, 14.

American private foreign investment since the war has been in the form of direct investment concentrated mainly in the petroleum industry. What investment has gone to poor countries has been mainly in agriculture and extractive industries, with only a small part in manufacturing. Most of the foreign direct investment in manufacturing has been made in countries already industrially well advanced. Public utilities and railways, principal objects for British foreign investment in the last half of the nineteenth century, now claim relatively little foreign capital. The purchase of foreign government bonds, an important form of international investment during the 1920's, has also been only on a very small scale. Finally, American private foreign investment has been characterized by cyclical instability, falling abruptly during depressions.

If external finance is to become a significant means of capital accumulation, the lending and borrowing countries alike must try to remove the impediments to private foreign investment. They must adopt methods for expanding the amount of private foreign capital, diversifying its character, making investment in the poor countries more attractive, and promoting a steadier flow of capital.

Perhaps some contribution to improving the flow of foreign private capital can come from promotional techniques. The lending country's government can collect information about investment opportunities abroad, make knowledge of these opportunities and the procedures of foreign investment more readily available to businessmen, and attempt to arouse interest in the overseas opportunities. But this approach is far too simple: businessmen will still not find the opportunities attractive unless they can be assured of higher returns or of lower risks than now exist. This is the crux of the problem, and measures are accordingly needed to make the potential returns of foreign investment sufficiently high to compensate for the risks of loss.

These risks are various. Foreign investors are acutely sensitive to signs of political and social instability, and are frequently uncertain about the jurisdiction of local courts and their status before the law. They also fear nationalization, expropriation, or public ownership and operation of a competitive industry. Foreign investment is also easily deterred by exchange controls and currency inconvertibility which impose limits on the transfer of earnings or capital sums. Moreover, activities that might otherwise be most likely to attract investors from abroad are frequently ruled out by barriers against the establishment of certain types of industry by foreign capital—"saturation laws" in many Latin American countries, the handicraft protection policy of India, the practice of screening for foreign exchange control or other purposes, or the principle of reserving basic industries or strategic production for domestic enterprises. Some countries also regulate the conduct of foreign business by setting maximum rates of earnings, subjecting foreign concerns to especially steep progressive taxes on profits, or by stipulating that a certain amount of the labor force employed be local labor, the proportion of indigenous personnel required being sometimes so high as to reduce efficiency and increase costs appreciably.

The Department of Commerce has summarized the factors limiting American private foreign investments as follows: (a) the imbalance and dislocation in trade and currency relationships leading to controls over the amounts of and purposes for which capital may be invested and the rate at which earnings and capital may be repatriated; (b) economic nationalism in the underdeveloped countries accompanied by unfavorable reactions on the part of the public and domestic business, and by an increasing stringency and number of controls by governments over the entry and conduct of foreign investments; (c) insecure and unstable political and social conditions which cause uncertainties and lack of confidence on the part of investors; (d) low levels of economic development as reflected in inadequate basic facilities, shortage of trained labor, lack of allied industries, and shortage of local venture capital.[4]

Various measures can be designed to minimize the risks of foreign investment—investment treaties, government guarantees, tax incentives, "joint ventures," relaxation of restrictions in the borrowing countries, and certain concessions granted by the borrowing countries.

Bilateral treaty arrangements may be used to afford reciprocal "national treatment" for the investments of either country in the other, thereby minimizing the risk of discriminations on businesses in foreign countries. The United States has signed investment treaties with Colombia, Ethiopia, Haiti, Israel, and Uruguay. The Treaty of Friendship, Commerce, and Economic Development with Uruguay accords American businesses free entry into and equal treatment in practically all lines of production. American companies are also given freedom in hiring personnel, are not subjected to higher taxes than local businesses, and have the same access to the courts and the same property rights as local enterprise. In the event of nationalization, the business is to receive prompt and just compensation. The transfer of earnings and capital in dollars is also assured except for the emergency imposition of exchange control.

Government guarantees on foreign investments can provide some insurance against the risks of foreign investment. The United States

---

[4] Department of Commerce, *Study of Factors Limiting American Private Foreign Investment,* Washington, D.C., July 1953; J. F. Gaston, *Obstacles to Direct Foreign Investment,* National Industrial Conference Board, New York, 1951.

government, for example, could make guarantees to Americans who invest abroad against the risks of expropriation, inconvertibility of local currency profits into dollars, and default. Although there have been some limited steps in this direction, there are numerous obstacles in the way of extending guarantees. There is some feeling that the cost is too high, delays are considerable in getting the guarantees, questions of definition are difficult, and the issue of equity arises as among different types of investments. Moreover, business interests have shown little enthusiasm for guarantees since the government would require access to corporation records, and the guarantees might lead to regulation of overseas operations. So far the American government has not offered guarantees to any significant extent.

Unlike guarantees, tax incentives have much more appeal to businessmen. Both capital-importing and capital-exporting countries could make tax concessions, but in practice capital-exporting countries are in a better position to act than are the importing countries. The lending countries are better able to absorb the resulting revenue loss, and countries that have a tax credit system, such as Canada, the United Kingdom, and the United States, can also be more influential with respect to tax concessions. A system of tax credits generally provides that the home country of a firm operating abroad will give the firm a tax credit for taxes already paid in the poor country in which it operates. Although substantial relief from double taxation, that is, in both country of origin and country of investment, has been provided since World War II, bilateral agreements for the elimination of double taxation could give additional tax relief by removing many of the complexities and uncertainties that still confront foreign investors in respect to their tax liabilities.

One of the most far-reaching proposals for tax relief, favored by the National Foreign Trade Council and the International Development Advisory Board, is to eliminate all United States taxes on business income earned abroad. At present there is only partial relief since foreign subsidiaries of American corporations pay a tax on foreign-source income but are granted a credit for the foreign income taxes paid by the subsidiary upon the income earned abroad. The advantage of outright exemption from the American tax is that it would provide an inducement to other governments to make tax concessions to American investors to attract them. It would also remove a competitive disadvantage which confronts the American investor when he is in direct competition with nationals of the foreign country who pay a lower tax. The disadvantages of this proposal are that it would give a windfall to companies already operating in countries with tax rates below those in the United States, would involve a loss in revenue for the Treasury, and is inequitable in so far as it favors the large corporation which is more likely to have foreign branches than is small business. Furthermore, it would give exemption to investors who would have invested abroad even without the tax incentives, and it would affect investment in rich countries as well as in poor countries: being non-selective, it is not designed to stimulate the flow of investment to particular countries or to particular industries. And, in so far as many capital-importing countries do not now tax profits that are reinvested in the country, there might actually be even an outflow of funds if general tax exemptions were granted.

It has also been suggested that the cost of capital investments overseas be allowed to be rapidly charged off to business expense. This privilege of accelerated capital amortization could stimulate investment by reducing the risks of capital loss; indeed, it is likely to be more of an inducement than tax concessions which are based on earnings and hence effective only after a new enterprise has become profitable.[5]

Another possibility of removing the risk of expropriation is to form "joint ventures" or "public-private partnership investments" in which foreign investors, local investors, and the government of the capital-importing country can all participate. Joint ventures of various types are becoming more widely accepted in Latin America and the Far East. In India, for instance, a number of foreign companies have licensed Indian firms to manufacture their products, some financing the process, others confining their activities to establishing local subsidiaries to market the goods; other companies have agreed with the Indian government on the gradual disposal of their shares in newly established factories to local investors. In Mexico, the Nacional Financiera has participated with private American business in the establishment of important enterprises. And the International Bank and International Finance Corporation have been especially active in promoting joint ventures in several countries.[6]

Even with guarantees, tax incentives, and use of the partnership principle, the "investment climate" in many poor countries will still not be sufficiently appealing unless restrictions and regulations on foreign investment are reduced further. In this connection, much more can be done by way of more general relaxations of exchange restrictions which would liberalize the transfer of interest and dividends and facilitate the repatriation of capital. Policies written into law, well-publicized and closely followed, would remove the arbitrary and uncertain character of the screening process through which foreign capital has to pass before being

[5] Cf. M. C. Conick, "Stimulating Private Investment Abroad," *Harvard Business Review*, Nov.–Dec. 1953, 104.

[6] Activities of the I.B.R.D. and I.F.C. are discussed in the next section.

admitted into a number of countries.[7]   Beyond avoiding or eliminating the various impediments to foreign capital, the poor countries can also take more positive steps to encourage a greater inflow of capital by granting exemptions from customs duties on plant and equipment and raw materials required by a new foreign industry, by granting exclusive rights for specified periods, or by assisting foreign firms with information and advice on legal matters, labor recruitment, site selection, capital raising, and other problems.

To remove impediments to private foreign investment action is clearly required from both lending and borrowing countries.   A Chilean law is a notable example of special concessions and inducements designed to attract foreign capital.   The law applies to foreign investment in export industries, industries that use 80 per cent or more national raw materials or goods to be sold in the home market, and credit institutions that will promote production.   The decree grants these privileges: the right to remit all interest and profits for at least 10 years; the right to repatriate, after 5 years, up to 20 per cent of invested capital annually; exemption from import duties and other charges on investment in the form of equipment and machinery; freedom from new taxes for 10 years; freedom from possible price fixing, control or freezing for 10 years if such controls are not already imposed on comparable domestic production; the right to revalue capital, if exchange rates change, without incurring liability for capital gains tax; and the right to treat reinvested earnings as new foreign capital, with full privileges.

Even if legislative or fiscal actions are taken, however, it is still doubtful if much of an increase in the international flow of private capital can be expected in the immediate future.   Many borrowers remain fearful that foreign investment means foreign control.   And, for the lenders, considerable time is needed before the political and economic risks are substantially reduced, ideological obstacles overcome, and sufficiently wide internal markets created in poor countries.   The Department of Commerce has concluded that a greatly increased flow of private investment from the United States cannot be expected in the next few years.   And the United Nations Economic and Social Council has observed that "a contract is not a climate and, accordingly, the promulgation of

---

[7] The purpose of the screening process is to ensure that maximum advantage occurs from the foreign investment in terms of technology and direction of the investment, as well as safeguarding the balance of payments. The process may, however, be self-defeating in so far as, when foreign investments are rejected, for payments purposes or to prevent a shift of demand away from local industries, demand may turn to products that require imports or interfere with exports. The whole question of screening foreign investments involves the major issue of how far government should go in interfering with market judgments.

investment codes, principles of contract obligations and commercial policy or bilateral treaties will not substantially promote the flow of private foreign investment . . . . It is the fruit of favorable experience of private investors and tangible economic results in under-developed countries that must be relied upon as the final assurance required by the investor to promote an accelerated flow of foreign capital. Time and increased familiarity by association are thus needed for a substantial acceleration of private investment."[8]

2. Public Foreign Investment

In view of the limited amount of private foreign capital that may be expected, and the fact that much of the investment in a development program must be undertaken by the government, poor countries must rely to a large extent on public foreign investment. The case of India is illustrative. India's national income in 1950–1951 was approximately $18 billion, of which about 5 per cent, or $900 million, was saved. This was barely enough, however, to maintain the capital stock intact and to keep up with the annual population increase. Even a doubling of the amount of capital available would not provide a very rapid rate of development in India; yet this would require another $900 million. The total United States direct private investment in India as of the end of 1954 was only $92 million.

If this type of calculation is extended to other poor countries, the magnitude of the problem will be readily realized. Indeed, a United Nations group of experts has estimated that the total capital required by the poor countries as a whole in order to increase per capita national income by 2 per cent per annum would require an annual investment of about $19 billion.[9] In 1949, domestic savings in this group of countries fell short of this amount by nearly $14 billion. After allowing for some increase in domestic savings, the group concludes that an annual capital import well in excess of $10 billion is required. In view of the

---

[8] Quoted in United Nations, *Processes and Problems of Industrialization in Under-Developed Countries,* New York, 1955, 89; also, cf. W. L. Thorp, "American Interest in Asian Development," in *The Changing Environment of International Relations,* Brookings Lectures 1956, Brookings Institution, Washington, 1956, 128, 143–144.

[9] The basis for this calculation may be seen in United Nations, *Measures for the Economic Development of Under-Developed Countries,* New York, 1951, 75–80. Assumptions are made about the annual amount of the transfer of population out of agriculture into non-agricultural employment, the amount of capital required for each person absorbed in non-agricultural employment, the amount of capital needed for industrialization and agriculture, the amount of net domestic savings, and increases in productivity. These assumptions are necessarily inexact, and at best the calculations indicate only the order of magnitude involved.

fact that the current inflow, including grants and loans, does not exceed $1500 million, the inflow of capital must be multiplied severalfold. It is thus apparent that, even if measures are successfully adopted to increase the flow of private foreign capital, considerable reliance will still have to be placed on public foreign capital.

Public foreign investment also has certain advantages over private foreign investment. A major advantage is that foreign loans for capital expenditure by governmental authority in the borrowing country can be used for domestic development in accordance with the country's over-all development program. To this extent it may more directly fill the needs of the debtor country and not be subject to the criticism that foreign investment serves mainly the needs of the lending country. If the loans come from an international agency, the borrowing country is also less likely to suspect and fear political interference with its domestic and foreign policies than it would if privately foreign-owned enterprises are established in the country. Many poor countries which have only recently lost their colonial status are now extremely nationalistic and view with fear any foreign capital that has any element of foreign domination attached to it. Furthermore, investment in public overhead capital involves such large amounts and so many risks that private investment cannot be expected to be attracted, and reliance must be placed on public loans for the basic requirements of overhead capital.

Special governmental institutions for foreign lending now exist in several countries. The Colonial Development and Welfare Act of 1929 enabled the British government to make loans or grants to Colonial governments for aiding agriculture and industry in an amount not to exceed £1 million in any one year. The Act of 1945 increased the sum to £120 million for the ten-year period 1946–1956. The Colonial Development Corporation, established in 1948, and the Commonwealth Development Finance Company, established in 1953, are also concerned with lending to British colonies. The Colonial Development Corporation is itself responsible for some projects; in other cases it lends to private enterprise; and in some instances it enters into partnership with private enterprise on undertakings that could not be carried out by either party alone.[10]

The Commonwealth Development Finance Company has an authorized capital of £15 million and borrowing powers amounting to twice its issued capital. As a lender of last resort, it supplements other sources of industrial capital overseas, and provides only a part of the funds required by the approved borrower. During its first year of operation

[10] For details of the Colonial Development Corporation's activities, see Colonial Development Corporation, *Report and Accounts,* H.M.S.O., London, annual.

it invested about £5 million in three major enterprises: electricity generation and cellulose pulp production in the Union of South Africa and natural gas development in Pakistan.

In the United States the Export-Import Bank was established in 1934 as a government agency to finance transactions and projects that would directly or indirectly promote United States foreign trade. It operates on a commercial basis and judges projects for which loans are requested "in the light of their worthiness as to self-liquidation and their benefits to the recipient foreign economies in respect to dollar earnings or savings."[11] The bank's lending authority was increased to $5 billion in 1954, and its loans have usually carried a rate of interest ranging from 3½ per cent to 6 per cent and have been for periods of 1 to 20 years. The loans are made for specific purposes, generally directly to governments or government corporations, although credits may also be advanced to private foreign banks and corporations. With Treasury consent, the bank may also use its resources to a limited extent to guarantee foreign loans made by private interests.

At the beginning of 1955, the Export-Import Bank had about $2767 million worth of loans outstanding, of which about $897 million were in Latin America, $110 million in Africa, and $346 million in Asia. Most of the loans to the poor countries have been for financing public works and utilities, but the proportion of loans for industrial purposes has risen; for example, the Bank financed the construction of steel mills (Brazil, Chile, Mexico, Turkey), iron working establishments (Brazil, Mexico), cement plants (Brazil, Indonesia, Venezuela), sugar mills (Mexico), and chemical and fertilizer plants (Egypt, Israel, Mexico, Turkey).

During the post-war period the United States government has also made other grants and loans to the poor countries. In the period 1946 to 1950, United States loans and grants to the poor countries amounted to about $2.6 billion, of which about $600 million went to Latin America.[12] In 1952, almost $815 million in grants and loans were made by the United States government to poor countries, and, in 1953, over $730 million.[13] This aid, however, was only a small part of total American foreign economic aid: in 1952, aid to poor areas amounted to only about 17 per cent of total foreign aid, and about 11 per cent in 1953.

[11] U. S. Congress, House Committee on Foreign Affairs, *The Mutual Security Act and Overseas Foreign Investment*, Washington, June 1953, 58.

[12] M. L. Weiner and R. Dalla-Chiesa, "International Movements of Public Long-Term Capital and Grants, 1946–1950," *International Monetary Fund Staff Papers*, IV, No. 1, 142 (Sept. 1954).

[13] N. S. Buchanan and H. S. Ellis, *Approaches to Economic Development*, Twentieth Century Fund, New York, 1955, 363.

Like private foreign capital, public foreign·capital has also been directed mainly to rich countries rather than to the poor countries for development purposes.

Of the American aid to poor areas, that provided by the International Cooperation Administration and its predecessors has been important, not so much because of the over-all sum involved as because of the character of the aid.   In 1953–1954 about $335 million was allocated for "economic and technical" assistance to poor areas.   The technical aid is diffused over a large number of countries, but the economic aid is mainly concentrated in India, Iran, Israel, and the Arab states.   The economic aid is designed to help the countries "carry out selected key activities in their own development programs" usually "when the country lacks the means to undertake such projects independently."[14]   This aid has been particularly important in providing specific imports and in offering aid on a grant basis or on a loan basis with much more lenient terms than those extended by the Export-Import Bank.

Another major source for the provision of public foreign capital is the International Bank for Reconstruction and Development.   The I.B.R.D. is authorized to make or guarantee loans for development projects, both with its own capital funds and through the mobilization of private capital, and is provided with a financial structure under which the risks of such investment are shared by all member governments (58 as of 1956).   The Bank's authorized capital is the equivalent of $10 billion; only 20 per cent of this, however, is required to be paid in, and only a portion of this is immediately available for lending.   The capital structure of the Bank is designed to provide the Bank with substantial loan resources from its own paid-in capital and with an even larger guaranty fund, consisting of the unpaid 80 per cent portion of all capital subscriptions, which enables the Bank to mobilize private capital for international investment, either through the sale of Bank obligations to private investors or through Bank guarantees of private international credits.   The Bank's charter stipulates that loans made or guaranteed by the Bank should be for productive purposes and must be to finance the foreign exchange requirements of specific projects; the merits of all projects financed must be carefully studied and arrangements made to assure that the most useful and urgent projects are dealt with first; the borrower may be a member government or a business, but, if the borrower is not the government, the loan must be guaranteed by the member government in whose territory the project is located; tied loans are prohibited; and the Bank must be satisfied, before making or guaranteeing any loan, that in prevail-

[14] Foreign Operations Administration, *Monthly Operations Report,* July 31, 1954, 8.

ing market conditions the borrower would be unable to obtain the loans from private sources under reasonable conditions.

As of the end of June 1956, the total amount of loans granted by the Bank during its 10 years of operation was $2720 million, consisting of 150 loans in 42 countries and territories. Total loans to some poor countries between 1947 and 1956 have been as follows: Rhodesia and Nyasaland, $122 million; Ceylon, $19 million; Chile, $37 million; Colombia, $111 million; El Salvador, $24 million; India, $200 million; Mexico, $141 million; Pakistan, $77 million; Peru, $36 million; Thailand, $37 million. As of mid-1956, the Bank's largest loan for a single project was the $80 million loan for the first stage of the Kariba hydroelectric power scheme in the Federation of Rhodesia and Nyasaland, and the largest loan for industry was the Tata iron and steel loan of $75 million in India.

Most of the developmental lending has been for electric power, transport and communications; only a small proportion has been directly for agriculture and industry. At the end of June 1956, the Bank's loans, classified by purpose, were distributed as follows: electric power, $789 million; transport, $656 million; communications, $26 million; agriculture and forestry, $228 million; industry, $331 million; and general development, $140 million.[15] This distribution reflects the immediate needs of the borrowing countries and the Bank's desire to emphasize projects that are designed to have a generally stimulating effect on production of all kinds, as distinguished from facilities designed for the production of particular final commodities.

Whether as guarantor or lender, the Bank has operated conservatively and has made prudent assessments of the prospects that loans would be repaid. The Bank has no single criterion by which it judges the relative urgency and productivity of various alternative investment projects. Its over-all aim is to select those projects that will contribute most to strengthening the economy of the borrowing country, and its general approach is first to determine what are or should be the important goals of a proper investment program and then gauge the relative priority of the various projects by the extent of their contribution to those goals. Considerations are also given to the prospects of suitable administration of the project and to the government's ability to withstand pressures.

The actual processing of a loan falls into two parts: a review of the general economic situation in the borrowing country, and then a more technical examination of the engineering, financial, and other aspects of the individual project considered. The Bank has stated that the object

[15] I.B.R.D., *Eleventh Annual Report,* Washington, 1956, 58.

of the economic investigation is to determine whether the country needs and can effectively use an addition to its investment resources and, if so, how much and at what rate; the extent to which and the currencies in which the country can afford to service additional foreign indebtedness, and whether the Bank can lend these amounts without undue risk; the development requirements of the country, the order of priority of the various fields of investment, the fields in which Bank financing can make the greatest contribution, and the place in these priorities of the particular project under consideration; and whether the economic and financial policies of the government are well adapted to the needs of the country or whether some modification of these policies would remove obstacles to the development process.[16] If the preliminary investigation is favorable regarding repayment prospects and the appropriateness of the particular project, the Bank then calls upon staff technicians or consultants to make a thorough examination of the technical plans, financial provisions, and administrative arrangements for the project.

The Bank's ability to finance private undertakings has been limited, however, because of the guarantee requirements and because the Bank does not engage in equity financing. To overcome these limitations, the International Finance Corporation was established in 1956 as an affiliate of the Bank. Membership in the I.F.C. is open to governments that are Bank members, but the agency is financially independent. If all member countries of the Bank joined the I.F.C., total subscriptions to the I.F.C.'s capital would be $100 million. It may recruit additional capital from private sources when suitable investment opportunities arise. The corporation began operating with 31 members and capital subscriptions of over $78 million.

The I.F.C. has more latitude than the Bank in financing private enterprise: it can invest in private undertakings, in association with private investors, in cases where sufficient capital is not available on reasonable terms, and it can provide not only fixed-interest loans but also venture capital without governmental guarantee. The corporation will not participate directly in management, but it may find experienced management, and it will seek to revolve its funds by selling its investments to private investors whenever it can appropriately do so on satisfactory terms.

Some assessment of experience with public foreign investment may now be made. Although the Export-Import Bank, United States government loans and grants, and the I.B.R.D. have been important in

---

[16] Cf. *The International Bank for Reconstruction and Development, 1946–1953,* Johns Hopkins Press, Baltimore, 1954, 61.

making up some of the deficiency of private foreign investment, the amount of public investment overseas is still only a fraction of what would be required for a full-scale program of development. Table 20.2 summarizes the flow of international investment to poor countries. Although the table does not include investments by the European colonial powers in their dependent territories, it is clear that the total sum of public and private international investment in poor countries is small:

TABLE 20.2.   FLOW OF INTERNATIONAL INVESTMENT
TO POOR COUNTRIES

Source	Amount $ Million Annual rate
United States	
Mutual Security Program	415
Export-Import Bank (net)	72
Private long-term investment (net)	500
I.B.R.D. (net)	98
Western Europe, public & private (net)	50
Total	1135

Explanations: (1) The "poor countries" are the independent, non-communist countries of Asia, the Middle East, Latin America, and Africa (excluding Japan and Union of South Africa).

(2) The Mutual Security Program figure represents estimated expenditure for fiscal year ending June 30, 1956. It consists of $162 million of "development assistance"; $153 million of "technical assistance," including the U. S. contribution to the U. N. Technical Assistance Program, and $100 million for the President's Fund for Asian Economic Development.

(3) The Export-Import Bank and I.B.R.D. figures are for calendar 1954.

(4) The figures for private long-term investment from U. S. and Western Europe are averaged for the years 1952 through 1954; these include reinvested earnings as well as new direct investments.

Source: Committee for Economic Development, *Economic Development Abroad and the Role of American Foreign Investment,* New York, Feb. 1956, 30–31.

only a little more than $1 billion from the United States, International Bank, and Western Europe. Nor is there must prospect for a substantial increase in the flow of international capital. The Gray Report concluded that the flow to poor regions would be only about $1.6 billion to $2.1 billion annually for the proximate future—composed of $500 to $800 million of private investment, $600 to $800 million from the I.B.R.D. and United States government loans and grants (including

Export-Import Bank credits), and $500 million in United States government grants and contributions to technical aid.[17]

To make much more public capital available, new international machinery may be necessary to provide funds for projects that cannot now meet the criteria of existing sources. Two new international bodies have been suggested to supplement the International Bank: an International Development Authority and a Special United Nations Fund for Economic Development (SUNFED). The recommendations for SUNFED envisage the establishment of a separate administration within the framework of the United Nations to make grants or long-term, low-interest loans to governments on terms more liberal than the best terms currently available either commercially or from the International Bank.[18] The I.F.C. still lacks what SUNFED seeks to be—a large-scale grant and long-range, low-interest lending agency for non-self-liquidating and other forms of social capital development projects. Creation of some kind of SUNFED probably depends on action by the United States. The United States can take the lead in supporting SUNFED, expand its own loans and grants, and broaden the role that the Export-Import Bank can play in aiding development in poor countries. The I.B.R.D. should also receive as much support as possible in obtaining funds to meet increased requirements for lending to poor countries. A United Nations group of experts has stated that "the Bank should set itself to reach, within five years, some such target as an annual rate of lending of not less than $1 billion a year to the under-developed countries. If it shows no signs of approaching this target, the whole question of the proper international organization for the provision of adequate amounts of loan capital to the under-developed countries should be reviewed by the United Nations."[19]

Another issue that is receiving considerable attention is the particular role of the different forms of financing. It is proposed by some that loans should be limited to self-liquidating projects where the criterion is ability to service the loan, but that grants, which do not require repayment or any interest charges, should be made for non-self-liquidating projects, such as education, health, and community development, where

[17] *Report to the President on Foreign Economic Policies,* Washington, Nov. 10, 1950, 72. Private direct investment may increase in the future because of the United States' need for increasing amounts of raw materials and because of more direct investment in manufacturing abroad to take advantage of wage differentials.

[18] For details, see United Nations, Department of Economic Affairs, *Report on a Special United Nations Fund for Economic Development,* New York, 1953.

[19] United Nations, *Measures for the Economic Development of Under-Developed Countries,* New York, 1951, 83–84.

the criterion is simply "need." The Export-Import Bank and the I.B.R.D., however, are not able to make grants. And, although the American Congress has made a few development grants for politically sensitive countries, the Congress has generally been reluctant to use grants for development on any widespread and continuing basis.

There are several arguments for making more capital available in the form of grants. First, there is the belief that development requires so much capital that if it all took the form of loans, the burden of interest and amortization charges would be greater than the poor countries could support or the creditor countries would admit within the expected patterns of foreign trade.[20] Certainly, international grants rather than loans would alleviate the transfer problem for borrowing countries. Secondly, it can be argued that the "idea of international grants-in-aid is essentially a consequence of the increased gaps in living standards and of the closeness of contact that is creating at the same time an increasingly acute awareness of these gaps—a situation without historical precedence . . . . Interest payments from poor to rich are now, it seems, not only basically unwanted by the rich countries but indeed are felt to be somehow contrary to the spirit of the age."[21] Thus, in so far as private international lending is not forthcoming, unilateral income transfers may be more in accord with the underlying situation as between the rich and the poor countries in international trade. And it can be maintained that the benefits that accrue to the capital-exporting country indirectly through higher real income overseas or improved terms of trade are more significant than any direct benefit in the form of earnings or interest on a foreign loan.

Grants-in-aid may be used directly or indirectly, however, for consumption or non-productive uses, and to this extent they will not help in relieving the problem of capital shortage. To avoid the use of funds that are received on a grant basis for purposes that do not conform to the requirements of development, it may be advisable to limit their use to such areas as were proposed in the establishment of an International Development Authority—grants for research and education, public health programs, subsidization of medium- or short-term farm credit, and improvement of rural public works. Further, grant assistance must be administered judiciously, lest it lead to frictions with the donor gov-

[20] W. L. Thorp, *Trade, Aid, or What?*, Johns Hopkins Press, Baltimore, 1954, 201–202.

[21] R. Nurkse, "The Problem of International Investment Today in the Light of Nineteenth-Century Experience," *Economic Journal, LXIV*, No. 256, 757 (Dec. 1954).

ernment attempting to use grant aid for political purposes, and the recipient government resenting any conditions attached to the grant or subsequent cuts.

In the last analysis, the contribution of foreign investment to development depends on whether the inflow of capital is accompanied by a relaxation of domestic saving efforts. If foreign funds are merely substituted for domestic saving, the country's consumption is increased, but there is no increase in the total rate of capital accumulation. The effectiveness of international investment thus depends basically on domestic policies designed to withhold resources from immediate consumption and to direct them into capital formation.

Chapter 21

Prospects

for Development

The discussion in this Part has considered the obstacles to development and has reviewed various policies for accelerating development. The question now arises as to whether the policies will be successful in overcoming the obstacles. What are the actual prospects for development in poor countries? Section 1 provides some general conclusions on this question. Beyond this, one must turn to specific case studies as furnishing the best approach for further study of the problems that the previous chapters have considered in only general terms. To facilitate such study, section 2 outlines some topics that might be investigated in case studies.

1. Development Potential

The simple fact that countries have developed at different rates indicates that conditions for development are more favorable in some countries than in others. In the poor countries conditions have remained decidedly unfavorable: development has been limited by all the obstacles included in the categories of market imperfections, vicious circles, and foreign repercussions. Yet, their persistent poverty does not mean that they have no development potential.

It cannot be maintained that there is no base for development in terms of natural resources. The supply of natural resources is a secondary factor from the viewpoint of development potential.[1] For there are historical examples of development in spite of a meager endowment of resources, for example, Japan, and more recently Israel. Further, the known resources in poor countries are generally not now being exploited at the same rate as in richer countries. The quality of domestic raw materials can be improved, the efficiency of the factors that produce them can be raised, and the costs of transporting and distributing the output can be reduced. There are in addition potential resources not yet discovered or utilized, and changes in technology may also increase the effective supply of resources by introducing new uses for existing resources.[2] Finally, it must be recognized that many countries have not yet developed in spite of the possession of valuable natural resources. Deficiency in natural resources cannot, therefore, be viewed as an insurmountable barrier to future development. If scarcities of capital and skill are overcome, resources may be opened up, and better resource utilization may be possible.

Nor is population growth in the poor countries an insuperable obstacle to their development. In the first place, not all the poor countries are overpopulated: parts of Africa and Latin America, for instance, would probably experience a higher rate of development if their populations were larger. It should also be remembered that in an earlier phase of their development some of the now rich countries had nearly as high birth rates as now exist in many poor countries. Moreover, historical cases have contradicted the Malthusian population theory which maintains that per capita income is the major determinant of the rate of population growth. Although population growth intensifies the need for development, one loses perspective if he succumbs in despair to neo-Malthusian fears. In a sense it is even possible to view excess population as actually being an asset from the standpoint of future development: if the disguised unemployed can be mobilized for more productive employment, the excess labor can be a means of capital formation. Given two countries with the same low per capita income, and arguing from the present position, it can be said that the country with excess population may have a better chance of development than the country with a labor shortage.[3]

[1] Cf. S. Kuznets, "Toward a Theory of Economic Growth," in R. Leckachman (ed.), *National Policy for Economic Welfare at Home and Abroad,* Doubleday & Co., New York, 1955, 101.

[2] Cf. R. L. Meier, *Science and Economic Development,* John Wiley & Sons & The Technology Press, New York, 1956, Chapters 2–4.

[3] H. W. Singer, "Problems of Industrialization of Under-Developed Countries,"

If the deficiency of natural resources and population growth are not insuperable obstacles to development, then the future rates of development in the poor countries will depend primarily on the success that they have in removing their shortages of capital, skills, entrepreneurship, and foreign exchange. At bottom, the rate of development will depend on increases in the quantity of productive factors, improvements in the quality of the people as productive agents, and advances in the level of productive techniques.

The strong national interests in accelerating development, and the international concern with promoting development, are also grounds for optimism. Particularly is this true in view of the variety of policies that a government can utilize to accelerate development. Especially significant may be such domestic measures as extension of educational and health facilities, provision of public overhead capital, introduction of agricultural improvements, use of fiscal and monetary policy, and the encouragement of entrepreneurship. Promise is also held out by additional international attempts to furnish external sources of capital, extend technical assistance, and strengthen the balance of payments position.

Historical experiences of the development of other countries also provide some encouragement on the prospects for development of poor countries. For countries that are now rich were, of course, at one time also poor; they too confronted at one time obstacles similar to those that now exist in the poor countries. Yet they subsequently developed. For instance, a century ago Japan confronted severe population pressures, inadequate raw material resources, and inadequate agricultural land, and was bound by a host of restrictive social and political traditions. Nonetheless, Japan succeeded in developing. Obstacles to development have not been immutable.

From the discussion in Part 2 and this Part, however, one may note many differences between the problems of development a century ago and now. Some of these differences have been seen to be less favorable to present development. Perhaps four broad differences are most significant: (1) the failure of many poor countries to have yet experienced an agricultural or commercial revolution which might provide a basis of preindustrial wealth before attempting to promote an industrial revolution; (2) the much more severe population pressures in many poor countries than were ever experienced in Western countries at the beginning of their industrialization, and the rapid rates of population growth which are due more to medical measures than to development itself;

in L. H. Dupriez (ed.), *Economic Progress,* Institut de recherches économiques et sociales, Louvain, 1955, 186.

(3) value systems that are substantially different from the general value system derived from Puritan and Presbyterian religious doctrines under which the development of some Western countries was inaugurated; and (4) as the gap between rich countries and poor countries grows wider, the "cost of catching up" increases, and the minimum cost per worker of modern equipment is much higher than in earlier periods.[4] Other differences, however, are more favorable to present development: for example, the strong conscious desire for development on the part of national leaders, and the ability of the poor countries to derive improved productive techniques and equipment from countries that have already developed.

Regardless of whether one interprets the historical comparisons as being on balance favorable or unfavorable, what ultimately matters from the standpoint of its prospects for development is whether a poor country is willing to bear the costs of development and is able to execute effectively the possible policies that might make its development potential realizable.

A major cost of development is associated with the necessity of increasing the rate of capital formation. To do this it is not so important to cut the present level of consumption as it is to transfer the redundant labor out of agriculture and services to more productive industries and to divert savings away from speculative and unproductive channels towards more productive investments. Once the capital formation process is organized, it is then necessary to plow back into additional investment part of the increased output resulting from the increase in capital. An increase in net savings is thus required. To abstain from consuming the increment in income is the type of cost that classical and neo-classical economists emphasized so much. If a country is not able to organize idle resources into the capital formation process in the first place, or if it is then unwilling to choose capital formation over present consumption so that the increased output is not plowed back into further investment, then the rate of development cannot be expected to accelerate. To increase investment without encountering inflation, there must be the mobilization of excess labor for capital formation, or an increase in voluntary saving, or greater taxation, or foreign borrowing.

If a country chooses to form a certain amount of capital by the inflationary method, or if the rate of capital formation exceeds the country's absorption capacity, then it will have to bear the costs of inflation. The danger here is that the costs of inflation can readily become excessive,

<hr/>

[4] H. Aubrey, "The Role of the State in Economic Development," *American Economic Review, Papers and Proceedings, XLI*, No. 2, 272 (May 1951).

and, if the inflation should spiral, the development process will then break down.

To suppress inflationary pressures and to coordinate the development program in general, a country may have to resort to direct controls. It must then be willing to bear the costs of planning—in particular, the negation of individual choice in some sectors of the economy.

Moreover, development necessitates changes and transformations which upset the *status quo*. If the class structure is such that one class, for example, absentee landlords or moneylenders, prevents economic gain by other groups, then this structure must be modified. To this extent, those with vested interests in the *status quo* will suffer. Thus land reform may be necessary to provide tenants with the incentives to make improvements, but as a result of such reform some individuals will be made worse off at the same time that it makes others better off. The country must then be willing to bear the costs of such institutional changes.

Finally, the changes associated with development may entail non-monetary costs in the form of social, ethical, and religious dislocations. Unless a country is willing to endure modifications in social demand, social institutions, habits, and beliefs, some of which will involve the costs of human unrest and discontent, development will not proceed very far. At least some groups in the society must become "achievement oriented," be concerned with the future, and believe in the rational mastery of nature.

Undoubtedly the domestic policies of the poor countries and their international relations will be dominated for a long time to come by this central problem of meeting the costs of development. To solve this problem, however, reliance cannot be placed on existing social, economic, and political institutions. There must be changes in the value pattern and the behavior pattern. To promote these changes, there must also be social and political transformations directed towards such core institutions as the family, the church, and the school if these support old values that resist innovation. If there is not this sociological development, then there cannot be much acceleration in economic development. For the development of a whole society requires, by its very nature, the fusing of both economic and non-economic means for achieving economic and non-economic objectives.

Conscious action, largely by the poor countries themselves, is needed. To a considerable extent, this action must come from their governments —at least in the initiation phase of more rapid development. For it would appear that the government is the only major existing institutional arrangement that is capable of meeting the wide scope of development problems. Among the decisions of the government, however, must be included the decision of whether development should be institutionalized mainly within the government or to a much greater degree within the private sector. The Western world hopes, of course, that the governments of the poor countries will aim for the private method, since it is believed that the maintenance of development over the longer run can best be accomplished by private enterprise, and that this method is more democratic.

Although, as Chapters 17 through 20 have shown, there are numerous policies that a government may follow to accelerate development, nevertheless, if they are to be effectively executed, there must first be improvements in the government itself. An adequate civil service has to be created. Antiquated conceptions of government functions will have to give way to efficient methods of public administration. Corrupt practices and sinecures must be eliminated. In some countries, government leadership will have to be acquired by groups that do not have vested interests in preserving the *status quo*. In short, many of the poor countries must first undergo political development before economic development can be accelerated. Political development, sociological development, and economic development are interdependent.

The path of development is an uphill one, but given the willingness to bear the costs of development, and given the prerequisites of sociological and political development, then it can be generally concluded that the prospects for development are hopeful. After the rate of development is accelerated, the obstacles to further development may then be more easily reduced, as social, political, and economic changes all have a reciprocal influence on each other. Once momentum is gained, the process tends to be cumulative: each advance creates the conditions for further advance.

2. Some Topics for Case Studies

Against the general background of the foregoing chapters, it would now be desirable to examine through case studies the particular development problems of individual countries, the specific policies designed to overcome these problems, and the actual prospects for accelerating development in individual countries. In the final analysis, the course of development must be investigated on such a country-by-country basis. Even though these studies cannot be undertaken here, their nature may at least be indicated by summarily listing some topics that may guide these studies, as in the following outline.

A: *Definition of "Economic Development"*

(1) Real national income.
(2) Real per capita income.
(3) Welfare implications.

B: *Development and Welfare*

(1) Definite and consistent social goals.
(2) Differences between increase in real per capita income and "economic welfare."
(3) Differences between "economic welfare" and "human welfare."
(4) Economic nationalism and neo-Mercantilism: national interests versus international interests.
(5) Issues of progress versus security.
(6) Value judgments of investigator.

C: *Sociocultural Features*

(1) Role of custom.
(2) Role of religion.
(3) Role of government.
(4) Level of education.
(5) Standards of health.
(6) Land ownership and attitudes.
(7) Motivations and attitudes.
(8) Value structure.
(9) Administrative, organizational, and technical abilities.
(10) Technological progress.
(11) Entrepreneurship.
(12) Technical and organizational innovations.

D: *Demographic Features*

(1) Population size.
(2) Trends in population size: estimated rate of increase or decrease of population; natural increase or decrease; net migration.
(3) Age distribution of population.
(4) Trends in age distribution of population.
(5) Indigenous and foreign elements; homogeneous population or multiracial problems.
(6) Population density: per unit of cultivated area; per unit of cultivable area.

E: *Demand and Supply of Labor*

(1) Labor supply in short term: size and composition of labor force.
(2) Labor supply in long term: potential labor force.
(3) Occupational distribution of the labor force.
(4) Continuity of employment: labor turnover; seasonal labor.
(5) Organization of labor.
(6) Public regulation of labor.
(7) Incentives and responses to them.
(8) Real wages.

F: Demand and Supply of Natural Resources

(1) Geographical and ecological background.
(2) Climate and soil: rainfall; irrigation; erosion and decline in fertility.
(3) Land utilization: techniques of utilization; law and custom governing land utilization.
(4) Mineral resources: what minerals present? how are they placed for transport purposes?
(5) Other raw materials? Foodstuffs?
(6) Survey of potential resources.
(7) Demand for products of the land.

G: Demand and Supply of Capital

(1) Domestic capital accumulation.
(2) Capital imports.
(3) Domestic savings.
(4) Pattern of investment.
(5) Return on investment.
(6) Investment opportunities.
(7) Investment criteria.
(8) Public investment: transportation facilities; communication facilities; public utilities.

H: Structural Characteristics of the Economy

(1) National income:
  (*a*) Size.
  (*b*) Trends in.
  (*c*) Consumption, investment, government expenditures.
  (*d*) Proportion of income saved and spent.
  (*e*) Proportion of spending on imports and home-produced goods.
  (*f*) Real income.
  (*g*) Distribution of income.
(2) Economic organization:
  (*a*) Public overhead capital.
  (*b*) Structure of production: plantation and/or peasant production; competitive or monopolistic markets; extent of commercialization of agriculture; extent of industrial activities.
  (*c*) Proportion of resources in primary, secondary, and tertiary activities; relations between industrial structure and occupational structure.
  (*d*) Proportion of resources in export and domestic industries.
  (*e*) Proportion of land, labor, and capital employed in production of national output.
  (*f*) Disguised unemployment and surplus labor.
  (*g*) Size of market and division of labor.
  (*h*) Currency and credit: money and non-money sectors; availability of credit; cost of credit; capital market; monetary policy.
  (*i*) Public finance: revenue structure; budgetary organization; fiscal policy.

(3) Market imperfections:
  (*a*) Product markets: foreign export-import enterprises; middlemen; retail trade.
  (*b*) Factor markets: labor mobility; incentives and response to price and income stimuli.
  (*c*) Knowledge: local markets; world markets; time horizon; custom; economic rationality.
(4) Foreign trade orientation:
  (*a*) Foreign investment.
  (*b*) Extraterritorial enterprises.
  (*c*) Export-oriented production.
  (*d*) Customs revenue.
  (*e*) Balance of payments position.

I: Relevance of Theories of Economic Development

(1) Classical: extent of market; division of labor; capital accumulation; Malthusian theory of population; stationary state.
(2) Marxian: primitive accumulation; surplus value; exploitation; economic structure as foundation of legal and political superstructure; imperialism.
(3) Neo-classical: optimum allocation of resources; capital accumulation; external economies; gains from international trade.
(4) Schumpeterian: innovations and the entrepreneur.
(5) Post-Keynesian: determinants of total demand and total supply of output; multiplier and accelerator.
(6) Interrelation of domestic and international aspects:
  (*a*) Leakage of demand into imports; multiplier and accelerator.
  (*b*) Infant industries or infant economies?
  (*c*) Distribution of gains from trade between rich and poor countries.
  (*d*) International transfer of factors: labor, capital, techniques.
  (*e*) Relevance of theory of comparative costs.

J: Obstacles to Development

(1) Market imperfections and less-than-optimum allocation of resources.
(2) Vicious circles.
(3) Foreign repercussions of international relations.
(4) Sociocultural limitations.

K: Development Measures

(1) General sequence of development: role of agriculture; role of industry; village-rural industrialization, heavy industrialization, induced industrialization?
(2) Creation of new economic, social, and political institutions or working through existing institutions?
(3) Growing points and balanced growth.
(4) Domestic measures: health and education; transport and communication; agricultural improvements; fiscal policy; monetary policy; direct controls; local credit facilities and mobilization of local savings; diversification of industries.

   (5) International measures: role of foreign investment—loans and/or grants; technical assistance; commercial policy.
   (6) Extent of government activity.

L: Prospects for Development

   (1) Obstacles to development.
   (2) Costs of development.
   (3) Requirements for development.
   (4) Political and sociological prerequisites.
   (5) Domestic policies to fulfill requirements for development.
   (6) International policies to fulfill requirements for development.

PART 4

Maintaining

Development

in

Rich

Countries

"... *to find the means by which prosperity may be lengthened out,
and the period of humiliation procrastinated to a distant day.*"

—WILLIAM PLAYFAIR

THE CHAPTER, STUDYING ECONOMIC DEVELOPMENT, stresses the view that the study of economic development should not be confined to poor countries. The problem of maintaining development in rich nations is equally relevant. To restrict the subject to poor areas alone is to lose an essential sense of continuity in the concept of economic development. For, although there are many political, sociological, and economic differences between rich and poor nations, the fundamental economic forces and processes involved in development are basically similar in the two cases. There is no sharp dividing line between theories of development as applied to poor and rich countries.

Part 4, therefore, examines development problems that confront nations near the top of the per capita income scale. Chapter 22 discusses the goal of economic development in relation to other economic objectives of rich countries and presents a brief survey of policy measures adopted during the nineteenth and twentieth centuries which affected the development objective. The chapter concludes with a summary of the development performance in some of the rich countries over the last 75 years. Economic characteristics and trends that affect the development rate in rich countries are examined in detail in Chapter 23. On the basis of these economic features and the analysis of Part 1, Chapter 24 then discusses the general requirements for maintaining development in rich countries. Finally, Chapter 25 outlines the major policy positions advocated for promoting development and discusses estimates of development prospects in the United States and Britain.

Chapter 22

Economic Development

as a Policy Goal

Although a satisfactory rate of economic development is an important economic goal, it should be viewed as only one objective of economic policy for the more advanced countries. In addition to the objective of continued development, these countries also seek: (1) high and stable levels of employment; (2) reasonable stability of the price level; (3) an equitable distribution of income and social security; (4) an efficient allocation of resources; and (5) satisfactory international economic relations.[1] Other objectives also could be mentioned, but the preceding list covers most of the economic goals of modern, rich countries.

As a background for better understanding the policy issues that face rich countries with respect to the maintenance of a satisfactory rate of development, the first section of this chapter examines possible conflicting and complementary relations between the development objective and the other goals mentioned above. The next two sections then discuss the emphasis upon the development goal compared to the other objectives in terms of the actual economic policies pursued by some

[1] See A. Smithies, "Economic Welfare and Policy," *Economics and Public Policy,* The Brookings Institution, Washington, 1955, 14.

rich countries. The last section summarizes the growth performance of these countries since about 1870.

1. Economic Development and Other Economic Goals

Consider first some of the possible conflicting and compatible inter-relationships between economic development and the twin goals of full employment and reasonable stability of the price level. Although virtually everyone opposes large-scale unemployment, there is a real question to what extent a full employment policy should be pursued. It can be argued (as some neo-classical economists do) that a small amount of unemployment is desirable. By giving the economy some flexibility, such unemployment may actually permit a more rapid long-run rate of development than "maximum" employment. Some Keynesians, however, contend that tight labor conditions are more favorable to rapid progress. With high levels of purchasing power, businessmen are optimistic and are more willing to expand their operations. Moreover, labor shortages may create an added incentive for technological improvements.

Similarly, two points of view can be presented with respect to the effect of a stable price level on development. A gradually rising price level (perhaps the necessary consequence of a vigorous full employment policy) may be more conducive to rapid growth than a stable level. Profit expectations are kept buoyant, and business is gradually relieved from its fixed money commitments. But rising prices may also encourage excessive emphasis on short-term and speculative projects to the detriment of long-run development. Thus, a stable price level may be a more favorable condition for rapid development. One might even advocate a gradually falling price level although, in view of wage and price rigidities in the rich industrial countries, few champion this policy.

Not only does a policy of full employment without unreasonable inflation affect the problem of maintaining a satisfactory rate of development, but the reverse is also true. The rate of development influences the achievement of the full employment and the stable price level objectives. As Schumpeter emphasizes, growth tends to occur in cyclical waves. And, the more rapid the surge of investment, the greater the difficulty of maintaining cyclical stability becomes. Post-Keynesian growth theorists also indicate the dangers of cyclical instability associated with development. Yet, equally apparent, as the stagnationists point out, is the fact that, unless growth is sufficiently rapid, the economy may be plagued by chronic unemployment.

Analogous interrelations between the development goal and a desire for an equitable distribution of income and social security exist. The classical writers, for example, stress the advantages of high profits and low wages for rapid development. According to Ricardo, taxation measures designed to attain a more equitable distribution of income invariably fall on profits and, consequently, dampen the rate of accumulation. Schumpeter, too, warns against redistributive measures. He contends that they may undermine the social conditions necessary for successful capitalistic development. Keynesian economists, however, generally support the opposite view: redistributive measures, by expanding consumption markets, encourage rapid development.

The rate of development, in turn, may affect the distribution of income in conflicting and complementary ways. Marxians stress the possible conflicts. Rapid development, they contend, widens the income gap between workers and capitalists and thus sharpens class antagonisms. But one can also argue convincingly that a rapid rate of growth lessens group tensions. According to Schumpeter, the real income of all groups generally rises in the process of development so that each group's desire for a better living standard need not be achieved at the cost of reducing the income level of other groups.

Consider next the problem of simultaneously achieving an efficient allocation of resources through the market mechanism and a rapid rate of development. According to classical and neo-classical writers, purely competitive market conditions not only produce an efficient resource allocation but also stimulate development. For these theorists, bigness is associated with monopoly power, and monopoly retards development. Opposing these authors are those like Schumpeter who emphasize the opportunity and ability of large corporations to exploit economies of scale, engage in extensive research, and secure capital funds. In other words, bigness, though it may entail a relatively inefficient allocation of resources at any moment of time, may encourage a more rapid, long-run development rate than purely competitive market conditions. The efficient allocation goal, therefore, becomes less significant with a rapid development rate.

Finally, international economic relations also affect and are affected by the rate of economic development. The relevance of tariff, quota, and exchange-control policies as well as of policies affecting international movements of labor and capital to the development goal is obvious. As noted in Part 1, there are development arguments both for and against such measures as tariffs. The rate of domestic development can also influence the type of policies necessary to maintain satisfactory international economic relations. For example, it may be easier for a rapidly growing rich economy to abandon protectionist policies and to increase its exports of capital to other nations. On the other hand, as some "dollar-shortage" economists stress, a high rate of domestic development may itself cause balance of payments difficulties for less rapidly growing economies. As a result, foreign aid programs by the rapidly growing nations and restrictive measures by the others may become necessary to maintain international equilibrium.

Possible conflicts and complementary relations among the goals thus make the simultaneous achievement of the various economic objectives difficult. As a result, a compromise is usually necessary. The most desirable compromise depends upon an evaluation of the relative importance of the goals and upon the economic repercussions of policy measures on the several goals. In considering a policy designed to achieve one particular objective, the repercussions of this policy on the other goals as well as the effect on this particular objective of policies designed to implement the other goals must not be forgotten. Otherwise a narrow and one-sided picture of policy formation emerges. Moreover, differences from country to country and changes over time within any one country in the nature of the economy and in economic attitudes imply that acceptable compromises among the goals as well as the economic measures appropriate to attain these compromises may vary widely from country to country and over time. What may be regarded as a satisfactory rate of development in one country may be considered quite inadequate or excessive in another country.

2. The Development Goal and Nineteenth-Century Economic Policy

The preceding section stresses the compromise that possible conflicts and complementary interrelations between the development goal and other major economic objectives usually necessitate. The next two sections consider actual compromises resulting from governmental actions directed towards the achievement of the development objective and these other goals. These sections examine salient policy attitudes of selected rich countries in both the nineteenth and twentieth centuries.

English industrial development in the nineteenth century, as Part 2 shows, took place largely within a framework of minimal government interference. The central government did not engage directly in production to any significant extent. Manufacturing industries and even such basic public utilities as the telegraph and telephone systems, railroads, canals, turnpikes, and waterworks were developed by private groups.[2] Strongly believing in the merits of competition, both the government and the public viewed monopoly power in the hands of the State

---

[2] The telegraph and telephone industries, however, were nationalized in 1868 and 1911, respectively.

or of private groups with abhorrence.[3] Many governmental actions in the early part of the nineteenth century therefore were directed towards removing vestiges of earlier governmental interferences in economic life. The Corn Laws were repealed in 1846; the Navigation Laws were gradually liberalized and completely repealed by 1853; the law prohibiting the emigration of artisans was repealed in 1824; restrictions on the exportation of machinery were eased in the same year; statutory apprenticeship was abolished in 1814, and the compulsory acceptance of apprentices in 1844; the monopoly of the East India Company in India and China was removed in 1813 and 1833, respectively; and exclusive privileges in the insurance and banking field were withdrawn in the 1820's.

In addition the government attempted to prevent excessive charges and inadequate service in the public utility field. The railroads, for example, were subject to maximum rate and minimum service requirements. Parliament also encouraged competition by allowing end-on amalgamations and by refusing combinations among competing parallel lines. Actions by the government with respect to the docking facilities for London offer another illustration of this type of practice. Parliament in 1823 refused to renew the monopoly of the West India Dock Company and in 1825 tried to increase competition by permitting the formation of a new company.

One field in which the law allowed a limited degree of combination was labor. In 1824, the Combination Acts, which penalized combinations of both workers and employers, were repealed. Another act was passed the following year "which nominally re-established the prohibition of combinations, but specifically exempted from prosecution organizations to regulate wages or hours of labor."[4] The common law of conspiracy, nevertheless, still restrained labor union actions except in so far as it was not modified by provisions in the 1825 Act. Since the courts generally interpreted the pro-labor provisions of the Act narrowly, unions continued to be treated harshly under the law.[5] Not until 1875 were measures passed that allowed peaceful picketing and exempted from criminal prosecutions union actions in connection with a dispute if such actions were legal when committed by one person. Collective bargaining, thereafter, was recognized as a legal way of establishing wages.[6]

Other important measures gradually enacted during the nineteenth

[3] C. R. Fay, *Great Britain from Adam Smith to the Present Day*, Longmans, Green and Co., London, 1948, 201.

[4] E. L. Bogart, *Economic History of Europe, 1760–1939*, Longmans, Green and Co., London, 1942, 206.

[5] H. A. Millis and R. E. Montgomery, *Organized Labor*, McGraw-Hill Book Co., Inc., New York, 1945, 492.

[6] Bogart, *op. cit.*, 438.

century to improve labor's position included limitations on the employment of women and children, the 10-hour working day, and safety and
sanitation regulations.   Tax changes during the period also favored the
working class.   An income tax was reintroduced in 1842, and indirect
taxes on basic foods were reduced to a minimum level.[7]

In the banking field some government controls to curb sharp cyclical
price fluctuations and periodic financial crises were deemed desirable
both from a short- and a long-run viewpoint.   The Bank Charter Act
of 1844, consequently, not only limited the quantity of banknotes that
could be issued but also tended to confine their issuance to the Bank of
England.   The joint stock company was another important financial
device sanctioned by the State.   After 1825, when the restrictions placed
on this form of business organization by the Bubble Act of 1719
were removed, the number of joint stock companies rose considerably.
Finally, in 1862 the principle of limited liability was extended to all types
of businesses (except the issuance of notes by banks).

In the United States, the Federal government likewise did not attempt
to accelerate development by engaging directly in production to any
significant degree during the nineteenth century.   To a small extent, however, it aided domestic development by partially financing turnpikes and
canals in the early part of the century.   Construction of the Cumberland
Road, to which the government contributed $7 million, was the most
notable project.   But Federal land grants were much more important in
promoting internal improvements than direct financial assistance.

In 1827, Congress passed legislation granting land to Indiana and
Illinois for the purpose of raising revenue to finance canal construction.
Each state was given alternate sections from a strip of public land 5 miles
wide on each side of the canal.   Besides granting liberal rights-of-way,
the Federal government also gave large amounts of public land from
1850 onwards to the states and later directly to private companies for
the purpose of stimulating railroad development.   Again, the principle
of granting alternate sections of land on each side of the road was followed.   In addition to rights-of-way and land grants, the Union Pacific
and Central Pacific railroads, as constructors of the first transcontinental
line, received a subsidy of national bonds which was repayable gradually
from the net earnings of these railroads.   By 1871, when the land-grant
policy expired, the area that had been awarded to the railroads was
about four times as large as New England or equal to the size of France.[8]

The Federal government in 1862 also made substantial land grants

---

[7] There had been a war-time income tax between 1799 and 1816.

[8] E. F. Humphrey, *An Economic History of the United States,* The Century
Co., New York, 1931, 287.

to the states for the purpose of establishing colleges. Funds accruing from the sale of this land formed a trust, the interest from which was to maintain these land-grant colleges. In addition, the Homestead Act was passed in 1862 to encourage internal settlements. This measure granted 160 acres of government domain to the head of a family, provided he resided upon or cultivated the land for 5 years.

In the international field the United States followed the advice of Alexander Hamilton rather than of the classical economists. The infant industry argument was widely accepted and implemented in America. From 1816 until 1832, tariffs on manufactures were high. The Act of 1833 inaugurated a period of tariff reduction, but this was reversed again with a strict protectionist measure in 1842. The Act of 1846, however, introduced a period of moderation which lasted until the Civil War. Thereafter a high protective tariff again prevailed for the rest of the century. There were, however, no restrictions placed upon the importation of capital; nor were there restrictions upon immigration until the 1880's.

Regarding business and labor, the Federal government adopted a "hands off" legislative policy. Efforts by labor unions to raise wages and improve working conditions were not treated with favor by the courts.[9] Unions were allowed to exist, but they were subject to the doctrines of conspiracy and restraint of trade. It was left to the states to enact measures beginning in the 1840's prohibiting the employment of children, regulating the hours of work, and imposing standards of health and safety upon employers. Business was not subject to federal anti-monopoly laws until near the end of the nineteenth century. Although the common law held unreasonable restraints of trade and contracts entered into to raise prices illegal, it was only with the passage of the Interstate Commerce Act (1887) and the Sherman Act (1890) that the Federal government took action in this field. The former Act provided for the control of railroad rates and services; the latter measure attempted to prevent industrial monopoly. Monopoly for a limited time period, however, was regarded as desirable in the field of invention. Congress passed patent laws which now provide an inventor exclusive rights to make, sell, or license an invention for 17 years.

Banking was another area where the Federal government exercised some control. The first and second Banks of the United States, lasting from 1791 to 1811 and 1816 to 1836, respectively, performed many central bank functions. But, after the second Bank lapsed, it was not until the National Banking Act in 1863 that the national government intervened again in this field. The Act established a system of banks that

9 See Millis and Montgomery, *op. cit.*, 503–508.

were chartered and controlled by the Federal government. By placing a 10 per cent tax on notes issued by state-chartered banks, the Congress in 1866 conferred a monopoly of note issuance on the national banks.

Although Federal efforts to stimulate growth by direct participation were modest during the nineteenth century, state activity was considerable.[10] Beginning with New York's Erie Canal in 1825, many states embarked upon large-scale programs of canal construction. Large sums were also spent on the construction of state roads. In some states the mixed enterprise in which both private interests and state governments purchased stock was common in the transportation field. Although state owned and operated railroads were not numerous, the states furnished substantial assistance by contributing cash and land and by purchasing stocks and bonds. By the last quarter of the century, however, state financial aid was minimal in these fields. Successive financial failures provoked constitutional provisions prohibiting this type of state activity.

In addition to assisting in the development of transportation facilities, the states tried to exercise charter control over rates, profits, and service performance. It was, however, only after the Civil War that serious and successful efforts were made by the states to regulate the railroads.[11]

Several states, particularly in the South, established state owned and operated banks. Banks jointly financed by the state and private interests also were common. And, of course, the states enacted banking regulations to prevent the excessive issuance of notes. But these measures were not very effective.[12]

In the manufacturing sector, direct state financial assistance was negligible. Some subsidies and rewards were offered for the establishment of certain industries in the last part of the eighteenth century, but these were not large. General incorporation Acts (beginning with Connecticut in 1837) and the gradual extension of the limited liability provision, however, benefited and encouraged industry in general. The states also tried to prevent monopoly abuses in manufacturing. By the time of the Sherman Act of 1890, twenty-one states had statutory or constitutional prohibitions of monopoly practices. But these measures also did not prove to be very effective.[13]

[10] For a discussion of economic activities undertaken by the state government in Pennsylvania, see L. Hartz, *Economic Policy and Democratic Thought,* Harvard University Press, Cambridge, 1948.

[11] E. S. Kirkland, *A History of American Economic Life,* F. S. Crofts and Co., New York, 1946, 557.

[12] H. F. Williamson (ed.), *The Growth of the American Economy,* Prentice-Hall, 1946, 265–268.

[13] *Ibid.,* 717.

In Germany and France, direct state-sponsored efforts to accelerate the growth of industry during the nineteenth century exceeded those in either Great Britain or the United States. The French government, for example, constructed an extensive road system. In 1818, the government also drew up a comprehensive plan of canal construction and improvement. The costs were met by private interests, but after 1850 most of the canals were nationalized. With respect to railroad transportation, the State contributed the land and built the roadbeds, but private companies operated the lines and provided the rolling stock, tracks, and working capital. In Germany, some railroads were constructed and operated by the State and others by private interests. By 1912, however, the railroads were almost completely government owned.

As in Britain and America, the government attempted to provide a sound banking system in both France and Germany. The Bank of France, which was established in 1800 with privately owned capital, in effect became a quasi-official organization. It was the depository for government funds; it distributed the interest payments on the government debt; and, after 1850, it was granted a complete monopoly of note issue. In Germany, private and semi-state banks were allowed to issue notes until 1836, when this privilege was restricted to the latter group. Finally, in 1875, the Reichsbank was created with the purpose of centralizing the issuance of bank notes. By 1914, only four semi-state banks possessed this privilege. The Reichsbank was privately owned but managed by government officials.

Two important financial enterprises sanctioned by the French government in 1852 were the Credit Foncier and the Credit Mobilier. The Credit Foncier, started with a government subsidy of 10 million francs, was designed as a national mortgage bank to make loans to peasants and townspeople on the security of their land. In 1900, the government also established the Credit Agricole to provide additional low-interest-rate loans to farmers. The purpose of the Credit Mobilier was to finance railroads and industrial enterprises. This company was permitted to issue bonds up to ten times the amount of its capital (which was raised from private sources). Although it collapsed in 1867, it was a forerunner of the type of industrial banking practiced by the private banks in Germany.[14] Credit to industry was extended for longer and longer terms in Germany until the banks, in effect, became controlling partners in many industrial firms.

The French and German governments also played a larger interventionist role in creating a favorable environment for development of man-

[14] J. H. Clapham, *The Economic Development of France and Germany, 1815–1914,* Cambridge University Press, Cambridge, 1951, 384.

ufacturing industries than the British or American governments did. The French government not only established schools of civil engineering and mining but also encouraged the development of new industries with generous rewards and subsidies. A liberal business organization law which permitted limited liability under certain conditions also facilitated French development.[15] Germany, although hampered by the slow disintegration of the guild system, likewise made some direct attempts to foster industry. The main effort was the creation of the Institute of Trades in 1821. Its purpose was to subsidize experiments, train individuals in the use of new industrial methods, and spread knowledge of these new techniques.

The attitude of the German government towards competition in the manufacturing sector differed sharply from the other countries considered thus far, particularly the United States. Whereas the United States enacted anti-monopoly legislation near the end of the century, the German government did nothing to curtail the cartel movement. Under German law cartel agreements were not only permissible but also enforceable.[16]

In the labor field French and German policy was not unlike that in Great Britain and the United States. Unions organized for the purpose of raising wages were not treated sympathetically under the law. Labor combinations were illegal in France until 1868 and in all the German states until 1869.[17] Thereafter, the union movement grew rapidly in France, but it received a sharp setback in Germany with the passage of restrictive legislation in 1878. Both countries gradually took steps, however, to limit the employment of children and to improve working conditions generally. In this respect, Germany took the lead in passing accident, health, and old age insurance programs.

In their international policies, neither of these two countries went as far as the British in establishing a policy of free trade. The Germans, however, started off in this direction with the creation of the Zollverein in 1834. Under this customs union, internal trade was free in most of Germany, even though Germany was a confederation of autonomous states. Modest external duties on manufactures were maintained, but raw materials were either admitted free or subject to very low duties. Between 1834 and 1848, however, there was a tendency towards slightly higher duties on manufactures. But this was checked and reversed in the 1850's and 1860's, and from 1873 to 1877 duties on manufactures

[15] *Ibid.,* 130–131.

[16] D. Day, *Economic Development in Europe,* The Macmillan Co., New York, 1942, 409.

[17] Bogart, *op. cit.,* 218 and 224–225.

almost disappeared. The trend towards free trade was changed, however, in 1879 and protection for manufactured goods was again imposed. This policy lasted until the 1890's, when some modest tariff reductions were made.

The French followed a strict protectionist policy from 1816 to 1848 with regard to both manufactures and raw materials. But by means of commercial treaties coupled with domestic subsidies there was a movement after 1850 towards freer trade. This trend, however, was reversed under the Tariff Act of 1892.

Japan is an illustration of a nation in which, during the late nineteenth century, the government pursued interventionist policies to foster industrial development on a scale considerably larger than even the French and Germans did. Between 1868 and 1882, the government financed and operated enterprises in both the public utility and manufacturing fields. Railroads and telegraph lines were constructed and operated by the government. Shipping also was subsidized. Moreover, the government established iron foundries, machine shops, silk and cotton spinning factories, and cement, paper, and glass factories.

After 1882, however, the government sold most of its projects in manufacturing to private groups. One exception was the iron and steel industry. Although the State encouraged the creation of private iron and steel companies by means of subsidies, the Yawata Iron Works, established by the government in 1896, dominated the industry. In the public utility area, however, the government continued its policy of state ownership. All trunk railways were nationalized in 1906. The telephone and telegraph industries also were controlled by the State.

Education was another field of widespread state activity. Students were sent abroad to study foreign industrial techniques, and hundreds of foreign specialists were brought to Japan to help establish new industries. Moreover, primary schools, technical schools, and universities were established on a grand scale.

To finance these industrial efforts the government relied heavily on land and consumption taxes. Large personal and business incomes were subject to only modest tax rates. The State also participated in banking. The Bank of Japan was established as a central bank of note issue and as a depository of government funds. Special banks also were organized under private auspices but with government control over the principal officers. These banks, as well as the private banks, lent to industry on both a short-term and long-term basis. Furthermore, the government encouraged the formation of enterprises under the joint stock principle.

The Japanese did not attempt to prevent concentration of economic power and monopolistic practices in the private sector. Under the law a firm could, by and large, make any decisions it wished with respect to price and output either alone or in conjunction with rival firms.[18]   As in the other countries already discussed, however, workers' efforts to raise wages did not fare very well.   In 1900, it was made virtually a crime to attempt to conduct a strike.[19]   Even by 1914, legislation on child labor and working conditions in general was almost non-existent.

Treaty agreements prevented Japan from using tariff protection to foster industry until 1899.   But, thereafter, the Japanese embarked on a decidedly protectionist policy.

3. Twentieth-Century Policy Towards Economic Development

Although the general economic policies adopted during the nineteenth century by the above countries differed widely, all of them were designed to give a high priority to the goal of economic development.   Other objectives that might have conflicted with development did not receive sympathetic consideration.   This was especially true of the goal of a more equitable distribution of income and social security.   As has been noted, labor received minimal governmental assistance in its attempt to improve its position.   Union efforts to raise wages through strikes were generally harshly treated; regulations on employment conditions were introduced only reluctantly; and the taxation systems employed by many governments were highly regressive.   Exclusive of the United States, efforts to control the private concentration of industrial wealth and to prevent free competition from deteriorating into monopolistic practices were either negligible or modest.   The tariff policies prevalent in most of the countries were also designed to subsidize industrial growth.

One striking change in the twentieth century is the increasing governmental attention to the goal of social security and greater income equality. Progressive income taxes and corporation taxes are commonplace.   Although the income tax long existed in Britain, it was not until around World War I that it became an important source of revenue.   The United States, by constitutional amendment, adopted the personal income tax in 1913.   Whereas the income tax contributed only 5 per cent of Federal tax revenues in 1913, its share of total Federal taxes rose to 82 per cent by 1952.[20]   In Japan, taxes on income, capital, and business enterprise amounted to 43 per cent of total national and local tax reve-

[18] W. W. Lockwood, *The Economic Development of Japan,* Princeton University Press, Princeton, 1954, 565.

[19] *Ibid.,* 557.

[20] J. F. Dewhurst and Associates, *America's Needs and Resources, A New Survey,* The Twentieth Century Fund, New York, 1955, Table 239, 584.

nues in 1933–1934 compared with only 13 per cent in 1893–1894.[21]

Comprehensive social security legislation also was enacted in this century. Great Britain and Germany passed national health insurance and old age pension laws before World War I. Since then, the British have inaugurated an extensive health program (the National Health Service Act of 1946), broadened their old age insurance programs, and sharply increased housing and education subsidies. The United States in 1935 established old age insurance and offered grants-in-aid to states for the assistance of needy persons. A Federal housing program for low-income families was also started in the 1930's. Even in Japan, a Health Insurance Act was passed in 1922 providing for worker benefits in case of illness, accident, maternity, or death.

Relatively depressed sectors in the economy received an increasing amount of state subsidization after the turn of the century. Agriculture was the main recipient of this type of aid. After abandoning its price support program for wheat and oats in 1921, the British government again introduced a price support program for wheat in 1931 and in 1937 extended it to oats and barley. Import quotas on beef and pork as well as marketing programs for hops, milk, and potatoes were also put into effect in the 1930's. The Agricultural Credit Act of 1928 provided for low cost, and in some respects subsidized, loans to farmers. Finally, the Agriculture Act of 1947 broadened the system of guaranteed agricultural prices.

The French and Germans pursued similar policies. After World War I France undertook a broad agricultural support program that included tariff protection, grants, direct price fixing, and aid for agricultural education. The German government fixed minimum wage rates in agriculture and organized market associations in an effort to control prices. In the 1930's, further tariff protection was secured, subsidies for certain commodities were granted, irrigation and drainage projects were undertaken—all in an effort to attain agricultural self-sufficiency.

The United States government established special credit facilities for the farmers in the 1920's and in 1929 also organized the Federal Farm Board to promote orderly marketing. Thereafter, a sweeping program of subsidization through production and marketing quotas, crop insurance, crop loans, direct subsidies, and Federal price supports was enacted.

Another legislative movement that emphasized the goal of a more equitable distribution of income occurred in the labor field after 1900. As already mentioned, after 1875 collective bargaining was recognized as a legal method of establishing wages in Great Britain. The Trade

21 Lockwood, *op. cit.,* 523.

Disputes Act of 1906 granted unions immunity from civil liability for those actions for which the 1875 measures had conferred criminal immunity. Machinery for settling disputes was set up under the Conciliation Act of 1896 and the Industrial Courts Act of 1919. Another measure passed in 1909 permitted the government to fix minimum wages for timework or piecework. The German Constitution after World War I not only ensured the rights of labor to combine and engage in collective bargaining but also provided for an 8-hour day and for labor dispute settlements. The United States in 1935 passed the National Labor Relations Act, which affirmed the rights of labor to organize and bargain collectively. The Fair Labor Standards Act of 1938 further improved labor's position by introducing minimum wage and maximum hours provisions.

The objective of full employment also became a national goal of primary importance during the twentieth century. Britain introduced unemployment insurance as early as 1911 in the National Insurance Act. Under this Act contributions made by the employers, employees, and the State provided unemployed workers with modest payments for a maximum of 15 weeks. Germany introduced unemployment insurance legislation in 1927. The scheme was financed by equal contributions from employers and workers, the latter being covered for a period of 20 weeks. The French established national unemployment insurance based on similar principles in 1928. Finally, under the Social Security Act of 1935 the United States adopted unemployment compensation legislation.

But more important than unemployment insurance itself is the willingness of governments in the industrial countries to use fiscal and monetary policies to promote full employment. A fiscal policy of tax reductions, coupled with an increase in expenditures, and a monetary policy of low interest rates and plentiful reserves are accepted means of combating unemployment.

Concern for unemployment in the United States is expressed in the Employment Act of 1946. Under this legislation, the Federal government assumes the responsibility "to promote maximum employment, production, and purchasing power." The British coalition government in a White Paper on Employment Policy (1944) accepted "as one of their primary aims and responsibilities the maintenance of a high and stable level of employment after the war." A "guarantee of full employment" was also expressed as a national objective in the post-war plan for modernization (the Monnet Plan) formulated by the French government.

Besides encouraging full employment, governments now take a more active role in maintaining price stability. Until the 1930's monetary policy was the major weapon for influencing price and employment levels. In the United States the Federal Reserve System was organized in 1913 and charged with maintaining "monetary and credit conditions favorable to sound business activity in all fields—agricultural, industrial, commercial." Although the Federal Reserve Banks are privately owned, the Board of Governors of the System is appointed by the President with the consent of the Senate. Governments in Great Britain long exercised some control over the Bank of England, but this control increased significantly after 1914. The same was true with respect to the Bank of France. Both of these central banks were nationalized after World War II. Besides exercising control over the banking system, governments have increasingly employed fiscal weapons to influence the general level of prices.

The attitude of the British government towards the goal of reasonable price stability is expressed in its White Paper on Employment Policy. "Thus, the stability of these two elements [wages and prices] is a condition vital to the success of employment policy; and that condition can be realised only by the joint efforts of the government, employers and organised labour. The government for their part are prepared to do what they can to stabilise prices so as to avoid or mitigate changes not rendered inevitable by higher costs either of imports or of production at home."[22] Similarly, in the United States this objective has been clearly stated in the President's Economic Report by both Democratic and Republican administrations.[23]

More government intervention also occurred during the present century in the area of resource allocation. Increasingly, public utilities were taken over by the State or subject to close state regulation. In the interwar period the British government nationalized broadcasting, established the British Overseas Airway Corporation, and operated part of the electrical power industry. During this same period the French government nationalized the railroads and part of the armament industry, including the aircraft industry; controlled the Bank of France (although it did not nationalize it); and purchased majority stock interest in a number of financially weak concerns. The German government also extended public ownership even in such manufacturing sectors as steel and automobiles as well as in the public utility field. The State railways, for example, were nationalized in 1920. In the

[22] Quoted in S. E. Harris, *Economic Planning,* Alfred A. Knopf, New York, 1949, 175.

[23] See, for example, *Midyear Economic Report of the President,* July 1950, 10, and *Economic Report of the President,* 1954, iii.

United States the growth of government enterprises on a Federal level during the interwar period was confined mainly to the fields of credit, electric power, and irrigation and flood control.

After World War II the pace of nationalization was especially rapid in Great Britain and France. Both countries nationalized the coal, gas, and electric power industries. The Bank of England and the Bank of France, together with four main commercial banks in France, were taken over by the State. The French nationalized the major insurance companies and extended state ownership in the steamship and air lines fields. The Renault automobile company and a few other industrial concerns also were nationalized.[24] In Britain all inland transport, civil aviation, telecommunications, and the iron and steel industry were nationalized.[25] In 1953, however, the iron and steel and the road haulage industries were denationalized.

Even in countries where state ownership in the public utility area is not general, the degree of state regulation has, nevertheless, increased. In the United States, for example, regulatory commissions to set rates and establish service requirements are used widely. Railroads, express companies, pipe lines, bus and truck lines, water carriers, telephone and telegraph companies, radio and television companies, and electric power concerns are all regulated by these agencies.

Government control over business outside of the public utility field also increased in this century. During the 1930's, the British government passed legislation establishing cartel arrangements in the coal industry and encouraged similar schemes in other industries. In Nazi Germany, the use of compulsory cartels and other devices enabled the State to control in detail almost every aspect of production in the private sector. The Japanese government also employed the technique of compulsory cartel agreements during the 1930's. Even in the United States, there was a short-lived attempt under the National Recovery Act of 1933 to combat the depression by setting up industry-wide agreements fixing minimum prices. In general, however, cartel-like agreements have been discouraged in the United States. Since the turn of the century measures such as the Federal Trade Commission Act (1914), the Clayton Act (1914), and the Robinson-Patman Act (1936) have been enacted to strengthen American domestic anti-monopoly laws. The British finally altered their long history of statutory neutrality on monopolies by passing an anti-monopoly act in 1948. After the war the occupation authorities

[24] See M. Einaudi, M. Bye, and E. Rossi, *Nationalization in France and Italy,* Cornell University Press, Ithaca, 1955, 81–86.
[25] See Central Statistical Office, *National Income Statistics,* H.M.S.O., London, 1956, 169–170, for a complete list of public corporations.

also endeavored to break up the high degree of industrial concentration in Germany and Japan. However, concentration in these countries increased after the occupation period ended.

The Germans, after the war, adopted a policy known as co-determination. This is a scheme by which labor participates in the management of private industrial corporations. In the steel and coal industries, the supervisory board of directors, who are responsible for long-run corporate policy, must be composed of five representatives of labor and five of the stockholders. An eleventh person is elected by the other ten. Furthermore, one of the three members of the managing board of directors (who direct the operations of the company) must represent labor. In 1952, a milder form of this co-determination concept was extended by the government to most other privately owned corporations. Under this law one-third of the members of the supervisory board are elected by the employees of the company. However, there is no provision for a labor director on the managing board. The 1952 measure also provides for a system of co-determination in the activities of the works councils which are elected in almost all public and private firms. In 1955, an even more limited form of co-determination was devised for government enterprises.

International trade is yet another area in which government intervention is much greater in this century than in the last. Britain, the great free trade power of the nineteenth century, began to abandon this policy after 1914. A definite shift to protectionism took place in 1932 with the Import Duties Act. Some quotas were also introduced in the 1930's. After leaving the gold standard the British created an exchange stabilization fund to moderate exchange rate fluctuations. Quantitative exchange control was not introduced, however, until 1939. France, which maintained its high tariff wall during the 1920's, resorted to an extensive quota system in an effort to cope with additional trade problems in the 1930's. In Germany, an extremely elaborate system of control over foreign trade was developed in the 1930's. Almost every foreign transaction became subject to detailed control by the State. After World War I, the United States established the highest tariff in its history with the Smoot-Hawley measure of 1930. Beginning with the Trade Agreements Act of 1934, however, these rates were substantially reduced.

Russian economic policy since World War I can be discussed best by considering it separately. The Soviet Union remains, of course, the foremost example of industrialization under detailed state control. But it should not be assumed that development lagged in the period before the Russian revolution in 1917. On the contrary, the period between the abolition of serfdom in 1861 and the begininng of World War I was characterized by rapid development towards which the State made important contributions. The government financed much of the railroad building and factory construction while state banks provided financial assistance to non-governmental enterprises. The inflow of foreign capital and the hiring of foreign technicians were also encouraged. The tariff policy of Russia, moreover, was designed to protect domestic manufacturing.

The Communists quickly nationalized most of the economy, and by 1921 banking, foreign trade, industry, domestic trade, and transportation became nationalized sectors. All land was also nationalized. For a few years thereafter the government eased its socialistic policy somewhat. During the so-called N.E.P. (New Economic Policy) period, private trade was allowed to flourish and the smaller workshops and factories were returned to private hands. Moreover, the peasants were allowed to sell part of their surplus commodities freely on the open market. By 1930, however, private trade and private industry again were negligible in importance. At the same time the government started its program of agricultural collectivization in earnest. By 1936 almost 90 per cent of the peasantry were employed on collective farms.

The first of the series of Five Year Plans, which establish economic goals and outline specific production targets for all commodities, was adopted by the Soviet Union in 1928. The Plan determines the division of national income between consumption and investment expenditures as well as the distribution of consumption and investment goods among the major income groups. It is, in short, a detailed scheme covering every aspect of economic activity. However, the Plan is not inflexible: the goals are frequently altered to meet changing circumstances. The most important economic characteristics of all the Plans are the emphasis on investment and the priority assigned to heavy industrial production. One estimate of the proportion of national income used for investment purposes is 24 per cent for the last year of the First Five Year Plan and 19½ per cent for the last year of the Second.[26] A study of Soviet capital formation places gross investment in 1955 at above 25 per cent of gross national product.[27] Rapid industrialization, and apparently the creation of a powerful military machine, are the prime goals.

Many of the measures discussed thus far in this section were, of course, introduced in part to facilitate a more rapid rate of development. Obvi-

[26] Maurice Dobb, *Soviet Economic Development Since 1917,* Routledge and K. Paul, Ltd., London, 1948, 268.

[27] G. Grossman, "Some Current Trends in Soviet Capital Formation," in *Capital Formation and Economic Growth,* National Bureau of Economic Research, Princeton University Press, Princeton, 1955, 176.

ously satisfactory growth cannot be achieved under conditions of mass unemployment or considerable inflation. Social welfare legislation also frequently was justified by growth arguments. Welfare measures improve the efficiency of the labor force and thereby tend to accelerate development. Government intervention in business likewise fits into this argument. State ownership in the public utility area was urged not merely to prevent monopoly practices by private firms but also to encourage general development by increasing public overhead capital. Policies directed towards other industries during the interwar period likewise were promoted on development grounds. The British government, for example, encouraged rationalization movements during the 1920's and 1930's on grounds that they improved the country's long-run competitive position. And, of course, the elaborate control of industry adopted in Germany and the Soviet Union was aimed at accelerating industrial development, with special attention given to armaments. The United States, on the other hand, continued the policy of discouraging monopolistic tendencies as one method of attempting to maintain a satisfactory development rate.

Nevertheless, the goal of economic development in the non-totalitarian countries was usually overshadowed during the interwar period by the objectives of full employment and a more equitable distribution of income coupled with social security. The problem of maintaining international equilibrium simultaneously plagued many of the rich countries. The great depression of the 1930's forced drastic action in regard to these matters. Although it was recognized that measures taken to achieve these other objectives might affect the rate of development, the development goal apparently was not the major consideration in policy formulation at that time. The quip by Lord Keynes, "We are all dead in the long run," typifies most governmental policies during this period. The prevalent tendency was to concentrate upon the short-run achievement of full employment and to let the long run take care of itself.

In effect, this policy position implied a continuation of the policy practiced just before World War I, namely, leaving the achievement of the development goal mainly in private hands. By World War I many of the direct nineteenth-century forms of governmental efforts to foster internal improvements and industry had ceased. In the public utility field government regulation or ownership existed, but governments no longer advocated a vigorous expansionist policy in this area. Industry, by and large, developed according to its own wishes and ability, although in some cases the government discouraged excessive monopoly power. Governments, in general, did not provide the financial assistance to industry which characterized earlier periods. In the monetary field governments attempted to facilitate private economic activity rather than actively to encourage long-run expansion in the private sector. And finally, the tariff policy of most countries was aimed more at maintaining the existing industrial structure than changing it drastically as continued development might require.

After World War II, however, the disappearance of the mass unemployment problem of the 1930's enabled governments to focus more attention upon the long run. In the United States both Democratic and Republican administrations emphasized the importance of continued economic growth as a national policy goal.

In order to promote economic development President Truman recommended:

> comprehensive housing and urban redevelopment legislation; further construction of multipurpose dams and related facilities; a comprehensive program of Federal aid to education; a comprehensive program [of research into scientific principles and their application] in which Federal aid should play a part; a comprehensive national health program; an expanded social insurance program; and checking the further excessive concentration of industrial control and, by protecting the position of smaller competing enterprises, of reversing the past trend towards concentration.[28]

In addition he proposed greater educational and financial aid to agriculture as well as increased Federal assistance for the purpose of developing transportation facilities.

President Eisenhower wrote: "Our economic goal is an increasing national income, shared equitably among those who contribute to its growth, and achieved in dollars of stable buying power."[29] According to President Eisenhower, the achievement of economic progress is primarily the function of the private sector. "It is Government's responsibility in a free society to create an environment in which individual enterprise can work constructively to serve the ends of economic progress; . . . ."[30] He argued, however, that some governmental measures are necessary to facilitate this effort. "To stimulate the expansive power of individual enterprise we should take action—by revising the tax laws so as to increase incentives and to remove certain impediments to enterprise, especially of small business; by improving credit facilities for home building, modernization, and urban rehabilitation; by strength-

---

[28] *Economic Report of the President,* Jan. 1948, United States Government Printing Office, 1948, 6–10 and 53–89.

[29] *Economic Report of the President,* Letter of Transmittal, United States Government Printing Office, Washington, 1954, iii.

[30] *Ibid.,* iii.

ening the highway system; and by facilitating the adjustments of agriculture to current conditions of demand and technology."[31]

Among the more advanced European countries the growth goal also was stressed after the war. In Great Britain the Labor Party victory at the polls in 1945 changed the traditional governmental policy towards the development objective. "The industrial goal set by the new Britain is the highest possible production per worker, since this alone will lead to increased living standards. In working towards this goal, many fundamental changes have already been made, or projected."[32] These changes involved more long-run economic planning by the State. First, of course, several basic industries were nationalized. Laborites argued that only through public ownership could these sectors be reorganized to work at full efficiency. They claimed that "without the obligation to attend to private interests, the new 'owners,' acting for the country as a whole, will be able to replan ruthlessly; and, with the Government behind them, will have all the capital they need."[33]

The government also established a number of Working Parties in industry: "To examine and inquire into the various schemes and suggestions put forward for improvements of organization, production and distribution methods and processes in the industry, and report as to the steps which should be taken in the national interest to strengthen the industry and render it more capable of meeting competition in the home and foreign markets."[34] The major result of these reports was the passage of the Industrial Organization and Development Act, whereby Development Councils for various industries could be established in order to put efforts to increase efficiency on a continuing basis. But these Councils did not have compulsory powers to institute changes within an industry.

A number of governmental measures were adopted, however, to control investment in the private sector. Almost all private building required permission of some kind from the government. A Capital Issues Committee had the power of approval and disapproval over large borrowing or new issues of capital, and, of course, the government used monetary and fiscal measures to control the volume of investment. By 1951, about one-half of all investment in the country was directly or indirectly under government auspices.[35] Another effort associated with

[31] *Ibid.,* v.

[32] *Labor and Industry in Britain,* British Information Services, *V,* No. 8, 162 (Sept.–Oct. 1947).

[33] *Ibid.,* 162.

[34] G. D. N. Worswick and P. H. Ady (editors), *The British Economy, 1945–1950,* Clarendon Press, Oxford, 1952, 455.

[35] *Labor and Industry in Britain, op. cit., IX,* No. 3, 129 (Sept. 1951).

long-run growth was the creation of the Economic Planning Board in 1947 "to advise His Majesty's Government on the best use of our economic resources, both for the realisation of a long-term plan and for remedial measures against our immediate difficulties."[36]

The British government, moreover, expanded its expenditures in the fields of education, housing, and health. Although many of these measures and programs of the government were aimed primarily at other objectives, the role of the government in actively promoting economic growth increased considerably in the period following World War II.

With the coming to power of a Conservative government in late 1951, there was a shift towards the more traditional policy, which minimizes direct governmental participation in the effort to achieve satisfactory growth. The Chancellor of the Exchequer pledged that the government "will seek to promote flexibility in those industries which have been brought under public management and to stimulate free enterprise by giving it a fuller share in our economic activity. They will be mindful of the great demands on our productive capacity, and will consider all methods for creating that spirit of partnership between management and workers on which industrial harmony and a higher level of productivity must depend."[37] As a result of the shift in power, the government gradually relaxed a number of direct control measures, cut taxes, and denationalized the iron and steel and road haulage industries.

As the Chancellor stated, "The fact that we have not been getting the best out of our production capacity springs in part from our terrible burden of taxation, which is about the highest in the world. Even after this Budget we shall not have 'let up' to a level which can be called even moderate. All reliefs are carefully designed for the prime purpose of giving the incentive for greater production."[38]

Efforts by the French government to accelerate economic development after the war centered round the Monnet Plan; this was a program for "the modernization and the economic equipment of Metropolitan France and her overseas territories."[39] Its objectives were to increase living standards, raise labor productivity, assure full employment, achieve international equilibrium, and alleviate the housing shortage. Six basic industries—coal, electricity, rail transport, iron and steel, cement, and agricultural machinery—were singled out for special emphasis. The Governmental Planning Commission, aided by modernization commis-

[36] Worswick and Ady, op. cit., 346.
[37] Labor and Industry in Britain, op. cit., IX, No. 4, 146 (Dec. 1951).
[38] Labor and Industry in Britain, op. cit., XI, No. 2, 52–53 (June 1953).
[39] Harris, op. cit., 395.

sions composed of representatives from labor, management, agriculture, and government, drew up specific investment programs for these industries.

The government attempted to achieve the planned investment programs by two methods. First, it employed controls over credit, raw materials, and imports to direct investment into the desired channels. Secondly, and most important, the government itself financed a large portion of the needed investment. In 1948, a Modernization and Equipment Fund was established by the government to centralize all state funds used for investment purposes under the Monnet Plan. This fund was used to channel the flow of modernization and equipment loans to both the nationalized and private sectors. During the period 1947–1950, 67 per cent of new investment was financed out of public funds.[40]

German postwar efforts to stimulate the rate of growth differed considerably from those adopted by the French and British. The private sector is relatively free from government control under Germany's development policy. As noted before, the policy of co-determination was followed rather than further government nationalization. This did not mean, however, that the government ceased to play a significant role in economic affairs. From 1950 to 1953, public investment accounted for about one-quarter of all German investment.[41] Much of this was in housing. Germany, moreover, continued its comprehensive governmental program of social security. In addition many sectors such as railroads, telegraph, telephone, radio, savings banks, and a number of industrial enterprises remained nationalized.

Nevertheless, as Wallich observes, the emphasis upon "fair shares" and full employment was considerably less than in Britain.[42] Instead growth by means of "the social free economy" was the main objective of the government.

In pursuing this policy the government attempted to create an environment favorable for a rapid increase of production in the private sector. The elaborate system of controls set up under the Nazi government was scrapped. Tight monetary and fiscal policies were adopted to avert the necessity for direct controls. Perhaps most interesting of all, a system of incentive taxation was employed to encourage development. First, a significant share of total government tax revenues was raised from

[40] H. Lubell, *The French Investment Program: A Defense of the Monnet Plan,* Ph.D. Thesis, 1951, Harvard University, 63.

[41] H. C. Wallich, *Mainsprings of the German Revival,* Yale University Press, New Haven, 1955, 169.

[42] *Ibid.,* 19.

turnover and sales taxes. Since these fell heavily on low-income groups, it meant that taxes on the major saving groups in the economy were not as high as they would otherwise be. Secondly, the government granted a number of tax exemptions to stimulate investment and incentives. Overtime earnings were virtually exempt from income taxes. Firms and individuals who made interest-free housing and shipbuilding loans deducted the loans from their taxable income. When, however, the loans were repaid they became fully taxable. Accelerated depreciation was allowed on capital expenditures for new plants, new residential property, and the repair of war-damaged equipment. Other tax provisions also reduced the tax rate on a part of the retained earnings of business.

4. Recent Development Performance

Postwar emphasis on policies designed to stimulate economic development emanates from many different factors. As already mentioned, much of it is associated with the attainment of other economic objectives. Governments which are committed to the goal of full employment know that it cannot be considered within a static framework. A growing labor force and capital capacity necessitate continual growth, if these productive means are to remain fully utilized. Moreover, in a country in which the foreign sector is very important, constant efforts are needed to keep up with the latest productive techniques so as to avoid market losses to other countries with resultant employment difficulties. Countries in which the goal of social security and a more equitable income distribution rank very high also appreciate the significance of a rapid rate of development for the achievement of this goal. It is much easier to afford extensive social services and to redistribute income in an expanding economy. Furthermore, policy leaders realize that at least a part of the pressure for redistribution can be eased by an absolute rise in the living standards of all groups.

But the goal of continued development is also endorsed for reasons other than the above objectives. One virtue of a progressive economy, which was demonstrated vividly during World War II and the Korean War, is its ability to undertake a large defense program more readily than is possible under stationary conditions. A desire to maintain the same relative position as a world economic power is another possible factor behind the emphasis on an expanding national income. And, if some European nations do not seem to stress the possibilities for a significant rise in per capita income levels as much as Americans do, they, nevertheless, do appear to emphasize the need for at least some steady upward movement in living standards. Certainly, all governments wish to avoid any actual decrease in per capita income. Those countries that rely upon manufacturing exports to pay for a large share of their food and raw material requirements are especially concerned about the dangers of declining living standards. With a growing population and increasing competition in export markets, the need for continued development efforts cannot be ignored.

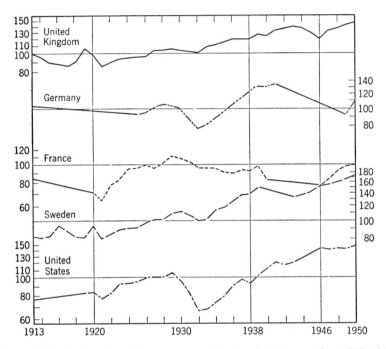

Figure 22.1. Real national income per capita in selected countries, 1913–1950. (Index numbers, 1925–1929 = 100.) Source: I. Svennilson, *Growth and Stagnation in the European Economy,* United Nations, Geneva, 1954, Chart 2, 29. A change in the nature of the line linking the various years for a particular country indicates the use of another national income estimate which is not exactly comparable to the previous estimate.

All countries are anxious to avoid the relative stagnation which prevailed during much of the interwar period. As Figure 22.1 indicates, the period from 1913 to 1929 was one of little growth for the United Kingdom and Germany. In 1929, British per capita income was only 6 per cent above the 1913 figure; in Germany it was 2 per cent higher. During the period from 1913 to 1929, there were only four years for the United Kingdom and two for Germany when per capita income exceeded its 1913 level. In contrast, per capita income rose in France and the United States 32 per cent and 38 per cent, respectively, from 1913 to 1929. The 1930's, on the other hand, were years of stagnation for the United States and France. Per capita income in 1939 fell below the 1929 level for both countries, and in no year during the decade was the 1929 figure exceeded. In 1939, British and German per capita income, on the other hand, was 20 per cent and 28 per cent, respectively, greater than the 1929 figure.

But the problem is not merely one of periods during the interwar years when the increase in real per capita income was negligible or when the change was actually negative. Compared to the last quarter of the nineteenth century, real per capita income in a number of the rich countries rose at a much lower rate from around the turn of the century to World War II. The statistics seem to indicate retardation in the long-run growth of these countries.

In the United States the changes per decade in real per capita income are: 1869–1878 to 1879–1888, 50.9 per cent; 1879–1888 to 1889–1898, 9.8 per cent; 1889–1898 to 1899–1908, 28.8 per cent; 1899–1908 to 1909–1918, 11.7 per cent; 1909–1918 to 1919–1928, 18.8 per cent; 1919–1928 to 1929–1938, −6.5 per cent.[43] The real per capita income changes for the United Kingdom as noted in Chapter 9, run as follows: 1870–1879 to 1880–1889, 17 per cent; 1880–1889 to 1890–1899, 25 per cent; 1890–1899 to 1900–1909, 8 per cent; 1900–1909 to 1910–1919, 3.5 per cent; 1910–1919 to 1920–1929, 6.1 per cent; and 1920–1929 to 1930–1939, 17.7 per cent.[44] Similar results hold for Germany where the real per capita income changes are: 1870–1879 to 1880–1889, 37.4 per cent; 1880–1889 to 1890–1899, 26.7 per cent; 1890–1899 to 1900–1909, 6 per cent. Between 1905–1914 and 1925–1934 real per capita income fell 4.3 per cent. From 1925–1934 to 1930–1938 it rose 6.5 per cent.[45]

Estimates of changes in real per capita income in Japan are 1883–1887 to 1893–1897, 32 per cent; 1893–1897 to 1903–1907, no change; 1903–1907 to 1913–1917, 21 per cent; 1913–1917 to 1923–1927, 44 per cent; and 1923–1927 to 1933–1937, 26 per cent.[46] The officially claimed Soviet increase in real national income between 1928 and 1937

[43] S. Kuznets, "Long-Term Changes in the National Income of the United States of America since 1870," *Income and Wealth,* S. Kuznets (ed.), Series II, Bowes and Bowes, Cambridge, 1952, computed from Table 4, 55.

[44] J. B. Jefferys and D. Walters, "National Income and Expenditure of the United Kingdom, 1870–1952," S. Kuznets (ed.), *Income and Wealth,* Series V, Bowes and Bowes, London, 1955, 14.

[45] P. Jostock, "The Long-Term Growth of National Income in Germany," *ibid.,* computed from Table III, 94.

[46] Lockwood, *op. cit.,* computed from Table 12, 135.

is 285 per cent.[47]   Real per capita income on the basis of official data, consequently, rose about 245 per cent between these years.[48]   The accuracy of Soviet statistics, however, is frequently questioned.   Recalculations by Western economists of the Soviet increase in national income during this period range from 50 to 98 per cent.[48a]   These changes correspond to an increase in real per capita income of 35 and 80 per cent, respectively, between 1928 and 1937.

Since World War II, the remarkable growth in national and per capita income in most of the rich countries has done much to allay the fears of secular stagnation.   As Figure 22.1 indicates, the war-time and postwar trends in per capita income varied from country to country, but the over-all picture of the period from 1938 to 1950 shows that real income increased significantly.   Whereas per capita income in the United States was 55 per cent higher in 1946 than in 1938, in the United Kingdom the 1946 figure was only equal to the 1938 level, and per capita income in France and Germany was actually below the pre-war level in 1946.   Between 1946 and 1950, the rise in the United Kingdom and France was greater than in the United States.   By 1950, real income per person exceeded the respective 1938 levels by 22 per cent in the United Kingdom, 9 per cent in France, and 61 per cent in the United States.   From 1950 to 1954 real per capita gross product rose about 6 per cent in the United States (9½ per cent from 1950–1953), and 35 per cent in Germany.   In France and Great Britain, the 1950 to 1953 rise was 3 per cent and 8 per cent, respectively.   Real per capita gross product in Germany surpassed the 1938 level in 1951 and was 24 per cent above this level by 1954.   In Japan, on the other hand, the 1954 level just equaled the 1938 level.[49]   Evidence for the period 1948 to 1950 indicates that Soviet development was at least as rapid as between 1928 and 1937.[50]

Despite the encouraging development performance of the last decade, the question of whether the rich countries can maintain rapid rates of development still persists.   Do these countries face retardation in their growth?   With respect to the United States, Abramovitz describes the situation as follows: "If we neglect this apparently remarkable decade

[47] A. Bergson (ed.), *Soviet Economic Growth,* Row, Peterson & Co., White Plains, 1953, 5.

[48] Population estimates for 1928 and 1937 computed from A. Bergson (ed.), *ibid.,* Table 3.1, 102.

[48a] *Ibid.,* Table 1.1, 7.

[49] The source of the figures for 1950–1954 is Statistical Office of the United Nations, *Statistics of National Income and Expenditure,* Statistical Papers, Series H, No. 8, New York, 20–27 (Sept. 1955).

[50] A. Bergson (ed.), *op. cit.,* 11.

[the late 1870's and early 1880's] and take into account the possibilities of error and bias, the rates of growth afford no significant indication of retardation until we reach the depression of the thirties. . . . Whether there has been a significant degree of persistent retardation in the growth of national product per capita would, therefore, seem to turn on the answers to two questions presently unanswerable. Do the various biases and weaknesses in the estimates make for an appearance of acceleration or retardation? Did the surge of the early years and the deep depression of the latter years represent fortuitous or persistent forces?"[51]   Similar questions, though for different periods, must be answered for countries like the United Kingdom and Germany.

To amplify the nature of the development problem in the rich countries, the next chapter presents the salient economic characteristics of the rich countries. On the basis of this presentation, the following chapter then discusses the requirements for maintaining development in these nations.

[51] M. Abramovitz, *Resource and Output Trends in the United States since 1870,* Occasional Paper 52, National Bureau of Economic Research, New York, 1956, 15–18.

Chapter 23

Economic Characteristics

and Trends

The economic structure within which the development process takes place influences the requirements and prospects for continued development. As in poor countries, however, this structure varies considerably among rich countries. It is just as difficult to select a "representative" rich nation as to locate a "representative" poor country. There are, nevertheless, a number of general economic characteristics that usually are associated with a high level of per capita income. The purpose of this chapter is to discuss these economic characteristics and their long-run changes.

1. Characteristics of the Productive Process

One important distinguishing economic characteristic that was noted previously is the relatively greater importance of manufacturing activities in rich countries than in poor nations. Both the distribution of the labor force by economic activity and the industrial origin of national income reflect this relationship. Manufacturing and construction pursuits (Table 23.1) engaged over 30 per cent of the economically active population in such rich countries as Australia, Canada, West Germany, the United Kingdom, and the United States around 1950. In most poor countries this share was below 15 per cent. Similarly, manufacturing and construction (Table 23.2) accounted for at least 35 per cent of the national income in 1954 in such countries as Canada, West Germany, Italy, the Netherlands, the United Kingdom, and the United States, whereas in countries near the bottom of the per capita income scale the proportion generally was below 20 per cent. Not only is the income

TABLE 23.1. OCCUPATIONAL DISTRIBUTION OF THE
ECONOMICALLY ACTIVE POPULATION
(Percentages)

	Agriculture	Manufacturing and Construction	All Other
Australia (1947)	15.4	32.5	52.1
Brazil (1950)	60.6*	13.0†	26.4
Canada (1951)	19.0	32.3	48.7
Egypt (1947)	50.6	9.2	40.2
France (1946)	36.5	26.8	36.7
Western Germany (1950)	23.2	38.9	37.9
India (1951)	70.6	10.1	19.3
Italy (1954)	39.7	28.2	32.1
Japan (1954)	44.5	20.4	35.1
Mexico (1950)	57.8	14.4	27.8
Netherlands (1947)	19.3	31.0	49.7
Philippines (1948)	65.7	7.9	26.4
Puerto Rico (1950)	36.8	22.5	40.7
United Kingdom (1951)	4.9	43.6	51.5
United States (1950)	12.2	33.1	54.7

* Includes mining.
† Includes electricity and gas.

Source: United Nations, Statistical Yearbook, 1955, Table 6, 56–70.

originating in the manufacturing sector relatively more important in rich than in poor countries, but the richer countries account for most of the world's supplies of manufactures. In 1954, for example, about 87 per cent of world industrial production (excluding the U.S.S.R., China, and Eastern Europe) originated in Western Europe and North America.[1]

The relationship between the level of per capita income and the importance of tertiary activities is not too clear. As Table 23.2 indicates, in 1954 at least 55 per cent of the net domestic product was derived

[1] United Nations, Monthly Bulletin of Statistics, IX, No. 4, viii (April 1955).

from trade, transportation, communication, and government services in such diverse economies as Egypt, Canada, Puerto Rico, and the United States. Between the 45 to 55 per cent range were such countries as Brazil, Japan, and the United Kingdom.

Employment data (Table 23.1) indicate a somewhat better positive correlation between the level of per capita income and the relative importance of tertiary industry. But, as noted in Chapter 9, the sig-

TABLE   23.2.   INDUSTRIAL ORIGIN OF
NET DOMESTIC PRODUCT
(Percentages)

	Agriculture	Manufacturing and Construction	All Other
Brazil (1952)	33.9	19.3*	46.8
Canada (1954)	8.8	35.1	56.1
Egypt (1953)	31.6	10.3	58.1
Western Germany (1954)	10.9	55.6*	33.5
India (1953)	50.9	16.0	33.1
Italy (1954)	24.6	38.7	36.7
Japan (1954)	22.0	27.6	50.4
Mexico (1950)	19.6	20.1	60.3
Netherlands (1954)	12.7	42.3	45.0
New Zealand (1952)	27.2	29.2	43.6
Philippines (1953)	39.3	19.4	41.3
Puerto Rico (1953)	17.1	18.2*	64.7
United Kingdom (1953)	5.4	44.0	50.6
United States (1954)	5.5	35.6	58.9

* Includes mining.

Source: United Nations, Statistics of National Income and Expenditure, Statistical Papers, Series H, No. 8, Table 3, 35–57.

nificance of these employment statistics is questionable. The discrepancy in the degree of occupational specialization between rich and poor countries makes it difficult to render occupational statistics comparable for these two types of economies. Although this difficulty restricts the possibilities of generalizing about the relative importance of any broad group of economic activities in rich versus poor countries, it seems to apply with particular force to generalizations about the comparative significance of tertiary industry. Tertiary industry also includes diverse types of activity. The importance of governmental services (including the armed forces), for example, differs widely among countries and is not necessarily related to the degree of development.

For countries near the top of the per capita income scale, however, long-run changes in income and occupational statistics show a rising trend in the relative importance of tertiary activities. These activities absorbed 24 per cent of the American labor force in 1870, 47 per cent in 1930, and 55 per cent in 1950.[2] The trend was also upwards in most other high per capita income countries.[3] The share of the labor force employed in the manufacturing, mining, and construction fields, however, has not changed significantly in many of the rich countries over the last 30 years. In the United States, for example, the proportion of the labor force engaged in these activities was approximately the same in 1950 as in 1920. Similarly, the percentage of industrial Europe's male population employed in industry was 44 per cent in 1920, 44 per cent in 1930, 44 per cent in 1940, and 46 per cent in 1950.[4]

Agricultural activities in the rich countries continued to decline in relative importance over the last 25 years. Whereas 22 per cent of the labor force was employed in American agriculture, forestry, and fishing in 1930, the share was only 12 per cent in 1950. The percentage for the industrial European nations fell from 24 to 20 between these years.[4,5] With the exception of New Zealand, where the proportion of the labor force in agriculture declined between 1861 and 1945 only from 24 per cent to 22 per cent, increases in per capita income generally were accompanied by a significant reduction in the relative importance of agriculture.[6]

The divergence in the productivity of labor also sharply differentiates rich from poor countries. Output per person in agriculture is 10 to 20 times greater in rich than in poor countries.[7] But even among the more advanced countries there is considerable disparity in labor productivity. Colin Clark's estimates of real product per man-hour in agriculture (measured in international units) for selected advanced countries are: New Zealand (1940–1941), 1.049; Australia (1938–

[2] J. F. Dewhurst and Associates, *America's Needs and Resources, A New Survey*, The Twentieth Century Fund, New York, 1955, 732.

[3] W. S. Woytinsky and E. S. Woytinsky, *World Population and Production*, The Twentieth Century Fund, New York, 1953, 432–433. Hereinafter cited as Woytinsky and Woytinsky, *World Population*. Svennilson, *Growth and Stagnation in the European Economy*, United Nations, Economic Commission for Europe, Geneva, 1954, 75–76.

[4] Svennilson, *op. cit.*, 75.

[5] This figure covers only occupied males.

[6] Burns, *Comparative Economic Organization*, Prentice-Hall, New York, 1955, 368. Also Clark, *The Conditions of Economic Progress*, second edition, Macmillan and Co., Ltd., London, 1951, Chapter 9.

[7] See p. 278.

1939), 0.676; United States (1934–1941), 0.282; Canada (1934–1935), 0.208; Great Britain (1937), 0.200; France (1938), 0.172; and Germany (1934–1935), 0.159.[8]

TABLE 23.3. REAL PRODUCT PER MAN-HOUR IN
MANUFACTURING IN SELECTED COUNTRIES
(In International Units)

United States (1939–1941)	1.070
New Zealand (1940–1941)	0.955
Canada (1934–1935)	0.687
Australia (1938–1939)	0.454
Sweden (1930)	0.380
Germany (1934–1935)	0.378
Britain (1937)	0.353
France (1938)	0.319

Source: C. Clark, *The Conditions of Economic Progress,* second edition, Macmillan and Co., Ltd., London, 1951, 316–319.

TABLE 23.4. REAL PRODUCT PER MAN-HOUR IN
TERTIARY INDUSTRY IN SELECTED COUNTRIES
(In International Units)

United States (1939–1941)	1.241
New Zealand (1940–1941)	0.636
Canada (1934–1935)	0.795
Australia (1938–1939)	0.736
Sweden (1930)	0.400
Germany (1934–1935)	0.448
Britain (1937)	0.669
France (1938)	0.420

Source: C. Clark, *The Conditions of Economic Progress,* second edition, Macmillan and Co., Ltd., London, 1951, 316–319.
The figures include small-scale manufacture.

Productivity in manufacturing likewise varies widely among rich countries. In 1948, output per worker in American manufacturing was about three times as high as in Britain and about four times as high as in Europe generally.[9] Pre-war productivity estimates are presented in Table 23.3. Manufacturing productivity in the poor countries, however, is considerably lower than in these economies. In 1948, for example, manufacturing output per worker in the United States was 8 and 15 times as great as in South America and Africa, respectively.[10]

[8] Clark, *op. cit.,* 316–319. An international unit is equal to the purchasing power of $1 in the United States over the average of the period 1925–1934.

[9] Burns, *op. cit.,* 163.

[10] Woytinsky and Woytinsky, *World Population,* 1012–1013.

Productivity data for tertiary industry (Table 23.4) also show significant differences among the rich countries. Nevertheless, in general, labor productivity is highest in tertiary industry; manufacturing and agriculture following in order. Australia and New Zealand, however, are notable exceptions. In these countries productivity in agriculture is greater than in manufacturing activities.

Post-war productivity measures do not indicate a more rapid growth in either agricultural or manufacturing productivity for the United States than for the advanced European nations. In agriculture, output per agricultural worker after the war probably increased about 4 to 5 per cent per annum in both the United States and Western Europe.[11]   As for manufacturing productivity (Table 23.5), the percentage increase

TABLE 23.5.   OUTPUT PER MAN-HOUR IN MANUFACTURING,
UNITED STATES AND WESTERN EUROPE
(1950 = 100)

	1948	1950	1952	1954	1955*
Austria	79	100	113	125	132
France	93	100	111	120	129
Germany	67	100	117	128	139
Italy	81	100	117	136	142
Netherlands	87	100	106	118	123
United Kingdom	91	100	98	107	110
Total O.E.E.C. countries	87	100	107	116	124
United States	90	100	101	107	112

* Provisional.

Source: G. D. A. MacDougall, "Does Productivity Rise Faster in the United States?" Review of Economics and Statistics, XXXVIII, No. 2, Table 11, 170 (May 1956).

in the United States and the United Kingdom since 1948 was about the same. Both of these countries, however, lagged behind Austria, France, Germany, Italy, and the Netherlands. But unlike the United States and the United Kingdom, where productivity was well above the pre-war level by 1948, some of these countries were still below their pre-war productivity levels in 1952.[12]   Consequently, the rapid rise in these countries was due in large part to the reorganization of war-disrupted industry.

Another important feature of the productive process in rich countries,

[11] G. D. A. MacDougall, "Does Productivity Rise Faster in the United States?" Review of Economics and Statistics, XXXVIII, No. 2, 170 (May 1956).

[12] See A. Maddison, "Industrial Productivity Growth in Europe and in the U.S.," Economica, XXI, No. 84, 311 (Nov. 1954).

which is difficult to appreciate merely from classification schemes based on broad economic activities, is the highly diverse and integrated nature of production. Most of the commodity production of the poor countries can be described adequately in terms of a relatively small number of primary commodities. These commodities, moreover, usually do not pass through any very elaborate processing stages. In industrial nations, on the other hand, one must list thousands of items to begin to appreciate the diversity of output and the high degree of specialization.

Input-output studies illustrate part of the complexity and interdependence of production in modern industrial economies.[13] An input-output table describes the manner in which each sector of the economy depends upon every other sector. A single column of such a table indicates, for example, how many dollars' worth of steel products the automobile manufacturers buy from the steel industry for every million dollars' worth of cars they produce. It also shows how many dollars' worth of upholstery material they need, how much paint from the chemical industry they require, etc. Similarly, the steel industry column describes the various kinds of inputs, such as coal, ore, etc., which the steel industry needs to produce its products. To produce an additional million dollars' worth of cars, automobile producers require more steel, upholstery, paint, etc. But to produce the additional steel, the steel industry requires more coal, iron ore, perhaps automobiles, etc. The other industries from which the automobile producers buy also require more inputs from these and other industries. An increase in output in one sector, consequently, has complex ramifications throughout the entire economy. In the case of an additional million dollars' worth of automobiles, the 1947 input-output structure for the American economy indicates that steel output would have to increase by $235,000; other fabricated metal products by $118,000; rubber products by $56,000; products of petroleum and coal by $47,000; and so on throughout most of the industrial structure.[14]

2. Consumption Expenditures

The great diversity of production in rich economies is also reflected in consumption patterns within these nations. In countries near the bottom of the per capita income scale, food expenditures comprise 70 per cent or more of total consumption outlays.[15] Food, liquor, and

[13] See W. Leontief, *Studies in the Structure of the American Economy,* Oxford University Press, New York, 1953.

[14] W. Leontief, "Domestic Production and Foreign Trade; the American Capital Position Re-examined," *Proceedings of the American Philosophical Society, XCVII,* No. 4, 334 (Sept. 1953).

[15] Woytinsky and Woytinsky, *World Population,* 279.

TABLE 23.6. CONSUMPTION EXPENDITURES BY MAJOR
GROUPS, UNITED STATES, PERCENTAGE DISTRIBUTION

	1914	1939	1950–1952
Food, liquor, and tobacco	35.0	31.2	34.9
Clothing, accessories, & personal care	14.1	13.6	12.7
Housing & utilities	23.6	17.9	14.2
Household equipment & operation	11.1	15.4	14.5
Consumer transportation	6.4	9.6	11.4
Medical care & insurance	2.7	4.3	4.3
Recreation	3.0	4.4	5.0
Education (private)	1.5	1.6	1.5
Religion	0.9	1.0	0.6
Welfare (private)	1.6	0.6	0.5
Total	100.0	100.0	100.0

Source: J. F. Dewhurst and Associates, *America's Needs and Resources,
A New Survey,* The Twentieth Century Fund, New York, 1955, 103.

TABLE 23.7. PERSONAL EXPENDITURES ON CONSUMPTION,
UNITED KINGDOM, PERCENTAGE DISTRIBUTION

	1938	1950
Food, alcoholic beverages, & tobacco	40.7	45.4
Clothing	10.3	11.1
Rents, rates, water charges, fuel, light	15.8	11.1
Durable household goods, communication services, & other household goods	7.3	8.2
Private motoring & travel	6.7	5.8
Entertainments, books, newspapers, & magazines	3.0	3.5
Other services	11.8	9.2
Other goods	4.1	4.5
Income in kind of armed forces	0.4	0.4
Less foreign tourists' expenditures in the U.K.	−1.0	−0.6
Personal expenditures abroad	0.8	1.2
Total	100.0	100.0

Source: J. E. Meade and R. Stone, *National Income and Expenditure,*
Bowes and Bowes, Cambridge, 1952, 27. For a detailed breakdown of food
expenditures from 1920 to 1938, see R. Stone, *The Measurement of Consumers' Expenditure and Behaviour in the United Kingdom, 1920–1938,* I,
Cambridge University Press, Cambridge, 1954.

tobacco expenditures in the United States and Great Britain (Tables
23.6 and 23.7), on the other hand, comprise only about 35 per cent
and 45 per cent, respectively, of total consumption outlays. The food
share in Germany before the war was also around 40 per cent.[16] In
rich countries, consequently, a much larger proportion of consumer

[16] *Ibid.,* 279.

outlays is available for clothing, housing, household equipment, and other consumer services than in poor nations.

As Table 23.6 shows, the shares of consumer transportation, household equipment, medical care and insurance, and recreation in American consumer outlays increased between 1914 and 1950–1952. On the other hand, expenditures for housing and utilities, private welfare, religion, clothing, accessories, and personal care declined in relative importance between these years. The food, liquor, and tobacco share has remained remarkably stable since 1900.

In the United Kingdom, the share of food, alcoholic beverage, and tobacco in consumer expenditures also remained about the same between 1900 and 1909 and 1940 and 1949. The proportion was 44.3 per cent and 46.5 per cent in 1900–1909 and 1940–1949, respectively.[17] Tobacco expenditures, however, increased sharply, particularly after World War II. Rents and utilities declined in relative importance, although not as much as in the United States. However, during the first half of this century total expenditures on services in the United Kingdom did not rise in relative importance as in the United States.[18] Apparently this is explained, at least partly, by the greater shift in Britain towards the public provision of many services.

3. International Trade

Significant differences between the economic structure of rich and of poor economies are also revealed in the field of international trade. In 1955, the industrial countries accounted for 63.7 per cent of total world exports.[19] Of this 63.7 per cent, 38.7 per cent represented exports to other industrial countries, and 25.0 per cent consisted of exports to non-industrial areas. Of the 36.3 per cent of world exports accounted for by the primary producing areas, 25.7 per cent represented exports to industrial countries, and 10.6 per cent exports to other primary producing areas. Thus, the trade between the industrial and non-industrial areas, i.e., the exports of industrial areas to primary producing areas plus the exports of primary producing areas to the industrial countries,

[17] Jefferys and Walters, "National Income and Expenditure of the United Kingdom, 1870–1952," S. Kuznets (ed.), *Income and Wealth,* Series V, Bowes and Bowes, London, 1955, 20.

[18] Jefferys and Walters, *op. cit.,* 22–23.

[19] The Contracting Parties to the General Agreement on Tariffs and Trade (GATT), *International Trade, 1955,* Geneva, 1956, 4. Industrial areas, according to this classification, are: Canada, United States, United Kingdom, France, Federal Republic of Germany, Belgium-Luxembourg, Denmark, Greece, Austria, Italy and Trieste, the Netherlands, Norway, Portugal, Sweden, Switzerland, Turkey, Iceland, Ireland, and Japan.

amounted to 50.7 per cent of world exports. Although there is some evidence of a decline in this figure since just before World War II, there does not seem to be any significant long-run trend.[20]

Among the major industrial countries (Table 23.8) the United States is by far the largest exporter. The United Kingdom, Germany, and France complete the list of the big four. In 1954, these four countries

TABLE 23.8. TOTAL EXPORTS OF SEVEN EUROPEAN
COUNTRIES, JAPAN, AND THE UNITED STATES,
1913, 1928, 1938, 1954

(Percentages)

	1913	1928	1938	1954
United States	22.7	30.0	27.4	37.1
United Kingdom	23.9	20.8	20.5	18.6
Germany	22.5	17.2	19.4	13.0
France	12.4	12.1	8.0	10.4
Belgium-Luxembourg	6.4	5.1	6.5	5.7
Italy	4.6	4.5	5.0	4.1
Japan	2.9	5.2	6.5	4.0
Sweden	2.0	2.6	4.1	3.9
Switzerland	2.5	2.5	2.7	3.0
Total	100.0	100.0	100.0	100.0

Source: Computed from trade returns of these countries.

accounted for about 42 per cent of total world exports. Since World War I, the most striking change in the relative importance of the countries listed in Table 23.8 was the rapid rise in the American export position. The United Kingdom's share of exports, on the other hand, gradually declined between 1913 and 1954. France and Germany likewise suffered in relative terms—though the German share was affected significantly by territorial changes. The shares of the smaller rich European countries either increased or else declined less than did the shares of the three largest European exporters.

The rich industrial nations also account for most of the world exports of manufactured commodities. In 1954, for example, the share of the nine countries in Table 23.8 plus Canada in total world exports of manufactures was 83 per cent.[21] This ratio remained remarkably constant between 1900 and 1954. There were, however, considerable changes in the composition of manufactured exports. Machinery and vehicle

[20] The Contracting Parties to the General Agreement on Tariffs and Trade (GATT), International Trade, 1954, Geneva, 1955, 7, 157–158.

[21] A. K. Cairncross, "World Trade in Manufactures Since 1900," Economia Internazionale, VIII, No. 4, 10.

exports amounted to 41 per cent of manufactured exports for the countries listed in Table 23.8 in 1952, as contrasted with only 12 per cent in 1900. Textile and miscellaneous exports, on the other hand, fell from 36 and 24 per cent to 13 and 19 per cent, respectively, between these two years. The other classes of manufactured goods, metals and chemicals, remained about the same in relative importance over the period.

The importance of manufactured exports for the nine countries above increased appreciably during the present century. The division of the exports of these countries between manufactures and primary products was 72 per cent and 28 per cent, respectively, in 1952 as contrasted with 54 per cent and 46 per cent, respectively, in 1900. However, compositional stability characterized the import side. Primary commodities accounted for 73 and 74 per cent of total imports for those countries in 1900 and 1952, respectively, and manufactured goods for 27 and 26 per cent, respectively.

Among rich countries there is no simple relationship between the value of foreign trade (imports and exports combined) and national income. For the United States, in 1955, the value of foreign trade (exports plus imports) was equal to only 9 per cent of national income.[22] The ratio for the United Kingdom, France, and Germany was 38, 21, and 21 per cent, respectively, in 1954. Even higher were the ratios (in 1949) for Canada (51 per cent), Australia (61 per cent), New Zealand (63 per cent), the Netherlands (63 per cent), and Belgium (71 per cent).[23]

Although such figures are only very rough indicators of the importance of foreign trade to a country, they do show that, as in the case of the poor economies, foreign trade plays a significant role in the total economic activity of most rich nations. The post-war balance of payment difficulties encountered by the Western European nations illustrate this point only too well. In 1938, Europe's current account was in balance. In 1947, however, Europe showed a deficit on current account of $7.5 billion. Although this is not the place to analyze the several causes and attempted cures of these difficulties,[24] the long-run forces underlying the problem should be emphasized. Two important long-run sources of adjustment difficulties for the older industrial countries are competition from younger industrial nations and changes in the composition of world trade. As already discussed in Chapter 12, Britain's relative position in world trade deteriorated, particularly after World War I,

[22] U. S. Department of Commerce, *Survey of Current Business,* Annual Review Number, Feb. 1956, 6, S21, S22.

[23] W. S. Woytinsky and E. S. Woytinsky, *World Commerce and Governments,* The Twentieth Century Fund, New York, 1955, 65.

[24] See the yearly *Economic Survey of Europe,* United Nations, Geneva.

when other industrial powers offered increasing overseas competition. In addition, Britain's traditional composition of exports was weighted heavily by a declining class of exports, namely textiles.

4. Government Expenditures and Revenues

Two outstanding institutional changes in the rich countries which accompanied the structural trends outlined thus far were the growth of "big" government and of "big" business. This section and the following one summarize these developments.

After World War I, the relative importance of government expenditures increased steadily in most rich countries. In the United States, for example, all government expenditures in 1913 amounted to only 6.4 per cent of the gross national product. By 1929, this proportion rose to 9.8 per cent; in 1937 and 1954, it was 16.3 and 30.7 per cent, respectively.[25] British public expenditures likewise rose from less than 15 per cent of national income before 1913 to around 30 per cent during the interwar period and to about 40 per cent of the national income after World War II.[26] The same upward trend developed in most other rich economies.[27]

Table 23.9 summarizes the growth in various types of governmental expenditures per person in the United States from 1913 to 1950. In 1913, the five major categories of per capita expenditure were: education, transportation, health and community facilities, postal service, and national defense. The largest percentage gains made during the period between 1913 and 1932 were for social insurance, interest on debt, agriculture and natural resources, transportation, and civilian public safety. The top five functions on a per capita basis in 1932 were: transportation, education, health and community facilities, public welfare and veterans' pensions, and national defense. With the war and the post-war defense programs, national defense rose to be the most important expenditure in both 1942 and 1950. Educational expenditures per person actually fell between 1932 and 1942, although they still ranked as the second most important activity in 1950. Per capita transportation expenditures dropped from 1932 to 1942 and from 1942 to 1950. They were only the fifth most important function in 1950. The continued rapid rise in social insurance expenditure throughout this period caused

[25] Dewhurst, op. cit., 578; Bureau of the Census, Summary of Governmental Finances in 1954, Bureau of the Census, Washington, Oct. 7, 1955, 25.

[26] U. K. Hicks, British Public Finances, 1880–1952, Oxford University Press, London, 1954, 12. Hereinafter cited as Hicks, British Public Finances.

[27] See W. S. Woytinsky and E. S. Woytinsky, World Commerce and Governments, The Twentieth Century Fund, New York, 1955, 695–699.

this activity to become the third most significant function by 1950. Interest on the debt ranked fourth in relative importance in 1950.

In Britain, a major reason for the growth of the public sector was the expansion of social services. These expenditures increased from 1.6 per cent of the national income in 1890 (or 14.4 per cent of total public expenditures) to 14 per cent of national income (or 38 per cent of

TABLE 23.9. PER CAPITA U. S. GOVERNMENT EXPENDITURES, BY FUNCTION, FISCAL YEARS 1913, 1932, 1942, 1950

(in 1950 dollars)

	1913	1932	1942	1950
All functions	99.58	217.15	633.52	459.74
National defense	8.62	15.00	328.27	83.19
International affairs	.20	.35	64.17	30.56
Civilian public safety	4.59	12.52	10.71	9.98
Education	22.79	39.74	34.76	68.19
Public welfare and veterans' pensions	7.26	19.64	35.06	36.07
Social insurance	.22	2.52	11.36	48.38
Health and community facilities	13.10	27.83	31.51	36.17
Transportation	17.74	50.77	40.13	38.05
Agriculture and natural resources	2.10	6.41	31.50	29.20
Regulation and promotion of business and labor	.72	1.52	1.84	1.79
Postal service	10.17	13.68	11.65	14.71
Liquor stores	—	—	3.57	4.41
Interest on debt	1.66	8.58	13.86	42.81
General control	7.77	12.76	10.60	11.24
Other	2.65	5.82	4.54	4.97

Source: J. F. Dewhurst and Associates, *America's Needs and Resources, A New Survey,* The Twentieth Century Fund, New York, 1955, Table 263, 632.

total public outlays) in 1950.[28] Of these services, education and assistance to the poor amounted to 52 and 41 per cent, respectively, in 1890. In 1951, the distribution among social services was as follows: education, 21 per cent; public health and national health service, 27 per cent; social security, 26 per cent; and such activities as non-contributory pensions, assistance to the poor, etc., 26 per cent.

[28] These figures and those that follow are from Hicks, *op. cit.,* 14–16, 31.

An equally dramatic increase took place in the economic expenditures of the British government. For example, in 1913, local trading services amounted to 2.3 per cent of the national income. In 1948, the total of gross current public outlays on trading and production was 18.4 per cent of national income. This large increase was attributable to the establishment of nationalized industries, the expansion of government trading activities, and state aid to agriculture and industry. Although expenditure for defense increased from 2.4 per cent to 6.9 per cent of national income between 1890 and 1950, its share in the budget actually fell from 38 to 25 per cent between these years.

The financing of the rapidly growing government outlays in the rich countries coincided with a sharp shift in the relative importance of various types of taxes. Much greater reliance was placed upon the income tax as a source of revenue. In 1913, only 1.6 per cent of all tax revenues in the United States was raised by the income tax, but the 1952 figure was 64 per cent.[29] Similarly, in Britain the proportion of revenue raised by the income tax increased from 19 to 43 per cent between 1913 and 1950.[30]

5. "Big" Business

A significant share of economic activity in most high per capita income countries is organized on a large-scale production basis. The United Kingdom's 1935 Census of Production indicated that 40 per cent of those working in manufacturing industries were employed by firms that had at least 500 employees. This proportion was 12 per cent in building and contracting, 87 per cent in mining, and 76 per cent in public utilities.[31] In 1951, 44 per cent of the employees in all United States private non-farm enterprises (except professional services) worked in firms employing at least 500 people. As in the British case, there was considerable diversity among industries. The percentage was: 59 in manufacturing; 74 in transportation, communication, and other public utilities; 48 in mining; 34 in finance, insurance, and real estate; 25 in retail trade; and 16 in wholesale trade.[32]

American data illustrate the rapid increase in the size of business

[29] Dewhurst, op. cit., 584.

[30] U. K. Hicks, The Finance of British Government, 1920–1936, Oxford University Press, London, 1938, 384; and Hicks, British Public Finances, 75, 79. The figures include surtax and profit taxes.

[31] Worswick and Ady (eds.), The British Economy, 1945–1950, Oxford University Press, London, 1952, Table 5, 80.

[32] U. S. Department of Commerce, Survey of Current Business, 34, No. 5, Tables 1 and 2, 18 (May 1954).

units. Between 1904 and 1952 the value added per establishment in manufacturing industries rose from $28,000 to $409,000.[33] During the same period the average number of employees per manufacturing establishment increased from 26 to 60.[33]

A considerable degree of business concentration also prevails throughout the industrial structure of the rich countries.[34] The following is a partial list of American manufacturing industries in which the four largest companies employed at least 50 per cent of the workers in that industry in 1950: cereal preparation (75 per cent); cigarettes (81 per cent); synthetic fibers (76 per cent); alkalines and chlorine (71 per cent); tires and inner tubes (78 per cent); flat glass (85 per cent); steel works of rolling mills (55 per cent); electrometallurgical products (86 per cent); aluminum rolling and drawing (89 per cent); tin cans and other tinware (77 per cent); steam engines and turbines (87 per cent); tractors (76 per cent); electric lamps (91 per cent); telephone and telegraph equipment (90 per cent); motor vehicles and parts (59 per cent); aircraft engines (54 per cent); and scientific equipment (68 per cent).[35]

The level of concentration in Britain is even higher, according to a comparison of the United Kingdom and the United States for 1935.[36] In that year the average of concentration indexes (percentage of employment in the three leading firms weighted by employment in each industry) was 20 per cent for the United States and 25 per cent for the United Kingdom. High levels of industrial concentration also exist in Germany, Canada, Japan, and Italy.[37]

In 1932, Berle and Means pointed out that in the United States the assets of the 200 largest non-financial corporations increased at the rate of 5.4 per cent annually between 1909 and 1928, whereas those of all

---

[33] Bureau of the Census, *Statistical Abstract of the United States, 1955*, U. S. Government Printing Office, Washington, 1955, 799.

[34] As noted before, the level of concentration in the industrial sectors of the poor countries also is frequently high.

[35] Federal Trade Commission, *Changes in Concentration in Manufacturing, 1935 to 1947 and 1950*, U. S. Government Printing Office, Washington, 1954, 132–136.

[36] Gideon Rosenbluth, "Measures of Concentration," *Business Concentration and Price Policy*, Conference of Universities—National Bureau Committee for Economic Research, Princeton University Press, 1955, 70–77. Also, see P. S. Florence, *The Logic of British and American Industry*, Routledge and K. Paul, Ltd., London, 1953, 130–135.

[37] See E. H. Chamberlin (ed.), *Monopoly and Competition and Their Regulation*, Conference of the International Economic Association, Macmillan and Co., Ltd., London, 1954, Part I; and R. Brady, *Business as a System of Power*, Columbia University Press, New York, 1943, Chapters 1–4.

other non-financial corporations gained only at the rate of 2.0 per cent per year in this period.[38]   Although the evidence for the 1909–1919 period was less conclusive than from 1919–1928, their findings caused considerable alarm.   For if this rate continued, practically all industrial activity would be absorbed by the 200 largest corporations by 1970.[39] But the trend has not continued—at least between 1931 and 1947.   Even excluding public utilities, a field where massive decentralization has taken place since the Public Utility Holding Company Act of 1935, and confining the study only to manufacturing industries, Adelman found that the 139 largest manufacturing corporations held 49.6 per cent of all assets of manufacturing corporations in 1931 and only 45.0 per cent in 1947.[40]   Moreover, concentration measures based on sales data do not show any significant upward trend.   One student of the problem found that in 1904 and 1939 the top one-tenth of the 185,000 largest manufacturing establishments accounted for 75.5 per cent and 78.2 per cent, respectively, of the total value of manufacturing products. The figures for the top one-half of these establishments were 96.2 per cent in 1904 and 97.1 per cent in 1939.[41]   Using "concentration ratios" —total sales of the four largest sellers divided by total sales of the whole group—Adelman's calculations showed even some decline in concentration between 1901 and 1947.[42]   In view of the imperfections of early data and the somewhat different results produced by various measures of concentration, the safest conclusion appears to be that the extent of concentration in the United States was approximately the same around the turn of the century and just after World War II.

The degree of concentration that is present in American manufacturing probably can be traced in large part to the great wave of mergers in the 1870's and 1880's and again from 1897 to 1904.   Technological advances favoring concentration, plus the promotional profits involved in mergers, were important reasons for this movement.   In the 1920's, another, though smaller, merger wave also evidently increased the extent of concentration.   Although the deep depression in the early 1930's increased concentration still more, recovery and the war-time boom seemingly worked in the opposite direction.   The

[38] A. A. Berle and G. C. Means, *The Modern Corporation and Private Property,* The Macmillan Co., New York, 1932, 35.

[39] *Ibid.,* 40–41.

[40] M. A. Adelman, "The Measurement of Industrial Concentration," *Review of Economics and Statistics, XXXIII,* No. 4, 289 (Nov. 1951).

[41] G. Warren Nutter, *The Extent of Enterprise Monopoly in the United States, 1899–1939,* University of Chicago Press, Chicago, 1951, Table 6, 34.

[42] Adelman, *op. cit.,* 290–292.   Adelman compared only those industries in which these concentration ratios were over 50 per cent.

effect of the wave of mergers in the post-war years on the extent of competition has not yet been fully analyzed.

Another aspect of "big" business in the major industrial countries is the separation of ownership and control.[43] Although the meaning of "control" is difficult to define satisfactorily, one definition frequently used is the possession of the power to select or change management. This of course relates the concept back to the degree of stock ownership. In the United States the Securities and Exchange Commission studied the nature of control in the 200 largest non-financial corporations (if subsidiaries of other corporations are eliminated, the number becomes 176) for the period 1937–1939.[44] With regard to management's, i.e., officers' and directors', share in the voting common stock of the corporation, it was found that in 1939 the median percentage of such stock ownership was only 2.11 per cent. It is clear, therefore, that neither the officers nor the directors of American big business exercised control by means of substantial ownership of voting stock. Nevertheless, the Commission concluded that control through stock ownership (usually minority) was typical in these corporations. The authors of the study judged that there was a dominant stockholding group (an ownership group able to "control" the company) in 118 of the 176 corporations. In the remaining 58 companies (representing 44 per cent of the total assets of the 176 corporations) they found no dominant stockholding group. In these companies the existing management group possessed considerable power to perpetuate itself by the proxy method.

6. The Distribution of Income

What shifts in the distribution of income accompanied the structural and institutional changes in rich countries described thus far? Although the distribution of income in rich countries presently appears to be more equal than in the poor economies, evidence concerning historical changes in the distribution of income by countries is scarce. Data for the United States from 1935 to 1950 (Table 23.10) indicate a gradual trend towards greater equality. Several factors accounted for the shift.[45] A lower percentage of unemployment in 1950 than 1935–1936 and a

[43] Brady, *Business as a System of Power*, Columbia University Press, New York, 1943, 228. For a discussion of this problem in Britain, see Florence, *op. cit.*, 202–203.

[44] This investigation is summarized and appraised in R. A. Gordon's *Business Leadership in the Large Corporation*, The Brookings Institution, Washington, 1945, 25–45.

[45] H. P. Miller, *Income of the American People*, John Wiley & Sons, New York, 1955, Chapter 9.

relatively greater increase in wage rates among the lower than the higher
paid occupations contributed to the greater equality in 1950. Disproportionately larger increases in the income of farm families (who tend
to be at the lower end of the income scale) and in the number of
earners per family among the middle-income families between these
years also had the effect of producing greater equality.

TABLE 23.10. DISTRIBUTION OF FAMILY PERSONAL
INCOME AMONG QUINTILES AND TOP 5 PER CENT OF
FAMILIES RANKED BY SIZE OF FAMILY INCOME

Quintile	1935–1936	1941	1944	1950	Per Cent Change 1935–1936 to 1950
Lowest	4.1	4.1	4.9	4.8	+17
Second	9.2	9.5	10.9	11.0	+20
Third	14.1	15.3	16.2	16.2	+15
Fourth	20.9	22.3	22.2	22.3	+ 7
Highest	51.7	48.8	45.8	45.7	−12
Total	100.0	100.0	100.0	100.0	—
Top 5 per cent	26.5	24.0	20.7	20.4	−23

Source: H. P. Miller, *Income of the American People,* John Wiley &
Sons, New York, 1955, Table 61, 112.

Prior to 1935, estimates of the distribution of income in the United
States are available only for the top 5 per cent of income recipients.
The share of aggregate income that this group received remained about
the same from 1919–1928 to 1929–1938 but fell sharply (both before
and after taxes) in the decade 1939–1948.

German statistics show a trend towards equality between 1913 and
1926, but a reversal of this shift during the depression of the 1930's.[46]
Unfortunately, post-war data for Germany are not available. The distribution of income in France, like the United States, became more
equal between 1938 and 1946.[47] However, much more information is
needed before any conclusions about long-term trends in the distribution
of income by size can be made.

Data concerning long-run changes in the distribution of income by
type are much more plentiful than by size of income. Table 23.11
shows the breakdown of aggregate payments into employee compensation, entrepreneurial income, and property income (dividends, interest,
and rent) for the United States.

[46] Woytinsky and Woytinsky, *World Population,* 408; and P. Jostock, "The
Long-Term Growth of National Income in Germany," *Income and Wealth,*
Series V, Bowes and Bowes, London, 1955, 112–117.
[47] Woytinsky and Woytinsky, *World Population,* 409.

Perhaps the most striking trend is the rise in the share of employee compensation throughout the period. Presumably this is the result of the shift from individual firms to corporations, which in turn was caused by the relative decline in agriculture and by the rising importance of the corporation in industries previously dominated by individual firms, e.g., manufacturing, trade, construction, and some service industries.[48] The same trend is clearly evident for Britain,[49] Germany,[50] and France.[51]

TABLE 23.11. DISTRIBUTION OF AGGREGATE PAYMENTS
BY TYPE, U. S. A., CURRENT PRICES 1909–1948

	Employee Compensation	Entrepreneurial Income	Property Income
1909–1918	56.2	24.6	19.2
1919–1928	61.7	19.5	18.8
1929–1938	64.1	14.7	21.2
1939–1948	69.6	18.4	12.0

Source: S. Kuznets, "Long-Term Changes in the National Income of the United States of America since 1870," Income and Wealth of the United States, Income and Wealth, Series II, S. Kuznets (ed.), Bowes and Bowes, Cambridge, 1952, 136.

The rise in entrepreneurial income in the United States between 1929–1938 and 1939–1948 apparently was caused by the sharp increase in agricultural prices during and after the war. Total service income, i.e., employee compensation and entrepreneurial income, remained roughly the same between 1909–1918 and 1929–1939 and even back to 1870. Between 1929–1938 and 1939–1948, however, a sharp rise in the share of service income (and fall in property income) occurred. Kuznets suggests that this was due to two factors: "a decline in the ratio of capital to product, caused largely by the tremendous expansion of output during the war years without a corresponding increase in capital stock; and the maintenance of low interest rates, and hence yields on capital, by government policy in connection with cost and marketability of government securities issued to finance the war."[52]

[48] S. Kuznets, "Long-Term Changes in the National Income of the United States of America since 1870," Income and Wealth of the United States, Income and Wealth, Series II, S. Kuznets (ed.), Bowes and Bowes, Cambridge, 1952, 138.

[49] Woytinsky and Woytinsky, World Population, 374–375; Meade and Stone, National Income and Expenditure, Bowes and Bowes, Cambridge, 1952, 33.

[50] Jostock, op. cit., 109.

[51] Woytinsky and Woytinsky, World Population, 375.

[52] Kuznets, op. cit., 137.

7. Capital Accumulation

Analyses of factor supplies (the capital stock, natural resource conditions, the size and composition of the population and the labor force) and the nature of technological progress disclose additional important differences in the economic characteristics of rich and poor countries. These subjects are discussed in the remaining sections of this chapter.

To decide just what should be counted as the capital stock is a difficult endeavor. Should, for example, investments in the education and training of people be included in the capital stock, or should the concept be restricted only to such items as buildings, tools and equipment, and working capital? In the final analysis, this problem turns out to be more apparent than real. Almost all the possible definitions are acceptable, if consistently followed. The main guide in the selection of a particular definition should be the nature of the problem under study.

Attempts to measure the supply of capital (whatever the definition) present more serious obstacles. If one wishes a dollar figure for the value of capital goods, the mathematically correct procedure is to compute the present discounted value of all future net receipts from the capital assets. But, in a dynamic world characterized by a high degree of uncertainty, such a procedure is neither very practicable nor meaningful. Most actual estimates, consequently, rest on the book value of capital assets after deduction of depreciation. There is, of course, always the alternative of actually enumerating the physical goods that compose the capital stock, but this is also highly impracticable.

Comparative figures on the supplies of capital in various countries are extremely rough and scarce. Colin Clark estimated the stock of capital (in international units) per head of persons in work as follows: United States (1939), 5820; Great Britain (1932–1934), 6660; the Netherlands (1939), 6320; Canada (1929), 5500; and Norway (1939), 2732.[53] The capital stock per worker in many poor countries is less than 10 per cent of the figure for such countries as the United States and Great Britain.[54]

Another imperfect but useful indicator of the quantity of equipment is the number of horsepower per employed person. In manufacturing activity this figure was as follows: the United States (1939), 4.8; the United Kingdom (1930), 2.4; Germany (1933), 2.4; France (1931), 2.2; Sweden (1938), 4.4; Norway (1938), 5.4; and Italy (1937–1940), 1.6.[55]

[53] Clark, *op. cit.*, 486–489.
[54] Cf. Chapter 14, section 3.
[55] United Nations, *Economic Bulletin for Europe, III*, No. 1, 27 (First Quarter, 1951).

A more recent study of the capital stock in the United States estimated that the value (in 1929 dollars) of reproducible tangible wealth per person in 1950 was $2370.[56] Although this figure in itself may not be very meaningful, its change over time is significant. According to Goldsmith,[56] it was (in 1929 dollars): $1321 in 1900; $1647 in 1912; $2361 in 1929; $2107 in 1939; $2047 in 1945; and $2370 in 1950. This growth in tangible wealth per person corresponded to a 1.44 per cent annual growth rate between 1900 and 1950 as contrasted with a 2.53 per cent annual growth rate between 1850 and 1900. A study of capital formation in the United Kingdom indicated that the per capita value of net fixed assets (in 1948 prices) increased about 10 per cent between 1947 and 1953.[57]

Still another survey based on a tabulation of the 100 largest non-financial corporations showed an average investment (including plant and equipment and current assets) per American worker of over $15,000 in 1952. This average, however, concealed a considerable degree of variability among industries. For example, investment per worker was $52,000 in electric and gas utilities; $46,000 in tobacco products; $38,000 in petroleum refining and distilling; $24,000 in railroads; and only $8000 in food, automobiles, tires, electrical equipment, and trade.[58]

The composition of net capital formation in the United States has shifted rather markedly since 1890. In the 1890's, about 77 per cent of capital goods expenditures consisted of payments for construction compared to only 23 per cent for equipment. During the 1920's, construction fell to 67 per cent of the expenditures for capital goods, and from 1948 to 1952 it was only 55 per cent.[59] Not only did the equipment share increase but machinery outlays within this category also rose.[60] In 1929, agricultural and non-agricultural machinery purchases

[56] R. Goldsmith, "The Growth of Reproducible Wealth of the United States of America from 1805 to 1950," *Income and Wealth of the United States,* Income and Wealth, Series II, S. Kuznets (ed.), Bowes and Bowes, Cambridge, 1952, 273. This figure excludes military tangible assets, subsoil assets, and civilian durable, semi-durable, and perishable assets.

[57] Value of net fixed capital from P. Redfern, "Net Investment in Fixed Assets in the United Kingdom, 1938–1953," *Journal of the Royal Statistical Society,* Series A, *CXVIII,* Table 7, 158 (Part 2, 1955). Population estimates from Central Statistical Office, *Annual Abstract of Statistics,* No. 91, H.M.S.O., London, 1954, Tables 6, 7, and Royal Commission on Population, *Report,* Cmd. 7695, H.M.S.O., London, 1949, 12.

[58] Dewhurst, *op. cit.,* 911.

[59] *Ibid.,* 1016–1018.

[60] The equipment category includes machinery, business motor vehicles, other transportation equipment, and other equipment.

in the United States were 8.1 per cent and 39.5 per cent, respectively, of total purchases of producers' durable equipment. In 1952, however, they were 9.7 and 48.1 per cent, respectively.[61]

Another significant change in the nature of the capital stock is the decline in capital-output ratios in the United States. In manufacturing the ratio was 1.65 in 1890, 2.56 in 1919, 1.81 in 1937, and 1.66 in 1948.[62] In mining, it was 1.66 in 1890, 2.89 in 1919, 1.59 in 1937,

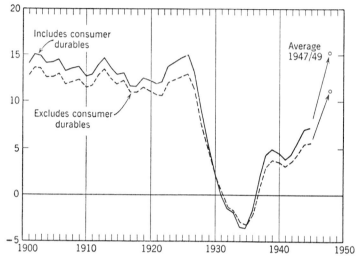

Figure 23.1. National saving-income ratio United States, 1897–1949. (Nine-year moving averages.)   Source: R. W. Goldsmith, *A Study of Saving in the United States*, Princeton University Press, Princeton, 1955, I, 78, Chart XIV.

and 1.55 in 1948.[63] The capital-output ratio in agriculture also declined after about 1912.[64] The downward trend in these ratios is also confirmed by comparing the stocks of privately owned plant and equipment with gross national product from 1910 to 1952.[65]

Behind the disparity in the capital stocks of rich and poor countries is the difference in saving habits. As noted in Chapter 14, the savings ratio is considerably higher in rich countries than in poor countries, and the gap in the stock of capital between advanced and poor countries

[61] Dewhurst, *op. cit.,* 482.

[62] D. Creamer, *Capital and Output Trends in Manufacturing Industries, 1880–1948,* Occasional Paper 41, National Bureau of Economic Research, New York, 1954, Table 8.

[63] I. Borenstein, *Capital and Output Trends in Mining Industries, 1870–1948,* Occasional Paper 45, National Bureau of Economic Research, New York, 1954, 60.

[64] W. Leontief, "Machines and Man," *Scientific American, 187,* 154 (Sept. 1952).

[65] Dewhurst, *op. cit.,* 832.

appears to be widening. The long-run trend of the saving-income ratio in the United States is not too clear. As Figure 23.1 indicates, the national saving-income ratio declined slightly from 1897 to 1949, if saving is defined to exclude consumer durables, but remained about the same if saving is defined to include consumer durables. In view of the imperfect nature of the data, Goldsmith concludes that "on the basis of the evidence now available absence of a long-run trend appears to be the most acceptable hypothesis."[66] The long-run behavior of the saving-income ratio in most other rich economies where statistics are available resembled that of the United States. In the United Kingdom, Canada, and Denmark, for example, the long-run ratio either declined slightly or remained stable from about the last quarter of the nineteenth century to the first half of the twentieth century.[67]

TABLE 23.12. PERCENTAGE SHARE OF MAJOR
SAVING GROUPS IN U. S. NATIONAL SAVING
FOR SELECTED PERIODS, CURRENT VALUES

	Personal	Corporations	Government
1897–1908	68.7	24.9	6.5
1922–1929	64.1	17.9	18.1
1946–1949	60.3	25.3	14.3
1897–1949 excluding: 1917–1918, 1930–1933, 1942–1945	72.1	20.4	7.4

Source: R. W. Goldsmith, *A Study of Saving in the United States,* Princeton University Press, Princeton, 1955, I, 271.

As Table 23.12 indicates, personal saving constitutes by far the largest part of national saving in the United States. During this century, however, government saving rose at the expense of personal saving. Not only did personal saving decline in relative terms, but—to use Goldsmith's term—personal saving increasingly took the form of "tied" saving, i.e., forms of saving that do not depend on a decision of the saver. When once begun, this form of saving must be carried through to the termination of the contract, often over a period of several decades,

[66] R. W. Goldsmith, *A Study of Saving in the United States,* Princeton University Press, Princeton, 1955, I, 75.
[67] S. Kuznets, "International Differences in Capital Formation and Financing," *Capital Formation and Economic Growth,* National Bureau of Economic Research, Princeton University Press, Princeton, 1955, 46; Jefferys and Walters, *op. cit.,* Table VII, 18.

unless part of the saver's contributions are to be lost.[68]   These types of saving principally comprise saving through insurance premiums, pension contributions, and repayments on amortizable urban residential mortgages.   They totaled about 7 per cent of personal saving before 1915, around 15 per cent in the 1920's, and well over 40 per cent of personal saving after World War II.[69]   A survey of personal saving in Britain for 1951–1952 indicated that tied saving was even larger than aggregate saving by private households.[70]

8. Natural Resources

In view of the high consumption rates of raw materials, many rich industrial economies face the problem of providing adequate supplies of natural resources to feed their industrial engines without a substantial increase in the real costs of these materials.   In the United States, the consumption of minerals, including oil, increased by five times between 1900 and 1950.   Experts, moreover, expect a rate of consumption roughly ten times the 1900 rate by 1975.[71]   American consumption of agricultural products rose about 130 per cent between 1900 and 1950, whereas the consumption of forest products remained approximately the same.[72]   The Materials Policy Commission predicts a 39 and 17 per cent increase, respectively, in these commodities between 1950 and 1975.[73]   Electric energy consumption increased more than 350 per cent between 1925 and 1950.[74]   The Commission concludes that, if the output of goods and services doubles in the United States between 1950 and 1975, an increase of 50 to 60 per cent in the supplies of all raw materials will be required.[75]

Similar rapid increases in materials consumption have occurred in other rich nations.   Between 1938 and 1950, for example, Western European consumption of solid fuels, petroleum, and hydropower increased 8 per

---

[68] Goldsmith, *op. cit.*, I, 159.

[69] *Ibid.*, 160.

[70] H. F. Lydall, "National Survey of Personal Incomes and Savings: Part IV, Personal Savings and Consumption Expenditures," *Bulletin of the Oxford University Institute of Statistics, XV,* Nos. 10–11, 349 (Oct. and Nov. 1953).   The saving account of private households in 1951–1952 was: contractual saving £ +513; change in liquid assets £ −323; miscellaneous saving £ +140; or a total saving of £ +330.   The figures are in millions of pounds.

[71] E. S. Mason, "Raw Materials, Rearmament, and Economic Development," *Quarterly Journal of Economics, LXVI,* No. 3, 329 (Aug. 1952).

[72] The President's Materials Policy Commission, *Resources for Freedom,* U. S. Government Printing Office, 1952, II, computed from Table II, 180.

[73] *Ibid.*, I, 24.

[74] *Ibid.*, III, Table I, 32.

[75] *Ibid.*, I, 59.

cent, 63 per cent, and 75 per cent, respectively.[76] Canada's consumption of these items rose 54 per cent, 134 per cent, and 76 per cent, respectively, between 1939 and 1950. The consumption of such minerals as copper, iron ore, aluminum, manganese ore, and sulphur also rose significantly for most rich countries between 1938 and 1950.[77] The Materials Policy Commission estimates that between 1950 and 1975 the demand for all materials will increase less than 50 per cent in Western Europe and over 50 per cent in Canada, Australia, New Zealand, and Japan.[78]

One consequence of this high rate of materials consumption is a greater reliance upon primary product imports on the part of industrial nations. Before World War I, the United States was a net exporter of both foodstuffs and raw materials, but during the 1920's it became a net importer of these commodities. More recently the United States became a net importer of such important raw materials as petroleum, copper, lead, zinc, iron ore, and lumber. In Europe, the story is much the same. In 1913, raw materials constituted 13 per cent of Great Britain's exports and 33 per cent of her imports. In 1954, the export share fell to 10 per cent, and the import share rose to 41 per cent. The same directional change took place in Germany and France.

Nevertheless, taking the poor and rich countries together, the question of sufficient *potential* supplies of natural resources does not appear to pose a serious problem for at least the next twenty to thirty years.[79] Rather the problems are: (1) whether certain industrial countries will be able to maintain a volume of exports of manufactured commodities sufficient to pay for their growing import needs of primary commodities; and (2) whether the poor countries will be able and willing to develop their large reserves of natural resources.

9. Population and the Labor Force

As in the poor countries, there is no simple relationship between per capita income and population density among the rich economies. Population in 1954 per square kilometer varied from 1 and 2 in Australia and Canada, respectively, to 289 and 245 in Belgium and the United Kingdom, respectively. For the United States, France, and Germany the figure was 21, 78, and 159, respectively.[80]

The annual rate of population increase, likewise, differs considerably

[76] *Ibid.,* III, computed from Table III, 29.
[77] *Ibid.,* II, 186–204.
[78] *Ibid.,* I, 59.
[79] Mason, *op. cit.,* 337.
[80] United Nations, Statistical Office, Department of Economic Affairs, *Statistical Yearbook, 1955,* New York, 1955, 21–35.

from one rich country to another. The population of the United States and Canada increased 15 and 21 per cent, respectively, between 1940 and 1950, whereas the population of the United Kingdom and France in this period rose only 5 per cent and less than 2 per cent, respectively.[81] Nevertheless, as indicated in Chapter 13, population growth in many poor countries exceeded that in most of even the fastest growing rich nations. Even more significant than the figures on population increases, however, is the fact that rich economies generally possess a low growth potential compared to the poor areas.[82] Both birth and death rates in rich economies, in other words, are low relative to those in the poor countries.

During the nineteenth century the combined population of Europe, Asiatic U.S.S.R., America, Australia, and New Zealand grew at a rate far above the world average. But in the first half of this century, the rate of growth declined in these areas and increased in the rest of the world. The net result was that between 1930 and 1950 the average annual rates of population growth in the so-called "European culture area" and the world as a whole were the same.[83] In explaining this development most demographers emphasize the lag in the decline of fertility rates compared with the decline in mortality rates. Although the same factors, such as the rise of industry and commerce, the spread of education, and the abandonment of traditional attitudes, operated on both mortality and fertility rates, "the mores governing fertility were less flexible than the conditions governing mortality."[84] Consequently, population in the European culture area grew rapidly in the nineteenth century, but the rate of increase then declined in the first half of this century.

Population growth in the United States and England and Wales illustrates the slackening population increase in many of the rich countries in the twentieth century. From 1801 to 1841, the decennial rate of increase in England and Wales averaged 15.5 per cent, and between 1841 and 1911 it varied between 11 and 14 per cent. In the decades 1931–1941 and 1941–1951, however, the rate of increase was only 4.50 and 4.78 per cent, respectively.[85] In the United States, population growth was over 35 per cent per decade between 1840 and 1860, around

---

[81] Woytinsky and Woytinsky, *World Population*, 44.

[82] See Chapter 13, section 2.

[83] United Nations, Department of Social Affairs, Population Division, *The Determinants and Consequences of Population Trends*, Population Studies, No. 17, New York, 1953, 10–20. Hereinafter cited as United Nations, *The Determinants and Consequences of Population Trends*.

[84] *Ibid.*, 150.

[85] I. Bowen, *Population*, James Nisbet and Co., Ltd., London, 1954, 54.

25 per cent per decade from 1860 to 1890, and about 20 per cent per decade from 1890 to 1910. Between 1910 and 1930, the decennial rate of increase was roughly 15 per cent. This rate declined still further to 7.2 per cent between 1930 and 1940, but rose to 14.5 per cent between 1940 and 1950.[86]

A great wave of overseas emigration accompanied the surge in European population growth—mainly to North America, as pointed out in Chapter 10. This reached a peak just before World War I and declined sharply thereafter. It was replaced to some extent, however, by a growing international movement of population within Europe. France was the principal country of this "normal" immigration in Europe.[87] Nevertheless, voluntary international movements to or from rich countries have been comparatively sluggish since 1930. Even though they increased after World War II, such movements remained considerably below the level of the 1920's.

To attempt to predict future population is a hazardous undertaking. Most population experts in the late 1930's and even the 1940's, for example, expected the population of the United States to reach a peak of between 140 and 160 million in the second half of this century and then to decline from this peak by the year 2000.[88] By July 1956, however, the population of the United States passed the 168 million mark. The Census Bureau has estimated that by 1975 the population of the United States will be 213 million.[89] Recent forecasts of British population predicted that in 1975 the population would be about the same size as it was in 1950.[90] Projections of the French population made in 1946 placed the 1975 population between 33.4 and 43.8 million.[91]

One important population difference between advanced and poor countries is the higher average age in the former economies. In most rich countries, an aging of the population occurred during the last 50 years or more. The median age in the United States in 1870 was about 20 years; by 1900, it was 23 years, and, in 1953, it was slightly over

[86] Dewhurst, *op. cit.,* 51.

[87] Population movements that represented chiefly refugee flights and forced transfers were extremely large during the interwar period and after World War II. These "non-normal" shifts, however, will not be discussed here. See Woytinsky and Woytinsky, *World Population,* 95–104.

[88] J. S. Davis, "Our Changed Population Outlook," *American Economic Review, XLII,* No. 3, 305–308 (June 1952).

[89] *New York Times,* August 8, 1956, 27.

[90] Bowen, *op. cit.,* 200–201.

[91] United Nations, *The Determinants and Consequences of Population Trends,* 155. In 1954, the population of France was already 43.0 million.

30 years.[92] In Britain, the average age of the population increased from under 27 years in 1891 to over 35 in 1947.[93] Similarly, population pyramids (percentages of the population in various age groups) for such countries as France, Germany, Belgium, and Sweden showed a relative rise in higher age groups and a fall in lower age groups since 1875.[94] Most population experts expect this aging to continue for several decades into the future.[95]

High standards of health and education also characterize the populations of the rich countries. Improvements in health are reflected in the steady increase in life expectancy. In the United States and the United Kingdom, for example, the expectation of life at birth for males rose from about 48 years around 1900 to over 65 years by 1952. The level of education also increased significantly over the last several decades. In the United States 62.6 per cent of the population 5 to 19 years of age was enrolled in school in 1910, but by 1950 the figure was 78.7 per cent.[96] The number of enlisted men in World War I who had completed high school and college was only 4.1 and 1.2 per cent, respectively. In World War II, these percentages rose to 23.3 per cent and 3.6 per cent, respectively.[97]

There is no simple relationship between the level of economic development and the ratio of the labor force to population. This ratio depends upon such complex factors as the age and sex composition of the population; the economic structure of the country; the mores of the community with reference to the status of women as wage earners, the age at which young people leave school, and the age at which older workers retire; the level of health of the population; the level of employment; the statistical classification by which the labor force is measured; etc.[98]

In the United States, the interaction of these various factors resulted in an increase in the proportion of the population in the labor force from 32.5 per cent in 1870 to 42.0 per cent in 1950. The percentage increase was, however, successively less over these decades, and in 1952 the proportion dropped to 41.7. The long-run decline in the importance of child labor and the trend towards earlier retirement tended to lower

[92] Dewhurst, *op. cit.,* 63.

[93] Royal Commission on Population, *Report,* Cmd. 7695, H.M.S.O., London, 1949, 12.

[94] Woytinsky and Woytinsky, *World Population,* 60.

[95] United Nations, *The Determinants and Consequences of Population Trends,* 253.

[96] Dewhurst, *op. cit.,* 379.

[97] *Ibid.,* 380.

[98] See United Nations, *The Determinants and Consequences of Population Trends,* Chapter 11.

this ratio. In contrast, the gradual aging of the population operated to increase it. In this regard, the ratio of the population between 15 and 65 years to the number in the dependent age groups (less than 15 years and over 65 years) rose from 1.4 in 1870 to 2.1 in 1940.[99] Population aging, of course, can also work to decrease the ratio of the labor force to population. This occurs in the "heavy old-age dependency" stage when in the advanced stages of aging the ratio of the aged to the producers is increasing at a rate that no longer is balanced by a decline in the ratio of children. However, a drop in the ratio of those in the working age to the dependent age group from 2.1 in 1940 to 1.7 in 1953 was not caused so much by the rising importance of the over 65 years age group as by a sharp increase in the relative importance of those under 15 years. This was reflected in the lower ratio of the labor force to the population in 1952. The gradual entrance of this young group into the labor force, however, will tend to reverse this recent trend.

Another factor that contributed to the long-run rise in the ratio of labor force to population was the rapid increase in the proportion of women seeking employment. In 1900 and 1950, the percentage of men over 10 years, who were in the labor force, was 79.8 and 75.3 per cent, respectively. The percentage of women 10 years and over, on the other hand, increased from 19.5 per cent to 29.4 per cent between these years. As a result, the percentage of women in the labor force rose from 18.8 to 28.5 per cent.[100] This trend also is expected to continue.

In Britain, the ratio of the occupied population to the total population declined slightly between 1861 and 1901 but rose gradually from 1901 to 1951.[101] As in the United States, the ratio of the population between 15 and 65 years to the rest of the population increased between the turn of the century and 1940 but diminished thereafter. It was 1.69 in 1901, 2.15 in 1931, 2.28 in 1939, 1.99 in 1951, and 1.96 in 1953.[102] And a Royal Commission has predicted that by 1977 this ratio would be between 1.79 and 1.96.[103]

One difference between the United States and Britain is that in Britain the proportion of women in the labor force did not rise to any significant

[99] Dewhurst, *op. cit.*, 63.

[100] *Ibid.*, 726.

[101] See Royal Commission on the Distribution of the Industrial Population, *Report*, Cmd. 6153, H.M.S.O., London, 1940, 22–23, and Central Statistical Office, *Annual Abstract of Statistics*, No. 91, 1954, H.M.S.O., London, 1954, Tables 6 and 13, 7, 15.

[102] Central Statistical Office, *Annual Abstract of Statistics*, No. 91, 1954, H.M.S.O., London, 1954, Table 7, 7.

[103] Royal Commission on Population, *Report*, Cmd. 7695, H.M.S.O., London, 1949, 84–85.

extent between 1910 and 1951. For example, the share of women in the British labor force in 1911 and 1951 was about 30 per cent.[104] There also was no significant increase in this percentage for other industrial European countries between 1910 and 1930.[105]

In advanced countries the rising trend in per man-hour productivity was accompanied by shorter working hours. The average work week in America, for example, was approximately 72 hours in 1850, 54 in 1910, 48 in 1930, and 40 in 1953. Hours of work in European countries likewise declined from about 84 hours in 1850 to 48 hours in 1950. The President's Materials Policy Commission predicts that weekly hours in the United States, Canada, Australia, and New Zealand will decline approximately 15 per cent between 1950 and 1975.[106] For the United Kingdom and the rest of free Europe the same group predicts a 10 per cent decline by 1975.

Another obvious factor affecting the rate of development is the extent to which the labor force is utilized. Between 1856 and 1920 the unemployment rate in British Trade Unions fluctuated between 2 and 8 per cent (except for 1879 when it was more than 10 per cent).[107] Between World War I and World War II, however, the unemployment rate increased significantly. In only one year (1927) from 1921 to 1938 did the general unemployment rate fall below 10 per cent. Moreover, it was over 15 per cent in seven of these years.[108] Similar high unemployment rates prevailed in most other advanced European countries between World Wars I and II.[109] Figures for the United States since 1900 indicate that until 1930 unemployment rates fluctuated between about 2 to 6 per cent (except in 1921 when the rate was over 11 per cent).[110] But during the 1930's unemployment rates rose sharply. The rate was 14 per cent or over in every year between 1931 and 1940 and was 20 per cent or more in four of these years.

The period 1948–1955 was one of reasonably full employment for most rich countries. In the United States, for example, unemployment did not exceed 5 per cent of the labor force in any of these years and

[104] Central Statistical Office, *op. cit.,* Table 13, 15; Woytinsky and Woytinsky, *World Population,* 354.

[105] Woytinsky and Woytinsky, *World Population,* 354.

[106] President's Materials Policy Commission, *op. cit.,* II, 111, 131.

[107] W. H. Beveridge, *Full Employment in a Free Society,* W. W. Norton and Co., New York, 1945, 42.

[108] *Ibid.,* Table 1, 47.

[109] Svennilson, *op. cit.,* Table 3, 31.

[110] W. S. Woytinsky and Associates, *Employment and Wages in the United States,* The Twentieth Century Fund, New York, 1953, 397.

was 4 per cent or less in five of the seven years.[111]   In Great Britain the unemployment rate did not exceed 2.1 per cent in any of these years.[111]

A general upgrading in the socioeconomic status of the labor force accompanied the industrial shifts in the composition of the labor force over the last 50 years in rich countries.   United States data (Table

TABLE 23.13.   SOCIOECONOMIC STATUS OF GAINFUL
WORKERS AND PERSONS IN THE LABOR FORCE,
U. S. A., 1910 AND 1940*
(Percentage Distribution)

	1910 (Gainful Workers†)		1940 (Labor Force)	
Professional persons	4.4		6.5	
Proprietors, managers & officials	23.0		17.8	
Farmers & farm managers		16.5		10.1
Others		6.5		7.6
Clerks and kindred workers	10.2		17.2	
Skilled workers & foremen	11.7		11.7	
Semiskilled workers	14.7		21.0	
Unskilled workers	36.0		25.9	
Farm laborers		14.5		7.1
Other laborers		14.7		10.7
Servants		6.8		8.0
Total	100.0		100.0	

* Excludes workers under 14 years of age in all years and new workers in 1940.

† "Gainful Workers" is a broader concept than the "Labor Force."   See U. S. Bureau of Census, *Comparative Occupation Statistics for the United States, 1870 to 1940,* United States Government Printing Office, Washington, 1943, 11–16.

Source: J. F. Dewhurst and Associates, *America's Needs and Resources, A New Survey,* The Twentieth Century Fund, New York, 1955, 730.

23.13) illustrate this trend.   The rising level of per capita income was associated with a sharp drop in the relative importance of unskilled workers and a rise in the significance of semiskilled workers, clerks and kindred persons, and professional workers.   Although the system of classification changed after 1940, a continuing rise in the importance of semiskilled and clerical work as well as professional persons was evident between 1940 and 1953.[112]

[111] Statistical Office of the United Nations, *Monthly Bulletin of Statistics, X,* No. 6, 18–20 (June 1956).

[112] Dewhurst, *op. cit.,* 731.

Most rich countries can be termed "laboristic" economies. By this is meant not only that the proportion of self-employed is lower in rich than in poor countries but that labor now expresses itself as a powerful force in the economy through the trade union movement. Both business and labor are "big." Indeed, perhaps as Galbraith suggests, "The economic power that the worker faced in the sale of his labor—the competition of many sellers dealing with few buyers—made it necessary that he organize for his own protection."[113]

By 1955, total union membership in the United States was 17.7 million, or 27 per cent of the civilian labor force.[114] In Great Britain, about 40 per cent of the working population were union members in 1952. Although these percentages are impressive in themselves, they underestimate the importance of unions in the industrial sector. Like "big" business, unionism is considerably more extensive in the manufacturing and public utility fields than in agriculture, retail and wholesale trade, and clerical and professional occupations. Industries in the United States in which at least 80 per cent of the wage earners were under union agreements in 1946 included agricultural equipment, aircraft and parts, automobiles and parts, clothing, electrical machinery, steel (basic), non-ferrous metals, railroads, trucking, meat packing, and electrical machinery. In Britain, the extent of union organization in selected industries was as follows in 1947: coal, 79 per cent; transport and shipping, 84 per cent; cotton, 61 per cent; wool, 59 per cent; metals and engineering, 52 per cent; and civil service, 57 per cent.[115] The figures were even higher in the Scandinavian countries. The degree of trade union organization in manufacturing, building, and transportation in 1950 was about 95 per cent in Sweden and 90 per cent in Denmark and Norway.[116]

A high degree of concentration among labor unions also exists. Fifteen of the 200 national and international unions in the United States, for example, accounted for about one-half of the total union membership in 1950,[117] and in Denmark 3 of the 72 national unions accounted for 53 per cent of the union membership in 1949.[118]

[113] J. K. Galbraith, *American Capitalism*, Houghton Mifflin Co., Boston, 1952, 121–122.

[114] U. S. Department of Labor, Bureau of Labor Statistics, *Bulletin No. 1185*, "Directory of National and International Labor Unions in the United States, 1955," U. S. Government Printing Office, Washington, 1955, 9.

[115] W. Galenson (ed.), *Comparative Labor Movements*, Prentice-Hall, New York, 1952, Table 2, 28.

[116] *Ibid.*, 119.

[117] Woytinsky and Associates, *op. cit.*, computed from Table 54, 643–646.

[118] Galenson (ed.), *op. cit.*, 122.

10. Technology

In some ways the most important characteristic of rich countries is that unlike poor economies they are technologically dynamic. The great technological discoveries that ushered in the Industrial Revolution together with those that propelled the increase in per capita income levels throughout the nineteenth century were discussed in some detail in Part 2. Rapid technological progress continued in the twentieth century. As the nineteenth century was the century of coal and the steam engine, the first half of the twentieth century was characterized by electrification, applications of the internal-combustion engine, and the development of industrial chemicals. The next 50 years are likely to be dominated by the century's most revolutionary accomplishment— the discovery of nuclear energy.

Electric-generating capacity in the United States increased from less than 1 million kilowatts to over 63 million kilowatts during the first half of the twentieth century.[119] This expansion of an easily controlled form of energy resulted in a shift to electricity as the main source of energy for power equipment in industry. Whereas less than 5 per cent of the horsepower for all power equipment in American manufacturing was supplied by electric motors in 1899, more than 80 per cent was furnished by electric motors in 1950.[120] In the last 50 years the electric furnace was greatly improved and used extensively in the production of steel, ferroalloys, aluminum, and a variety of metal compounds. Electricity for lighting purposes, refrigeration, and air conditioning also spread rapidly in this century. Moreover, the great advances in radio, television, ultrasonics, electric computers, and other automatic instruments and controls were associated with the utilization of electric energy.

Advances based on the use of the internal-combustion engine were equally dramatic in this century. The development of the gasoline, Diesel, and turbojet engines revolutionized transportation techniques. Not only did motor vehicles and aircraft become a major form of transportation but even the railroads abandoned the steam engine in favor of the Diesel engine. The use of internal-combustion engines to operate tractors and other specialized agricultural machinery, to provide the motive power for the heavy work in road building and construction, and to supply the energy for portable tools were other important applications of the internal-combustion engine in this century.

Chemistry was yet another field of tremendous progress in the first half of this century. Plastics, synthetic fibers, synthetic rubber, artificial

[119] Dewhurst, *op. cit.,* 857.
[120] *Ibid.,* 857.

dyestuffs, synthetic soil conditioners, and insecticides were just a few of the new materials from chemistry.   New and improved ways of utilizing metals were other signs of substantial technological progress.

The above list of improvements, however, represents only a few examples of progress in this century.   Better managerial techniques, new distribution methods, new medical products, improved mechanical methods, etc., were also introduced.   With the discovery of nuclear power the next 50 years seem likely to be ones of even greater progress as its applications spread throughout the economy.

Another highly significant development in the field of technology has been the growth of organized research activities.   In 1952 total outlays on scientific and industrial research in the United States were $3 billion —$1.2 billion by industry, $1.6 billion by government (mainly the Defense Department and the Atomic Energy Commission), and $.2 billion by universities and foundations.[121]   By 1954, research outlays climbed to $5 billion.   This compared with only about one-half billion dollars spent in 1938.[122]   Industrial research and technological progress have thus become increasingly important in the rich countries.

[121] The President's Materials Policy Commission, *op. cit.,* I, 141.
[122] *New York Times,* January 22, 1956, section 3, F-1.

Chapter 24

General Requirements
for Maintaining Development

From the previous chapters' discussion of the general characteristics of rich countries and from an analytical knowledge of the development process, it is possible to suggest a number of broad economic requirements for the maintenance of economic development. These will be discussed under four general headings: (1) technological progress and capital accumulation; (2) natural resources; (3) population; and (4) resource flexibility.

1. Technological Progress and Capital Accumulation

In rich countries, the capital stock is increasing at a faster rate than the population. This growing quantity of capital per person is highly important in contributing to a rising per capita income. Such a state of affairs means, however, that diminishing returns to capital tend to develop unless technological progress occurs at a sufficiently rapid rate.[1] And diminishing returns to capital, of course, tend to retard the process of capital accumulation.

---

[1] An increase in natural resources is regarded as reflecting an improvement in technology.

Just how rapidly the rate of accumulation would decline in modern industrial countries if technological progress and population growth ceased is debatable. In view of the relatively high uncertainty premium of investors and the price rigidities in advanced market economies, the neo-classical description of a gradual and smooth movement to a stationary state seems overly optimistic. It appears more likely that any persistent tendency towards diminishing returns would precipitate a complete cessation of net investment within a considerably shorter period than neo-classical economists visualize. In addition, a slackening of investment may well cause serious unemployment problems. Although population growth in itself tends to offset diminishing returns to capital, in most advanced industrial countries population growth seems likely to stimulate at best only enough investment to prevent per capita income from falling. These matters cannot be firmly established one way or the other, however. But, if it is true that the rate of net investment falls abruptly in the absence of technological progress, then, in order to prevent the upward trend in per capita income from stopping within a relatively short time and to avoid serious unemployment difficulties, continued technological progress is required.

To conclude, however, that technological progress must be sufficiently rapid to avoid any persistent tendency towards diminishing returns does not imply that to achieve a reasonably smooth rate of development technological progress must be so rapid and steady as to satisfy the rigorous requirements of the Harrod-Domar growth model. There is no flexibility in this model. As Fellner notes, in the Harrod-Domar analysis "the implied constancy of relative [factor] shares, and the implied constancy of the interest-plus-profit rate needed for growth, leads to constructing a model in which *growth can continue only with a constant (not rising) capital requirement per unit of output-increment.* . . . In the Harrod-Domar model the offsets to diminishing returns must hold the output-increment per unit of new investment *constant* when the total amount of new investment is of the size needed to match savings. This is their condition of smooth growth."[2]

The neo-classical model of capital accumulation, on the other hand, assumes there is a sufficient degree of flexibility to produce uninterrupted growth under conditions of full employment without continuous technological progress.[3] The interest rate and the wage rates respond in

---

[2] W. J. Fellner, *Trends and Cycles in Economic Activity,* Henry Holt and Co., New York, 1956, 144.

[3] Given, of course, an interest rate high enough to induce net saving.

such a way that the capital-output and saving-income ratios which are required in the Harrod-Domar model for full employment growth are always achieved.

A position somewhere between the Harrod-Domar and the neo-classical views seems more realistic. The model of the former type appears more useful in short-run analyses. The further the time horizon extends, however, the better it seems to regard the Harrod-Domar constants as values that can adjust within limits and thereby produce a reasonably smooth rate of growth of national income. Yet these limits probably are not as wide as neo-classical economists believe possible. Hence, it appears likely that a fairly rapid rate of technological progress is necessary to maintain continued and reasonably smooth economic development.

Are there any characteristics of rich countries that suggest that technological progress may be either more or less rapid in the future than in recent times? Schumpeter's remark that, "Technological progress is increasingly becoming the business of teams of trained specialists who turn out what is required and make it work in predictable ways," expresses one view on this question.[4] Those holding this position reason as follows. In an environment of many small, highly competitive business units the progress of technology is highly uncertain. Individual firms usually cannot finance the large, highly trained staff necessary for balanced and varied research programs. Without monopolistic protection in the market place, moreover, a small firm is not able to reap extra profits for a sufficiently long period to cover the risks and costs of research activities.

Big businesses, on the other hand, can provide the basis of rapid technological progress through systematic research within their profit-and-loss framework.[5] Research expenditures can be treated as a normal and continuing phase of business activity. Although any one project may not produce a profitable invention, experimental activities as a whole can be conducted on a sufficiently large scale to predict an over-all rate of return on these endeavors.

Others suggest, however, that widespread monopolistic power in rich countries acts as an obstacle rather than an aid to technological progress and growth. This has already been discussed in Chapter 5. Not only

[4] Schumpeter, *Capitalism, Socialism, and Democracy,* second edition, Harper and Brothers, New York, 1947, 132.

[5] For a general survey of the possible effects of monopolistic powers on progress, see P. Hennipman, "Monopoly: Impediment or Stimulus to Economic Progress?" in E. H. Chamberlin (ed.), *Monopoly and Competition and Their Regulation,* Macmillan and Co., Ltd., London, 1954, 421–456.

does the existence of excess capacity in oligopolistic industries tend to restrain investment but it also tends to misallocate investment by forcing personal savings into relatively less productive channels.

The decline in population growth is another factor that some writers contend affects technological progress adversely. As noted in Chapter 5, some argue that a rapid growth in population creates expanding markets and thereby encourages experiment and research. In contrast, others maintain that such an outcome is far from necessary or inevitable. The rising proportion of college graduates in the population of advanced countries and the improving levels of education generally are other developments that frequently are stressed as improving the prospects for technological progress.

Well-organized labor unions in the advanced countries also may affect the rate of technological progress either adversely or favorably.[6] Union wage pressure stimulates management to seek new low-cost production techniques in order to maintain profits. On the other hand, the resistance of unions to labor-saving devices discourages improvement efforts.

Finally, the economic effects of a big-business environment and of growing governmental activity are relevant to a discussion of technological progress. These factors, however, will be considered later in the chapter.

Although there seems to be a greater degree of flexibility in rich economies than the Harrod-Domar growth model postulates, there are some qualitative aspects of technological progress that are required of the improvement process for satisfactory development.[7] "It is not enough to state that improvements must be sufficiently plentiful. Within reasonable limits, the character of improvements must adjust to the resource scarcities in the system."[8]

Suppose inventions raise the marginal productivity of capital significantly compared to the marginal productivity of the existing labor force, i.e., inventions are highly labor-saving. Under these conditions, the capital stock may not grow at a sufficiently rapid rate in relation to the labor force to prevent wage rates from falling. And, if wage rates are rigid, unemployment may arise. There may not be enough capital, in other words, to employ the labor force at the rigid wage level. This, it will be remembered, is the kind of unemployment Ricardo and Marx discuss. Since development under conditions of falling wage rates or rising unemployment usually is considered unsatisfactory in modern,

[6] G. F. Bloom, "Wage Pressure and Technological Discovery," *American Economic Review, XLI*, No. 4, 603–617 (Sept. 1951).

[7] The following is based on Fellner, *op. cit.*, Chapter 8, sections 5–6.

[8] *Ibid.*, 209.

rich economies, one requirement of the nature of the improvement process is that inventions must not be too labor-saving.

Consider next the case where improvements significantly raise the marginal productivities of the existing labor force and natural resource supply in relation to the marginal productivity of the prevailing capital stock, i.e., inventions are highly capital-saving. These circumstances mean that the demand for labor and natural resources increases considerably compared to the demand for capital. Consequently, if more capital is accumulated and the supplies of the other factors do not rise, the return on capital may fall. This tends to slow down the rate of accumulation. Furthermore, unemployment of the Keynesian variety may arise because of an insufficiency of investment in relation to full employment saving. Another requirement of satisfactory development, therefore, is that improvements must not be too capital-saving.

Whether these qualitative requirements for the improvement process present any very real problem for rich countries is questionable. Labor groups have expressed fears that a widespread and rapid trend toward automation will create severe hardships for particular labor groups and perhaps even generate general technological unemployment or lower wage rates.[9] Whether improvements in automatic technology will be too labor-saving cannot be forecast at this stage. But this outcome appears unlikely. Automation has not taken place thus far with any alarming rapidity. Fairly steady growth seems in prospect, but no economy-wide revolution.[10] If this proves true, the outlook seems favorable for the major income groups, especially in view of business's high marginal propensity to save out of profits.

Fellner asserts that the improvement mechanism in the United States actually is not sufficiently labor-saving.[11] He concludes, somewhat tentatively, that a slight increase in labor's relative share of national income has been associated with a mild long-run decline in rates of return to investors. These trends are not too disturbing, however. "By and large, the improvement mechanism has tended to adjust to requirements in the long run."[12] The reason, he suggests, is that there is a market mechanism for inducing the required types of improvements. In imperfectly competitive factor markets, firms are likely to take current relative factor

[9] Modern innovations in automatic technology can be grouped into four types: (a) automatic machinery; (b) integrated materials handling and processing equipment; (c) automatic control systems; and (d) electronic computers and data-processing machines. See E. Weinberg, "A Review of Automatic Technology," *Monthly Labor Review, 78,* No. 6, 638 (June 1955).

[10] *Ibid.,* 643.

[11] Fellner, *op. cit.,* 217.

[12] *Ibid.,* 218.

scarcities (as reflected by their prices) directly into account in their schedule of improvements. Similarly, previous factor-price experience is likely to condition atomistic factor buyers towards seeking the right kinds of improvements.

So far very little has been said about the saving requirement for continued growth. Obviously technological progress is of limited use (except in so far as output can be increased with a given capital stock) unless the economy is willing to save in a net sense. Rapid development requires a high propensity to save. Just how high this must be depends upon what is regarded as a satisfactory development rate in relation to the rate and character of technological progress and the increase in the size and efficiency of the labor force.

As previously mentioned, some evidence suggests a lower saving-income ratio in some rich countries now than several decades ago. No clear-cut trend is discernible, however. But if investment opportunities decline significantly, the long-run saving ratio is likely to fall, especially since internal business savings seem to be geared largely to investment prospects. The assumption of a constant saving-income ratio which is completely independent of investment opportunities appears inappropriate for long-run analysis.

Aside from the question of technological possibilities, it is usually suggested that the aging of the population, the trend towards urbanization, and the increasing efforts by governments to equalize the distribution of personal income may lower the saving-income ratio in the long run.[13] In contrast, such factors as the increasing importance of organized saving institutions and the rising ratio of the labor force to the population may raise the saving-income ratio in the future. The influence and relative importance of these various factors, however, still are not understood completely.

Even if the saving ratio declines somewhat in the rich countries, this need not reduce current rates of development. For, as was pointed out, evidence for the United States suggests a downward trend in the capital coefficients of both manufacturing and agriculture. In other words, the output increment per unit of new capital formation appears to be higher now than in earlier periods.

2. Natural Resources

Every few years the cry goes up that a growing scarcity of natural resources threatens to halt development. As Osborn contends, "This

[13] For a study of the relation between saving and some of these factors, see R. W. Goldsmith, D. S. Brady, and H. Mendershausen, *A Study of Saving in the United States,* III, Princeton University Press, Princeton, 1956, Chapters 3 and 4.

is that other, silent world-wide 'war.' Its spawn are armed conflicts such as World Wars I and II. Its eventual results, if present ways remain uncorrected, point to widespread misery such as human beings have not yet experienced, and threaten, at the end, even man's very survival."[14] Opposing this pessimistic position is Mather's view: "There is no prospect of the imminent exhaustion of any of the truly essential raw materials, as far as the world as a whole is concerned. Mother Earth's storehouse is far more richly stocked with goods than is ordinarily inferred."[15] No economist dismisses the natural resource problem as trivial. Continued development clearly requires an adequate supply of natural resources. Few economists, nevertheless, regard the problem as an almost insuperable obstacle to continued growth.

As the discussion of natural resources in Chapters 14 and 23 indicates, the problem is twofold: more complete utilization of existing technological knowledge and continued discovery of new technology. If progress in these directions continues, then development should not be stifled by natural resource shortages in the foreseeable future. Nevertheless, there is the question of how well these requirements for adequate natural resource supplies actually will be met. It is frequently suggested that rich countries that rely extensively upon foreign supplies of food and raw materials must expect a gradual long-run deterioration in their terms of trade.

3. Population

As Chapter 13 points out, many of the poor areas contend with the problem of such a rapid increase in population accompanying their efforts to accelerate development that per capita income actually falls below the previously existing low levels. In general, this is a much less serious matter for nations near the top of the per capita income scale. The maintenance of prevailing rates of national income growth seems unlikely by itself to cause excessive rates of population growth.

Indeed, insufficient population growth may exist in some of the sparsely populated rich countries (e.g., Australia and New Zealand). If such economies are in the range of increasing returns to labor and capital, then a higher rate of population increase facilitates rapid development by enabling these countries to take greater advantage of the economies of large-scale production. On the other hand, a slackening of domestic population growth or more restrictive immigration policies conceivably could lessen their rate of per capita income growth.

[14] F. Osborn, *Our Plundered Planet,* Grosset and Dunlap, New York, 1948, ix.
[15] K. F. Mather, *Enough and to Spare,* Harper and Brothers, New York, 1944, 29.

In other rich countries, however, population growth under conditions of full employment may tend to depress per capita income. These economies may be in the range of diminishing returns to capital and labor. Consequently, a decline in population growth releases resources for use in supplying the labor force with a larger per capita quantity of materials and equipment. In this connection, the problem of obtaining the natural resources required by an ever-expanding population is especially stressed. Some writers assert that a growing population in countries that rely extensively upon foreign sources for food and raw materials tends to increase the degree of dependence on international trade.[16] They fear that this development increases the likelihood of a long-run deterioration in the trading terms of these countries.

Aside from the above points, the rate of population growth is pertinent to the full employment problem. A growing population creates heavy demands for investment goods in the form of dwellings, public overhead capital, etc. Since a sizable part of the labor force produces these commodities, unemployment may result from a reduction in the rate of population increase. This, of course, is what the stagnationists claim occurred in the 1930's. As previously mentioned, however, others contend that adequate alternative investment outlets exist to compensate easily for any gradual decline in population growth.

It would be idle to speculate on just what rate of population growth is most desirable for the maintenance of satisfactory development rates. Conditions vary widely from one country to another as well as from one period to another. Yet it seems reasonable to suggest that a positive rate of population growth is desirable in most rich countries. The alleged advantages of some population growth, i.e., the stimulation of investment and technological progress, the encouragement of large-scale production, the increase in the degree of flexibility in the economy, etc., appear to outweigh the major alleged disadvantage, i.e., the larger resources needed to maintain a given standard of living. Even if this conclusion is accepted, however, there is still the question whether this rate should be high or low. On this matter, no generalization seems possible for the rich countries.

Although "the will to progress," "the spirit of capitalism," etc., are elusive phrases to interpret or define, most economists agree that the drives and goals reflected in these terms have played a vital role in the economic success of the progressive economies. Consequently, the maintenance of growth-oriented attitudes within the population is essential for continued economic development.

[16] Royal Commission on Population, *Report*, Cmd. 7695, H.M.S.O., London, 1949, 108.

Business management is the primary sector to which economists direct their attention in discussing these attitudes. If the rich economies are to continue their long-run rates of development, those who direct production must be aggressive in their managerial capacities. They must seek out innovational possibilities and assume the risks associated with them. In short, what Schumpeter terms "entrepreneurial spirit" is necessary for maintaining a high rate of development.

Some economists question whether the big-business environment, which now is so important in the typical advanced economy, is capable of producing the requisite type of aggressive leadership over the long run.[17] The bureaucratic nature of large-scale organization, it is suggested, may breed inefficient and unimaginative management which stresses conformity and the security of tenure. Sluggish action and inflexibility, which may be the by-products of bureaucratic big business, also impede rapid growth.

Quite apart from the drawbacks of mere size, observers also point to the impact of the separation of ownership and control upon business leadership qualities. In companies where ownership is so diffused that management can easily perpetuate itself in power, the management may become overly cautious about promoting technological progress. Since they do not share directly in profits of the company and are likely to lose their control only if the company's profit performance is extremely poor, business leaders may hesitate to exploit new lines of investment activity. They may adopt a "play it safe" attitude. In addition, professional business leaders, driven by power and prestige motives, may pursue activities inconsistent with the goal of an efficient allocation of resources.

The growing influence of the government upon the private sector is another factor frequently stressed as a possibly serious obstacle to entrepreneurship. The steeply progressive income tax structure in many rich countries, in particular, is viewed with alarm by some. Such a tax, it is argued, weakens the incentive to work and to assume risks. Thus there may be a danger that governmental efforts to redistribute income more equitably and to provide social and economic security seriously weaken the risk-taking attitudes so essential to continued economic progress. As Wright states, the epitaph of our civilization may be:

From freedom and science came rapid growth and change.
From rapid growth and change came insecurity.

[17] For example, David E. Lilienthal, *Big Business: A New Era,* Harper and Brothers, New York, 1952, and Gordon, *Business Leadership in the Large Corporation,* The Brookings Institution, Washington, 1945, 326–340.

From insecurity came demands which ended growth and change. Ending growth and change ended science and freedom.[18]

There are, however, arguments that suggest that entrepreneurial capacity is increasing rather than declining in rich countries. The existence of large business units permits a much greater degree of managerial specialization than is possible in a small firm. Large staffs of highly trained individuals, who are experts on some particular aspect of the management process, enable large-scale business units to discover and undertake profit possibilities that would escape the notice of smaller firms. The large unit, moreover, can undertake a much more careful and extensive training program for developing new management talent.

Instead of hampering entrepreneurship, the growing activities of the government, particularly in the field of countercyclical fiscal policy, may encourage businessmen to undertake more aggressive development policies. Without governmental intervention, a high degree of cyclical economic instability is likely. This, in turn, increases the risks of expansion. With modern governments pledged to maintain high employment levels, however, businessmen need not fear disastrous decreases in the demand for their products and, therefore, can plan with more confidence. As a result, they are likely to expand their productive facilities more rapidly than in the absence of a vigorous countercyclical policy on the part of the government.

This stability argument is often used by big business itself. The operation of a purely competitive industrial structure may create so much uncertainty that businessmen are reluctant to undertake new ventures. "A dose of monopoly has, according to some, a balancing, steadying effect, permitting the economy to progress less erratically, more steadily, and, as a net result, faster than under unlimited competition. If a mechanical analogy may be used, monopolistic devices may act as shock absorbers without which investors would not dare to travel the rough and bumpy roads to higher levels of national production."[19]

The managerial group is not the only sector in the economy where attitudes conducive to continued development are necessary. A desire for varied consumption goods, a demand for change even for its own sake, a willingness to take risks, a readiness to work in order to achieve higher living standards, and a desire to become better trained are the kinds of growth-oriented attitudes needed on the part of all the major economic groups in order to maintain development.

[18] D. M. Wright, *Democracy and Progress,* The Macmillan Co., New York, 1948, 81.

[19] Fritz Machlup, "Monopoly and the Problem of Economic Stability," in E. H. Chamberlin (ed.), *op. cit.,* 395.

In addition to the maintenance of general attitudes favorable to continued development, rich countries must preserve and improve their already high standards of labor efficiency. The tremendous difference in labor efficiency between rich and poor countries is by no means merely a matter of different attitudes towards economic achievement. Larger and more balanced diets, better medical service, and higher levels of education and skill explain much of the greater efficiency in the progressive economies.

As noted in the preceding chapter, technological progress and shifts in demand as per capita income rises require a better educated and trained labor force. If the advanced countries are to realize their full development potential, they must plan for education facilities to meet this requirement. Fortunately, the outlook for improving the general level of education as well as the standards of health appears to be favorable. Both private groups and governments recognize the importance of these factors and are devoting increasing efforts to raise labor efficiency through enlarged educational and health programs.

There is some concern, however, about the effects on labor efficiency of the aging of the population in rich countries. The decline in the proportion of young workers, who probably are superior in strength, energy, adaptability, and speed, may reduce the efficiency of the labor force. This may be compensated, on the other hand, by the greater dependability, skill, and wisdom that come with old age. More important than these effects, however, is the likelihood that this aging will reduce the efficiency of the population by eventually reducing the ratio of the labor force to the total population.

Some economists also are concerned over the effects of the growing labor union movement on labor efficiency. They fear that union emphasis on seniority and security schemes may weaken worker efficiency. Others argue, in contrast, that unions give workers a greater sense of participation in economic decisions and thereby improve morale and efficiency. A similar two-sided argument is often made concerning the impact of government fiscal policy. Some claim that the highly progressive income taxes in rich countries weaken incentive not only within the managerial group but within the labor force in general. Others maintain that this effect is more than offset by the higher levels of health, education, and social security that government expenditures provide.

4. Resource Flexibility

Economic development is not just a problem of increasing the capital stock, the size and quality of the population, the supply of natural resources, and the level of technological knowledge. It is also the problem of utilizing existing resources in an efficient manner. A particular structure of production which yields a high per capita income cannot be developed and then merely proportionately enlarged. Development is a dynamic process of adaptation. Changing demands and technological progress frequently involve replacing old capital equipment by completely different types of equipment, increasing the capital stock in one sector and decreasing it in another, retraining the labor force, shifting labor from one industry to another, etc.

Svennilson emphasizes this requirement when he concludes that the low rate of development in European countries during the interwar period "is to a large extent explained by the formidable transformation problem which they had to face after the first World War, and by the slowness with which the necessary adjustment took place. If this interpretation is correct, the interwar period can be regarded as a prolonged transformation crisis for the European economy."[20] The interdependent nature of production in modern industrial economies makes resource flexibility especially essential for development. The inability of one sector to adapt to changing conditions may act as an important deterrent to development by impeding growth in other dependent sectors.

As has been repeatedly stressed, the problems of increasing resource supplies and of utilizing them in an efficient manner are closely related. An inefficient use of existing resources serves not only to keep national income below its potential level but also to retard the growth of the productive factors. Growing resource supplies, on the other hand, can improve the degree of flexibility within the economy and thus facilitate a more efficient utilization of these resources.

An expanding population, for example, may ease the problem of adjustment to changing demands and new technological conditions. Workers already well established in a declining industry find it difficult to move into other industries and occupations, especially if employment opportunities do not exist nearby. With a growing population, however, the demand for the products of this industry may remain sufficiently high so that only a relative rather than an absolute decline in the industry is required. Furthermore, since young workers entering the labor force are more mobile geographically and occupationally, a growing supply of such workers enables an expanding industry to take advantage more easily of its economic opportunities.

Capital accumulation likewise increases an economy's ability to undertake new opportunities. Since capital equipment wears out only slowly, the composition of a given capital stock cannot be changed quickly. An

[20] Svennilson, *Growth and Stagnation in the European Economy*, United Nations, Geneva, 1954, 44.

expanding economy which is accumulating capital can exploit higher-yielding investment opportunities more rapidly.

Quite apart from the effects of growing resource supplies, a number of institutional arrangements influence the flexibility of an economy during the development process. One of the most important is the nature of market structures. Classical and neo-classical writers from Smith to Marshall praise the purely competitive market as a unique social institution where everyone is, in a sense, free and yet under the strict discipline of market forces. Although sellers can legally choose any price and output they wish, there is only one price-output relation in the long run at which they can avoid bankruptcy. The rewards (profits) and the punishments (losses) are determined by impersonal and spontaneous market forces rather than by bureaucratic or political judgments. This market arrangement, consequently, is highly responsive to resource shifts under the impact of changing technological and demand conditions.

Some writers contend that the flexibility requirement for successful development is imperiled by the high degree of concentration in the industrial sectors of the rich countries. Monopolistic tendencies may hamper the reallocation of existing resources just as they may adversely affect net investment and entrepreneurship. An oligopolistic industry faced with a declining demand for its products is likely to release its supply of resources for alternative employments only very slowly. High profit margins protect the weak and inefficient firms. Growing signs of overcapacity also may lead to intra-industry agreements regarding market sharing and price maintenance rather than to a prompt movement of resources out of the industry. Absence of the ruthless rules of pure competition, in other words, enables excess capacity to exist for prolonged periods. The difficulties of entry, characteristic of oligopolistic industries, likewise may prevent a rapid flow of resources into an industry possessing expansion opportunities. And those already established in the field may proceed cautiously to avoid upsetting the existing pattern of investment returns.

Another institutional factor that may diminish flexibility in industrial countries is the growth of well-organized labor unions with monopolistic power. By changing the nature of the labor supply curve, individual unions can impair the free flow of labor among industries that would otherwise take place in a purely competitive market. For example, unions may prevent falling wage rates in declining industries. They thereby slow down the rate of resource adaptation by retarding the flow of labor into expanding industries.

A flexible money supply is also required for the maintenance of rapid development. In view of existing price rigidities in rich economies, it is highly improbable that the rate of development can be as rapid with a fixed money supply as with an expanding supply. The difficulty of lowering prices as output expands is likely to be associated with unemployment and consequently a general decline in the development rate. Falling prices, moreover, may generate adverse investment expectations. As a permissive condition for rapid development, therefore, the monetary system must be organized in such a manner as to permit the monetary authorities to expand the money supply.

On the other hand, monetary arrangements that permit rapid, long-run inflation should be avoided. As was stressed in the discussion of the poor countries, there are serious disadvantages in inflation. Consequently, monetary authorities should be able and willing to take appropriate steps to counter any strong long-run inflationary pressures.

One issue frequently raised in connection with the relation between price level changes and development is the alleged tendency of labor unions to initiate a long-run wage-price spiral.[21] The argument runs as follows. Union leaders under the competitive pressure of rival leaders and the general membership are forced to press year after year for substantial money wage increases. To the extent that productivity gains are exceeded, the wage increases give rise to compensating price increases, since big business easily passes the higher costs on to consumers. The outcome is a rising price level which penalizes the recipients of relatively fixed incomes, creditors, many small businessmen, and even some groups within the ranks of labor. This, in turn, tends to cause a malallocation of investment.

Others contend that inflationary pressure from unions is not to be feared as much as inflationary measures taken by governmental and monetary authorities to implement the full employment goal.[22] Rather than risk recessions modern governments may initiate extensive demand-generating programs which later prove to be irreversible and, therefore, contribute towards long-run inflation. An opposing argument is that some long-run inflation is beneficial to economic development. It keeps expectations buoyant and shifts income from the passive saver and rentier elements to the active, risk-taking groups. In general, however, economists assert that an approximately stable price level is most favorable for continued development.

Rapid development also requires mobility of investible funds. Al-

[21] For a discussion of this price problem, see J. M. Clark, "Criteria of Sound Wage Adjustment, with Emphasis on the Question of Inflationary Effects," in D. M. Wright (ed.), *The Impact of the Union*, Harcourt, Brace and Co., 1951, 1–33.

[22] M. Friedman, "Some Comments on the Significance of Labor Unions for Economic Policy," *ibid.*, 229–231.

though this problem is by no means as serious in rich as in poor countries, there is still room for considerable improvement. Compared to the well-known large firms, small business enterprises encounter difficulty in raising funds for expansion purposes in capital markets. Both bank and non-bank lenders are reluctant to provide funds to firms with weak profit and asset positions. Since they find exhaustive investigations concerning the potential profitability of a proposed investment program too expensive, lenders determine their willingness to lend on the basis of simple rules of thumb, such as the ratio of debt to equity and previous performance. This capital-rationing system hampers borrowing by small firms and forces them to finance expansion programs with internal funds. Funds channeled through capital markets, consequently, may not flow towards the highest-yielding investment projects. Restrictions on the types of economic activity that lending institutions can finance and different tax levies on the earnings from various types of financial investment are additional obstacles to the efficient allocation of investment funds available through capital markets.

Financing expansion programs from internal sources of funds is also a widely followed practice by large business units. Because of inadequate knowledge of profit possibilities in other industries and a reluctance to undertake completely different activities, firms that normally retain a significant share of their earnings may not direct these investible funds towards the highest-yielding investment opportunities in the economy. In part, of course, this is offset by raising funds in capital markets and by a growing willingness to enter new production lines. There are, however, probably many cases of reinvesting earnings in relatively declining firms instead of directing these funds towards higher-yielding projects in expanding enterprises.

Just as monopolistic power in domestic market structures hampers resource mobility, national barriers to international trade may thwart the process of resource adaptation. As was pointed out in Chapters 12 and 23, the composition and pattern of world trade have undergone considerable change. Similar shifts probably will occur in the future.

To counteract declines in demand associated with these shifts, it is tempting for a country to impose protective measures. Such action tends to shift part of the adjustment burden onto other countries. But, when all countries follow this procedure, the collective effect can seriously depress the potential rate of development. Protected industries retain resources needed to achieve the full growth potentials of other expanding lines of production. The longer this policy is followed, the more serious the consequences are likely to be. If the older industrial countries block the resource adjustments indicated by changes in international demand, new and rising industrial powers may capture a larger and larger share of their foreign markets.

The adjustment problem may then implicate the whole economy, not just a relatively small part, as chronic balance of payments difficulties develop. At this stage, the required adjustments can be extremely painful. Thus, an apparently sensible short-run policy may merely aggravate the long-run problem. The misallocation of resources not only reduces the rate of development but also weakens the capacity for further growth.[23]

Therefore, a system of international trade that minimizes the barriers to the free flow of commodities must be endorsed by the rich countries. Certainly, as in the poor countries, there are grounds for arguing that some attempts must be made to mitigate the domestic effects of rapid shifts in international demand. Such measures, however, must not seriously hamper the long-run mobility of resources. Otherwise the older industrialized countries may find the general upward movement of world incomes has left them behind.

International movements of labor and capital are equally important for maintaining development. Referring to Europe in the interwar period, Svennilson observes, ". . . the effects of the structural changes of international trade on national growth could have been alleviated by international capital movements. It would then have been easier to utilize national resources, including labour, fully and effectively by expanding in a process of long-term growth the respective national economies. Alternatively, labour could have moved to countries where conditions for expansion were more favorable. The conditions for European expansion could in this way have approached those of a more completely integrated national unit like the United States."[24]

An expanded flow of capital to poor countries is especially important for continued development in the rich economies. In particular, since industrialized countries are importing an increasing quantity and variety of raw materials, they should give increased attention to the development of natural resource potentials in the poor countries. Sufficient investment funds and trained labor to exploit these potentials should be made available. But, much more than this, the expansion in world markets accompanying successful development in the poor countries can act as a powerful stimulator of development in the rich nations.

[23] Kindleberger, *The Terms of Trade,* John Wiley & Sons, New York, 1956, 311–312, stresses the need for flexibility in industrial Europe if this area is to cope adequately with long-run changes in its international economic position.

[24] Svennilson, *op. cit.,* 42.

Chapter 25

Policies and Prospects

for Maintaining Development

Although widespread agreement exists with respect to the general requirements for maintaining development in the rich countries, opinions differ widely about the relative importance of the various requirements and the ability to meet these requirements. There is, consequently, a wide range of views concerning the proper economic policies for implementing development. The first section of this chapter describes the prominent policy positions advocated for promoting development and contrasts the arguments used to support them. The following section then discusses estimates of development prospects over the next few decades, using the United States and the United Kingdom as examples. The final section considers the institutionalization of the development process in the rich economies.

1. Policy Approaches for Maintaining Development

Among the diverse policy proposals for achieving satisfactory development as well as other desirable economic and non-economic goals, at least five positions stand out as especially relevant at the present time. They range from complete public control over the means of production and production itself to drastic measures designed to restore effective competition in private markets. Most proposals that currently receive serious consideration in the rich countries fall somewhere between these two policy extremes. This section discusses these two positions first and then considers three intermediate policy approaches. The list is not exhaustive in any sense, but merely illustrative of the approaches to development policy frequently advocated.

One extreme approach to the problem of maintaining or accelerating development is socialism.[1] An important alleged advantage of this policy is that it successfully answers the monopoly problem of the modern free enterprise economy. According to socialists, economies of scale are so significant with modern technology that on efficiency grounds alone a relatively small number of large firms inevitably dominate wide areas of manufacturing, mining, and distribution. If, say these writers, monopolistic firms are free from government regulation, they exercise their monopoly power to retard the rate of innovation. A declining rate of development and increased instability ensue. Under non-socialist approaches, society can forestall this outcome by drastic anti-trust policies only at the cost of losing the economies of scale. However, state ownership of business, the socialists claim, enables the economy to exploit the benefits from economies of scale at no risk to the rate of technological innovation.

Since the State determines the rate of investment under socialism, supporters of this policy also argue that the rate of development is more rapid, smoother, and better balanced than under capitalism. Investment can be set by the State at a higher rate than is likely to emerge in a free market economy even under full employment conditions. Because they contend that the factors of production always are fully utilized under socialism, socialists claim that the rate of development is not subject to the sharp declines associated with cyclical depressions under capitalism. This implies a much steadier rate of investment over the long run. They also maintain that technological progress proceeds at a faster pace with governmental encouragement, financing, and control of research activities.

In addition to the higher and smoother rate of investment and innovation, socialists argue that, in a planned economy, development occurs

[1] Economists who have stated the case for socialism in recent years include: M. Dobb, *On Economic Theory and Socialism,* International Publishers, New York, 1955; O. Lange and F. M. Taylor, *On the Economic Theory of Socialism,* The University of Minnesota Press, Minneapolis, 1938; A. P. Lerner, *The Economics of Control,* The Macmillan Co., New York, 1944; and P. Sweezy, *Socialism,* McGraw-Hill Book Co., New York, 1949.

more rapidly because resources are more flexible than in a free enterprise system. Under socialism this greater resource flexibility is achieved by means of either price manipulations by the government or direct controls. But even more important, according to this group, the rate of development is faster because central planning eliminates the distortions and maladjustments that arise in the investment process in the unplanned economy. "One may express the crux of the matter by saying that the quintessential function of planning as an economic mechanism is that it is a means of substituting *ex ante* co-ordination of the constituent elements in a scheme of development . . . for the co-ordination *ex post* which a decentralised pricing-system provides . . . ."[2] Socialists maintain that not only does this planning lessen the degree of uncertainty facing any one producer but also the economy is able to secure the full benefits of the external economies which are so vital in the development process. Planning "will open the door to certain types of development which would not be possible at all (or at least be extremely unlikely) for an unplanned capitalist economy. . . . This fact is attributable to the existence of relations of interdependence between various productive units and sectors of the economic system, which cause cost or productivity at one point to be dependent, not only on the scale of production at that point, but on the scale of production in other production units and in other industries as well."[3] These writers contend, in other words, that an efficient balance among all sectors in the economy is attainable only under socialism.

At the other end of the scale of policy positions is a school of thought that contends that economic progress is furthered best by policy measures that make competition truly effective.[4] Like the socialists, those who hold this view strongly emphasize the retarding effects of monopoly practices on development. But unlike the socialists, who endorse state ownership, the adherents of the "effective competition" position propose measures to establish a high degree of competition among privately owned enterprises. It is not, however, merely more vigorous enforcement of the existing anti-trust laws which they advocate. They desire drastic measures to eliminate private monopoly in all its manifestations.

[2] M. Dobb, *op. cit.*, 76.

[3] M. Dobb, *Soviet Economic Development Since 1917,* Routledge and K. Paul Ltd., London, 1948, 9–10.

[4] Economists who hold this view include: F. A. Hayek, *The Road to Serfdom,* The University of Chicago Press, Chicago, 1944; L. Robbins, *The Economic Problem in Peace and War,* Macmillan and Co., Ltd., London, 1947; and H. C. Simons, *Economic Policy for a Free Society,* The University of Chicago Press, Chicago, 1948.

Large business corporations and trade unions must be broken down;[5] incorporation laws should be changed to prevent such practices as intercorporate stock ownership and directorship; all attempts to restrain trade must be prosecuted unremittingly; the patent laws should be revised to provide for a greater degree of free access to technical knowledge; tariffs should be removed; etc.

This school differs from the socialists in maintaining that technological economies are not the major reason for the prevailing concentration in industry but rather collusive business agreements and government policies which foster monopoly power.[6] Those who hold this position argue, therefore, that the economy would not lose any substantial benefits in the form of economies of scale by dismantling most of big business. Free competition, they contend, is by far the best arrangement to promote rapid development within a framework of political democracy. It provides the only satisfactory basis for the high degree of resource flexibility that is so essential for continued rapid development. They maintain, moreover, that the successful operation of free competition is compatible with an extensive system of social services.

Like almost all writers on the subject of development, this group realizes that reasonably full employment and the avoidance of excessive inflation are essential for rapid progress. Without these conditions, resource rigidity and uncertainty on the part of investors handicap the attainment of a satisfactory rate of growth. According to this school, an environment of effective competition by itself eliminates a large part of the employment and inflation problems, since monopolistic practices are the main causes of these problems. But competition in itself is not entirely sufficient. The government must take positive steps to moderate economic fluctuations. In this regard, one writer proposes radical monetary reforms which would give "the central government complete control over the quantity of effective money and its value."[7] However, others who also strongly favor the competitive approach prefer the use of existing monetary and fiscal weapons to control aggregate employment and the price level.

Countercyclical endeavors do not exhaust the list of activities that this group regards as proper for the government to undertake. Efforts to improve resource mobility by facilitating labor migration through financial assistance and by providing extensive information services to

---

[5] Simons, *op. cit.*, 319, suggests "that in major industries no ownership unit should produce or control more than 5 per cent of the total output."

[6] For a statement of this position, see W. Adams and H. M. Gray, *Monopoly Power in America*, The Macmillan Co., New York, 1955.

[7] Simons, *op. cit.*, 65.

workers and employers concerning economic opportunities are supported. Government research programs to ensure an adequate flow of
new techniques are also proposed. These writers, however, are not
particularly concerned about a lack of technological progress. They
contend that an effectively competitive environment usually yields
sufficient technological progress and innovation to guarantee rapid
development.

They also acknowledge that some activities, which are highly desirable
for development from a social point of view, are not likely to be performed by the private sector. These, they concede, should be undertaken directly by the State or partly subsidized. Moreover, in cases
where economies of scale are significant, mainly the public utility sector,
they urge either rigid government control or outright state ownership.
Writers in this group maintain, however, that these governmental activities need not imply the kind of extensive and detailed state control advocated by the socialists.

Socialism, whether decentralized or centralized, as a method of achieving rapid development is rejected for the following reasons by this group
—as well as most other groups. Decentralized planning of the Lange-
Lerner variety is not likely to prove very efficient, even if serious attempts
to practice it are made.[8] But it is not likely to be practiced—or, at any
rate, for very long. Centralized planning is almost inevitable. Because
of the elaborate bureaucracy necessary for central planning, there are
also serious doubts about the efficiency of this type of socialism. It is
difficult to select the best qualified individuals, to weed out inefficient
personnel, to prevent uneconomic "empire building" on the part of
officials, to maintain adequate incentives and free discussion within this
type of organization, to prevent corruption and political patronage, to
provide for flexibility in the decision-making process, etc. Much more
important than these economic drawbacks, however, are the political
and social dangers to individual freedom under central planning. The
strongest bond that unites all the writers who favor the competitive order
is their strong assertion that central planning is incompatible with
democracy.

Supporters of "dynamic competition," the next policy position to be
considered,[9] are distinguished from the other groups by (1) their greater

[8] For the kinds of criticism on grounds of efficiency which are made concerning
this type of socialism, see M. Friedman's essay "Lerner on the Economics of
Control" in *Essays in Positive Economics,* The University of Chicago Press,
Chicago, 1953, 301–319.

[9] Examples of writings that illustrate this general policy approach are: Committee for Economic Development, Research and Policy Committee, *How to
Raise Real Wages,* Committee for Economic Development, New York, 1950;

willingness to accept elements of "bigness" in the structure of private markets and (2) their stronger emphasis on the possible unfavorable repercussions on development of governmental efforts to redistribute income and stabilize aggregate demand.

Like all groups, those who advocate this approach note the evils of widespread monopoly practices. They reject, however, proposals that entail the wholesale dismantling of big business and big labor. They contend that this cannot be accomplished without sacrificing substantial technical efficiencies in business and necessary bargaining power for labor. "Big" business and "big" labor, they insist, do not necessarily imply general restrictive practices. Moreover, according to these writers, market structures approaching the purely competitive ideal contribute to economic instability, lead to large social wastes, and retard the rate of technological progress. These economists, consequently, favor an anti-trust policy which does not penalize bigness *per se*. Of course, they argue, anti-trust measures which prevent large firms from destroying smaller firms by monopolistic means and from retarding the entry of new units into an industry are necessary, as well as special credit and information aids to small businesses. Obvious cases of restrictive practices in business and labor also are not to be tolerated either in domestic or international markets. These economists, therefore, favor a greater degree of free trade.

Unlike the effective competition economists, who prefer large numbers of producers throughout the various sectors of industry, this group argues that a "big" business and a "big" labor environment is compatible with a high degree of competition. They particularly stress the competition which is associated with the process of innovation. In their view, the stifling effects of oligopolistic markets on technological progress are greatly exaggerated, both by the socialists and by those who represent the effective competition school of thought.

Although the dynamic competition economists minimize the negative effects of "bigness" on the development goal, they are concerned about the adverse repercussions on development of governmental activities designed to redistribute income and stabilize aggregate demand. Not that they disapprove of these goals—rather they question the emphasis on these goals and the methods by which they are achieved. Highly progressive income taxes are regarded as especially detrimental to rapid

Economic Report of the President under the Eisenhower Administration; H. G. Moulton, *Controlling Factors in Economic Development,* The Brookings Institution, Washington, 1949; S. H. Slichter, *The American Economy,* Alfred A. Knopf, New York, 1948; and D. M. Wright, *Democracy and Progress,* The Macmillan Co., New York, 1948.

development by these economists. They argue that such taxes not only seriously weaken the incentives for risk-taking but lower the level of saving in the economy. Reducing the degree of progressivity, they claim, not only accelerates development but, by increasing the tax base, avoids the necessity for raising other tax rates to maintain the volume of tax revenue. Indeed, they assert that in the long run a greater volume of tax revenue can be secured by this method. More liberal tax provisions with respect to capital gains, depreciation policy, and dividends are also advocated. In short, this group contends that the best way to stimulate rapid development is to moderate those provisions of the tax structure that tend to discourage private investment.

The government, however, must take an active part in stabilizing aggregate demand. In this regard, the dynamic competition adherents stress the merits of flexible monetary policy and of automatic stabilizers in the government budget. If these prove inadequate to cope with severe depression or serious inflationary pressures, they prefer to ameliorate these conditions, if possible, by variations in tax rates rather than by large-scale, non-automatic changes in Federal expenditures. Such policies represent to them the best compromise for maintaining economic stability without hampering the development potential of the private sector.

In addition to these countercyclical policies, this school supports governmental activities designed to provide better information for workers and employers concerning economic opportunities and to facilitate the migration and retraining of workers. Moderate government programs to develop natural resources and to provide greater financial aid for the improvement of certain public services, e.g., transportation, are also proposed. A modest program of public investment in the poor countries is another policy that this group accepts. Furthermore, most of the social service programs that are in existence in the United States are supported. What these economists are concerned about is that welfare programs will be extended at the cost of a greater tax burden on those types of income that serve as a financing source and a stimulus for investment. They argue that the best way to obtain the funds necessary for larger welfare programs is to minimize restrictive tax rates and thereby obtain both a more rapid growth of national income and a larger tax base.

Writers favoring "guided capitalism" are somewhat less optimistic than the last two groups about the ability of the private sector to provide the mainsprings of economic progress.[10] Like the dynamic competition

---

[10] Economists whose views are close to this position include: *Economic Report of the President* under the Truman Administration; A. Hansen, *Economic Policy and Full Employment*, McGraw-Hill Book Co., New York, 1947; J. M. Keynes,

supporters, they do not argue that disaggregation of large business and labor units is the major reform necessary to promote rapid economic development. Although they favor a more vigorous anti-trust policy aimed at large-scale firms than the preceding group, the guided capitalism adherents are willing to give more serious consideration to the actual performance of large business and labor units than the effective competition group. Unlike the dynamic competition economists, however, they maintain that the creation of a more favorable climate for private risk-taking and private saving by means of reductions in the progressive income tax is not sufficient to stimulate the high rate of investment required for the simultaneous achievement of full employment and rapid development. These economists fear that long-run, private investment opportunities are not sufficient for the attainment of these goals. They, therefore, place a greater reliance upon government expenditures. Moreover, they are willing to accept a greater degree of progressivity in the tax structure in order to finance expenditure programs than the former group.

The importance of external economies receives more attention from these writers than from those in the last two groups. Substantial government programs to improve transportation facilities, to furnish hydroelectric power, to develop peaceful uses of atomic energy, and to conserve natural resources are deemed proper and necessary for an adequate rate of development. In addition, this group advocates more extensive aid by the government for education, research, and urban redevelopment than presently exists in the United States.

The need for public social security measures is also endorsed more vigorously by these economists than by those in the dynamic competition school. Advocates of the guided capitalism position argue that these measures are not only highly beneficial in themselves but on balance actually stimulate a faster rate of development. Low tariffs and large public investments abroad are also supported as effective methods for stimulating development by expanding export markets. When deflationary tendencies exist, they favor the immediate increase of government expenditures to stimulate employment. Furthermore, under these conditions, this group stresses the need for tax reductions that directly stimulate consumption rather than saving. Above all, according to this group, the best way to secure rapid economic development is for the

---

The General Theory of Employment, Interest and Money, Harcourt, Brace and Company, New York, 1936; United Nations, Report of a Group of Experts (J. M. Clark, A. Smithies, N. Kaldor, P. Uri, E. R. Walker), *National and International Measures for Full Employment,* United Nations, New York, 1949; and S. E. Harris (ed.), *Saving American Capitalism,* Alfred A. Knopf, New York, 1948.

government to ensure a high level of aggregate demand by a substantial long-run program of public expenditures. In such a buoyant economic environment, private enterprise can make its greatest contributions to economic development.

Between complete state planning of almost all economic activities (socialism) and the kind of partial long-run planning involved in the position just outlined, lies the final policy position to be discussed. The essence of "planned capitalism" is that the State's role is sufficiently important to determine the over-all rate and the general direction of development.[11] More specifically, the government prepares national plans establishing the volume and the general composition of consumption, private investment, and public expenditures which it believes are both desirable and attainable. The State then formulates action to implement these objectives. Proponents of this position do not argue that complete public ownership of all production units is necessary. On the contrary, they reject complete state planning on grounds of inefficiency and of its threat to democracy. Instead, they usually propose government ownership of public utilities and basic industries. This policy, they contend, not only solves much of the monopoly problem but also provides a manageable area for efficient planning on a detailed basis.

The rate of development in the private sector is influenced by somewhat less direct methods. Writers who hold this view advocate the use of monetary and fiscal policies to control the volume of saving and consumption in the economy. Such policies, they maintain, can also be employed to influence the channels of investment activity. When necessary, however, the use of direct price and allocation controls in the private sector is recommended. These controls are especially necessary with respect to the location of new industries and international transactions.

The case for extensive planning is based upon the conviction that a predominantly private enterprise system is not capable of achieving a rapid rate of development and, at the same time, attaining what those who hold this position regard as sufficient satisfaction of other economic goals. Since these writers maintain that the case for some expenditure

[11] Writings that illustrate this general viewpoint are: W. Beveridge, *Full Employment in a Free Society,* W. W. Norton and Company, New York, 1945; Sir Oliver Franks, *Central Planning and Control in War and Peace,* Harvard University Press, Cambridge, 1947; C. Landauer, *Theory of National Economic Planning,* University of California Press, Berkeley, 1947; W. A. Lewis, *The Principles of Economic Planning,* Dennis Dobson Ltd., London, (no publishing date); and B. Wootton, *Freedom under Planning,* The University of North Carolina Press, Chapel Hill, 1945.

programs by the State to promote development is obvious, they argue that it is ridiculous not to plan on a general scale. Indeed, they assert that piecemeal planning is not sufficient to offset the strong tendency towards secular stagnation and chronic unemployment.

Planned capitalism economists concede that there are dangers of inefficiency under planning, but they hold that the extensive use of decentralized planning methods and indirect controls can overcome any serious difficulties with regard to this problem. Similarly, in their opinion, planning of this variety is compatible with political freedom. In short, these writers contend that, in the search for methods to secure rapid economic progress, planned capitalism achieves the main advantages and avoids the worst disadvantages of complete planning or free enterprise.

As Chapter 22 indicates, the actual post-war development policies followed by rich countries illustrate most of the above positions. The Soviet Union represents the case of central planning under socialism. France and the United Kingdom, to some degree, illustrate the policy that has been termed planned capitalism. Post-war policy in the United States exemplifies an approach nearer the dynamic competition and the guided capitalism positions. German policies since the war also illustrate certain aspects of these two approaches.

The purpose here is not to attempt to judge the comparative merits or drawbacks of these various policy approaches. Judgments on these policy positions are considerably influenced not only by their implications for the achievement of development as well as other economic objectives but also by their non-economic repercussions. For example, the possible effect of these policies on individual liberty and political democracy must receive serious attention. The relative importance attached to economic goals other than development, and the connections between measures designed to achieve rapid development and these goals, are highly relevant in judging the different policy approaches. Estimates of the prospects for continued development under existing policies also play a large part in evaluating the various policy alternatives.

There are some consistencies, however, among these policy positions regarding the general types of action necessary to maintain development. Almost all the writers emphasize the need for substantial government activity in the field of education and job training. Representatives of every position also urge more government subsidization of pure and applied research than exists in most rich countries. Greater government efforts to increase the mobility of labor by providing more extensive information services and facilitating migration are also approved by practically all economists. As a minimum, the various writers advocate a somewhat more vigorous anti-trust policy for the private sector than is practiced currently in most rich countries. In particular, there is agreement that entry into an industry must not be hampered by restrictive practices on the part of existing firms. More liberal credit facilities for small businesses are also generally proposed.

An expanding volume of international trade as a necessary condition for rapid development is stressed by all these approaches, but the techniques for achieving this prerequisite vary. Economists favoring development policies that rely mainly on private enterprise strongly recommend free trade and the removal of impediments to private capital movements. Those advocating extensive government planning, however, prefer a more conscious manipulation of the foreign sector. The writers also concur on the desirability of some governmental projects in areas where external economies are important. But there is a wide diversity of opinion about the proper scope of these activities. In addition, most economists urge some welfare programs designed to improve the efficiency of the labor force. Finally, the use of monetary and fiscal policies to maintain full employment without unreasonable inflation is accepted by almost all the various writers.

Even though there is agreement among the various writers regarding some aspects of government development policy, nevertheless, this common base does not cover what each group regards as most essential for rapid growth. The effective competition group stresses the necessity for a much greater degree of competition, in the sense of large numbers in each market. Those representing the dynamic competition position maintain that the key to a faster rate of development is lower taxes on business and on the higher-income groups. The guided capitalism position emphasizes substantial government expenditures for creating a favorable economic environment in which private enterprise can flourish. Writers who advocate planned capitalism argue that development is best fostered by selective government ownership of industry and by a firm control over the private economy. Finally, socialist economists contend that only with complete control over all parts of the economy can rapid, smooth, and integrated development take place.

2. Prospects for Maintaining Development

An appraisal of the prospects for development in the rich countries is even more complex than an attempt to evaluate the various policy approaches for promoting growth. A number of writers, however, have made specific estimates of the possibilities for development in the not too distant future.[12]   Needless to say, all of them emphasize the rough nature of their predictions.[13]

In general, these estimates of growth prospects are highly optimistic. This is especially true with respect to those dealing with the United States.   One of the best-known American appraisals, which also illustrates the type of forecasting method generally used, is the projection of gross national product for 1975 by the President's Materials Policy Commission.   On the basis of recent historical experience, this so-called Paley Commission suggests that a 2½ per cent annual increase in product per man-hour is a reasonable assumption.   It also predicts a 15 per cent decrease in the number of working hours per worker between 1950 and 1975.   Using these productivity and man-hour relationships and an estimate of the 1975 labor force (derived from the historical ratio of the labor force to the population multiplied by the Census Bureau's estimate of the 1975 population), the Commission concludes that a real gross national product level "twice that of 1950 is almost certain to be reached at some point in the decade 1970–80."[14]

The crucial estimate in so far as per capita income is concerned is productivity per man-hour.   The long-run historical average of this figure in the United States is about 2 per cent.   Few observers, however, accept this rate in forecasting national income for the next 10 to 25 years.   Forecasts usually assume a rate closer to 2½ per cent per year, which is approximately equal to the average annual rate for the decade 1940–1950.   Some writers even state that a rate closer to 3 per cent

[12] Attempts to project national income in the United States include: C. Clark, *The Economics of 1960,* Macmillan and Co., Ltd., London, 1942; G. Colm, *The American Economy in 1960,* National Planning Association, Planning Pamphlets, No. 81, 1952; Dewhurst and Associates, *America's Needs and Resources, A New Survey,* The Twentieth Century Fund, New York, 1955; the President's Materials Policy Commission, *Resources for Freedom,* U. S. Government Printing Office, Washington, 1952, II, Chapter 22; S. H. Slichter, "How Big in 1980?" *Atlantic Monthly,* Nov. 1949, 39–43.

For a discussion of various projections by the United States Department of Agriculture, see J. P. Cavin, "Projections in Agriculture," *Long-Range Economic Projection, Studies in Income and Wealth, XVI,* National Bureau of Economic Research, Princeton University Press, Princeton, 1954, 107–130.

For a recent, non-statistical analysis of the development possibilities in the United States, see J. S. Davis, "Economic Potentials of the United States," in R. Lekachman (ed.), *National Policy for Economic Welfare at Home and Abroad,* Doubleday and Company, Garden City, 1955, 104–148.

[13] The problems and hazards of long-run projections are discussed in *Long-Range Economic Projection,* National Bureau of Economic Research, Princeton University Press, Princeton, Part I, 9–104.

[14] President's Materials Policy Commission, *op. cit.,* II, 112.

per year is well within the range of possibility.[15]   Ignoring changes in the number of hours worked, a 2½ per cent rate and a 3 per cent rate imply that output per worker increases about 85 per cent and 109 per cent, respectively, in 25 years.

Estimates of development prospects for Britain vary considerably in their degree of optimism.   One analysis of the Chancellor of the Exchequer's comment in 1954, that it should be possible to double living standards, i.e., per capita consumption and government welfare expenditures, between 1954 and 1979, concludes that such an accomplishment is feasible.[16]   This projection assumes as reasonable a "rise in output per head of 15 per cent per six years,"[17] or slightly under a 2½ per cent annual rate.   Another estimate of British national income concludes that the annual rate of productivity increase under full employment conditions in peace-time should be at least 2 per cent per year.[18]   The Paley Commission's 1975 projection for the United Kingdom (and non-Communist Europe as a whole) assumes that productivity increases at the same rate as in the United States, i.e., 2½ per cent per year.[19]

Pessimism over future British development is based largely upon an unfavorable appraisal of British prospects in the international sector.[20] Several writers argue that Britain faces increasing competitive pressures in its export markets from both rich and poor countries.   These writers also maintain that the long-run terms of trade are likely to move against the United Kingdom.   The existing pattern of development may, therefore, be associated with severe balance of payments difficulties.   Rapid development, in other words, may be inconsistent with international equilibrium.   This, in turn, may encourage policy measures that sacrifice a high rate of development.   On the other hand, if appropriate changes in the exchange rate are made to maintain balance of payments equilibrium, the United Kingdom may lose most of the benefits of a high rate

[15] Slichter, op. cit., 43; W. S. Woytinsky and Associates, Employment and Wages in the United States, The Twentieth Century Fund, New York, 1953, 85.

[16] A. A. Adams and W. B. Reddaway, The British Economy—A Longer View (Reprint Series, No. 90), University of Cambridge, Department of Applied Economics, Cambridge, 1955, 5.

[17] Ibid., 4.

[18] Beveridge, op. cit., 397.

[19] President's Materials Policy Commission, op. cit., II, 131.

[20] For a general discussion of this problem, see P. D. Henderson, "Retrospect and Prospect: The Economic Suryey, 1954," Bulletin, Oxford University Institute of Statistics, XVI, Nos. 5–6, 137–177 (May and June 1954); and the comments on this article by H. G. Johnson, P. Streeten, J. R. Sargent, R. L. Morris, D. Seers, R. Nurkse, C. Kennedy, W. A. Lewis, N. H. Leyland, and G. D. N. Worswick, ibid., XVII, No. 1, 1–69 (Feb. 1955).

of productivity increase through adverse movements in its terms of trade.

This kind of reasoning leads to several different conclusions. Some suggest that the United Kingdom either should not attempt to achieve a high rate of growth or should seek higher real income levels for its people by shifting its resources to other countries through migration and foreign investment.[21] Others argue that the best procedure is to concentrate upon the development of industries that tend to decrease the need for imports.[22] Still others maintain that special emphasis on increasing productivity in export industries is necessary.[23]

3. The Institutionalization of Economic Development

When commenting upon the prospects for development within the not too distant future, many economists, in effect, assume that the major requirements for maintaining development are institutionalized within the social framework of the rich countries. This does not imply that they do not advocate policy changes to accelerate development nor that they are not concerned about obstacles to development. But, by and large, they seem to assume the existence of a powerful, quasi-automatic development mechanism for at least the next 10 to 25 years.

The differences in the nature of recent discussions of development prospects in the poor and the rich countries illustrate this attitude. In analyzing the development problem in poor countries, economists stress the importance of immediate policy measures to create a system of attitudes in which the desire for material improvement is an important motivation of economic action; to improve the level of education and health; to maintain reasonable political stability; to establish adequate credit facilities; to develop an entrepreneurial spirit; to increase the level of saving; etc. Although these factors are also mentioned in considering the long-run development prospects of the rich countries, a reasonable current achievement of these requirements for continued development usually is accepted as given.

Many economists, moreover, believe that, at least for the next 25 years or so, these and other requirements for development can be maintained within a capitalistic framework. An examination of the economic trends in rich, capitalistic countries appears to support this view. The pros-

[21] H. G. Johnson, "Economic Expansion and the Balance of Payments," *ibid.,* 8–10.

[22] E. A. G. Robinson, "The Changing Structure of the British Economy," *Economic Journal, LXIV,* No. 255, 443–461 (Sept. 1954).

[23] G. D. N. Worswick, "Flexibility and the Stimulation of Investment," and R. Nurkse, "Internal Growth and External Solvency," *loc. cit.,* 63–69 and 38–50, respectively.

pects for technological progress, for example, seem favorable. The evidence does not suggest a rapid trend towards greater business concentration, which might result in a stifling of invention and innovation. On the contrary, the relatively greater research efforts by government, business, and other private groups indicate that rapid technological progress is becoming increasingly "institutionalized" within the economic structure of these countries. Research, in other words, is becoming a large and well-established industry which tends to turn out innovations on a regularized basis. Moreover, the problem of satisfying the qualitative requirements of the improvement process does not appear to be serious. The behavior of the long-run saving-income ratio also does not give grounds for concern with respect to development prospects in the near future. As noted, this ratio seems to be approximately constant in the rich countries. Furthermore, as in the case of technology, saving is regularized to a greater extent than in the past.

The prospects for population growth and natural resource supplies likewise are not considered by most writers to be serious obstacles to maintaining development within the next 25 years. Nor is there convincing evidence to indicate that in the near future the economic environment of "big" business, "big" labor, and "big" government may seriously weaken incentives for growth. Indeed, a major reason why many take an optimistic development position is that they assume that, under existing government policies, the problem of maintaining full employment without unreasonable inflation is largely solved. Given this condition (and the absence of a major war), they foresee no serious reason why investment cannot continue to expand and produce a satisfactory rate of development.

Most of the doubts concerning development in the near future appear to involve some aspect of the resource flexibility requirement rather than such general factors as technological progress, population growth, and natural resource conditions. The question is: can the pattern of resource allocation adapt to the strong forces underlying development in such a way that these potentials for satisfactory growth are realized? This is a serious problem, but most economists do not believe that its solution requires the abandonment of capitalism.

Although many are prepared to assert that the prospects for economic development within the next 10 to 25 years are favorable, they are reluctant to make longer-run predictions. There appear to be convincing reasons, however, for modern economists to abandon the pessimistic predictions of such writers as Ricardo and Hansen. To these economists, a rapid rate of development seemed to depend on fortuitous and exceptional circumstances. Consequently, as they saw particular forces that had stimulated development wane, they tended to assume that the rate of development would also decline.   In their minds the burden of arguments concerning development prospects rested upon those who were optimistic about the future.   But, in view of the current institutionalization of many requirements for development within the rich countries, it might be suggested that at present the burden of these arguments should rest upon the pessimists.   In other words, under existing conditions one can expect continued development in the rich economies.   Pessimists must establish a case showing that changes in the prevailing economic and social structure are undermining the present institutionalization of development requirements.   Viewing long-run development prospects in this manner may be more realistic than the rather negative outlook of many earlier economists.

$$For$$

$$Further$$

$$Study$$

Abbreviations of Periodical Titles

Amer. Anthro.	*American Anthropologist*
Amer. J. Econ. Soc.	*American Journal of Economics and Sociology*
Amer. Soc. Rev.	*American Sociology Review*
A.E.R.	*American Economic Review*
A.E.R.P.P.	*American Economic Review, Papers and Proceedings*
Annals	*The Annals of the American Academy of Political and Social Science*
A.P.S.R.	*American Political Science Review*
C.J.E.P.S.	*Canadian Journal of Economics and Political Science*
Caribbean Econ. R.	*Caribbean Economic Review*
Col. J. Int. Aff.	*Columbia Journal of International Affairs*
Econ. Bull. A.F.E.	*Economic Bulletin for Asia and the Far East*
E.H.R.	*Economic History Review*
Econ. Hist.	*Economic History*

Econ. Internaz.	*Economia Internazionale*
Econ. J.	*Economic Journal*
Explorations	*Explorations in Entrepreneurial History*
Econ. Record	*Economic Record*
Harv. Bus. R.	*Harvard Business Review*
I.M.F. Staff Papers	*International Monetary Fund Staff Papers*
Indian Econ. J.	*Indian Economic Journal*
Indian Econ. R.	*Indian Economic Review*
Indian J. Econ.	*Indian Journal of Economics*
Int. Aff.	*International Affairs*
Int. Lab. R.	*International Labor Review*
Int. Soc. Sci. Bull.	*International Social Science Bulletin*
J. Econ. Hist.	*Journal of Economic History*
J.P.E.	*Journal of Political Economy*
Lloyds B.R.	*Lloyds Bank Review*
Manchester School	*Manchester School of Economic and Social Studies*
Mid.E.J.	*Middle East Journal*
O.U.I.S. Bull.	*Bulletin of the Oxford University Institute of Statistics*
O.E.P.	*Oxford Economic Papers*
Q.J.E.	*Quarterly Journal of Economics*
Rev. of Econ. Stat.	*Review of Economics and Statistics*
R. Econ. Stud.	*Review of Economic Studies*
Rural Soc.	*Rural Sociology*
Soc. Res.	*Social Research*

Sociocultural Aspects

of Development:

Select Readings

The following readings relate anthropological, sociological, and psychological aspects of cultural change to problems of economic development. They provide an understanding of the nature of culture and cultural conditioning and some analysis of motivational phenomena. In general terms, the readings discuss to what extent development requires change in institutions and values, and to what extent development can be accelerated within the existing institutional framework and value structure. More specifically, they consider the effects of particular institutional and environmental factors on mobility, productivity, and entrepreneurship in different countries, and they appraise institutions, values, and motives in terms of the requirements for accelerated development.

Anderson, C. A., and M. J. Bournan, "A Typology of Societies," *Rural Soc., XVI,* No. 3, 255–271 (Sept. 1951).

Bauer, C., "The Pattern of Urban and Economic Development: Social Implications," *Annals, CCCV,* 60–69 (May 1956).

Barnett, H. G., "Invention and Cultural Change," *Amer. Anthro., XLIV,* 14–30 (Jan.–March 1942).

Belshaw, C. S., "The Cultural Milieu of the Entrepreneur," *Explorations, VII,* No. 3 (Feb. 1955).

Boulding, K., "Religious Foundations of Economic Progress," *Harv. Bus. R., XXX,* No. 3, 33–40 (May–June 1952).

Browne, G. St. J. Orde, *The African Labourer,* Oxford University Press, London, 1933.

Brozen, Yale, "Social Implications of Technological Change," *Social Science Research Council Items, 3,* 31–34 (Feb. 15, 1951).

Clark, S. D., "Religion and Economic Backward Areas," *A.E.R.P.P., XLI,* 259–265 (May 1951).

Comhaire, J. L., "Economic Change and the Extended Family," *Annals, CCCV,* 45–52 (May 1956).

Cox, R. W., "Some Human Problems of Industrial Development," *Int. Lab. R., LXVI,* No. 3, 246–267 (Sept. 1952).

Davis, J. M., *Modern Industry and the African,* Macmillan Co., London, 1933.

———, "A Conceptual Analysis of Stratification," *Amer. Soc. Rev.,* 217–229, Dec. 1940.

Davis, K., "Population and Change in Backward Areas," *Col. J. Int. Aff.,* 43–49, Spring 1950.

———, *Population of India and Pakistan,* Princeton University Press, Princeton, 1951.

———, "The Unpredicted Pattern of Population Change," *Annals, CCCV,* 53–59 (May 1956).

Dube, S. C., *Indian Village,* Cornell University Press, Ithaca, 1955.

Entrepreneurship and Economic Growth, Conference, Social Science Research Council and Harvard University Research Center in Entrepreneurial History, Cambridge, Mass., Nov. 1954.

Firth, H., "Some Features of Primitive Industry," *Econ. Hist., I,* No. 1, 12–22 (Jan. 1926).

Fisher, S. N. (ed.), *Social Forces in the Middle East,* Cornell University Press, Ithaca, 1955.

Gerschenkron, A., "Social Attitudes, Entrepreneurship and Economic Development," *Explorations, VI,* No. 1, 1–19 (1953).

Gerth, H. H., and C. W. Mills, *From Max Weber,* Routledge and K. Paul, London, 1947.

Greaves, I. C., *Modern Production among Backward Peoples,* Allen and Unwin, London, 1935.

Helleiner, K. F., "Moral Conditions for Economic Growth," *J. Econ. Hist., XI,* No. 2, 97–116 (Spring 1951).

Herskovits, M. J., *Acculturation: The Study of Social Contact,* Augustin, New York, 1938.

Hoselitz, B. F., "Entrepreneurship and Economic Growth," *Amer. J. Econ. Soc., XII,* No. 1, 97–110 (Oct. 1952).

———, "Non-Economic Barriers to Economic Development," *Economic Development and Cultural Change,* March 1952.

———, "The Role of Cities in the Economic Growth of Underdeveloped Areas," *J.P.E., LXI,* 195–208 (June 1953).

Hoyt, E. E., "The Impact of a Money Economy on Consumption Patterns," *Annals, CCCV,* 12–22 (May 1956).

Hoyt, E. E., "Want Development in Undeveloped Countries," *J.P.E., LIX,* 194–202 (June 1951).

Hsu, F. L. K., "Cultural Factors," in *Economic Development* (Williamson and Buttrick, eds.), Prentice-Hall, New York, 1954, 618–664.

———, "Incentives to Work in Primitive Communities," *Amer. Soc. Rev., VIII,* No. 6, 638–642 (Dec. 1943).

International Labor Organization, *Basic Problems of Plantation Labor,* Committee on Work on Plantations, First Session, Bandoeng, 1950, Geneva, 1950.

———, *Industrial Labor in India,* P. S. King and Staples, London, 1938.

Kardiner, A., *Psychological Frontiers of Society,* Columbia University Press, New York, 1945, Chapter XIV.

Levy, M., "Some Sources of the Vulnerability of the Structures of Relatively Non-Industrialized Societies to Those of Highly Industrialized Societies," in *The Progress of Underdeveloped Countries* (B. Hoselitz, ed.), University of Chicago Press, Chicago, 1952.

Linton, R. (ed.), *Most of the World: The Peoples of Africa, Latin America, and the East Today,* Columbia University Press, New York, 1949.

Lipset, S. M., and R. Bendix, *Class, Status and Power: A Reader in Social Stratification,* Free Press, Glencoe, 1953.

Lorimer, F., et al., *Culture and Human Fertility,* UNESCO, Paris, 1954.

Malinowski, B., *The Dynamics of Culture Change,* Yale University Press, New Haven, 1945.

Matthews, C., "Agricultural Labor and Mechanization," *Caribbean Econ. R., III,* Nos. 1 and 2, 48–57 (Oct. 1951).

McClelland, D. C., et al., *The Achievement Motive,* Appleton-Century-Crofts, New York, 1953.

Maunier, René, *The Sociology of Colonies,* Routledge and K. Paul, London, 1949.

Mead, M. (ed.), *Cultural Patterns and Technical Change,* UNESCO, Paris, 1953.

Meek, C. K., *Land Law and Custom in the Colonies,* 2nd ed., Oxford University Press, London, 1949.

Merton, R. K., *Social Theory and Social Structure,* Free Press, Glencoe, 1949.

Moore, W. E., *Industrialization and Labor,* Cornell University Press, Ithaca, 1951.

———, "Primitives and Peasants in Industry," *Soc. Res., XV,* 44–81 (March 1948).

Nash, M., "The Recruitment of Labor and Development of New Skills," *Annals, CCCV,* 23–31 (May 1956).

Orchard, J., "Social Background of Oriental Industrialization," in *Explorations in Economics,* McGraw-Hill Book Co., New York, 1936.

Parsons, K. H., R. J. Penn, and P. M. Raup (eds.), *Land Tenure: Proceedings of the International Conference on Land Tenure and Related Problems in World Agriculture,* University of Wisconsin Press, Madison, 1956.

Parsons, T., "The Motivation of Economic Activities," in *Essays in Sociological Theory, Pure and Applied,* Free Press, Glencoe, 1949, Chapter IX.

———, *The Social System,* Free Press, Glencoe, 1951.

———, *The Structure of Social Action,* McGraw-Hill Book Co., New York, 1937.

———, *Toward a General Theory of Action,* Harvard University Press, Cambridge, 1951.

Redfield, R., *Peasant Society and Culture,* University of Chicago Press, Chicago, 1956.

Ryan, B., *Caste in Modern Ceylon,* Rutgers University Press, New Brunswick, 1953.

Ryan, B., "Ceylonese Value Systems," *Rural Soc., XVII,* 9–28 (March 1952).

Salter, Sir Arthur, *Modern Mechanization and Its Effects on the Structure of Society,* Oxford University Press, London, 1953.

Sawyer, J. E., "The Entrepreneur and Social Order," in *Men in Business* (W. Miller, ed.), Harvard University Press, Cambridge, 1952, Chapter 1.

———, "Social Structure and Economic Progress," *A.E.R.P.P., XLI,* 321–329 (May 1951).

Schapera, I., *Migrant Labour and Tribal Life,* Oxford University Press, London, 1947.

Singer, M., "Cultural Values in India's Economic Development," *Annals, CCCV,* 81–91 (May 1956).

"Social Implications of Technical Change" (Collected Papers), *Int. Soc. Sci. Bull., IV,* Summer 1952.

Sorokin, P. A., "Social Mobility," in *Encyclopedia of the Social Sciences,* Macmillan Co., New York, 1934.

———, *Society, Culture, and Personality: Their Structure and Dynamics,* Harper and Bros., New York, 1947.

Spengler, J. J., "Sociological Value Theory, Economic Analyses and Economic Policy," *A.E.R.P.P., XLIII,* 340–349 (May 1953).

Spicer, E. H. (ed.), *Human Problems in Technological Change,* Russel Sage Foundation, New York, 1952.

Taueber, I. B., "Ceylon as a Demographic Laboratory," *Population Index,* Oct. 1949.

Tawney, R. H., *Religion and the Rise of Capitalism,* 2nd ed., John Murray, London, 1937.

Tax, S., "Selective Culture Change," *A.E.R.P.P., XLI,* 315–320 (May 1951).

Thompson, S. H., "Social Aspects of Rural Industrialization," *Milbank Memorial Fund Quarterly,* July 1948.

Thurnwald, R., *Economic Activities in Primitive Communities,* Oxford University Press, London, 1932.

United Kingdom Colonial Office, *Bibliography of Published Sources Relating to African Land Tenure,* Colonial No. 258, London, 1950.

United Nations, *The Determinants and Consequences of Population Trends,* New York, 1953.

———, *Proceedings of the World Population Conference, 1955, XIII,* 8.

———, *Social Progress through Community Development, 1955, IV,* 18.

———, *Special Study on Social Conditions in Non-Self-Governing Territories,* New York, 1953.

University of Natal, Department of Economics, *The African Factory Worker,* Oxford University Press, London, 1950.

Warriner, D., *Land Reform and Economic Development,* National Bank of Egypt Fiftieth Anniversary Commemoration Lectures, Cairo, 1955.

Wilson, G., and M. Wilson, *The Analysis of Social Change,* Cambridge University Press, Cambridge, 1945.

Wolf, C., "Institutions and Economic Development," *A.E.R., XLV,* No. 5, 867–883 (Dec. 1955).

Development Programs

and Plans:

Select Readings

The following readings discuss the specific development programs and plans of various poor countries.   They range from an examination of comprehensive and detailed programs, such as the Five-Year Plan of India, to specific policy measures, such as fiscal policy or agricultural improvements.   Some of the readings are more general and consider policies from a more analytical viewpoint in terms of objectives and purposes.

Adler, J. H., "The Fiscal and Monetary Implementation of Development Programs," *A.E.R.P.P., XLII,* 584–600 (May 1952).

Akhtar, S. M., "The Colombo Plan with Special Reference to Pakistan," *Econ. Internaz.,* 134–147, Feb. 1952.

Aubrey, H. G., "Deliberate Industrialization," *Soc. Res., XVI,* 158–182 (June 1949).

———, "Small Industry in Economic Development," *Soc. Res., XVIII,* 269–312 (Sept. 1951).

———, "The Role of the State in Economic Development," *A.E.R.P.P., XLI,* 266–273 (May 1951).

Baster, J., "A Second Look at Point Four," *A.E.R.P.P., XLI*, 399–406 (May 1951).

Bauer, P. T., "The United Nations Report on the Economic Development of Under-Developed Countries," *Econ. J., LXIII*, 210–222 (March 1953).

———, and F. W. Paish, "The Reduction of Fluctuations in the Incomes of Primary Producers," *Econ. J., LXII*, 750–780 (Dec. 1952).

Benham, F., "Deficit Finance in Asia," *Lloyds B.R.*, 18–28, Jan. 1955.

Bernstein, E. M., and I. G. Patel, "Inflation in Relation to Economic Development," *I.M.F. Staff Papers, II*, 363–398 (Nov. 1952).

Bhattacharyva, K. N., "Fiscal and Monetary Policies in Planning—A Study of Indian Problems," *Indian J. Econ., XXII*, 395–401 (April 1952).

Bingham, J. B., *Shirt-Sleeve Diplomacy: Point Four in Action*, John Day Co., New York, 1953.

Bohr, K. A., "Investment Criteria for Manufacturing Industries in Underdeveloped Countries," *Rev. of Econ. Stat., XXXVI* (May 1954).

Brown, W. A., "Treaty, Guaranty, and Tax Inducements for Foreign Investments," *A.E.R.P.P., XL*, 486–494 (May 1950).

Caldwell, L. K., "Technical Assistance and Administrative Reform in Colombia," *A.P.S.R., XLVII*, 494–510 (June 1953).

Carnegie Endowment for International Peace, "An Approach to Economic Development in the Middle East," in *International Conciliation*, No. 457, New York, 3–32 (Jan. 1950).

Carr-Gregg, J. R. E., "The Colombo Plan: A Commonwealth Program for South-East Asia," *International Conciliation*, No. 467, New York, 1–55 (Jan. 1951).

Ceylon, Six-Year Program of Investment, Government Publications Bureau, Colombo, 1955.

Cohen, J. B., "The Colombo Plan for Cooperative Economic Development," *Mid. E.J., V*, No. 1, 94–100 (Winter 1951).

Commonwealth Consultative Committee, *The Colombo Plan for Co-operative Economic Development in Southeast Asia*, H.M.S.O., London, 1950.

Food and Agriculture Organization, *Activities of the F.A.O. under the Expanded Assistance Program, 1950–52*, Rome, May 1952.

Frankel, S. H., "United Nations Primer for Development," *Q.J.E., LXVI*, 301–326 (Aug. 1952); also included in *The Economic Impact on Underdeveloped Societies;* see also comments by W. A. Lewis and others, *Q.J.E., LXVII*, 267–285 (May 1953).

Hambridge, G., *The Story of F.A.O.*, D. Van Nostrand Co., New York, 1955.

Hicks, J. R., and U. K. Hicks, *Report on Finance and Taxation in Jamaica*, Government Printer, Kingston, 1955.

Hicks, U. K., "The Search for Revenue in Underdeveloped Countries," *Revue de Science et de Législation Financières*, 6–43, Jan.–March 1952.

India, Government of, *Five Year Plan Progress Report for 1953–1954*, New Delhi, Sept. 1954.

———, *A Plan for Community Development*, New Delhi, Dec. 1951.

International Bank for Reconstruction and Development, *The Agricultural Development of Uruguay* (with F.A.O.), Washington, 1951, mimeo.

———, *The Agricultural Economy of Chile* (with F.A.O.), Washington, 1952, mimeo.

———, *The Basis of a Development Program for Colombia*, Washington, 1950.

———, *The Economic Development of British Guiana*, Johns Hopkins Press, Baltimore, 1953.

International Bank for Reconstruction and Development, *The Economic Development of Ceylon,* Johns Hopkins Press, Baltimore, 1953.

———, *The Economic Development of Guatemala,* Johns Hopkins Press, Baltimore, 1951.

———, *The Economic Development of Iraq,* Johns Hopkins Press, Baltimore, 1952.

———, *The Economic Development of Jamaica,* Johns Hopkins Press, Baltimore, 1952.

———, *The Economic Development of Malaya,* Johns Hopkins Press, Baltimore, 1955.

———, *The Economic Development of Mexico,* Johns Hopkins Press, Baltimore, 1953.

———, *The Economic Development of Nicaragua,* Johns Hopkins Press, Baltimore, 1953.

———, *The Economic Development of Nigeria,* Johns Hopkins Press, Baltimore, 1955.

———, *The Economic Development of Syria,* Johns Hopkins Press, Baltimore, 1955.

———, *The Economy of Turkey—An Analysis and Recommendations for a Development Program,* Washington, 1951.

———, *Report on Cuba: Findings and Recommendations of an Economic and Technical Mission to Cuba,* Washington, 1951.

———, *Surinam: Recommendations for a Ten Year Development Program,* Johns Hopkins Press, Baltimore, 1952.

"The International Labor Organization and Technical Assistance," *Int. Lab. R., LXVI,* 391–418 (Nov.–Dec. 1952).

Iversen, Carl, *Report on Monetary Policy in Iraq,* Ejnar Munksgaard Publ., Copenhagen, 1954.

Kahn, A. E., "Investment Criteria in Development Programs," *Q.J.E., LXV,* 38–61 (Feb. 1951).

Keenleyside, H. L., "Administrative Problems of Technical Assistance Administration," *C.J.E.P.S., XVIII,* 345–357 (Aug. 1952).

Kindleberger, C. P., "Planning for Foreign Investment," *A.E.R.P.P., XXXIII,* 347–354 (March 1943).

Lewis, W. A., "Developing Colonial Agriculture," *Three Banks Review,* June 1949.

———, "Issues in Land Settlement Policy," *Caribbean Econ. R., III* (Oct. 1951).

———, "Planning in Backward Areas," in *The Principles of Economic Planning,* Public Affairs Press, Washington, D. C., 1951.

Malenbaum, W., "Colombo Plan: New Promise for Asia," *United States Department of State Bulletin, XXVII,* 441–448 (Sept. 22, 1952).

Naidu, B. U. N., "Planning in Underdeveloped Countries," *Indian Econ. R., I* (July 1953).

Pakistan Ministry of Economic Affairs, *Pakistan Looks Ahead, the Six-Year Development Plan,* Karachi, 1951.

Pazos, F., "Economic Development and Financial Stability," *I.M.F. Staff Papers, III,* No. 2, 228–253 (Oct. 1953).

Political and Economic Planning, "International Capital for Economic Development," *Planning, XIX,* 169–184 (April 13, 1953).

———, "Planned Development in the Less-Developed Countries," *Planning, XIX,* 153–168 (Feb. 16, 1953).

Political and Economic Planning, "The Strategy of World Development," *Planning, XVII,* 233–268 (April 23, 1951).

Prasad, P. S. Narayan, "The Colombo Plan," *India Quarterly, VIII,* 158–169 (April–June 1952).

Rao, V. K. R. V., "The Colombo Plan for Economic Development: An Indian View," *Lloyds B.R.,* July 1951, 12–32.

———, "An International Development Authority," *India Quarterly, VIII* (July–Sept. 1952)

Riggs, F. W., "Public Administration: A Neglected Factor in Economic Development," *Annals, CCCV,* 70–80 (May 1956).

Ruopp, P. (ed.), *Approaches to Community Development,* W. van Hoeve, The Hague, 1953.

Salant, W., "Some Basic Considerations of Public Finance in the Development of Underdeveloped Countries," International Institute of Public Finance, London, Sept. 1951.

Schlesinger, E. R., *Multiple Exchange Rates and Economic Development,* International Finance Section, Princeton, 1952.

Sharp, W. R., "The Institutional Framework for Technical Assistance—A Comparative Review of U. N. and U. S. Experience," *International Organization, VII,* No. 3, 342–379 (Aug. 1953).

———, *International Technical Assistance, Programs and Organization,* Public Administration Service, Chicago, 1952.

Singh, B., *Federal Finance and Underdeveloped Economy,* Hind Kitabs, Ltd., Bombay, 1952.

Staley, E., *The Future of Underdeveloped Countries—Political Implications of Economic Development,* Harper and Bros., New York, 1954.

Stone, D. C., *National Organization for the Administration of Economic Development Programs,* International Institute of Administrative Sciences, Brussels, 1954.

Teaf, Jr., H. M., and P. G. Franck, *Hands across Frontiers: Case Studies in Technical Cooperation,* Cornell University Press, Ithaca, 1956.

Thorp, W. L., "Some Basic Policy Issues in Economic Development," *A.E.R.P.P., XLI,* 407–417 (May 1951).

Tinbergen, J., "Capital Formation and the Five Year Plan," *Indian Econ. J., I* (July 1953).

Tirana, R., "Government Financing of Economic Development Abroad," *J. Econ. Hist.,* Supplement, 1950, 92–105.

United Kingdom, "Colonial Development Corporation Annual Reports and Accounts," H.M.S.O., London, annual.

———, Colonial Office, *The Colonial Territories,* H.M.S.O., annual reports.

———, "A Review of Colonial Marketing Organizations and Related Bodies," H.M.S.O., London, 1952.

United Nations, *Analysis and Projections of Economic Development, I: An Introduction to the Technique of Programming,* 1955, II.G.2.

———, *Domestic Financing of Economic Development,* New York, 1951, II.B.1.

———, *The Economic Development of Latin America and Its Principal Problems,* New York, 1950, II.G.2.

———, *The Expanded Program of Technical Assistance for Economic Development of Under-Developed Countries,* New York, 1953, TAB/1/Rev. 1.

———, *Formulation and Economic Appraisal of Development Projects,* Lahore, Pakistan, 1951, II.B.4.

United Nations, "Inflation and Mobilization of Domestic Capital in Underdeveloped Countries of Asia," *Econ. Bull. A.F.E., II,* No. 3, 21–34 (Feb. 1952).

———, *International Cooperation in a Latin American Development Policy,* New York, 1954, II.G.2.

———, *Land Reform, Defects in Agrarian Structure as Obstacles to Economic Development,* New York, 1951, II.B.3.

———, *Measures for the Economic Development of Under-Developed Countries,* New York, 1951, II.B.2.

———, *Measures for International Economic Stability,* New York, 1951.

———, *Methods of Financing Economic Development in Under-Developed Countries,* New York, 1949, II.B.4.

———, *Mobilization of Domestic Capital: Report and Documents of the Second Working Party,* Bangkok, 1953, II.F.2.

———, *Progress in Land Reform,* New York, 1954, II.B.3.

———, *Report of the Commission on Community Organization and Development in South and Southeast Asia,* New York, 1953.

———, *Report on a Special U. N. Fund for Economic Development,* New York, 1953, II.B.1.

———, *Rural Progress through Co-operatives,* New York, 1954, II.B.2.

———, "Some Financial Aspects of Development Programs in Asian Countries," *Econ. Bull. A.F.E., III,* Nos. 1–2, 1–12 (Nov. 1952).

———, *Standards and Techniques of Public Administration with Special Reference to Technical Assistance for Underdeveloped Countries,* New York, 1951, II.B.7.

———, *Taxes and Fiscal Policy in Under-Developed Countries,* New York, 1955, II.H.1.

———, *Technical Assistance for Economic Development,* New York, 1949, II.B.1.

United States, Committee of the Senate on Foreign Relations, Subcommittee on Technical Assistance Programs, *Multilateral Technical Assistance Programs,* Staff Study No. 1, March 11, 1955.

———, House of Representatives, *Staff Memorandum on Increasing the Flow of Private Investment into Underdeveloped Areas* (Committee Print), 82nd Congress, 2nd Session, March 27, 1952.

———, International Development Advisory Board, *Guidelines for Point Four,* Washington, D. C., June 5, 1952.

———, State Department, Division of Library and Reference Services, "Point Four, A Selected Bibliography of Materials on Technical Cooperation with Foreign Governments," Bibliography No. 54, Supplements Nos. 55, 56, 57.

Wilson, J. S. G., "Problems of Commonwealth Economic Development," *Westminster Bank Review,* 5–8, May 1954.

Wu, Y. L., "A Note on the Post-War Industrialization of 'Backward' Countries and Centralist Planning," *Economica, XII,* No. 47, 172–178 (Aug. 1945).

Appendix C

Case Studies
of Development:
Select Readings

The following readings consider the course and problems of the development process in various countries. All the countries are now among the poor countries of the world, with the exception of Japan and Russia, which are included because they are classic cases of "forced development." Only a few of the readings, however, constitute full-scale case studies, since these are unfortunately still limited in number. But all the readings illuminate at least some aspect of the historical course of development in the country being examined. In combination they provide considerable scope for a comparative study of the historical causes and problems of development in different countries. Although they are mainly concerned with policy recommendations, the I.B.R.D. mission reports, listed in Appendix B, are also useful contributions as case studies; they offer fairly comprehensive surveys of the present structural features of the various countries considered, and they provide more detailed information on contemporary conditions than is readily available elsewhere. Particular attention is also called to United Nations Headquarters Library, *Bibliography on Industrialization in Under-Developed Countries*, Bibliographical Series No. 6, New York, 1956, II.B.2.

Abramson, A., "The Economic Development of the Soviet Union under the Second and Third Five-Year Plans," *Int. Lab. R., XLI*, 177–201 (Feb. 1940).

Adler, J. H., E. R. Schlesinger, and E. C. Olson, *Public Finance and Economic Development in Guatemala*, Stanford University Press, Stanford, 1952.

Agrawal, A. N. (ed.), *Industrial Problems of India*, Ranjit Printers & Publishers, Delhi, 1952.

Akhtar, S. M., *Economics of Pakistan*, 2nd ed., Arthur Probsthain, London, 1951.

All-India Rural Credit Survey, Report of the Committee of Direction, Vol. II, *The General Report*, Reserve Bank of India, Bombay, 1954.

Allen, G. C., *Japanese Industry: Its Recent Development and Present Condition*, Institute of Pacific Relations, New York, 1940.

———, *A Short Economic History of Modern Japan, 1867–1937*, Allen & Unwin, London, 1946.

———, and A. G. Donnithorne, *Western Enterprise in Far Eastern Economic Development*, Allen & Unwin, London, 1954.

American Academy of Political and Social Science, "Puerto Rico: A Study in Democratic Development," *Annals, CCCLXXV*, 1–166 (Jan. 1953).

Anstey, V., *The Economic Development of India*, 4th ed., Longmans, Green and Co., New York, 1952.

Aubrey, H. G., "Structure and Balance in Rapid Economic Growth: The Example of Mexico," in *Papers of the Conference on Strategic Factors in Periods of Rapid Economic Growth*, Committee on Economic Growth of the Social Science Research Council, New York, April 1954.

Banerjea, P., *A Study of Indian Economics*, 6th ed., University of Calcutta, Calcutta, 1951.

Batten, T. R., *Problems of African Development*, Oxford University Press, London, *I*, 1947, *II*, 1948.

Baykov, A., *The Development of the Soviet Economic System*, Cambridge University Press, Cambridge, 1945.

Bergson, A. (ed.), *Soviet Economic Growth: Conditions and Perspectives*, Row, Peterson & Co., White Plains, 1953.

Boeke, J. H., *The Evolution of the Netherlands Indies Economy*, Institute of Pacific Relations, New York, 1946.

Bonné, Alfred, *The Economic Development of the Middle East*, Oxford University Press, New York, 1945.

———, "Land and Population in the Middle East," *Mid. E. J., V*, No. 1, 39–56 (1951).

———, *State and Economics in the Middle East: A Society in Transition*, K. Paul, London, 1943.

Borton, H., *Japan's Modern Century*, Ronald Press Co., New York, 1955.

Britnell, G. E., "Factors in the Economic Development of Guatemala," *A.E.R.P.P., XLIII*, 104–114 (May 1953).

———, "Some Problems of Economic and Social Change in Guatemala," *C.J.E.P.S., XVII*, 468–481 (Nov. 1951).

Buchanan, D. H., *The Development of Capitalistic Enterprise in India*, The Macmillan Co., New York, 1934.

———, "Japan vs. Asia," *A.E.R.P.P.*, *XLI*, 359–366 (May 1951).

Carlson, R. E., "Economic Development in Central America," *Inter-American Economic Affairs*, *II*, 5–29 (Autumn 1948).

Carus, C. D., and C. L. McNichols, *Japan: Its Resources and Industries*, Harper and Bros., New York, 1944.

Cohen, J. B., "Economic Development in Pakistan," *Land Economics*, *XXIX*, 1–12 (Feb. 1953).

Crouchley, A. B., *The Economic Development of Modern Egypt*, Longmans, Green and Co., London, 1938.

Dobb, M., *Soviet Economic Development Since 1917*, Routledge & K. Paul, London, 1948.

Dobby, E. H. G., *Southeast Asia*, University of London Press, London, 1950.

Ellsworth, P. T., *Chile: An Economy in Transition*, The Macmillan Co., New York, 1945.

———, "Factors in the Economic Development of Ceylon," *A.E.R.P.P.*, *XLIII*, 115–125 (May 1953).

Fage, J. D., *The History of West Africa*, Cambridge University Press, Cambridge, 1955.

Fairbank, J. K., et al., "Influence of Modern Western Science and Technology on Japan and China," *Explorations*, *VII*, No. 4, 189–204 (April 1955).

Frankel, S. H., *Capital Investment in Africa: Its Course and Effects*, Oxford University Press, London, 1938.

Furnivall, J. S., *Colonial Policy and Practice: A Comparative Study of Burma and Netherlands India*, Cambridge University Press, Cambridge, 1948.

———, *Netherlands India: A Study of Plural Economy*, The Macmillan Co., New York, 1944.

Galbraith, J. K., R. H. Holton, et al., *Marketing Efficiency in Puerto Rico*, Harvard University Press, Cambridge, 1955.

Gayer, A. D., P. T. Homan, and E. K. James, *The Sugar Economy of Puerto Rico*, Columbia University Press, New York, 1948.

Gourou, P., *The Tropical World*, Longmans, Green and Co., London, 1953.

Grad, A. J., *Land and Peasant in Japan*, Institute of Pacific Relations, New York, 1952.

Hailey, Lord, *An African Survey*, Oxford University Press, London, 1938.

Hicks, J. R., and U. K. Hicks, *Report on Finance and Taxation in Jamaica*, Government Printer, Kingston, Jamaica, 1955.

Joint Brazil-United States Economic Development Commission, *The Development of Brazil*, Institute of Inter-American Affairs, Washington, D. C., 1953.

Kuznets, S., W. E. Moore, and J. J. Spengler (eds.), *Economic Growth: Brazil, India, Japan*, Duke University Press, Durham, 1955.

Lewis, W. A., "The Industrialization of the British West Indies," *Caribbean Econ. R.*, *II*, No. 1, 1–61 (May 1950).

———, *Industrialization and the Gold Coast*, Government Printer, Accra, 1953.

Lockwood, W. W., *The Economic Development of Japan*, Princeton University Press, Princeton, 1954.

Madan, B. K. (ed.), *Economic Problems of Underdeveloped Countries in Asia*, Geoffrey Cumberlege, London, 1954.

Malenbaum, W., "India and China: Development Contrasts," *J.P.E.*, *LXIV*, No. 1, 1–24 (Feb. 1956).

May, S., *Costa Rica: A Study in Economic Development,* Twentieth Century Fund, New York, 1952.

McPhee, A., *The Economic Revolution in British West Africa,* G. Routledge & Sons, London, 1926.

Morgan, T., "The Economic Development of Ceylon," *Annals, CCCV,* 92–100 (May 1956).

Mosk, S. A., *Industrial Revolution in Mexico,* University of California Press, Berkeley, 1950.

———, and M. Burgin, *Economic Problems of Latin America,* University of California Press, Berkeley, 1953.

Nanjundan, S., "Economic Development of Malaya," *India Quarterly, VIII,* 289–311 (July 1952).

Nathan, R., et al., *Palestine: Problem and Promise, an Economic Study,* American Council on Public Affairs, Washington, D. C., 1948.

Nelson, L., *Rural Cuba,* University of Minnesota Press, Minneapolis, 1950.

Neuman, A. M., *Industrial Development in Indonesia,* Students' Bookshop, Cambridge, 1955.

Nicholls, W. H., "Domestic Trade in an Underdeveloped Country—Turkey," *J.P.E., LIX,* 463–480 (Dec. 1951).

Norman, E. H., *Japan's Emergence as a Modern State,* Allen & Unwin, London, 1940.

Perham, M. (ed.), *The Economics of a Tropical Dependency,* Faber & Faber, London, 1947.

———, *Mining, Commerce, and Finance in Nigeria,* Faber & Faber, London, 1948.

Perloff, H. S., *Puerto Rico's Economic Future,* University of Chicago Press, Chicago, 1950.

Pim, Sir Alan, *The Financial and Economic History of the African Tropical Territories,* Oxford University Press, London, 1940.

Puerto Rican Planning Board, *Economic Development of Puerto Rico,* San Juan, 1951.

Rao, V.K.R.V., *The Structure of Asia's Economy,* Indian Council of World Affairs, New Delhi, 1953.

Reubens, E. P., "Foreign Capital in Economic Development: A Case Study of Japan," in *Modernization Programs in Relation to Human Resources,* Milbank Memorial Fund, New York, 1950.

———, "Small Scale Industry in Japan," *Q.J.E., LXI,* 577–604 (Aug. 1947).

Robequain, C., *The Economic Development of French Indo-China,* rev. ed., Oxford University Press, New York, 1944.

Royal Institute of International Affairs, *The French Colonial Empire,* Royal Institute of International Affairs, New York, 1940.

———, *The Italian Colonial Empire,* Royal Institute of International Affairs, New York, 1940.

———, *The Middle East,* Royal Institute of International Affairs, New York, 1950.

Sarda, J., "Some Aspects of Economic Development in Venezuela," *Inter-American Economic Affairs, VI,* 29–39 (Summer 1952).

Schumpeter, E. B. (ed.), *The Industrialization of Japan and Manchukuo; 1930–1940,* The Macmillan Co., New York, 1940.

Seers, D., and C. R. Ross, *Report on Financial and Physical Problems of Development in the Gold Coast,* Government Printing Office, Accra, 1952.

Simey, T. S., *Welfare and Planning in the West Indies,* Oxford University Press, New York, 1947.

Singer, H. W., "Capital Requirements for the Economic Development of the Middle East," *Middle Eastern Affairs, III,* 35–40 (Feb. 1952).

Smith, T. C., *Political Change and Industrial Development in Japan—Government Enterprise, 1868–1880,* Stanford University Press, Stanford, 1955.

———, *Population Growth in Malaya,* Royal Institute of International Affairs, London, 1952.

South African Institute of International Affairs, *Africa South of the Sahara,* Oxford University Press, Capetown, 1951.

Spiegel, H. W., *The Brazilian Economy: Chronic Inflation and Sporadic Industrialization,* Blakiston, Philadelphia, 1949.

Stamp, L. D., *Africa: A Study in Tropical Development,* John Wiley & Sons, New York, 1953.

Thompson, C. H., and H. W. Woodruff, *Economic Development in Rhodesia and Nyasaland,* Dennis Dobson, London, 1955.

Thorogood, C. B., *Ceylon,* H.M.S.O., London, 1952.

Thornburg, M. W., et al., *Turkey: An Economic Appraisal,* Twentieth Century Fund, New York, 1949.

United Kingdom, *Overseas Economic Surveys,* Board of Trade, H.M.S.O., London (various countries annually).

United Nations, *Economic Bulletin for Asia and the Far East,* issued three times annually by the Research and Statistics Division, Economic Commission for Asia and the Far East, *I,* No. 1, issued Aug. 1950, Bangkok.

———, *Economic Development in Selected Countries: Plans, Programs and Agencies, I* (Sales No. 1948. II.B.l), New York, 1947, *II* (Sales No. 1950. II.B.l), New York, 1950.

———, *The Economic and Social Development of Libya* (Sales No. II.H.8), New York, 1953.

———, *Economic Survey of Asia and the Far East, Annual, 1949–* , New York, 1949–

———, *Economic Survey of Latin America, Annual, 1948–* , New York, 1948– .

———, *Enlargement of the Exchange Economy in Tropical Africa* (Sales No. 1954. II.C.4), New York, 1954.

———, *Final Report of the United Nations Economic Survey Mission for the Middle East* (Sales No. 1949. II.B.5), New York, 1949.

———, *A General Economic Appraisal of Libya* (Sales No. 1952. II.H.2), New York, 1952.

———, *Report of the United Nations Economic Mission to Chile, 1949–1950* (Sales No. 1951. II.B.6), New York, 1951.

———, *Review of Economic Conditions in the Middle East,* Supplement to the *World Economic Report, 1953–* , New York, 1953– .

———, *Scope and Structure of Money Economies in Tropical Africa* (Sales No. 1955. II.C.4), New York, 1955.

———, *United Nations Mission to Haiti* (Sales No. 1949. II.B.2), New York, 1949.

———, *World Economic Situation: Aspects of Economic Development in Africa,* New York, March, 1953.

Uyeda, T., et al., *The Small Industries of Japan: Their Growth and Development,* University of Chicago Press, Chicago, 1938.

Wallich, H. C., and J. H. Adler, *Public Finance in a Developing Country: El Salvador,* Harvard University Press, Cambridge, 1951.

Warriner, D., *Land and Poverty in the Middle East,* Royal Institute of International Affairs, London, 1948.

Weinryb, B. D., "International Development of the Near East," *Q.J.E., LXI,* 477–499 (May 1947).

Whetten, N. L., *Rural Mexico,* University of Chicago Press, Chicago, 1951.

Wythe, G., et al., *Brazil: An Expanding Economy,* Twentieth Century Fund, New York, 1949.

Index

Abramovitz, M., 250, 476
Acceleration principle, 103, 104, 106, 107, 110, 128, 133, 137, 187, 224, 226, 253, 328, 332
Adams, A. A., 539
Adams, W., 530
Adelman, M. A., 492
Adler, J. H., 346, 389
Ady, P., 408, 469, 470, 490
Afghanistan, 279, 284
Africa, agriculture, 274, 275, 278, 280
  capital stock, 280, 304
  foreign investment in, 208, 214, 222, 429
  government policy, 365
  income, 9, 10, 247
  international trade, 243, 253
  manufacturing, 481
  natural resources, 291–293, 380
  population, 10, 58, 283, 284, 286, 289, 438
  saving, 305
  technical assistance to, 411, 414
  see also Africa, Central; Africa, East; Africa, West; and under names of individual countries

Africa, Central, 284
Africa, East, 278, 328
Africa, West, 278, 407
Agriculture, in balanced growth, 348, 350, 400
  capital-output ratio in, 498
  classical analysis of, 19, 24–27, 30–39, 40, 43, 124, 128, 130
  collectivization, 378, 379
  consumption of foodstuffs, 11, 201, 483–485
  credit facilities for, 379, 381–383, 393, 461
  demand for products of, 198, 201, 500
  education and extension services for, 368, 369, 375, 376, 381–383, 410, 411, 415, 461
  fertilizers, use of, 280
  foreign investment in, 422, 428, 431
  in gradual development approach, 363–366
  income originating in, 199, 201, 275, 479
  irrigation and drainage projects in, 292, 364, 376, 379–383, 461, 464

561